The Encyclopedia of Unbelief

The
Encyclopedia
of
Unbelief

GORDON STEIN, Ph.D., *Editor*

VOLUME TWO, L-Z

PROMETHEUS BOOKS
Buffalo, New York

Published in 1985 by
Prometheus Books
700 East Amherst Street
Buffalo, New York 14215

91 90 89 88 87   5 4 3 2

Printed in the United States of America

Library of Congress Catalog Card No. 85-43327
ISBN: 0-87975-307-2

L

LAFFITTE, PIERRE (d. 1903), French positivist, successor to AUGUST COMTE. See **Positivism.**

LAMARCK, JEAN-BAPTISTE DE (1744–1829), French natural philosopher. See **Evolution and Unbelief.**

LA METTRIE, JULIEN OFFRAY DE (1709–1751), French philosopher, was, during his lifetime, probably the Enlightenment's leading exponent of MATERIALISM and ATHEISM. Born in Saint-Malo, Brittany, the son of a merchant, he studied medicine in Paris before taking his doctorate at Rheims in 1733. He continued his training under the celebrated Boerhaave in Leiden. Strongly influenced by the latter's iatromechanistic doctrine, La Mettrie later translated most of Boerhaave's work into French. After practicing medicine for several years in his native town, he became a medical officer in the French army during the War of the Austrian Succession.

La Mettrie's first philosophical work, the *Histoire naturelle de l'âme* (1745), aroused hostility among defenders of orthodoxy in France and was condemned to be burned by the Parliament of Paris, prompting its author to seek refuge in Holland. There he wrote his most important and notorious book, *L'Homme machine* (1747), which again excited a furor. Luckily, he was saved from renewed persecution when Frederick the Great of Prussia summoned him to Berlin, where he became a member of the Royal Academy of Sciences, as well as "reader" and "physician ordinary" to the philosopher king.

Among La Mettrie's writings during this last phase of his career, the *Discours sur le bonheur* (1748) in particular raised the hackles of his pious critics, who denounced him untruthfully as a debauched and cynical immoralist. To counter such slander, Frederick II personally composed Le Mettrie's eulogy on the occasion of his premature death.

The main thesis of the *Histoire naturelle de l'âme* is that the soul and its various faculties, such as sensation, memory, imagination, emotion, reason, and language, are exclusively products of organic structures and functions located primarily in the brain and nervous system. La Mettrie made extensive use of medical and biological knowledge in order to base this radical opinion on empirical evidence. He qualified his psychophysiological definition of man by claiming further that matter was not the passive substance described by traditional metaphysics but was endowed with an innate *force motrice*. This dynamic principle made the organism, and the psychic activity dependent on it, a self-sufficient entity, thus eliminating the need for an immaterial substance, or soul, to animate, direct, and control it.

La Mettrie's aim was to reject philosophical dualism, especially of the Cartesian type; but along with this, he also intended—though he refrained from attacking religion openly—to discredit the theological dogma of a supernatural and immortal soul. Because such a negation struck at the heart of Christian belief, he had to take precautions, particularly since he was still subject to French censorship. He therefore masked his materialist thesis, somewhat confusingly, with a conceptual scheme and terminology that were meant to be reassuringly scholastic. This evasive maneuver failed, however, to deceive the authorities, who easily recognized the work's underlying materialism and irreligion.

His Thought. In *L'Homme machine* La Mettrie, encouraged by the freedom and security of Holland, presented the same ideas without veiling their true sense. The work expounded, rather bluntly and even recklessly, a mechanistic and deterministic theory of the mind and of all its modalities and manifestations—a daring and (since THOMAS HOBBES) a novel position to take, at least in print. La Mettrie admitted only a difference of degree, not of essence, between the Cartesian animal-automaton, which he interpreted materialistically, and the man-machine, which he viewed as a better organized and thus a more intelligent and educable animal.

La Mettrie drew upon new data, concerning especially the phenomenon of irritability, to prove that the man-machine was capable of behaving normally without benefit of a soul. *L'Homme machine* had, moreover, a polemical edge, for its author foresaw the angry reaction that such a picture of man would provoke in devout circles and sought to parry it in advance. He therefore stated that relevation was no trustworthy guide to understanding human nature, inasmuch as revelation was itself a datum of sense-perception, and must, like all objects of knowledge, be judged by empirical standards as to its truth or falsity.

It is the medical scientist, not the theologian, La Mettrie asserted, who relies on his senses to learn what a human being is. By contrast, the notion of an immaterial and immortal soul is merely a theological invention, with no basis in experience or reason. Although *L'Homme machine* did not explicitly affirm atheism—an act that apparently even La Mettrie found too risky—the work was generally considered atheistic, and rightly so, for its materialism, then as now, implied atheism. It pointed out the futility of positing the existence of a divine creator, because the formation of the world and the causation of all natural events could be attributed more plausibly to the laws governing matter in motion.

Le Système d'Epicure (1750) would sketch, along these lines, a naturalistic theory of the "evolutionary" origins of all living things, including man. La Mettrie's anticreationist speculation in deliberately opposing science to theology, expressed a fundamental challenge to religion—even to DEISM. Religious apologists tried hard at the time to demonstrate, not only the existence and providence of God, but also the truth of Christianity, by means of rational arguments that often turned to science for corroboration. It was in this context that La Mettrie's thought, by citing scientific arguments which rejected spirituality and the supernatural, dealt a severe blow to religion in the faith-versus-unbelief debates that typified the French Enlightenment.

L'Homme machine asserted other opinions that also signified atheism to 18th-century readers, such as the denial of free will, the preference of godless virtue to fanatical piety, the classing of all ritual as superstition, and the allegation that religion, not irreligion, had throughout history brought civil strife, cruelty, and oppression into the world.

In the *Discours sur le bonheur,* La Mettrie's heterodoxy showed a different face, as he vehemently took the side of hedonism against stoicism. While his immediate target was Seneca, the dismissal of Stoic virtue in favor of Epicurean *volupté*, that is, of self-denial in favor of self-gratification, was equally a dismissal of Christian ethics, built largely on the transcendent moral value of continence, self-sacrifice, suffering, and remorse. La Mettrie linked happiness, or *le souverain bien,* to the freest possible exercise of the pleasure-principle, claiming further that, contrary to popular wisdom, evil-doers are not necessarily made unhappy by their actions, and that remorse, being against nature and mentally unhygienic, ought to be avoided in all situations. Misunderstood as an advocacy of immoral and criminal behavior, the *Discours* offended La Mettrie's contemporaries (including many of the *philosophes*), who accused the author of subverting public morality and order.

La Mettrie answered those charges in *Discours préliminaire* (1751). Its chief purpose was to justify "philosophical freedom," or the right to publish opinions that ran counter to established religious and moral maxims. La Mettrie distinguished sharply between philosophy, which sought objective knowledge about nature (both human and non-human), and religion, which, together with morality and politics, was essentially a means of protecting the interests of society by fabricating and inculcating socially useful myths or *préjugés* that disguised the real nature and condition of man.

Thus religion had intrinsically nothing to do with truth; and philosophy, which had to do only with truth, was socially quite harmless because people were in fact ruled, not by philosophical truths, but by the religious and moral fictions they had been taught since childhood. La Mettrie did not mean, by this explanation, to defend religion as a beneficial delusion. Instead, he went on to suggest that in the long run political power, when enlightened by philosophy, could be expected to promote the common good much better than it had in the past when aided by religion. La Mettrie thus envisioned the modern alliance between science and the state that has replaced ecclesiastical pressures on government. In this respect, the *Discours préliminaire* reflected official policy under Frederick II's enlightened and anticlerical rule.

Despite persistent efforts to denigrate or suppress his ideas, La Mettrie significantly influenced the growth of unbelief in the Enlightenment, especially the atheistic materialism of DENIS DIDEROT and PAUL HENRI HOLBACH, who, however, chose to keep silent about their debt to him.

Other articles of interest: **Enlightenment, Unbelief During the. God, Existence of. Revelation, Unbelief in.**

Bibliography

Baruzzi, Arno. *Mensch und Maschine.* Munich: Fink Verlag, 1973.

Boissier, Raymond. *La Mettrie, médecin, pamphlétaire et philosophe.* Paris: Les Belles Lettres, 1931.

Falvey, John. *J. O. de La Mettrie: "Discours sur le bonheur."* Banbury, England: Voltaire Foundation, 1975.

Lemée, Pierre. *J. O. de La Mettrie, médecin, philosophe, polémiste; sa vie, son oeuvre.* Mortain: 1954.

Poritzky, J. E. *J. O. de La Mettrie, sein Leben und seine Werke.* Berlin: 1900.

Thomson, Ann. *Materialism and Society in the Mid-Eighteenth Century: La Mettrie's "Discours préliminaire."* Geneva: Droz, 1981.

Vartanian, Aram. *La Mettrie's "L'Homme machine": A Study in the Origins of an Idea.* Princeton, N.J.: Princeton U. Press, 1960.

ARAM VARTANIAN

LATIN AMERICA, PHILOSOPHICAL BASES OF UNBELIEF IN.

The roots of unbelief in Latin America are many. From a philosophical standpoint, however, three basic sources of such an attitude can be identified: liberalism, POSITIVISM, and Marxism (see KARL MARX). All three are to be understood broadly to include what can only be regarded sometimes as conflicting positions but which on the whole originated within a well-defined historical and ideological tradition, even though they may not always adhere to a strict doctrinal code. Moreover, it should also be noted that a clear-cut historical distinction between these three movements in Latin America is not possible. The dividing line between them is not sharp, and many of the participants of one can also be considered adherents of the other. Liberalism and positivism share many doctrinal points in common, as do positivism and Marxism. In addition, there were also liberals influenced by socialist ideas, although not always by the ideas espoused by Marx and his followers.

In spite of the differences among these three movements, they share, except in a few cases that we shall examine later, a basic antireligious and anticlerical attitude, even if its intensity varies substantially from individual to individual. This hostile attitude is directed primarily against Catholicism and the Catholic clergy, a fact that is to be expected, given the dominance of the Catholic church in Latin America and its historical, doctrinal, and political affiliations.

For liberalism, whose main aim was the political and ideological liberation of the colonies from Spain and Portugal, Catholic doctrine and the hierarchy constituted an obstacle that had to be removed. The church, with its political ties to the imperial powers and its ideological justification of their authority, represented a formidable stumbling block on the road to independence and other plans the rationalist-inspired liberals had for Latin America. It should be noted, however, that despite liberalism's antireligious emphasis, not all Latin American liberals were antireligious. Their opposition was more to clerics and the institutional church than to religion per se.

For the positivists, who came later, church doctrine was viewed as a dogmatic and antiscientific force that stood in the way of progress that could be achieved through social evolution. Finally, for Marxists, the church and religion in general are seen as pacifying instruments used by the upper classes, who desire to preserve the status quo, to prevent social revolution and their own demise. Religion had been regarded by V. I. LENIN as "the opium of the people," and in Latin America, according to Marxists, the Catholic church in particular has played a very effective role in this regard.

In short then, religion, which in the Latin American context usually means Catholicism, has been seen as an instrument of foreign domination, an obstacle to progress, and a means of preserving an enslaved proletariat. It is, therefore, not surprising that liberals, positivists, and Marxists have spent considerable energy opposing the Catholic church.

To these three philosophical positions should be

added a fourth factor that also contributed substantially to the development of an antireligious and anticlerical attitude in Latin America. This is the growing prestige and progressive dissemination of scientific knowledge, particularly that related to the biological sciences, all of which tended to emphasize and support materialistic views of reality. Indeed, Charles Darwin's theory of evolution played an important part in the disenchantment of Latin American intellectuals with religious ideas. (See EVOLUTION AND UNBELIEF.)

Moreover, the traditional and open opposition of the church to scientific views that seemed well established undermined the credibility of the clergy and contributed to the growth of an anticlerical attitude. The role of science in this, however, was not direct. It found expression in and became a part of the three philosophical positions we have outlined. For this reason we do not give science separate consideration. But it should be kept in mind that a large part of the ammunition that Latin American liberals, positivists, and Marxists have used to oppose religious ideas and the organized church is taken from science. In some cases, moreover, scientific knowledge has been instrumental in developing the very positions that are the philosophical bases of unbelief in Latin America.

LIBERALISM

The aftermath of the wars of independence in Latin America in the early 19th century posed tremendous problems of political and social organization throughout the continent. The same Enlightenment ideas that supported the platforms of the movements for independence proved no longer useful after the Spanish and Portuguese colonial regimes were overthrown. Such ideas, which basically defended "freedom" from the religious, political, and economic tenets of the Spanish crown, could not provide an alternative model of social organization with which to replace the three-centuries-old institutions established by the empire.

As we have said, one of the most influential institutions was the Catholic church, which retained considerable economic power, as well as the loyalty of most of the population, after liberation. Not only was the church able to survive the wars of independence, but the hierarchy subsequently posed significant challenges to attempts at undermining its political and social influence. Although the monarchy had been overthrown, its social and cultural structures survived through the still-powerful church.

In order to counter such influence, politicians and intellectuals embraced models of political organization that they believed could effectively restrict religious interference in national affairs. The most important of these models was liberalism, which came to Latin America from Spain, France, and Britain. Spanish liberalism, although short-lived, had been characterized by an unprecedented openness to the principles of mercantilism and political diversity, as well as restrictions on the power and influence of the church.

In particular, the celebrated Cortes (legislature) of Cádiz in 1812 influenced Latin Americans. The Spaniard José Joaquín Mora, a former member of the Cortes, traveled to Chile and in 1828 drafted one of the country's first liberal constitutions. The influence of the Cortes was also considerable in Argentina, Ecuador, and Mexico. French liberalism, which had evolved as a response to the aftermath of the 1789 Revolution, was characterized by a bourgeois-based and antidemocratic ideology. Especially influential in Latin America were Montesquieu and Edgar Quinet, among others. British liberalism, in addition to the principles of laissez faire in economics, was characterized by the establishment of parliamentarianism. Such philosophers as JOHN LOCKE and JEREMY BENTHAM were widely read and translated, and their ideas were applied to the emerging Latin American legal and educational systems.

Latin American followers of liberal ideas adopted the basic philosophical principles of liberal doctrine, namely, freedom of the individual and a critical attitude toward religion in its cultural and social implications. They understood liberalism eclectically and chose to emphasize different aspects of it in different circumstances. They often cited and defended contending tenets within the liberal tradition; indeed, no one tenet can be considered a genuine representative of the doctrine. This is to be expected, however, for even European liberalism lacked unity and consistency of purpose.

Followers of liberal ideas in Latin America embraced those aspects that most closely served their intention of building national states. Such an endeavor entailed conflicts with the church, and Latin American liberals found themselves, at one point or another, in open conflict with the hierarchy. The creation of a republic, a system of laws, and a sense of national identity all posed threats to the corporate interest and status of the church. Major conflicts followed in such areas as education, land and property rights, and other economic and social issues, which often triggered the many civil altercations between liberals and conservatives that characterize the history of 19th-century Latin America.

Ultimately, liberals succeeded in secularizing the state in most of the Latin nations, but they never managed to draw as much popular support for their tenets as the church had done for its own. Indeed, much of the cultural history of Latin America after independence reflects the tension between secular and religious institutions, RATIONALISM and faith, belief and unbelief.

The most important liberals resided in the major cities of 19th-century Latin America. Members of a privileged elite, they were often far removed from the needs and demands of the larger population. Moreover, most of them spent considerable periods of time in Europe, some in exile, some voluntarily. Their preoccupations and culture were derived from European sources, and little, if at all, from indigenous ones. They shared allegiances to the new urban middle class that was generated by the process of industrialization after independence, and they had little contact with the social and ethnic complexities of the constituencies they claimed to represent.

Their contributions to the social, political, and cultural life of the continent, however, were significant and should not be underestimated. Their influence, which covered the period ranging from the wars of independence to the advent of positivism, proved to be the most powerful challenge to Catholic-inspired thought and institutions. The movement experienced particular success during the 1840s and 1860s.

Chile. One of the most noted liberals was the Chilean José Victorino Lastarria (1817–1888), who founded the Liberal party and published perhaps the most important liberal newspapers of his time. As a representative of the Chilean Congress, Lastarria was instrumental in promoting the mandate to secularize education, and he was active in attempting to abolish the *fueros* (privileges) of the church. His lifelong struggle against religion is summarized by his comment to Domingo Faustino Sarmiento in 1876: "There is nothing worse for our societies than Catholic morality." Such writings as Lastarria's *Investigaciones sobre la influencia social de la conquista i del sistema colonial de los españoles en Chile* (1844) and his *Recuerdos literarios* (1868) are examples of anticlericalism.

Similarly—although closer to the tenets of utopian socialism—Francisco Bilbao (1823–1865) shared the feelings of his fellow countryman and articulated one of the sharpest attacks against the Catholic church. In such books as *La sociabilidad chilena* (1844) and *Evangelio americano* (1864), Bilbao opposed Catholicism, suggesting that it denied the most fundamental principles of the republic, which in his view were the sovereignty of men and reason. For this and other attacks, the Chilean church accused him of blasphemy and brought him to trial.

The Argentineans Domingo Faustino Sarmiento (1811–1888) and Juan Bautista Alberdi (1810–1884) were perhaps less outspoken against Catholic doctrine, but they were equally radical in their opposition to that institution. Favoring the economic doctrine of liberalism, they sought to diminish the influence of the church by promoting a policy of Anglo-Saxon immigration and investment in Latin America. In this way, they believed that a national spirit based on enterprise and industriousness, which they felt characterized Europe and the United States, could be attained. These two thinkers are, in fact, immediate predecessors of positivism, and in many points they herald it. They believed Catholicism could best be opposed by removing its economic foundations that were based on feudal structures and by promoting the principles of free enterprise and laissez-faire economics. "Will the clergy," asked Alberdi, "give to our young generations the instinct for mercantilism and industriousness which ought to characterize the South American man? Will they instill the fever of activity and enterprise which would make him a Hispanic American yankee?" (*Bases y puntos de partida para la organización de la confederación argentina*, 1852).

Both Alberdi and Sarmiento made substantial contributions to the creation of contemporary Argentina and to the erosion of church influence in economics and education. Alberdi was the main architect of the constitution in 1853, and Sarmiento was president of the nation, 1868–74. Sarmiento is perhaps the best representative of the brand of Latin American liberalism which, in addition to anticlericalism, was strongly committed against the despotism of the *caudillos* during the period and against the legacy of Spain. His *Civilización y barbarie* (1845) well exemplifies such commitment.

Sarmiento's influence on the Argentinean educational system was also substantial. The well-known "Ley de Educación Común," in force until recently, was engineered by the liberals. This established secular, free, and mandatory education in Argentina and eliminated religious instruction in primary schools. Another important law approved under the liberal government established civil marriage as the only legal marriage in Argentina.

In Mexico, José Luis María Mora (1794–1850) understood the corporate interests of the church to be the biggest stumbling block in the creation of the Mexican Republic. He felt that its many franchises and *fueros* prevented any serious attempt at creating national unity. Mora suggested that the corporatism of the church, as well as the army, weakened public morality. He consequently set out to promote the redistribution of church property and to defend the individual property holder as the bulwark of a free society. His most significant writings are *México y sus revoluciones* (1836) and the essays collected posthumously as *Obras sueltas* (1937).

Mora provided the basis for subsequent attacks on the power and influence of the church that were carried out by liberals such as Ignacio Ramírez (1818–1879). It was Ramírez who passed the reform laws that suppressed monasteries in Mexico; this earned him the name *El nigromante* (the necromancer) for his alleged ATHEISM.

The Remainder of Latin America. Liberal activity in other areas was not as rich as in Chile, Argentina, and Mexico, with no 19th-century intellectuals of the stature of the men discussed, but it was no less significant. In Cuba, Félix Varela (1787–1853), a priest, and José Luz y Caballero (1812–1862), successfully attacked scholasticism, promoted liberal principles, and introduced the rationalist philosophy that would enrich the intellectual life of their country.

In Ecuador, Juan Montalvo (1832–1889) produced some of the sharpest attacks against the regime of Gabriel García Moreno (1860–1875) and his alliance with the church, in such books as *Siete tratados* and *Mercurial eclesiástica*. His anticlerical stands eventually earned him the accusation of heresy. Also in Ecuador, Presidents Vincente Rocafuerte (1783–1847) and Eloy Alfaro (1864–1912) implemented significant anticlerical reforms, particularly in the field of education. In Honduras (but also representing the many Central American nations that came under his leadership between 1821 and 1823) Francisco Morazán (1792–1842) introduced the Lancasterian system of education, abolished tithing, and established freedom of worship.

In Colombia, José María Samper (1828–1888)

was the best representative of the "Generation of 1849," which created the Liberal party and brought José Hilario López to power between 1849 and 1856. This administration enacted the most sweeping anticlerical reforms of the century, the first that truly separated church and state in Latin America. "Until 1848," Samper suggested in 1853, "Bogotá had been held in almost complete subjection by the clergy. The Jesuits and the other friars and clerics dominated most of the families with the power of superstition, and they had been able to fanaticize the masses and make them into blind instruments of absolutistic propaganda" (*Apuntamientos para la historia política y social de la Nueva Granada desde 1810*).

Liberal reforms, although successful in separating church and state, did not achieve the support of the masses, which remained highly religious. Samper himself became a devout Catholic and later suggested that liberalism and Catholicism were not incompatible, urging his followers to moderate their attacks on the church, for "man does not live on science, work, freedom and acquisitions alone, but also on love and religion; that is, on feelings and faith, abnegation and sacrifice, charity and poetry" ("La libertad y el catolicismo," 1873).

Samper's withdrawal from militant anticlericalism provides one of the earliest examples of liberals' recognition of the failure of their movement. Liberalism could remove the political influences of the church on the state, but it could not remove the roots of people's belief. It also illustrates the fact that not all anticlericalism was antireligious. There were many liberals who, although opposed to the institutionalized church, were not antireligious; their opposition was only to those aspects of the church that were in conflict with their liberal political and economic ideas. (The enlightened despot Charles III, who can be considered in some ways the founder of liberalism in Spain and its colonies, is a case in point.)

In summary, then, the liberal struggle against the church took place on different, although intimately connected, levels—economic, political, and cultural. Economically, liberals sought to undermine the power of the church by questioning and attempting to abolish its franchises and claims to landed property. Politically, they sought to reduce the influence of the church on the state, and they established constitutions that emphasized secular principles and institutions. Culturally, they opposed RATIONALISM to superstition and sought to create a national ethos based on the former. In all of this, liberals were successful only to the extent that positivism inherited such concerns and continued the fight with the church for dominance in the field of education. Yet, after the last liberal was gone, the church still retained considerable influence.

POSITIVISM

Positivism has been by far the most pervasive philosophical movement in Latin America to date. Its influence began around the middle of the 19th century and extended to the first quarter of the 20th. The period of greatest popularity occurred between the years 1880 and 1900, although the work of its two most important figures, José Ingenieros of Argentina (1877–1925) and Enrique José Varona of Cuba (1849–1933), extended well into this century.

Positivism means something different in the Latin American context from what it has meant in the history of European and North American philosophy. It cannot be identified exclusively with the positivism of AUGUSTE COMTE (1793–1857), although Comte's thought is one of its most important foundations. In Latin America, positivism includes such diverse elements as the evolutionary naturalism of HERBERT SPENCER (1820–1903), the utilitarianism of JOHN STUART MILL (1806–1873) and JEREMY BENTHAM (1748–1832), and the monistic evolutionism of THOMAS HENRY HUXLEY (1825–1895) and ERNST HAECKEL (1834–1919).

All these perspectives were combined in different ways and with different emphases. Isolated for the most part from others, each country and thinker developed a particular brand of positivism, depending on the sources available and the surrounding circumstances. Latin American positivism, then, is not a monochromatic philosophy; nor is it a close reflection of European positivism. Rather, it is a general attitude that emphasized science to the detriment of metaphysics and theology; indeed, it may be called a "scientism" rather than a philosophy.

All knowledge is to be based on empirical evidence and never on theoretical speculation. In the words of Ingenieros: "Future philosophers will leave to the poets the beautiful privilege of every legitimate hypothesis in order to get closer to less and less inexact forms of expression" *(El hombre mediocre,* 1942).

Positivists also held fast to the principle that society was evolving toward a humanistic stage in which all social evils were to be eradicated. Comte had identified the three stages through which society passes: theological, metaphysical, and scientific or positive. The theological stage is dominated by prejudice and superstition, the metaphysical by speculation, and the positive by knowledge based on experience. This evolution is to be spurred through education, one of the reasons why Latin American positivists did so much to reform their educational systems. This is also the root of positivistic antireligiosity and anticlericalism. The church and its doctrine, with its traditional monopoly on education and what the positivists perceived as its antiscientific spirit, was a colossal obstacle to the positivists' plans for Latin America.

In holding this position they were following Comte's view that traditional religion constitutes an obstacle to human progress, promoting, as it does, superstition, slavery, and militarism. Consequently, Latin American positivists, in accordance with the attempts already made earlier by liberals, tried to separate church and state and to develop secular systems of education based on the scientific principles of Comte, Mill, and others.

The appeal of positivism to Latin American intellectuals can be explained easily in terms of their desire to develop their countries and their unlimited faith in positivistic thought's contribution to orderly progress. As José Echeverría put it, there was "posed a sort of choice between a past, characterized by the presence of the Indian, by the Spanish Catholic colonial theology and culture, and by the oscillation between anarchy and despotism on the one hand and on the other a future that was thought of as the triumph of liberty within order, of democracy, lay education, of science and general welfare, and of the civilized city confronting a retrograde and barbarous countryside" *(La enseñanza de la filosofía en la universidad hispanoamericana,* 1965). Under these conditions the temptation to embrace the positivist philosophy was irresistible.

The practical effects of positivism were felt in almost every country in Latin America that had any claim to intellectual life, but it is in Brazil and Mexico in particular that one can see the pervasive influence of positivism on society.

Brazil. The influence of positivism was felt in Brazil in the middle of the 19th century. In 1856 there appeared the first important work of the movement, *A escravatura no Brasil* by Benjamin

Constant Botelho de Magalhães (1836–1891). It was Luis Pereira Barreto (1840–1923) who popularized positivism with the publication of the first volume of *As tres filosofías* (1874). Constant, as an influential teacher in the Military School of Brazil, trained a whole generation of army officers in the principles of positivism. Both Pereira Barreto and Constant saw in positivism a way of eradicating the influence of traditional scholastic doctrine. As minister of education in the newly established Brazilian republic, Constant worked hard to implement positivist views concerning the separation of church and state and a scientific, nonreligious education.

The influence of Comte in particular was substantial in Brazil. To this day the Brazilian flag carries the motto "Order and Progress," which was one of Comte's favorite slogans. It is well known that Comte, although critical of traditional religion, favored the establishment of a positivist version of the church. Brazil was one of the few places where this idea flourished. Miguel Lemos and Raimundo Teixera Méndez led in founding the Apostolado Positivista do Brasil, which became in all respects a church, with temples, services, and dogma. Elsewhere in Brazil, however, in the so-called School of Recife, positivism maintained its nonreligious, theoretical character. Here the influence of Comte was not so pronounced. Writers like Tobias Barreto, Silvio Romero, and Clovis Brevilaqua favored instead the evolutionism of Spencer. Barreto (1839–1889) in particular maintained a strong and antireligious attitude, equally rejecting miracles, theology, and metaphysics.

The influence of positivism in Brazil extended to thinkers who cannot be classified strictly as positivists. Ruy Barbosa (1849–1923) is a good example. Early in his life he took a strong anticlerical stance that earned him the reputation of being an atheist, even though later in his life he emphasized the importance of man's relation to God. All the same, as the principal author of the first constitution (1891) of the Brazilian republic and minister of justice in the provisional government, he put into effect several anticlerical measures: the separation of church and state, freedom of worship, and church decontrol of marriage, public education, and cemeteries.

Mexico is the Latin American country where positivism became more closely identified with the political establishment, although paradoxically, no positivist work of note was published there in the 19th century. Gabino Barreda (1818–1881)

introduced a Comtean variety of positivism in Mexico. Put in charge of educational reform by the republican government of Benito Juárez in 1867, he introduced drastic changes that reflected his antischolastic views.

Later, during the dictatorship of Porfirio Díaz, it was Justo Sierra who led the intellectual life of the country, although he was inspired more by Mill and Spencer than by Comte. He presented the Porfirian ideal of evolution without revolution in his work *Evolución política del pueblo mexicano.* He served as secretary of the Supreme Court for a time, but his greatest contribution was in the area of education. Porfirio Díaz named him minister of education, and Sierra used this post to reestablish the National University, which had been abolished 50 years earlier as a result of a church-state controversy. Like most positivists, Sierra's anticlericalism is based on his opposition to what he regarded as religious superstition.

Other Locales. The impact of positivist ideas, in education in particular, is evident in other countries as well. Uruguay is a case in point, owing to Alfredo Vázquez Acevedo's influence as president of the university. In Cuba, Enrique José Varona, as minister of education, put into effect drastic reforms that remained in place until Fidel Castro's revolution. As a result, for example, classical languages were dropped from the secondary-school curriculum and the study of science was emphasized. A similar thing happened in Honduras, where the positivist Ramón Rosa (1848–1883) was named minister general by Aurelio Soto, his friend and president. These men carried out ecclesiastical and educational reforms of note.

As with liberals, not all positivists were equally anticlerical and antireligious, and some, like José Manuel Estrada (1842–1894) of Argentina, who adhered to some positivistic ideas in his younger years, rejected positivism later in life and defended the church.

Other positivists that deserve to be mentioned are the Chileans Valentín Letelier (1852–1919) and the Lagarrigue brothers (Jorge, d. 1894; Juan Enrique, d. 1927; and Luis, d. 1948), who maintained positivism in Chile until the 1940s. Also important are Mariano H. Cornejo (1866–1942) in Peru and J. Alfredo Ferreira (1863–1935) in Argentina.

MARXISM

Marxism, like positivism, interprets religion as

superstition and an obstacle to social advancement. They also share an emphasis on science, a deterministic and materialistic view of reality, and the goal of social progress. Both positivism and Marxism attempt to develop a science of society while rejecting, at least on the surface, metaphysical speculation; the basis of all knowledge is experience. Indeed, in many ways Marxism is a type of positivism, and it will become evident that many Latin American positivists were influenced by Marxist ideas. In some cases the church identified the two, accusing positivism of being an evil mixture of liberalism, Marxism, and Freemasonry. But there are differences, some of which are of degree.

Marxists, for example, are more antireligious and anticlerical than positivists, and indeed some positivists adopted religious beliefs in spite of their anticlerical perspective. But in other areas there are qualitative differences as well. For Marxists, the fundamental science is economics, and they believe economic realities determine the course of history. Moreover, while positivism adheres to the basic principle of *evolutionary* change—that is, progress within order—Marxism believes change is possible only through revolutionary upheaval and class struggle, which follows a well-established dialectical process. Finally, some positivists, following Comte, attempted to substitute a positivist religion for what, according to them, were the superstitious forms of established religion. Orthodox Marxism, on the other hand, rejects all religion and replaces it with a secular HUMANISM (unless the government adopting Marxist doctrine becomes repressively totalitarian).

The influence of Marxist ideas in Latin America, particularly in recent times, cannot be underestimated. According to Harold Eugene Davis: "By mid-twentieth century, Marxism had penetrated the liberal and reforming social thought of the Latin American reform movements much as positivism had penetrated the liberalism of the nineteenth century. Marxism slowly found acceptance in the intellectual middle class, in university circles (in the student movement for university reform in the 1920s), and among immigrant and native labor leaders, appearing in an emerging labor press. Limited to a small minority among the professional classes in the early years of the century, it came to be the most common pattern among professionals by the 1960s" (*Latin American Thought*, 1972; see Bibliography below).

The ground for the eventual growth of Marxism in Latin America was prepared by a number of European socialists throughout the 19th century who were widely read in the Hispanic countries and Brazil. Their ideas, however, were often mixed with other views, such as liberalism and positivism. The influence of the utopian socialism of Claude Henri de Saint-Simon (1760–1825) and Charles Fourier (1772–1837) are evident in the *Dogma socialista* of Esteban Echeverría (1805–1851), for example. Through him and the Association of May, which he founded to oppose the dictatorship of Juan Manuel de Rosas (1793–1877) in the 1830s, they influenced the young intellectuals who came to be known as the Generation of 1837.

Utopian socialism, which Domingo Miliani considers to be the "transitional thread from Romanticism to Positivism" in Latin America, can also be found outside Argentina, particularly in the work of the Chilean Francisco Bilbao. He founded, in 1850, a society of young intellectuals committed to the criticism of clerical institutions and thought, which he called the Society of Equality.

In the later part of the 19th century, working-class Marxism was introduced by the leaders of an incipient labor movement who were influenced by Marx and the Russian anarchists Michael Bakunin (1814–1876) and Prince Peter Kropotkin (1842–1921). The most important center of this movement was Argentina, where its leader, Juan B. Justo, and a group of his followers, such as Americo Ghioldi, Nicolas Repetto, and Alfredo Palacios, constituted the leadership of the Socialist party of Argentina.

José Ingenieros, one of the most important positivists in Latin America, became associated with this group for a brief period. It must be remembered that his father was an Italian immigrant who became a labor leader and journalist and defended Marxist socialism. Some of these socialist ideas can be seen in Ingenieros' *Sociología argentina,* inspired by the evolutionary social thought of Spencer and the sociological psychologism of Gabriel Tarde (1843–1904). Later in his life Ingenieros abandoned many of his socialist ideas and followed a more clearly defined positivist course, although he continued to emphasize the role of economic forces in social change. This led A. Zum Felde to remark that he "makes economics the omnideterminant factor and the key to the entire process of social evolution" (*Indice crítico de literatura hispanoamericana,* Mexico, 1954). But Ingenieros did not maintain his youthful devotion to Marxism.

In other countries there was also Marxist activity. Diego Vicente Tejera (1848–1903) founded the Cuban Socialist party at this time, and in Uruguay, Emilio Frugoni (1880–1969) founded the Karl Marx study center in 1904.

In Peru, the influence of Marxist theory can be seen in Manuel González Prada (1848–1918), the main ideological source of the Peruvian Popular Alliance for American Revolution (APRA), and his followers Victor Haya de la Torre (1895–1979), founder of APRA, and José Carlos Mariátegui (1895–1930). Prada himself cannot be considered a Marxist; he can be viewed better in terms of the rationalism he borrowed from Ernest Renan (1823–1892) in order to attack the clergy, what he considered to be the superstitions of the church, and the system which, according to him, enslaved the Indian.

Prada was also strongly influenced by the positive sociologism of Comte. Nevertheless, his emphasis on economic conditions over education reveals to some extent his reliance on Marxist principles. His anticlericalism and opposition to Catholicism are part of a general rebellion against traditionalism. As he put it: "Positivistic science . . . in only one century of application to industry has produced more good for humanity than have thousands of years of theology and metaphysics" (*Páginas libres,* Lima, 1946). As expected, he argued for the complete separation of church and state.

20th-Century Marxism. In spite of these developments, it was not until this century that Marxist thought acquired sufficient importance to be regarded as a respectable ideological and political force. Comtean and evolutionary forms of positivism were too strong in the 19th century to allow Marxism to develop significantly—not that Marxism and positivism were regarded as opposed. As we have seen with Ingenieros and Prada, positivism and Marxism were frequently allied. Still, it was the positivist strain that dominated 19th-century thinkers.

By the beginning of the 20th century the positivist ideology had run its course, and the atmosphere was ripe for new ideas. Some of these took the form of a vitalist rebellion against positivism, which was inspired by Henri Bergson, while others consisted of a revival of Thomism and scholastic thought. But along with these came Marxism. Scholastics saw their main task as the defense of traditional Christian ideas and the authority of the church. Many of those who led and participated in the vitalist rebellion against positivism were also devout Christians. But most Marxists and Marxist-influenced authors considered Catholic doctrines superstition and opposed the power and privileges the church had accumulated through centuries of colonial rule and which it still claimed a right to have.

Marxist thought has played an important role in several political movements in Latin America: the Mexican Revolution, the APRA movement in Peru, the Cuban Revolution of Fidel Castro, and the liberation movements in several countries, most recently in El Salvador and Nicaragua. Some of its ideas have also been adopted by members of a group of radical clergy and proponents of "theologies of liberation," although the debate as to how much Marxism is contained in liberation theology, first expounded by the Peruvian priest Gustavo Gutiérrez, has continued into 1985.

After the Mexican Revolution of 1910, the situation was favorable for the development of a Marxist and anticlerical current in Mexico, encouraged and aided by the government. The country was secularized and the economic and political power of the church broken, although its spiritual hold on the population continued unabated. Vicente Lombardo Toledano (born 1894), labor leader and former disciple of Antonio Caso, was one of the first who adopted Marxism. In his major work, *Escritos filosóficos* (1937), he addresses the problems of social reform along orthodox Marxist lines. Also important for the movement are Narciso Bassols (1897–1959), Eli de Gortari (born 1918), and Adolfo Sánchez Vázquez (born 1915). Bassols put his ideas into effect as minister of state in what has been called "socialist education" in Mexico in 1934. Sánchez Vázquez is part of the generation of Spanish emigrés who settled in Mexico after Franco's victory in Spain in the late 1930s. Both he and Gortari have written a great deal about social issues.

In Peru, after González Prada's death, his two disciples and heirs, Haya de la Torre and Mariátegui, parted ideological company. Mariátegui embraced communism, while Haya de la Torre developed a peculiar brand of socialist thought, which he wanted based on autochthonous conditions. According to Haya de la Torre, the Marxist interpretation of European history is not valid for America, because Latin America may not have to go through the revolutionary stage prescribed by Marxism.

Mariátegui, on the other hand, followed a Marxist line, although his ideas were far from being orthodox. Indeed, unlike most Marxists and Communists, he explicitly proposed a religious and spiritual conception of man, and his world view was nonmaterialistic. He had his first-born child baptized in the Catholic church and refused to join Haya de la Torre in his campaign for a complete separation of church and state. In his *Siete ensayos* (Lima, 1928) he writes: "The days of anticlerical a priori reasoning have been completely surpassed— that period when freethinking criticism contented itself with a sterile and cursory dismissal of all dogmas and churches . . ."

The Cuban Revolution has not produced any theoretician of note thus far; nevertheless the actions of the government show strict adherence to orthodox Marxist ideology. The results are strong antireligious and anticlerical measures. Although at the beginning of the revolution there seemed to have been an alliance between the leaders of the revolutionary government and some members of the Catholic clergy, all appearance of cooperation soon ended. Castro expelled hundreds of members of the clergy, secularized education, abolished private education, which until then had been dominated by religious orders, and in general relegated the role of the church to a purely spiritual one. Indeed, Catholicism is discouraged, although not persecuted. The same has happened to the less important Protestant churches, although in the beginning they were spared and were often used in the regime's struggle against the Catholic church.

There are also Marxist and Communist nuclei in other countries of Latin America, which militate against the power of the established church in particular and religious ideas in general. Among the intellectual leaders of these groups (which are not always orthodox) have been Caio Prado Junior, Artur Gianotti, and Joâo Cruz Costa in Brazil; Luis Carranza Siles and Rolando Requena in Bolivia; Rómulo Betancourt (who turned anti-Communist in later years) in Venezuela; Cayetano Betancour and Alfredo Trendall in Colombia; José Portuondo and José Marinello in Cuba; Julio César Jobet, Salvador Allende, and Luis Recabarren in Chile; José Revueltas in Mexico; and others, like Che Guevara, who defy geographical classification.

In summary: Liberalism, positivism, and Marxism developed to some extent in Latin America as challenges to the predominance of Catholic thought and influence. In spite of periods of popularity and power, these movements have not been successful in attaining large popular support for their platforms. With the exception of Marxism, the challenges to Catholicism have been restricted to relatively small, although often powerful, groups of intellectuals. Moreover, in some cases, even members of the church have adopted some of the tenets of liberalism, positivism, and Marxism. As a result one can only conclude that orthodox Catholicism has perhaps seen its influence diminished through the efforts of these movements but that the bases of religious faith in the area, inspired by Catholic doctrine, remain strong.

Other articles of interest: **Enlightenment, Unbelief During the. Spain, Unbelief in.**

Bibliography

Aguilar, Luis, ed. *Marxism in Latin America*. New York: Knopf, 1968.

Crawford, William Rex. *A Century of Latin American Thought*. 2nd ed. Cambridge: Harvard U. Press, 1961.

Davis, Harold Eugene. *Latin American Social Thought*. Washington, D.C.: U. Press of Washington, 1961.

——. *Latin American Thought: A Historical Introduction*. New York: Macmillan, 1972.

Frondizi, Risieri, and Jorge J. E. Gracia. *El hombre y los valores en la filosofía latinoamericana del siglo xx*. Mexico: Fondo de Cultura Económica, 1975, 1981.

Jorrin, Miguel, and John D. Martz. *Latin American Political Thought and Ideology*. Chapel Hill: U. of North Carolina Press, 1970.

Pike, Frederick B., ed. *The Conflict Between Church and State in Latin America*. New York: Knopf, 1964.

Stabb, Martin. *In Quest of Identity: Patterns in the Spanish American Essay of Ideas, 1860–1960*. Chapel Hill: U. of North Carolina Press, 1967.

Whitaker, Arthur, et al. *Latin America and the Enlightenment*. 2nd ed. Ithaca, N.Y.: Cornell U. Press, 1961.

Zea, Leopoldo. *The Latin American Mind*. Trans. James H. Abbott and Lowell Dunham. Norman: U. of Oklahoma Press, 1963.

JORGE J. E. GRACIA
IVÁN JAKSIĆ

LAW, HARRIET, in full, Harriet Teresa Frost Law (1831–1897), an English FREETHOUGHT and women's-rights lecturer and a magazine editor. She was born on Nov. 5, 1831, in Ongar, Essex. After her father's business fell upon hard times, the family moved to London. She ran a school to help her parents and, as a strict Baptist, taught Sunday School. But in London she came in contact with open-air, freethought lecturers, and at first attempted to defend her faith against the onslaughts of the anti-Christian lecturers. She also attended freethought lectures in the Philpott Street Secular Hall, where she debated with GEORGE JACOB HOLYOAKE, CHARLES SOUTHWELL, and CHARLES BRADLAUGH in an informal way, mostly away from the audience.

Harriet Frost's views about religion began to change as a result of her contact with freethought. She also met her future husband, Edward Law, at the Secular Hall. They were married in January 1855. Shortly after her marriage, both she and her husband became secularists. Harriet began to lecture for freethought in 1859. She is described as a short, stout woman with a low voice, which became rather harsh in her later years. Although not an intellectual, Mrs. Law had a profound knowledge of the Bible and a great deal of courage in dealing with hostile reactions from audiences.

In 1860 Harriet Law made her first lecture tour for freethought. She was called the best female lecturer since EMMA MARTIN, and her reputation was soon established. She then began to tour regularly, leaving her husband to care for their children. As a woman lecturer, she was a novelty. The fact that she was opposing religion and advocating women's rights put her in the select company of FRANCES WRIGHT, Emma Martin, and ERNESTINE ROSE. When ANNIE BESANT became popular, the novelty had worn off; by about 1876 Mrs. Law had been displaced by Annie Besant.

During the 1860s and 1870s Harriet Law lectured under the auspices of the secularists, the republicans, and the Reform League. She showed political leanings toward the left, once offering KARL MARX the only forum he could find. She printed his writing in her *Secular Chronicle* magazine, which had been founded by George Reddalls of Birmingham in 1872. She purchased the magazine from the Reddalls estate in 1876, and published it as a penny weekly until 1878, when it ceased publication. Mrs. Law estimated that she lost 1,000 pounds on the magazine during those three years.

Mrs. Law began to suffer from bronchitis, which forced her to retire from the lecture platform at the close of the 1870s. She died of a heart attack in July 1897.

Other article of interest: **Women and Unbelief.**

Bibliography

Foote, G. W. "Harriet Law." *The Freethinker.* July 4, 1915.

Moss, Arthur B. "Famous Freethinkers I Have Known—Mrs. Harriet Law." *The Freethinker.* June 6, 1915.

Royle, Edward. *Radicals, Secularists and Republicans: Popular Freethought in Britain, 1866–1915.* Totowa, N.J.: Rowman & Littlefield, 1980.

Secular Chronicle, The. Birmingham: 1876–78. Ed. Harriet Law.

Wheeler, J. M. "Death of Harriet Law." *The Freethinker.* Aug. 1, 1897.

GORDON STEIN

LAW AND UNBELIEF, THE. This article is a brief historical review of instances in which religious unbelievers have been singled out for unfair or less than equal treatment under the law. The cause of such unfair treatment may be a law passed by the U.S. Congress or a state legislature. It may be that an unfair principle was embodied in a state constitution. Often the unfairness is historically rooted in common law, which originated in England centuries ago.

A distinction must be made here between laws or court rulings that single out the unbeliever specifically and laws requiring that all people comply with the beliefs or personal moral convictions of one or more religious groups. Examples of the latter are BLASPHEMY LAWS and laws that require all or some places of business to refrain from operating on Sunday because some Christians believe everyone should be worshiping "their" god on the day of the week he allegedly arose from the grave. While the second type of laws obviously infringe on individual liberty, they do not single out the unbeliever specifically, and this variety of legal/religious, antifreedom measure will not be covered in this article.

The Colonies and Unbelief. The laws enacted in some of the American colonies were unsurpassed in their discrimination against unbelievers, when compared with anything since the American

Revolution. In colonial America, being an unbeliever (or a believer in the wrong religion) was hazardous not only to health but also to life.

In Massachusetts (1641) and Connecticut (1650) anyone who worshiped the wrong god (or presumably no god at all) was to be put to death. The Massachusetts law quoted Exodus and Deuteronomy in its support. Virginia decreed the death penalty for speaking impiously of the Trinity or any one of the divine persons or for speaking against any article of the Christian religion. Apparently one could break the Sabbath twice or curse twice and live, but upon the third conviction for either the penalty was death.

The famous so-called "Toleration Act" of Maryland (1649) is taught to school children as the first law granting religious freedom in the colonies. What is not taught is that the law prescribed toleration only for Christians. Death was the punishment for blasphemy and denying the Trinity. For good measure the executed party was to have his or her property confiscated by the state, thus impoverishing the deceased's heirs.

The remarkable group of deists (see DEISM) who were primarily responsible for founding the United States saw to it that the laws just cited would never again be promulgated in their country. But the founders were not perfect. As will be shown, many avenues were left open by which the legal system mistreated unbelievers.

The Witness and Unbelief. Perhaps the most notorious mistreatment of unbelievers after the American Revolution was the disqualification of a person to testify in a court of law if that person did not express belief in a deity or a belief in divine retribution for perjurers. The last cases of disqualification fall within the memory of many freethinkers living today. The root of judicial discrimination against unbelievers is the idea that if an individual does not believe that he or she will be punished by God in an afterlife for lying on the witness stand, he or she cannot be trusted to tell the truth.

No one has ever produced evidence that theists are more honest under oath than atheists or that Christians who believe in hell are more likely to tell the truth than Christians who do not believe in hell. However, even in the extremely unlikely event that such evidence is presented, there would still be no basis for disqualifying a witness. Every person has the right to present testimony and be judged as to its credibility. This idea is embodied in the Equal Protection Clause of the Fourteenth Amendment

to the Constitution; adoption of this amendment following the Civil War should have ended the witness disqualifications at once. But while some judges recognized the amendment's application to witnesses, many judges simply disregarded it.

The legal root of discrimination against unbelieving witnesses can be traced back to the British jurist, Edward Coke. Lord Coke was one of the great legal minds of all time, developing and refining countless principles of the English common law. Many of his principles still survive today in England, the United States, and countries that were once part of the British Empire. However, in the realm of religion, Coke was a bigoted product of his time.

In 1607, relying in part on previous court decisions, Coke formulated the common-law principle that for a person to be competent as a witness, he or she must believe in both orthodox trinitarian Christianity and in a future state of divine rewards and punishments. Coke felt perfectly justified in declaring this rule on both scriptural and legal bases.

By the next century, it was becoming apparent that it was against the self-interest of England to enforce Coke's rule against Jews and foreign nations whose citizens were not Christians. It was bad for trade, and if it was bad for trade it was bad for England. Thus Coke's rule was modified in 1745 in the case of *Omichund* v. *Barker,* with no real concern for individual rights. The *Omichund* judges did not even honestly admit that they were overruling Coke's 1607 rule; they pretended that their new rule had always been the common-law rule.

Of course, the new rule was only marginally better, and by the end of the 18th century it was not even certain exactly what the new rule was. The first report of the *Omichund* case was published in *Atkyns' Reports* in 1765. According to Atkyns, Chief Justice Willes stated in his opinion that a witness must believe in some god and in divine rewards and punishments in the presumed afterlife. Willes' alleged manuscript of this decision was published in 1799 in *Willes' Reports.* According to this version, Willes required witnesses to believe in a god and believe that this god would punish them in this world or the next if they were sinful.

When American courts started looking at the issue, they found that they had a choice of two different common-law rules to follow. Of course there was a third alternative. The courts could have applied basic principles of individual rights and fairness and thrown out both rules completely. It is likely that some lower courts did just that and ignored the rule. Some states adopted laws or constitutional provisions that no one could be prevented from testifying because of religious belief. But, for many courts the only argument was over which version of the *Omichund* rule to follow.

Most early American decisions followed the rule as reported by Atkyns. This was true in the federal case of *Wakefield* v. *Ross* (1827) and in two state cases, *Atwood* v. *Welton* (1828) and *Jackson* v. *Gridley* (1820). However, some judges were embarrassed by the fact that the Atkyns version of the rule disqualified Universalists, who did not believe in post-mortem punishments and thought everybody would be saved. (See UNIVERSALISM.) Still, Universalists could be said to believe in some measure of rewards and punishments during natural life. Furthermore, in a later North Carolina case, *State* v. *Pitt* (1914), it was pointed out that the Atkyns version would also disqualify Jews.

In order to avoid disqualifying Jews, Universalists, and other "respectable" religious people, most state courts eventually adopted the Willes rule. While there was strong historic evidence for preferring Willes to Atkyns, the primary motivation of the courts seems to be that they thought Universalists and Jews were respectable and should not be disqualified. Again, as in *Omichund,* a marginal advance was made, albeit through rationalization rather than rationality.

One state, South Carolina, interpreted the *Omichund* rule more liberally than either the Atkyns or Willes ruling. The court, employing even more rationalization than other courts, used language written by one of the other judges in the *Omichund* case, Lord Chancellor Hardwicke. In *Jones* v. *Harris* (1846), the court decided that to be a competent witness, one must "only" believe in "the being of a God, and his providence." This decision is odd in that the philosophical basis for requiring religious belief for testifying was that unless people believe some supernatural power would punish them for lying, they could not be trusted to tell the truth. If the South Carolina court could dispense with the need for belief in divine punishments, it might as well also have scrapped the requirement of belief in a God who would let a witness lie and get away with it.

Almost all states now have either constitutional or statutory provisions forbidding witness disqualifications on the basis of religious belief or disbelief. (Restrictions still exist in North Carolina and Maryland, but they could never be enforced.) It would be unthinkable today for a court to attempt to enforce such a provision. However, judicial scruples concerning this matter were not always as strong, as is evidenced by a disgraceful case, *Clinton* v. *Ohio* (1877). As Frank Swancara (see Bibliography below) reported in *Obstruction of Justice by Religion:*

"The Constitution of 1851 of that state [Ohio] provided that no person should 'be incompetent to be a witness on account of his religious belief.' In spite of that clear clause the Supreme Court Commission in 1877 held that to be a competent witness one must have 'a belief in a Supreme Being, who will certainly, either in this life or in the life to come, punish perjury.' The opinion reasoned that since the constitution also preserved 'oaths and affirmations' it intended to continue the requirement of the common law of a religious belief for the competency to take an oath or affirmation. Such reasoning ignores the purpose of the clause relating to witnesses; the latter clause could not have been intended merely to remove some imaginary disqualifications. Its obvious purpose was to remove a disability which the common law imposed on persons not believing in Divine punishments."

While we have seen that many judges have little regard for individual rights, it is most surprising to see a court blatantly ignore a constitutional provision that clearly recognizes the existence of such a right. Fortunately, this kind of extreme judicial lawlessness has been the exception rather than the rule. Other courts in the 19th century in states such as Illinois, Virginia, and Kentucky recognized the rights of unbelievers to testify.

While rules barring the testimony of unbelievers existed, there were many bad results. The cases are too numerous to receive individual mention, and it is suggested that interested readers see Swancara's book. One particularly disgraceful case reported by Swancara is *Beason* v. *Alabama* (1882). In this case, an eleven-year-old girl was raped. The defendant was indicted, tried, and convicted for the crime. The Supreme Court of Alabama reversed the conviction on the grounds that the trial court erred in allowing the little girl to testify. Although the child proved that she understood the difference between right and wrong and that she knew it was wrong to tell a lie, the court ruled that she should have been disqualified because "she manifested an entire want of instruction as to the nature and effect of an oath, of all religious training, and utter ignorance of the existence of a Supreme Being, the rewarder of truth and the avenger of falsehood."

ROBERT G. INGERSOLL summed up the injustice of disqualifying unbelieving witnesses in a scathing comment on a case cited by Swancara: *The Central Military Tract R.R. Co.* v. *Rockefeller* (1856). Ingersoll said: "The Supreme Court of Illinois decided, in the year of grace 1856, that an unbeliever in the existence of an intelligent First Cause could not be allowed to testify in any court. His wife and children might have been murdered before his very face, and yet in the absence of other witnesses, the murderer could not have even been indicted. The atheist was a legal outcast. To him, Justice was not only blind, but deaf. He was liable, like other men, to support the government, and was forced to contribute his share towards paying the salaries of the very judges who decided that under no circumstances could his voice be heard in any court. That was the law of Illinois, and remained so until the adoption of the New Constitution. By such infamous means had the Church endeavored to chain the human mind, and protect the majesty of her God."

The Dying Witness and Unbelief. As with the living witness, there was a time when the declarations of a dying person (often a murder victim) were inadmissible in court if the deceased did not hold the "correct" religious beliefs. The rationale was parallel to the disqualification of witnesses: if the dying person did not believe in some sort of god who would punish him or her for lying, he or she could not be trusted to tell the truth.

The English common-law rule was that if the dying person did not believe in a future state of rewards and punishments (either because he lacked belief or was too young to have learned of it), that person's declaration was inadmissible in court. The extent of injustice under this rule is illustrated by the British case of *Rex* v. *Pike* (1829). A four-year-old child was fatally beaten by blows to her head. As she was dying, she identified her murderers to her mother. Since it could not be proved that the child had any understanding of an afterlife, the alleged assailants, although they were indicted, apparently were never tried.

The key case in 19th-century American jurisprudence appears to have been *Donnelly* v. *New Jersey* (1857). Here we find a marginal improvement over the British rule. The *Donnelly* court placed the burden of proof upon the accused murderer to show that the victim did not hold the required belief. Albert S. Moses, having been stabbed in the throat, named James P. Donnelly as his assailant before he bled to death. Donnelly attempted to prove that Moses did not believe in a future state of rewards and punishments, and the jury was instructed to disregard Moses' dying words if it was convinced by the evidence of Moses' unbelief.

Incredibly, the U.S. Supreme Court, in *Carver* v. *U.S.* (1867) stated the following about dying declarations: "They may be discredited by proof that . . . [the victim] did not believe in a future state of rewards and punishments." Although this dictum did not even have anything to do with the case, it gave lower courts an excuse to be unjust toward the unbelieving murder victim.

Nevertheless, the Oregon Supreme Court, in *Oregon* v. *Yee Gueng* (1910), upheld the judge in the trial court who refused to instruct the jury with the *Carver* dictum. Alabama modified *Carver* to require "only" a belief in rewards and punishments in this life or the next. And it appears that the *Carver* dictum was never applied against Unitarians or Universalists. Finally, the Alabama Supreme Court, in *Wright* v. *Alabama* (1931), ruled explicitly that an atheist's dying declaration was admissible. Occasionally, the U.S. Supreme Court has been defied when its declarations are perceived to be unjust. Although the *Carver* dictum has never been formally repudiated by the Court, it would be unthinkable for any lower court to follow its rule on dying declarations today.

The Testator and Unbelief. The dying unbeliever, even if not a murder victim, sometimes had his or her right to bequeath property to whomever or whatever he or she chose taken away by judicial bigotry. This was likely to happen when it was perceived that the bequest would somehow be antireligious. In the case of *Zeisweiss* v. *James* (1870), Levi Nice left real estate to the Infidel Society of Philadelphia to build a hall for the free discussion of religion and politics. The court held that, being "an association of infidels and unbelievers," the society could not receive the bequest.

Ten years later, the Pennsylvania Supreme Court struck again in *Manners* v. *Library Company* (1880). Dr. James Rush was the testator and an "infidel." His father was Dr. Benjamin Rush, an orthodox Christian famous for his contributions to the American Revolution. James, in his will, left most of his estate to the Philadelphia Library to erect a new building and to purchase any books for it as long as they did not contain "ribaldry or indecency." He wanted nothing excluded on the grounds that it was not in agreement with conventional views on several subjects, including theology. Robert Manners filed a suit contesting the will in 1878, although it had been admitted to probate nine years earlier. The lower court upheld the will and Manners appealed to the state Supreme Court. While the court upheld the will because it did not require the library to include any book, it was made clear that if Dr. Rush had expressly directed the library to include antireligious books, the entire will would have been declared invalid.

The will of John Bryan never reached the courts, but it received a great deal of attention from the other two branches of government in Ohio. Bryan died in 1918, leaving 500 acres of land to the state for a natural-history preserve, providing there should never be a church or religious exercises on the land. The state legislature kept accepting the gift but three governors vetoed the acceptance. Finally, in 1923, the legislature overrode the governor's veto.

Vidal v. *Girard's Executors* (1844) is notable for going all the way to the U.S. Supreme Court and for the famous lawyer who argued the case against the will—Daniel Webster. Stephen Girard's will established a "college" for orphaned boys. He directed that no religion be taught in the college, no religious exercises be held there, and no members of the clergy be allowed on the premises. He wanted the boys to be brought up in a nonreligious atmosphere so they could choose or reject religious beliefs in maturity. Webster attacked the will with an unsurpassed viciousness as being anti-Christian and anticlergy. The ultimate irony was his contention that the boys, not having been taught about a future state of rewards and punishments, would not then be qualified to testify in a court of law. To the great Daniel Webster, two wrongs did make a right.

The Supreme Court, making a fine distinction, upheld the will, saying it did not actually aid infidelity or attack Christianity, since it only required that Christianity not be taught. If Girard had, however, directed that Christianity be impugned or repudiated, the will would not have survived.

Custody of Children and Unbelief. Swancara relates two cases of famous persons in England whose children were taken away from them merely because they were atheists. Although the United States seems not to have had any comparable cases, the British cases are fascinating examples of some of the most cruel legal treatment of un-

believers on record. Swancara justifiably calls it "judicial kidnapping."

The first case involves one of the greatest English poets, PERCY BYSSHE SHELLEY (*Shelley* v. *Westbrook*). Shelley's wife, the 19-year-old Harriet, drowned herself in 1816 (only six years before Shelley himself died at the age of 30). A custody battle took place over the Shelley children, with Shelley having to fight Harriet's parents. Shelley was an avowed atheist who was expelled from school for writing *The Necessity of Atheism,* a pamphlet that remains a minor freethought classic to this day. He had also written a poem called "Queen Mab," which was declared blasphemous by British courts. The Westbrooks objected to the fact that Shelley was an atheist, and his liaison with Mary Wollstonecraft Godwin may also have angered them. He was not shown to be unfit as a parent, but for a bigoted court, Shelley's ATHEISM made him unfit, and his children were taken from him.

The second case involves a less famous figure but one well known in FREETHOUGHT history, ANNIE BESANT (*In re Besant,* 1879). Annie and the Reverend Frank Besant had two children, a son born in 1869 and a daughter, Mabel, born in 1870. Annie, at one time a believer in the Church of England in which her husband was a minister, fell away from her faith. This broke up the marriage. In 1873 the couple separated and an apparently amicable custody arrangement was made. Annie had custody of Mabel for 11 months a year and of the boy for one month. Apparently, as long as Annie remained "in the closet" the arrangement was acceptable to Frank. Annie was of the highest moral character, and there was no reason to accuse her of being unfit. But Annie soon went public with her views, publishing several books advocating atheism and going into business with the outspoken British atheist, CHARLES BRADLAUGH. Frank sued to have Mabel taken away.

The court ruled that Annie could not be faulted as a parent but then engaged in an incredible series of rationalizations, ostensibly showing how Mabel's welfare would be in danger if she stayed with her mother. It was said that Mabel might grow up to write the same kinds of books as her mother. It was said that no minister's wife would associate with Annie and the same dire fate of being unliked and shunned awaited Mabel if she remained with her unpopular mother.

The "judicial kidnapping" was carried out when Mabel was recovering from scarlet fever. The girl physically resisted but the law of course prevailed over a fit mother, a child who wanted to stay with her mother, and justice.

Later in life, Annie Besant left atheism and became a Theosophist. She took over leadership of that unorthodox, mystical group upon the death of its cofounder, Madame Helena Blavatsky. An interesting question is whether Annie would have lost her child if she had been a Theosophist rather than an atheist at the time of the custody battle. No one can doubt that she at least would have had a better chance; Theosophists, after all, believe in God.

The Draft and Unbelief. Whenever the draft has been in effect in the United States, in order to be declared a conscientious objector a young man has had to base his case on religious beliefs, specifically a belief in a supreme being. While many people believe that any draft is involuntary servitude and should not exist, all should wonder how those who advocate the draft could justify the requirement of religious belief for conscientious objectors.

There is a common misconception that the case of *U.S.* v. *Seeger* (1965) overturned the religious requirement. But Seeger did not claim to be an atheist, and his unorthodox religious beliefs were merely found to qualify under the law as it is written. The court refused explicitly to deal with the questions of whether an atheist could qualify as a conscientious objector and whether the law itself should be declared unconstitutional. It is difficult to speculate what the rules will be now that registration is being strictly enforced, but it is safe to say that there is, at the very least, some doubt that the unbeliever will be treated equally with the believer.

The Religious Test and Unbelief. Often a religious test has been required for a person to hold a public office. One of the most famous cases was *Attorney General* v. *Bradlaugh* (1885). Bradlaugh, the atheist, was elected to the House of Commons in England, in 1880. But he refused to take the religious oath required for being seated. He was reelected several times and finally took the oath. He began his duties as a member of Commons, including voting. As soon as he cast a vote, the government prosecuted him for having voted without taking the required oath. The court held that, although he had said the required words, he had not taken the oath because he did not believe what he said.

In spite of this setback, Bradlaugh ultimately triumphed. In 1888, Commons passed his bill allowing nonbelievers to affirm rather than take the oath, both for membership in Parliament and to be a witness in court.

Article 6 of the United States Constitution forbids the requirement of any religious test for public office. However, this provision was not applicable to the states. Surviving into the 20th century were constitutional provisions in eight states requiring a person to believe in a god to hold public office (Ark., Md., Miss., N.C., Pa., S.C., Tenn., and Tex.).

These state religious tests were overturned by a landmark case before the U.S. Supreme Court in 1961, *Torcaso* v. *Watkins.* Roy Torcaso applied for the position of notary public, a position virtually anyone can hold if qualified. Torcaso's employer had asked him to become a notary for the convenience of having one in the office.

Torcaso applied and the commission was apparently granted. But when he was asked to declare his belief in God, he refused and he was denied the commission under Article 37 of the Declaration of Rights of the State of Maryland: "That no religious test ought ever to be required as a qualification for any office of trust or profit in this state, other than a declaration of belief in the existence of God. . ."

Torcaso brought suit in the Maryland courts charging that Article 37 violated Article 6 and the First and Fourteenth Amendments of the Constitution. The state courts rejected his argument on the grounds that Torcaso would not be punished for his beliefs or be compelled to believe in God. The Supreme Court found that Article 37 violated Torcaso's freedom of religion (First Amendment) and that the First Amendment was applicable to the states through the Fourteenth Amendment. The court found this sufficient reason for Torcaso to win and thus did not consider the Article 6 argument.

It is unfortunate that the *Torcaso* case was not decided on Article 6 by simply saying that the Article 6 prohibitions against religious tests apply to the states. In basing its decision on Torcaso's religion, the court wrote a strange footnote declaring certain nontheistic beliefs to be religions: BUDDHISM, TAOISM, ETHICAL CULTURE, and, incredibly, secular HUMANISM. This rationalization was necessary because the court did not have the courage to declare that freedom of religion includes freedom *from* religion.

Philosophically, it seems absurd to consider secular humanism, a nontheistic and nonsupernatural belief system, to be a religion. In practical terms, this has given many religious believers, particularly fundamentalists, ammunition against nonbelievers. Whenever identification as a religion is somehow disadvantageous, religious believers claim that secular humanism and atheism are religions also (if the Supreme Court said it, it must be true). But when religion brings an advantage, the "nontheistic religions" are conveniently forgotten.

While the *Torcaso* case would appear to have overturned all state requirements of religious tests and despite its less than satisfactory reasoning, it is surprising to find that the religious test remains in the constitutions of Maryland, North Carolina, Pennsylvania, and Texas. A note in the Maryland statute book points out that the requirement has been found unconstitutional. In North Carolina, a 1972 opinion of the attorney general was that the religious test was unconstitutional.

Although it would seem that religious-test requirements are nothing but pieces of dead wood that have not yet been thrown out, the question surfaced in 1981 in Texas in *O'Hair* v. *Hill*. MADALYN MURRAY O'HAIR, in a series of complicated legal maneuvers, challenged the Texas state constitution's requirement that a person believe in a supreme being to hold office. A three-judge panel of a federal appeals court dismissed all of O'Hair's arguments with judicial rationalizations. However, one of the three judges dissented in part, and two months after the decision O'Hair was granted a rehearing before the entire appeals court. In July 1984 Texas state officials admitted that the state constitutional requirement violates the U.S. Constitution. Thus ended what will probably be the last religious-test case in the U.S.

Other article of interest: **Church, State, and Religious Freedom.**

Bibliography

Hartogensis, B. H. "Denial of Equal Rights to Religious Minorities and Non-believers in the United States." *Yale Law Journal* 39 (1930).

Holdsworth, W. S. "The State and Religious Non-conformity: An Historical Perspective." *Law Quarterly Review* 36 (1920).

Kauper, Paul G. *Religion and the Constitution.* Kingsport, Tenn.: Louisiana State U. Press, 1964.

O'Hair, Madalyn Murray. *Freedom Under Siege.* Los Angeles: J. P. Tarcher, 1974.

Pfeffer, Leo. *Church, State and Freedom.* Boston: Beacon Press, 1953.

Swancara, Frank. *Obstruction of Justice by Religion.* Denver: W. H. Courtright, 1936.

———. *The Separation of Religion and Government.* New York: Truth Seeker Co., 1950.

HOWARD L. GLICK

LEIBNIZ, GOTTFRIED WILHELM VON (1646–1716), German philosopher. See **German Literature, Unbelief in Modern.**

LEICESTER SECULAR SOCIETY, THE, enjoys a special place in the annals of British secularism, for though it is a provincial society, it has established a reputation that reaches far beyond the bounds of the industrial city in the east Midland region of England which is its home base and from which it takes its name.

Leicester has always enjoyed something of a radical reputation, and its people have given their support to many progressive causes. The works of THOMAS PAINE exercised considerable influence, and the townspeople rallied financially to support RICHARD CARLILE in his fight to have Paine's writings published. The radicalism of Carlile sowed the seeds for a ready reception to political Chartism, essentially a movement for electoral reform, and then to the ideas of ROBERT OWEN. It was supporters of Owen who gave birth to Leicester's first Secular Society in 1853.

The present Leicester Secular Society claims to have been founded in 1851, though documentary evidence to establish the validity of this is not available. Still, the possibility that it was founded then cannot totally be ruled out. The 1853 society does not appear to have flourished, but clearly people continued to give organized secularism support in the town, for it reappeared publicly in 1861; however, it was not until 1867 that the society was firmly established. It has continued as an active freethought body since.

Unlike most local FREETHOUGHT societies the L.S.S. did not merge its identity with the NATIONAL SECULAR SOCIETY, and in the 1870s the two became involved in a bitter quarrel, the L.S.S. standing as moderate and positive, as distinct from the negative and militant ATHEISM of the N.S.S. under CHARLES BRADLAUGH. The controversy led to the formation of an N.S.S. branch in

Leicester to compete with the L.S.S.; however, the latter proved to be the more attractive group, and eventually when the controversy was resolved the N.S.S. branch disappeared. By 1881 full accord reigned between the L.S.S. and the N.S.S., and when in March of that year the society's new hall was opened, Bradlaugh shared the platform with his rival GEORGE JACOB HOLYOAKE, whom Leicester had supported, as well as a galaxy of leading British secularists.

The Secular Hall in Humberstone Gate, in the heart of Leicester, is perhaps the L.S.S.'s greatest claim to fame, for it is now the only Secular Hall in Great Britain—and perhaps the world—still occupied and used (though used only in part) by the society for which it was built. In actual fact, the hall is not owned by the L.S.S.; ownership is vested in the Leicester Rationalists Trust, for which the society provides the trustees. The hall is the focal point for society activities, and while financial conditions have forced the organization to lease out the main hall and the shop that forms part of the front of the building, it uses a large room on the ground floor for public functions and a smaller room as a members' lounge. There is also a large display window that carries the secularist message to the multitude of people who pass the Secular Hall daily.

The building was designed by the architect Larner Sugden, himself a secularist, who used a style he described as a "free treatment of Flemish Renaissance." It looks typically Victorian, being built mainly of red glazed bricks and ornamented stone. The outside front of the building carries five terracotta busts, the "five saints" as they were soon dubbed—Socrates, VOLTAIRE, Paine, Robert Owen, and Jesus. The local Christians could not have been more upset had the secularists included a bust of the devil, and pulpits thundered with outraged condemnation. But the Leicester secularists argued that in his day Jesus was a freethinker, and so the bust remained. In this day and age it arouses no comment, let alone condemnation, and most people, even secularists, pass the bust without a glance.

In March of 1981 the main hall was brought back into use for a secularist meeting on a Sunday afternoon, the first time it had been used by the secularists for some years. It was a glimpse of past glory, for the meeting was packed to capacity to hear one of Britain's leading political figures, Michael Foot, a member of Parliament and leader of the official opposition to the Conservative government. Unlike many politicians, Foot has never hidden the fact that he is an atheist, having been a member of the National Secular Society for many years. He spoke on the contribution freethinkers had made to British life.

The work of the L.S.S. has revolved around three headings: agitational, educational, and social. Of these the latter has declined considerably in recent years, the hall no longer being central in the social life of most members. However, the agitational work continues unabated with campaigns against various forms of repressive legislation such as the BLASPHEMY LAWS, which remain on the books in Britain. The educational side of the society's work consists in the main of regular lectures and discussions held throughout the autumn and winter. There has probably been no leading British secularist over the past hundred years who has not graced the society's platform one or more times. The range of subjects covered at meetings has been immense, and speakers have been drawn from all professions and shades of opinion, for the society has always made a point of ensuring that its members and the general public (meetings are open to all at no charge) hear all points of view.

Some secularists have, of course, had closer connections with the society than others. It was the L.S.S. who gave JOSEPH MCCABE his first employment after he left the priesthood of the Roman Catholic church, appointing him resident manager. This help was never forgotten by the famous rationalist, who regularly addressed meetings and eventually was elected an honorary member. Another celebrated freethinker and author employed by the society was F. J. Gould, who wrote a history of the organization. The Leicester Secular Society must be one of the few, if not the only, English provincial secularist groups to have had its history published.

The past century saw the rise and fall of English secularism, and there can be no doubt that the L.S.S. is now but a pale shadow of its former self; nevertheless it remains an active society, and its membership has started to increase. It faces major problems, not the least of which is having a historic building to maintain. Changing population patterns in Leicester, which has included a massive influx of Asian immigrants, most of them Muslim, also present challenges to the L.S.S. It is attempting to make contacts with these newcomers in order to introduce them to secularist ideas.

Bibliography

Gould, F. J. *History of the Leicester Secular Society.* Leicester: Leicester Secular Society, 1900.

Royle, Edward. *Radicals, Secularists and Republicans: Popular Freethought in Britain, 1866–1915.* Totowa, N.J.: Rowman & Littlefield, 1980.

ROBERT W. MORRELL

LENIN, VLADIMIR ILYICH (1870–1924), Russian revolutionary, born V. I. Ulyanov in Simbirsk, where he spent his early years. The namesake of the Russian czar who converted pagan Russia to Christianity by decree in the 10th century, Lenin was born into the family of a highly successful czarist bureaucrat. For his diligent efforts to promote education in vast portions of the Russian empire, Ilya Nikolayevich Ulyanov, Lenin's father, was eventually awarded the title and status of a hereditary nobleman. Thus Lenin, the founder of the Soviet state, was a "scion of the landed gentry," as he put it himself on one occasion in 1904.

Religion in the Early Life of Lenin. According to all the available accounts, Lenin grew up in an exceptionally harmonious family environment. There is no evidence to suggest that religion ever became a major issue in the Ulyanov home. Nevertheless, it stands to reason that the differences in religious upbringing and outlook of the parents must have resulted in an undercurrent of tension.

Lenin's father had been raised in the Orthodox faith; he was devoutly religious and scrupulous in church attendance. His mother had been brought up by a Lutheran aunt and reportedly did not like to go to church. While religious rites and ceremonies were observed in the Ulyanov home and Lenin's family regularly celebrated what Pushkin in *Eugene Onegin* called the "customs of dear ancientry," only Lenin's father retained a deep religious faith to the end of his life.

Lenin's mother, by contrast, was not a religious person. Whether her indifference to religion was due to skepticism, apathy, or dislike of the ritual of the Russian Orthodox church is not known. In any event, only during times of extreme stress and despair is she reported to have turned to prayer. The Ulyanov children were allowed to decide for themselves in matters of religion. When Alexander Ulyanov, Lenin's older brother, announced one day that he would no longer attend church, his father—though wrought with anxiety—accepted the decision of his son, and the issue was not raised again.

According to his own admission, Lenin broke with religion at the age of 16. By the winter of 1885–86, his sister recalls, Lenin began to throw off authority, developing a "very oppositional attitude towards the high school authorities, his high school studies, as well as religion," a portent of things to come. Lenin nevertheless continued to earn top grades in all his subjects, including religion, at the Simbirsk Gymnasium.

Lenin's "religious upbringing" figured importantly in the strong recommendation for admission to the University of Kazan he received a year later from his high school principal, F. M. Kerenski, who—such are the vicissitudes of history and the irony of fate—was the father of Alexander Kerenski, whose government Lenin would overthrow in 1917. His ATHEISM notwithstanding, Lenin went through a full-scale Orthodox wedding ceremony when he was married to N. K. Krupskaya in Shushenskoye, his place of exile at the time.

Lenin's attitude toward religion, a distinct type of political atheism, was a *Zeitgeist* phenomenon reflecting, on the one hand, his hostility toward the established church and its interdependence with the autocracy, and, on the other, his preoccupation with issues ranging from an extreme anticlericalism to spiritual slavery, which suggest the influence of such seminal Russian radical thinkers as Bakunin, Belinski, Chernyshevski, Herzen, and Pisarev. To the extent to which Lenin saw in the autocracy his mortal and implacable enemy, his hostile attitude toward religion and the established church in Russia was a foregone conclusion. To him, the members of the clergy were "gendarmes in cassocks." Along with the bureaucracy and police, he regarded the Russian Orthodox church as an integral part of the autocracy, destined to be "smashed" in the revolution.

In spite of the claims by various Soviet writers, Lenin's theoretical contributions to the understanding of religion were neither original nor particularly profound. Part of the reason for this, no doubt, was Lenin's conviction that the nonexistence of God had been conclusively demonstrated by science. The problem of religion, as far as Lenin was concerned, reduced itself to popularizing LUDWIG FEUERBACH's insight into the nature and origin of the "religious illusion" and to drawing the practical and political consequences from the exposure by KARL MARX and Friedrich Engels of the social function of religion as an instrument of class exploitation.

Unlike his erstwhile teacher and mentor, G. V. Plekhanov, Lenin did not regard religion as merely a kind of intellectual error that could be overcome by intellectual and scholarly methods. To Lenin, religion was "one of the most odious things on earth," a moral outrage and a social disease, whose elimination from human life required an active struggle and persistent campaign. The abusive and venomous language employed by Lenin is a measure of his hatred of religion:

"All worship of a divinity is necrolatry [worship of the dead]," he wrote to Maxim Gorki in 1913. ". . . any religious idea, any idea of any god at all, any flirting with a divinity even is the most inexpressible. . . [and] dangerous foulness, the most hideous 'infection.'" He continued: "A million physical sins, obscenities, acts of violence [including the corruption of young girls by Catholic priests] and infections," Lenin told Gorki, are infinitely preferable to, and much less dangerous than, the "*subtle* spiritual idea of god, dressed up in the most attractive 'ideological' garbs."

Lenin's neo-Marxist conception of religion centers around two basic assumptions regarding the *source* and the *function* of religious beliefs and institutions. In his essay, "The Attitude of the Workers' Party to Religion" (1909), he wrote that the roots of religion "in modern capitalist countries are mainly *social*." The origin of religion, according to Lenin, must be sought in the "social oppression of the working masses," in their "complete helplessness before the blind forces of capitalism, which daily and hourly inflicts upon ordinary working people the most horrible sufferings and the most terrible torments—a thousand times greater than those inflicted by extraordinary events, such as wars, earthquakes, etc."

Religion, in short, has its source in the fear and insecurity generated by capitalism. "Fear made the gods," Lenin wrote. The belief of the masses in a better life after death, he confidently asserted, is nothing but the result of their impotence in the struggle with their exploiters. "Religion," according to Lenin, "is one of the forms of spiritual oppression which everywhere presses heavily on the masses of the people, crushed by their endless work for others, by destitution and isolation," a form of oppression, moreover, which cannot and must not be separated from the class struggle.

Lenin's second assumption concerning religion is that it always functions as an instrument of exploitation in the hands of the ruling classes. He repeated with approval Marx's celebrated dictum that "religion is the opium of the people," elaborating further that "religion is a kind of cheap spiritual booze, in which the slaves of capital drown their human image, their demands for a life more or less worthy of man." Once again joining issue with Gorki on the subject of religion, Lenin pointed out that in practice the idea of God helps the exploiters to keep the people in slavery. Therefore, any attempt to beautify the idea of God is tantamount to the beautification of the chains by which ignorant workers and peasants are fettered.

"In history and in real life," Lenin lectured Gorki, "God is first of all the complex of ideas generated by the brutish subjection of man both by external nature and by class oppression—ideas which *consolidate* this subjection and *lull to sleep* the class struggle." The idea of God, Lenin argued, always serves to bind "the oppressed *classes* with a faith in the *divinity* of their oppressors." In modern times, Lenin concluded, "*any,* even the most refined and best-intentioned defense or justification of the idea of god is a justification of reaction."

Lenin was adamant that the struggle against religion cannot be separated from the class struggle but must always be subordinated to it. So far as the state is concerned, religion must be declared a private matter. In other words, there must be complete separation of church and state in modern society. But as far as the party of the socialist proletariat is concerned, religion is not and cannot be a private affair. "Our party is an association of class-conscious and leading fighters for the emancipation of the working class. Such an association cannot and must not be indifferent to the lack of consciousness, ignorance or obscurantism in the form of religious beliefs." "A Marxist must be a materialist, i.e., an enemy of religion." For "Marxism is materialism" and "as such. . . relentlessly hostile to religion."

Religion in the Class Struggle. Unlike Plekhanov, who regarded religion as a pseudoscience, a kind of innocent superstition, Lenin perceived a pernicious purpose and sinister design behind all religion, namely, its function as an instrument of class oppression. Religion, in Lenin's view, had a class character; the struggle against religion, therefore, was an important and inseparable aspect of the class struggle. Lenin's conception of religion as a class phenomenon made it impossible for him to accept the classical Marxist view of religion as a transient historical phenomenon, inextricably linked to socioeconomic exploitation and destined to "wither away" as the classless and stateless society, devoid of all exploitation, becomes a reality.

Lenin, in short, did not believe in the automatic "withering away" or the self-liquidation of religion that is implicit in classical Marxism. He called for the organization of "the most widespread scientific education and antireligious propaganda" while at the same time cautioning against "insulting the [religious] feelings of believers since this would only lead to the strengthening of religious fanaticism." But reliance on "untiring atheist propaganda and an untiring atheist fight" are not enough.

The most important thing is "to awaken in the still undeveloped masses an intelligent attitude towards religious questions and an intelligent criticism of religion." The elimination of religion ultimately requires the severing of its socioeconomic roots, freeing the worker "from his belief in a life after death by rallying him to a genuine struggle for a better life here on earth . . . for the creation of paradise on earth."

Thus, in religion as in politics, Lenin in the end refused to place his trust in the determinism of the Marxist doctrine; in religion as in politics, he ended up advocating a voluntarist solution to the problem of social change. The revolutionary, he concluded, would be foolish to wait idly and passively for the "withering away" of religion and also could not afford to rely exclusively on antireligious propaganda. Lenin's prescription for dealing with religion is strikingly similar to his militant call for political action in *What Is to Be Done?* (1902): the creation of an organization of dedicated men to provide leadership in the struggle for the realization of the socialist vision, which—by definition—includes the abolition of religion.

It is one of the great ironies of history that Lenin, who had such a deep hatred and contempt for religion in any form and throughout most of his adult life, argued forcefully against the "God-building" of Lunacharski, Bogdanov, and Gorki, and that he should after his death in January 1924 become the subject of a grotesque cult in his native land—a cult that has transcended the dimensions of many religious cults in the world today. It is doubly ironic that this cult transformed Lenin into a godlike figure, because throughout his life Lenin, like Marx and Engels, had adamantly rejected any form of leadership adulation or worship. But perhaps in a strange sort of way the fantastic dimensions of the Lenin cult in the Soviet Union and the rest of the Communist world constitute a measure of the Promethean task to which Lenin dedicated his life.

Other articles of interest: **Propaganda, Antireligious. Yaroslavski, Emel'yan M.**

Bibliography

Besançon, Alain. *The Rise of the GULAG: Intellectual Origins of Leninism.* New York: Continuum, 1981.

Eissenstadt, B. W., ed. *Lenin and Leninism.* Lexington, Ky.: Lexington Books, 1971.

Fischer, Louis. *The Life of Lenin.* New York: Harper & Row, 1964.

Harding, Neil. *Lenin's Political Thought.* Vol. 1: *Theory and Practice in the Democratic Revolution.* Vol. 2: *Theory and Practice in the Socialist Revolution.* New York: St. Martin's Press, 1977–81.

Kline, George L. *Religious and Anti-Religious Thought in Russia.* Chicago: U. of Chicago Press, 1968.

Krupskaya, N. K. *Memories of Lenin (1893–1917).* London: Lawrence and Wishart, 1942.

Lenin, V. I. *Collected Works.* 40 vols. Moscow: Foreign Languages Publishing House, 1960–68.

Meyer, A. *Leninism.* Cambridge: Harvard U. Press, 1957.

Schapiro, Leonard, and Peter Reddaway, eds. *Lenin: The Man, the Theorist, the Leader.* New York: Praeger, 1968.

Shub, David. *Lenin.* Garden City, N.Y.: Doubleday, 1948.

Theen, Rolf H. W. *Lenin: Genesis and Development of a Revolutionary.* Princeton, N.J.: Princeton U. Press, 1979.

Tucker, Robert C., ed. *The Lenin Anthology.* New York: Norton, 1975.

Ulam, Adam B. *The Bolsheviks.* New York: Macmillan, 1965.

Valentinov, Nikolay. *Encounters with Lenin.* Trans. P. Rosta and Brian Pearce. London: Oxford U. Press, 1968.

———. *The Early Years of Lenin.* Trans. and ed. Rolf H. W. Theen. Ann Arbor: U. of Michigan Press, 1969.

Wolfe, Bertram D. *Three Who Made a Revolution.* Boston: Beacon Press, 1962.

ROLF H. W. THEEN

LESSING, GOTTHOLD EPHRAIM (1729–
1781), German dramatist and critic. It is doubtful
at best whether Lessing deserves a high place
among the famed unbelievers of Western spiritual
history. In contrast to VOLTAIRE and the *philosophes*, who were so lucid that they did not perceive
the complexities of the theological problems of
their time, Lessing confronted Christianity on its
own grounds by painstakingly asking its very
"realities" for their truths: the Gospel, divine
revelation, God's claim on man, the manifestations
of this claim in the Judeo-Christian tradition, and,
above all, God's covenant with man through
Christ.

The son of a Lutheran pastor, Lessing had been
destined for the ministry and "heard" theology for a
few semesters. Although he gave up these studies
for the vocation of a literary critic and dramatist, he
nevertheless remained throughout his life an amateur in theological matters, one who questioned
Christian orthodoxy—especially its Lutheran
variety—from within. This position distinguishes
him from his deistic predecessors in England and in
France (see DEISM), most of whom had nothing
but scorn for the Bible and the church, as well as for
the church's traditions and paraphernalia. For this
reason Lessing, "the great Lord's dear bastard" as
he called himself, has frequently been designated
"a deist with a difference." Two of his most
significant literary works, the play *Nathan the Wise*
(1779) and the tract *The Education of Mankind*
(1780), reflect this crucial difference in theological
attitude.

Lessing's Theological Stance. Yet it is generally acknowledged that Lessing's ultimate theological position is far from definitely established.
The most recent *Forschungsbericht* still depicts
him as wavering between rationalist (see RATIONAL-
ISM) and irrational positions. Critics of theological
rationalism see him as *the* 18th-century believer in
the autonomous growth of reason, for whom the
"God of history" is nothing but a temporary, albeit
useful, adjunct; while orthodox apologists portray
him as a committed Lutheran. For others, he was a
daringly independent thinker, a truth-seeker of
indomitable courage, one of those *heretics* whose
quest expresses the deepest religiosity, that "genuine religious reverence for the infinite." A judicious
literary critic has put the problem of Lessing's
enigmatic religiosity quite succinctly: "Lessing
refers often and energetically to the Christian faith
and calls himself a good Lutheran, and yet there is
no Christian dogma that he did not question, and

none that he professed *expressis verbis*."

The reasons for Lessing's vacillations between
extreme theological positions derive from the
German constellation—unique to the 18th century—
of a self-assured Lutheran church in the central
and northern German states, the subversive intellectual bustle of the ENLIGHTENMENT, and reform
movements within Lutheranism. These reform
movements, which had been prompted by the
spirit of the age to "humanize" theology, took two
forms in Germany. In the first place, there was the
rationalist attempt of the neologists to incorporate
God into the human capabilities, that is, to reduce
God in order to make him comprehensible to
human understanding. The other religious force
was Pietism. Although rationalism and Pietism
seem to stand at the opposite ends of the emotional-
intellectual spectrum of religion, the two did spring,
as Ferdinand Baur, Albrecht Ritschl, and Karl
Barth have shown, from similar, if not identical,
origins. Their common denominator was individualism, the notion that the "*in-dividium*, as un-
divided and indivisible, . . . recognized himself as
a being who is at least similar, at least related to the
ultimate reality of God."

Eighteenth-century individualism meant not
only "the enthronement of man" as the highest
terrestrial authority, but it also signified "the
making inward of what is external, objective to
man, by which it is robbed of its objectivity, . . .
[and] made into something within man." With
their eyes fixed on the individual, his human potent
ial, and his "happiness," the rationalist theologians
thus had set out to recast religion into a form
amenable to man by making it "reasonable and
natural," while the Pietists emphasized the individual religious experience.

It is hardly surprising that Lessing absorbed
more of the neologists' suppositions than he would
have cared to admit, particularly elements of J. F.
W. Jerusalem's and Johann Semler's teachings,
which meshed quite oddly with his orthodox
heritage and with his temperamental inclination
toward Pietism. These disparate spiritual influences were increased by his intensive readings in
G. W. von Leibniz and BENEDICT SPINOZA. Even
though there is no inexorable causal link between
these influences and critical positions Lessing
assumed on different occasions, it is an indisputable
fact that the theological views he held do not coa-
lesce into anything approaching a system. Not only
are there glaring contradictions within the body of
his theological work, but in some instances in-

consistencies can even be found within a single treatise. An additional complication regarding Lessing's theological position stems from his decision to adapt, as he wrote to his brother Karl, his weapons to his opponents. In no way, he asserted, would he accept all he had said in the manner of an intellectual exercise ("gymnastically") as dogma. It must, of course, also be kept in mind that such "gymnastics" were often necessitated by the intransigence of a militant, if not triumphant, Lutheran church that was not prepared to surrender the hard-won gains it had made a century earlier at the conclusion of the Thirty Years War.

Nevertheless, there are a number of *constants* characterizing Lessing's theological work. In *Nathan the Wise* and a number of his essays he displays his preference for a Christian disposition over speculative thought and dogmatic rigidity. Yet foremost among these constants is his ever-present readiness to challenge accepted ideas, to rush to the defense of the embattled (as for instance in his vindications of heretics), and to espouse seemingly hopeless causes. Since he thrived on combat, he embarked on many of these campaigns for the sheer sake of engendering intellectual debates, but in some cases he did indeed risk his own security in order to draw out his adversaries, to force them to assert intellectually indefensible positions, and to cleanse spiritual life of compromising ambivalence.

Publication of the Reimarus Fragments.
The general uproar Lessing created with the publication of the *Fragments* (1774–78) is an instructive case in point. With this venture Lessing, who up to then had primarily been engaged in literary pursuits and had kept his theological views mostly to himself, suddenly—in the manner of Sören Kierkegaard's Mephisto—leapt onto the public stage of religious controversy. In *Contributions to Literature and History,* he printed excerpts from an unpublished work, *Apology for Rational Worshippers of God,* by Samuel Reimarus (1694–1768). The first piece, "On the Toleration of the Deists: Fragment of an Anonymus Writer," appeared in 1774 and attracted little attention. In 1777, however, Lessing published five more installments, the second of which, "Impossibility of a Revelation Which All Men Can Believe on Rational Grounds," together with a further fragment released in 1778, "On the Intentions of Jesus and his Disciples," squarely addressed *the* theological problem of the age.

In this second fragment, Reimarus denied the plausibility of biblical Christian revelation when juxtaposed with the conception of a "reasonable, natural" religion. Regarding Jesus and the disciples, Reimarus began by separating the teachings of the historical Jesus from those of the apostolic church, and went on to "prove" that Christian articles of faith have little in common with the convictions of the Galilean "apocalyptic," who had no conception of a cosmopolitan church of those who believe in eternal spiritual salvation through his redeeming death.

Although Lessing wrote a series of commentaries on the *Fragments* entitled *Editor's Contrasts,* wherein he took exception to most of Reimarus' propositions, his assertion that the questions Reimarus raised were signficant for their substance and methodology was understood by the orthodox establishment as a challenge to its essential tenets. Lessing was met with no less than 32 rebuttals, the most substantial of which were those of Pastor Melchior Goeze of Hamburg. In contrast to his partisans, Goeze did not turn on the *Fragments* but on Lessing himself, reproaching him for two cardinal transgressions, one substantive, the other formal. He accused Lessing of sacrificing the Bible in order to save religion; furthermore the religion he was trying to save was no longer that of Christ. In the second place, Goeze held that Lessing would have observed good form if he had published the *Fragments* and his *Contrasts* in Latin, that is, for the educated reader, rather than in German for public consumption. Before the censor's office in Brunswick forbade Lessing to protract the dispute, the attacks by the orthodox had given him the opportunity to answer his detractors in a brilliant series of polemics.

The central issues of the dispute over the *Fragments*—the relationship between biblical revelation and reason, the place of revelation in history, and the divinity of Christ—are also the focal points of Lessing's theological interests. In "New Hypothesis Concerning the Evangelists Regarded as Merely Human Historians" (1777–78), which Lessing considered his finest theological accomplishment, he had once more taken up the question of the Gospels. He found that the first three are closely tied to Judaism and portray Jesus as an inspired, wonder-working *man,* whereas John's Gospel had been conceived as a guidebook for the emerging Christian church and therefore presents a different, sanctified image of Jesus. Yet Lessing was, in contrast to Reimarus, sufficiently circumspect to realize that in order to find answers to the historical

Jesus, the "sources" must first be critically examined. Because of the controversy still smoldering about the *Fragments*, Lessing transferred his investigation of theological questions to the realms of dramatic literature and the philosophy of history. As a result, the play *Nathan the Wise* and the treatise *The Education of Mankind* revolve around the same central theme found in the dispute over the *Fragments:* the problem of positive or revealed religion.

Nathan the Wise. It is a testimonial to Lessing's prudence that he wrote *Nathan the Wise*, his gospel of religious tolerance, in blank verse and set it in the Jerusalem of the Crusades, thus removing its thought and action in tone, place, and time from the battleground of the *Fragments*, over which it arches like "a rainbow after the thunderstorm." In *Nathan the Wise*, Lessing not only expands the conventional 18th-century family comedy into a family comedy of mankind but he also gives the traditional dramatic form unprecedented depth by turning the play into a forum where the claims and suppositions of revealed religion are on trial.

In act 3, scene 6—the middle of the play—the Jewish merchant Nathan, the hero, is asked by the powerful sultan which of the three faiths—Judaism, Christianity, Islam—is the true revealed religion. The gist of Nathan's response, the celebrated ring-parable, has become a paradigm of enlightened sagacity. According to Nathan, it is no longer possible to discern the religion originally revealed. Rather the adherents of each of the three faiths have the opportunity to prove that theirs is the true religion, particularly since, in the words of the parable, its followers are beloved in the sight of God and man. Crucial in Nathan's elucidation is the implicit acknowledgement that there *is* one faith, and that the spirit and the power of this true faith will reveal themselves in the *moral* conduct of its devotees. In the play there is only one wholly negative figure, the Patriarch of Jerusalem, a caricature of orthodoxy, who distinguishes himself through his intolerance and inaccessibility to reason. In the end his claims are rendered ineffective since the "natural" and "spiritual" family bonds of all major characters supersede the dogmatic "rights" of the church.

The important element in *Nathan*—which characterizes Lessing's theology as well as that of the rationalists and Pietists—is the conviction that the true faith will bear the fruits of morality. In this assertion one finds a significant element of continuity in Lessing's religious deliberations, since he already had disclosed a comparable view in his first theological essay, "Thoughts on the *Herrenhuter*" (1750), published posthumously. There, as in *Nathan the Wise*, he holds that "man was created to do deeds, and not for the purpose of rationalizing." The spirit of this early essay, which exalted the Christian *vita activa* of fellowship, love, and compassion, thus also informs his last dramatic creation. The same applies to the "The Testament of St. John" and its legacy, "Children, love one another!" The fact that Nathan is a widely traveled and successful merchant, who acquired his wisdom not from books but from practical experience, reinforces this constant in Lessing's religious criticism. The other tenet of Lessing's belief, that the true faith will manifest itself through time, makes revelation a dimension of history and constitutes a thematic bridge to *The Education of Mankind*.

The Education of Mankind. The relationship between revelation and reason—the two antipodes of 18th-century thought representing orthodox Christian dogma and the intellectual tenor of the Enlightenment—underlies the historical analyses and projections of Lessing's last great philosophical-theological work. By fusing this relationship with the idea of historical development, he achieved in *The Education of Mankind* a justification of positive religion that sets him apart from all representatives of the Enlightenment. His equation of revelation and education was the decisive measure: "What education is to the individual man, revelation is to the whole human race." The treatise shows that educational contents and methods must be in agreement with the maturity of the learner.

For the primitive Hebrews, whom God had chosen to demonstrate his pedagogy upon, revelation constituted the only means of guidance. Yet in order to become permanently useful, "the development of revealed truths into truths of reason, is absolutely necessary." Revealed truths were "certainly not truths of reason, but they were revealed in order to become such." Under Persian rule in Babylonia (538–332 B.C.), exposed to the influence of a more advanced culture, the Hebrews not only ennobled their conception of the divine by becoming familiar with the idea of God as the One, but they, whose reason had up to then been guided by revelation, suddenly began to use their reason in order to give cogency to their revelation. This, Lessing states, was "the first reciprocal influence which the two [reason and revelation] exercised on one another; . . . without it either of them would have been useless."

Nevertheless, the relationship between revelation and reason remains ambiguous in *The Education of Mankind*. In one section he disparages revelation; in another, reason. Inspired by Spinoza's thought, he not only demonstrated that historical truths, which are unprovable by their very definition, had to turn into truths of reason to be valid, but he also asserted that there is no definitive truth whatsoever. Rather, all truths are conditioned and limited by the culture and the time that formed them. The theological consequence of this position follows in Section 72: we not only have dispensed with the Old Testament, but "We are gradually beginning also to be less dependent on the New Testament." Lessing's view that even the four Gospels are nothing but pedagogical catalysts that will, like all other revealed truths, become unnecessary in due course, leads to the question of how he envisioned the future of mankind.

Like J. G. von Herder, Lessing attributed to mankind an inner force, the "smaller, faster wheels" of Section 92, that will propel it forward on a course prescribed by its own genius. In order to intimate the dynamic essence of human history, its process of *becoming*, Lessing relies on Spinoza's concept of *divine immanence*, a concept that—paradoxical as it may sound—allows for an explanation of reality in worldly terms. Lessing's acceptance of the idea *hen kai pan* (one and all) links him with Goethe and his contemporaries, whereas his prediction of the destiny of mankind, which rests on the belief in the perfectibility of man, characterizes him as a representative intellectual of the Enlightenment. What he foresaw was nothing less than another chiliasm. Thus he sounds almost hymnic when he presents *his* vision in Sections 85 and 86 of the treatise: "It will come! it will assuredly come! the time of perfecting, when man . . . will do right because it *is* right, not because arbitrary rewards are set upon it . . . . It will assuredly come! the time of a new eternal gospel, which was promised us in the primers of the New Covenant itself."

History has refused to honor Lessing's prophecy. Events and developments in the 19th and 20th centuries have not only refuted his notion that mankind is continually becoming wiser; on the contrary, they have seen "advanced" forms of man's inhumanity to man. Lessing's outlook had built on the optimistic philosophy of Leibniz, on the belief that what is best must be, and what must be is best, and that the history of mankind is unfolding itself according to the plan of providence. The same optimism motivated Lessing's preoccupation with Freemasonry, which he embraced in order to probe the possibility of a society distinguished for genuine tolerance.

Yet a suggestion of the causes of the disasters of modern history can already be found between the lines of Lessing's own reflections. Regarding his simultaneous struggle against Lutheran orthodoxy and the neologists, he wrote on Feb. 2, 1774, to his brother: "We are one in our conviction that our old religious system is false. But I cannot agree with you that it is a patchwork of bunglers and half-philosophers. I know nothing in the world upon the study of which human intelligence has been more acutely shown and exercised. What really is a patchwork of bunglers and half-philosophers is the religious system which they now want to put in place of the old; and with far more influence upon reason and philosophy than the old arrogated to itself."

In another letter to his brother, Lessing compared orthodoxy to "impure water" that was being poured out for the "manure" of neology. In contrast, it was Lessing's purpose to purify the faith. In spite of this noble intention the question must be asked whether Goeze was right after all when he accused Lessing of sacrificing Christianity in order to save religion. To satisfy the requirements of "enlightened" reason, Lessing did indeed give up much, perhaps too much. In Section 73 of *The Education* he suggests that the concept of original sin and the conception of Jesus as the son of God are only metaphors that are useful in making the unfathomable intelligible to the common mind. Thus Lessing not only denied the reality and eternal validity of biblical truths, but he also thought that by making the concrete truth of the Gospel relative, he could be all the more certain of salvaging its spirit and *inner truth*: "The letter is not the spirit, and the Bible is not religion," he had claimed in *Contrasts* to the *Reimarus Fragments*. Although Luther had insisted on the irrefragability of the scriptural word, Lessing invoked the reformer's spirit to bear witness against one of the cornerstones of Lutheranism: "You have freed us from the yoke of tradition: who will free us from the unbearable yoke of the letter!"

Is it possible to preserve and uphold the spirit of something once the "realities" have been discarded that engendered it? Can, in other words, the divine attributes of perfection and love, justice and mercy, survive in a world that considers itself emancipated from God, a world that has loosed upon itself as many subjectivities as there are individuals and that is no longer capable of conceiving one truth but only partial truths, perspectives, and relations? As full of promise as Lessing's vision was, mankind has proved in the 20th century that it does not fare well without certainties.

But was it Lessing's fault that his fellow men failed to actualize his lofty conception of the human race and its destiny? His Faustian impulse to question all established truths, to accept nothing at face value, to search earnestly and untiringly for new answers to old questions—these characteristics made him at once one of the great subversives in the spiritual odyssey of man and a "believer." In *A Rejoinder* he formulated his credo and his legacy most eloquently: "If God were holding all the truth that exists in his right hand, and in his left just the one ever-active urge to find the truth, even if attached to it were the condition that I should always and forever be going astray, and said to me: 'Choose!' I should humbly fall upon his left hand and say: 'Father, give! Pure truth is surely for thee alone!'"

Other articles of interest: **German Literature, Unbelief in Modern. Germany, Unbelief in. Jesus, Historicity of.**

Bibliography

Allison, Henry E. *Lessing and the Enlightenment.* Ann Arbor: U. of Michigan Press, 1966.

Barth, Karl. *Protestant Theology in the Nineteenth Century.* Trans. Brian Cozens and John Bowden. London: SCM Press, 1959.

Chadwick, Henry, ed. *Lessing's Theological Writings.* London: Adams and Charles Black, 1959.

Guthke, Karl S. *Der Stand der Lessing-Forschung.* Stuttgart: Metzler, 1965. Pp. 88–95.

Harris, Edward P., and Richard E. Schade, ed. *Lessing in heutiger Sicht.* Bremen and Wolfenbüttel: Jacobi-Verlag, 1977.

Hazard, Paul. *European Thought in the Eighteenth Century.* Trans. J. Lewis May. London: Hollis and Carter, 1954. Pp. 416–34.

Nigg, Walter. *Das Buch der Ketzer.* Zürich and Stuttgart: Artemis, 1962. Pp. 401–17.

Pons, Georges. *Gotthold Ephraim Lessing et le christianisme.* Paris: Didier, 1964.

Thielicke, Helmut. *Offenbarung, Vernunft und Existenz: Studien zur Religionsphilosophie Lessings.* 3rd ed. Gütersloh: Bertelsmann, 1957.

VOLKER DÜRR

LEWIS, JOSEPH (1889–1968), American author, editor, and publisher of atheist and sex-education books. Born in Montgomery, Ala., on June 11, 1889, into a large Jewish family, he quickly abandoned all religious notions. His father was a struggling merchant. Joseph was compelled to quit school at the age of nine to go to work. Determined to educate himself, he quickly absorbed the writings of ROBERT G. INGERSOLL and other great freethinkers of the English-speaking world. Undoubtedly, THOMAS PAINE was his ideal from American history from his early youth. In ensuing decades he would demonstrate his astonishing command of American history and constitutional law. His ambitions spurred him to relocate in New York City, around 1920. There, he sought the company of fellow atheists, with the plan to publish the daring ideas of freethought as his life's mission. Always mindful of Southern poverty and the bigotry underlying it, Lewis became phenomenally successful by turning FREETHOUGHT publishing into a lucrative business.

Early in his New York days, Lewis was elected president of Freethinkers of America, first organized in 1915. He remained its president for the rest of his life—allegedly employing devious means at times to retain his position—and saw to the group's incorporation in 1925. Establishing his own publishing house, the Freethought Press Association, he wrote and printed more than a score of books. His first was *The Tyranny of God* (1921); probably his most famous was *The Bible Unmasked* (1926), a shocking book in its time which was reprinted for many years. Lewis had an unflagging faith in the durability of his own words. His volume of public addresses, *Atheism* (1930), was reissued for decades, each time in an expanded edition with added tracts, until 1960.

Sexology. In the early 1930s, Lewis opened a subsidiary publishing operation, the Eugenics Publishing Company, specifically to disseminate books of sexology. Those volumes, all written by medical specialists—many of them like-minded Freethinkers—might never have been accessible to the American reading public at low cost, except for Lewis' enterprise. Assuming the rights to the sex manuals of William J. Robinson, M.D., when that pioneer of contraceptive information was grappling with critical financial problems in his own book outlet, Lewis kept the Robinson volumes in print into the era of the popular newsstand paperback. Those sexologists in need of a forum, such as Maurice Chideckel and Frederick M. Rossiter, found a home in the Eugenics Publishing Company. Lewis probably accorded the widest distribution for the once infamous work by Marie Stopes, *Married Love*, which was banned for many years in the U.S.

With his main product line—freethought literature—Lewis sought to expose the sham and obscurantism of church dogma and practice, champion the separation of church and state, and assure readers that religious faith was unnecessary to the moral life of an individual or equal justice under law to the citizenry. Notable in this connection are some of his own works: *Voltaire, the Incomparable Infidel* (1929), *The Bible and the Public Schools* (1931), *Should Children Receive Religious Instruction?* (1933), and *In the Name of Humanity* (1949), his memorable excoriation of the practice of circumcision. His most complete statement of a rationalist's ideal lifestyle was *An Atheist Manifesto*, published in book form in 1954.

Lewis' other thrust as author and publisher was to dispel the mirage that ATHEISM was unpatriotic and to set forth a mass of evidence that the nation's founders and heroes were themselves freethinkers. Among his own books on great Americans were *Lincoln, the Freethinker* (1925), *Jefferson, the Freethinker* (1925), *Franklin, the Freethinker* (1926), and *Burbank, the Infidel* (1929). In his 644-page magnum opus, *The Ten Commandments* (1946), Lewis sought to unravel the Judeo-Christian code, with allusions throughout to the skepticism of statesmen and heroes in American history.

Paine's Avatar. Lewis' monthly magazine, varying in number of pages but printed from cover to cover, undertook the same revisionist and ideological tasks. Inaugurated in January 1937, its first title was *Bulletin, Freethinkers of America*. In the mid-1940s its title was changed to the *Freethinker*. With the coming of the 1950s it was renamed the *Age of Reason*. Lewis maintained this title until the publication folded after his death in 1968. The leading freethought journalists and essayists of this century, including William J. Fielding, Franklin Steiner, and Corliss Lamont, were regular contributors.

The title change to the *Age of Reason* reflected Lewis' obsession with Thomas Paine. He saw his own industrious output as an extension of Paine's, to the point that he virtually adopted a Paine persona. In 1947 he published *Thomas Paine, Author of the Declaration of Independence*, in which he sought to prove that the conception and authorship of that document were Paine's. In 1954

he wrote *The Tragic Patriot*, a play dramatizing the deeds and persecution of his hero in America and France.

For half his lifetime, Lewis was a publicist for Paine's worldwide recognition. In 1936, Lewis prevailed upon the Socialist government of Leon Blum in France to erect a Gutzon Borglum sculpture of Paine in Paris. This dedication had to wait until 1948. Lewis dedicated two other Paine statues: one in Morristown, N.J., in 1950, and one in front of Paine's birthplace in Thetford, England, in 1964.

The dapper, well-dressed Joseph Lewis cut an exceptional figure in public life and caused much visibility for the freethought movement. A combative individual, he was not beyond jousting with windmills in the name of church-state separation and the quelling of church power. With the help of Joseph Wheless, rationalist author and attorney, Lewis filed numerous suits in the federal courts, most of them unsuccessful. He tried to have the phrase *under God* stricken from the Pledge of Allegiance, and he protested such government actions as the official celebration of Thanksgiving and the Post Office Department's annual issue of Christmas stamps. In 1935 he sought $5,000 in punitive damages from New York's Trinity Church, because the metal plaque at St. Paul's Chapel was allegedly engraved with a prayer attributed to George Washington. The case was carried to appeal, but lost. For several years he led the campaign against New York's "released time" policy, which allowed public-school children weekly periods for religious instruction.

Lewis the Gadfly. When Lewis admonished Jews to cease their observance of Yom Kippur, six honorary vice-presidents of Freethinkers of America resigned in protest. Such actions rarely troubled him. Joseph Lewis is also remembered as having conducted some poorly announced board meetings alone in New York restaurants, acting as chairman and sole voting member.

His home was in Purdys, a suburb of New York. Later he resided for a time in Miami, Fla., where he broadcast freethought lectures over the local radio. Lewis was married twice: to Fay Jacobs, in 1914; and to Ruth Stoller Grubman, in 1952. He had one daughter.

On Nov. 4, 1968, shortly after Lewis arrived at his office in New York City, he was stricken with a heart attack, collapsed, and died at his desk. No funeral was held, but there were memorial services in New York and Philadelphia.

Bibliography

Howland, Arthur H. *Joseph Lewis—Enemy of God.* Boston: Stratford, 1932.

Martin, Martin J. "*Repartee:* Mourns the Loss of a Great and Noble Leader, Joseph Lewis 1889–1968." *Repartee* (n.d. 1969?).

"Joseph Lewis, Publisher, Dead; Crusader for Atheism Was 79." *New York Times.* Nov. 5, 1968.

Lewis, Joseph. *Ingersoll the Magnificent.* New York: Freethought Press Association, 1957.

———. *Spain: Land Blighted by Religion.* New York: Freethought Press Association, 1933.

———. *Atheism and Other Addresses.* New York: Freethought Press Association, 1960.

Ryan, William F. "The Later Years—Radical Energy and Stormy Seas." *Humanist* 36, no. 2 (March/April 1976).

WILLIAM F. RYAN

LEWIS, SINCLAIR (1885–1951), American novelist. See **American Literature, Unbelief in.**

LIBERALISM IN LATIN AMERICA. See **Latin America, Philosophical Bases of Unbelief in.**

LIBERATOR, THE, was published in Melbourne, Australia, from June 1884 to March 1904. This famous—and in orthodox quarters notorious—weekly paper was launched a few months after the arrival in the colony of Victoria of JOSEPH SYMES. From the outset the *Liberator* had its own printing press, which was presented to Symes by members of the Australasian Secular Association.

The paper was very much Symes' personal mouthpiece, devoted to militant freethought, republicanism, anticolonialism, popular science, poetry (including contributions from the young Bernard O'Dowd) and occasional excursions into fiction (by Symes). It also advocated contraception and political radicalism, sometimes spiced with anticlerical cartoons. It resembled both the FREETHINKER (London), to which Symes contributed, and to a lesser extent CHARLES BRADLAUGH's NATIONAL REFORMER.

"If blasphemy," warned Symes in the first issue, "is the equivalent of fearless truth and the exposure of consecrated shams and pious imposture, our course is clear. We shall crowd our paper with all the blasphemy its pages can carry."

No blasphemy charge was ever brought against the *Liberator,* but in 1885 Symes was prosecuted for failing to deposit securities against printing blasphemy and sedition. Fines and costs totalled 125 pounds. Symes promised to pay "at the resurrection, if you make demand." Other methods of muzzling the paper, such as a six-month boycott by the Victoria post office, were singularly unsuccessful. In its heyday it ran to 20 pages a week (perhaps a freethought record), and unverified claims of a circulation as high as 20,000 have been made.

Symes' success in Melbourne resulted in the arrival in Sydney of WILLIAM WHITEHOUSE COLLINS, who ran a short-lived paper of his own, the *Freethinker and N.S.W. Reformer.* Collins was coeditor of the *Liberator* during parts of 1886 and 1887 before launching another Sydney paper, *Freedom,* and later becoming a politician and prominent freethought advocate in New Zealand.

The *Liberator*'s success ended at the end of the 1880s when Melbourne's prosperity ceased. The city's population declined by 46,000 between 1891 and 1893, and in the latter year Nonconformist churches and even banks closed their doors in the economic slump. Organized freethought collapsed, but Symes and his devoted second wife, Agnes (A. T. Wilson), kept the paper going throughout the 1890s, despite their dire poverty and the animosity of personal enemies. Often they depended on last-minute help from loyal friends in order to have enough paper to go to press. The *Liberator* ran at a loss for perhaps a decade before Symes, exhausted and in poor health, was finally persuaded to retire and rest.

Not only is the *Liberator* a detailed chronicle of Australian freethought from the 1880s to the early years of federation, but it also contains valuable accounts of British secularism in the 1870s and 1880s (as seen through the eyes of Symes) and various autobiographical articles by Symes. Its regular appearance, over a period of 20 years, was a remarkable labor of love, perseverance, and self-sacrifice. In 1884 the *Bendigo Evening News* predicted that the *Liberator* would have only "a month's existence"; instead it became a classic of late 19th-century atheist journalism.

Bibliography

Pearce, Harry H. "Some Notes on Freethought Journals." Ms., National Library of Australia, 1965.
See also Bibliography for Joseph Symes.

NIGEL H. SINNOTT

LIBRARY COLLECTIONS ON UNBELIEF.
Throughout history the books and magazines that have survived have been only a small percentage of those that were originally published. In general, those that survived were those which were collected, either by libraries or by private individuals. Many thousands of books, pamphlets, and magazines by unbelievers have been published all over the world, yet today it is very difficult to locate even one copy of many of them. The reasons for this are complex, but partly involve the fact that many were published by small publishers in small numbers, that few libraries were courageous enough to order copies of some of the more openly propagandistic works, and that those that did often found them missing from the shelves soon afterwards. How many private collections of materials on unbelief have been refused as gifts by libraries or not donated by relatives of a deceased unbeliever who had wanted them donated is anyone's guess.

Yet a good number of the books and magazines of unbelief *have* survived in isolated libraries around the world. A few libraries even have special collections of unbelief or "freethought" books. In the United States, the three best collections are at the Library of Congress, the New York Public Library, and the University of Wisconsin. The Library of Congress collection was an unplanned one. As a copyright depository, that library simply received and retained one copy of every book copyrighted in the United States. The New York Public Library, in addition to many smaller donations, received the Irving Levy collection of hundreds of volumes of bound FREETHOUGHT books and pamphlets. The University of Wisconsin, on the other hand, has made a determined effort to collect freethought materials.

The next best collection is at the University of Michigan, in its Labadie Collection on Social Protest Movements. Yale University has a fine collection of freethought periodicals, whose source is unknown. Harvard has a fairly good, general freethought collection. There are also a number of more specialized collections within the general area of unbelief. For example, Northwestern University has the Kaye collection on DEISM, Southern Illinois University has the Stein collection on ROBERT GREEN INGERSOLL, and many of the books of THEODORE SCHROEDER. The rest of Schroeder's books are in the Library of the Wisconsin State Historical Society. There is also the superb Gimbel collection of THOMAS PAINE materials at the American Philosophical Society in Philadelphia.

Other specialized American collections are the ethnic freethought materials in the Immigration History Research Center at the University of Minnesota, at the Chicago Historical Society, at the Balzekas Library of Lithuanian Culture in Chicago, at the Czechoslovak Society of America Library in Chicago, and the FREIEN GEMEINDEN materials at the Milwaukee County Historical Society Library.

Other specialized collections are the Gilmour Victorian freethought pamphlets at the Lilly Library at Indiana University; the RICHARD CARLILE manuscripts at the Huntington Library in San Marino, Calif.; the Ingersoll papers at the Library of Congress, at Southern Illinois University, and at the Illinois State Historical Library in Springfield; the ROBERT DALE OWEN and FRANCES WRIGHT papers at the Workingman's Institute at New Harmony, Ind. Many of the papers of MONCURE CONWAY are at Columbia University Library in New York City. At Southern Methodist University in Dallas, there is a collection of freethought magazines, which is listed only in the periodical catalog. The Meadville-Lombard Theological School Library in Chicago has the freethought book collection of William Berrian in the stacks.

In Canada, a collection formerly belonging to Marshall Gauvin has recently been given to the library at the University of Manitoba in Winnipeg.

In the United Kingdom, the British Museum has a superb collection of freethought materials although some of them are scattered at different locations, such as the Collindale newspaper library. Also in London are the small but important libraries of the NATIONAL SECULAR SOCIETY, now at the Bishopsgate Institute, and the Rationalist Press Association; others are in Manchester at the Central Library and the Library of the Co-operative Union. The public library of Northampton has the Barker collection of materials about

CHARLES BRADLAUGH. The Thetford Public Library has a collection of Thomas Paine materials. The Public Record Office has the files of many of the blasphemy trials that were held in England. The manuscripts division of the British Museum has the papers of Francis Place, containing much on the freethinkers of the early 19th century, and the Manchester Cooperative Union has the papers of ROBERT OWEN and most of GEORGE JACOB HOLYOAKE's. The other Holyoake papers are at the Bishopsgate Institute Library in London. The National Secular Society has the papers of Charles Bradlaugh. Most of ANNIE BESANT's papers are at the Theosophical Society Library in Madras, India.

Many of the papers of important unbelievers are missing today. It is known what happened to some of them. Thomas Paine's papers, for example, were lost when a barn in which they were being stored in Pennsylvania caught fire and burned down. There is a mystery surrounding the papers of GEORGE WILLIAM FOOTE and those of JOHN M. ROBERTSON. Both groups of papers have disappeared without a trace. JOSEPH MCCABE's papers were mistakenly hauled away by the garbage man and destroyed. CHARLES WATTS', JOSEPH MAZZINI WHEELER's and ROBERT TAYLOR's papers are also missing.

VOLTAIRE's papers have been largely reassembled by Theodore Besterman at the Voltaire Museum in Geneva. Many of Voltaire's books are in the Lenin Library in Moscow, where they were sent after the Empress Catherine bought the library containing them. Most of BERTRAND RUSSELL's papers are at the library of McMaster University in Hamilton, Ontario.

In Australia and New Zealand, there are the following collections and archives. The large freethought book collection of Harry H. Pearce is in the National Library of Australia in Canberra. The papers of ROBERT STOUT are in the Turnbull Library in Wellington, New Zealand. There is a small freethought library at the headquarters of the New Zealand Rationalist Association in Auckland. The La Trobe Library in Melbourne has a good collection of freethought materials that came in the Bosher gift, and in Sydney the Mitchell Library also has a good collection of Australian materials.

In India, there are small freethought collections at the Indian Rationalist Society in Madras, the Atheist Center in Vijayawada, and at the World Headquarters of the Theosophical Society near Madras. The latter has 19th-century materials.

Following are the locations of the largest collections of the papers of other people whose biographies appear in the Encyclopedia. Most were freethinkers or unbelievers, but may have made their major contributions in another field: Sigmund Freud, New York Psychoanalytic Institute; Karl Marx, many of which are in the International Institute of Social History, Amsterdam; Friedrich Nietzsche, Friedrich-Schiller University, Jena, East Germany; Samuel L. Clemens, University of California, Berkeley; Clarence Darrow, Library of Congress; John Dewey, Southern Illinois University; Denis Diderot, Bibliothèque Nationale, Paris; Benjamin Franklin, Yale University; Emanuel Haldeman-Julius, Kansas State College at Pittsburg; David Hume, Royal Society of Edinburgh Library, Scotland; Thomas Jefferson, Library of Congress; H. L. Mencken, Enoch Pratt Free Library, Baltimore, Md.; Thomas Henry Huxley, Imperial College Libraries, London; Auguste Comte, Maison Auguste Comte, Paris; and Jeremy Bentham, British Museum and University College Library, London.

Catalogs of some of these collections have been published: Bertrand Russell Archives at McMaster University, the *Catalogue of the Charles Bradlaugh Papers* at the National Secular Society, the *Catalogue of the George Jacob Holyoake Papers* at the Cooperative Union and elsewhere, the *Catalogue of the Thomas Paine Collection of Richard Gimbel at the American Philosophical Society,* the *Catalogue of the Thomas Paine Collection at the Thetford Public Library.* There also exist published catalogs of the private libraries of the following freethinkers (in many cases these were auction catalogs of the library, prepared after the death of the owners): ANTHONY COLLINS, PAUL HENRI HOLBACH, Charles Bradlaugh, Thomas Jefferson, G. W. Foote, J. M. Robertson, Edward Truelove, and Hypatia Bradlaugh-Bonner (along with freethought book collectors Ambrose Barker and Herbert Cutner) in the published catalogs of the freethought bookseller David Collis.

A number of private collections of books on unbelief exist. Some of these are better than any of the public collections. Most of the private collections are open to scholars only under special conditions. [A letter to the editor of the *Encyclopedia of Unbelief,* stating the research topic and needed materials will be referred to the owners of private collections, if appropriate. A private collection sometimes made available to the public on a limited basis is the American Atheists' collection,

P.O. Box 2117, Austin, Tex. 78768.]

Other articles of interest: **Appendix 1: Bibliography of Unbelief. Appendix 4: Publishers of Unbelief. Appendix 5: Periodicals of Unbelief.**

Bibliography

Anonymous. *Catalogue of Books from the Library of the Late Edward Truelove, Now on Sale by His Executors.* London: Estate of E. Truelove, 1899.

Anonymous. *A Catalogue of the Extensive Library of the Late Rt. Hon. J. M. Robertson, P.C. For Sale by Auction on Wednesday, April 26, 1933.* London: Hodgson & Co., 1933. Catalogue #14 of the 1932–33 season.

Anonymous. *Preliminary Check List of the Kaye Deism Collection at Northwestern University.* Evanston, Ill.: Northwestern U. Library, n.d. Typescript.

Anonymous. *The Thomas Paine Collection at Thetford: An Analytical Catalogue.* Norwich, U.K.: Norfolk County Library, 1979.

Bonner, Hypatia Bradlaugh. *A Catalogue of the Library of the Late Charles Bradlaugh.* London: Mrs. H. Bradlaugh Bonner, 1891.

Brown, Marshall, and Gordon Stein. *Freethought in the United States.* Westport, Conn.: Greenwood Press, 1978. Appendix contains additional information about libraries that have smaller collections of freethought material.

Dobell, P. J., and A. E. Dobell, compilers. *A Catalogue Chiefly of Books in English Literature from the Library of the Late G. W. Foote.* London: P. J. and A. E. Dobell, 1916. Catalogue #251.

Gillett, Charles Ripley, ed. *The McAlpin Collection of British History and Theology.* 5 vols. New York: Union Theological Seminary, 1927–1930.

Rationalist Press Association. *Catalogue of the Library of the Rationalist Press Association.* London: Watts, 1937.

Royle, Edward, compiler. *The Bradlaugh Papers: A Descriptive Index.* Wakefield, U.K.: E. P. Microfilm, 1975.

Stephans, Hildegard, compiler. *The Thomas Paine Collection of Richard Gimbel in the Library of the American Philosophical Society.* Wilmington, Del.: Scholarly Resources, 1976.

Stein, Gordon. *Freethought in the United Kingdom and the Commonwealth.* Westport, Conn.: Greenwood Press, 1981. Appendix.

GORDON STEIN

LIFE, ORIGIN OF, AND UNBELIEF. How, where, and when did life begin? Questions concerning the origin of living things on this planet and elsewhere in the cosmos have intrigued scientists as well as philosophers and theologians, especially in light of the implications of the theory of evolution (see EVOLUTION AND UNBELIEF) and the possibilities inherent throughout the material universe. From rational speculations among the ancient thinkers to the recent discoveries in the earth sciences (particularly geopaleontology) along with astrochemistry and astrophysics in modern cosmology, naturalists have sought for an explanation that accounts for the existence of organic matter without referring to theology or metaphysics.

The origin of life is no longer such an elusive problem in modern biology and chemistry, since scientific experimentation and philosophical scrutiny in this century have shed considerable doubt on the credibility of earlier attempts to explain organic existence on earth as due to, for example, divine intervention, a series of special creations, pervasive vitalism, spontaneous generation, and the panspermia hypothesis.

Mechanistic materialists claim that living things first emerged on our planet from inorganic matter according to physical laws and have subsequently evolved for several billion years, while some philosophers and religionists argue that life itself is the result of a metaphysical force or a theistic creation separate from the physical world. The naturalist approach to the problem of the origin of life is, in fact, diametrically opposed to the supernaturalist attitude. Within the evolutionary continuum, however, the distinction between inert matter and life is not clear. Yet there are problems that involve raw materials, monomers, polymers, isolation, replication, photosynthesis, and sexual reproduction (among others).

Speculations about the origin and nature of life as we know it probably go back to prehistoric times when early humans could not as yet account for birth, growth and development, sexual reproduction, diseases, and the inevitability of death in terms of empirical evidence and logical deliberation. As the result of increased awareness, men recognized the distinction between inorganic objects and living things. To account for the organic world, thinkers referred to a supernatural power or forces immanent and/or transcendent, dynamic concepts or principles and, later, naturalistic explanations derived from critical observations and rational reflection.

In general, three major accounts have been given to explain the origin of life on earth: the creation of all living things by unobservable magico-religious entities, the sudden appearance of plant and animal forms from inanimate matter through spontaneous generation, or the gradual emergence of life from matter as demonstrated by the ongoing accumulation of facts and relationships in the special sciences (e.g., geology, paleontology, taxonomy, genetics, and biochemistry) which support the biological theory of organic evolution.

Likewise, various philosophical positions from hylozoism and vitalism to the panspermia hypothesis and an organismic view of the earth or cosmos have been offered as plausible explanations for the seemingly elusive phenomenon of life in the universe. Scientific findings and rational speculations continue to shed light on the origin of life from a planetary framework and more recently, due to the developing science of exobiology, within a cosmic perspective. Seriously considering the documented evidence of the special sciences, a critical thinker may interpret life within a naturalist viewpoint without recourse to theology or metaphysics. In fact, in our times it needs to be demonstrated that the supernatural realm is even *necessary* for a sound understanding of and clear appreciation for life within physical reality.

A precise definition of life is not possible at this time, especially if it is to include all living things both past and present as well as exclude all nonliving things. For example, it may be debated whether a virus (which cannot replicate on its own) is a living or nonliving entity, since it exists at the borderline between complex megamolecules and simple organisms.

Living things as we know them generally exhibit the following properties or characteristics: metabolism, self-replication or sexual reproduction, growth and development, irritability, and (less often) mobility, mutability, and heterocatalysis. The elemental foundation of all life on earth is based on the carbon atom, although organic phenomena elsewhere in the cosmos may be structured around silicon, ammonia, or some other molecule. Likewise, all living things on this planet consist of the same naturally occurring 20 amino acids as the building blocks of structural proteins and enzymes. The materialistic viewpoint accounts for the historical continuity and essential unity of life in terms of biochemistry and organic evolution (see MATERIALISM).

Before philosophy and science, explanations for organic phenomena relied upon appeals to myth, legend, magic, religion, and personal opinion. Evidence suggests that, even in prehistoric times, early man recognized the significance of life: Neanderthal men deliberately buried their dead with ritual; Cro-Magnon man painted magnificent cave murals; and technologically primitive, nonliterate peoples believed in various forms of animism and animatism before the emergence of institutionalized religion and, later, science and reason.

During the Pre-Socratic period (600–400 B.C.), several naturalist cosmologists offered rational speculations to account for the origin of living things: Thales wrote that life originated in water, the basic element of all reality; Anaxagoras claimed that cosmic seeds pervade the entire universe; and Empedocles gave a bizarre explanation to account for the origin of the first organisms from the haphazard synthesis of free-floating organs of various sizes and shapes (this view implied the principles of variation, adaptation, survival, and reproduction, since monstrosities perished and only those plants and animals compatible with their environments lived long enough to reproduce themselves).

In their steadfast appeal to the critical observations of nature itself and the rigorous use of reason (logic and mathematics), these early philosophers found no need to rely upon supernatural beliefs (see ANCIENT WORLD, UNBELIEF IN).

Later, Aristotle (384–322 B.C.) as the father of biology held every plant and animal form to be eternally fixed in its natural place within the static hierarchy of organic nature. He did not concern himself with the origin of things and, consequently, never anticipated the idea of organic evolution. He did, however, resort to spontaneous generation to account for the sudden appearance of some simple organisms from inanimate matter. This Greek thinker believed that, among living things, the established development from potentiality to actuality is caused by the existence of an eternal and perfect unmoved mover as pure thought thinking about itself beyond the fixed ceiling of stars; man as the rational animal occupies the terrestrial apex of this ascending ladder of increasing complexity and sensitivity.

18th and 19th-Century Views. Interestingly enough, two millennia later, Charles Darwin did not speculate on the origin of life (although his paternal grandfather, Erasmus Darwin, had held that all living things on earth had evolved from a single living filament that existed millions of years ago). Charles apparently thought the question to be beyond the comprehension of the human mind and the domain of the empirical sciences. Even today, the origin of life remains one of the central problems in evolutionary science and natural philosophy.

Some thinkers have claimed that life is actually material in origin, having arisen and evolved naturally as a result of the physico-chemical processes of nature. Following the successes of science and mathematics during the Italian Renaissance (particularly in astronomy), early biologists and philosophers attempted to understand and appreciate life by comparing organisms to machines. Mechanistic materialism was supported by JULIEN OFFRAY DE LA METTRIE in his major work *L'Homme machine* (1747) and was advocated later by Frederick Engels in his speculative volume *Dialectics of Nature* (1925).

However, some thinkers still believe that at a specific moment in earth's history the divine action of a supernatural creator caused the origin of life and, as a result, this unique event sharply separated inorganic nature from the organic world. In the Judeo-Christian tradition, the living God may be interpreted as an intelligent and personal creator who also sustains and nourishes organic evolution. In sharp contrast to this liberal religious view, fundamentalist creationists continue to preach that God created each plant and animal species once and only once less than 10,000 years ago. (Although some are willing to accept microevolution below the species level, all reject macroevolution in their dogmatic belief in the eternal fixity of floral and faunal types.)

Naturalist Views. Although there are numerous religious accounts for the creation of life, a rigorously naturalist explanation for the emergence of the organic world rejects any appeal to religious interpretations and the assumed existence of a supernatural realm transcending material nature. An appeal to supernatural powers in order to explain the origin of living things is, in principle, outside the realm of scientific investigation. There is no evidence to support the belief that life is

contingent upon the existence of a divine will and its intervention into the natural order of all things. Such a religious view is grounded in blind faith rather than science and reason.

Through the extensive use of analogy, both Leonardo da Vinci and Alexander von Humboldt interpreted our earth as a living organism. They did not separate life from matter and, therefore, perceived this planet in terms of a pervasive metabolism. Recently, Lewis Thomas has written that the earth resembles nothing so much as a single living cell. The organismic philosopher Alfred North Whitehead even envisioned all of reality as a process field of interacting feelings, an idealist position giving preference to rational speculations rather than the empirical sciences. Although stressing an animated conception of nature, these thinkers did not concern themselves with the origin of life.

It is possible to hold that, in the physical universe, life is actually coextensive and coeternal with nonliving matter and therefore had no origin as such. From this viewpoint, even though inorganic and organic structures are interrelated, neither preceded the other in cosmic history. This curious position was supported by those cosmologists who appealed to the steady-state theory, which claims that the universe presents the same characteristics in all places and times throughout reality. However, according to the big-bang theory, which accounts for an evolving and expanding universe, modern scientific evidence demonstrates that our dynamic cosmos originated about 20 billion years ago. Nevertheless, this planet has been able to harbor life only during the past four billion years.

One hypothesis even suggests that all cosmic matter is in fact merely the residue of universal life that preceded it.

Philosophers advocating forms of vitalism or idealism assert that life originated as the result of the creative act of a personal God, spiritual source, higher intelligence, or cosmic intelligences. From Aristotle and Galen to Henri Bergson and Driesch, some biologists and natural philosophers have explained life in terms of a theory that supposes the necessary existence of a metaphysical force autonomous from inanimate matter.

From this standpoint, living organisms are claimed to be something more than merely the systematic organization of nonliving parts, since only the vital force is able to infuse matter with life. This dynamic entity is held to account for the increasing complexity and sensitivity, diversity and continuity, and essential unity of all life on earth. (Hylozoism is the doctrine that all matter is active with life, or that life is inseparable from matter; panpsychism maintains that mind or consciousness pervades all nature.)

Some natural philosophers from Lamarck to Teilhard de Chardin have appealed to such an active principle to explain the origin and evolution of life as we know it. Teilhard, a geopaleontologist and Jesuit priest, even believed that a personal God plays a key role in directing the organismic character of the unfolding universe. Although an irrefutable position in principle, vitalism remains a pseudoexplanation to account for the origin of life; it is grounded in intellectual obscurantism that may take the form of unwarranted religious—if not mystical—beliefs.

Early biologists thought that worms, eels, fish, toads, rats, flies, and insects (among other organisms) suddenly arise from substances such as mud, slime, and decaying matter. Clearly misunderstanding the causal relationships between matter and life, these naturalists offered spontaneous generation as an explanation for the emergence of living things. Following the Italian Renaissance, the physician Francesco Redi (1626–1697) offered experimental evidence to discredit the prevailing Aristotelian concept of the spontaneous generation of visible organisms. He correctly concluded that fly larvae are not suddenly formed from decaying meat. Instead, adult flies lay their eggs on unprotected meat; later, these eggs give rise to maggots.

The Dutch lens-grinder and naturalist Anton van Leeuwenhoek (1632–1723) used his single-lens microscope to see microorganisms, which were held by some to be spontaneously generated from inorganic matter. The discovery of microorganisms revived the idea of spontaneous generation, criticized by Lazzaro Spallanzani but supported by John Needham.

In 1864, the French chemist Louis Pasteur (1822–1895) performed several ingenious experiments to demonstrate that organisms are not spontaneously generated from inanimate matter but, on the contrary, are produced from other existing organic forms. For a few decades following Pasteur's work, the origin of life was no longer considered to be a legitimate scientific question worthy of empirical inquiry. Of course, the discrediting of spontaneous generation does not require that all organic entities must be generated only by other life forms.

Instead, in modern science, spontaneous generation has been superseded by the *theory of abiogenesis*, which maintains that, under primitive terrestrial conditions very different from those now prevailing on the surface of our earth and over vast periods of time, chemical evolution slowly led to the emergence of the first primordial organic systems from complex preliving protein macromolecules. But there is a crucial distinction between the spontaneous generation of those complex forms of flora and fauna on our planet today from nonliving matter (as was believed by early biologists), and the gradual abiogenetic emergence of the earliest entities of life under the environmental conditions of the primitive earth as a result of chemical evolution. In short, although Pasteur contributed to the refutation of the former, he did not discredit the claim of the latter or the biological theory of organic evolution.

There are those who maintain that a naturalist argument for the origin of life in terms of random events in chemical evolution is not plausible in light of the assumed extremely improbable occurrence of protolife substances (eobionts) when considering statistical calculations and the age of the earth. However, life does exist on our planet, and one must distinguish between empirical evidence and formal reasoning. For the scientist and natural philosopher, a very improbable event may be certain to occur given enough time as well as the required chemical substances in a suitable environment. In fact, considering the vast age and uniformity of the cosmos, the presence of life may even be a natural imperative on other worlds throughout the material universe.

The Work of Oparin. A major breakthrough in the systematic attempt to scientifically account for the emergence of living things on earth was first offered by the great Russian biochemist A. I. Oparin in his classic volume *The Origin of Life* (1938). He argued that the atmosphere of the primitive earth contained almost no free oxygen and had no upper ozone layer to act as a shield against ultraviolet radiation. At that time in planetary history, the surface of our earth contained both seas and pools of so-called probiotic soup, rich in chemical elements that reacted to the intense radiation from outer space as well as terrestrial sources of energy. As a result of prolonged photochemical activity, these inorganic mixtures give rise to organic compounds (including amino acids). Through time and chemical selection, these eobionts or organic systems increased in complexity and stability, becoming the immediate precursors of living things.

Oparin conceived of coacervate molecules as precursors to molecules that could reproduce themselves. He was successful in separating prebiotic coacervate liquid molecules from aqueous solutions of several organic polymers. These prebiotic molecules were able to absorb energy from the external environment and, consequently, grow slowly or rapidly depending upon the surrounding conditions. In fact, microspheres may have first formed in ice, mud, or the primitive atmosphere of our planet instead of emerging as surface films on the primordial waters of the earth.

On the basis of empirical facts accumulated in this century, one may consider the origin of life on earth to be a natural process of the evolution of carbonaceous compounds, which are present not only on this planet but also throughout interstellar space (including existence in the chemical composition of comets, meteors, and cosmic dust/gas clouds).

Thus, the beginning of life is an event that may have occurred at a single time or different times, at the same location or different locations. The presence of carbonaceous compounds throughout the sidereal regions of the universe suggests that organic substances originated from inanimate matter even before the appearance of life on earth and, in fact, before the earlier formation of our planet. This gives credence to the abiogenetic hypothesis for the origin of organic substances from inanimate matter. The hypothesis is empirically strengthened by recent discoveries in both biochemistry and geopaleontology.

Modern Experimenters. The American chemist Harold C. Urey theorized that the primitive reducing atmosphere of our earth must have contained water vapor and gaseous hydrogen as well as carbonaceous compounds of methane and cyanogen, along with nitrogen in the form of ammonia, as well as carbon monoxide and carbon dioxide. This atmosphere slowly changed through time, with the evolution of simple anaerobic forms contributing their waste product, free oxygen, to the environment. As a result, the atmosphere gradually acquired oxidative properties that eventually made possible the emergence of plant and animal life.

In 1953, urged by Urey, Stanley L. Miller conducted studies on abiogenetic synthesis. Under laboratory conditions, he succeeded in producing several organic compounds (including 25 amino acids) by introducing an electrical charge through a gaseous mixture presumed to be more or less analogous to the atmosphere of the primeval earth. His subsequent experiments produced glycine, adanine, uracil, porphyrins, and adenosine triphosphate (among other things).

In 1956, the Russian scientists A. G. Pasynskii and T. E. Pavlovskaia demonstrated that it is possible experimentally to create amino acids as the result of irradiating a gaseous mixture containing ammonia salts and formaldehyde with ultraviolet light. These experiments gave further credibility to the mechanistic materialist theory of protobiogenesis (the origin of life from nonlife).

Sidney W. Fox, in 1957, obtained complex organic molecules similar to proteins from a heated dry mixture of various amino acids. Twelve years later, through abiogenetic synthesis, he formed proteinlike substances and polypeptides. In 1960, the Spanish scientist J. Oró had even abiogenetically synthesized the components of the DNA and RNA molecules (purines, pyrimidines, ribose, and deoxyribose).

In 1970, Cyril Ponnamperuma produced ATP (adenosine triphosphate), which is the immediate source of metabolic energy in living organisms. His experiments further supported the idea of the origin of organic compounds from inorganic substances in the universe through the stimulation of various cosmic energies. Probionts may have been synthesized on the subvital surface of the primitive earth through the natural transition from chemical development to biological evolution as an inevitable occurrence. If so, the transition from matter to life was the necessary consequence of ongoing environmental circumstances rather than due to accidental changes producing a chance event.

Dating the Origin of Life. In sharp contrast to the other hypotheses, modern science continues to support the theory that the chemical evolution of matter paved the way for the slow emergence of life in the hydrosphere of this world. The earth formed about five billion years ago and, extrapolating from recent fossil evidence, the earliest forms of life probably appeared less than a billion years later: chemical transformations formed first simple and then complex organic substances (prebionts through probionts to protocells). Still a puzzle is whether proteins or nucleic acids emerged first, or if they appeared jointly. Apparently viruses, being reproductively parasitic, have shed no light on the origin of life. The emergence of genetic information imperative for the synthesis of amino acids into structural proteins and enzymes remains a crucial area of scientific investigation.

In brief, organic molecules may be synthesized from inorganic matter: amino acids are the essential constituents of life as we know it (the DNA and RNA molecules as the code of life are nucleic acids distinct from free-floating amino acids).

The most primitive yet complex microorganisms on earth are the anaerobic bacteria, found where there is little or no free molecular oxygen (e.g., in the depths of the oceans and in specific areas of living organisms). In evolution, these anaerobic bacteria preceded both the autotrophic and heterotrophic bacteria and other simple organisms, for although viruses are simple, composed only of a protein sheath and a nucleic acid core, their parasitic nature prevents them from being the earliest form of life since they require a living host cell for mutation and reproduction.

Exobiology. The natural events that occurred throughout earth history have probably happened (are happening or may happen) on other worlds elsewhere in the universe. This is the primary assumption underlying the emerging science of exobiology. The existence of life on other planets among the galaxies is inferred by statistical probability and the fact that organic molecules are found in outer space, although no concrete empirical evidence has yet confirmed the presence of life or intelligence in different regions of our solar system or beyond in the cosmos.

In the 19th century, both Kelvin and Helmholtz hypothesized that the first germs of life came to our earth from deep space through the arrival of meteorites carrying organic particles (or bits of cosmic dust with living germs propelled through the material universe by such forces as light quanta or the pressure of radiation). Early in this century, S. A. Arrhenius and J. B. S. Haldane defended the panspermia hypothesis.

Recently, astronomer Fred Hoyle and mathematician Chandra Wickramasinghe hypothesized that life was first brought to our earth by comets or meteors, which allegedly carry simple organic forms throughout an eternal steady-state universe. At present, there is no empirical evidence to suggest that cosmic seeds or living spores pervade outer space. Likewise, their notion does not account for the actual origin of life but merely places its existence elsewhere in the universe.

Francis H. C. Crick and Leslie E. Orgel have suggested that the sterile earth might have been deliberately seeded by intelligent beings living in other solar systems of the cosmos whose planets are billions of years ahead of our own in their stages of evolutionary development. Crick argues for the directed panspermia hypothesis in his book *Life Itself* (1981).

However, there are difficulties with this approach to explaining the existence of life on the earth. To begin with, it does not account for the appearance of those first living things presumed to inhabit the depths of outer space. Likewise, no irrefutable empirical evidence of such organic entities as cosmic seeds or biospores has yet been found in regions beyond our earth. In fact, the intense cold and radiation of the universe propose serious threats to any life as we know it (not to forget the vast emptiness of the cosmos). These facts make it extremely improbable that viable organic germs or spores or seeds could ever reach our planet from the abysses of the universe; Crick's hypothesis requires a bacteria-carrying rocket.

At this time in scientific inquiry, any theory of how life first came into being must necessarily be speculative without disregarding the established facts of various relevant fields and the need for logical consistency. One needs to distinguish among inorganic chemistry, organic chemistry, and biological evolution (although there is no clear separation between plants and animals, or between matter and life).

How Life Originated. The atmosphere of the primitive earth was an open system containing methane, ammonia, and water vapor; and later carbon monoxide, carbon dioxide, and free oxygen. Free energy came from volcanic heat, electrical discharge, and both cosmic and terrestrial radiation. The origin of life was a natural process that occurred at least four billion years ago with the first living things appearing gradually after a long period of chemical evolution. Controversy still surrounds the biochemical explanation for the origin of life on earth, particularly as to whether something analogous to the DNA or RNA molecule arose first or, instead, basic amino acids necessary for protein synthesis. Living things emerged when organic systems became capable of metabolism and reproduction; the development of inorganic syntheses in chemical evolution paved the way for biological evolution and subsequently the adaptive radiation of more and more complex and diversified forms.

Life may have first appeared in the atmosphere and/or in slightly acidic aqueous environments such as the seas (if not in pools or clays or ice crystals). The development of eukaryotic cells and subsequent multicelled organisms from prokaryotic cells took longer than the relatively short time necessary for the emergence of monomers (e.g., sugars, organic bases, and amino acids) and, later, polymers (e.g., proteins, nucleic acids, lipids, and ATP as the primary molecule of energy storage and exchange in all living organisms on earth). Today, according to some taxonomists, there may be as many as seven separate organic kingdoms (each having had a distinct origin). Nevertheless, diverse anaerobic bacteria are the earliest known organic inhabitants of our globe as evidenced by the discovery of Precambrian microfossils and stromatolites.

Although various explanations have been offered to depict how life could have begun, not one of these has as yet been sufficiently documented and experimentally tested. The law of parsimony, however, dictates that neither religious nor metaphysical assumptions are necessary for a sound understanding of and valid appreciation for the origin of life as we know it. Nevertheless, it is even possible that organic phenomena elsewhere in the universe are beyond technological detection and human cognition. At present, the naturalist theory of biochemical evolution to account for the emergence of life from prelife is the best explanation in terms of science and reason. Indeed, the problem of the origin of life continues both to excite and to challenge scientists as well as natural philosophers and enlightened theologians.

It is debated whether life emerged once or several times, and if this process could occur again in light of the changes in our atmosphere and on the surface of our earth. Also, it is debated whether mere chance or necessity was the predominant factor in the origin of life. Supernaturalists may argue that divine intervention caused the transition from inanimate matter to living things, while naturalists may conceive of the first appearance of life in terms of statistical probabilities and chemical evolution.

Biologists are still far from explaining all the awesome complexities of the terrestrial origin of living things, although the chemical emergence of life on earth is now the most widely accepted explanation for the beginning of organic history. Today, an interdisciplinary team of scientific specialists is needed to continue the search for the direct evidence of life's origin on our planet if not also in deep space. In the future, one may even anticipate scientists synthesizing under natural conditions complex organisms in test tubes where neither theology nor metaphysics need be required.

Other article of interest: **Universe, Origin of the, and Unbelief.**

Bibliography

Buvet, R., and C. Ponnamperuma, eds. *Chemical Evolution and the Origin of Life.* New York: Elsevier, 1971.

Dickerson, Richard E. "Chemical Evolution and the Origin of Life." *Scientific American* 239, no. 3.

Folsome, Clair Edwin. *The Origin of Life: A Warm Little Pond.* San Francisco: W. H. Freeman, 1979.

Fox, Sidney W., and Klaus Dose. *Molecular Evolution and the Origin of Life.* San Francisco: W. H. Freeman, 1972.

Hoyle, Fred, and Chandra Wickramasinghe. *Lifecloud: The Origin of Life in the Universe.* New York: Harper & Row, 1978.

Margulis, Lynn. *Early Life.* Boston: Science Books International, 1982.

Miller, Stanley L. and Leslie E. Orgel. *The Origins of Life on the Earth.* Englewood Cliffs, N.J.: Prentice-Hall, 1974.

Oparin, A. I. *The Origin of Life.* New York: Dover, 1953.

Orgel, Leslie E. *The Origins of Life.* New York: John Wiley, 1973.

Wald, George. "The Origin of Life." *Scientific American* 191, no. 2.

H. JAMES BIRX

LOCKE, JOHN (1632–1704), English philosopher, was born at Wrington in Somerset, on Aug. 29. He came from Puritan stock on both sides of his family. Through a paternal connection, he gained admission to the Westminster School, whence he was elected to a studentship at Christ Church, Oxford. Locke successfully graduated B.A. (Feb. 1655/6) and M.A. (June 1658), and worked his way up the academic ladder, achieving the Censorship of Moral Philosophy in December 1663.

Locke's Career. After rejecting a career as a clergyman, Locke embarked upon medical studies. It was because of his medical training that Locke made the acquaintance of Anthony Ashley Cooper, later first Earl of Shaftesbury, and Lord High

Chancellor, who introduced the young scholar to London's virtuoso culture, wealth, affairs of state, and religious toleration. But it was also because of links with Shaftesbury that Locke was forced to flee England in February 1682/3, when his patron was detected plotting subversion.

Locke settled in Holland, where he remained until after the Glorious Revolution, bringing to completion his philosophic masterpiece, *An Essay Concerning Human Understanding.* Upon his return to London, he saw through the press, in addition to the *Essay,* the *Two Treatises of Government* and *A Letter Concerning Toleration.* In 1691, he took up residence with Sir Francis Masham and his wife, Damaris, daughter of Ralph Cudworth, the Cambridge Platonist, in Essex. Though Locke hated public controversy, he was repeatedly involved in it as the result of the publication, albeit anonymous, of *The Reasonableness of Christianity* (1695). He was appointed a charter Commissioner of the Board of Trade, set up in 1695, and performed his duties assiduously until his retirement in 1700. In Essex, Locke maintained his contact with the outside world through a steady stream of visitors and correspondence until his death, Oct. 28, 1704.

His Thought. Though the works mentioned above do not begin to exhaust the range of Locke's publications, it is fair to say that from the time of his youthful tracts on the civil magistrate's authority over things indifferent, his thought revolves around the twin axes of politics (including economics) and religion (embracing morals). The *Essay* originated in discussion about the principles of morality and revealed religion. Locke shared the consensus of 17th-century Englishmen that morality and civil order depended upon general acknowledgement of God and his purposes for man. Man, as God's handiwork, provides the paradigm for the relationship between man and his property in Locke's political thought. The *Letter on Toleration,* so ample in its defense of liberty, stops short of countenancing atheists, who allegedly would not be bound by the oaths and covenants Locke regarded as the mortar binding society.

Where Locke differed most from contemporaries was how he sought to defend and justify Christianity. In a chapter of the *Essay* devoted to an examination of the relation between faith and reason, he defines the former as "the assent to any proposition, not thus made out by the deductions of reason, but upon the credit of the proposer as coming from God, in some extraordinary way of communication. This way of discovering truths to men we call revelation." Though many proper matters of faith may be above reason because we can have no natural knowledge of them, as that the dead shall rise and live again, none can be contrary to reason.

In *Reasonableness,* Locke seeks to show that belief in the revealed truths of the Christian faith is reasonable, given the fulfillment of prophecies foretelling the advent of a Messiah, and his performance of miracles. Locke's asseverations are markedly latitudinarian. All that a Christian needed to believe was that Jesus is the Messiah. Locke seems to have been a thinker who wished to delimit faith and reason, in order to preserve the integrity of both.

In the face of religious obscurantism, Locke added to the fourth edition of his *Essay* an additional chapter, "Of Enthusiasm," which concludes that "Reason must be our last judge and guide in everything." At about the same time, however, Locke was defending himself in his *Second Vindication of the Reasonableness of Christianity* against the charge of rejecting revealed religion by saying that he sought to correct misunderstandings of Christianity, not to deny revelation.

In spite of these protestations of faith, Locke deserves a place in the history of unbelief. His contemporary critics fastened on features of Locke's thought which, they maintained, tended to undermine the belief he professed to defend, whether he intended or realized it or not. By denying the innateness of speculative or practical principles, they charged he had destroyed the foundations of religion and morality. By denying any possible knowledge of the real essence of substance, he had called into question the nature of God, his incarnation, and the relation of the incarnate God to the other two persons of the Trinity. By speculating about thinking matter, he had opened the door to SKEPTICISM concerning the nature and immortality of the human soul.

Furthermore, though Locke himself undoubtedly was not a deist, he was related to the deists in a variety of ways (see DEISM). With some, like ANTHONY COLLINS, Locke maintained the closest personal relations. In the case of others, like JOHN TOLAND, whose *Christianity Not Mysterious* (1696) appeared in the year following Locke's *Reasonableness,* the basic doctrines and principles are avowedly drawn from Locke's epistomology, and are employed to denude religion of all mystery. But more generally, Locke's philosophic approach, the way of ideas, and the empirical phenomenalist analysis exemplified in the *Essay* were used by the most radical elements among the deists to dispel mysteries and abandon traditional jargon.

Modern readers of Locke have focused on Locke's novelties in isolation from the moral and religious concerns that gave rise to them. By attending to his distinction of first-order science and second-order philosophy, his adaptation of the resolutive-compositive method, his employment of the way of ideas, his defense of the new science, and his preoccupation with the limits of human knowledge, readers have discovered in Locke a watershed in English intellectual history, the beginning of modernity. Locke's place in the history of unbelief is not the less important for being unintended.

Bibliography

Modern editions of works by Locke include: *An Essay Concerning Human Understanding*, P. H. Nidditch, ed., Oxford, Clarendon Press, 1975; *Two Treatises of Government*, P. Laslett, ed., 2nd ed., Cambridge, Cambridge U. Press, 1967; *Epistola de Tolerantia*, R. Klibansky and J. W. Gough, eds., Oxford, Clarendon Press, 1968; *Correspondence*, E. S. de Beer, ed., Oxford, Clarendon Press, 1976–84.

Aaron, R. I. *John Locke*. 3rd ed. Oxford: Clarendon Press, 1971.

Bourne, H. R. Fox. *The Life of John Locke*. 2 vols. London: Henry S. King, 1876.

Brandt, R., ed. *John Locke Symposium Wolfenbuttel*. Berlin and New York: Walter de Gruyter, 1981.

Cragg, G. R. *From Puritanism to the Age of Reason*. Cambridge: Cambridge U. Press, 1950.

Cranston, M. *John Locke: A Biography*. London: Macmillan, 1957.

Redwood, J. *Reason, Ridicule and Religion: The Age of Enlightenment in England 1660–1750*. London: Thames and Hudson, 1976.

Schouls, P. *The Imposition of Method*. Oxford: Clarendon Press, 1980.

Yolton, J. W. *Locke and the Way of Ideas*. Oxford: Clarendon Press, 1956.

———, ed. *John Locke: Problems and Perspectives*. Cambridge: Cambridge U. Press, 1969.

———. *Thinking Matter*. Minneapolis: U. of Minnesota Press, 1983.

ROSS RUDOLPH

LITERATURE, UNBELIEF IN. See the following: **American Literature, English Literature, French Literature, German Literature, Russian Literature, Scandinavian Literature, Spanish Literature.**

LOGICAL POSITIVISM AND UNBELIEF. The name *logical positivism* was introduced by Albert Blumberg and Herbert Feigl in 1931 to refer to the basic ideas of a group of philosophers, mathematicians, and scientists known as the Vienna Circle. The same or very similar ideas were advocated by other groups in Europe in the 1920s and 1930s, notably in Germany, Scandinavia, and Poland. The leading figures of the movement in its early years were Moritz Schlick, Rudolf Carnap, Hans Reichenbach, Otto Neurath, Friedrich Waismann, Hans Hahn, Phillip Frank, Alfred Tarski, Kurt Gödel, Karl Menger, Richard von Mises, Carl Hempel, and Feigl. Except for Hahn and Schlick, who died before the Nazi invasion of Austria, all the other leading logical positivists emigrated to England and the United States in the 1930s.

In Central Europe the logical positivists were soon forgotten, but their influence on the intellectual life of the Anglo-Saxon world has been immense. Even before the exodus from Central Europe, the logical positivists had won a number of adherents and sympathizers in English-speaking countries. These included W. V. Quine, ERNEST NAGEL, and Charles Morris in the United States, and Frank Ramsey, Gilbert Ryle, R. B. Braithwaite, Susan Stebbing, ALFRED JULES AYER, and the biologist J. H. Woodger in England.

Ayer spent several months in 1932 and 1933 in Vienna, where he was one of the few foreigners allowed to participate in the meetings of the Vienna Circle. On his return to England he wrote a lucid, systematic, and remarkably comprehensive account of the major doctrines of the new movement. This was *Language, Truth and Logic* (1936), which, more than any other single publication, succeeded in bringing the new ideas to a general audience.

Wittgenstein. No mention was made in the preceding paragraphs of Ludwig Wittgenstein, who has often been described as the "founder" of logical positivism. It is true that Wittgenstein's book *Tractatus Logico-Philosophicus* (1921) was greatly admired by members of the Vienna Circle and that it contained several of its most characteristic doctrines. Wittgenstein also remained in close contact with Waismann and Schlick, who championed his views at meetings of the Circle and who repeatedly referred to his influence on them in their publications. However, Wittgenstein had a distaste for labels and programs, and he never considered himself part of any movement. With the sole exception of Schlick, Wittgenstein was not known to make complimentary remarks about any members of the Vienna Circle, but his posthumously published works of this period show close affinities to the view of the logical positivists. At the same time Wittgenstein was temperamentally far removed from the spirit of the movement.

Like the logical positivists, Wittgenstein did not believe in God or any metaphysical system, but from the time of his service in the Austrian army during World War I there was a strong mystical streak in him. Emotionally he was much closer to such gloomy Christian believers as Blaise Pascal and Sören Kierkegaard than to the thinkers of the ENLIGHTENMENT revered by the Vienna Circle.

The Verifiability Principle. One of the basic goals of the logical positivists was the formulation of a criterion that would enable us to discriminate between intelligible and unintelligible statements and questions. The criterion they proposed was the Verifiability Principle (VP), which became the basis of their rejection of speculative metaphysics as "nonsense."

The earliest explicit formulation of the principle is found in an article by Waismann: "If there is no way of telling when a proposition is true, then the proposition has no sense whatever; for the sense of a proposition is the method of its verification. In fact, whoever utters a proposition must know under what conditions he will call the proposition true or false; if he cannot tell this, then he also does not know what he has said" ("A Logical Analysis of the Concept of Probability," 1931).

Ayer's formulation in *Language, Truth and Logic* dispenses with any reference to "method of verification," a phrase that has led to a great deal of misunderstanding. A statement, he writes, is "factually significant" to a person if he knows how to verify it, that is, "if he knows what observations would lead him under certain conditions to accept it as true or reject it as being false." If the assumption of its truth or falsehood, on the other hand, "is consistent with any assumption whatsoever concerning the nature of his future experiences," then it is a mere pseudostatement. It may be "emotionally significant to him, but it is not literally significant."

Following Schlick, Ayer sharply distinguishes between "verifiability in practice" and "verifiability in principle." To say that a statement is verifiable in practice is to say that we can actually subject it to a test. The statement "there are brains inside the heads of human beings" can actually be tested, and hence it is verifiable in practice. The same cannot be said of "there are iron deposits at the center of the earth." We cannot at the present time subject this statement to a test, since we cannot travel to the center of the earth. This statement is, however, verifiable in principle. We can describe what a test of it would be like—we can specify where an observer would have to be placed and what observations would show the statement to be true and false respectively.

According to the VP, a statement must be verifiable in principle if it is to be meaningful. It does not have to be verifiable in practice. It is evident that statements about the world at periods before there was any life, or after life will have ceased, do not violate the VP. The statement "4.2 billion years ago mountains and oceans existed on the earth" is clearly verifiable in principle although, according to scientists, there were no living things on the earth at that time. We *can* describe what *would* have been observed at the time and places in question if the statement is true and what would have been observed if the statement is false. The fact that nobody was around to carry out the appropriate tests in no way affects our capacity to describe them. Similar remarks would apply to statements about the frozen surface of the earth after the last animate being has died.

What is excluded by the VP? Certainly a great many statements in the writings of metaphysicians from Parmenides and Plato to G. W. F. Hegel, ARTHUR SCHOPENHAUER, F. H. Bradley, and contemporary existentialists. Almost any of the statements made by the German philosopher, Martin Heidegger, about Being will serve as an illustration.

In his "Letter on Humanism" Heidegger declared that man is "the shepherd of Being." This pronouncement has been hailed as a major insight by Heidegger's numerous followers, but the VP makes short shrift of it. Let us suppose that a rival existentialist were to say "No, man is not the shepherd of Being." How could such a dispute be resolved? What observations, actual or possible, would count as evidence for or against either statement? The answer seems to be that there are none, and if this is so, the VP rules out Heidegger's statement as meaningless.

It might be said that perhaps Heidegger had something in mind when he made the statement, namely the fact that human beings are the only entities in the universe that ask questions about the meaning and purpose of things. Perhaps he did have this in mind, but it cannot be all that he intended to assert. For, according to Heidegger, Being is a reality that transcends all observable entities (all "beings"), and he meant to make an assertion about man's relationship to this transcendent reality. He repeatedly insists that when he writes about man's relation to Being, he is not making empirical statements but "ontological" claims, and he would agree that these ontological assertions are not even in principle verifiable.

To those familiar with the work of earlier empiricists, it will be apparent that the VP is not altogether new and that anticipations can be found in a number of earlier philosophers. DAVID HUME's doctrine of impressions and ideas, although couched in a misleading psychological idiom, is evidently a forerunner and so is William James' pragmatism, understood not as a theory about truth, but about meaning. James speaks of the "concrete" and "practical" consequences of theories and ideas and not of their verifiability or testability, but the intent of his "pragmatic method" is much the same as that of the VP. In the second chapter of *Pragmatism* James approvingly quotes from a letter sent to him by the famous German chemist Wilhelm Ostwald: "I am accustomed to put questions to my classes in this way: In what respects would the world be different if this alternative or that were true? If I can find nothing that would become different, then the alternative has no sense."

James comments that if rival views make no difference, they "mean practically the same thing, and meaning, other than practical, there is for us none." Very much in the spirit of the logical positivists, he remarks a little later that "it is astonishing to see how many philosophical disputes collapse into insignificance the moment you subject them to this simple test of tracing a concrete consequence."

Logical Positivism and God. Returning to statements about God, let us suppose that during a violent storm at sea, somebody remarks that God is angry with the world. He may employ these words simply as a colorful way of speaking about the intensity of the storm in the same way as somebody who says that the sea is angry is speaking

metaphorically and is not literally endowing the sea with emotions. However, this is *not* the kind of thing most religious believers intend to do when they assert that certain phenomena or events—e.g., the adaptation of organisms to their environment or disasters befalling their enemies—are the work of God. Similarly, when believers say that God created the universe, they are not merely saying that the universe exists. In all such statements they intend to refer to an entity transcending all natural or observable facts. The word *god* as used by traditional believers is not, according to Ayer, "a genuine name," and statements in which it occurs are not even in principle verifiable. We can at least in principle observe the various alleged empirical manifestations of God's activities, but we cannot even describe what it would be like to observe God himself. It follows, Ayer concludes with evident relish, that statements about the existence or nature of such a transcendent god "can possess no literal significance."

Carnap briefly discusses statements about God in "The Elimination of Metaphysics Through Logical Analysis of Language" (1931), one of the basic texts of logical positivism. He distinguishes between the "mythological" and the "metaphysical" use of *God,* and he points out that theologians tend to oscillate between these uses. In the mythological use, *god* stands for "physical beings which are enthroned on Mount Olympus, in Heaven or in Hades" and that are endowed with various human attributes. In the "metaphysical" use, the word refers to something "beyond experience." It is now "deliberately divested of its reference to a physical being or a spiritual being that is immanent in the physical."

Statements about God or gods in the mythological sense are empirical and hence they are intelligible, but they suffer from the disadvantage of being "subject to the judgment of empirical science." Theological statements using the word *god* metaphysically do not suffer from this disadvantage but only because they are pseudostatements asserting nothing at all. The word *god,* as used in them, has been deprived of the meaning it has for the mythological believer and it has not been given a new meaning.

It is noteworthy that a number of theologians have made similar distinctions, and most of them would accept the first of Carnap's conclusions. The eminent German theologian, Paul Tillich, who was a contemporary of Carnap, distinguished between the anthropomorphic and the metaphysical uses of the word *god*. Believers in the anthropomorphic god tend to think of God as a "cosmic policeman," a king on his heavenly throne, or as a superhealer, who is like a human physician except that he can cure any conceivable illness. Tillich repeatedly expresses contempt for the anthropomorphic belief, declaring that the "protest" of atheism is absolutely justified against such a theology, if only because there is no cosmic policeman, no heavenly king, and no superphysician.

Tillich's own God "infinitely transcends" every finite being. Between it and the finite objects of experience there is "an absolute break, an infinite 'jump.'" To avoid the anthropomorphic associations that have come to surround the word *god,* Tillich in his later years frequently dropped the word *god* altogether and instead spoke of "Being-itself," the infinitely transcending reality whose nonexistence is in no way implied by the nonexistence of cosmic policemen, heavenly kings, or superphysicians. Tillich's God is so far removed from the observable world that predicates taken from ordinary experience cannot be applied to his God in any of their literal senses. We cannot say that God is "good" or "loving" or that he "cares" for man unless we use these terms metaphorically. Tillich's God is of course not available to sense-observation, but he or it also "transcends both mysticism and the person-to-person encounter." Carnap would undoubtedly have commented that Tillich purchased invulnerability from "the judgment of empirical science" by escaping into statements that are not even verifiable in principle and hence are devoid of meaning.

It might be instructive to see how logical positivists would treat statements about God's presence in our midst. In his poem, *Lepanto,* G. K. Chesterton speaks about "the hidden room in man's house where God sits all the year." Similar statements about God's presence constantly occur in religious literature and conversation. When Chesterton's statement is read to students, most of them react skeptically—they do so whether they are believers or unbelievers. They raise the question how Chesterton could possibly know this. After all neither he nor anybody else has seen God in his apartment. An atheist would say that since there is no God to begin with, he cannot be sitting in anybody's house and hence Chesterton's statement is false. A logical positivist, by contrast, would argue that Chesterton's statement is empty, that it has no real content.

Let us consider the situation of a teacher who makes his living by giving courses in his apartment.

He has exactly 21 chairs, 20 for the students enrolled in his courses and one for himself. He and they would be put out if even one of them had to stand or sit on the floor. After reading the statement in *Lepanto,* the teacher asks Chesterton for advice: Should he buy a 22nd chair, since one of his chairs is evidently occupied by God? There is no doubt that Chesterton's answer would be in the negative. It would turn out that God's occupation of a chair is of a most peculiar kind. Not only can God not be seen or touched the way human beings can be seen and touched, but God's sitting is so peculiar that it does not at all preclude a human being from occupying the same chair, just as if it were empty.

A logical positivist would maintain that such a response would show Chesterton's statement to be factually meaningless. It *seems* to assert a fact about the occupation of rooms and chairs similar to everyday statements about the occupation of rooms and chairs by human beings or animals, but when pressed it turns out that Chesterton is making no such claim. Furthermore, there is every reason to believe that his expectations of what he would find in people's houses and apartments are no different from what they would be if he did not "believe" that God is sitting in every house.

Expressive, Directive, and Pictorial Meaning. From the beginning, the logical positivists called attention to the fact that language is used not only to make assertions about the world but also to express feelings and attitudes and to influence people. In lectures given in London in 1935 entitled "Philosophy and Logical Syntax," Carnap distinguished at some length between what he called the "expressive" and the "cognitive," or "descriptive" or "theoretical" functions of language. He pointed out there that if in a lyrical poem the poet uses the words *sunshine* and *clouds* she is not trying to inform us of meteorological facts. A lyrical poem has expressive meaning, but it does not have "assertive sense" or cognitive meaning. "All arts," Carnap wrote, "have this non-theoretical character without thereby losing their high value for personal as well as for social life."

Like lyrical poetry, metaphysical statements have expressive meaning, but they have no theoretical or cognitive content. Unlike the author of lyrical poetry, however, the metaphysician believes that his statements describe the world and in this he is deluding himself. Carnap would certainly not have denied that statements about God may have deep expressive meaning for certain people. If they believe that God is always with them or that he keeps a "protective eye" over their affairs, such beliefs may have highly important effects on their lives even though examination shows them to be devoid of literal or cognitive content.

Carnap mentioned only cognitive and expressive meaning. Later writers who agreed with him that metaphysical statements have expressive meaning called attention to other senses in which these statements are also meaningful. One of these is the sense in which recommendations, requests, and commands have meaning. "Please shut the door!" and "Make an appointment with my secretary for early next month!" are not assertions about the world, they are not true or false, but they are nevertheless perfectly intelligible: a person understands such an imperative if he knows what conduct is requested or suggested by its use. If we adopt Feigl's terminology and say that in such a case the sentence has "directive meaning," it is plain that metaphysical statements or, better, metaphysical systems, frequently possess meaning in this sense. This is particularly obvious in the case of those metaphysical systems that are connected with the promotion of a quietist and conservative outlook, and it is also evident in the case of many statements about God. When a religious preacher tells his congregation that God will punish those who act in certain immoral ways, his goal is to prevent them from acting in the ways of which God is said to disapprove.

When metaphysical statements contain everyday words, these at once produce images or mental pictures in the reader. They do this even if the author of the statement is quite willing to add that the words in question are not used literally. Let us say that a statement has "pictorial meaning" insofar as it has a tendency to be associated with mental images. This is, of course, a relative notion, and one and the same statement may have pictorial meaning for one individual but not for another. It must be emphasized that if a statement has pictorial meaning, this is no guarantee at all that it also possesses cognitive meaning. When challenged about her tardiness in preparing papers for the Aristotelian Society, Susan Stebbing once defended herself by saying, "My trouble is that I sleep more slowly than other people." This is a perfect example of a nonsense-sentence, at least as the English language is presently used. It nevertheless takes a little while to realize this because the presence of the familiar word *sleep* calls up certain pictures in most people. When Heidegger says such things as "the Region regions" or the "Nothing

nothings," one at once suspects nonsense because these expressions are not for most people associated with any mental pictures. One is less apt to do this in the case of such a statement as "Man is the shepherd of Being" because the word *shepherd* produces pictures of meadows, sheep, and real shepherds.

Returning to statements about God, there can of course be no doubt that just as they frequently have powerful expressive meaning so they also usually have more or less vivid pictorial meaning for most people. This fact helps the metaphysical theologian who, a logical positivist would argue, is mistakenly thought to make cognitively meaningful pronouncements because some of the words he uses tend to be associated with certain pictures and because both he and his readers do not clearly distinguish between pictorial and cognitive meaning.

Everybody knows how most children are taught the use of the word *God*. The god they are taught to worship is a thoroughly anthropomorphic god—a being like their daddy or granddaddy, who is most emphatically not a pure mind or spirit. Children are taught to pray to the all-powerful "Heavenly Father" for special blessings, and they are warned that the same all-seeing person will punish them for transgressions committed in the absence of their parents and teachers. They may thus develop deep feelings of love, fear, and guilt in relation to this Heavenly Father.

It cannot be sufficiently emphasized that in the text of prayers, hymns, and also in the Bible, God is generally spoken of as if he were a magnified human being with whom we may at some time come "face to face." Even children do not assign a definite location to God, but everybody habitually thinks of him as being "up above" and not "down below," and people regard the picture of a dignified elderly man with a white beard, looking perhaps like Tolstoi, as more appropriate than that of a young man with a moustache or perhaps a voluptuous young woman.

If God were really regarded as a purely spiritual being this should not be the case, and all pictures should be dismissed as equally inappropriate. When a child grows up and as a result of reflection or instruction shifts or tries to shift to belief in a metaphysical god, the old associations remain. They are so deeply entrenched that no amount of critical reflection can ever fully eliminate them. It is safe to say that even the most metaphysically oriented believer who prays in a time of acute personal distress is addressing the anthropomorphic

Heavenly Father and Superphysician, who is taken to be good and to care for his creatures in the ordinary literal sense of these words and not to the infinitely transcending Being-itself of Tillich. Unbelievers sometimes resist the conclusion of the logical positivists quite as strenuously as believers. The logical positivists would maintain that this is due to the fact that they too have very concrete pictorial associations with the word *god* and that they too confuse pictorial with cognitive meaning.

This is perhaps the place to explain why William James, in spite of the similarity of his "pragmatic method" to VP, did not reach the conclusion that statements about God are cognitively meaningless. Aside from purely emotional obstacles to reaching such a conclusion, this was due to a failure on his part to distinguish between cognitive meaning on the one hand and expressive and directive meaning on the other. It seemed clear to James that belief in God can make a great deal of difference to a person's life; and if it makes a difference then it has "practical" or "concrete" consequences and hence it is meaningful.

The answer to this is that these practical consequences of belief in God show only that the statements which the believer accepts have expressive and possibly directive meaning. They do not show that these statements have cognitive meaning. Belief in God would have been shown to have cognitive meaning only if statements about actual or possible observations could be logically derived from the statements the believer accepts that would contradict observation-statements derivable from the statements accepted by a person who denies the reality of God. If belief in God brings a person consolation during a period of mourning or if it gives him confidence when confronting a dangerous situation or if it turns him into a persecutor of heretics, the belief certainly makes a difference, but not in the sense that would show that the statement he believes has cognitive meaning.

Other Religious Doctrines. Liberal Protestant and Jewish theologians no longer believe in the devil, but the pope and fundamentalists in all religions do. Most of those who reject belief in demons would say there are no such beings, that statements asserting their existence are false. Logical positivists would disagree. Such a verdict, they would say, is semantically naive and does not do justice to the situation.

One of the foremost experts on demons and their nefarious activities is the Reverend Billy Graham. In a detailed study of Graham's life and work,

Marshall Frady quotes Billy Graham's diagnosis of the downfall of Richard Nixon, who, in pre-Watergate days, had been his close friend: "I think it was sleeping pills. Sleeping pills and demons. I think there was definitely demon power involved. . . . All through history, drugs and demons have gone together—demons have always worked through drugs."

If such statements about demons doing their destructive work inside the human body had been made in the Middle Ages the speaker might have been seriously referring to certain *visible* little beings—beings having the shape, tail and all, familiar from religious art. It is clear, however, that although he *suggests* something of the same kind, this is not what Graham is asserting. He is not asserting that when Richard Nixon took sleeping pills, a *visible* little demon invaded his body along with each pill. He is not asserting that, if we had opened up Richard Nixon's body, we would have found, in addition to the traces of the sleeping pills, a number of little manlike creatures with tails. Nor is he asserting that when a person dies as a result of taking an overdose of sleeping pills, the autopsy discloses such entities in his body. If this is a correct interpretation, then Billy Graham is not guilty of making a false statement but *one that has no content.*

What about survival after death? Are statements about survival intelligible by the principles of logical positivism? It is disconcerting to find Ayer and Schlick offering diametrically opposite conclusions, both of them supposedly derived from the VP. At the time of writing *Language, Truth and Logic,* Ayer had no doubt that statements about life after death are meaningless. To say that people do not ever die, meaning by this that their bodies never cease to live is intelligible (and false), but this is not what the believer in the afterlife affirms. He believes that "there is something imperceptible inside a man, which is his soul or his real self" and that this soul or real self goes on living after the death of the body.

The "content of this belief is not a genuine hypothesis," and the believer's assertion is no less metaphysical than the statement asserting the existence of God. Like the latter it has "no factual content." Moreover, even if there were a metaphysical self or soul that survives the death of the body, it would not be what anybody means when he uses the word *I.* When we use this word, we refer to the "empirical self"—the succession of impressions and ideas Hume opposed to the unobservable substance postulated by metaphysicians. This empirical self is also ruled out as a candidate for survival, but not by appealing to the VP. In discussing the criteria of personal identity—what makes perceptions at different times the experiences of the same person—Ayer rejects both memory and continuity of character and opts in favor of bodily identity. If this is granted, it becomes "self-contradictory to speak of a man as surviving the annihilation of his body."

For Schlick the survival hypothesis is not metaphysical at all but an "empirical statement which owes its meaning to its verifiability." Schlick is evidently talking about the survival of the empirical self. In all probability he would have agreed with Ayer that statements about the metaphysical self *are* meaningless. There are two ways in which the survival hypothesis could be put to the test. One of them is a "private method of verification," which is prescribed in the sentence "wait until you die." If the survival hypothesis is true, the experiences we will have after death will constitute its verification.

However, there seems to be trouble verifying the hypothesis if it should turn out to be false. If it is false we will of course have no experiences, and having no experiences does not seem a method of verification in the sense in which Schlick was using this term. Schlick did not pursue this puzzle. Instead he concentrated on the public evidence that might settle the question. "It is easy to describe experiences," he writes, "such that the hypothesis of an invisible existence of human beings after their bodily death would be the most acceptable explanation of the phenomena observed."

What Schlick has in mind is the kind of thing that goes on at seances. He expresses his contempt for the "ridiculous happenings alleged to have occurred in meetings of the occultists," but one can imagine more extensive and far better authenticated phenomena of the same kind that would render the survival hypothesis highly probable. Schlick is not fazed by the more specific hypothesis that "the souls of the deceased inhabit some supercelestial space." This statement would be nonsensical if *supercelestial* space is defined in such a way that it becomes *logically* impossible ever to obtain access to it and perceive what goes on there. If, however, it is only empirically impossible to get there so that we could describe "some means of overcoming the difficulties" of reaching it, then we are dealing with a perfectly intelligible theory. Lest Schlick be mistaken as a forerunner of such explorers of "the Beyond" as Elisabeth Kübler-

Ross and Raymond Moody, it should be emphasized that he did not have the slightest belief in the *truth* of the survival hypothesis, but merely defended its intelligibility.

The mere existence of the disagreement between Ayer and Schlick is not without significance. It seems to indicate that the application of the VP may turn out to be a tricky affair. The authors of the principle had evidently hoped that it would be an easy and sure guide to the resolution of disputes about intelligibility. At least in the present instance, however, it did not prove to be such a guide.

The Empiricist Language. Before going any further a few words are in order about difficulties encountered by the early versions of the VP. As a result of criticisms by opponents of the movement but for the most part discussions among the logical positivists themselves, it soon became apparent that all the earlier formulations were unsatisfactory. It was shown that they were either too narrow or too broad—too narrow in excluding as meaningless statements like scientific laws that were quite certainly meaningful, or too broad in letting in all kinds of statements that seem quite obviously meaningless.

One of the major difficulties that may be mentioned briefly concerned statements about the experiences of mental states of other people. If I say "I feel dejected" my experience of my own mental states will serve as verification (or falsification) of this statement. If I go on to say about another person, X, that he feels dejected, I am making a statement that is, in principle, unverifiable by me. It is in principle and not merely in practice unverifiable by me since it is logically impossible for me to experience somebody else's dejection.

The supporter of the VP seems to be faced with the following dilemma: He can say that the statement "X feels dejected" is meaningless although "I feel dejected" is perfectly meaningful. This is surely preposterous. Or he can say that "X feels dejected" is not about X's private feeling of dejection but about the publicly observable behavior on the basis of which others maintain that X feels dejected. This was in fact the course adopted by Ayer in the first edition of *Language, Truth and Logic*. He offered a behavioristic analysis of statements about other people's experiences and stuck to a "mentalistic" analysis of statements about one's own mental states. This alternative is also wildly paradoxical. It seems plain that there is no such asymmetry in the meaning of statements about one's own and other people's experiences. Ayer, it should be noted, was quick to retract this view in the second edition of his book.

Carnap and Hempel were prominent among those who tried to find more satisfactory formulations of the VP. It is impossible to do justice to their work in a brief and nontechnical summary, but perhaps one of their basic ideas can be mentioned here. The goal, as explicitly stated by Hempel in his article "The Empiricist Criterion of the Meaning" (1950) was the construction of an "empiricist language." A statement was then said to have cognitive meaning if it could be translated into such a language while it would be classified as meaningless if no such translation could be effected. The predicates of an empiricist language will consist of observation predicates and predicates introduced by being linked to observation predicates in certain ways. It can be shown that statements about other people's mental states are translatable into such a language.

The same is true of scientific statements involving dispositional terms and "theoretical constructs" (such as gravitational potential, electric field, or unconscious motive), which had proved troublesome. Statements about mythological physical deities like Zeus and Jupiter can also be translated into an empiricist language. On the other hand, various statements by metaphysicians like Hegel and Heidegger cannot be translated into it; and the same is true of Tillich's statements about Being-itself and Graham's statement about demons.

It may be interesting to note that the basic idea of Hempel's paper, though without any of the ingenious and careful technical elaborations, had been suggested in two articles by W. T. Stace ("Metaphysics and Meaning," *Mind,* 1935, and "Positivism," *Mind,* 1944). Stace was not a logical positivist but was sympathetic to some of the goals of the movement. He formulated what he called the "empirical theory of meaning": "Any statement, to have meaning, must symbolize experiencible characters of the world; or, what is the same thing, every concept employed in it must have empirical application."

Stace then proceeds to show how statements about other minds are entirely meaningful by this criterion. He points out that a person experiences her own conscious states. Statements about other people's conscious states present no problems since the individual will be attributing to other people the same experiencible conscious states—dejection, joy, the awareness of a loud noise—which she has experienced herself.

Attempts at Reconciliation. In the early days of logical positivism the usual response of pro-religious philosophers was to attack the VP, and no doubt this is still a fairly widespread reaction. Later on it became more common to say that the VP was basically sound, but that it was not fatal to religious belief. We will consider three prominent attempts at such a reconciliation.

1. One of these which was particularly popular in the 1950s and 1960s is usually referred to as "noncognitivism." Accepting the VP either in its original or in some modified version, these philosophers concede that statements about God would indeed be meaningless if taken as claims about a supernatural reality. The same statements are entirely meaningful if they are regarded as having some noncognitive function; and the latter is the proper way of interpreting them.

Perhaps the best-known and the most widely discussed defense of such a position is that by R. B. Braithwaite, the distinguished philosopher of science, in his Eddington Memorial Lecture, *An Empiricist View of the Nature of Religious Belief* (1955). According to Braithwaite religious statements are declarations of the asserter's intention to act "in the particular sort of way specified in the assertion."

"God is love (agape)" "epitomizes" the assertions of the Christian religion and is misconstrued if interpreted as a statement about the character of an unobservable transcendent being. Its real meaning consists in a declaration to follow "an agapeistic life." Such a way of life includes not only "external behavior," but also an "agapeistic frame of mind." Christianity requires not only that you should behave towards your neighbor as if you loved him as yourself; it requires that you should love him as yourself." Braithwaite believes that linguistic usage about what makes a person a "truly religious man" and a "real Christian believer" supports this interpretation. What constitutes a "religious conviction" is not belief in a supernatural creator but "the intention to behave in a certain kind of way, the allegiance to a set of moral principles."

Braithwaite realizes that not only Christians but also Buddhists, Jews, and believers not belonging to any denomination may be committed to the same "behavior policies, both of inner life and of outward conduct." The difference between Christians and non-Christians is that they are attached to different "stories." The Christian, but not the Jew or the Buddhist, finds stories about the life and death of Jesus a fortifying source in his or her intention to lead an agapeistic life. A religious assertion does possess a "propositional element which is lacking in a purely moral assertion, in that it will refer to a story as well as to an intention."

The stories that form part of the religious view need not be accepted as true. Some believers will indeed do so, but others will regard them as allegories, fables, or myths. In this connection, Braithwaite points out that works of fiction may also play a significant role in the adoption of a policy of action although they do not report any facts. A person can be a Christian believer even if she does not believe that Jesus worked any miracles and even if she does not believe that Jesus ever lived, so long as Christian stories help her to persist in an agapeistic policy.

Braithwaite's account contains one sound observation. It is perfectly true that, as many people use the term *religious* and more specific labels like *Christian,* a person does not qualify as a religious believer or as a Christian unless he acts or at least intends to act in a certain way. Belief in a supernatural God or adherence to certain rituals is not enough. This does not, however, mean that belief in a supernatural God is irrelevant. The most that Braithwaite has shown is that commitment to a certain morality *may* be part of what we mean by religious belief. It does not show that it is the whole of it, and in fact it clearly leaves out an essential element.

Theistic religions like Christianity and Judaism involve very definite supernaturalistic assertions, and Braithwaite has simply chosen to ignore them. When Christian and Jewish believers assert that the universe was created and is governed by an all-powerful, perfectly good, and perfectly wise God they may indeed be mistaken. It is also not incredible that what they say fails to have cognitive meaning. What is utterly and totally incredible is that they do not even *intend* to make a statement about the world; and yet this is what Braithwaite's thesis implies. It should be remembered that Braithwaite professes to give an account of what actual religious belief consists in and that he is not just telling us what he thinks it should be.

The same point can be brought out by considering what an unbeliever is challenging. When an unbeliever says such things as "there is no God" or "the universe has always existed and hence there is no need for a Creator," he is most certainly *not* opposing the adoption of any ethical policy. He is opposing supernaturalistic assertions about the existence of a transcendent God and the creation of the universe by such a God. From the disagreement between the believer and the unbeliever nothing whatever can be deduced about disagreement in the moral outlook of the contending parties; and in fact there frequently is none. In 1948 the B.B.C. featured a debate on the existence of God between Father F. C. Copleston and BERTRAND RUSSELL. Nobody reading this debate could for a moment deny that there was a fierce and extensive disagreement between the disputants; and yet there was not a word about moral policies. Read against the background of such a debate Braithwaite's thesis is simply ludicrous.

2. Unlike Braithwaite and the noncognitivists, John Hick, a leading Protestant theologian, insists that theological statements *are* factual claims. Hick grants that statements about God could not comply with the conditions laid down by the VP if the verification or test-experiences had to be confined to this life. Hick postulates a "Resurrection World" in which human beings who have died on earth will be supplied with healthy replicas of their previous bodies, and he thinks that certain of the experiences in these resurrection lives would give content to statements about God.

We shall here ignore all the obvious difficulties connected with the notion of a resurrection world populated by survivors from the earth who possess special resurrection bodies. The basic question is whether Hick can supply a description of *what* we would have to observe in the next life in order to test such statements as "God exists," "God created the universe" or "God cares for human beings." We cannot travel to the center of the earth but we can describe what observations would constitute verification and falsification of the statement "there are iron deposits at the center of the earth." Does Hick succeed in supplying anything that would correspond to these descriptions?

Hick begins by telling us that he is going to invoke the Christian doctrine of the Incarnation—the teaching that God revealed himself to human beings in the person of Jesus. We could verify theism if, in the next life, we could have "an experience of communion with God." Hick does not, however, maintain that we can directly observe God even in the next world. For our experience will be a "communion with God as He has made Himself known to men in Christ." Although we cannot observe God in the next life, we can obtain decisive evidence that the teachings of Jesus about God are authoritative: "God is the transcendent

Creator who has revealed himself in Christ. Now Jesus' teaching about the Father is a part of that self-disclosure, and it is from this teaching (together with that of the prophets who preceded him) that the Christian knowledge of God's transcendent being is derived."

Statements about God are "susceptible of indirect verification" if "rational doubt" about the authority of Christ could be removed by experiencing "the reign of the Son in the Kingdom of the Father." Such a "post-mortem experience" would indirectly confirm "the validity of Jesus' teaching concerning the character of God in His infinite transcendent nature."

There are two objections to this "eschatological" attempt to reconcile theism with the VP. The first and less important concerns the implication, of which Hick seems to be oblivious, that Christians (and by no means all Christians but only fairly conservative ones) are talking sense when they talk about God, but that other believers (Muslims, Jews, liberal Christians, unaffiliated believers and for that matter agnostics and atheists) are talking nonsense when they discuss the existence of God. Surely this is a totally unacceptable consequence. Jews and Christians disagree about the divinity of Christ, but they agree about the existence of God and if the theistic assertion is intelligible, it ought to be possible to explain its meaning independently of assumptions peculiar to Christians.

The more fundamental objection is that Hick totally fails to meet the challenge of the logical positivists to describe what it would be like to observe God—God *himself* as distinct from an embodied representative or "son" of God. Hick in one place uses the phrase "communion with God," but in doing so he muddies the waters. For in his view there will *not* be a meeting with God even in the next life. Instead we will experience the "reign of Jesus" and this experience will validate Jesus' teachings about the "transcendent Creator" who is his Father and who "reveals" and "discloses" himself in the Son.

Hick has evidently forgotten what the problem is. The problem is not whether statements about God are true, but whether they have any content and, if they have any, what this content is. If we already knew what these statements mean, then perhaps an appeal to the authority of Jesus would be a reason for accepting them as true. Such an appeal, however, most assuredly does not tell us what they mean and it does not show that they mean anything. As previously pointed out, the word *god* is familiar and for this reason most people assume that it means something, but in the present context this is what is questioned. If we substitute *girod,* a nonsense word, Hick would have seen that appeals to the authority of Jesus, or anybody else, are totally beside the point. It is clear that Hick has not succeeded in specifying post-mortem verifying data that correspond to the logically possible observations constituting the verification or falsification of the statement about iron deposits at the center of the earth.

It should be added that Hick uses the words *reveal* and *disclose* in a thoroughly misleading way when he tells us that God has "revealed" himself in Christ and that the teaching of Jesus is part of the "self-disclosure" of God. We know what these words mean in various familiar situations. A critic might observe that Kiri Te Kanawa's singing of the songs of Richard Strauss clearly "reveals" the influence of Elisabeth Schwarzkopf. A historian might report that John Dean disclosed the content of Richard Nixon's conversations with his henchmen on how to obstruct the Watergate investigation. We understand *reveal* in the first of these statements, because we can at least in principle identify or describe the features of Elisabeth Schwarzkopf's singing, whose influence is supposed to be revealed in the performances of Kiri Te Kanawa. Similar remarks apply to John Dean's "disclosure."

However, we cannot, independently of the actions and teachings of Jesus, describe what God is like. In contrast to the familiar cases, we do not really understand what it is that Jesus and his teaching are supposed to "reveal" and "disclose," but Hick, in using crucial terms as if their meaning were not at all problematic, suggests just the opposite. The question-begging nature of his procedure recalls the lady who, in the company of a friend, tried to cash a check in a bank in which she did not have an account. When the teller referred her to the manager and the manager pointed out that nobody in the bank knew her, she answered "My friend here will vouch for me." To this the manager responded, "But I don't know your friend either." The lady was not taken aback and said, "Allow me to introduce her to you."

3. What may at first seem the most promising attempt to reconcile the intelligibility of statements about God with the VP was first suggested in W. T. Stace's article "Metaphysics and Meaning" mentioned earlier. Stace thought that the logical positivists had been unduly restrictive in what they

counted as "experience." Why should sense observation or, as some logical positivists allowed, sense observation and introspection be the only kinds of experience we can use for testing statements? It is undeniable that some people have religious experiences and just as statements about the physical world are meaningful because they are verifiable in sense-experience so statements about God may be meaningful because they are testable in religious experience. The religious experiences *may* include post-mortem experiences, but Stace was evidently thinking primarily of religious experiences during the present life.

Somebody urging this objection might add that the exclusion of religious experiences as a mode of testing is itself an a priori prejudice which is inconsistent with the empiricism espoused by the logical positivists. It is tempting but illegitimate to reply to this attempt at reconciliation by claiming that it reduces theological statements to statements about the psychology of the people having religious experiences. In the present context this would be begging the question: it would assume without discussion that people who have religious experiences never apprehend an extramental divine reality.

However, there is another reply which seems decisive. In the case of empirical disputes it is always in principle possible to decide who is right and who is wrong, but this is not possible in the religious case. When Arthur Rodzinski, a great conductor but an exceedingly difficult man, took over as music director of the New York Philharmonic in 1943, his first act was to dismiss 15 of the players. Arthur Judson, the manager of the orchestra, urged Rodzinski to move slowly. Rodzinski agreed to talk it over with God. The next morning he told Judson that he had discussed the question with God and that God had advised him to "fire the bastards" (Rodzinski lasted just one season as director of the Philharmonic).

Let us suppose that Judson, as well as Rodzinski, was in the habit of seeking God's advice and that God had told Judson that the musicians should not be dismissed. Assuming that God does not issue contradictory advice, how can we tell who was really communicating with God? Statements about the physical world are testable in sense experience not simply because we *have* sense experiences, but because we have *criteria* for distinguishing between what counts as confirmation and disconfirmation respectively. We have no such criteria in the religious case.

What is substantially the same point can also be brought out in the following way. In the case of sense observations there comes a stage when any further doubt or question is absurd if not completely nonsensical. In the spring of 1981 there was an attempt to assassinate President Reagan. After the President was taken to the hospital two physicians removed a bullet from his lung. Conceivably there could have been a time at which the physicians may have wondered whether their patient was really the President and also whether the bullet was really in his lung, but eventually all doubt on these matters became absurd. The corresponding doubt in the religious case would *never* be absurd. Let us suppose that both Rodzinski and Judson reported that God had told them to "fire the bastards." It would not at all be absurd to question whether God really appeared either to Rodzinski or to Judson.

Let us go further and assume that in 1943 the world contained 500,000 mystics who habitually consulted God and that all of them sought his opinion on the Philharmonic issue. Let us assume that all of them reported God's advising the dismissal of the 15 musicians. It would still not be absurd to question whether all of them were deluded the way in which it *is* absurd to question whether Ronald Reagan was really shot and whether a bullet was really removed from his lung.

"Moderate" Metaphysical Theology. Carnap's distinction between the "mythological" and "metaphysical" varieties of theology does not do justice to all the major kinds of belief in God. There are two rather different positions, both of which would qualify as "metaphysical" by Carnap's definition, but about which an empiricist may reach quite different conclusions. One of these is the position of theologians who maintain not only that God is an unobservable reality but who also declare that this reality is so utterly different from human beings that terms like *intelligent, wise, powerful,* and *good* cannot be applied in a literal sense. Tillich exemplifies this viewpoint.

The other, more moderate position also holds that, not being a physical entity, God is unobservable. On this view, however, God is similar to human beings in being a mind and hence we can apply terms like *intelligent, wise, powerful,* and *good* in their literal senses to him. God is indeed vastly more intelligent, vastly more powerful, very much better and very much wiser than any human being, but the differences are in degree and not in kind. This is the position advocated by Cleanthes, the character in Hume's *Dialogues Concerning Natural Religion* who defends the viewpoint of the liberal believer against the skeptic Philo on one side and the orthodox believer Demea on the other. Turning to actual philosophers, it was clearly JOHN STUART MILL's view in "Theism," in which, on the basis of the argument from design, he regarded it as probable that organs like eyes and ears were produced by a superhuman intelligence, preferring this theory to the nonteleological explanation of Charles Darwin. It was also the position of unorthodox believers like W. P. Montague and the Boston personalists. What is perhaps more significant, however, is that *in practice* it seems to be the position of many educated believers who may not verbally acknowledge it. They in effect believe in a god who is a combination of protector, healer, and judge on a superhuman scale but who, unlike his human counterparts, operates without a body. Unbelievers, too, often think of God in this way. The great 19th-century physiologist Emil Dubois-Reymond argued against the existence of God on the ground that no cosmic brain can be discovered that would serve as the physiological foundation of a divine mind. "Before he can allow a psychical principle to the universe," Dubois-Reymond wrote, the student of nature "will demand to be shown somewhere within it, embedded in neurine and fed with warm arterial blood under proper pressure, a convolution of ganglionic globules and nerve-tubes proportioned in size to the faculties of such a mind." The fact that many believers are upset by arguments of this kind indicates that they do think of God as a supermind and not as a totally uncharacterizable reality like Tillich's Being-itself. Let us refer to this position as "moderate metaphysical theology" as contrasted with the "extreme" metaphysical theology of writers like Tillich.

As we saw earlier, the VP tells us that the statements of the mythological believer are meaningful, while those of the extreme metaphysical theologian are cognitively meaningless. Does it give us any guidance about the "middle" position, the statements of the moderate metaphysical believer? In any event, it is an intrinsically interesting question—at least to people concerned with the existence of God—whether these statements are intelligible. It is the theological counterpart of the question that has been widely discussed by philosophers in recent years: whether talk about disembodied consciousness is intelligible on the human level. Antony Flew has argued that psychological predicates are introduced in connection with the behavior of "flesh-

and-blood" persons and that they lose their significance as soon as the flesh-and-blood subject is removed. The same message seems implicit in several of the writings of Gilbert Ryle and in various passages of Wittgenstein's *Philosophical Investigations*. Wittgenstein does not discuss the question of disembodied consciousness, but in his dismissal of talk about the consciousness of a stone and chairs as nothing but "image mongery," he evidently took the view that all our talk about conscious states and processes is *logically* tied to the behavior of biological organisms like human beings. It would seem to follow that it makes no sense to talk about the thoughts, feelings, or sensations of a disembodied mind. It is interesting to note that P. T. Geach, a leading supporter of Wittgenstein's views on this subject who is also a Christian believer, has openly endorsed the notion of human survival in the form of bodily resurrection, arguing that statements about a pure mind would be meaningless.

On the other side of this issue, P. F. Strawson, A. Pap, A. Quinton, and H. H. Price have argued that it is entirely intelligible to talk about the sensations, feelings, and thoughts of a disembodied being. Schlick, too, it will be remembered, held this view when he argued that the notion of disembodied survival is intelligible. Although Ayer regarded such statements as self-contradictory in *Language, Truth and Logic,* he now holds the view that "disembodied spirits" in the sense of "disembodied streams of consciousness" are logically conceivable. It should be emphasized that, with the sole exception of Schlick, none of the philosophers on either side of this dispute appealed, at least not in any obvious way, to the VP in support of his position. The arguments are about what is logically involved in the concept of a person, in the concepts of seeing, hearing, feeling, thinking, dreaming, etc. One of the prime issues is the question of whether experiences require an "owner"; on the face of it the VP has no bearing on this question at all. As for Schlick, his appeal to the VP was couched in very general terms, and he never attempted to specify the observations in "super-celestial space" which would verify or falsify statements about the survival of the disembodied mind.

Let us suppose that analysis of the various concepts listed a moment ago can yield an answer to the question at issue and, for the sake of definiteness, let us assume that the Strawson–Quinton–(late) Ayer side is right. In that case we would have determined, without the use of the VP, that statements about disembodied consciousness are intelligible. If we have grounds for retaining the VP we will *then* conclude that these statements, since they are intelligible, must be verifiable in principle or translatable into an empiricist language. What this means is that, even allowing the VP to be "correct" or "valid" (in whatever sense a defender would regard it as "correct" or "valid"), it does not prove to be helpful in this case.

Let us now return to the position of the moderate metaphysical believer in God. It is evident that if the VP is of no use in deciding whether statements about disembodied consciousness are intelligible on the human level, it will also not help us decide the same question concerning statements about the divine mind. If we reached the conclusion that statements about disembodied consciousness on the human level are intelligible it would not be unreasonable to conclude that the theological assertions of the moderate metaphysical believers are intelligible. If we concluded that such talk is meaningless on the human level, then the same conclusion could be extended to moderate metaphysical theology.

To avoid misunderstandings it should be added that if statements asserting the existence of the supermind are intelligible, they are probably false for the very reason given by Dubois-Reymond: all our evidence indicates that consciousness cannot exist without a brain or at least a brainlike structure and, as far as we can tell, no such cosmic brain structure exists. Furthermore, the supermind would have to be limited in various ways, and there is no suggestion that it would be the creator of the universe.

VP as a Method of Challenge. Aside from the difficulty of determining in some cases whether a statement is verifiable or translatable into an empiricistic language, the VP ran into difficulties even in its later and more cautious formulations. Hempel (*Aspects of Explanation*) and Ayer eventually concluded that the quest for a "general and precise" criterion separating meaningful from meaningless statements should be abandoned. It is not clear how much comfort a metaphysician is entitled to derive from this conclusion. It most emphatically does not follow that certain statements are not definitely meaningful and certain others definitely meaningless. Nor does it follow that the VP is not frequently a useful instrument in determining whether a given statement is meaningful.

In 1966, more than a decade after reaching the conclusion that we cannot obtain a general and

precise criterion of cognitive significance, Hempel did not hesitate to apply the VP to the pretensions of a contemporary Thomist who had "explained" the mutual gravitational attraction of bodies as a manifestation of certain "appetites or natural tendencies" (closely related to love), which are inherent in these bodies. Hempel shows that neither this "explanation" nor the theory of an imaginary opponent, who explains gravitational attraction as due to a natural tendency in bodies akin to hatred which inclines them to hit and destroy other bodies, yields any testable consequences. The dispute between such natural philosophers is not "too deep" for scientific adjudication. It is not a genuine dispute, because the conflicting statements are "pseudo-hypotheses," which "make no assertions at all" (*Philosophy of Natural Science*).

Perhaps it would be best to use the VP as a method of challenge of statements and systems of statements whose intelligibility or coherence is not obvious. If somebody makes a statement that purports to describe the world but which does not have a clear meaning, we will demand to be told what, if any, verifiable consequences can be derived from it or how it could be translated into an empiricist language. If the author of the statement can give a satisfactory answer, we will know that he has made a genuine assertion and we can pass on to the question of whether his assertion is true. Sometimes, as in the case of statements about disembodied consciousness, it will not be easy to answer our question, but on many occasions the answer will clearly be that the statement has no verifiable consequences. In that event we have a "suspect" on our hands who requires further investigation, and we will not offer a definite opinion about the intelligibility or lack of intelligibility of the statement until our further investigation is concluded.

This more circumspect procedure has numerous advantages over the sledgehammer approach of the logical positivists of the 1930s. Among other things, it makes one see, in the case of those statements and systems that further investigation reveals to be incoherent, just what the confusions are that drove the author into meaninglessness. It also not infrequently turns out that, on the way, he or she made some valuable (and entirely intelligible) observations which the more drastic procedure of the earlier period was liable to miss.

Other articles of interest: **Devil, Unbelief in the Concept of. God, Existence of.**

Bibliography

Ayer, A. J. *Language, Truth and Logic.* London: Victor Gollancz, 1936, 1946.

———, ed. *Logical Positivism.* Glencoe, Ill.: Free Press, 1959.

———. *The Central Questions of Philosophy.* London: Weidenfeld and Nicolson, 1973.

Braithwaite, R. B. *An Empiricist View of the Nature of Religious Belief.* Cambridge: Cambridge U. Press, 1955.

Carnap, Rudolf. "The Elimination of Metaphysics Through Logical Analysis of Language." 1931. Reprinted in *Logical Positivism* (op. cit.).

———. *Philosophy and Logical Syntax.* London: Kegan Paul, 1935.

Edwards, Paul. "Professor Tillich's Confusions." *Mind.* 1965.

Feigl, Herbert. "Logical Empiricism." *Readings and Philosophical Analysis.* H. Feigl and W. Sellars, eds. New York: Appleton Century Crofts, 1949.

———. "The Wiener Kreis in America." *Perspectives in American History.* Vol. 2. Cambridge: Harvard U. Press, 1968.

Hempel, Carl G. "The Empiricist Criterion of Meaning. Reprinted in *Logical Positivism* (op. cit.).

Hick, John. "Theology and Verification." *Theology Today.* 1960.

Klein, K. H. *Positivism and Christianity.* The Hague: Martinus Nijhoff, 1974.

Mises, Richard von. *Positivism.* Cambridge: Harvard U. Press, 1951.

Nielsen, Kai. "Eschatological Verification." *Canadian Journal of Theology.* 1963.

Pap, A. *The Elements of Analytic Philosophy.* New York: Macmillan, 1949.

Passmore, J. "Christianity and Positivism." *Australian Journal of Philosophy.* 1957.

Schlick, Moritz. "Meaning and Verification." 1936. Reprinted in *Readings in Philosophical Analysis* (op. cit.).

Stace, W. T. "Metaphysics and Meaning." *Mind.* 1935.

Waismann, Friedrich. "A Logical Analysis of the Concept of Probability." 1931. Reprinted in Waismann, *Philosophical Papers.* Dordrecht: Reidel, 1977.

PAUL EDWARDS

LUCRETIUS, in full, Titus Lucretius Carus (about 99 or 94–55 B.C.). Almost nothing is known or seems knowable about the life of Lucretius, beyond what little may be inferred from his unfinished epic poem *On the Nature of Things (De Rerum Natura).* One view is that he was a Roman, from a moderately distinguished family. Others have suggested he was a freedman attached to the Lucretii family.

There is also a story, enthusiastically retailed by St. Jerome, that Lucretius produced his didactic masterpiece—six books totaling 7,400 hexameter lines—in a fit of madness culminating in suicide. Thoughtfully, the saint added that this affliction was the result of taking a poisoned love philtre.

What Jerome held against Lucretius was that *On the Nature of Things* expounds the most coherent system of MATERIALISM in the ancient world, that of Epicurus. When Jerome was writing, this was only the most readable account; the studiously prosy prose of Epicurus himself was no match for the passion and eloquence of the poet. But the accidents of loss and survival have since made it by far the richest and fullest source of Epicurean ideas. There is also some reason to believe that Lucretius actually improved a little on Epicurus, not only in presentation but also in content; and this notwithstanding that the pupil was always at pains to express the most fawning devotion to his master.

The fundamental principle of the poem, as is later found in the philosophy of THOMAS HOBBES, is that stuff is all there is; while everything which is not stuff is nonsense. Stuff consists in atoms. All our knowledge of all there is must, therefore, be based upon sensory perception. And, furthermore, our universe of atoms is and must be, in the last analysis, mechanical. Both Epicurus and Lucretius would have felt at home with Lord Kelvin (Sir William Thomson), who protested that he could not understand anything of which he was unable to construct a working model.

But Epicurus had introduced a peculiar new twist into the original Classical Greek atomism of Leucippus and Democritus. This was the doctrine of *parenklisis* (Latin, *clinamen*). The natural state of all bodies was supposed to be uniform motion in a straight line, downwards; a kind of gravity being taken to be characteristic of the entire universe or, as we might say, of spacetime. (Compare this with the modern Newtonian First Law of Motion.) But the doctrine of *parenklisis* added that there are also equally natural, occasional deviations. Sometimes one atom departs from its set, straight way without having been previously pushed off course by another.

The argument which led Epicurus to introduce this theoretical innovation, and which Lucretius faithfully followed, was twofold. In the first place, something of this sort appeared to be necessary if every atom in the universe was not to be left endlessly and uniformly moving downwards. Second, since choice between open alternatives is one of the most manifest and inescapable facts of human experience, we must, in order to accommodate it, introduce some indeterministic element into our basic physics.

On the Nature of Things develops these ideas, and applies them to explain both present, everyday experience and past origins. Seeing, for instance, is a matter of atomic transactions between the objects seen and the eyes of the creature seeing. Again, the adaptation of living organisms to their various environments is a consequence of the survival of those fittest to survive in a struggle for existence, although no one was able to anticipate Charles Darwin and his successors by providing any more or less adequate account of the emergence of variations for such natural selection to be selections between.

Lucretius sees his Epicurean teaching as the sovereign prophylactic against everything that DAVID HUME would dismiss as "religious fears and prejudices." Above all, Epicureanism was valuable because it removed the basis for fear of death. For if indeed death is final, then it must be as silly to be moved by hopes or fears for a life after death as it would be either to pine about the sufferings suffered or to exult in the joys enjoyed in the infinite period of nonexistence before we were conceived.

The Lucretian line here is that the soul, or *anima,* by which human organisms are animated or made alive, is composed of peculiarly small and delicate atoms. The *anima* is, therefore, something that cannot but be irreparably destroyed in the trauma of death. Lucretius specifically considers, but rejects, the alternative and surely stronger mortalist position, which starts from the insistence that people are merely creatures of flesh and blood, refusing to accept the far-fetched and utterly

unwarranted assumption that we are the invisible and maybe even the incorporeal occupants of our bodies. Death and dissolution for such flesh and blood creatures cannot but be irrevocably final.

It has been suggested that in crusading against the promise of the delights of paradise or the threat of hell's torments, Lucretius was crusading against enemies who had long since withdrawn from the field. Certainly his contemporary Cicero, in the Tusculan *Disputations,* does dismiss such promises and such threats as matters that no longer troubled any halfway-educated person. But, before taking this as the last word, we should remind ourselves of two things. First, in those days there were more people who were not halfway educated than there are now. Second, it is both possible and common for in-groups to congratulate themselves on their own enlightenment while nevertheless being themselves surrounded by unnoticed and far-from-enlightened outsiders.

Nor should we forget that with the revival of classical learning in the 16th and 17th centuries *On the Nature of Things* became, after a long period of neglect in the Middle Ages, a widely read source of secular ideas. As an acknowledged masterpiece of ancient literature, it was studied then by people who would never have opened a book by a notorious modern infidel.

Other article of interest: **Ancient World, Unbelief in the.**

Bibliography

Recent complete translations are: in prose, by R. E. Latham (Harmondsworth: Penguin, 1951); and in verse, by A. D. Winspear (New York: 1955). Perhaps the best attempt to convey the poetic force of the original is found in extracts "in the metre of *Omar Khayyam*" in W. H. Mallock, *Lucretius on Life and Death* (London: Adam & Charles Black, 1900). About the influence Lucretius exercised, see G. D. Hadzsits, *Lucretius and His Influence* (New York: Longmans, Green, 1935) and A. D. Winspear, *Lucretius and Scientific Thought* (Montreal: Harvest House, 1963).

ANTONY FLEW

M

McCABE, JOSEPH MARTIN (1867–1955). In his autobiography *Eighty Years a Rebel* (1947), the Englishman McCabe described himself as a "pedlar of culture." His chief American publisher, EMANUEL HALDEMAN-JULIUS, repeatedly called him the world's greatest scholar. In truth McCabe was both. An immensely prolific author (by his own estimate at the age of 80, he had written over 200 books, "more than any other living author," he said), he did some hack work, often under pseudonyms.

In the fields of religion and history, McCabe was a prodigious scholar, although he was largely self-taught. He had an encyclopedic curiosity, was indefatigably interested in all aspects of human culture, and usually was engaged in research and writing seven days a week 52 weeks a year. Unlike most scholars, McCabe did not write only or even primarily for other scholars. He carried on into the 19th and 20th centuries the cause of public enlightenment championed by such 18th-century *philosophes* as DENIS DIDEROT and VOLTAIRE. To him knowledge was not an end in itself but a means for promoting SKEPTICISM, unbelief in all the dogmas that keep men from realizing the finer, happier social order that is in their power to create. His writings, particularly the more polemical ones, sold in the millions; he lectured and debated around the world before audiences sometimes numbering in the thousands.

Early Life and the Priesthood. Joseph McCabe was born on Nov. 11, the second son of a poor family on the outer fringes of the working class in Macclesfield, England. His Roman Catholic father of Irish extraction, William Thomas, was a weaver; his Scots-English mother, born Harriet Kirk in a Protestant family, was a convert to Roman Catholicism who "never lost her zeal." Following a brief period as an errand boy and then a clerk in a Manchester merchant house, the 16-year-old entered preparatory college at the Gorton Franciscan monastery.

McCabe was ordained a Roman Catholic priest at 23 and appointed professor of philosophy, a subject in which he had taken an unusual interest. By the age of 27 he had become the Very Reverend Professor Father Antony of the Order of St. Francis. However, during these years the young McCabe increasingly doubted the truth of the fundamental tenets of his religion. Characteristically, in 1895 he shut himself up in his cell, took a sheet of paper and divided it into two columns for arguments for and against God and immortality. After weighing the evidence for many days and nights, on Christmas Eve he wrote "Bankrupt" at the bottom of the sheet and gave up his sacerdotal career forever.

McCabe's writing career was launched through his becoming a friend of the skeptical Sir Leslie Stephen, then dean of British letters, who encouraged him to write his autobiographical *Twelve Years in a Monastery* (1897). The book was a success, attracting more than 100,000 readers. He opened his serious literary career with *Peter Abelard* (1901) and *St. Augustine and His Age* (1902), and began a long series of biographies including ones of Goethe (1912), GEORGE BERNARD SHAW (1914), ROBERT OWEN (1921, 1948), GEORGE JACOB HOLYOAKE (1922), *The Hundred Men Who Moved the World* (1931), and Edward Clodd (1932).

Although McCabe was to produce about 50 translations of various works, it was his translation of ERNST HAECKEL's *Riddle of the Universe* (1902) that spread his name throughout the English-speaking world. McCabe also wrote popularizations of science emphasizing the concept of evolution. In his writings on history and religion, McCabe applies the same evolutionary perspective; for, in his view, history is a science. Indeed, history, evolutionary history, provides the only genuinely scientific understanding of the development of human culture and of human social institutions. All scientific understanding is the understanding of evolutionary processes, of their course of development or "histories," whether one is considering the birth and death of stars or the rise and fall of the gods.

His Ideas. For McCabe MATERIALISM, in the sense of unbelief in any nonempirical, spiritual, or supernatural causes, is the only scientific philosophy. Therefore, a truly scientific history must rest on a deterministic materialism. While generally sympathetic with the deterministic materialism of KARL MARX, he rejected dialectical materialism as idealistic verbiage left over from Hegel and the economic determination of history as too narrow a version of the materialistic determination of history.

McCabe argued that in the 20th century it was religion, particularly Roman Catholicism, that appealed to nonempirical, spiritual, supernatural causes and thus was the chief opponent of materialism and, therefore, of science. What gave a polemical, anticlerical edge to his writings on religion was his conviction that this religious opposition was dishonest, a rationalization to preserve and augment the power of the churches and the men who control them. A scientific history of religion, McCabe contended, shows that religion and religious institutions, like that of monarchy, are on the road to extinction in the 20th century.

McCabe's historical thesis of the doom of religion perhaps received its best and fullest presentation in his *The Story of Religious Controversy* (1929) and *The Rise and Fall of the Gods* (1930). By the close of the 19th century, science had deposed religion from its old position of sovereign intellectual authority; in the following century science would be applied to all of human life and usher in an age of unprecedented peace, prosperity, happiness, and cultural advance. The dreams of the 18th-century *philosophes* would become reality for all mankind. The chief adversary of the progress of science, religion (with Roman Catholicism as the most formidable and die-hard opponent) was everywhere in decay.

By the early 1930s it was clear that the development of a fully scientific civilization had been slowed, even though the churches had suffered a severe decline in membership. In McCabe's view, what had produced this setback was the threat to economic privilege posed by the rise of socialism and communism. Capitalism had smashed the old alliance of king and priest. But now alarm at the advance of socialism and communism was driving the liberal bourgeoisie into an alliance with clerical-

ism and the Vatican to defend private enterprise and religion. In practical terms, McCabe felt, this new "Holy" Alliance resulted in the rise of fascism and the launching of a grand assault on the Soviet Union in World War II. Once communism was destroyed, socialism would be next. At the end of the year, however, the Soviet Union emerged victoriously as a world power, and three years later China passed under Communist control. The Cold War ensued, with the United States the world leader of the capitalist-clerical opposition.

McCabe argued the foregoing thesis in a long series of works including *The Papacy in Politics Today* (1937, 1943, 1951), *A History of the Second World War* (1946), *The Epic of Universal History* (1948), and *The Origin and Meaning of Ideas* (1951). In *The Next 50 Years* (1950) he reaffirmed his belief that the socialists and communists would give up their old quarrel, reunite, vanquish their old foes of wealth, religion, and militarism, and establish a new and superior world civilization by 1999.

Although McCabe seems to have been at least on speaking terms during the first quarter of the 20th century with nearly everyone in English intellectual and political life even slightly tinged with religious skepticism, his personal life was one of increasing isolation, dwindling to his living alone like a secular priest with his housekeeper. His 1899 marriage to Beatrice Lee, which resulted in two sons and two daughters, failed in 1925.

McCabe's aggressive frankness and skepticism seem to have offended nearly everyone. The final breach with the British Rationalist Association came in 1928; he was expelled from the association and ostracized from rationalist circles. McCabe contended this was engineered by CHARLES BRADLAUGH's daughter and other admiring Bradlaughites angered by his criticism of Bradlaugh and praise of Holyoake. The bulk of McCabe's writings after 1928 were published in paperbound form in America by Haldeman-Julius, who wrote in 1949 that McCabe had authored 121 Little Blue Books and 122 larger books totaling 7,600,000 words and earning him over $100,000.

In spite of his personal calamities, as McCabe called them, until his death on Jan. 10, 1955, at the age of 88, he remained an optimist, atheist, materialist, socialist, and admirer of the Soviet Union, contending that communists had a right to exist and were superior to "bishops, preachers, exploiters of the poor, millionaires, parasites, dictators and liars and crooks generally." He wished his epitaph to be: "He was a rebel to his last breath."

Other articles of interest: **Enlightenment, Unbelief During the. Evolution and Unbelief. God, Existence of. Immortality, Unbelief in.**

Bibliography

Cook, Freda. "Joseph McCabe at Home." In Joseph McCabe. *Cybernetics—The New Science of the Electronic and the Human Brain.* Girard, Kans: Haldeman-Julius, 1950.

Goldberg, Isaac. *Joseph McCabe: Fighter for Freethought.* Girard, Kans.: Haldeman-Julius, 1936.

Haldeman-Julius, E. *My Second 25 Years.* Girard, Kans.: Haldeman-Julius, 1949. Passages about McCabe are scattered throughout Haldeman-Julius' writings.

Haldeman-Julius, Marcet. *Talks with Joseph McCabe and Other Confidential Sketches* Girard, Kans.: Haldeman-Julius, n.d.

McCabe has not received the attention his life, ideas, and writings deserve, and no full studies of him have been published.

JOHN R. BURR

MAGAZINES OF UNBELIEF. See Appendix 5: Periodicals of Unbelief.

MALRAUX, ANDRÉ (1901–1976), French author and art historian. See **French Literature, Unbelief in.**

MARÉCHAL, SYLVAIN (1750–1803), known as "*l'homme sans Dieu,*" was probably the most articulate and militant atheist of the French Revolution. The son of a Parisian wine merchant, he was trained as a lawyer before he decided to make a career of literature. His prolific writing includes, not only the attacks on religion for which he is chiefly remembered, but also Anacreontic verse, pastoral tales, moral maxims, political tracts, plays, and erudite works on history and archeology.

His Life as an Activist and Writer. Being already before 1789 a republican at heart, Maréchal welcomed the Revolution, and took an active role in it as a journalist and pamphleteer. He was intransigently anticlerical, a fervent partisan of dechristianization, and voiced strongly antimonarchistic, plebeian, and egalitarian sentiments. This, however, did not turn him into a Jacobin, because he was also opposed to dictatorship.

Maréchal's political views, which are best revealed in the *Correctif à la Révolution* (1793), advocated a semianarchistic, agrarian type of socialism founded on the imperative, not of popular sovereignty, but of patriarchal authority. Since this visionary opinion did not coincide with the actual program of any party, it made him something of an iconoclast and "outsider" in revolutionary politics. Hoping, under the Directory, to wed at last dream and reality, Maréchal composed the *Manifeste des égaux* (1796) as his contribution to François Émile Babeuf's abortive conspiracy to set up a "communist" government. The following year he published a *Correctif à la gloire de Bonaparte,* in which he shrewdly foresaw and courageously denounced the future tyrant of France. The last phase of his life, during which he continued to write on the many subjects that interested him, was uneventful.

Although Maréchal's hostile remarks on religion derived generally from the literature of the French ENLIGHTENMENT (especially JEAN MESLIER, DENIS DIDEROT, and PAUL HENRI HOLBACH), the ultimate use he made of it was distinctly his own. His ATHEISM represented an original synthesis of several components: a "Rousseauistic" nostalgia for a lost Arcadian age when, according to Maréchal, the expression of natural piety had been patriarchal and social, instead of theistic and church-oriented; the moral and practical superiority of a simple cult of virtue to a mystifying worship of God; and a utopian socialism, resembling that of Morelly, which idealized a just and peaceful society based on the principle of civil and economic equality. These different elements of Enlightenment thought were combined by Maréchal in a nonsystematic, aphoristic, rhetorical, and polemical manner, as befitted the political concerns and strident tone of his times. To form a more accurate notion of his attitude as an unbeliever, it is necessary to describe in some detail his principal works on religion.

Culte et loix d'une société d'hommes sans Dieu (1797). Consisting of slogan-like axioms, this curious text codifies a "cult of atheism." What seems to be a paradox is really proof that Maréchal was opposed, not to the practice of religion, but to one centered on God and ecclesiastically organized. The object of his own cult, in which God would be replaced by such interchangeable abstractions as Virtue, Nature, Reason, and Justice, is solely to consecrate and promote the common good. To do so, Maréchal thinks it is indispensable to have an institution whose express purpose will be to combat belief in God, which he regards as "the pretext for all crimes and the source of all calamities."

The *hommes sans Dieu* (H.S.D.) would have their own "Bible," but it would contain only models of virtuous behavior to be revered and emulated. Their cult would be celebrated in a "temple," where young and chaste women would burn incense and sing hymns to the self-sufficiency of Virtue and the uselessness of God. At these "services," a white cloth separating initiates from postulants would bear the inscription: "Of all errors, the greatest is God." The H.S.D. would carry out "pastoral duties" among their "congregation"; would "baptize" infants in the name of Reason and Virtue; and would perform marriage ceremonies.

The cult's printing press would publish *Mémoires* devoted to the advancement of atheism. Each year a prize would be awarded for the best essay refuting belief in God, and a course of lectures would be established at which famous scientists argue against the existence of God and in favor of "almighty Nature." No one would be admitted to the cult if his atheism is prompted by the wish to escape punishment for his bad actions, or if his fortune is more than three times what he needs to live on. The H.S.D. would respect the principle of toleration and patiently endure persecution for their beliefs.

There are other rules, but these suffice to characterize Maréchal's zealous and elaborate "religion of atheism." The latter should be understood in the context of the various non-Christian civic cults that sprang up in that period of improvisation for the purpose of securing the political and social goals of the Revolution. It differs from the others, however, in that it is based, not on the acceptance, but on the rejection of an impersonal Supreme Being.

Le Lucrèce francais (1798). This work in verse was preceded by two shorter versions: *Fragments d'un poème moral sur Dieu* (1780) and *Dieu et les prêtres* (1793). It evokes many of the themes that underlie Maréchal's atheism. In particular, a Diderotian-Holbachian kind of naturalism pictures the universe as an eternal self-contained whole, in which everything changes by necessary

physical laws and outside of which there is nothing. On the human-historical scale, it is stated that when the happy, primitive life of mankind gave way to competition, violence, and finally tyranny, the gods were invented by an "imposter" to keep the unhappy victims of inequality and injustice subservient to those in power.

For Maréchal, religion has ever since been an instrument of oppressive government and socio-economic exploitation, so that reform of those great evils absolutely requires the triumph of atheism. The sage does not regard this world as a place of exile, but performs, without recourse to God, his obligation as a faithful husband, tender father, and loyal friend; the evil which God permits to exist, he tries to correct; he has no desire for a Lord in heaven, because there are already too many lords here on earth. The atheist is an elitist, not a democratic republican, for he separates himself from the common people, whom superstition renders obedient to God and tyrants.

Dictionnaire des athées anciens et modernes (1799). In this work, an atheist is defined as someone who practices virtue for its own sake, or whose life is meaningful and fulfilled through his social relations alone, or who has expressed any opinion on religion, morality, or politics that may be interpreted as consistent with atheism. A definition so extremely broad allows Maréchal to include in his *Dictionary* not only those whom one expects to find in it, but many others whom one does not.

The different categories of "atheists" he lists may be distinguished as follows: (1) more or less true atheists like Democritus, Epicurus, LUCRETIUS, GIORDANO BRUNO, GIULIO CESARE VANINI, THOMAS HOBBES, Meslier, JULIEN DE LA METTRIE, DAVID HUME, Diderot, and Baron d'Holbach; (2) possible atheists such as Cicero, Averroës, Campanella, Michel de Montaigne, RENÉ DESCARTES, Molière, PIERRE BAYLE, and BENEDICT SPINOZA; (3) those who seem atheists only from the standpoint of the strictest religious orthodoxy: Plato, Aristotle, Sir Francis Bacon, Pierre Gassendi, JOHN LOCKE, Nicolas Malebranche, Sir Isaac Newton, G. W. Leibniz, Jean Jacques Rousseau; and (4) those who are the very opposite of atheists: Saint Augustine, Jansenius, Jacques Bénigne Bossuet, Blaise Pascal, François de La Mothe-Fénelon, and even Jesus.

This controversial "reference-book" may be explained as an incident in the contemporary struggle between the partisans of religion and those of unbelief, which was to end with the official reinstatement of the Catholic church under Napoleon I. Maréchal's work was a polemical ploy meant to forestall that event by giving its readers to understand that a national religion was unnecessary because the best and wisest men of all ages had been unbelievers. His paradox of universal atheism also pointed to a deeper truth, namely, that if the test for belief in God is made stringent enough, it could well turn out that practically everyone is, consciously or unconsciously, an atheist.

Pour et contre la Bible (1801). Although much of this work echoes the biblical criticism of the Enlightenment, its originality is that Maréchal's judgments often derive from aesthetic criteria. What he says in praise of the Old Testament (which he prefers to the New) is usually based on its sublime rhetoric and narrative skill. This literary appreciation does not prevent him, however, from insisting on the "unevenness" of the Bible, and on the obscenities, immoralities, absurdities, puerilities, and atrocities with which it is replete. His final verdict is that a prudent government should ban it altogether as a dangerous book; for while many excellent things may be found in the Bible from which mature and reasonable readers can profit, it contains too many precepts and examples which the average reader, always credulous and not especially virtuous, could only be expected to abuse, finding in them encouragement for his worst passions.

Bibliography

Aubert, Françoise. *Sylvain Maréchal: passion et faillite d'un égalitaire.* Paris: Nizet, 1975.

Dommanget, Maurice. *Sylvain Maréchal, l'égalitaire, "l'homme sans Dieu."* Paris: Spartacus, 1950.

Fusil, Casimir. *Sylvain Maréchal, ou l'homme sans Dieu.* Paris: Plon, 1936.

ARAM VARTANIAN

MARTIN, EMMA (1812–1851), a shadowy figure in the history of English freethought, was born in Bristol and brought up as a strict Baptist. Her religious doubts began in 1839 after she heard a lecture given by Alexander Campbell (1796–1870), an early trade-union agitator and political reformer. The trials for blasphemy of GEORGE JACOB HOLYOAKE and CHARLES SOUTHWELL during the early 1840s stimulated her interest in freethinking, and she became a lecturer for the cause. *Baptism a Pagan Rite,* published in 1843, was the first of several tracts she wrote.

Among her brushes with the law was an arrest in 1845, shortly before a public debate on Christianity, in which she was to engage Robert Lowery in Scotland. Later, when she left placards round a Glasgow church announcing that she would publicly criticize the contents of the Sunday sermon, she was fined three pounds for creating a disturbance.

Emma Martin was the author of several pamphlets, but it was as a public lecturer that her principal contribution to freethought was made. She was much in demand, and an extended lecture tour almost certainly exacerbated the tuberculosis that led to her early death. She was buried in Highgate Cemetery, London, leaving four daughters. Holyoake described her as "a handsome woman, of brilliant talent and courage."

Other article of interest: **Women and Unbelief.**

Bibliography

The only biographical study of Emma Martin appeared in the Second Series of *Half-Hours with the Freethinkers,* ed. John Watts; and *Iconoclast,* 23 (Feb. 2, 1865). This study is, however, curiously uninformative, and further research is needed on her life.

After her death Holyoake wrote *The Last Days of Mrs. Emma Martin, Advocate of Freethought,* first published in the *Reasoner* 282 and reprinted in 1852.

VICTOR E. NEUBURG

MARX, KARL (1818–1883), 19th-century revolutionary thinker who created and disseminated what he called a "scientific socialism," was born in Trier in the Prussian Rhineland on May 5, 1818, the son of Heinrich Marx and Henriette Pressburg Marx. Both his father and mother were descended from a long line of rabbinical families. Marx's father converted to the Protestant faith in 1816 or 1817. Karl attended the Trier secondary school, the Friedrich Wilhelm Gymnasium, and later matriculated as a law student at the University of Bonn. While there, Marx accumulated debts and got into trouble for his hell-raising. In 1836, he left Bonn and secretly became engaged to Jenny von Westphalen, whom he married and who remained his wife from 1843 until her death in 1881. His daughter, Jenny Longuet, died a few months before he did. Marx was buried in northern London, in Highgate Cemetery. His friend and long-time collaborator, Friedrich Engels, presented the eulogy in English, describing Marx as one who "discovered the law of development of human history."

Early Work. Marx presented his dissertation, "The Difference Between the Democritean and Epicurean Philosophy of Nature," to the philosophical faculty at the University of Jena and was awarded a doctorate in philosophy. From 1836 to 1838 he studied law and some philosophy and history at the University of Berlin. It was there that he began his lifelong habit of "scribbling down reflections." Marx's hopes for a teaching post were dashed after his friend and supporter, BRUNO BAUER, was dismissed from his lecturing post at Bonn. After contributing a few articles to radical journals, Marx began writing for the *Rheinische Zeitung.* He became editor of the newspaper and remained in this position for about six months. It was this experience, he later said, that drew him to economic problems.

In 1843 Marx went to Paris, where he wrote essays for the *Deutsch-Französische Jahrbücher.* At this time, he was drawn closer and closer to communism, even managing to elicit the sympathies of the poet Heinrich Heine. Sometime in 1841, he worked on a critical analysis of Hegel's *Philosophy of Right.* As a result of his articles for the *Jahrbücher,* Marx was accused of high treason by the Prussian government and under its instigation he was banished from Paris by the French government. In the same year, 1845, he renounced his Prussian citizenship.

Marx traveled to Manchester and Brussels, and he and Engels took part in the Second Congress of the Communist League in London in 1847. After the publication of the *Communist Manifesto* (1848), he and Engels went to Germany and took part in the revolution of 1848–49. After a brief stint of coediting, with Engels, the *Neue Rheinische Zeitung* in Cologne, Marx settled in London with his family in 1849, resuming his economic studies (primarily in the British Museum). He was supported at this time, in part, by Engels (who was a partner in a manufacturing firm) and by his work as a contributor to the *New York Daily Tribune* (1851–61).

Mature Work and View of Religion. The first

volume of Marx's most famous work, *Das Kapital,* appeared in 1867. From then until 1880, Marx continued work on the remaining volumes of *Kapital.* From 1849 until his death in 1883, he suffered from a number of physical complaints and lived, for the most part, in poverty or semi-poverty. Aside from persistent financial worries, his marriage was often stormy. At one point, he fathered an illegitimate child born to Helene Demuth. Despite his poverty, his domestic and health problems, Marx managed to maintain his productivity during this period of his life.

Although nominally a Christian, Marx seems to have had virtually no religious sentiments. In his doctoral dissertation he quotes with obvious approval lines from Aeschylus' *Prometheus Bound*: "I shall never exchange my fetters for slavish servility. It is better to be chained to the rock than bound to the service of Zeus." This Promethean defiance is echoed in many of his writings. In one of his earliest books, Marx proclaimed that the "criticism of religion" is the premise of all criticism." He argues that it is not religion that makes man, but man who makes religion. In general, Marx proclaimed that religion has often defended the established socioeconomic forces. He continued to espouse this view even though he concurred with Engels' view that the Peasants Revolt in 16th-century Germany (led by Thomas Münzer) reflected protocommunist sentiments in the guise of Christian principles. Nonetheless, Marx held that the "social principles of Christianity" encourage renunciation in "the proletariat" and offer the hope of a heavenly reward.

In the *Economic and Philosophic Manuscripts of 1844,* Marx declared that ATHEISM, as the *negation* of God, "postulates the existence of man through this negation." He sought to abolish religion in order to liberate man, in order to encourage a HUMANISM that would no longer accept as a consolation "the opiate of the people." In his most controversial work, *On the Jewish Question* (1843), he argued that Judaism and Christianity were "stages in the development of the human mind" that had to be surpassed if man was to attain genuine "political emancipation."

Marx accepted Hegel's dialectical conception of actuality, but he turned it right-side up: the evolution of the modes of production and the consequent social and economic relations in society at a particular stage of development were the substructures that conditioned the legal, religious, and philosophical superstructure that emerges in a historical period. A "genuinely human" society requires not only the overcoming of the "alienation" and "exploitation" of the workers but also the overcoming of a deeply rooted religious "alienation." Even though Marx agreed with LUDWIG FEUERBACH (in his *Theses on Feuerbach)* that religious belief entailed man's "self-alienation," he also argued that the "contradictions" in the secular world that gave rise to the projection of an ideal, "imaginary" world in religion must be eliminated.

The "earthly family," Marx said, is the secret of the "holy family," the "family" that must be "criticized in theory and revolutionized in practice." An atheistic humanism suffused Marx's writings, giving them an antireligious, moralistic coloring that infiltrated his ideal of a communal, cooperative society of the future. He believed that man no longer needed to depend upon belief in God, that he had already begun to master nature and now lived in an "anthropological Nature" that he could shape and form into a "realm of freedom."

The enormous powers generated by the capitalistic economy or "system" were to be coopted, Marx suggested, by the proletariat by means of an "expropriation of the expropriators" that would negate the negations and contradictions that Marx believed were inherent in the capitalistic system and its "social relations." Previous philosophers, he said in his notes of 1845 (subsequently published by Engels as *Theses on Feuerbach)* "have only interpreted the world": his aim was "to change it."

Marx's contributions to philosophy, sociology, economic theory, and philosophy of history are important and numerous. He began with a polemical attitude towards egoism, "greed," dehumanization and "alienation" in work, thought, and religious belief. He began and ended his productive life with a few basic assumptions: (1) that religious beliefs channel human energy and hope into another, ethereal world and thereby divert man's efforts from the improvement of his earthly estate; (2) that the capitalist economy, especially in the form of political economy, is unjust and encourages egoism and selfishness, breeding "social atoms" that are only interested in their own welfare; (3) that there are "laws" governing human history, principles of economic evolution, and dialectical opposition that derive from the historical pattern of "class conflict"; (4) that a truly human society of communal cooperation toward a common end is possible; (5) that man must overcome both religious and economic alienation if he would attain genuine emancipation; and (6) that the capitalist system of economy entails basic "contradictions" (especially that engendered by the collective production of goods and the unequal benefits of the distribution of these goods) that will eventually lead to its negation.

The description and analysis of 19th-century capitalism remains a remarkable piece of socioeconomic "phenomenology." Marx's contributions to sociology, especially his analysis of classes, class relations, and class conflict, are lasting contributions to that discipline.

For better or worse, Marx has had greater impact on the world than any other modern thinker. Although he once said, "I am no Marxist," he gave rise to two major revolutions and a number of minor revolutions undertaken under the banner of Marxism. The theoretical conceptions of Marxism, in many shapes and forms, have spread throughout the world. He did for economic reality what SIGMUND FREUD did for the "unconscious mind": he uncovered, analyzed, described, dissected, and laid bare the elements of economic life in a way that few had done before him. Although Marx prided himself on seeing that social classes are intimately associated with "definite historical developmental struggles of production," describing the movement of "class struggle" and pointing to the promise of a "classless society," he probably will be remembered, most of all, as a passionate and radical humanist whose faith in the fundamental goodness of man, once he was freed from the nets of alienation, was his overriding faith.

For his daughter, Eleanor Marx, see EDWARD AVELING.

Bibliography

Biographies: Isaiah Berlin, *Karl Marx, His Life and Environment,* rev. ed. London, 1970. W. Blumenberg, *Portrait of Marx,* D. Scott, trans., New York, 1972. Vladimir I. Lenin, *Karl Marx,* Peking, 1967. Franz Mehring, *Karl Marx: The Story of His Life,* New York, 1957. David McLellan, *Karl Marx: His Life and Thought,* New York and London, Macmillan, 1973. D. Riazanov, *Karl Marx, Man, Thinker and Revolutionist,* London, 1927. M. Rubel and M. Manale, *Marx Without Myth,* New York, Oxford U. Press, 1975.

Studies and Commentaries: Harry B. Acton, *The Illusion of the Epoch,* London, 1955. Georg Adler, *Die Grundlagen der Karl Marxschen Kritik der bestehenden Volkswirtschaft,* Tübingen, 1887.

Shlomo Avineri, *The Social and Political Thought of Karl Marx,* Cambridge: Cambridge U. Press, 1970. M. Bober, *Karl Marx's Interpretation of History,* Cambridge: Harvard U. Press, 1950. Jean-Yves Calvez, *La Pensée de Karl Marx,* Paris, Editions de Seuil, 1956. Louis Dupré, *The Philosophical Foundations of Marxism,* New York, 1966. Erich Fromm, *Marx's Concept of Man,* New York, 1961. Sidney Hook, *From Hegel to Marx,* new ed. Ann Arbor, U. of Michigan Press, 1962. Georg Lukács, *History and Class Consciousness,* R. Livingstone, trans., Cambridge, Harvard U. Press, 1971. A. G. Meyer, *Marxism: The Unity of Theory and Practice,* Cambridge, Harvard U. Press, 1954. Melvin Rader, *Marx's Interpretation of History,* New York, 1979. Robert Tucker, *Philosophy and Myth in Karl Marx.* Cambridge, Cambridge U. Press, 1961.

GEORGE J. STACK

MASTERS, EDGAR LEE (1869–1950), American poet. See **American Literature, Unbelief in.**

MATERIALISM may be defined in either a weak or a strong sense. In its weak sense, it maintains that whatever is real is either purely physical in its properties or is ultimately dependent upon something that is purely physical. In its weak sense, the doctrine implies that although there may be things that are *not* entirely physical in their character, such things, if any, are entirely dependent on other things that *are* entirely physical. The destruction of the physical world would result in the destruction of everything as a consequence.

In its stronger form, the doctrine implies that whatever is real is purely physical. It is not conceded that anything is, to any extent or in any way, nonphysical.

Both forms of materialism are metaphysical theses—in other words, theses about what the universe ultimately consists of. Both entail ATHEISM, and in particular the rejection of Christianity and Judaism, for God is held to be a nonphysical being. They also imply the rejection of an afterlife unless it literally involves a reconstituted physical body, a doctrine that is surely implausible on general scientific grounds. The idea of a soul as a spiritual substance capable of existing independently of the body is also rejected. It should be noted that although materialism entails atheism, the converse is not true; there are many contemporary atheists who maintain that there are simple facts about the character of our experience of consciousness that are possibly compatible with materialism in the weak sense but are irreconcilable with materialism in the stronger sense, the sense in which the term is more commonly used today.

The question on which the debate about materialism essentially centers today is the nature of the human mind. Materialism (in the weak sense), of which Marxist dialectical materialism is a special case, maintains that mental phenomena are essentially dependent upon physical phenomena. The Cartesian belief that the human person is composed of two distinct substances interacting with each other, a body and a mind, each with their own distinguishing properties—bodies being spatially extended but not conscious, minds being conscious but not extended—is rejected. One motive for rejecting it is the growth in our knowledge of the brain and central nervous system. Neurophysiological knowledge does not seem to require us to postulate two distinct entities in interaction with one another but points instead to a physical basis for every mentalistic occurrence. The direction of dependence seems to be not two ways, as RENÉ DESCARTES believed, but one way, the mental being invariably dependent upon the physical.

Materialism in the strong sense goes further and denies the separateness of any mental realm, even a mental realm with a highly or entirely dependent status. This denial however has to be interpreted with great care. The rejection of the mental realm means in some cases the elimination of mind and the mental as an obsolete fiction to which all reference should be dropped, just as the idea of God is commonly held to be an obsolete fiction. For others, rejection of the mental realm means reduction of the mental to, or identification of the mental with, entities with purely physical properties. Eliminationists maintain that, strictly speaking, there is no such thing as mind or the mental. Identificationists and reductionists continue to affirm the existence of mind and the mental but insist that it is nothing but, nothing more than, or nothing over and above the physical entities or properties with which they identify—or to which they reduce—mind and the mental.

Contemporary philosophers attracted to materialism in the strong sense have been reluctant to embrace eliminative materialism in general, because of the continuing influence of the common-sense and ordinary-language traditions in contemporary philosophy. To say that mind does not exist would be to outrage the common-sense recognition that we often have to make up our minds, keep someone's name in mind, keep a clear mind, and so on. It seems unduly provocative to say that all these sorts of claims are literally false. The preferred alternative is to say that such claims are really about something which is physical, not that they are false.

One type of reductionist materialism popular in the third quarter of this century was *analytic behaviorism,* according to which statements about the mind and the mental were analyzed as really statements about actual or potential behavior. To say that Mary is angry is, on this view, not to refer to some mental state of a nonphysical sort within Mary but rather to say that she is disposed to display characteristic anger behavior (go red in the face, snap, gesture in certain ways, and so on) and would display such behavior given certain specifiable conditions.

One advantage of this overt stimulus-response analysis was that it fitted in with the newly recognized need to provide an account of the mental consistent with the fact that the words we used to characterize what had been regarded as mental phenomena must be learnt in relation to publicly observable phenomena. The main disadvantage was that it seemed implausible when applied to the self-ascription of mentalistic terms. When I describe myself as angry, or in pain, or as thinking of Vienna, I do not do so on the basis of observations of or inferences to my actual or probable behavior.

In the fourth quarter of this century greater attention has been given to another type of materialism known variously as *central-state materialism* or *physicalism.* Unlike the behaviorists, materialists in this sense do not reduce the mental to its behavioral expression but rather identify the mental with those inner states, many of which we can be aware of through introspection, which characteristically cause the overt behavior with which the behaviorist identifies the mental. For the central-state materialist, to say that Mary is angry is to say that she is in a certain state, a state likely to cause her, given certain conditions, to behave in certain ways (the ways to which the analytic behaviorist wrongly reduces anger).

It turns out, as a matter of contingent fact, that the state in question happens to be a state of the brain and mental nervous system. Hence Mary's anger may be identified, contingently, with that neurophysiological state. There is no need to postulate a Cartesian mind substance to wear the state, nor to postulate nonphysical dependent properties of the inner neurophysiological processes to account for the reality of the mental. Common sense is preserved for we continue to speak of and refer to the mental; it just turns out that the mental of which we speak is in fact perfectly and fully physical.

Against materialism in this sense some have argued that it flies in the face of the phenomenological facts. In particular they have claimed that the data of introspection reveal that the content of consciousness is decidedly nonphysical. While it may be true that what data introspection reveals is ultimately dependent upon purely physiological processes, it is absurd to suggest that those things that I am directly aware of in introspection are the very same states and processes that a brain surgeon could, in principle, be aware of if I were subjected to an appropriate brain probe.

In reply it is argued that introspection is a mode of access to the brain and central nervous system in the way that vision and touch are both modes of access to the external physical world. From the data of touch or sight alone (assuming that one had no use of the other senses) it would not be possible to work out a priori what it could be like to be aware of the relevant objects of perception by the other sense. A person who sees the circularity of a coin is aware of exactly the same property of the coin as a person who feels its circularity. But if we had never learnt to coordinate our senses of sight and touch, we would probably find the claim that we could see the same property that we feel quite extraordinary.

This analogy is intended to suggest that it is fallacious to conclude from the fact that the data of introspection strike us as utterly unlike anything we are aware of through those senses we use to explore the external physical world, that therefore they are nonphysical. The apparent difference is no greater than the difference between circularity as seen and circularity as felt.

There are still many issues associated with central-state materialism that make it controversial. Some find the contingency of its identification of the mental with the physical troublesome. Others believe that the intentionality of the mental—that we can think of, imagine, or have feelings about absent or unreal objects—renders it unidentifiable with anything physical. Current uncertainty about the evidentiary status and the interpretation to be placed on parapsychology and alleged paranormal phenomena in general indicates an area of potential difficulty. Nonetheless it is now fair to say that strong materialism of this sort is a widely held and respected thesis about the mental, something that certainly would not have been true until well into the second half of this century.

Other article of interest: **Indian Materialism, Ancient.**

Bibliography

Armstrong, David M. *A Materialist Theory of the Mind.* New York: Humanities Press, 1968.

Cornman, James W. *Materialism and Sensations.* New Haven: Yale U. Press, 1971.

Lange, Frederick A. *The History of Materialism.* 3 vols. Boston: James Osgood, 1877–81.

La Mettrie, Julien O. *Man a Machine.* La Salle, Ill.: Open Court, 1953.

O'Connor, John, ed. *Modern Materialism: Readings on Mind-Body Identity.* New York: Harcourt, Brace, 1969.

Rosenthal, David. *Materialism and the Mind-Body Problem.* Englewood Cliffs, N.J.: Prentice-Hall, 1971.

LAUCHLAN CHIPMAN

MEETINGS OF UNBELIEVERS. See **Appendix 2.**

MENCKEN, HENRY LOUIS (1880–1956), or H. L. Mencken, as he preferred, was an American journalist, editor, and author. He was born Sept. 12 in Baltimore, Md., into a worldly scene that was to inexhaustibly fascinate him. Both of his parents were of German stock and his ancestors included not only merchants but also professors, lawyers, theologians, historians, philosphers, and government officials. August, his father, was a prosperous cigarmaker.

Early Life and Religious Upbringing. His father and paternal grandfather, an 1848 immigrant from Saxony, were total agnostics or, perhaps more accurately, atheists since they appear to have been without any religious belief whatever. Although grandfather Burkhardt enjoyed drinking beer and disputing theological points with the Xaverian Brothers, August was anticlerical. Henry's mother attended the English Lutheran church, more or less as "a social gesture," according to her son. However, he not only was baptized but in 1895 was confirmed in his mother's church.

Young Henry also attended Sunday School because, as he later wrote to Will Durant, his father wanted him to learn what Christian theology was but never thought his son would believe any of it. In the same letter Mencken said all he got from Sunday School was an extensive familiarity with Christian hymnology and "a firm conviction that the Christian faith was full of palpable absurdities, and the Christian God preposterous." He insisted that his having grown up devoid of religious belief left him free of any hatred of religion, so that he could scrutinize it untroubled by bad conscience and with the dispassionate curiosity of a good reporter or scientist.

A precocious boy, Mencken was privately educated and graduated valedictorian from the Baltimore Polytechnic Institute in 1896. Yet he appears to have been largely self-taught; by the time he was eight he had become a steady and omnivorous reader, saying many years later that he doubted anyone had ever read more than he did between his 12th and 18th years. Although he had seriously wanted to become a chemist, by the time he graduated he was determined to be a newspaperman. Nevertheless, an interest in exact science remained strong throughout his life. He claimed his knowledge and appreciation of science gave a unique character to his literary criticism and criticism of ideas generally, since other such critics in America were usually ignorant of science.

Career in Journalism. Mencken's father died unexpectedly when H. L. was 18. Shortly thereafter he landed a job on the *Baltimore Morning Herald.* In 1906 he joined the *Baltimore Sun,* beginning a working association that was to last, with the exceptions of World Wars I and II when he stopped writing for the paper because of wartime censorship, until Nov. 23, 1948, when a stroke destroyed his ability to read and write. He was successful almost immediately. By 1902 he was city editor of the *Herald.* By 1910 he was contributing two editorials and a column to the editorial page of the *Baltimore Evening Sun,* outraging readers and eliciting a barrage of denunciations.

The head "The Free Lance," soon to be famous or infamous, appeared in 1911. Baltimore had never experienced such free and forthright journalism; nor probably has any quality American newspaper since. Mencken excoriated the Anti-Saloon League, the vice crusaders, the town boomers, politicians, and "other such frauds." Mencken, in effect, enjoyed a private editorial column in which he was free to write almost anything he wanted.

At the start of the series Charles H. Grasty, the publisher, had obtained a promise from Mencken that he would not aim his howitzer prose at any church or clergymen as such. However, when the Methodist ministers of the city denounced the young iconoclast, Grasty released Mencken from his pledge. Although a skeptic generally, Mencken held an unshakeable faith in the value of free speech for himself and for all others as an absolute good. He also was convinced that most Americans were intellectual cowards and therefore did not share his faith.

His great journalistic output, which Mencken believed contained some of his best writing, was accompanied by immense productivity as author and editor. Not counting revisions and new editions, from 1903 to 1956 Mencken was the sole author of 28 books, part author of 5, editor of 8, and translator of 1. In addition, he wrote introductions to other books, book reviews, magazine editorials and articles, pamphlets and brochures, and compiled selections from the writings of authors he admired. He achieved his greatest popular renown as a literary critic and magazine editor of the *Smart Set* and then of the *American Mercury* magazines.

Concerning religious unbelief. Mencken's most important books are: *The Philosophy of Friedrich Nietzsche* (1908), *Treatise on the Gods* (1930), and *Treatise on Right and Wrong* (1934). He considered his *Treatise on the Gods* (revised in 1946) the best statement on agnosticism since THOMAS HENRY HUXLEY. However, his skeptical views on religion were scattered through nearly all of his writings.

Mencken's complete rejection of all religious belief whatever resulted from his scientific SKEPTICISM. In his view, religion by its very nature was adamantly opposed to free inquiry and thereby checked human progress. Mencken praised the Austrian philosopher Karl Popper for his conception of science as the disinterested, incessant search for the truth. Conceived as ceaseless inquiry into the truth of all beliefs, as systematic doubt of all beliefs, science and skepticism are the same. Indeed, such doubting of all beliefs is human intelligence in operation. However, every religious belief claims to be indubitable truth; consequently, religious belief and human intelligence are intrinsically opposed to one another.

In Mencken's view, the conflict between scientific skepticism and religious belief was not only a conflict over the truth of religious beliefs; nor was it primarily a struggle between doubt and dogma. Fundamentally, it was a conflict of values. For scientific skepticism claims that doubt is *better* than belief. All beliefs should be held tentatively and repeatedly subjected to critical scrutiny; to call a belief true is to say that it has not yet been falsified. For religion, on the contrary, faith is superior to doubt; the skeptic is a heretic, a sinner.

In reality, this conflict of values is a conflict between two ethical systems, between what FRIEDRICH NIETZSCHE called a master morality and a slave morality. An ethics of skepticism, or, as Mencken preferred to call it, an ethics of honor, approves of whatever promotes doubt; whereas Christian ethics—or mere morality, as Mencken disparagingly called it—approves of whatever promotes belief and faith. Consequently, an ethics of honor exalts struggle, courage, freedom, rebellion, honesty, and individual enterprise. The noble man fights God and triumphs over him. Christian ethics, on the contrary, praises peace, obedience to God, security, humility, childlike pliancy, and resignation.

In Nietzsche, Mencken found corroboration of another thesis. Skepticism, an ethics of honor, is too demanding, too difficult for most men, who find it unendurable. Sooner or later they lapse into belief in order to escape the pain of doubt. The majority prefer belief and all it entails to doubt. Thus Christian ethics is a mob ethics. Consequently, he opposed democracy and its extension from government to economics, called socialism and communism, as secularized forms of Christian ethics. Only a minority of human beings, so abnormal as to almost constitute another species, possesses a strength of intelligence that not only can endure skepticism but also can delight in doubting, finding in the free functioning of the mind an end in itself. The conflict between scientific skepticism and religious belief, therefore, is a conflict between a minority and a hostile, uncomprehending majority. Mencken rejected any hope that the majority could be won over to skepticism. Nevertheless, he was no pessimist. To be a skeptic is to live decently, even nobly, to win the only victory possible for an intelligent human being.

Mencken was not a cynic in any true sense. He set forth a positive ideal, although his attacks on opponents of skepticism often obscured it. Nor was he a social Darwinist. His hero was not the successful businessman but Huxley, the embodiment of scientific skepticism. The immediate task was to preserve and increase the liberty necessary for future Huxleys to function freely. In comparison with the majority of men, Huxley was a kind of *Übermensch* ("beyond-man") shorn of the mystical overtones with which Nietzsche had endowed his ideal.

Bibliography

In accordance with Mencken's will, in 1981 at the Enoch Pratt Free Library, Baltimore, the following unpublished writings by Mencken were taken out of time lock and are available to interested scholars: his five-volume diary from 1930 through 1948; "Additions and Corrections" to *Happy Days, Heathen Days,* and *Newspaper Days,* 3 vols.; and "Letters and Documents Relating to the *Baltimore Sunpapers 1892–1941,"* 4 vols. In 1991 two unpublished Mencken manuscripts will come out of time lock: *Thirty-five Years of Newspaper Work* and *My Life as Author and Editor.*

Bode, Carl. *Mencken.* Carbondale: Southern Illinois U. Press, 1969.

Dorsey, John, ed. *On Mencken.* New York: Knopf, 1980.

Fecher, Charles A. *Mencken: A Study of His Thought.* New York: Knopf, 1978.

Fitzpatrick, Vincent, ed. *H. L. M. The Mencken Bibliography: A Second Ten-year Supplement, 1972–1981.* Baltimore: Enoch Pratt Free Library, in preparation.

Forgue, Guy J. *H. L. Mencken: l'Homme, l'Oeuvre, l'Influence.* Paris: Minard, 1967.

Rasmussen, Frederick N., ed. *Menckeniana.* Baltimore: Enoch Pratt Free Library. A quarterly devoted to material on Mencken.

Stenerson, Douglas C. *H. L. Mencken: Iconoclast from Baltimore.* Chicago: U. of Chicago Press, 1971.

JOHN R. BURR

MESLIER, JEAN (1664–1729), the most remarkable apostate of his age, was also one of France's foremost advocates of ATHEISM and MATERIALISM. He was born at Mazerny, a village of Champagne, the son of a modest wool merchant. He had already lost his religious faith as an adolescent, but, wishing to obey his father, he pursued a clerical career. After attending the seminary of Rheims, he was ordained in 1688, and soon thereafter was appointed to the parish of Etrépigny, in the Ardennes, where he remained until his death.

His Life as a Cleric. Outwardly, Meslier's obscure life was that of the average country priest serving the needs of his flock of simple souls. There were no signs that, behind his prudent exterior, a total and passionate revolt was taking place against the civil and religious institutions of France. To be sure, he began a bitter quarrel, in 1716, with the *seigneur* of Etrépigny, which caused him finally to be disciplined by his archbishop. But while such an incident was in itself not unusual, it is significant that, in Meslier's case, the dispute sprang from his desire to protect the villagers from unfair exactions by their feudal lord.

Frustrated and incensed by the hypocritical role he felt condemned to play during his lifetime, Meslier resolved to avenge himself by drawing up a document in which he would expose without restraint the "lies" and "deceptions" of Christianity (as of all religions), together with his hatred of the social and economic inequities of the *Ancien Régime.*

To this end, he prepared three copies of a very lengthy *Mémoire* (known also as his *Testament*), to be made public posthumously. Addressing his parishioners, he begged their forgiveness for having confirmed them in the errors and superstitions of the Catholic church, and offered at last to make amends by disabusing them. The ecclesiastical authorities covered up the immediate scandal of Meslier's "counter-confession," but all three copies of the *Mémoire* survived, and after some years his act of apostasy became notorious.

A thoroughgoing critique of Christianity forms the major part of the *Mémoire.* Christianity is described, like all other religions, as a mere human invention. The various "proofs" advanced in its support are methodically refuted. The miracles cited in the New Testament fail to substantiate that Christianity is of divine origin, because every religion has its miracles, and yet these cannot all be taken as authentic. In that respect, the Gospels merit no particular credence; far from being the manifest word of God, they are full of contradictions, inconsistencies, outright fantasy, and textual corruption. Moreover, the inclusion of some texts as canonical and the exclusion of others was an arbitrary choice. The "visions" and "communications" that certain biblical figures supposedly had from God also prove nothing, not only because all religions make such spurious claims but also because anyone imagining that he receives messages directly from God must be demented.

The scriptural prophecies are likewise worthless as evidence, for few of them can be shown, in any plausible sense, to have been fulfilled. Apologetic attempts to save the prophecies by interpreting them in a figurative and far-fetched manner, are futile, because by such techniques any prediction or promise whatsoever, regardless of how baseless, could be said to have come true. The dogmas central to Christianity, such as the trinity, the incarnation, the eucharist, original sin, eternal punishment, and so forth, cannot withstand rational examination, which reveals them to be self-contradictory and unintelligible. From the accounts of Christ's actions given in the Gospels, we must conclude that he was a *fou et fanatique,* for that is exactly how someone acting as he did would now be judged.

Meslier's sweeping attack on religion is solidly buttressed by a philosophical construct of materialism and atheism. He argues against the idea of creation, pointing out its inherent difficulties. In place of God as the "unmoved mover"—a patently absurd notion—he postulates the existence of an eternal and universal matter constantly in motion. Nature, including natural reason, is the sole ground of Being, and outside of a rational understanding of physical objects and events there is nothing but illusion. All phenomena, from the formation and arrangement of planetary bodies to the emergence and behavior of animal species and the human race, have resulted necessarily from combinations of the particles of which matter is composed. Furthermore, there is no "soul" separate from corporeal structure. The mental activities specific to human beings and to higher animals can be defined as functions of their organisms. Historically, Meslier's materialism derived largely from a "radical" interpretation of RENÉ DESCARTES' science divorced from its accompanying metaphysics— a Cartesianism that reached him mainly through his unorthodox reading of Nicholas Malebranche.

Social and political convictions are expressed uncompromisingly in the *Mémoire.* Meslier saw the world of the *Ancien Régime* as made up of the poor and the rich, the weak and the strong, the oppressed and their oppressors. This polarized view of society reflected the rural milieu he knew from personal experience more than it did the overall, especially urban, class relations of 18th-century France. Meslier sided fervently with the "downtrodden masses" against their feudal masters, so much so that, despite his contempt for Christ and Christianity, he often sounds like a choleric Jesus. He regarded government as a cynical alliance between shrewd exploiters and ambitious priests, made at the expense of the common people. While religion disarmed and subdued the latter by means of superstition and ritual, by false hopes and fake threats, the monarch and nobles could oppress them economically and politically without fear of retaliation or revolt.

If no one had as yet denounced this reprehensible scheme of domination by church and state working as accomplices, it was because no one had dared to do so, and also because many had expected, by keeping silent, to gain something for themselves from the general game of deceit. All religions, continues Meslier, are nothing but "*erreurs, abus, illusions, et impostures.*" If, despite this, they have always flourished, the reason is that their usefulness to governments has always consisted in the clever manipulation of just those negative traits.

In contrast to the unjust and exploitative society he condemns, Meslier calls for a socialistic order of things, in which the fruits of the earth and the pleasures of life will be distributed as equally as possible among everyone. Being neither an economist nor a political scientist, he provides no analysis of existing institutions for the purpose of clarifying how the envisioned goal is to be attained. His criticism keeps to the level of generalities; but what it lacks in concrete proposals for change is compensated by its moral earnestness, vehemence of tone, and prophetic scope. Although Meslier had no blueprint for revolution, his rhetoric, by its violent impatience with the status quo, conveys a revolutionary meaning. Nor does he hesitate even to recommend regicide as a practical remedy for France's ills.

One way to explain his fulminations against the *Ancien Régime* is to set them in the context of the crushing taxation and extreme misery that provoked a series of peasant uprisings in the last decades of Louis XIV's reign. The *Mémoire* would thus be the literary counterpart of those *jacqueries.* But its great originality ought not to be overlooked. This lay in the fact that Meslier's thought, for the first time, joined a socialist ideal to a materialistic and atheistic philosophy—a synthesis that was destined to have a momentous future, though not until the advent of KARL MARX.

From the 1730s on, the *Mémoire* circulated in manuscript copies. While in this form it had relatively few readers, it may have helped to shape the atheistic materialism of such thinkers as JULIEN DE LA METTRIE, DENIS DIDEROT, and PAUL HENRI HOLBACH, with all three of whose ideas it exhibits close parallels. Meslier's opinions were most widely disseminated in the 18th century through the text published by VOLTAIRE in 1762 with the title *Extrait des sentiments de Jean Meslier.* In this version, the devastating case against the Christian religion was preserved, but given a deistic turn; at the same time, Voltaire expurgated the materialist and atheist doctrines, in addition to the entire sociopolitical critique that were logically associated with it.

In 1790, SYLVAIN MARÉCHAL brought out a *Catéchisme du curé Meslier,* which in fact was written by himself. The following year, a digest of Baron d'Holbach's philosophy appeared under Meslier's name. Known as *Le bon sens du curé Meslier,* it had innumerable editions in French, as well as English, German, and Spanish translations during the 19th century, so that the great majority of those who believed they were reading Meslier were actually reading Holbach.

The full and authentic text of the *Mémoire* did not become available in print until 1864. It is therefore not easy to measure Meslier's real influence in the 150 years after his death. No doubt, his impact on later generations would have been more important if the *Mémoire* had been published intact in the 18th century. Yet, though his message was distorted and sidetracked, enough of it apparently got through to the *philosophes* and the public to make Meslier one of the most challenging voices of unbelief in the ENLIGHTENMENT and afterwards.

Bibliography

Dommanget, Maurice. *Le Curé Meslier, athée, communiste et révolutionnaire sous Louis XIV.* Paris: Les Lettres Nouvelles, 1965.

————. *Etudes sur le curé Meslier.* Actes du Colloque international d'Aix-en-Provence. Paris: Société des Etudes Robespierristes, 1966.

————. *Le Curé Meslier et la vie intellectuelle, religieuse et sociale: fin 17ᵉ–début 18ᵉ siècles.* Actes du Colloque international de Reims. Reims: Bibliothèque de l'Université, 1980.

Meslier, Jean. *Oeuvres complètes.* 3 vols. Prefaces and notes by J. Deprun, R. Desné, A. Soboul. Paris: Editions Anthropos, 1970–72.

————. *Le Testament de Jean Meslier.* 3 vols. Ed. Rudolf Charles. Amsterdam: La Librairie Etrangère, 1864.

Verona, Luciano. *Jean Meslier, prêtre, athée, socialiste, révolutionnaire.* Milan: 1975.

ARAM VARTANIAN

MILL, JOHN STUART (1806–1873), the principal utilitarian philosopher and moralist, was also an economist, an administrator of the East India Company, a member of Parliament briefly, and, throughout, an indefatigable writer. Educated at home under the dominating influence and constant superintendency of his father, the well-known intellectual James Mill, John Stuart experienced not a scintilla of religious influence during his formative years. Never having been a Christian, he exhibited none of the contempt that often accompanies its later rejections, nor had he been bored with it as had so many children of his time. Thus, he was able to approach Christianity (and other religions too) on their merits with an uncommonly even temper. Like JEREMY BENTHAM before him, he refrained from professing ATHEISM, held Jesus in the highest esteem, and looked upon St. Paul as the principal perverter of original Christianity.

Though Mill touched upon religion briefly and episodically throughout his vast literary production, he devoted relatively few pages to its sustained analysis, these being principally three essays, "Nature," "The Utility of Religion," and "Theism." These are presented, along with an essay on Coleridge, in the 10th volume of his *Collected Works* (22 vols. projected; Toronto: University of Toronto Press, from 1963; hereafter referred to as CW).

Possibility of Design. Although Mill knew the Darwinian theory of evolution and wrote of the adaptions of various organisms to their different environments, he did not fully comprehend nor wholly accept what is now commonly taken to be the creative role of environmental factors in the selection and shaping of surviving organisms. Thus, he was not prepared to abandon the idea of design in nature. However, taking the first law of thermodynamics seriously, he saw no reason to believe that the designer, if any (the evidence for that not being conclusive), was also the creator or first cause of matter and energy. Since he took these to be, most likely, eternal in their own right, he believed all arguments for the necessity of God based on the idea of a first cause to be failures. In any case, of one point he was supremely confident; the designer of such a world as we experience it to be cannot be all-powerful and all-good. It is "too clumsily made and capriciously governed" for that (CW, X, p. 423).

God, Neither Perfect nor Omniscient. Mill not only denied the orthodox Christian conjunction of perfect power and perfect goodness in God but he also denied each conjunct. Design implying a designer in any sense comprehensible to human beings also implies that the designer had preexisting and to some extent intractable materials with which to work. If a designer is at all thwarted by his materials and has to resort to various means to gain his ends, then he cannot be all-powerful. A truly all-powerful being could accomplish anything and everything instantaneously by fiat. Moreover, the designer of this universe cannot be all-good as we understand goodness. Since experience shows that the order of nature "cannot have had for its sole or even principal end, the good of human or other sentient beings," and since nature gives even shorter shrift to justice than to benevolence, there is no evidence of a moral end of the universe. "In sober truth," wrote Mill (CW, X, p. 385), "nearly all the things which men are hanged or imprisoned for doing to one another, are nature's every day performances."

In summation, Mill wrote: "These, then, are the net results of Natural Theology on the question of divine attributes. A Being of great but limited power, how or by what limited we cannot even conjecture; of great, and perhaps unlimited intelligence, but, perhaps, also more narrowly limited than his power: who desires, and pays some regard to, the happiness of his creatures, but who seems to have other motives of action which he cares more for, and who can hardly be supposed to have created the universe for that purpose alone. Such is the Deity whom Natural Religion points to; and any idea of God more captivating than this comes only from human wishes, or from the teaching of either real or imaginary Revelation" (CW, X, p. 459).

Dubeity of Revelation. Although Christianity has relied on natural theology whenever convenient, it has always claimed to be based on revelation. If this were true, it could validly assert more about the God of revelation than Mill's limited conclusions, based on experience and reason, allow. But, how firm a basis for such a claim does revelation provide? In analyzing the subject, he concludes that there are two types of warrant for revelation, the internal and the external. By the internal warrant he means either empirical experience or dependable testimony.

The internal warrant is not sufficient to Mill to justify the Christian claim to revelation. Although the "Author of Christianity" is a more benign figure than the "Author of Nature" (CW, X, p. 423), and although some of Jesus' teachings carry moral goodness to the highest pinnacle, much in them is equaled by Stoicism, the latter having a merely human origin, as all would agree. Furthermore, Jesus, on the one hand, offers eternal bliss to believers, thus bribing belief, and, on the other hand, threatens unbelievers with eternal punishment.

Mill found it most repugnant in Christianity that the object of its highest worship was also the "Author of Hell" and pictured in theology as one who had perfect foreknowledge that generations upon generations of his human creatures were doomed to suffer there. Any moral enormity, he thought, could be justified by a deity capable of this. Even without these objections, Mill believed that no internal warrant could suffice to establish the reality of revelation. For that, external warrants were required.

However, claims of revelation made by virtue of external warrants fare no better. If there are any supernatural facts that can be taken as proof of a deity, Mill sees no reason why they should not be accessible to empirical experience. But, there are no such facts presently available about which informed observers can agree. Hence, one is thrown back on various testimonies respecting alleged miracles that are presumably revelatory. For Mill, a miracle would have to be an event produced by "the direct volition" of God without or in spite of natural law. There is not, however, a "farthing's" worth of evidence for any biblical miracles, and there is much evidence against miracles in general. Moreover, there may be, and most likely is, a natural, though hitherto unrecognized explanation for any alleged miracle, and even if there were events that occurred without or in spite of natural law, they could not prove the existence of God.

When Mill concluded his analysis of miracles, nothing was left of them but their logical possibility. The same was true of the idea of the soul's immortality. To him, only an "express revelation duly authenticated" could support this notion. Lacking that, neither the existence of God by itself nor the human desire to live forever, alleged by some to be instinctive and thus implanted by God, could suffice to establish the fact of human immortality. "The whole domain of the supernatural," he wrote (in CW, X, p. 483), "is thus removed from the region of Belief [it never was a matter of Knowledge] into that of simple Hope. . . ."

Mistakes of Religious Ethics. Even apart from numerous well-known cruelties perpetrated throughout history because of religion, Mill found much to deplore in it. Religious ethics are one-sided and incomplete. They fall short of disinterestedness, emphasizing self-interest instead, and alter the focus from social well-being to personal good. People enthralled by religion, even when otherwise moral, often ascribe immorality to their God, worship a being who by their own admission has unknown attributes, believe in contradictory doctrines, and lodge their beliefs in a realm beyond rational criticism.

Mill did not wish to win over to his skeptical position on religion any but those of superior intelligence and character. Respecting lesser mortals, he was content to try to improve their religion, certainly not to deprive them of it altogether. Nevertheless, he thought the time had come to argue for free expression in and against religion and to dissent from it as the occasion demanded.

The improved religion he had in mind for the masses is now recognizable as a kind of liberal Christianity approximating the religion of humanity.

Bibliography

Bain, Alexander. *John Stuart Mill: A Criticism with Personal Recollections.* New York: Augustus M. Kelley, 1969.

Hayek, F. A. *John Stuart Mill and Harriet Taylor.* Chicago: U. of Chicago Press, 1951.

Mill, John Stuart. *Autobiography.* Indianapolis: Bobbs-Merrill, 1959.

———. *Theism.* Ed. Richard Taylor. Indianapolis: Bobbs-Merrill, 1957.

Packe, Michael St. John. *The Life of John Stuart Mill.* London: Secker & Warburg, 1954.

Randall, John H., Jr. *The Career of Philosophy,* Vol. 2. New York: Columbia U. Press, 1965.

Stephen, Leslie. *The English Utilitarians,* Vol. 3. New York: Augustus M. Kelley, 1968.

Willey, Basil. *Nineteenth Century Studies.* New York: Columbia U. Press, 1949.

DELOS B. MCKOWN

MIRACLES, UNBELIEF IN. Some years ago there used to be talk at Oxford of a "new cure for atheism." Eager youngsters going to the university as convinced atheists found themselves suffering, under the impact of the then prevalent academic philosophy, a progressive loss of unfaith. They would, in lost confusion, confess that they were atheists no longer. They did not know, they complained, in what an atheist was supposed to disbelieve.

What Would a Miracle Have to Be? People often give to the word *miracle* senses giving no scope for unbelief. Suppose, for instance, that someone is using it strictly and solely in the relativistic understanding proposed by JOHN LOCKE in his *Discourse on Miracles.* Then no one but a fool could deny that there have always been and always will be miracles innumerable. For Locke had defined the word to mean "a sensible operation, which, being above the comprehension of the spectator, and in his opinion contrary to the established course of nature, is taken by him to be divine."

A conception of this sort that makes no claim about what actually is the case, as opposed to what is believed to be, might well be acceptable to our sociologists of belief. But to introduce anything thus purely relativistic into a discussion of the existence of God and the structure of the natural order must be diversionary and obscurantist.

This first false move is attractive to believers. It offers them a sure way of keeping any and every miracle story safe beyond the reach of skeptical inquiry, albeit at what ought to be the unacceptable cost of emptying belief in those stories of substantial and disputatious content. A second false move offers a similar delusive appeal to unbelievers. This move is to make it true by definition that miracles, being exceptions to genuine laws of nature, cannot occur. To speak, in this interpretation, of the occurrence of a miracle is to contradict yourself. Miracles so conceived are, to employ another terminology, logically impossible. The position of the unbelievers thus becomes impregnable.

Nevertheless the price of such security is too high. For, so construed, the assertion that there are no miracles is no more and no less exciting and controversial than the assertion that there are no unmarried spouses or that perfect circles cannot be perfect squares. To quote one characteristically gnomic saying from Ludwig Wittgenstein's *Tractatus Logico-Philosophicus*: "All the propositions of logic say the same thing, that is, nothing."

If believers and unbelievers are to meet in head-on conflict over the same contested ground, then they have to agree to employ a traditional concept of the miraculous. Any notion of that sort contains two essential elements. On the one hand there has to be a strong natural order, an order that cannot be broken or upset by any person or power (or combination of persons or powers) within the universe. On the other hand, we have to have an occasional and essentially exceptional overriding of that strong natural order, by a supernatural power conceived as lying beyond or behind that universe. Such interventions from outside would either constitute or endorse revelations of that supernatural power(s).

This sort of idea carries two paradoxical implications with which we must come to terms. First, miracles in this understanding will be (not logically but) contingently impossible. The occurrence of such miracles, that is to say, will not be ruled out by definition; talk about such properly conceivable occurrences will be neither self-contradictory nor in any other manner without meaning. Yet these miracles, if they were to occur, could not but be impossible in that second sense—the sense in which in fact it is (the world being as we now think we know it to be) impossible to produce either a runabout vehicle running about without needing any fuel or a spaceship traveling faster than the speed of light. This is to say only and precisely that miracles must be impossible to both man and nature, though not, of course, by the same token to a God or to any other putative supernatural power.

The second paradoxical consequence is that believers wanting to claim that miracles do happen and unbelievers affirming that they do not are both equally committed to defending the idea of a strong natural order. They differ only in this: whereas believers say that, no doubt very rarely and exceptionally, some supernatural power(s) does override this order, unbelievers maintain that, since there in fact are no such powers, they never do.

Of course some variations upon this central theme are found. Some, for instance, insist that the term *miracle* should always be so used that it becomes necessarily true that a miracle can only be worked by either the Judeo-Christian God or his specially deputed plenipotentiaries. Others would even build into their definition reference to the purposes for which Authority is supposed to be prepared to consider the making of such an exception. Certainly too, most theist theologians are at pains to maintain that a miraculous event could not be rated an irregular violation; it would not represent any infringement of the fundamental and divinely sustained hierarchical order: "It is not against the principle of craftmanship," Thomas Aquinas writes, "if a craftsman effects a change in his product, even after he has given it its first form." (*Summa contra Gentiles*, III, 100).

Yet these very labors to show that and how such "violations" need involve no ultimate irregularity, still admit and presuppose the essentially overriding character of the miraculous. There would be no point in trying to show that a miracle must ultimately be one thing unless it were taken for granted that immediately it is another.

The point is fundamental. So it needs to be stressed more heavily today than in the past. For in addition to the traditional theist reluctance to ascribe to the Deity anything savoring of unseemly irregularity, it is nowadays usual to find a certain shyness about any ostentatious repudiation of scientifically accepted modes of explanation. Aquinas, earlier in the same chapter, gives a perfectly clear and unequivocal definition: "Those things are properly called miracles which are done by divine agency beyond the order commonly observed in nature." In the same forthright tradition, Eric Mascall insists in his article in *Chamber's Encyclopaedia* that the term "signifies in Christian theology a striking interposition of divine power by which the operations of the ordinary course of nature are overruled, suspended, or modified."

Reasons for Believing That Miracles Have Occurred. In the first volume of his *History of the Rise of the Spirit of Rationalism in Europe*, W. E. H. Lecky remarks: "Credulity in antiquity varied with the vigour of religion"; although he does also allow "that at least in some respects Christians were far less credulous than their contemporaries, at least in the period before Augustine." Lecky then proceeds to trace a development by which stories of the ostensibly miraculous, from being accepted as a chief guarantee of the authenticity of the Christian revelation, become instead "a scandal, a stumbling block, a difficulty."

By the time we reach the 19th-century we find the radical biblical critic DAVID FRIEDRICH STRAUSS in the introduction to his *Life of Jesus* (Tübingen, 1837) announcing: "We may summarily reject all miracles, prophecies, narratives of angels and demons, and the like, as simply impossible and irreconcilable with the known and universal laws which govern the course of events."

In the 20th century a scientifically educated Anglican bishop of Birmingham, England, was perhaps only a few years ahead of his flock when he wrote of the author of the Gospel of Mark: "He was credulous inasmuch as the miracles, as they are narrated, cannot, in the light of our modern knowledge of the uniformity of nature, be accepted as historical facts."

Any professing Christian who is tempted to concur needs to be reminded of the two different reasons why Christianity cannot afford to repudiate commitment to the miraculous. First, it is if, and perhaps only if, suitable endorsing miracles have occurred, and even still do occur, that a Christian has sufficient grounds for believing that the so-called revelation is indeed of God. Second, at least one crucial miracle—the alleged resurrection of Jesus—is not merely external evidence for but also itself constitutive of that revelation. It is, that is to say, the very heart and essence of the Gospel message that the second person of the Trinity became a man. He was born of woman (if not necessarily of a virgin); he preached the word of God in Galilee; he was crucified, died and was buried; and he rose again on the third day.

It was, therefore, entirely fitting—in those now so far-off days when believers still offered evidencing reasons for their faith—that the traditional apologetic consisted of two stages. The first attempted to establish the existence and certain minimal characteristics of God by appealing only to natural reason and experience. The second tried to supplement this rather sketchy religion of nature with a more abundant revelation. This program, in its characteristically 18th-century form, achieved archetypal fulfillment in Archdeacon William Paley's *Natural Theology* (1802) and *Evidences of Christianity* (1794).

The weight of the first part of Paley's case was borne primarily by the argument to design: if from a watch we may infer a watchmaker, then, surely, the orderliness of the universe entitles us to infer, by parity of reasoning, a universe maker. The

second part of the case rested on the claim that there is ample historical evidence to show that the biblical miracles, including crucially the physical resurrection of Jesus, did in fact occur; and that this in turn proved the truth of the main Christian claims.

The general validity of this two-stage apologetic, although not that of any particular putative proof of natural theology, was defined in 1870 by the First Vatican Council as a dogma necessary to salvation. However we have to realize that, since the Second Vatican Council touched off the progressive Protestantization of the Roman church, this defined dogma appears to have become one item rather rarely picked by those professing Catholics who insist on choosing out of the historic deposit of the faith their own individual anthologies of credibility. The relevant canon dealing with the second stage neither hesitates nor compromises: "If anyone shall say . . . that miracles can never be known for certain, or that the divine origin of the Christian religion cannot properly be proved by them: let them be cast out."

It was against this whole traditional apologetic that DAVID HUME in sections 10 to 12 of the first *Enquiry* fired his most devastating broadside. With regard to stage two the contention was, in his own words, "that a miracle can never be proved so as to be the foundation of a system of religion." For him all other questions about the miraculous are, officially at least, merely incidental to this. A miracle he defines as "a transgression of a law of nature by a particular volition of the Deity, or by the interposition of some invisible agent," a definition of a kind equally suited, as we have seen, both to his own purposes and to those of his opponents.

Notice next that in the present context it would be worse than useless to appeal to revelation to provide criteria by means of which genuinely miraculous events may be identified, and thus distinguished from the unusual, the untoward, or the merely ordinary. For, if the occurrence of a miracle is to serve as the endorsement of a revelation, then we have to find some means entirely independent of that revelation by which this guarantee may be recognized.

Exactly the same point applies, of course, if one urges that miracles are essentially not overridings but signs. If a sign is to signify *to the unbeliever,* then there must be some means independent of the doctrinal system itself by which the signs may be identified and read as such. Maybe there is something to be said for interpreting many of the references in the New Testament to wonders and signs in this way, rather than as mainstream miracle stories. But then it is necessary to insist, because this is often overlooked, that part of the price of such a defense is losing the support these stories might provide as independent evidences of the genuineness of the alleged revelation.

Another immediately consequential point is that if any occurrence is to be rated a miracle and to constitute, as such, evidence for the truth of "a system of religion," then it has to be possible to identify it as miraculous without reference to that system. The difficulty of meeting this requirement is frequently concealed by accepting what seems to many an almost unquestionable assumption. Protagonists of the supernatural, and opponents too, take it for granted that we all possess some natural (as opposed to revealed) way of knowing that and where the unassisted potentialities of nature (as opposed to a postulated supernature) are more restricted than the potentialities that we find to be in fact realized or realizable in the universe around us. We do not.

Seductive though this assumption seems to be, it nevertheless remains entirely unwarranted. We simply have not got, nor could we have, any natural (as opposed to revealed) criterion to enable us to say, in the face of something that is found actually to happen, that here we have an achievement which nature, left to her own unaided devices, could never compass. The natural scientist, confronted with some occurrence inconsistent with a proposition previously believed to express a law of nature, can find in this disturbing fact no ground whatsoever for proclaiming that the law, while remaining effective, has nevertheless been supernaturally overridden.

On the contrary, the new discovery is simply a reason for conceding that the scientist had previously been wrong to think that the proposition thus confuted did indeed express a true law, as well as a reason for resolving to search again for the law that really does obtain. We certainly cannot say, on any natural (as opposed to revealed) grounds, that anything which actually happens is beyond the powers of unaided nature, any more than we can say that anything any man has ever succeeded in doing transcends all merely human powers. For our evidence about the powers of nature in general, and of men in particular, is precisely and only everything that things and people do. For a scientist to insist that some recalcitrant fact constitutes an overriding of a still inviolably true law of nature is,

to borrow Rudolf Carnap's mischievous analogy, as if a geographer were to maintain that the discrepancies between his maps and their objects show that there is something wrong with the territories thus mismapped.

All this, however, notwithstanding that it is both relevant and—in spirit at least—thoroughly Humean, falls rather beside the line of argument Hume chose to develop. This line is just as methodological. But it treats the question as it arises for history, rather than as it might impinge upon natural science. Hume is concerned primarily not with the question of fact but with that of evidence. The problem is how the occurrence of a miracle can be proved, rather than whether any such events ever have occurred. Consequently, even if Hume is successful, the way will still remain clear to believe in miracles simply on faith. Hume permits this, although insisting always that "a wise man proportions his belief to the evidence."

Hume hoped to have discovered "a decisive argument . . . which must at least silence the most arrogant bigotry and superstition, free us from their impertinent solicitations . . . an argument which . . . will . . . with the wise and learned, be an everlasting check to all kinds of superstitious delusion . . ." It is sometimes thought there is no more to this "everlasting check" than a trite reminder that, because the occurrence of a miracle must be very improbable, it needs to be exceptionally well evidenced.

But C. S. Peirce, who seems never to have exploited it fully, had the vital clue in his hands when he remarked: "The whole of modern 'higher criticism' of ancient history in general, and of Biblical history in particular, is based upon the same logic that is used by Hume."

For what, with certain lapses and hesitations, Hume is contending is that the criteria by which we must assess historical testimony, and the general assumptions which alone make it possible for us to interpret the detritus of the past as historical evidence, must inevitably rule out any possibility of establishing upon purely historical evidence that some genuinely miraculous event has occurred.

Hume's fundamental theses are: (1) that the present detritus of the past cannot be interpreted as historical evidence at all, unless we presume that the same basic regularities obtained then as obtain today; and, (2) that in trying as best he may to determine what actually happened, the historian must employ as criteria all his present knowledge or presumed knowledge of what is probable or improbable, possible or impossible.

In his first work, *A Treatise of Human Nature*, Hume argued that it is only on such presumptions that we can justify the conclusion that ink marks on old pieces of paper constitute testimonial evidence. Earlier in his first *Enquiry* he argues the inescapable importance of having such criteria. In a footnote to section 10 he quotes with approval the reasoning of the famous physician De Sylva in the contested case of a Mlle. Thibaut: "It was impossible she could have been so ill as was proved by witnesses, because it was impossible that she could, in so short a time, have recovered so perfectly as he found her."

Deficiencies in Hume's Critique. Two very serious faults in Hume's whole treatment may obscure the force and soundness of De Sylva's reasoning, and the fact that this sort of application of canons to evidence is absolutely essential to the very possibility of critical history. The first is a rather wooden dogmatism of disbelief, which left Hume wide open to Hamlet's rebuke to overweening philosophy: "There are more things in heaven and earth, Horatio, than are dreamt of in your philosophy."

Against all his own high skeptical principles Hume tends to take it for granted that what in his own day he and all his fellow men of sense firmly believed about the order of nature constituted: not just well-grounded yet always humanly fallible opinion but the definitive and incorrigible last word. He is thus betrayed into dismissing categorically as downright impossible certain reported phenomena which the later progress of abnormal psychology and of psychosomatic medicine has since shown to have been perfectly possible.

The second major fault is both more serious and more excusable. Hume is unable to provide an adequate account of the logical character of a law of nature. Hence he cannot offer any sufficiently persuasive rationale for the employment as canons of exclusion in historical inquiry of propositions which express, or which are believed to express, such natural laws.

Casting back to the reasoning of De Sylva, we can now see that and how it constitutes a paradigm of critical history. For it is only and precisely by presuming that the laws that hold today held in the past, and by employing as our canons all our knowledge (or presumed knowledge) of what is probable or improbable, possible or impossible, that we can rationally interpret the relics of the past as evidence and from them construct our account

of what actually happened. But in this context what is impossible is what is contingently, as opposed to logically, impossible. And contingent impossibility is, and surely has to be, explicated in part by reference to inconsistency with a true law of nature. Or rather, since this sense of *impossible* is prior to the development of science proper, let us introduce a new expression and say: What is contingently impossible is whatever is inconsistent with a true nomological proposition.

Both causal propositions and those expressing laws of nature fall under this genus. Although Hume himself concentrated on the causal species, what he said can easily be extended to cover the entire genus. Yet once these easy extensions have been made we are still left with an account that does not begin to do justice to the ideas of contingent necessity, contingent impossibililty, and contingent (or causal) connection. This is no place to try to fill these enormous gaps; it must suffice to point out that Hume's analysis was ultimately in terms of mere brute fact, observed but not experimentally tested, constant conjunctions.

In effect—and discounting the misguided psychologizings—Hume attempted to reduce nomological propositions to statements of what modern logicians so misleadingly insist on dubbing material implications, to statements, that is to say, of the form: *Never as a matter of fact this and not that.* But all nomological propositions entail, what can never be legitimately deduced from any elaboration of material implications, contrary-to-fact conditional statements, that is to say, of the form: *If this had happened, then that would have.*

Something of the cash value of all these somewhat formidable technicalities can be brought out through a homely illustration. Suppose that someone, referring to an automobile, utters the nomological proposition: The cause of the trouble is a fault in the ignition. Then this statement entails the contrary-to-fact conditional proposition: If all other things had remained the same, and if there had been no fault in the ignition, then there would have been no trouble.

To assert any such contrary-to-fact conditional is to assert the subsistence of some contingent connection and to imply the associated presence of both contingent necessity and contingent impossibility. If the cause of the trouble was a fault in the ignition, then there is, necessarily, a contingent connection between the state of the ignition and the owner's inability to get the machine going. Given that state, with all other things as always remaining the same, then it must be contingently necessary that it will not run and contingently impossible to get it to do so. And, furthermore, anyone who has observed some constant conjunction, without either attempting or yet referring to the experience of others who had attempted to disrupt it, has no business to infer that the elements of that conjunction are not merely constantly conjoined but also connected. A creature who was always and only an observer, never an actor, could surely not acquire nomological concepts. Even if he did, miraculously, he certainly would not be evidentially entitled to employ them in describing the nonlinguistic world.

In the light of all this, consider again the question of historical evidence for the miraculous. The critical historian confronted with some story of a miracle will usually dismiss it out of hand, although maybe asking whether it can be used as evidence not for the occurrence reported but for something else. To justify his procedure he will have to appeal to precisely the principle Hume advanced: the "absolute impossibililty or miraculous nature" of the events attested must, "in the eyes of all reasonable people . . . alone be regarded as a sufficient refutation."

Our sole ground for characterizing the occurrence reported as miraculous is at the same time a sufficient reason for calling it contingently impossible. Contrariwise, if ever we became able to say that some account of the ostensibly miraculous was indeed veridical, this can only be because we now know that the occurrences reported were not miraculous at all.

To this representation of the procedure of the critical historian two main objections arise. First, it will certainly be argued that such an approach to what purports to be historical evidence for the miraculous is irrationally dogmatic. The historian seems to be represented as dismissing all evidence that conflicts with his own fundamental prejudices—that is, defending a closed system in which his professional predilections are guaranteed against falsification by a "Heads-I-win-tails-you-lose" argument. Second, it will be argued that there is something arbitrary, or at least optional, about the appeal to the canons provided by the sum of our knowledge, of what is probable or improbable, possible or impossible.

To the first objection the reply is that, as Hume himself was from first to last insisting, it is a matter of overwhelming evidence, not of dogmatism. For—and from this point we are beginning to

improve on Hume—the nomological propositions providing the historians canons of exclusion are open and general of the form: *Any this must be, or be followed by, that*. The proposition reporting the (alleged) miraculous happening will be singular and in the past tense, of the form: *This particular, or that occasion, was, or was followed by, that*.

But now, whereas it must in the nature of the case be too late to put the truth of any proposition of the second sort to a direct test, propositions of the first kind can in principle, if not in practice, be so tested by everyone, anywhere, and at any time. And it is only and precisely to the extent that any such proposition actually assumed or asserted by historians has in fact been strongly and widely tested, and always confirmed, that they are warranted to assume the subsistence of the natural law which, were the other and so much weaker proposition to be true, would presumably have been overridden.

Suppose that in some quite extraordinary case the evidence for asserting that a miracle did, in fact, happen seems extremely strong. Then historians may perhaps ask themselves whether the nomological precluding the natural occurrence of any such event is true after all. This nomological could, in principle at any rate, be tested further and more severely. Suppose, as might happen, it turned out to be false. Then maybe the exceptional past event did in fact occur. But the prior falsification of the original nomological robs historians of their only reason for entertaining the suggestion that there might have been a miracle.

Suppose now, alternatively, that the nomological survived, still unfalsified, all further tests. Then all these additional tests must be accepted as providing yet more evidence that the miraculous occurrence never happened. Only if it were conceded that we had sufficient reasons to make probable the occurrence of a miracle of that kind on that occasion—reasons presumably of natural or revealed religion—only then could we begin to consider returning any verdict more supportive than an agnostic, and appropriately Scottish, "not proven."

The second objection sees something arbitrary, or at least optional, about appealing to canons provided by the sum of our knowledge, or presumed knowledge, of what is probable and improbable, possible and impossible. Certainly we can choose whether to try to act as critical historians or not. But once that fundamental choice is made there is nothing arbitrary and nothing optional about insisting on the employment of these preferred canons. For the essential aim of the historian is to get as near as he can to a full knowledge of what actually happened and why. To do this he must find and interpret evidence. Belief unsupported by evidence may of course be true. But it cannot constitute knowledge. To interpret the detritus of the past as evidence, and to assess its value and bearing as such, we must have canons.

For the rational inquirer these can only be derived from the sum of available knowledge, or presumed knowledge. It is not the insistence on the systematic employment of these always corrigible canons that is arbitrary. What is arbitrary is, while eschewing wholesale rejection, to pick and choose among the available mass of miracle stories; to urge, for instance, that, since it is (psychologically) impossible that these particular witnesses were lying or misinformed, therefore we must accept that on this occasion the (biologically) impossible occurred. Once we have departed in such arbitrary ways from these canons of critical history, then everything goes and anything goes. Outside of unbelief there is no systematic rationality; and no salvation either.

Only Brute Faith Remains. Nothing said in this article closes the door on faith. We have been concerned only with questions about the possibilities of having good reasons for belief in the miraculous. Again, nothing has been said to preclude the production of nonhistorical and nonscientific considerations that might, either by themselves or with the aid of historical evidence, justify us in believing that certain miracles did indeed occur.

Perhaps one might develop some defensible system of rational theology that would provide criteria both for identifying particular occurrences as miraculous and for separating true miracle stories from false. Hume tried in section 11 of his *Enquiry* and elsewhere to rule this out. But it has been no part of our present assignment to examine arguments against natural theology. Finally, it is perfectly possible to develop a fresh concept and to apply to it the word *miracle*. There is never anything to stop anyone from simply changing the subject.

Other articles of interest: **God, Existence of. Jesus, Historicity of. Voltaire** ("Miracles").

Bibliography

Development of Ideas About the Miraculous

Grant, R. M. *Miracle and Natural Law in Graeco-Roman and Early Christian Thought.* Amsterdam: 1952.

Lecky, W. E. H. *History of the Rise of the Spirit of Rationalism in Europe.* London: Longmans Green, 1890. First three chapters.

Stephen, Leslie. *English Thought in the Eighteenth Century.* Vol. 1. 3rd ed. London: Murray, 1902.

Logical and Methodological Analysis

Aquinas, Thomas. *Summa contra Gentiles.* Trans. A. C. Pogis. New York: Doubleday, 1955.

Augustine. *The City of God.* Ed. V. S. Tasher. Trans. J. Healey. New York and London: Dutton, Dent, Everyman's Library, 1945.

Flew, Antony. *Hume's Philosophy of Belief.* Chap. 8. London: Routledge & Kegan Paul, 1961.

Hume, David. "An Enquiry Concerning Human Understanding." In *Hume's Enquiries.* Ed. L. A. Selby-Bigge; rev. P. Nidditch. 3rd ed. Oxford: Clarendon Press, 1975.

Swinburne, R. G. *The Concept of Miracle.* London: Macmillan, 1970.

Tennant, F. R. *Miracle and Its Philosophical Presuppositions.* London: 1928.

Historical Investigations of Christian Miracle Stories

Middleton, Conyers. *A Free Inquiry into the Miraculous Powers Which Are Supposed to Have Subsisted in the Christian Church from the Earliest Ages Through Several Successive Centuries.* London: 1748. This work was pivotal in the 18th-century controversy described by Stephen. Compare also both Hume and J. H. Newman, "Essay on the Miracles Recorded in Ecclesiastical History." In *The Ecclesiastical History of M. L'Abbé Fleury.* Oxford: 1842.

Perry, M. C. *The Easter Enigma.* London: Faber and Faber, 1959.

Schweitzer, Albert. *The Quest for the Historical Jesus.* Trans. W. Montgomery. New York: Macmillan, 1966.

Thompson, J. M. *Miracles in the New Testament.* London: Arnold, 1911.

ANTONY FLEW

MONTAIGNE, MICHEL DE (1533–1592), French essayist and skeptical writer. See **French Literature, Unbelief in.**

MORAL JUDGMENTS, IMPACT OF UN-BELIEF ON. World War I may mark the time when Christianity in the United States, like other religious traditions elsewhere, started its descent into limbo, or into what is more politely called "cultural pluralism." Before the war the term *free-thinker* was an epithet; after it, honor and respect began to be paid to the "open mind" in the "open society."

James Truslow Adams, in the *Atlantic Monthly* (1926), spoke not only of "the decay of the Christian theology" then plainly in evidence but he also tied it to "the loss of Christian ethics." When one ends, the other does too. Adams' perception is the heart of the matter.

Although our focus here is on the American experience, it may be taken as a prototype of what is going on in most other parts of the world. As religious beliefs weaken, whatever doctrinaire morality is built on them loses credibility. In their place an "autonomous" ethics takes shape—ethics with humanistic rather than theistic presuppositions.

Objections to religion are of two kinds. One is intellectual, the other moral. The core of the intellectual objections is that there are no good grounds in reason to think any religion is true. The moral objection is that the ethical precepts of religion are outmoded and cruel, compared to contemporary standards of humane conduct.

The Background. Even though we shall be examining quite specific instances of religious morality, it seems worthwhile, first, to look at the philosophical and theological background. What we find is that theology, understood as a rational reflection on the tenability and implications of religious beliefs, is itself a major contributing factor to the weakening process, which emancipates conscience from various notions of what the "divine will" commands or requires of human moral agents. Traditionally, the assumption was that religious belief is essential and necessary to morality, both as the sufficient reason for it and as its effective sanction.

This idea was at least part of what lay behind the remark of VOLTAIRE: "If God did not exist it would be necessary to invent him." It also explans why BENJAMIN FRANKLIN, himself an unbeliever, asked: "If men are so wicked with religion, what would they be without it?" In North and South America, as well as in Western Europe, this necessary foundation was supposed to lie in Christianity in particular, not just any religion; in the Middle East it lay in Islam; in Southeast Asia, Hinayana Buddhism, and so on. JOHN LOCKE, tolerant though he was, wrote out of an Anglican environment that we are not morally obliged to keep faith with Roman Catholics or atheists.

It is to be expected, therefore, that evangelists and churches will cry havoc as religious reservations, doubts, tolerances, and denials come more and more rapidly into play in universities, public affairs, and the mass media.

Not so long ago it was a fair assumption that practically everybody in our society was either a Christian or a Jew, at least nominally. The essentials of Christian doctrine were exactly those which the "fundamentalists" still stubbornly refuse to retreat from: the inerrancy of scripture, the deity of Jesus, his virgin birth, a substitutionary atonement (that is, eternal salvation won for mankind when the Roman soldiers executed Jesus), his physical resurrection from death, and a visible second coming. This is the set of beliefs proclaimed in the papal *Syllabus of Errors* issued by the Vatican in 1864 and sounded steadily from Protestant pulpits.

Some faith propositions are of a factual kind and vulnerable therefore to empirical and scientific falsification. For example, in 1950 Pope Pius XII issued his bull *Humani generis*, requiring Catholics to believe that all men are inheritors of sin from one man. This, the bull explained, was actually true, not merely metaphysically. Thus it threw aside biology's theory of the human species as polygenic, in favor of a monogenic doctrine. Furthermore, it asserted the inheritance of acquired characteristics, thus flatly contradicting evolution by natural selection. It is not surprising that both Catholic and Protestant fundamentalists still wage a rearguard fight for "special creation."

Except among the fundamentalists or "Bible Christians," the theology now taught and preached for the most part is "reinterpreted" as "metaphorical truth," rather than actual or historical fact. This is the weakening process. Science and scientific method have put speculative metaphysics aside in favor of rational cognitive principles, and the consequence is a progressive weakening of belief in classical Christian doctrines—even in those not vulnerable to empirical discredit.

Demythologization. In their own circles theologians call this growing weakness "dehistorization" and "demythologization." Demythologized and metamorphized beliefs no longer provide an effective back-up for Christian ethics, as the old simple, matter-of-fact faith did. Nominal believers, who are in the great majority, have weakened most. The average church member professes belief for social reasons, not out of conviction. The strongest binders are ethnic and family ties, and in some areas (for example, the Bible Belt) prudence is a strong motivator. But the ethics of even the most serious believers—"true believers," to use Eric Hoffer's apt phrase—is steadily eroded.

Take an actual case. In a southern university's school of medicine, at a grand-rounds discussion of a problematic case in which the physician's moral obligation was the question, one student said the right thing to do was what the Bible says, and to trust in God's approval either in this life or the next. There was a gale of laughter; his opinion was treated as comic relief.

It is the common feeling nowadays that a thoroughly religious person is not fit to conduct public affairs. Before his election John Kennedy had to assure the voters that he would not let his Catholicism influence his judgment (incidentally raising the question what it is worth if it does not influence his judgment).

The issue between ethical autonomy (man-based) and ethical heteronomy (God-based) is by now nearly a nonissue. The great majority of philosophers, scholars, scientists, and legislators (these last being committed constitutionally to the separation of church and state) now see moral concern and judgment as something all human beings can engage in without any supernatural validation or sanction whatsoever.

The Pelagian Heresy. This humanist morality is known in theological circles as the Pelagian heresy. Pelagius (about 360–431) held that ethical action is a human initiative and that men can achieve goodness without the special help ("grace") of God. He therefore rejected the doctrine of original sin—the sin of Adam, believed by the orthodox to be (1) inherent in human nature, (2) following the "fall" (when Adam was tempted to eat the forbidden fruit, which represented knowledge of good and evil), thus (3) losing to himself and all of his descendants their aboriginal amorality or "innocence," and (4) requiring baptism as an exorcist release from the hold of Adam's sin on infant human beings. This religious package is of

the kind that led BERTRAND RUSSELL to coin the term *superstitious ethics*.

The principle of human ethics in Pelagianism was described by a distinguished modern apologist, William Temple, as "the only intrinsically damnable heresy." Temple appreciated its significance as a radical departure from the classical Christian faith, as a big factor in the weakening process of theology. When Dostoevski cried, "If God is dead all things are possible," he gave tongue to his loyalty to the dying notion of heteronomous or grace ethics, but when FRIEDRICH NIETZSCHE, said it, he was congratulating men on their emancipation.

Theologians, scrapping their "received" doctrine, now acknowledge that ethical autonomy is tenable. Some even welcome it. W. G. Maclagen's *The Theological Frontier of Ethics* (1961) provides the most competent treatment of the question in recent times. The Glasgow philosopher offers as his conclusion that morality is possible without religion, although he prefers to keep them wedded. Then he confesses, "the insistence that morality depends extraneously on religion debases both" since "it may rather drive men from morality than bring them to religion." Furthermore, he adds, "it could even lead to the corruptest forms of fanaticism."

Maclagen's fear of fanaticism is borne out by the Moral Majority, to take one example. Its fierce drive is in character, to impose on all Americans a fundamentalist morality on abortion, betting, school prayers, special creationism, sexual ethics, the subjection of women, racial segregation, and the like. They pit their Bible ethics flatly against the American consensus of moral pluralism, a part of which is that an atheist (who, John Buchan said, has no invisible means of support) is a moral agent equally with any religious believer.

Society now holds that an atheist is as answerable morally for what he or she does as believers are. It not only concedes but protects the freedom to *not* believe. The forum of conscience is no longer assumed to be supported by one notion or another of transcendental knowledge or power. This is both the official (constitutional) and cultural policy of the United States, as well as of many other countries.

Our consensus was well put by Gunnar Myrdal: "There is no country on earth which has more of a common, explicit ideology—more of a common explicit morality, I might say. This is the old Enlightenment ideal; dignity of the human individual, justice between people, liberty, equality of opportunity, and brotherhood."

This dereligionized morality got its start firmly with IMMANUEL KANT. In the 18th century he built an epochal case against the very idea of "religious knowledge"—and therefore against any ethics supposedly derived from it. Indeed, he actually turned things around 180 degrees by showing how belief in God could be derived (though it need not be) from ethics. He reversed the medieval fundamentalism that claimed that ethics is derived from religious belief, by propounding the moral argument for the existence of God.

The age of reason was taking shape, reaching farther than Kant did. It is marked by a humanist reliance on moral struggle guided by reason, in place of the old theistic belief in redemption attained by divine grace. As Crane Brinton used to say, the source of morality changed from "the transcendental God-determined Christian otherworldly heaven" to "this-world *transformed* by human reason guiding human action."

Thomas Aquinas had already faced the question, raised first in Plato's *Euthyphro,* that if the gods approve of an act it cannot be because it is good, for in that case the good would be established prior to the gods' approval. "Does God will it because it is good," St. Thomas asked, "or is it good because God wills it?" He supported the first view (realism), as Duns Scotus did the second (nominalism). Plato long ago made the case for ethical autonomy, whereas Scotus took as his starting point the very essence of all genuinely religious ethics, namely, heteronomy or "divine-command" morality.

Our modern culture's assignment of moral responsiblity to unbelievers is tantamount to acceptance of their nonreligious values, as well as their judgments. Except for professedly religious thinkers, who still appear but only in a minor role in the literature (outside of their own doctrinaire publications), contemporary philosophers and social scientists deal with values and valuation entirely in secular terms. Value perceptions are dealt with in an ethics-related discipline called *axiology.*

Value is taken to mean the worth of a thing. As William Frankena explains, in *The Encyclopedia of Philosophy* (8:230), there are various kinds of value or goodness: instrumental (a good knife), technical (a good driver), utilitarian (good advice), hedonic (a good dinner), and conventional (a good citizen). The main point here is simply to say that religiosity is inessential on any of these scores of value, except for a diminishing minority who choose to relate them to religious beliefs in one way or another. Just as moral judgments about right and wrong are commonly determined independently of a "divine" imperative, so are value judgments (preferences) about good and evil.

Students of comparative religion often remark that "theology stands at the bar of ethics." They mean that beliefs that carry morally repugnant prescriptives are sooner or later discarded. Most unbelievers disbelieve on moral grounds; they reject gods and doctrines that fall short of their human perceptions. While there is no way to prove that religious beliefs are false (nor, for that matter, true), there is plenty of evidence that the morality of believers, if they are compliant, can be very cruel and inhumane. Religion has blessed war and slavery, encouraged the subjugation of women, favored ignorance and intellectual stasis, and, as we shall see, it continues these traits right down into the present.

Specific Problems of Moral Judgment. When we turn to these we can contrast the two approaches: one from religious premises and the other from secular (nonreligious) premises. We shall look closely at six controversial questions, made so by religious moralists who condemn what is already being done or what is acceptably innovative.

The six policies or practices are: abortion, birth control, medically assisted human reproduction, earth burial of the dead, human initiatives in death and dying, and prayers in public schools. There are many others we might have taken but these have the virtue of being familiar, intimately personal, and yet also with substantial impact on society's interests. We shall try to put them in historical perspective as well as examine their contemporary shape.

Looking at these issues we can readily see why Russell, in *Why I Am Not a Christian,* summed it up with the observation: "The more intense has been the religion of any period, and the more profound has been the dogmatic belief, the greater has been the cruelty and the worse has been the state of affairs." The religious input in these controversies is marked by a bitterness sometimes frightening because Christians' "love of the brethren" easily leads to hatred of others. As the Irish clergyman and wit Jonathan Swift said, "We have just enough religion to make us hate but not enough to make us love one another."

(Something else ought to be said, however. Critics of the emotional tone of dogmatic morality are imperceptive if they fail to appreciate how those who advocate moral imperatives based on dogma, rather than upon human needs, never wholly rid themselves of a nagging self-doubt, which causes them to become strident easily.)

Abortion. "Religion," as Remy de Gourmont, the French novelist, put it, "revolves madly around sexual questions." The abortion debate at the end of the 20th century illustrates this insight. The demand of Catholics (right-to-life agitators) and the Protestant, self-styled Moral Majority to outlaw abortion as "murder" and to gain legal standing (even by inserting an amendment to the Constitution) in their drive to impose compulsory pregnancy, has been carried on in the face of poll after poll of public opinion showing that the majority of people disagree with them. Most of the clergy and laity suppose, mistakenly, that their view of the question has always been the Christian one.

In fact, it was not until a century ago, in an 1869 decree, that Roman Catholic authorities declared abortion *for whatever reason* to be wrong, regardless of human needs. In the Middle Ages many authorities followed Aristotle's opinion that it was all right to abort an "unformed" fetus (prior to "quickening"). Theologians (Thomas Aquinas, for example) allowed abortion if a fetus was "inanimate," meaning if it had not yet received a "soul." They were never able, however, to agree as to when the soul was "infused."

In 1869 the Holy Office under Pius IX decided to squash the debate; it decreed excommunication for all Catholics involved in abortion, *on the ground of prudence.* It was admitted, however, that there is no way to know when a fetus becomes a person, but to avoid any *risk* of murder they decided that it cannot "safely" be taught that abortion at any time after conception is licit, not even to save the mother's life. (Many "liberal" theologians now argue intricately that abortion is "permissible" to save a pregnant woman's life—some adding "if she is married.")

Contrary to popular belief, therefore, the Vatican's official position was that abortion might be murder, not that it is. Typical of such religious moralism, however, what was originally only prudence has already been converted into dogmatic prohibition. The Second Vatican Council (1965) condemned abortion as "an unspeakable crime," with no ifs, ands, or buts about it. As this history shows, what we may call a "hardening of the oughteries" is characteristic of dogmatic ethics.

The religious prohibition on abortion is a universal negative; it pontificates that to terminate a pregnancy is immoral, no matter how misbegotten the pregnancy nor how good the consequences of an abortion might be, and this is the case always, everywhere, and at all times. There is good reason to think that fundamentalist Protestants are not as absolutistic in this matter as Catholics, neither in their utterances nor their practice, but however that may be everybody knows that both groups tolerate abortions frequently; this is especially the case when fetal disease or disorder is revealed by prenatal diagnosis. Nevertheless, in spite of growing lay revolt, church spokesmen and the militants hold fast to the newly simplified prohibition: Since we cannot be sure when a fetus becomes a person, thereby making abortion murder, let all abortions at any time and for any reason be declared to be murder.

Not only has the timing of abortion been debated but there has also been a fierce debate about what constitutes the "person" who must be predicated to make a charge of murder. Some have held that life *simpliciter* is all that is needed. Others have said that a minimum of physical and/or mental development is what gives personal status (eliminating, for example, the anencephalic). But the dominant religious tradition has taken a third view, that the individual is a person when the soul (*animus*) has been infused into the body and that this occurs before, not after, birth. Moreover, Catholics, and some Protestants, hold that the soul is not a byproduct of the body (the traducian theory) but a special gift of God to each fetus (the creationist theory). As we have seen, we cannot pinpoint the event on the embryonic continuum; hence, abortion is prohibited at any time after fertilization takes place.

Since only speculative or "faith" answers may be given to questions as to the personal status of a fetus, most people, contrary to the dogmatists, follow the Supreme Court, Plato, Jewish rabbis, and others, by assigning personhood to the live-born rather than to prenatal life.

The antiabortionists, nearly all of whom are religiously motivated, stand firmly and often angrily against the law in America, and against the moral consensus. The consensus regards abortion as a private and personal matter of choice. Nobody should be forced to have an abortion or to forego one. Most people who support selective abortion in principle see it as a sad and even tragic action, yet one which carries only regret, not remorse or moral guilt. Often it is thought to be the best thing to do on balance, if human need and happiness—not a speculative belief—is what should determine right and good.

The Jewish position comes nearer to the contemporary norm. Rabbinic law says human life begins at birth, as Plato and the U.S. Supreme Court have held. On this view there is a right to life but not a right to be born; abortion is allowed, but only for the gravest reasons (to preserve a woman's life or health). Abortion without medical indication, however, violates the *mitzvah* (commandment) to "replenish" the population; this Talmudic, pronatalist imperative means, they say, that to fail in this respect makes one "guilty of bloodshed." Obviously this is an ethical teaching widely ignored even by professedly *religious* Jews.

Birth Control. Whoever is indiscriminately opposed to abortion as such should, one would think, be in favor of contraception—that is, of preventing unwanted pregnancies, thus reducing the number of medically indicated interruptions of pregnancy (as in the case of fetal illness or disorder) or terminations due to a considered choice against parenthood. Nevertheless, no matter how sane and responsible such a position might seem, the fact is that many religious people disapprove both things; they are not only opposed to ending unwanted pregnancies but they are also opposed to preventing them. This is precisely the official morality of the Vatican, although, as we shall see, many of its adherents are in revolt—because they are revolted by it.

The religious condemnation of birth control has been presented in a practically united front of all Christians up and into the present century. The official Catholic moral rule opposes all methods except abstinence from intercourse and "rhythm"—a maneuver which tries to calculate the "infertile period" in the menstrual cycle. But by this time only a few of even the fundamentalists agree—and no Protestant church does. Only those who are positively antisexual remain loyal to the classical Augustinian opinion that sex is "ordered" solely for reproduction, not for human need. The moral consensus in America clearly sides with Margaret H. Sanger (1833–1966), birth control's major prophet, who was herself a Catholic in revolt.

Protestant fundamentalists are somewhat at a loss, since as biblicists they can find no teaching by Jesus on the ethics of sex. This hiatus in the Gospel is, of course, no obstacle to Catholic opinion, which is more apt in any case to appeal to "natural law" than to holy scripture.

This nature-law argumentation is mixed up with traditional magniloquence, and the mixture results in amusing inconsistencies. Rhythm, for example, is now allowed on natural-law grounds, but St. Augustine explicitly denounced rhythm in his diatribe *On the Morals of Manichees,* in which he lays down the rule that baby-making must always be the end sought in lovemaking. Classical moral teaching has always followed Augustine, the logic of whose teaching is that if (as they say) nature does not "intend" conception during the infertile period, then it follows that contraceptives are morally permissible whenever the rhythm method is—and contraceptives are far more reliable.

Nothing has sobered ecclesiastical theocrats more in modern times than the by now open defiance of these anticontraception edicts, including the encyclical *Casti connubii* of 1930 that restricted sex to reproductive purposes. In the U.S. it was a Catholic physician and research scientist, John Rock, who helped to develop the oral "pill" and in 1963 defended its use in *The Time Has Come,* a book challenging the papal rule. The revolt of the rank and file grew so strong that in the sixties a papal commission of clergy and laity was set up to review the question. Their majority report favored contraceptive intercourse.

Nevertheless, in his role as the infallible vicar of Christ on earth and the last word in matters of faith and morals, Pope Paul VI rejected the commission's findings in the encyclical *Humanae vitae.* The result of his decision was an almost open disobedience. The hierarchy still follows the "line" but minor clergy and lay people generally ignore it. Within their penitential system of confession and penance clergy simply instruct Catholics that if they do not think contraceptive intercourse is immoral there is no reason why they should make their practice of it a matter of confession, or even bring it up.

This revolt is a step in the direction of rational ethics but for some people another means of fertility control, that is, sterilization, is outside the pale. Millions of Americans now use this way of preventing unwanted pregnancies; it is the most reliable form of contraception. And within the ranks of the fundamentalists, both Catholic and Protestant, even though they use birth control their opposition to abortion causes them mixed feelings. Biologically, some of the contraceptives are in fact abortifacients. They prevent nidation, not fertilization. Thus far most "good" Christians have seemed somehow able to ignore this contradiction; many students of the cultural scene are convinced that in a fairly short time all but the most fanatical of them will change their attitude toward abortion, as they have done toward birth control.

Reproductive Medicine. Perhaps the saddest of the issues we must look at lies in reproductive medicine. The angry attacks of Catholics and Moral Majoritarians on medical assistance to reproducers in trouble seem sad as well as silly, because their effect so often is to deny both reproducers and their progeny any help when disease or disorder threatens. They act out of obedience to their religious ethic—a situation often called "the immorality of morality" because of their insistence on unalterable rules based on "eternal" principles.

Medicine has learned how to assist people who are infertile or suffering from infectious diseases or who are for whatever reason unable to procreate in the normal coital way. Among the modalities which can help are artificial insemination and enovulation, *in vitro* fertilization and implantation, and surrogate pregnancy. Other procedures to surmount obstacles to reproduction will soon become clinically feasible, including artificial gestation (in a synthetic uterus rather than one of human tissue), and asexual methods such as germ-cell fusion, parthenogenesis, and "cloning."

These procedures are expensive, cumbersome, and uncomfortable; only a few people will resort to them and then only because they have to if they are unwilling to remain childless. The normal or typical process of baby-making will ordinarily be preferred, for obvious reasons.

From the very start, as soon as medicine began to find ways to assist production, the religious moralists have condemned them. They have been denounced as artificial (that is, not "natural"), especially by Catholic theologians. The notion behind this concept of naturality is that God as creator has ordered certain ways of doing things; this is the "natural" way—an "objectively" valid "moral order" of things. Any departure of human innovation, for whatever reason, and no matter how great the human benefit, is a demonic pretension of the sort that only "secular humanists" would try to defend. Whatever is "artificial," if it prevents or circumvents the natural, is *ipso facto* impious and immoral.

One example will serve to make the point. Recent success in the use of *in vitro* for women whose Fallopian tubes have been blocked irreversibly by disease has been well covered in the press, in part because of the moral controversy the Christian fundamentalists have created. In 1981 the Erie County Medical Center in Buffalo, N.Y., announced it would open an *in vitro* clinic; already there had been 83 applications. The local Catholic bishop promptly denounced it, and it was shut down out of fear of political reprisals. Asked for his reason, he made the mistake of giving one; he said that it is murder to discard a blastocyst (a fertilized ovum), and this—abortion—is what is done with all conceptuses left over after the procedure attains success. The fact is that *all* conceptuses are implanted at each trial. It is a further fact that far more embryos are lost (aborted) in "natural" conceptions than in medically contrived conceptions.

Jerry Falwell, Moral Majority leader, was shrewder. When he condemned the opening of an *in vitro* clinic in Norfolk, Va., where they simply ignored him and his cohorts, he too was asked his reason. He gave no tangible reason whatever and thus avoided discredit factually; he simply said that the clinic was "delving into an area that is far too sacred for human beings to be involved in." It was an objection without a reason; there was no way to take hold of it because it was empirically vacuous.

A year later, a young family-practice physician in a midwest university medical center was offered a faculty appointment, which he accepted, at a prominent eastern university under Catholic management. When he arrived to take up his duties, sitting in the midst of the unpacked boxes in his new apartment, he learned his appointment had been cancelled. Why? Because he had done an A.I.D.—artificial insemination from a donor—for a patient, which moral theologians characterize as both an unnatural act and adultery. (In their eyes, presumably, it was heinous enough to justify breaking a promise or contract, on the "lesser evil" principle).

Religious morality is either mistaken as to the facts, as in the bishop's case, or it takes care to ignore factual data altogether, as in Jerry Falwell's case. Most of the time religionists make moral judgments based on premises that are neither verifiable nor falsifiable. Human need and benefit do not determine what is right; the key to their rules is either in general revelation ("nature") or special revelation (scripture). For most people that kind of ethics ends up being quite unethical.

Disposal of the Dead. Another revealing moral issue arises in disposing of the dead, which has always been a "rite of passage" surrounded by religious theory and practice. The burial of the dead in the ground, letting human tissue rot away or destroying it through cremation are practices no longer morally tolerable.

Modern medicine can save life by transplanting tissue and organs by graft from one body to another. Not long ago the bodies of the dead were quite properly disposed of to the worms or flames, but in our day "spare-parts medicine" has made cadavers supremely precious because of their life-saving value.

Bodies have always been needed for anatomy study and research autopsy, but they had to be stolen or found in potter's fields. But now they are more urgently needed in order to save lives. Corneas, kidneys, and other organs, bones, skin, blood— any and every part of the human body at or after death can be used to save life and give health to waiting recipients. Cadaver materials are needed not only for transplants but also for medical research, and to yield therapeutic extracts (such as pituitin to treat dwarfism in newborns), serum-based solutions, cell cultures, and vaccines. In actual fact, thousands of patients die every year for lack of supplies. Hospital requests on admission or prior to it for transplant permission are constantly ignored.

A major cause for this shameful waste and callous disregard of human need is religion. It plays up the body taboo for ceremonial purposes: "do not go into the next life blind, maimed, or halt." The sense of identity is largely somatic, especially for the simple-minded. Belief in the physical resurrection of Jesus is still common among Christian fundamentalists, and its imagery still holds for the individual believer and his or her own "triumphal ascent." Leonardo da Vinci was forbidden by the pope to enter a hospital in Rome because he had once engaged in human dissection.

The Catholic opposition to transplant medicine has nearly ended. Its last condemnation came from Pius XII in 1956 and even he objected only to transplants *inter vivos*, from living donors, not from cadavers. Orthodox Jews still attack autopsies, so much so that they often fear to enter hospitals for treatment because their bodies might be "violated" if they die.

In short, religious influence builds up on the psychic and subrational body taboo, thus denying life to literally thousands of human beings every year. Appeals to ministers to recommend memorial services for the dead instead of funerals and burials get nowhere. This would obviously be "bad for business," for the clergy as well as the undertakers. The moral claim weighs very little against the Christian ideology and ceremony of death. The religiously indifferent, on the other hand, are usually willing to give up all or part of their bodies for medical use.

Right-to-Die. Religion is a hurdle in the way of ethical sensitivity before death comes, as well as after. Modern resuscitative medicine has increased our ability to preserve and prolong life, but often to the point of prolonged dying rather than living. Will we ever look upon death as a friend, welcome enough to be invited? We are all familiar with heartbreaking stories of prolonged suffering and disastrous hospital bills. Because of this, and in spite of right-to-life protesters and the Catholic hierarchy, right-to-die or death-with-dignity laws have been passed in 23 state legislatures, and are pending in many more.

Advocates of quality-of-life judgments are prepared to favor release sometimes, while the sanctity-of-life religionists insist on "life" no matter how much a person may be suffering pointlessly. None of the major religious bodies teaches that we are morally obliged to preserve life in all terminal illnesses, but the question calls for a closer look.

The key term is *terminal.* That is to say, religious leaders are willing to let treatment be stopped when the medical evidence is that the patient is dying anyway, whether treated or not. Letting the dying die hardly seems to be a real problem of moral judgment. Even so, Catholics and other fundamentalists vigorously oppose the passage of laws giving social expression, as a legal right, to the Living Will, which records a person's wish to be allowed to die when death is at hand. Spokesmen for the National Council of Catholic Bishops appear sedulously in opposition at all public hearings when legislatures invite comment on proposed right-to-die laws. The mounting success of right-to-die advocates shows again, of course, the tension between the moral norms of our society and the traditional morals of religion.

The real problem is not what we ought to do in terminal illness. Moral judgment becomes significant only when a patient is, alas, *not* dying; when death is not imminent yet treatment cannot help alleviate the suffering or arrest the loss of personal integrity. And the patient decides he or she wants out. What then?

Religionists charge that to choose to die, no matter how evil the foreseeable consequences of going on living would be, is "playing God." God, they believe, is the lord of both life and death and to take any human initiative or responsibility (whether in birth control or death control) is gravely sinful. This means, of course, that the human being as a moral agent is without responsibility, and thus the "conscience" is boxed off; it is solely a command ethic ("yours not to reason why, yours but to multiply" or "yours but to endure whatever 'nature' does to you").

Arguably, the real question is whether we may ever help someone else to die at their request. This is what SIGMUND FREUD's doctor did when Freud's jaw cancer got too bad. The British Suicide Act of 1961 decriminalized suicide, but it still holds that assisting it is a felony. The statute is hardly ever enforced by the courts, however, showing the conscious hypocrisy of the law. The same is true in most of the United States. Can we not say that what is morally right for persons to do for themselves is right and good for another to do for them? This is the problem of "assisted suicide" in the health context. The happy fact that such situations do not arise very often is irrelevant to the moral question.

Prayer in Public Schools. Thus far we have been looking at biologically oriented issues. Before we end we ought to look at an issue in another area—the place of prayer in education—as the final illustration of the tension between secular and religious ethics. (The fundamentalist campaign for "equal time" in the schools for the biblical doctrine of creation would serve our purpose just as well.)

Historically, ever since the Land Ordinances of 1785 and 1787 provided for common-school funds, "public" education has meant not only that it is free of financial charge but free also of control by special interests. The chief special interests that manipulated the schools in the pre-Constitution colonies were doctrinaire religious elements of various kinds. Religious groups wanted the schools to promote their own beliefs. Roman Catholics fought the establishment of public schools. Protestants wanted them to teach either sectarian or nonsectarian Protestantism. The struggle was vitriolic, especially in New York, Massachusetts, and Pennsylvania from 1820 to 1860, when the policy of secular control and secular instruction was finally settled upon. Private institutions were left free to teach whatever religions they believed in, if they paid for it themselves.

Believers continued to fight a rearguard war. For a long time they demanded prayers and Bible readings, then they devised a "released time" plan for in-school religious instruction, until the courts stopped that. Finally, after much controversy and a long struggle, the Supreme Court (in decisions in 1962 and 1963) declared that prayer, Bible reading, and religious teaching in public schools are unconstitutional. It was a slow but predictable victory for the secular principle's rule in public affairs. (Still left are some curious vestigial deposits such as presidential swearings-in or the Senate's "opening prayers," even while they are passing legislation to protect secular rule.)

Religious reactionaries of the "radical right" have lately undertaken to make a Custer's Last Stand, in order to get prayers back in the schools. Usually, as with Falwell's vocal minority, school prayers are linked with antiabortion. In patent contempt for the principle of majority rule they even talk of trying by political maneuvers to get amendments to the Constitution in order to outlaw the Supreme Court's decisions on school prayers and abortion. Polls have shown that what the Moral Majority wants is not wanted by the real majority of people, but the Moral Majority is undeterred for a simple strong reason: they are doing "God's work," and what weight has democracy against that? *Vox populi non est vox dei* has always been the maxim of the churches and the preachers.

The evangelical "electronic" churches of television raise huge, unaccounted-for funds sent in $10 and $20 cash donations by millions of religiously aroused listeners. Not only are the Bible pounders on the airwaves indifferent to the views of others but the victims of the preachers are too. After all, it seems to follow logically, does it not, that if you know God exists and if you know his eternal truth and what he wills, how dare you abide by the "errors" of the unbelievers? You owe it to *them* to do anything you can get away with to save them from themselves. "Truth has rights which error may not claim" is another old religious maxim, Protestant as well as Catholic.

As to ethics itself, the "bottom line" is between those who think moral principles are intrinsically valid and absolute, not subject to change, and those who think values and therefore moral judgments made in the interest of values are relative, not absolute. The religious temper inevitably embraces the first view; the rational and scientific (or "secular") temper embraces the second.

Religious ethics makes its moral judgments by rules drawn deductively from faith premises about what God wills; secular ethics is based on human needs and hopes, its judgments drawn inductively from the facts of each case or situation. It is this contrast that is always the essential difference and source of tension between believers and unbelievers.

Other articles of interest: **Church, State, and Religious Freedom. Ethics and Unbelief. Law and Unbelief, The.**

Bibliography

For a full discussion of the two approaches to moral judgment, see *The Encyclopedia of Bioethics,* vol. 1 (1978), pp. 400–437. Compare Joseph Fletcher, *Humanhood: Essays in Biomedical Ethics* (1979) and Bernard Haring, *Medical Ethics* (1973).

JOSEPH FLETCHER

N

NAGEL, ERNEST (1901–   ), American philosopher and teacher, was born in Czechoslovakia to a family that emigrated to the United States in 1911. He became an American citizen in 1919. Nagel obtained an M.A. in mathematics at City College, New York, before proceeding to Columbia University for a Ph.D. in philosophy. It was there that he spent his entire academic career, as a professor of philosophy.

A contemporary of SIDNEY HOOK, who was also educated at Columbia, Nagel was, with Hook, one of the two philosophically most distinguished, former pupils and lifelong admirers of JOHN DEWEY. Both are, as Dewey was, atheistic naturalists. Much less publicly and politically involved than Hook, Nagel is most renowned as a teacher and expositor.

Nagel's gifts for and dedication to this role were best expressed in *An Introduction to Logic and Scientific Method* (New York, 1934), written in collaboration with Morris Cohen. Unlike so many other textbooks of logic, both before and since, this does not concentrate upon the quasi-mathematics of abstract symbolic manipulation. Instead it demonstrates a broad concern with the fundamental principles of all rational inquiry and with enabling students to understand these principles, as well as encouraging them to apply those principles in every field.

The Structure of Science. The same commitments to advancing both theoretical enlightenment and the practical application of that enlightenment on the broadest possible front are seen also in Nagel's massive treatise *The Structure of Science* (New York, 1961). Its central thesis is the unity of science. Nagel, like the members of the original Vienna Circle of logical positivists (see LOGICAL POSITIVISM AND UNBELIEF), construes this as requiring that the methods of investigation and the forms of explanation possible and proper in the physical sciences be, in the end, equally applicable to the study of history and to the social sciences generally. Hence, everyday explanations of human conduct in terms of the motives, intentions, and beliefs of the agents have to be somehow—and in fact with enormous patience, care, sympathy, and understanding—either assimilated to or replaced by nonteleological hypothetico-deductive explanations of the type familiar in the traditional hard sciences.

In the final paragraph of the final chapter, "Problems in the Logic of Historical Inquiry," after disclaiming certain unfortunate formulations, Nagel concludes: "Nevertheless, to abandon the deterministic principle itself is to withdraw from the enterprise of science."

Usually Nagel's consistently atheistic naturalism has been seen in what he does not say rather than in what he says. But when occasion has called, he has stood up to be counted. There was, for instance, his contribution to the collection *Basic Beliefs: The Religious Philosophies of Mankind* that was reprinted as "Philosophical Concepts of Atheism" (in Peter Angeles, ed., *Critiques of God*, Buffalo, 1976). From time to time Nagel has stepped forward with a quietly devastating review of some trendy book of obscurantism—for example, Aldous Huxley's *The Perennial Philosophy*. Some of these occasional pieces were reprinted in the collection *Sovereign Reason* (New York, 1954).

Nagel has expounded and defended his naturalism in various essays and addresses, some reprinted in *Logic Without Metaphysics* (Glencoe, Ill., 1956). He espouses two contentions: (1) The familiar universe, sometimes called nature, is in truth all there is; and its manifest plurality is no sort of false front for any hidden or transcendent unity. (2) "Organized matter" is primary "in the executive order of nature." This is a more sophisticated version of THOMAS HOBBES' MATERIALISM, the doctrine that, since stuff alone can significantly be said to exist separately, and in its own right, the only real causes are pushes. Nagel's naturalism, similarly, admits no incorporeal, purely spiritual agents.

ANTONY FLEW

NATIONAL REFORMER, THE, was the single most important freethought periodical in Britain in the second half of the 19th century. It was the weekly mouthpiece of CHARLES BRADLAUGH and organ of the NATIONAL SECULAR SOCIETY under his leadership from 1866 to 1890.

Early Days. The paper was established in the West Riding of Yorkshire in February of 1860 by secularists from Sheffield and Halifax. A company was formed under the presidency of James Dodworth, a knife manufacturer, and the first monthly issue appeared on April 14, 1860. It was a demy-folio newspaper of eight pages, sold for twopence. Joseph Barker, a prominent West Riding figure who had successively been a Methodist preacher and a Chartist lecturer before becoming a secularist, was invited to coedit the paper with the young Bradlaugh, who had recently emerged as a powerful advocate of FREETHOUGHT and had attracted favorable notice in Sheffield. Barker, an experienced journalist, was to edit the first four pages; and Bradlaugh, who was relatively inexperienced, the last four pages.

The paper was a success, and publication became weekly from June 2, 1860. A year later circulation had reached 5,500 but the editorial arrangements were a disaster. Bradlaugh began using his half of the paper to advocate the neo-Malthusian views expressed in George Drysdale's *The Elements of Social Science,* which had been reissued in 1861. Barker found this morally repulsive, and soon the first half of the paper was criticizing the second half. At the end of August 1861 Barker left the paper to start *Barker's Review,* after the company had decided to appoint Bradlaugh as sole editor. An agreement was then reached at the end of the year, for GEORGE JACOB HOLYOAKE, the founder of the secularist movement in the 1850s, to close his own paper and become chief contributor with sole control over the first three pages. John Watts, who had worked as a printer with Holyoake, became subeditor.

This new arrangement fared no better, for Bradlaugh and Holyoake were soon at loggerheads. The directors and Holyoake wanted to turn the newspaper into a foolscap periodical; Bradlaugh, the largest shareholder, did not. When the directors appeared willing to go behind his back he resigned as editor and then successfully stood for reelection. Two days before the election meeting, on March 21, 1862, Bradlaugh had informed Holyoake that his status was reduced to that of contributor of two columns only. Holyoake immediately withdrew his copy, and each man attacked the other for breach of contract. Holyoake won an arbitration decision, but Bradlaugh refused to pay damages. The company was ended on Sept. 7, 1862, and Bradlaugh became sole proprietor, transferring the paper to London, where it was printed by John Watts.

When Bradlaugh was suffering from ill-health in 1863, he transferred the *National Reformer* to Watts' control. Watts, who was more a disciple of Holyoake than of Bradlaugh, made William Maccall chief contributor, and the following year reduced the paper to a 16-page foolscap folio periodical, rather like the *Saturday Review.* His brother, CHARLES WATTS, became subeditor. The new venture was not a success, John Watts fell ill, the paper lost money, and the circulation fell to around 2,500. Before John Watts died of consumption (Oct. 31, 1866), Bradlaugh resumed ownership on April 29, keeping Charles Watts as subeditor.

Bradlaugh's vigorous hand made itself felt at once. While keeping the format of a periodical, he increased the political content of the paper and its circulation began to recover. By August 1867 the average circulation was 3,000, though 4,000 was needed for the paper to pay its contributors, and 4,500 for a profit; this was more than achieved by 1872. Copies were being sent to Europe, and as far away as the United States, Australia, and India, but domestic circulation was hindered by the refusal of a major distributor to handle the paper at its bookstalls. Bradlaugh also met legal problems in 1867, when he was prosecuted for failing to deposit sureties against the commission of blasphemous and seditious libels. He refused to pay and challenged the law until it was repealed in 1869.

Bradlaugh's greatest achievement through the *National Reformer* in these years was the creation of the National Secular Society (N.S.S.). A strong, national organization had eluded the secularists, but in September 1866 Bradlaugh used the *Reformer* to announce a provisional program for the N.S.S. and thereafter to maintain its vitality. Control of the paper made Bradlaugh the central figure in British freethought, just as Bradlaugh's personal position appeared to guarantee success to his paper.

Content of and Writers for the National Reformer. The content varied somewhat over the years, usually reflecting contemporary preoccupations. After the passing of the Reform Act in 1867 the emphasis given to politics declined; in the early 1870s republicanism and European affairs were important issues. Bradlaugh's personal campaigns were always well covered, and in the 1880s this again meant that about half the contents were political. There was also a gradual turnover of contributors.

One of the leading writers for the paper in the 1860s, George Sexton ("Melampus"), joined the First International in 1871 and so became an anti-Bradlaughite; James Thomson, whose powerful and despairing atheistic poem "The City of Dreadful Night" was published in the *National Reformer* in 1874, quarreled with Bradlaugh the following year; and in 1877 Charles Watts was dismissed for refusing to defend the publication of Dr. CHARLES KNOWLTON's birth-control pamphlet, *The Fruits of Philosophy*. But others were added to Bradlaugh's team, notably J. H. Levy, who taught political economy at the City of London College and whose economic conservatism coincided with Bradlaugh's own; EDWARD AVELING, who from 1879 wrote on a wide range of themes, including Darwinism; and, above all, ANNIE BESANT, who replaced Watts as subeditor in 1877 and became coeditor in 1881.

The subtitle of the paper was changed from "Secular Advocate and Freethought Journal" to "Radical Advocate and Freethought Journal" in July 1877, and during the early 1880s it was given over increasingly to reports of Bradlaugh's parliamentary struggle, legal contests, and personal campaigns. Frequent special issues devoted entirely to law reports were published.

Though of interest to those who identified themselves with Bradlaugh's cause (the circulation reached an undisclosed peak in 1882–83), this was not light reading. Bradlaugh admitted in 1886 that the "*National Reformer* has, for this last twenty-six years, been a sort of personal diary in which those who cared had companionship in our life. This has identified it very much with the career of one man, but we trust not to the detriment of the cause in which that man's work has been done."

In the later 1880s as Bradlaugh's name fell from public attention and he became increasingly absorbed in parliamentary work, secularism languished in the country and the circulation began to fall. The caliber of the writers, though, remained high, with JOHN M. ROBERTSON replacing Aveling in 1884. Annie Besant was increasingly taken up with socialism and reverted to subeditor in October 1887. With Levy retiring in ill-health in 1890 and Bradlaugh handing the N.S.S. presidency to GEORGE WILLIAM FOOTE, the circulation now reached its lowest point while it was under Bradlaugh's control. When he died in 1891, Mrs. Besant severed her connections with the paper, and Robertson was left to take over the editorship.

Robertson was able to revive the *National Reformer's* flagging fortunes for a while, but on Oct. 1, 1893, he closed it as being uneconomic. He attributed its failure to changing patterns of leisure: the working classes preferred the pub and the music hall, and the middle classes (to whom the paper had increasingly appealed) wanted something lighter after a hard day's work. Robertson's own preference was to aim at a higher market, and he began the *Free Review*, which was a heterodox version of the *Fortnightly Review* and the other "heavy" monthlies.

Hypatia Bradlaugh Bonner, Bradlaugh's only surviving child, attempted to revive the old traditions in 1897, when she started the *Reformer*. But, although it lasted until 1904 and attracted contributions from many former writers for Bradlaugh and Robertson, it was never able to recapture the success enjoyed by the *National Reformer* when it was identified with Bradlaugh's personal campaigns for freethought, republicanism, birth control, and the right of the atheist to sit in Parliament.

EDWARD ROYLE

NATIONAL SECULAR SOCIETY, THE, was founded in London in 1866 on the initiative of CHARLES BRADLAUGH and CHARLES WATTS.

The society's principles are: "Secularism affirms that this life is the only one of which we have any knowledge and human effort should be directed wholly towards its improvement. It asserts that supernaturalism is based upon ignorance and assails it as the historic enemy of progress.

"Secularism affirms that progress is possible only on the basis of equal freedom of speech and publication; that the free criticism of institutions and ideas is essential to a civilised State.

"Affirming that morality is social in origin and application, Secularism aims at promoting the happiness and well-being of mankind. Secularism demands the complete separation of Church and State and the abolition of all privileges granted to religious organizations. It seeks to spread education, to promote the fraternity of all peoples as a means of advancing universal peace, to further common cultural interests, and to develop the freedom and dignity of mankind."

The concept of SECULARISM came from GEORGE JACOB HOLYOAKE, who adopted the word to describe a radical approach that combined ATHEISM and social reform. The tradition stretches back to those influenced by the writings of THOMAS PAINE and ROBERT OWEN.

After the failure of the Chartists to achieve radical reform in 1848, energy was channeled into some Owenite groups, which began to give themselves a secularist title. During the 1850s, without gaining wide support or political power, secularist groups spread atheist arguments and agitated over matters such as the BLASPHEMY LAWS and Sunday observance. There had been unsuccessful attempts at forging a federation or greater cohesion between secularist groups before 1866, but when the National Secular Society (N.S.S.) was founded, membership was on an individual basis. Bradlaugh was the first president and Watts the first secretary. After several years of vigorous lecture tours, membership began to grow. At first the N.S.S. was seen as one of the many secularist societies, but its close association with Bradlaugh, whose forceful personality was giving him public prominence, enabled it to become and remain the predominant secularist organization. Many secularist groups affiliated and became branches, although a strong tradition of independence of thought and organization remained within the branches into the 20th century.

The N.S.S. was closely identified with the individual campaigns and style of Charles Bradlaugh during its first two decades. Its activities were reported in detail in the NATIONAL REFORMER. In 1872 ill health and other political activities caused Bradlaugh to withdraw from the society, and, although Sir Arthur Trevelyan was nominally the president for a few years, the N.S.S. was almost in abeyance.

Bradlaugh resumed N.S.S. activities and ANNIE BESANT became vice-president. Public debates were a favorite form of countering theologians. Not all members were happy with Bradlaugh's autocratic style and the extent to which he gave prominence to Mrs. Besant.

In 1877 the trial of Bradlaugh and Mrs. Besant brought the N.S.S. national attention. A birth-control pamphlet, *The Fruits of Philosophy* by Dr. CHARLES KNOWLTON of New England, was among the book stock acquired by Charles Watts. After a case against a Bristol bookseller who sold the pamphlet, Watts was charged with publishing an obscene work. He decided not to defend the case, but Bradlaugh and Mrs. Besant thought it was an important free-speech issue and republished the Knowlton pamphlet under the imprint of their own Freethought Publishing Company. They defended themselves skillfully, but were found guilty and given prison sentences. The judgment and sentences were set aside upon appeal.

The Knowlton case brought the issues of free speech and birth control before the public and gave Bradlaugh and the N.S.S. some notoriety. Birth-control literature was not supported by all secularists, and Charles Watts and others quarreled with Bradlaugh and formed a breakaway group called the British Secular Union. They also resented Bradlaugh's dominant influence, but the B.S.U. only survived as an anti-Bradlaugh caucus until about 1884. Bradlaugh's force of personality and public activities ensured him the allegiance of the majority.

Bradlaugh was elected a member of Parliament for Northampton in 1880 and spent the following six years struggling to take his seat in the House of Commons. He had asked if he was entitled to affirm instead of taking an oath but was willing to be sworn in if affirmation was not permissible—in fact, he made repeated attempts to be sworn in. Parliament denied him affirmation *or* oath taking, and the Bradlaugh struggle became a national cause célèbre. The N.S.S. was active in support of Bradlaugh, collecting petitions on his behalf and assisting in the organization of public meetings in St. James's Hall and Trafalgar Square.

The peak of N.S.S. activities came in the early 1880s, which also saw the prosecution and imprisonment of GEORGE WILLIAM FOOTE for publication of blasphemous material in the FREE-THINKER. Secularism briefly became an important aspect of national politics. At its peak the N.S.S. claimed the affiliated support of 6,000 members, with much wider unaffiliated support. There were over one hundred branches, with particular regional strength in Lancashire and Yorkshire. As well as lectures, debates, and political action, secularist groups engaged in education, music (including secular hymns), and leisure outings. Support came largely from the skilled and artisan sections of the working class.

In 1890 Foote succeeded Bradlaugh as president of the N.S.S. because of the pressure of the latter's parliamentary work and his health problems. It was agreed that decline had set in by that time. Foote acknowledged, at the time of Bradlaugh's death in 1891, that "the 'heroic period' of English freethought" was at an end. Decline may be attributed to the absence of Bradlaugh's personal dynamism and to the development of new political ideas and changing recreational patterns. The N.S.S. disqualified itself from seeking political power by taking a neutral stance toward socialism, which was attracting the energy of younger radicals.

The N.S.S. found a new role as a pressure group on specific issues and as a focus for atheist views in society. Under Foote's presidency, which continued until his death in 1915, secular education, opposition to the blasphemy laws, and the legalization of bequests to freethought organizations remained matters of importance. Links with international freethought organizations had been established, and the society took an interest in the separation of church and state in France and the martyrdom of FRANCISCO FERRER in Spain.

Under Foote, the N.S.S. and the *Freethinker* became more closely associated. The link was maintained by CHAPMAN COHEN, who was president of the N.S.S. from 1915 until 1949. Cohen was a tireless lecturer and prolific writer of great lucidity. He emphasized the philosophical and sociological analysis of the phenomenon of religion. Under Cohen the N.S.S. regularly criticized the extent to which the British Broadcasting Association was used for religious propaganda. Cohen warned as early as 1919 that the League of Nations could only be successful if nation-states were prepared to relinquish power, and the N.S.S. was forthright in its denunciation of fascism and nazism in the thirties. The society staunchly opposed militarism and defended free speech in time of war and spoke for the rights of atheists in the armed forces. The N.S.S. offices were bombed during the 1941 Blitz.

F. A. Ridley, a well-known socialist writer, succeeded Cohen as president, but he was more of a scholar and writer than leader and administrator. The public meeting and open-air orations, which had remained important secularist platforms, gave way in the 1960s to attempts to put across secularism by press releases and appearances on radio and television. David Tribe, as president, did much to establish the N.S.S. presence in the media. During the 1960s notable social reforms took place, and the N.S.S. supported the liberalizing of laws on divorce, abortion, and homosexuality.

The N.S.S. remains a small but active pressure group. Barbara Smoker became its president in 1972. A decade later she defended its continuing role: "The N.S.S. is often charged with being 'negative' in its outlook—and, certainly, it is vigorous in its opposition to the forces of superstition, obscurantism, and illiberalism; but that is merely another way of looking at its vigorous support for progressive, liberal causes. When it campaigns against censorship, it is campaigning for freedom of expression; when it campaigns against denominational schooling, it is campaigning for educational impartiality in the controversial area of religious belief; when it campaigns against sabbatarian laws, it is campaigning for freedom of choice; and when it campaigns against any of the social and fiscal survivals of religious privilege, it is campaigning for equality in a pluralist society."

Bibliography

Budd, Susan. *Varieties of Unbelief.* London: Heinemann, 1977.

Cohen, Chapman. *Almost an Autobiography.* London: Pioneer Press, 1940.

Herrick, Jim. *Vision and Reform, the Freethinker 1881 to 1981.* London: G. W. Foote, 1982.

Royle, Edward. *The Infidel Tradition from Paine to Bradlaugh.* London: Macmillan, 1976.

———. *Radical Politics 1790–1900, Religion and Unbelief.* London: Longmans, 1971.

———. *Radicals, Secularists and Republicans.* Manchester: Manchester U. Press, 1980.

———. *Victorian Infidels.* Manchester: Manchester U. Press, 1974.

Stein, Gordon. *An Anthology of Atheism and Rationalism.* Buffalo, N.Y.: Prometheus, 1980.

———. *Freethought in the United Kingdom and the Commonwealth, A Descriptive Bibliography.* London and Westport, Conn.: Greenwood, 1981.

Tribe, David. *100 Years of Freethought.* London: Elek, 1967.

———. *President Charles Bradlaugh.* London: Elek, 1971.

JIM HERRICK

NETHERLANDS, UNBELIEF IN THE.

In 1980 the Kingdom of the Netherlands had 14,500,000 inhabitants. For the greater part, the Dutch are descendants of Germanic tribes (Franks, Saxons, and Frisians), which, in the Middle Ages, were converted to Christianity and Roman Catholicism. In the 16th and 17th centuries, however, a considerable number of them became Calvinists. In 1581 the Hapsburg king of Spain, who was also regent of the Netherlands, was forced to abdicate, and the Republic of the United Provinces was proclaimed. The republican governments, though Calvinist until 1795, had a liberal attitude toward minority groups. Approximately one-third of the population of the time, mainly in the south, remained Roman Catholic. The French Huguenots, immigrants who had fled their country because of Louis XIV's Catholic absolutism, were indeed Calvinists, and the Jewish newcomers, partly from Spain and Portugal, partly from Eastern Europe, still professed their Jewish faith, if they professed a religion at all. The numerous German immigrants of the 18th century increased the number of Lutheran Protestants.

This diversity of religions had two consequences. On the one hand, there were many theological disputes, in which Catholicism in particular was continually attacked, and many dogmas that had once been sacred were sometimes ridiculed. On the other hand, this same atmosphere generally created a more moderate attitude toward all religions. The authorities, although formally Calvinist, allowed—more than anywhere else in the Europe of that day—dissenting religious communities that had been loyal to republican authority and were of economic importance to profess their unorthodox faiths. When, in 1795, after the invasion of French revolutionary troops, a new republic was established in which church and state were separated, the minority groups (Catholics, Jews, and a number of dissenting Protestant sects of brotherhoods) emerged as equals. In 1813 the French protection came to an end; clerical reaction temporarily prevailed, but from 1848 onward, when the liberal constitution came into effect, the actual equalization of all religious (and soon nonreligious) communities began.

Dechristianization. Since 1848, censuses—and later, official inquiries and public polls—have provided information for establishing the number of Dutch people not belonging to any religious community. In 1859 only a thousand people dared admit this openly. This number increased to 115,000 in 1899, and in 1939, 1,250,000 people—nearly 15 percent of the population—declared that they did not belong to a religious community. After World War II this trend accelerated. On the one hand, believers and unbelievers, who together had offered resistance to the German occupying forces, had put their religious quarrels aside. As a consequence, after 1945 there was less opposition to religion than before.

On the other hand, the war had led to a religious crisis within the church. Where had God been during this horrifying tragedy of murder, persecution, genocide, and destruction? Of the Dutch Jewish population, which consisted of 125,000 people, 100,000 were annihilated by the Nazis. Many of them perished in the gas ovens of Auschwitz, the notorious concentration camp. In Protestant churches, belief was losing more and more of its foundation. "Demythologization" could be heard. Miracle tales were much less believed than before.

People also wondered why the organized churches had not offered more resistance to the German occupiers. "Emancipation of the laity" was being discussed in Catholic churches. Formerly pious believers, who until then had not had any influence on the substance of traditional Christianity, desired to have their say in religious matters, and they did so in a very critical way. All Christians propagated more than ever the idea that social services should be extended, that one should occupy oneself with worldly rather than heavenly affairs. They no longer conceived of war as a necessary judgment to which one ought to submit. The "God is dead" theory was accepted in all its extremity by some people. This theory proposed reconsideration of the ancient images of God and suggested that the old theology had come to an end. During this turbulent evolution, more and more people abandoned the church and said farewell to traditional Christianity.

From the 1960 census the conclusion could be drawn that 18 percent of the population no longer belonged to a religious community. But this figure was much too favorable toward the church, since many indifferent people still indicated that they belonged to their parents' religion, without ever visiting a church themselves.

In 1971, 23 percent of the Dutch no longer professed any Christian belief. More than a dozen years later no new census had been taken, but from various inquiries it was possible to conclude that about 30 percent of the Dutch consider themselves unbelievers. As a result of the population growth, this meant about 4,350,000 people. Can we conclude, then, that ten million still profess a religion? In reality, the number of people who had become non-Christian is considerably greater because, relying on church attendance, one could ascertain that only one-third of those recorded as believers obey their religious duties; two-thirds of them live without any bonds to a church or religion and might therefore be regarded as unbelievers. Thus, one must conclude that only one-third of the population—3,500,000 people—could still be called Christian in the Netherlands.

In Protestant churches, attendance at services has become quite small. The Catholic clergy, who complain about the shortage of young priests, monks, and nuns, increasingly speak of dechristianization. An orthodox bishop, Monsignor Simonis of Rotterdam, declared on Jan. 21, 1978: "We still keep the church upright now, but shortly she will crumble and her facade will collapse completely."

Meanwhile the population structure had changed. In 1980 one million out of a total of 14.5 million inhabitants consisted of new groups of immigrants. Four chief groups could be distinguished, each of them having increased to approximately 250,000 people in 1980. (1) From the former colony of Netherlands East Indies (Indonesia) came Indo-Europeans who were formally Christian and partly irreligious. (2) From Surinam, which became an independent South American state in 1975, a group arrived consisting of three different religious communities—as far as they could be considered to profess a genuine religion at all. These immigrants were all descendants of Africans and Asians, who in the past had been put to work in South America. Their religions were originally (a) Christianity (as far as the blacks were concerned), (b) Hinduism, professed by immigrants from former British India, and (c) Islam, professed by Javanese and some workers from British India. These traditional religions had become decadent in the New World, but they played a special role in the manners and customs of the 250,000 Dutchmen concerned.

The two remaining groups of immigrants consisted of Muslims from (3) Turkey and (4) Morocco. Several buildings were converted into mosques by them, for, although having come as temporary workers, they remained in the Netherlands with their families. These foreign communities suffered serious crises. Dechristianization had gone hand in hand with greater liberty and cultural emancipation for women, whereas many Islamic men demanded submission and obedience from their wives and daughters. In a religious sense, the new immigrants constituted reactionary centers in Dutch society. It was their turn now to go through the evolutionary stages in which theological dogmas and antiquated hierarchy lost their power—an evolution already experienced by the Christian world. Immigrants who had not so far been able to assimilate were confronted with situations entirely alien to them, such as the celebration of Christian holy days and food regulations. It was quite peculiar that orthodox Christians asked Hindus and Moslems for help in their fight against unbelief and in the attempt to reestablish archaic rituals.

Sources of Unbelief. To some extent, sources of unbelief could be found within Holland's borders. Heretics, individually avowing their doubts, had always lived there. In some respects Desiderius Erasmus of Rotterdam (1469–1536) was a pagan rather than a Christian, for he frequently cited Greek and Roman authors and philosophers, as well as moralists. He depended upon the human conscience and believed that, in spite of all religious conflicts, an objective, hence universally human, notion of good and evil existed for all nations and all times. He rarely relied on ecclesiastical dogmas, preferring on the moral duty of making peace among all people. He appealed to the monarchs of his day to be enlightened despots.

The same spirit of the Renaissance could be found in François Rabelais and Michel de Montaigne in 16th-century France. They wrote in French, whereas Erasmus made use of Latin, but they all were humanists within the Catholic church. In Holland, Erasmus' legacy is important for its accentuation of the existence of ethical judgment that went above and beyond all religious bounds. People gradually began to realize what was at stake: the instinct of the human race to survive through the solidarity of all its members. "Do unto others as you would have them do unto you"—the emphasis on the necessity of peace increasingly brought this notion to light. To Erasmus, Jesus had been a preacher of the good: "Since Christ commanded the swords to be put back into the scabbards the Christian has absolutely been forbidden any fight except for the most virtuous fight against the most vicious foes of belief: avarice, wrath, ambition, frightful death."

In this philosophy the ethical commandment exists within the self and does not come to us from the outside world. In the same spirit, BENEDICT SPINOZA (1632–1676) would later say: "God's word has been inscribed in the human heart"—God's word meaning nothing else but the law of nature within ourselves. The philosopher, who was born in Amsterdam and died in The Hague, had broken with Judaism without converting to Christianity. He was truly an irreligious humanist who was quite satisfied with grinding lenses (a new and specialized craft), writing treatises, and being in his small circle of friends.

Spinoza renounced the image of God as a humanlike individual. Universal laws inside man and in his surrounding world revealed themselves as laws of nature and laws of thought. Matter and thought correspond to one and the same notion, the nature of reality, which he called "substance." Hence, miracles cannot be true, and body and soul form a unity, two manifestations of one substance. This philosophy left no room for the doctrines of the churches or synagogues. Essential were human relations and mutual conduct. Harmony would prevail among mankind if reason were followed. Only reason was capable of governing one's passions, increasing knowledge, and promoting human understanding. It was this Stoic principle that was eventually to lead to self-consciousness, self-control, and freedom, that is, freedom from external authority. In the 19th century, Spinoza would become the great inspiration of Dutch freethinkers.

Ethics. In Erasmus' and Spinoza's wake, much attention was paid to ethics. It is only possible to speak of good and evil if individual, rational choice is at issue, a self-reliant attitude. If man is to obey a dogma, the Bible, a church, or a state, it would not be just to speak of ethics, but simply of unworthy servitude.

It is remarkable to observe how in the 19th century this philosophy had already influenced modern Protestant circles, for whom, among others, the French Spinozist, Ernest Renan, was an example. Later, two lecturers at the University of Groningen, G. Heymans and Leo Polak, were to develop this autonomous ethics. Polak (1880–1941) was an atheist and patron of the Dutch freethinkers.

Besides Erasmus' ethics and Spinoza's philosophy there was a third, typically Dutch source of unbelief, rooted in the exegesis of the Bible. Erasmus had edited the Greek text of the Bible and included critical notes. He was suspected not to have believed wholeheartedly in what had been

written about Jesus in the Gospels. To quote the much devouter Martin Luther: "Erasmus of Rotterdam regards the Christian religion and its doctrine as a comedy or as a tragedy, in which the events described never truly happened but had been invented in order to teach the people virtuous conduct and discipline."

Spinoza had not stated his opinion about the New Testament, but his criticism of the Old Testament was the first scholarly disavowal of its "truth." He wrote: "The so-called Word of God is false, maimed, falsified and in contradiction with itself." And he showed numerous errors, myths, legends, and misinterpreted statements.

Especially in the 19th century, modern Protestantism led to a disgraceful exegesis of the Bible. If there remained anything at all of the old religion, then it could hardly be called Christian. It was, indeed, accepted that Jesus had been a historical being, but he was divested of all miraculous qualities. By the end of the 19th century, a school of philosophy arose that chiefly consisted of followers of the German philosopher G. W. F. Hegel (1770–1831). They argued that the first Christian authors had adopted many symbolic images from the Jewish-Greek religion and from Roman mythology. People believed in these tales, but to the authors of the Bible these tales had a much deeper meaning. The principal Dutch scholars following Hegel's thought were G. J. P. J. Bolland (1854–1942) and G. A. van den Bergh van Eysinga, who wrote penetrating books on the origin of Christianity in a pagan world.

Foreign Contributions. Besides these three domestic, intellectual movements, two movements of foreign origin contributed to the increase in unbelief. The French ENLIGHTENMENT of the 18th century, with which the names of VOLTAIRE, Jean Jacques Rousseau, and DENIS DIDEROT were associated, encompassed provocative ideas that were in no respect in harmony with Christianity. The philosophers mentioned were not outspoken atheists, but could no longer be called Christians either. Their guide was DEISM, which taught that God had been the impetus of the motion of the universe and the evolution on earth, and that he had created the natural laws. This had been the only part he had played in reality, which was to be controlled by its own powers and order.

Deism also repudiated belief in miracles. The idea of "first origin" was contradictory by nature, since it should have had an origin itself. What actually remained in this line of thought was the perpetual motion of the universe and nature. But deism had still preserved the notion of God. In practice, Spinozism and pantheism often had a great influence on the deistic school of thought.

A second foreign movement in the 19th century reached Holland chiefly through Germany. There, LUDWIG FEUERBACH had argued that the image of God was extremely human (anthropomorphic) and that this God represented what people wanted to see in themselves and from which, consequently, their images of God had sprung. It might have been said that people created their gods after their own ideal image and desire. In deed, however, people showed that they did not believe this honestly: they acted as people without trust in God but with much trust in nature, power, money, science, and violence.

The best-known form of philosophical MATERIALISM emanated from this German ATHEISM. Scholars like Vogt, Moleschott, LUDWIG BÜCHNER, and ERNST HAECKEL had a great influence in the Netherlands. Their ideas were sometimes quite Spinozistic. In their view, human consciousness was an instrument of nature. The human mind caused nature to become conscious of itself, the human mind thus providing a pure image of reality. Materialism has had enormous influence on the empirical sciences as well as on the applied science of technology.

It must be added that Charles Darwin's theory of evolution (having become widely known after 1859) increased unbelief considerably. (See EVOLUTION AND UNBELIEF.) The scripture stories seemed more improbable against the background of Darwin's theory. The Dutch translator of Darwin's works, Dr. Hartog Heys van Zouteveen (1841–1891), an active member of the Freethinkers' Association, was noted for his refusal to take a religious oath.

Notwithstanding the advance of unbelief in the 19th and 20th centuries, Christian worshipers in Holland had maintained an unusually great political and economic influence. In 1980, two-thirds of the charity organizations, hospitals, and institutions of cultural and social education were still in their hands. Clergymen were to be found in extraordinary numbers in the army, in prisons, and in hospitals. The Christian social, medical, and educational foundations received from the state virtually all the funds necessary for buildings, personnel, teachers, and so forth. In spite of the substantial dechristianization, the churches and their affiliated Christian organizations retained their disproportionate political-economic power. This had been made possible by virtue of legislation. Among the bureaucrats, in the army, and in governmental offices, the devout were on duty at such influential posts that they were in a position to favor their kindred spirits. This also occurred in many big companies. The conviction that Christians as soldiers, authorities, and businessmen were exceptionally reliable was still valid to the state.

Organizations of Unbelief. The first Freethinkers' Association in the Netherlands was founded in 1856, after the many European revolutions and after the constitution of 1848, which had given the Dutch political system a liberal appearance. Already in 1855 the physician Franz Junghuhn (1809–1864), who was of German origin, had initiated a monthly called *Dageraad* (daybreak or dawn). Junghuhn had worked in Java, the most densely populated island of the Netherlands East Indies, cultivating quinine, an excellent medicine against fever. He had written a book in which he accused Europe and Christendom of being jointly responsible for wars, misery and disease. His opinion of colonization was exceedingly critical as well.

In 1856 a political tragedy took place in Java, when a government official, E. Douwes Dekker (1820–1887), who wrote under a pseudonym, Multatuli ("I have borne much"), revolted against colonial rule. He resigned and returned to Holland to continue—in serious poverty—his struggle against abuses of his time. In 1859 he renounced his faith in a personal God.

Like Junghuhn, Dekker might be called a "naturalist," nature for them being the supreme power. They felt that man is capable of understanding nature and thus capable of influencing nature for the benefit of humanity. In social life, people ought to let themselves be governed by their conscience in full freedom and responsibility. Dekker wrote an autobiographical novel, *Max Havelaar*, which is still considered a literary masterpiece, and he published numerous writings against narrow-minded belief, theology, colonization, poverty, and discrimination against women. Without any intention of being a socialist, he fostered rebellious conduct in various spheres of life. No wonder that he was nominated an honorary member of the Freethinkers' Association.

This association, which initially had been a society for the study of natural science, soon became a center of RATIONALISM, ethics, and social reform. In the 19th century it directed the people's attention to the following: emancipation of the workers—still without pretending to adhere to socialist principles; militant pacifism; the fight against colonialism; equal rights for men and women; birth control; cremation; substitution of a simple promise to tell the truth for the religious oath; nonreligious education; separation of state and church. A century later such ideals were encompassed in most people's philosophy of life.

After 1914 the struggle for universal peace, and after 1930 the struggle against fascism and National Socialism came to the forefront. The Freethinkers' Association never ceased to rouse protest against racial discrimination and the persecution of the Jews. With the German Occupation (1940–45), the association was dissolved, but it arose again immediately after Holland's liberation in 1945. In 1980 it published a monthly and had its own publishing company. Moreover, it had the right to broadcast radio and television programs. Scores of books and pamphlets were published in large runs, as well as three memorial volumes in 1906, 1956, and 1981, which provide a vivid picture of the fundamentals and growth of unbelief in the Netherlands.

A notable personality was the chaplain F. Domela Nieuwenhuis (1846–1919), who left the church in 1879. He became the first important socialist propagandist. During the last 20 years of his life, he was an anarchist and he served freethinking through innumerable writings. He was an educator, more than a politician, a preacher of complete freedom of thought and deed. Nieuwenhuis left the people his *Handbook for the Freethinker*, wherein all arguments against the church and in favor of socially conscious atheism were summarized.

After World War II, a need was felt for a new organization. In 1946 the Humanistisch Verbond (Humanist Union) was founded. Its great inspiration was Dr. J. P. van Praag, who graduated from the Faculty of Literature and Philosophy of the University of Amsterdam. Whereas the Freethinkers' Association traditionally paid much attention to the fight against religion, the Verbond's chief aim was to protect the rights of unbelievers and to achieve equality with Christians in as many areas as possible.

In the meantime different views on oath taking and cremation had been recognized. Legalized, free abortion, reform of marital law, and the emancipation of homosexuals have been advanced by the Verbond, always in close cooperation with organizations that specialize in these fields. At a few universities, professorial chairs have been instituted for the advancement of the principles and aims of humanism. Governmental funds have been acquired for the education and wages of humanist counselors in the army, in prisons, in hospitals, and in institutions for the aged. The Verbond has the opportunity to broadcast radio and television programs, and through HIVOS (Humanist Organization for Development Cooperation), its own state-funded organization, humanists participate in developmental aid to Africa, Asia, and Latin America; hence they can be active in areas that in former days were virtually monopolized by Christian institutions.

One of the aims of the Verbond is to rouse the interest of unbelievers in ethical and philosophical issues, especially in order to unite intellectual power in favor of the equality of unbelievers and Christians. This can be achieved through activities within the sphere of state and legislative influence. The Verbond is more reformist than the Freethinkers' Association, and it reaches and mobilizes much larger groups of people.

There is a third humanist institution called Humanitas, which occupies itself especially with social and medical care. These three associations jointly established an organization for the management of homes for the aged that have been erected in many districts.

In summary: Unbelief in the Netherlands increases rapidly, not only through the activities of organizations of freethinkers and humanists, but especially through the dechristianization of science, philosophy, and culture in general. Science, philosophy, art, sexual life, and politics are becoming more and more irreligious. Social life takes place outside the churches. And, despite the existence of a few hundred churches and the presence of non-Christian sects among minority groups, the rules that conduct daily life are predominantly based on humanist principles.

Bibliography

Constandse, Anton L. *Geschiedenis van het humanisme in Nederland.* 2nd ed. 1978.

Noordenbos, O., and P. Spigt. *Atheisme en vrijdenken in Nederland.* 2nd ed. 1976.

van Praag, J. P. *Grondslagen van het humanisme.* 1978.

See also three memorial issues of *Dageraad:*

1906. *Geschiedenis, herinneringen en beschou-
wingen* (history, memories and essays) by A. H.
Gerhard, F. Domela Nieuwenhuis, Ernst
Haeckel, Hypatia Bradlaugh Bonner, Charles
R. Drysdale, M. Bertholet, G. Renard, G. Sergi.

1956. *Bevrijdend denken* (liberating thought) by C.
Bradlaugh Bonner, A. L. Constandse, J. Presser,
O. Noordenbos, P. Spigt, J. M. Romein, Ber-
trand Russell, G. A. van den Bergh van Eysinga,
F. Grewel, S. de Wolff.

1981. *125 jaar vrijdenken* (125 years of freethought)
by J. Vis, A. L. Constandse, J. Baars, C. van
Oostrom, M. Paulissen, H. Visman, S. Radius.

ANTON L. CONSTANDSE

NEWSPAPERS OF UNBELIEF. See **Appendix
5: Periodicals of Unbelief.**

NEW ZEALAND, UNBELIEF IN. In the early
days in the colony, unbelief covered a wide range
of associated unorthodox positions, out of which
an organized FREETHOUGHT movement ultimately
emerged by 1881. These unbelievers included those
who called themselves freethinkers, secularists,
liberals, rationalists, deists, spiritualists, and even
Unitarians. The common denominator was that all
held unorthodox views about the supernatural
doctrines of Christianity.

Freethinker was the most popular term, but
secularist was, to the writer's knowledge, the
earliest term used. *Rationalist* came into more
frequent use in modern times; *liberal* went out of
use because it became associated with political
activity and particular parties.

Auckland (1853-60). The earliest reference to
organized unbelief in New Zealand (known to the
writer) is to a "Secular Society" associated with
CHARLES SOUTHWELL in Auckland. GEORGE
JACOB HOLYOAKE printed in the *Reasoner* (Jan.
3, 1857) a letter from Southwell (Auckland, March
9, 1856), which said: "The *Reasoner* is read here by
a considerable number of worthy people, and the
Secular Society meets from time to time. We have
also a Young Men's Christian Association, which
beats the Secular Society hollow—if not in pure-
ness of intention or reasonableness of dogma, at

least in wealth and numbers . . . . My discourses
on education and other topics created a stir."

The "considerable" readers of the *Reasoner,* in
association with the existence of a Secular Society
so highly spoken of by Southwell, indicates that he
then had no intention of recanting his unbelief in
Christianity, as Holyoake charged.

Southwell arrived in New Zealand Jan. 30, 1856.
From Holyoake's account, he went there to cover
up personal differences. On Dec. 11, 1856, he
founded and edited his own *Auckland Examiner,*
modeled on Leigh Hunt's London *Examiner.* Its
last issue was June 25, 1860, Southwell dying from
consumption on Aug. 7, 1860. His "farewell" in the
last issue is a moving piece.

It is difficult to estimate the real influence
Southwell may have had on the early freethought
movement in New Zealand. From the *Examiner*
we learn that he visited Gisborne on North Island
and from a letter by a "Mr. Russell" to Holyoake
that he visited Otago (Dunedin?) on South Island
for three months in the summer of 1860 before he
died. It is difficult to believe that a man such as he
could have been inactive. In other respects, he
reports having traveled among the Maori and we
know that he wrote articles on them. Was his
presence in Otago a germinating influence in that
outburst of freethinking a few years later, out of
which came the Dunedin Freethought Association?
Were the elements of that flowering too elitist and
"respectable" to acknowledge any such association?
We may be able to evaluate this as we examine
unbelief in Dunedin.

Dunedin (1870-95). The next distinct organization of unbelievers called themselves freethinkers. By this time great advances had taken place in
the scientific world following the publication of
Charles Darwin's *Origin of Species* in 1859, creating an intellectual revolution that had a profound
influence in consolidating and expanding the whole
range of unbelieving positions, which did not take
long to filter throughout the world.

In the 1870s there was at Dunedin a young
migrant lawyer from the Shetland Islands named
ROBERT STOUT (1844–1930), who had arrived in
1864. A grammar-school teacher who knew Greek,
Latin, and French, he was called to the bar in 1871.
He became a member of Parliament, attorney
general, and twice prime minister of New Zealand,
being knighted in 1886. Stout declared himself a
"new liberal" and an "agent in the uplifting of
humanity." He was an admirer of CHARLES
BRADLAUGH.

Stout was the driving force and guiding mind behind the formation of the Dunedin Freethought Association in February and March of 1878. Later, in a Sydney Unitarian journal, *Modern Thought*, edited by the Rev. George Hughes, he wrote about the organization: "The first step in heterodoxy was taken by the Spiritualists, and Dunedin was the first place in which there were any regularly organised Freethinking Associations. [This ignores Auckland in Southwell's time.] The lectures delivered by Mr. James Smith of Melbourne, Mr. Charles Bright and Dr. Peebles, had the effect of creating an organisation in Dunedin. The Association which is now called the Freethought Association is the result of other organisations that preceded it" (Aug. 1885).

Those other organizations included the Mutual Improvement Society (founded in 1870), which lent aid to many traveling "liberal theological lecturers" and was stigmatized by one Christian clergyman as that "coterie which met in the Atheneum and drew its inspiration from the *Fortnightly* and *Westminster Reviews*, won honours in heresy, and reached the lowest depths of Atheism." This body was dissolved and replaced by the Spiritual Investigation Society, formed by the spiritualists. Stout was a member and, at one stage, served as president.

Meetings advertised as freethought were run "under the auspices of a Committee of Gentlemen." At one such meeting (March 30, 1876) Charles Bright, although a spiritualist, suggested that an Eclectic Society be formed. And on Feb. 11, 1878, Bright again initiated a move to found an Eclectic Institute on a "more *popular* basis."

Bright had been a journalist in Australia and edited the Melbourne *Punch*. He was associated with the Eight-Hour movement, and later with the political Labor movement in Australia. He rejected orthodoxy at 16 (before becoming a spiritualist). Bright was born in Yorkshire in 1832 and was eight years older than Stout, with whom he got on very well. He married the widow of the Rev. J. Pillars, a Unitarian of Sydney, and died there on July 17, 1903.

For four nights in 1879, in Dunedin, Bright debated the Rev. M. W. Green on the topic "The Divine Origins of Christianity." Two of Bright's freethought lectures were published as *Rationalism v. Dogma* (Sydney, 1879). He was said to have had respect for "all fighters for freedom" such as VOLTAIRE, THOMAS PAINE, ROBERT OWEN, ROBERT G. INGERSOLL, and Bradlaugh. His

freethought lectures always provoked wide protest among the orthodox. One elderly freethinker in Dunedin who knew him said that Bright was "a second edition of Bradlaugh," having a "mellifluous voice, a courteous and whimsical style."

Among those forming the new institute suggested by Bright in 1878 was a group who next formed the Dunedin Freethought Association, prominent among whom were Robert Stout and R. Rutherford, father of Sir Ernest Rutherford. Charles Bright's prominence eventually receded, as Stout came to the fore.

Before the Freethought Association was founded, Stout had already published two periodicals that seem to have been of a freethought nature: a fortnightly *Day Star* and a monthly *Truth Seeker*. Both lasted only a short time in the 1860s. Then he started a weekly newspaper, the *Echo*, which was militantly freethought. It lasted from Feb. 1, 1869, until March 8, 1873. Then Bright proposed starting a freethought journal to be called the *Freethinker*. But Stout restarted his *Echo* on Feb. 28, 1881, and it continued until Nov. 17, 1885.

An indication of how the *Echo* was regarded in orthodox circles comes from a clerical outburst at a Presbyterian synod, where it was characterized by "rank and virulent opposition to religion and advocacy of spiritism and infidelity of the grossest kind" (*Otego Daily Times*, Oct. 17, 1881).

And of Stout the same paper said: "There is something of arrogance in all Mr. Stout's utterances of Freethought. He evidently feels that he looks down from a height of wisdom immeasurably above the level occupied by us poor Christians groping down below."

The various elements of unbelief became sorted out when the three aforementioned groups existed separately for a time: the Eclectic Society, the Eclectic Institute, and the Freethought Association. The last survived the others, but it carried with it an influential spiritualist group. A Lyceum Hall and Freethought Sunday School was built in October 1881 at an estimated cost of $7,000. In the same year a *Lyceum Guide* was published, based on spiritualist ones in the United States, such as Andrew Jackson Davis' *Children's Progressive Lyceum Manual* (Boston, 1865).

Ultimately disintegration set in. Joseph Braithwaite, a vice-president and a spiritualist, suddenly resigned and repudiated his reasons for belonging to the association in a self-contradictory letter to President Stout, who replied. Both letters were printed in the *Freethought Review* (Feb. 1884,

Wanganui). Stout confesses that in founding the Freethought Association, "we" were careful *not* to proselytize because of the various opinions and beliefs among the founders, who included Braithwaite.

However, many things caused the Dunedin Freethought Association to break up, a process that seems to have developed rapidly. An old member, Henry Gore, said that finances, especially interest payments on the Lyceum Hall, were a burden. Another old member, a Mr. McLellan, said that one of the prominent founders, John Logan, was a spiritualist. And there have been suggestions that Stout's wife also had "leanings" that way. Mr. McLellan said that the spiritualists began to drift away and hold their own separate meetings, causing the more "secular" freethinkers to "soft pedal" their stronger radicalism. Another factor was Stout's increasing absences in Wellington on political matters and his acceptance of a knighthood, which produced strong criticism. Coinciding with these events was the onset of a severe economic depression in New Zealand.

It is impossible to fix a date for the actual winding up of the Dunedin Freethought Association. It simply faded away sometime in the early 1890s. WILLIAM WHITEHOUSE COLLINS from Australia gave six lectures in Dunedin in 1890, but no mention is made under whose auspices. JOSEPH SYMES also came to Dunedin from Australia, in 1893–94, but there is no indication that he lectured at the association.

Sir Robert Stout remained a firm freethinker, of the agnostic or rationalist type, all his life. Isaac Selby, a secretary and lecturer of the Dunedin Freethought Association (although he later recanted) told the writer that Stout, in a letter only 13 months before Stout died, said: "I have been, as you know, a Rationalist all my life."

In the Sydney Unitarian publication, *Modern Thought*, Stout gave (March 1885) census figures for 1881 on religious beliefs, or lack of them, in a population of about 535,000. Nearly one-third were outside orthodox Christianity. The population of New Zealand only reached its first million in 1908. So the country seemed ready for the widespread growth of freethought throughout the main centers and country towns, triggered by events in Dunedin, to which people looked for guidance. Yet other locations also seemed to suffer, except for Christchurch, from the same defects and problems, including internal dissension and economic depression.

Traveling professional lecturers, either by invitation or choice, soon invaded New Zealand and found it a fruitful field for their various "gospels." The uninvited did not create too favorable an impression—to the detriment of genuine unbelief. Legitimate freethinkers who traveled throughout the country by invitation were Bright, Gerald Massey, Professor W. Denton, Dr. James York, a Dr. Hughes, MONCURE DANIEL CONWAY, Professor R. A. Proctor, and, before they recanted, Isaac Selby and Joseph Evison ("Ivo").

Most of the information about freethought activities of that period can be found in freethought journals published at the time in Dunedin, Wanganui, Auckland, and Christchurch.

Christchurch (1881–present). The Canterbury Freethought Association at Christchurch took its name from the province it is situated in. It is said to have originated from a fund-raising event to assist in bringing Bradlaugh on a visit to Australia and New Zealand. This also motivated other associations even though ultimately Bradlaugh did not come, since he was heavily involved in his parliamentary struggles. The Canterbury association was formed on Sept. 4, 1881, with 120 members, and it soon established a lyceum with 50 children.

W. W. Collins, after lecturing in Dunedin in 1890, proceeded to Christchurch, where he settled. The association does not seem to have had the trouble with spiritualists that Dunedin had, and this probably impressed Collins. He was appointed secretary and lecturer almost immediately. From 1893 to 1896 and again from 1899 to 1902 he served in Parliament as a Liberal. Collins published a periodical, the *Tribune* (Feb. 1894 to Jan. 1895), whose content, however, was more political than freethought.

From March to August in 1898 Collins published a more freethinking periodical, *Modern Thought*. Then from April 1907 to June 1917 he published and edited, apart from the association, the *Examiner*, a radical and atheistic journal. It was scientific and literary in content, and from an editorial and a production standpoint, it was of the highest order. Collins had been trained for the church, knew the latest advances in all fields of science, was familiar with the philosophy and history of secularism, and was certified by Bradlaugh as an official lecturer of the British NATIONAL SECULAR SOCIETY.

World War I, increasing costs, and ill health forced Collins to cease publication, resign from the

Christchurch association, and return to Sydney, where he had originally been appointed by the freethinkers and where he worked in freethought and labor politics until he died on April 12, 1923.

It seems clear that it was Collins' *Examiner* and his service as secretary and lecturer of the Canterbury Freethought Association that kept this organization going when all others had faded out. After his departure, the association continued to function but with reduced influence, and it was at a low ebb when the writer was there in 1932.

At that point it was held together by its president, J. G. Bryce, and secretary, A. R. Sadler, who formed part of a three-man committee (of which this writer was asked to be a member). Bryce claimed that the condition of the association was because people were afraid to join from fear of social and political ostracism and persecution. He proposed turning the association into a secret body with a secret creed, signs, hand clasps, passwords, and so forth. The writer condemned this idea, pointing out that it was completely contrary to all principles historic freethought stood for, especially the notion of having a formulated "creed" that members were required to accept.

However, Bryce went on with his proposal, and notices were sent of an annual meeting on Feb. 11, 1932, with information that the business would include "Proposals to Reorganise the Association." But it was not brought up until a presidential notice dated Sept. 22, 1932, advocated the "necessity for a more virile Rationalist activity," saying: "The scheme requisite to providing an effective constructive policy has been evolved [not saying by whom] and will be submitted for your approval at a special meeting to be held in the Orange Hall on Tuesday 27th at 8 p.m."

A fairly good audience attended and heard Bryce give an elaborate exposition of his scheme. The writer spoke at some length, historically, philosophically, scientifically, and rationally, pointing out that such a vital and important matter should be given time for members to consider. It was moved that copies of the proposal be sent to all members and another meeting be called to make a decision. This was seconded and carried by one vote. When the next meeting was held on Dec. 15, 1932, with about the same sized audience, a far stronger and more penetrating argument was presented against Bryce's plan, and it was defeated by six votes. Nothing more was heard of it.

A previous change had taken place when the name Canterbury Freethought Association was changed to the Rationalist Association, which Collins announced in the *Examiner* (Feb. 1910). He felt this change would mark an important new stage in rationalism for all of New Zealand, but up until the writer's time no difference was noticeable. Christchurch, for all practical purposes, was still a local organization.

Wanganui (1883–85). The Wanganui Freethought Association was started June 3, 1883, with six members, and by January 1884 it had 85.

The *Freethought Review* was founded and edited by JOHN BALLANCE, one-time prime minister of New Zealand. In the formation of the Wanganui association particular reference is made to "the services of a gentleman of ability and influence who has ever stepped forward with first class lectures and carried its meetings to a successful issue." He is not named, but there is a suspicion that it is Ballance himself. With A. D. Willis from a Wanganui newspaper Ballance began the *Review*, a monthly, in October 1883; it continued until September 1885, printed and published by Willis, who was also a local bookseller.

Ballance was born in Belfast, Ireland, of Protestant parents, in 1839. His father was a tenant farmer. Educated at a National School and apprenticed to an ironmonger, he went at 19 to Birmingham to follow his trade. During eight years there he became secretary to a literary and debating club, attended political meetings, and listened to Richard Cobden and John Bright speak against the Corn Laws. Birmingham was a strong center for ROBERT OWEN's ideas and radical SECULARISM, and young Ballance attended classes at the Midland Institute. He went to New Zealand via Australia in 1866, when he was 27, and he entered politics in 1875, becoming prime minister in 1891 after holding a number of portfolios. Before he died in office in 1893, he had introduced many pioneering social reforms as a Liberal.

Ballance's Owenite and secularist backgrounds were displayed in Wanganui with the founding of both the Freethought Association and the *Freethought Review*. He could not have helped but be influenced by Owen's ideas on "rational religion," which held that "all religions are so many geographical insanities." The *Review* was well written and carried a wide range of rationalist, scientific, social, and educational articles, as well as reprints of articles by Bradlaugh, Robert G. Ingersoll, and others. Ballance seems to have been more of a radical, "people's" unbelieving reformer than Stout, perhaps because of the former's radical, grass-roots experiences and self-education. The *Review* was published at perhaps the height of freethought organizing in New Zealand. It carried reports from all over the islands of the formation of freethought associations. They held local meetings; traveling speakers visited them; and they sent reports to the *Review*. But nothing is heard of them after the *Review* ceased publication.

Auckland (1883–1886). A second attempt, following the first in Southwell's time, to form a freethought body at Auckland was successful in 1883. (The writer has no knowledge of any organization in between.) Alexander Campbell, who knew Southwell, took part in forming the Auckland Rationalist Association, of which the *Freethought Review* reported (Jan. 24, 1884): "At the invitation of Mr. A. Campbell, Mr. W. H. Webbe, and a few other friends . . . fifty-six gentlemen met on Monday, 15 December, 1883," and formed the association. Campbell, the president, was a bookseller in Queen Street.

Among those present in 1883 were William Cooper and William Dennes. Webbe had been active in the National Secular Society in England and personally knew Bradlaugh; he was an advocate of "aggressive freethought." Cooper, more moderate, was a lawyer and became a magistrate afterwards in Samoa, where he partnered Robert Louis Stevenson in a newspaper. Dennes was a solid freethinker who did not trust Isaac Selby and had little time for him, a suspicion that proved correct when Selby turned Christian.

Eric Craig was first secretary, followed soon by Dennes and then S. Phillpot, who in January 1885, wrote to the *Review*: "We have not yet resumed our Sunday Night meetings owing to the Opera House lectures being continued." This was the first indication of a cleavage in the camp. In the *Review* for July 1885, he wrote that he regretted "The manner in which the A.R.A. has been put into the background," although he does not say by whom. Still he continues that he "is grateful that the principles of Freethought are being maintained." Thus, two bodies of freethought activists were apparently operating.

That same month in 1885 the first issue of the *Rationalist* appeared; it was printed and published independently (from the Rationalist Association) by the Rationalist Syndicate. That syndicate consisted of members of the association, and it also ran the lectures at the Opera House. Members of the syndicate were William Cooper, William Dennes, and John McKinlay. Eric Craig seems to

have joined them later.

Joseph Evison ("Ivo") was editor. He was born in England June 3, 1841, and educated at the Royal Naval School. He joined the Merchant Service and made voyages around the world, spending many years in India and China, where he saw the Taiping Rebellion. He commanded various vessels, owning one that was captured by pirates. Evison went to New Zealand in 1880, lecturing and practicing journalism. Well-acquainted with freethought and its literature, he was a fluent speaker and writer, so much so that the Dunedin Freethought Association prohibited distribution of the *Rationalist* at its meetings.

The Rationalist Association had existed less than two years before the *Rationalist* appeared. There was obviously a sharp division between the militants and the moderates, or those who advocated forebearance.

After three months the printers refused to print the *Rationalist*. The syndicate then bought its own press but ran into financial difficulties. A company was floated that bought the syndicate's assets. The *Rationalist*'s last issue was Aug. 8, 1886; "Ivo" had been the editor until the end. With the company a "new" *Rationalist* and a new policy was announced —freethought with political and social issues.

Then on July 27, 1886, various mysterious signs and notices were published that indicated secret meetings and penalties for nonattendance, by order of "H" or "ICL" and "D," directed to "Comrades" to meet at "midnight by command of "G Craft, BN2 and USS." An editorial dealt with corrupt government and the helplessness of electors because the "people who could be of use dare not join any organisation or lend the weight of their names." The answer to this was: "Organise secretly."

With that, no more issues appeared. Stout's Dunedin *Echo* and Ballance's *Freethought Review* had ceased, so nothing was published about these events at Auckland.

The similarity between the proposals of Bryce to alter the constitution of the Rationalist Association at Christchurch in 1932 and what we find in the *Rationalist* at Auckland in 1886 is too strong not to suggest a common origin, even though there were 46 years between them. Both were inspired by the activities of an American organization called the Knights of Labor, which, at its peak, had an immense popularity in the U.S. It invaded both New Zealand and Australia in the 19th century. In the U.S. the Knights of Labor was replaced by the American Federation of Labor, mainly because the former was too "secret." (*The History of Capital and Labour: An Encyclopedia of Australian and Foreign Statistics*, Sydney and Melbourne, 1888. Also, *Encyclopedia of Social Reform*, New York and London, 1898.)

The Rationalist Association does not seem to have existed long after the demise of the *Rationalist*. The problems in Auckland appear to have been irreconcilable ideological differences, economic depression, and the introduction of widening interests.

"Ivo," who had toured New Zealand as a professional lecturer before editing the *Rationalist*, continued to do so afterward. Eventually he became a Catholic.

End of the Early Period of Freethought. At this point it may be said that the early phase of organized unbelief ended, with the notable exception of the Canterbury Freethought Association, which continued into modern times. Just how bad things had become we may discover by letters in Joseph Symes' Melbourne LIBERATOR. E. Syles of Wellington wrote: "Support is languishing for the want of good leaders," and he asks if Symes or Collins could visit New Zealand (April 12, 1887). Charles Rae of Auckland wrote: "I cannot see as yet any chance of renewing the Freethought organisation in Auckland . . . (Christchurch) still holds its own, while those at Auckland, Dunedin, Wanganui, Wellington, Palmerston North and Picton, are defunct or dying" (Sept. 23, 1888). Other letters paint the same picture. According to Collins' *Examiner* (July/Nov. 1910), an effort was made for a revival at Auckland, but it came to nothing. Collins toured the North Island in April 1911 and gave some lectures at Auckland, but he does not mention any association being there.

Auckland (1923–present). In 1923 some freethinkers sponsored a visit by JOSEPH MCCABE (in conjunction with the Rationalist Society of Victoria), presumably with the object of forming another Rationalist Association in Auckland. James Hanlon has described his memory of the event: "Early in 1923 an advertisement appeared in the Auckland press announcing that, in view of the approaching visit of Joseph McCabe . . . a meeting was to be held in Auckland with the object of forming a Rationalist Association." He attended, and an association was indeed formed. He continues: "About May Joseph McCabe arrived . . . [but] interest in Rationalism sagged . . . and the

Association went into recess" (*New Zealand Rationalist and Humanist*, May 1977). The late A. E. Carrington took up the story: "Early in 1927 [four years later] I attended a meeting called to revive it [the one of 1923]" (Ibid., Aug. 1977). This revival was really a new association, since these remarks were made in conjunction with the 50th anniversary of the present association in 1977, which the association itself counts from 1927, not 1923.

The first important step was to establish a monthly periodical the *Truthseeker*. I arrived in New Zealand in 1924 from Australia, where I had been a member of the Victorian Rationalist Society of which J. S. Langley was secretary and lecturer. Reaching Auckland late in 1927, I joined the Auckland Rationalist Association and published an article in the *Truthseeker* (Feb. 1928), and thereafter was a regular contributor as "Profanum Vulgus" and "H.H.P." I was a committee member and, for a time, acting secretary. As "Profanum Vulgus" I engaged in continuous, militant rationalist controversies in Auckland, Gisborne, Christchurch, and Dunedin until I returned to Australia.

The Auckland association and the periodical have changed names, as have the officials of the association; Jim Hanlon and I may be the last of the old executives. Of the original executives, A. E. Carrington was the outstanding individual. His undying and untiring energy, organizing ability, and intellectual and historical grasp of freethought philosophy inspired all who knew him. I arranged for a lecture tour of New Zealand after a discussion with Carrington.

Rationalist associations exist again in Wellington, Wanganui, Palmerston North, and Hamilton. The movement at Christchurch (of Sept. 1881) gave to the Auckland association the right to call itself the New Zealand Rationalist Association with the groups in Christchurch and other centers becoming branches of it.

In the decade following the foundation of the association in 1927, its executive pioneers were Harry Major, president; A. E. Carrington, secretary and treasurer; and Fred Way, John Sim, James Hanlon, Messrs. Boardman, Chadwick, and Scott, myself, and later George Rawson. All of us were more or less militant freethinkers.

A little later Henry Hayward, who had been a member, became president. He came from an English theatrical and music-hall family, retaining those associations all his life and controlling a number of theaters in New Zealand. He became a convinced freethinker early in his life, and claimed

Bradlaugh as one of his political heroes. He also knew Oscar Wilde. Hayward ran the Empire Theatre in Auckland, in which he let the Rationalist Association hold Sunday-night lectures. These drew full houses but raised howls of protests from the clergy until the municipal council withdrew permission. I was an usher and sold rationalist literature.

The suspension of the Sunday-evening programs led to a reorganization of the association, which was renamed the New Zealand Rationalist Association and Sunday Freedom League.

The *Truthseeker* had ceased with the issue of August 1939, but a new publication began as the *N.Z. Rationalist*, incorporating the *Truthseeker*. Later, when HUMANISM began to spread through the world as a watered-down form of freethought, proposals were made to change the name again to one incorporating *humanist*. This met with strong opposition. The association took a referendum in February 1958 on the issue, the result being 70 for a name change versus 12 against; for changing the name of the journal, 69, with 13 against.

But the idea that the rationalist "battle" has been won is still alive in the association and colors its general propaganda, under the old names.

Over the years the association has been active in countering Christian attempts to introduce the Bible into the schools. It has also worked on the issue of freedom of the air on radio and T.V. and freedom of choice for women to obtain abortions. In 1953 the association was fined 20 pounds for mailing an "indecent" publication on sex education. For many years the association was licensed to marry couples; this was withdrawn in 1951 but reinstated in 1977.

In 1940 a building fund was established; by 1960 the association was able, by taking a mortgage of 6,000 pounds, to purchase a three-story building costing 12,000 pounds. Rationalist House stands at 64 Symonds Street, Auckland, close to the Symonds Street Cemetery, where Charles Southwell is buried.

Other article of interest: **Australia, Unbelief in.**

Bibliography

Aldritt, Charles. "Early Rationalist Journals." *N.Z. Rationalist & Humanist.* May 1977.

Carrington, A. E. "Rationalism in Auckland—Struggles and Achievements." *N.Z. Rationalist & Humanist.* Aug. 1977.

Campbell, P. "Early New Zealand Freethought."

N.Z. Rationalist & Humanist. Jan./Feb. 1963.

Pearce, H. H. "Early Dunedin Freethought." *New Zealand Rationalist.* Dec. 1938–Oct. 1941.

Trower, J. "The Beginning and the End of the Dunedin Freethought Association." *N.Z. Rationalist & Humanist.* Nov. 1977.

HARRY H. PEARCE

NIETZSCHE, FRIEDRICH WILHELM (1844–1900), revolutionary 19th-century German philosopher, born in Röcken in Prussian Saxony on Oct. 15, the son of a Protestant clergyman (Carl Ludwig) and the younger daughter (Franziska) of a rural pastor. A younger brother, Joseph, died at the age of two; his younger sister, Elisabeth, later played an important role in his life, presenting her version of his life and thought in a biography (see Bibliography) that exploited his writings and presented a distorted impression of his "doctrines."

Early Life. The death of his 36-year-old father when Nietzsche was four years old left an indelible impression on him, causing him to fear that he would die at the same age at which his father died. He incorporated into one of his major works his reaction to his father's brain injury from a fall. In *Thus Spake Zarathustra* (the most poetic presentation of his philosophy), there is a poignant and disturbing allusion to the dreadful howling of a dog that is related to the vision of the unconscious body of a man lying in the moonlight. This terrible dream is presented at a crucial point in the development of the work (Part 3, "On the Vision and the Riddle"), at which, among other things, the difficult process of overcoming pity is emphasized.

As a result of his father's death, Nietzsche was raised in a home dominated by women. This has sometimes been adduced as an explanation of his sometimes ambivalent, sometimes hostile, attitude toward women. Although Nietzsche had close relationships with Richard Wagner's wife, Cosima, and a young writer, Lou Salomé, his relationships with these women and others were typically unsatisfying and finally abortive.

Soon after his father's death, the family moved to Naumberg, and Nietzsche was enrolled in the Gymnasium. In 1858, he entered the prestigious Pforta School, where he excelled at classical studies and made a number of friendships that lasted most of his life. Although much is made of his later "isolation" and loneliness, Nietzsche did have many friends in his youth, and his voluminous correspondence indicates a fairly wide range of acquaintances. In 1864 he enrolled at Bonn University, and the next year moved on to Leipzig University, primarily in order to study with Friedrich Ritschl, a leading classics professor who had taken a position there.

It was in 1865 that Nietzsche shocked his mother by refusing to take the sacrament at Easter services. In the same year, he had written to Elisabeth, telling her that religious faith provides no guarantee of "objective truth," that one must choose either to seek comfort and consolation in faith or, like himself, pursue truth to the fullest, no matter how "abhorrent or ugly" it may be. At this time, Nietzsche's break with the Christian faith was complete.

Professional Life. Nietzsche excelled in Greek literature and culture and gravitated toward philology. His extraordinary talents were recognized by Ritschl, who recommended him for a position as a professor of philology at the University of Basel, a position he assumed in May 1869 at the age of 24. Without examination, he had been awarded a Ph.D. by the University of Leipzig.

While still in Leipzig, Nietzsche came across a copy of ARTHUR SCHOPENHAUER's *The World as Will and Representation.* He consumed it avidly, becoming an overnight convert to the philosophy of the German pessimist. It was during this same eventful period that he met the composer Richard Wagner and developed a close friendship with him. He became an advocate of his music, a supporter of his Bayreuth project, and a champion of Wagner's vision of a new cultural renaissance in Germany. During the following years, Nietzsche's friendship with Wagner waxed and waned and stimulated praise and criticism of the man Nietzsche once called "the master." *The Birth of Tragedy out of the Spirit of Music* (1872) was written, in part, under the influence of Wagner, and the fourth of his *Untimely Meditations, Richard Wagner in Bayreuth,* as well as a later work, *The Wagner Case* (1888), dealt with various aspects of Wagner's music, his place in German culture, and his conception of the meaning and function of the artist.

While fulfilling his military obligation as a member of an equestrian, field-artillery regiment in 1867, Nietzsche suffered a severe injury to his chest when he was thrown from a horse against a saddle. He was relieved of his military duties. Later, in 1870, at the outbreak of the Franco-Prussian War, he volunteered for ambulance duty.

While caring for seriously wounded soldiers, he contracted diphtheria and dysentery. Shortly thereafter, he resumed his teaching at the University of Basel and remained there for 10 years. His experiences during the Franco-Prussian War left two legacies: a hostility toward Prussian militarism and a tendency toward illness which, when combined with the poor eyesight he inherited from his father, made the remainder of his life often painful. At one point, his physical suffering was such as to lead him to contemplate suicide. Considering his frequent bouts with emotional and physical suffering, his creative productivity was astounding.

As if the years from 1865 to 1870 were not eventful enough, it was probably during this period, in Leipzig, that Nietzsche contracted the syphilitic infection that resulted in the outbreak of general-paresis insanity in 1889. Ironically, the exceedingly rare sexual experiences that cost him so much were atypical in a life that was virtually ascetic.

In 1869, Nietzsche resigned his post as professor of philology at the University of Basel. From then until his collapse in 1889, he lived on a modest pension from the university, traveling from place to place, preferring the Engadine and northern Italy, and frequently suffering from eye pains, headaches, stomach ailments, insomnia, and assorted complaints. Despite his enormous creativity, he remained, for most of his life, virtually unknown except to a small coterie. From 1889 to 1900 he was mentally ill, but he was released from the Jena Asylum in 1890 to live with his mother in Naumburg. Having contracted a fever, he died at home on Aug. 25, 1900.

His Work. Nietzsche is rightly considered one of the finest stylists in German literature. His first major work, *The Birth of Tragedy out of the Spirit of Music* (1872), impressed a select group of readers and was commended by F. A. Lange in the second edition of *The History of Materialism* (1873). However, it was attacked by a man who was to become one of Germany's leading philologists, Ulrich von Wilamowitz-Moellendorff, in such a devastating way as to destroy Nietzsche's reputation as a philologist. For the rest of his productive life he devoted himself to an ambitious philosophical "task."

The Birth of Tragedy sought to uncover the irrational, Dionysian spirit in Greek culture and to examine its relationship to the coeval tendency toward Apollonian order, symmetry, and artistic idealization. Dionysian passion and energy, the energetic affirmation of existence in face of the contradictions, pain, and suffering of existence, remained a central theme throughout Nietzsche's philosophical life. Although Nietzsche was criticized at the time and subsequently for his emphasis upon the irrational tendencies in Greek culture that were masked by rationality and artistic transformation, studies such as E. R. Dodds' *The Greeks and the Irrational* (1951) have vindicated Nietzsche's insight into the antithetical orientations in Greek culture.

Human, All-Too-Human (1879), a long sequence of aphorisms, emphasized the value of the precision of the exact sciences and contrasted it with the vagaries of metaphysical, "romantic" speculation. This work represented the so-called "positivistic" stage of Nietzsche's thought and was under the influence of the naturalistic orientation found in the writings of his friend Paul Rée—so much so, that in a letter he acknowledged that his philosophical orientation at the time could be called "réealism."

Dawn or *The Dawn of Day* (1881) inaugurated Nietzsche's attack upon traditional, conventional morality by means of what he called, in a preface added later, a "self-suppression of morality." In this work Nietzsche had begun the task of clearing the way for his own "naturalistic morality" or "morality of growth."

Sprinkled throughout *Human, All-Too-Human* and *Dawn* are numerous criticisms of religious consciousness, religiously rooted morality, and the Christianity of St. Paul. Nietzsche presents a variety of protopsychoanalytical interpretations of religious attitudes and values and critically examines the unseemly psychic origin of negative or "slave" morality. *The Genealogy of Morals* (1887) explores the origin of morality, describes the distinction between a "slave morality" and a "master morality" and offers a kind of phenomenological description of the "ascetic" personality. *Beyond Good and Evil* (1886) is a work in aphoristic form that deals with a variety of issues, including the question of truth, the nature of willing, the "hypothesis of the will to power" and the "problem," as Nietzsche sees it, of the rise of mass man.

His Masterpiece. Between 1883 and 1885 Nietzsche published his poetic-philosophical work, *Thus Spake Zarathustra*. Most of the central themes of his philosophical vision are found in this lyrically presented "edifying" work. At the core of *Zarathustra* is the gospel of the *Übermensch* ("overman," sometimes translated "superman").

The goal of the man that Nietzsche proposes as a replacement for God is to establish the "table of values" and the conditions for the emergence of the "overmen" of the future. Such suprahuman beings will affirm existence and life even in the face of the dreadful thought of "the eternal recurrence of the same," for which Nietzsche poetically and dramatically presents a meaningful rationale.

Zarathustra introduces the idea of a "will to power" pervading all living beings and suggests the harnessing of this energistic *nisus* toward power in order to create beyond ourselves. The overman is depicted as one who is powerful and capable of all things, but who is confident and relaxed while exuding a quiet courage. Because of its evocative power and intense imagery, *Zarathustra* is probably Nietzsche's best presentation of his aesthetically conceived ideas.

The three central notions that Nietzsche emphasized were: the cultural ideal of the "overmen" of the future, the thought of the eternal recurrence of the same, and the "interpretation" of actuality as pervaded by a universally immanent will to power. In addition, one of his aims was to liberate man from the "spirit of revenge," from a negative, repressive morality, from the debilitating effects of pity and the "pessimistic will" that he saw pervading German thought. True *Existenz* involves, among other things, liberation from the "human, all-too-human" way of thinking, feeling, and acting, the courage to embrace life despite its negativities, the endeavor to strive for "self-overcoming."

His Atheism. Although in his autobiographical and, in part, eccentric work *Ecce Homo* (1889) it is suggested that ATHEISM came instinctively to Nietzsche, this does not jibe with his intense desire to find a replacement for the loss of God, to create a new, meaningful cultural ideal for Western civilization; it is also inconsistent with his obviously strenuous attempt to overcome his basically "religious" sentiments. Nietzsche thought through and felt deeply the implications of atheism for man.

In *The Gay Science* (1882) a madman announces that "God is dead" and then realizes that he has come too soon. Nietzsche sees the death of God as a liberating idea that sets man free to explore vast possibilities, but he also indicates that the consequences of the loss of religious faith in God will be a 100-year period of "nihilism." Nietzsche's atheism was both passionate and intellectual: he called God (if conceived of as a "providential" being) "the greatest immoralist in deeds that has ever existed." He lashed out at the religious "explanation" and "justification" of human suffering and condemned religions that construed the sufferings of man as deserved "punishment."

The Antichrist (1889) is the culmination of Nietzsche's long-held, anti-Christian sentiments and ideas. In it he attacks the value of a "faith" that does not entail effort, that undermines striving and self-overcoming, and that passively awaits its reward. He charges Christendom with encouraging a hostility towards life and equates it with anarchism and nihilism. Polemical in the extreme, *The Antichrist* points to the "vampiric" effect that Christendom had on the Roman Empire and castigates its reversal of the "noble" values of the Greco-Roman world. Nietzsche spares Jesus, however, saying that there was only one Christian and he died on the cross. Against the life-denial, the hostility toward nobility and creativity that he finds in Christianity, Nietzsche opposes his Dionysian ideal of the affirmation of existence, the passionate acceptance of the joys and sufferings of life that is strong enough to will the eternal recurrence of the same. Against the Christian imperative to "die unto life," Nietzsche opposes his own imperative: "Live in such a way that you would will to have your life eternally repeated."

The voluminous notes that Nietzsche left behind, the *Nachlass,* contain a series of insights and condensed philosophical analyses. He had intended to write a magnum opus to be called *The Will to Power,* a work that would attempt a "transvaluation of values." Nietzsche never completed this project, and the various notes that have been brought together under the title *The Will to Power* do not comprise a work prepared for publication by him. Nonetheless, the notes (especially of the late 1880s) include an analysis of the origin of nihilism, a description of the forms of nihilism, as well as critiques of (Christian) morality, and rudiments of a critical theory of knowledge. In these same notes Nietzsche tries to define and depict the meaning of "the will to power" from a number of perspectives.

His Ideas. Nietzsche's polemical writings powerfully attack metaphysical, religious, and ethical valuations that he believes have been ruinous to Western civilization; they expose the negative, debilitating aspects of Socratic, Christian, and utilitarian ethical values. His positive and constructive philosophical conceptions are relatively weaker in their thrust even though they are aesthetically impressive and stimulating. The central question he struggled with throughout his creative life was the *problem of value,* the search for new cultural ideals that would reverse what he considered the "decadent" and nihilistic tendencies inherited from the past, that arose in his own time, and that he saw extending into the 20th century. Against the leveling tendencies of the age, Nietzsche opposed an "aristocratic radicalism" that would, he hoped, promote life-affirmation, courage, artistic creativity, and the creation of a human meaning for the earth.

Although critics of Nietzsche see him as a 19th-century "ideologist," whose ideas have had a detrimental effect on the Western world, he was, in many respects (especially in terms of the compelling and complex themes he examined with unsparing honesty) the first post-metaphysical, post–Judeo-Christian, 20th-century thinker. Because he clearly saw that the 20th century would be a period of intense conflict of values, he has been called a prophet of the 20th century.

Bibliography

Andler, Charles. *Nietzsche: Sa vie et sa pensée.* 6 vols. Paris: Bassard, 1920–31.

Bertram, Ernst. *Nietzsche: Versuch einer Mythologie.* Berlin: G. Bondi, 1918.

Danto, Arthur. *Nietzsche as Philosopher.* New York: Macmillan, 1965.

Deleuze, Gilles. *Nietzsche et la philosophie.* Paris: Presses Universitaires de France, 1962.

Förster-Nietzsche, Elisabeth. *Das Leben Friedrich Nietzsches.* 2 vols. Leipzig: Naumann, 1895–1904.

Granier, Jean. *Le problème de la vérité dans la philosophie de Nietzsche.* Paris: Editions du Seuil, 1966.

Hayman, Ronald. *Nietzsche: A Critical Life.* New York: Oxford U. Press, 1980.

Heidegger, Martin. *Neitzsche.* 2 vols. Pfüllingen: Neske, 1961.

Hollingdale, R. J. *Nietzsche: The Man and His Philosophy.* Baton Rouge: Louisiana State U. Press, 1965.

Jaspers, Karl. *Nietzsche.* Trans. C. Walraff and F. J. Schmitz. Tucson: U. of Arizona Press, 1965.

Kaufmann, Walter. *Nietzsche: Philosopher, Psychologist, Antichrist.* 3rd ed. Princeton: Princeton U. Press, 1968.

Magnus, Bernd. *Nietzsche's Existential Imperative.* Bloomington: Indiana U. Press, 1978.

Morgan, George A. *What Nietzsche Means.* Cambridge: Harvard U. Press, 1941.

Salter, W. M. *Nietzsche, the Thinker.* New York: Henry Holt, 1917.

Simmel, Georg. *Schopenhauer und Nietzsche.* Leipzig: Duncker and Humblot, 1907.

Stack, George J. *Lange and Nietzsche.* Berlin and New York: Walter de Gruyter, 1983.

Stern, J. P. *A Study of Nietzsche.* Cambridge: Cambridge U. Press, 1979.

Strong, Tracy B. *Friedrich Nietzsche and the Politics of Transfiguration.* Berkeley: U. of California Press, 1975.

Wilcox, J. T. *Truth and Value in Nietzsche.* Ann Arbor: U. of Michigan Press, 1974.

GEORGE J. STACK

O

O'HAIR, MADALYN MURRAY (1919–   ), American atheist activist and publicist. Madalyn Mays was born in Pittsburgh. She attended several colleges before receiving her B.A. from Ashland College in Ohio in 1948. She also received a law degree from South Texas College of Law in 1953.

There is some dispute about whether Madalyn was ever married to William Murray and whether he was the father of both of her sons. She worked for many years as a psychiatric social worker for the Baltimore city and county government and for the federal government in a similar capacity. Madalyn had become an atheist upon reading the Bible from cover to cover when she was in the sixth grade.

Her Lawsuit. Madalyn Murray's son, William J. Murray, was a student in the Baltimore public schools. Claiming that her son was discriminated against when he asked to be excused from the "voluntary" Bible readings in his school, she filed suit in the local courts, asking that Bible readings and recitation of the Lord's Prayer be declared unconstitutional. She claimed that even though the Bible verses and the prayer were read without comment, their presence was a violation of both the First and Fourteenth Amendments to the Constitution. The case was appealed all the way to the U.S. Supreme Court, which joined her case with that of *Schempp* v. *School District of Abington Township* (Pa.).

In its ruling in the October term of 1962, the court held, in a single decision (but dealing largely with the facts of the Schempp case) that Bible reading aloud and the recitation of the Lord's Prayer by the students constituted a religious exercise. Exercises of this type were declared unconstitutional under the First and Fourteenth Amendments as an establishment of religion.

Although Madalyn Murray has often taken credit for singlehandedly banning Bible reading and *all* prayer from the public schools, a reading of the court decision will show that (1) she was only partly responsible for the decision, which would have occurred without her case, and (2) that only the Lord's Prayer (not all prayer) was banned by this decision. In a related case (*Engel* v. *Vitale*), a state-composed prayer was banned by the court. Voluntary prayer has never been banned from the public schools.

Problems for the Family. As the case was being tried by the Supreme Court, Bill Murray was subjected to a lot of abuse by his schoolmates in Baltimore. After the decision, the Murrays were not popular in the city. When Bill fell in love with a 17-year-old Jewish girl and had her come to stay at his house, against her parents' wishes, the police were notified. A policeman came to the Murray house on a tip that the girl was there. A scuffle broke out between the Murrays and the police. As a result, Madalyn and Bill Murray were arrested and charged with assault and disorderly conduct. After they were released on bail, the Murrays and the young woman (now married to Bill Murray), thinking they could never get a fair trial in the area, fled to Hawaii. Madalyn chose Hawaii because she thought it was overwhelmingly Buddhist, and therefore more hospitable to her anti-Christian views.

When extradition orders arrived from Maryland and were unsuccessfully appealed to the Hawaiian Supreme Court, the Murrays fled to Mexico. There she met Richard O'Hair, supposedly a former C.I.A. agent. She and O'Hair crossed the border into Texas, and took up residence in Austin. Maryland again tried to extradite her. She fought extradition on two grounds. The first (in Texas courts) was that she was being persecuted for her ATHEISM, putting her life in danger if she were sent back to Baltimore. This fight she lost.

The second court battle was waged in Maryland with the help of her son, who had been arrested in West Virginia and extradited to

Maryland. Madalyn claimed that the six counts of assault returned against her by the grand jury were invalid, because Maryland law specifically excluded atheists from being judges or serving on juries. (A Buddhist also raised this issue.) She won this case, and all outstanding grand jury indictments from this period were thrown out. Maryland finally dropped the one remaining count of contempt of court, just as Texas agreed to her extradition.

Madalyn Murray O'Hair, as she was known after marrying Richard O'Hair, remained in Austin, where she formed an organization known as the Society of Separationists, later renamed American Atheists. After a long battle with the Internal Revenue Service, she won tax exemption for her group. She published a magazine, *American Atheist,* conducted a series of radio programs (later published as the book *What on Earth Is an Atheist!*), and instituted a number of lawsuits. These ranged from a suit to stop U.S. astronauts from reading the Bible in space to an attempt to end the tax exemption of churches. All of these suits failed except her suit to overturn the Texas requirement that officeholders have a belief in God.

O'Hair also appeared on numerous radio and television shows, often facing a clergyman. From her lawsuits and wide media publicity, she has come to be taken as the only spokesperson for atheism, a misleading notion. She is obviously the most accessible spokesperson, and is unafraid to give colorful comments. She moved into a large modern building in Austin in 1977, from which she continues to propagandize for atheism, separation of church and state, and against religious discrimination toward unbelievers. Her son, Bill, has broken with her and become a Christian, documenting much of his early life with his mother in *My Life Without God.*

Other articles of interest: **Church, State, and Religious Freedom. United States, Unbelief in. Women and Unbelief.**

Bibliography

Bozarth, G. Richard. "Madalyn Murray O'Hair: The Mouth That Roared." *American Rationalist.* Jan./Feb. 1983.

Frazier, Raywood. *Religious Persecution U.S.A.: The Case of Bill Murray.* Los Angeles: Heritage Manor, n.d.

Insider's Newsletter, The. Austin, Tex.: Society of Separationists, 1966–1984.

McClain, Virgil. "Know Madalyn Murray." *American Atheist* (Baltimore) 6, no. 7 (July 1964). Also contains other important articles on the Baltimore fight.

Murray, Madalyn E. "Madalyn Murray for Miscreant." *The Realist* 53 (Sept. 1964).

Murray, William J. *My Life Without God.* Nashville: Thomas Nelson, 1982.

Murray Newsletter, The (Baltimore and Honolulu), 1962–64.

Negri, Vitali. "Freethought Leadership and the Paranoid Personality." *American Rationalist.* Nov. 1964.

O'Hair, Madalyn Murray. *An Atheist Epic: Bill Murray, the Bible and the Baltimore Board of Education.* Austin: American Atheist Press, 1970.

———. *Freedom Under Siege: The Impact of Organized Religion on Your Liberty and Your Pocketbook.* Los Angeles: J. P. Tarcher, 1974.

"Playboy Interview: Madalyn Murray." *Playboy.* Oct. 1965.

United States Supreme Court. "School District of Abington Township, Pennsylvania *v.* Edward Lewis Schempp/William J. Murray III *v.* John N. Curlett et al." 374 U.S. Reports 203.

GORDON STEIN

ORGANIZATIONS OF UNBELIEF. See Appendix 3.

ORIGIN OF LIFE. See Life, Origin of, and Unbelief.

OWEN, ROBERT (1771–1858), British industrialist, philanthropist, polemicist, and prophet, gained fame for advocating improvement in the treatment of workers and the poor. He also suffered notoriety for asserting that traditional religious beliefs and institutions hindered his work of social reform. Praised for his practical schemes of improving the morals and education of workers in his New Lanark factories, Owen was condemned for advocating secular education and the inculcation of morality based not on church attendance but on individual education and loyalty to communal groups.

Early Life and Career as an Industrialist.
Owen was born on May 14 in Newtown, Wales, to
Anne Williams Owen and Robert, an artisan
saddler and ironmonger. Owen recounts in his
autobiography that he was a precocious child, who
became an usher in his school at age seven. At nine,
he went to work as a clerk in a grocery and
haberdashery in Newtown, and at ten he left to join
his brother William, a saddler in London.

Owen's training in the newly developing textile
trade was begun almost immediately, when he was
placed with McGuffog, a cloth merchant in Stamford, Northamptonshire. The McGuffog family
also encouraged Owen's SKEPTICISM, providing a
model of religious heterodoxy coupled with social
benevolence and reading in classical philosophy.
After four years in Stamford and a brief stint with
a haberdasher in London, Owen joined a similar
firm, that of a Mr. Satterfield, in Manchester.
Observing the fluid opportunities in the new textile
industry, Owen borrowed money from his brother
to open his first business, with a mechanic named
Jones, to manufacture machinery for cotton
spinning.

Between 1790 and 1795, Owen organized his
own cotton-spinning shop, became manager of a
larger spinning factory owned by a Mr. Drinkwater
in Manchester; ultimately he left Drinkwater to
form a partnership at nearby Chorlton, the Chorlton Twist Company, which he managed. Meanwhile, he continued his self-education as a member
of the Manchester Literary and Philosophical
Society, where he met the chemist John Dalton
and the writer Samuel Taylor Coleridge.

On business trips to Glasgow, Owen met Anne
Caroline Dale, daughter of David Dale, a prominent cotton manufacturer who had established
mills at New Lanark in partnership with the
inventor Richard Arkwright in 1785. The Dales
were devout Christians and Owen already an established skeptic, but he wooed the daughter by offering to buy the father's mills. In 1799 he married
Caroline, and in 1800 took over management of
Dale's New Lanark properties.

**Owen's later influence in advocating re-
form** of industrial policies, building communities,
establishing cooperative stores and labor exchanges, and organizing a union of workers derived
from his successful direction of the New Lanark
mills and town. Believing that industrialists had
paid more attention to their "dead" than to their
"living" machinery—the workers—Owen set out to

transform the character of uneducated, uncoopera-
tive workmen. He established stores with good
merchandise for low prices, paid the workers
wages when the mills were closed during the 1806
embargo, and inaugurated a public evaluation
system, placing colored labels to indicate "superi-
or," "good," and "bad" work next to each worker's
post.

Although the New Lanark mills regularly made
a profit, Owen's original partners objected to his
plan of setting up a model school for children.
Joining with other philanthropists, notably the
Quaker William Allen and the utilitarian philosopher JEREMY BENTHAM, Owen bought out his
original partners in 1814 in order to expand the
reform elements in the mill town. The most important of these Owen believed to be schools that
would train children from infancy to adulthood,
providing them with the basic character to be good
workers and good people, and all based on his now
constantly reiterated notion that human character
was formed by "circumstances" in the environment
and not by individuals themselves. On Jan. 1, 1816,
schools with three grades opened in New Lanark.

Having earned the fortune that would subsidize
the remainder of his career and provide a small
annuity even after large investments in experimental communities and journals, Owen was not
present regularly at New Lanark after 1816. In
1824, he allowed his partner, Allen, to give religious
training in the schools, and in 1829 Owen gave up
his shares in the mills.

After 1816 Owen developed his career as theorist, publicist, and builder of various communities
and cooperative ventures. Becoming a prophet, he
was listened to largely because of his earlier success
as an industrialist. Because Mrs. Owen remained
with her four sisters in the family residence at
Braxfield House, Scotland, from 1808 until 1828,
when they moved to a smaller house at Hamilton,
Scotland, Owen saw his wife irregularly from about
1816 until her death in 1831. Owen's concern for
his six children, who were raised largely by Mrs.
Owen and her sisters, was sincere, however, and his
four sons joined him in his reform efforts, attesting
to their fondness and respect for him.

The close of the Napoleonic Wars that had
engulfed Europe in the wake of the French Revolution, from the 1790s until 1815, created two crises
of which Owen took advantage. The first was the
economic depression that followed the collapse of
war production and the reopening of trade with
countries that began producing their own goods

again. This threw English workers out of jobs and closed factories. The second was the disappointment of the hopes bred by the political reforms in France, which collapsed in 1815 and saw the restoration not only of European monarchs but also of social conservatism bolstered by religious revivals throughout the Western world.

Various religions, from Roman Catholicism to American evangelical Protestantism, sought to restore traditional morality, order maintained by social hierarchy, leadership by the clergy, and conventional behavior. The only difference was that the new order would not be controlled by monarchs and aristocrats but by newly enriched manufacturers and merchants devoted to free trade and laissez-faire competition. Religion became the supporter of respectable leadership and diminished the impetus for political and social reform.

Owen persisted as a radical, because he had ceased to be interested in maximizing the profits of a manufacturing concern. He became obsessed with using profits to raise the level of workers' intelligence and character rather than reinvesting them in more "dead" machinery. His initial response to the economic crisis of 1815 was to call a meeting of manufacturers in Glasgow to petition the government to remove the import tax on cotton to enable British textiles to be more profitable.

Owen faced his first disappointment when the manufacturers, enthusiastic about the tax proposal, refused to support his corollary resolution to limit hours for children's labor in the mills. Rebuffed by the mill owners, Owen urged parliamentary legislation to prohibit employment of children under the age of ten, to restrict the hours of those under 18 to ten and a half hours a day, and to require inspection. A much-reduced Factory Act was passed in 1819, and Owen henceforth recognized the employers as opponents.

Cooperative Villages. Owen's second remedy for the economic crisis, which he attributed to overproduction of goods made possible by machinery that displaced workers, was equally unpopular with manufacturers: to establish "villages of unity and cooperation," in which workers would share the profits of production. Owen called a meeting at the City of London Tavern on Aug. 14, 1817, sending out 30,000 copies of his proposals. Owen was challenged at this meeting to give his religious views, and at a reconvened meeting on the 21st, he enunciated the principles that filled the rest of his life with notoriety: that the poor were degraded not by innate moral defects but by bad education; that

cooperation was a more effective and humane means of production than competition; that all religions contained gross errors; and that, as quoted by Margaret Cole in *Robert Owen of New Lanark:* "By the errors of these systems, he [man] has been made a weak, imbecile animal; a furious bigot and fanatic; or a miserable hypocrite; . . ."

Urging that money be raised to carry out his schemes for cooperative villages, Owen then left England for the Continent, to spread the message and to visit sites of experimental education— Johann Friedrich Oberlin's at Freiberg, Johann Heinrich Pestalozzi's at Yverdun, and Philipp Emmanuel von Fellenberg's at Hofwyl, Switzerland. He returned to New Lanark to stand unsuccessfully for Parliament. The election produced his *Report to the County of Lanark* (1820), a fuller exposition of his notion that cooperatively run villages could be healthy, self-supporting (with even a surplus for exchange), and rationally governed by a committee of elders. Such a village, organized around a parallelogram of apartments, with communal kitchens, nurseries and schools, agriculture and small factories for 2,000 people, would also free women from household drudgery. With basic education and income shared, there would be no need of religious authority, because those deficiencies that drove men to crime would no longer exist.

With the enunciation of his cooperative scheme, Owen lost interest in the actual management of New Lanark. Instead he turned to the encouragement of communitarian ventures, and later to publicizing the theory that labor was the basis of all profit, which laborers should control for the benefit of themselves and their families.

Owen's report inspired one venture in England, at Orbiston, which lasted from 1825 to 1827. While Owen, disenchanted by the selfishness of English manufacturers, undertook the establishment of a model community in the United States, at New Harmony, Ind., a site he bought already cleared from George Rapp in 1825. The U.S. seemed less class-ridden and altogether a more attractive location for a communitarian experiment, and Owen was invited to deliver two speeches in 1825 before the combined houses of Congress. However, New Harmony quickly deteriorated into a squabble over the ownership of the land, sharpened by Owen's avowal of common rights. In addition, Owen's anticlerical statements aroused hostility in a country where evangelicism was a dominant moral and social force.

Bequeathing the New Harmony property, which had been a great drain on his wealth, to his sons, ROBERT DALE OWEN and William Owen, in return for an annuity, Owen then sailed for Mexico, where the government had offered land. Finding a new regime and no land, he returned to England in 1830 to discover that his pronouncements had been more popular with urban workers than with employers.

Newspaper Publisher. Owen began to publish a series of newspapers under a variety of titles; this would remain his most consistent activity until his death. The first, the *Crisis,* announced in 1832 the opening of a "labor exchange" in London, at which workers could deposit articles for exchange in receipt for "labor notes," with which they could purchase goods. This model, although it was unsuccessful, spawned a movement for consumer cooperatives in addition to labor exchanges, and eight cooperative congresses met between 1831 and 1835.

In 1834, Owen defended the Tolpuddle Martyrs, a group of Dorset laborers who were being transported for taking union oaths. He began publication of the *New Moral World,* which became the journal for laborers organizing craft unions that unified briefly in 1834 as the Grand National Consolidated Trades Union. Although the journal lasted until 1841, British organized labor after 1834 opted for political reform under Chartism rather than Owenite cooperationism.

For one moment in the early 1830s, Owen's critique of the new industrial order was appealing to large numbers of skilled workers. Despite his anticlericalism, or perhaps because of its explicit attacks on the moralism of middle-class employers, more radically inclined workers were attracted by Owen's defense of their rights to education and decent wages. But once the economic crisis of the postwar period had passed, and once the middle class had shown its effective use of the franchise granted in the 1832 Reform Act, workers turned to direct political action to gain the suffrage and to influence national politics.

Owen continued to lecture and publish on the same themes he had developed: education, cooperation, and the necessity of charity. A weekly *Journal* (1850–52) and the *Rational Quarterly* (1853) preceded his conversion to spiritualism in 1854. In 1855, he published the *Millennial Gazette,* and in 1857–58, his autobiography appeared. Since he was still interested in all movements to organize society justly through rational planning, he attended the first two meetings of the new Social Science Association at Birmingham in 1857 and at Liverpool in 1858. He died in his birthplace of Newtown in 1858, and was buried there next to his parents.

In summary: All who met Owen during his long career attested to his good humor and humanitarian decency. He was not a caricature philanthropist devoted more to an idea than to actual people. Having himself risen from the provincial obscurity of an artisan family through hard work, canny investments in the new industrial order, and self-training, he sought to share the benefits of the new production techniques and of education. Unable to comprehend why his fellow industrialists lacked his charity, he could only attribute their selfishness to the wrong-headed doctrines taught by religious leaders. He was not a man without faith, but he believed that religious dogma had obscured the true meaning of charity. His own success supported his belief in the capacity of workers and employers to learn and to improve. He could not accept religious tenets that rationalized poor planning and justified the poverty that accompanied early industrialization.

Bibliography

Bestor, Arthur. *Backwoods Utopias. The Sectarian Origins and the Owenite Phase of Communitarian Socialism in America, 1663–1829.* Philadelphia: U. of Pennsylvania Press, 1970.

Cole, G. D. H. *The Life of Robert Owen.* 3rd ed. London: Frank Cass, 1965.

Cole, Margaret. *Robert Owen of New Lanark.* New York: Augustus M. Kelley, 1969.

Harrison, J. F. C. *Quest for the New Moral World. Robert Owen and the Owenites in Britain and America.* New York: Scribner's, 1969.

Owen, Robert. *The Life of Robert Owen, Written by Himself.* New York: Augustus M. Kelley, 1967.

———. *A New View of Society or Essays on the Formation of the Human Character.* Clifton, N.J.: Augustus M. Kelley, 1972.

———. *Report to the County of New Lanarck.* New York: AMS Press, 1975.

Podmore, Frank. *Robert Owen. A Biography.* New York: Appleton, 1924.

PHYLLIS PALMER

OWEN, ROBERT DALE (1801–1877), Anglo-American writer, communitarian, and politician, was the eldest son of the British industrialist and reformer, ROBERT OWEN, and Caroline Dale Owen. Born in Glasgow, Scotland, on Nov. 7, he was educated in his father's model school in New Lanark and by private tutors before entering Philipp Emmanuel von Fellenberg's school at Hofwyl, Switzerland, at the age of 18. There, his father's faith in human perfectability through education and in human progress through cooperation were confirmed. Returning to New Lanark in 1823, Robert relieved his father from the management of the family mills for a time.

New Harmony. In 1825 Owen made his first trip to the United States to join his father's newly established community at New Harmony, Ind. Teaching in the community's school and editing the *New Harmony Gazette,* Owen improved his skills as a publicist and fell under the influence of FRANCES WRIGHT, whose own colony at Nashoba, Tenn., sought to use Owenite cooperative techniques to educate slaves and enable them to purchase their freedom. Fleeing the rancorous New Harmony debates about whether his father should turn over ownership of the property to its inhabitants, Owen joined Wright at Nashoba and traveled with her to Europe in 1827.

The trip, also intended to recruit new members for Nashoba, resulted in only one potential recruit, Frances Trollope, but it did allow Wright to introduce Owen to Lafayette in France and to Mary Shelley and Robert Owen's former supporter, JEREMY BENTHAM, in London. In the meantime, Nashoba had gained public disrepute due to the publication of a notice that it no longer recognized the artificial tie of marriage and that one of its white members was cohabiting with a mulatto.

Journalism and Writing. On their return to the U.S. in 1828, Owen immediately resumed editorship of the *New Harmony Gazette,* and Wright joined him as coeditor in the summer. In the fall she began a lecture tour to attack clerical authority, and in 1829 Owen joined her in New York, where they continued the old *Gazette* under a new title, the *Free Enquirer.*

As Wright pursued her lecturing, Owen filled most of the editorial duties. The journal, already freethought and hostile to the evangelical clergy, quickly found an additional political cause and outlet in the Working Men's party of New York. Owen was six years Wright's junior, but he became more influential as their emphasis shifted to the need for free public education, a demand they hoped would give them leadership among working-men. As Wright's notoriety grew, Owen became more circumspect. When Wright left for Europe in the summer of 1830, Wright took full responsibility for their paper and also provided secret financial and editorial backing for the *Sentinel,* ostensibly a workingmen's journal.

Owen also began composition of *Moral Physiology,* an informative tract on contraception, which he defended on grounds that women, especially, should not be burdened with the ignorance that led to unwanted pregnancies. *Moral Physiology* (1830) made Owen's name as antipathetic to the clerical upholders of moral respectability as was Frances Wright's. Even though the work was a logical Owenite application of rational human planning, it offended propriety even more than his notions of public education for workers' children.

Owen's most personal public statement on behalf of women came in 1832, when he married Mary Jane Robinson, daughter of one of the *Sentinel's* supporters. After a brief civil ceremony, they signed a declaration, in which Owen forfeited the unfair rights granted to husbands over wives by law and religious dogma. Immediately the couple sailed for Europe, where young Owen helped his father edit the *Crisis* and organize a labor exchange in London. With his mother dead and the parental Owen home broken up, Robert Dale now saw the necessity to turn his attention to his father's land holdings at New Harmony and the remnants of his father's fortune, and to build a secure estate there for himself and his siblings. In 1833, he returned to New Harmony, which would become the center of his and his brothers' activities for the next decade.

Political Career. After 1833, Owen's career changed, due to the need to support his own family. He stayed in the U.S. for the next 20 years, becoming a citizen, making a living from farming and land speculation in southern Indiana, raising a family, holding public office, and from among his early reform interests focusing upon education, antislavery, and women's rights.

From 1836 to 1838, Owen was a Democratic member of the Indiana legislature, where his major acts were to apply part of the federal revenues returned to the state to public education and to increase the widow's intestate inheritance from one-third to two-thirds of the estate. In 1838, on the eve of his candidacy for the U.S. House of Representatives, he half-conceded, to continued charges of radicalism, that his youthful enthusiasm had been the necessary prelude to a more sensible, albeit essential reform commitment in middle age. This concession is the only explanation, in addition to rumored quarrels over an early loan, of Owen's estrangement from Wright, who had returned to the U.S. in 1835, and from other former free-thought allies.

Owen was defeated in his campaign for Congress in 1839, partially due to publicity about his earlier radicalism and partially to the Whig party sweep. For the next two years, he mended fences and defended his past, and in 1843, he was elected as a Democratic candidate from Indiana, beginning a long career in national politics. He supported his party's expansionist policy to annex Texas and to rescind the agreement for joint Anglo-American occupation of Oregon.

In Congress, Owen's interest in the Smithsonian Institution illustrated both his continuing commitment to public education and his new willingness to accommodate political and ideological differences. He authored the House version of the incorporation charter in 1845, advocating that the bulk of the bequest be used to establish a national normal school to provide scientific training beyond that available in the states, in addition to the publication of inexpensive tracts on agriculture, scientific innovation, and educational methods. When this ambitious proposal was pared down by House support solely for a scientific library, Owen acceded, and the measure passed Congress in 1846. Owen afterward became a regent of the new institution. Between 1838 and 1851, he also served intermittently on the board of the new Indiana University in Bloomington, which, his biographer Richard William Leopold suggests, was congenial to him as a nonsectarian, state-supported institution of learning.

Serving in the Indiana constitutional convention of 1850–51 and in the legislature in 1851, Owen again gave support to a constitutional amendment to protect the property of married women (over which their husbands had legal authority) and to a legislative act to collect taxes in support of public education. He failed in the former and succeeded in the latter.

Espousal of Emancipation and Spiritualism. Having failed to win reelection to Congress, Owen was willing to accept the reward for Democratic loyalty with a diplomatic appointment, in 1853, as chargé d'affaires to the Kingdom of the Two Sicilies in Naples. His return to America in 1858 coincided with drift toward the Civil War.

Owen opposed the Republican Lincoln's election, but he supported the new president's defense of the union. Being a war Democrat, Owen urged Lincoln in 1862 to announce emancipation as a means of shortening the war. In 1863, Secretary of War Edwin Stanton appointed Owen a member of the American Freedman's Inquiry Commission to formulate policies towards freed slaves; Owen implicitly recommended granting equal civil and political rights.

Owen's many publications in favor of emancipation were well received despite the notoriety of his conversion to spiritualism, revealed in *Footfalls on the Boundary of Another World* (1859). Although the book was condemned by American freethinkers, it did not endear Owen to evangelical Christians either. Indeed, *Footfalls* is a rationalist's appeal to empirical evidence for existence outside the corporeal realm. While Owen appealed to an existence after death and seemed to accept the existence of a personal deity, in many ways his spiritualism was as antithetical to evangelical Christianity as his freethought had been. Inspired perhaps by the death of his beloved wife, Mary Jane, in 1871, Owen's next spiritualist book, *Debatable Land Between This World and the Next* (1871), confirmed him as a leader in the movement.

From 1871, until his death at his summer residence at Lake George in 1877, Owen continued to write, publishing his autobiography, *Threading My Way,* in 1874. His progress from notoriety to respectability was confirmed by a respectful obituary in the *Nation*.

In summary: Less charismatic and less of a practical businessman than his father, Robert Dale Owen nonetheless fulfilled his father's hopes for the rationally educated man. A dedicated public servant, an intelligent and prolific publicist, and a devoted son and husband, Robert Dale combined the RATIONALISM of his father's generation with the practical, reform politics of 19th-century America. His early freethought principles gave way to a secular humanitarianism less at odds with the American temper, and even his late devotion to spiritualism did not completely dispel his scientist's desire for empirical proofs. He was a respectable Victorian, albeit without the religious beliefs that generally accompanied such a character.

Bibliography

Bestor, Arthur. *Backwoods Utopias. The Sectarian Origins and the Owenite Phase of Communitarian Socialism in America, 1663–1829. Philadelphia: U. of Pennsylvania Press, 1970.

Leopold, Richard William. *Robert Dale Owen, A Biography*. New York: Octagon Books, 1969.

Owen, Robert Dale. *Threading My Way. An Autobiography*. New York: Augustus M. Kelley, 1967.

Palmer, Phyllis Marynick. "Frances Wright: Case Study of a Reformer." Ph.D. dissertation, Ohio State University, 1973.

PHYLLIS PALMER

P

PAINE, THOMAS (1737–1809), Anglo-American writer and political theorist. The history of modern unbelief cannot be written, or even understood, without reference to the influence of Paine and, in particular, his book *The Age of Reason*, first published in 1794. (An earlier essay, entitled "La Siècle de Raison" and attributed to François Lanthenas—which appeared in 1793 but was either withdrawn or suppressed soon after—may have been by Paine, thus foreshadowing his later work; however, doubts about the authorship of this work remain, and only one copy appears to have survived.)

His Life. Paine came from a humble background, the only son of a master stay-maker who practiced his trade in the small town of Thetford, England, where his son was born on Jan. 29. Educated at the local boys' school, young Paine was forced to leave early and enter his father's trade, which he later practiced with little enthusiasm in various places before trying his hand at several other professions. Finally he settled in the town of Lewes as an exciseman, where he married for a second time, his first wife having died a year after marrying him. Paine ran a small business in addition to his excise duties.

As a government employee, Paine possessed a measure of security (even if the salary was low) that many others in England of the time did not have, yet he was prepared to sacrifice this by leading a public campaign for better pay for his fellow excisemen. The resulting agitation failed to attain its aim, and Paine was dismissed from the service, though the official reason given did not specify that he was fired for leading the campaign. This may also have been the reason why his second marriage failed and he was forced to sell his business. All of this happened in 1774, the year Paine left England for the American colonies.

For all the fame Paine was to achieve, his life remains something of an enigma, since not only do we know tantalizingly little about his early life but the earliest biography of him was written by George Chalmers, using the pseudonym "Francis Oldys," for the express purpose of damaging his reputation. All too many of Paine's foes record every fault and failing, real or imaginary, but no one close to him wrote a biographical study; his personal papers were lost in a fire after his death. However, after Paine arrived in the colonies he quickly became editor of the *Pennsylvania Magazine* and proved to be outstandingly successful, seemingly having found a profession suitable to his talent and taste. Yet with a career in journalism opening up to him, he thrust safety and security aside and plunged into the political discontent then simmering in the colonies. In doing this, Paine the obscure became Paine the famous.

His Writings. The contribution that signaled Paine's arrival on the political scene was a little pamphlet that did not carry his name on the title page: *Common Sense*, which appeared in January 1776. It was an immediate and dramatic success, and its author's name was soon a household word. An unqualified plea for total independence from Britain, *Common Sense* had an estimated sale of 150,000 copies (in a population at the time of only three million men, women, and children).

Paine went on to play an active role in the American Revolution, being particularly valued for his ability as a writer and propagandist, with his *Crisis* letters being read out to the troops. In one of these letters there occurs the first use of the name "United States."

At the end of the war it would have been natural for Paine to settle down, resume his role as a journalist, and bask in the prestige his work had brought him. Instead he left America in order to promote his ideas on the use of iron for bridge building, since he had been advised this could best be done in France or Britain. Yet once in Britain, where he was courted by the top elements in society for his celebrity, he soon put himself in danger again by openly giving support to the revolutionaries in France.

This occurred with his book, *Rights of Man,* a telling reply to Edmund Burke's criticism of the events on the Continent in *Reflections on the Revolution in France* (1790). Paine's book caused considerable alarm, and the publisher was pressured to prevent it from appearing in 1791. But if the first part of the book caused alarm, the second, which appeared in 1792, almost caused a panic, for it was an open demand for a new social and political system based firmly upon republican sentiments. Both parts of *Rights of Man* were received with considerable jubilation by those campaigning for reform. The government took steps to have the book suppressed, but Paine left for France before his trial in order to assume a seat in the French Convention, to which he had been elected.

The Age of Reason. Trouble and Paine always seemed to go together. He wanted recognition for his work, and certainly entertained a high opinion of himself; yet again and again he adopted a course of action that appeared to have been deliberately planned to cause him maximum trouble. In France he spoke out for the ex-king and thus made himself a marked man. Arrested late in 1793, he managed to pass the last of Part One of the manuscript of *The Age of Reason* to a friend while on the way to prison. We know from Paine that it was his intention to publish his views on religion late in life, so it would seem he considered his chance of leaving prison alive as being remote. In fact, the mark indicating execution was chalked on his cell door, but on the wrong side, so that when the door was closed the chalk mark was not visible.

Paine did leave prison ten months later, but he was broken in health from the poor conditions in which he had been housed and the mental torment he must have suffered. Without realizing it at the time, he was to have good reason for regretting having written the book, for it created antagonism and animosity, even among those who had been close friends and colleagues in the fight for American independence.

Paine constantly appealed for differences to be discussed in a reasoned manner, but his many enemies were quite prepared to employ an emotive irrationalism against him. In *The Age of Reason,* Paine placed in their hands a weapon that allowed them to do just this. By any standard, the campaign of vilification against Paine was vicious and sustained, but it was effective, as Paine discovered when he returned to the U.S. in 1802. He found that memories were short and that the role he had

played in the struggle for independence was largely forgotten. He was described in the press as an "outrageous blasphemer" and "this loathesome reptile." Many who had sought his company in the past pointedly ostracized him, although some, notably President THOMAS JEFFERSON, warmly welcomed him.

The last seven years of Paine's life were years of sadness. He was to write much of value, but little notice was taken of him unless it was to pour further scorn upon him. Even his citizenship and thus his right to vote was questioned; indeed this was the excuse used by Gouverneur Morris, American minister in Paris when Paine was arrested. His political enemy, Morris had failed to take strong action to have Paine released in France. He died on June 8, 1809, and was refused interment in a Quaker cemetery, being buried in a plot on his own farm at New Rochelle, N.Y. Few people attended his funeral, and of these none represented the American government. Ten years later William Cobbett removed his remains and took them to England, but their whereabouts are unknown.

Paine's Religious Views. Paine has been described as an unbeliever who wrote *The Age of Reason* to destroy religion. Nothing could be further from the truth, for he wrote to promote what he envisioned as true religion, a point the subtitle of his book stresses: "An investigation of true and fabulous theology." Paine was above all a reformer; *Reason* is a continuation of his political ideology, for in advocating his ideas on religion, he was seeking to remove a major obstacle to achieving social and political reform. The obstacle was the entrenched power of the Christian cult, which he had seen used to counter all attempts at reform no matter how modest they were. Paine felt he had to undermine the source of authority for Christianity, and, being from a Protestant background, he saw this authority as being the Bible. An Episcopalian theologian, William Chillingworth, had summed up his own Protestant belief accurately when he wrote that "the Bible and the Bible only is the religion of Protestants." Thus if the Bible could be shown to be suspect in respect to its central tenet, that it was the word of God, any authority based upon it would fall. In place of the revealed religion of the Bible—or any other revealed religion—Paine offered a faith he considered to accord firmly with science and with what could be learned from nature insofar as it applied to religious concepts. The faith he advocated was DEISM, a system in which God was credited with creation but after which God left mankind to get on with things themselves. Paine felt men could do this through the application of reason.

The Age of Reason consists of an analysis of the claims of the Bible, which Paine shows will not stand up. The authorship traditionally attributed to various books he showed to be highly doubtful if not impossible, a conclusion he maintained destroyed the authority and authenticity of those books. He accepted revelation as a possibility, but rejected it as a fact, holding that it was only such to the recipient; to everyone else it was hearsay. He cited aspects of the Bible that he claimed were shocking to both humanity and moral justice, even though ascribed to God. He noted the antagonism shown by Christianity to science, and commented upon the links between pagan and Christian ideas. Christianity he categorized as "a species of atheism," though he held Jesus in high regard as an individual but not as the Son of God. Paine rejected the resurrection on the grounds that if Thomas could doubt, so could he.

Summarized, Paine's case is that revealed religion is harmful to humanity and as such should be rejected. To him the Bible was the product of human beings and should be subject to the same critical norms as any other work. In a second part to *The Age of Reason*, written by Paine after his release from prison and designed to lend more specific support to his case against the Bible, he offers a book-by-book analysis of the scriptures that flesh out the more generalized comments in the first part, written, Paine claimed, without access to a Bible. Part Two of *The Age of Reason* has been described, quite accurately I feel, as an elaborate footnote to Part One.

Although Paine's book met with considerable hostility, many individuals responded favorably to it, and as time wore on this appreciation and support grew considerably, often in the face of massive repression, particularly in Britain. Critics such as Bishop Richard Watson were forced to agree that the case presented by Paine carried weight; thus as the 18th century gave way to the 19th, the influence of *The Age of Reason* grew. Throughout America, Britain, parts of the British Empire, and certain European countries, particularly Germany, the unbelief of individuals coalesced into organized groups, and FREETHOUGHT presented various religious bodies with a real challenge.

The influence of *The Age of Reason*'s ideas among these groups is tellingly illustrated in their books, pamphlets, journals, debates, and meetings, which frequently present Paine's work either as he put it down or as freethought scholars developed it. Paine's deism received short shrift and, if acknowledged, it was only to show that freethinkers could give support to one who not only did not share their unbelief but campaigned against it. When asked for their reasons for losing religious belief, many 19th-century freethinkers cited their reading of Paine.

When Paine wrote *The Age of Reason*, the ideas found in the Bible dominated many areas of thought—not least those of science—but by the time the freethinker MONCURE CONWAY wrote his epic life of Paine in the 1890s, the Bible had lost its old dominance even among churchmen. At all levels of debate the Christian cult was in full retreat from what most people had once assumed was an unassailable position, and Christianity had been forced to take refuge in a position from which its proponents argued not on grounds of biblical fact but from faith and morality. The struggle between belief and unbelief, between science and religion was integral to the intellectual life of the era, and in this debate the ideas Paine had advanced in *The Age of Reason* played an important part.

But the fall of the Bible from its position of eminence had other consequences, one being the decline of organized freethought, something that became increasingly evident as the 20th century wore on; as a result there was a decline in the influence of Paine's theological ideas, though there has been a significant increase of interest in Paine's political views. This has brought with it more interest in Paine as an individual and a growing volume of academic study, which has certainly enhanced Paine's reputation. But leaving this aside (also the fact that much of *The Age of Reason* is, in scholarly terms, dated), it remains a simple truth that when anyone who is unfamiliar with the world of biblical controversy and who imagines it to be nothing more than sterile disputes between rival sects reads Paine's book, it opens for him or her a whole new dimension in critical thought. Furthermore, when set against any biblically oriented thesis, *The Age of Reason* still packs a considerable punch.

Bibliography

Aldridge, A. Owen. "Thomas Paine: A Survey of Research and Criticism Since 1945." *TPS Bulletin* 5, no. 3 (1976).

Hawke, David Freeman. *Paine*. New York: Harper

& Row, 1974.

Paine, Thomas. *The Complete Writings of Thomas Paine*. Collected and ed. Philip S. Foner. 2 vols. New York: Citadel Press, 1969. Vol. 1 is available in paperback as *The Life and Major Writings of Thomas Paine*. Citadel, 1974.

Williamson, Audrey. *Thomas Paine, His Life, Work and Times*. London: Allen & Unwin, 1973.

Wilson, Jerome D. "Thomas Paine in America, An Annotated Bibliography 1900–1973." *Bulletin of Bibliography* 31, no. 4 (1974).

ROBERT W. MORRELL

PALMER, ELIHU (1764–1806), not only was the most notorious of the militant American freethinkers in the generation of THOMAS PAINE and THOMAS JEFFERSON, but also was by far the most advanced in his philosophical views. The only sympathetic, contemporaneous source of biographical information is a memoir written by his friend John Fellows and enclosed with a letter to the London publisher RICHARD CARLILE. Carlile published the memoir, together with three chapters of Palmer's unfinished book on politics and some brief writings, under the title *Posthumous Pieces* (1824).

His Life. Born on his father's farm in Canterbury, Conn., Palmer entered Dartmouth as a somewhat older student, was elected to Phi Beta Kappa, and graduated in 1787. After reading theology with the Rev. John Foster in Pittsfield, Mass., he went through a quick succession of Presbyterian and Baptist pulpits on Long Island and in Philadelphia. His first discourse as a deist "against the divinity of Jesus Christ" provoked such a reaction from the Episcopal bishop of Philadelphia, William White, and others that Palmer was "induced to quit the city."

Palmer and his first wife spent the next two years in western Pennsylvania, where he read law with his brother. Returning to Philadelphia in 1793, he was admitted to the bar, but yellow fever struck almost at once. Mrs. Palmer died, and he was left blind. After a brief stint expounding DEISM in Augusta, Ga., he was prevailed upon to organize the Deistical Society of New York, a base from which he operated for the rest of his life. He lectured frequently to freethinking groups in small towns along the Hudson River, in New Jersey, and as far south as Baltimore. He died while on a speaking tour in Philadelphia in 1806, at the age of 42.

His Works. Palmer's written works are understandably slim. They consist of a number of orations; editorials in the *Temple of Reason*, which he took over from Dennis Driscol in 1801, and in *Prospect*, which he founded and published 1803–05; and one book, *Principles of Nature; or, A Development of the Moral Causes of Happiness and Misery Among the Human Species* (1801–02).

For all of the inconsistencies in Palmer's occasional writings, one can discern a momentum of thought that carried his scientific RATIONALISM beyond deism. He became one of the first tentative voices of philosophical naturalism in America. His views were unified by the anthropology of his confident HUMANISM. His thought and work were inspired by the conviction "that the powers of man are competent to all the great purposes of human existence" (*Prospect*, Dec. 17, 1803).

Palmer's striking originality in the context of American deism can be made plain by a few comparative observations. It was a consensus among leading deists that an important distinction should be made between the respective roles of Jesus and of organized Christianity in the history of the West. By this means they exonerated Jesus from responsibility for the record of ecclesiastical history, which they denounced. Palmer challenged this convention. He maintained that there were flaws of personality and teaching in the founder of Christianity that poisoned the springs of Western religious history.

Palmer preferred "the correct, the elegant, the useful maxims of Confucius, Antoninus, Seneca, Price and Volney" because they were based on "principles from the physical and moral organization of human beings." (Unless otherwise noted, all quotations are from *Principles of Nature*.) By contrast, New Testament morality was antinatural. One of Palmer's most popular writings was a Christmas discourse of 1796, which circulated first in pamphlet form and was later incorporated into his book. In that piece he reached the unambiguous conclusion that from "every moral point of view, the world is infinitely worse" as a consequence of mankind's devotion to the model of Jesus.

The singularity of Palmer's philosophy was manifested also on the matter of immortality. (See IMMORTALITY AND UNBELIEF.) Most deists hedged the issue but retained some tepid belief in the traditional doctrine. The most eloquent passages penned by Palmer are those in which he reinterprets the meaning of death. (On this and many other points he is far closer to the more materialistic *philosophes* than to his countrymen. It is not accidental that he was one of the very few Americans of his generation to read PAUL HENRI HOLBACH with comprehension and sympathy.)

Palmer's anthropology and his political philosophy were linked on this point. He argued that mankind "must be reconciled to that kind of immortality which nature prepares for her children, and which diffuses through the intelligent world a sentiment of equality, terrifying to every species of spiritual or political aristocracy."

In sum, "nothing is immortal but matter." This insight should not terrify us but furnish us "with instinctive lessons of sympathy, justice, and universal benevolence." In this way he voiced the naturalist's counter to the claim that a belief in an afterlife is necessary to ensure socially responsible behavior. "It is in vain for a man to deceive himself; a knowledge of his true condition in nature, and his relationship with all existence, will furnish a consolation far superior to all the theological reveries of antiquity."

Palmer's most decisive step toward outright SECULARISM was the hypothesis that a sound system of ethics could be developed without any theistic presuppositions. This marked him off from virtually all of his more famous American contemporaries, who could never convince themselves that morality was possible without divine aid—certainly not for the masses of ordinary men and women.

Palmer announced in the preface to *Principles* that the aim of the book was "to render the sentiment of virtue as far as possible independent of all the theological reveries of antiquity." His main objective was to lay the basis for a totally naturalistic ethic. "If a thousand Gods existed, or if nature existed independent of any—the moral relation between man and man would remain exactly the same in either case. Moral principle is the result of this relation" and "it is founded in the properties of our nature."

Palmer was a vocal leader of that very small set of citizens who believed that the fulfillment of the promise of the Revolution of 1776 entailed a combined program of rationalism in religion and republicanism in politics. Palmer was convinced that human progress and Christianity were utterly "incompatible with each other." He called for the extension of the franchise to females and found the perpetuation of slavery in the new republic intolerable. He believed the opponents of rational and

democratic progress were "interested in keeping up a privileged system of plunder and robbery."

The tide went against Palmer's ideas, both among the general populace and in the universities, but he remained constant. Palmer and his second wife were virtually the only friends of Thomas Paine who remained loyal to the old man through his last years in disgrace. Mrs. Palmer served as his maid and nurse as the old revolutionary shifted from one lodging to another. She used part of Paine's hundred-dollar bequest to her to publish his reply to Bishop Richard Watson in 1810.

Palmer also was forgotten—or despised, if remembered—by the majority of his fellow citizens. But the next generation of freethinkers, in the 1820s, who braved the stigma of infidelity were quick to salute Palmer for the contribution he had made to the clarification of their thinking. At the 1827 celebration of Paine's birthday in New York, one celebrant proposed this toast: "The memory of Elihu Palmer, Voltaire, Hume and all those deceased philosophers who, by their writings, contributed to subvert superstition, and vindicate the rights of humanity" (*The Correspondent*, Feb. 3, 1827). There was other evidence of the continuing provocative power of Palmer's works here and abroad. In 1819 an English court imposed a one-year imprisonment and a fine of 500 pounds on Carlile for having republished *Principles of Nature*.

Bibliography

French, R. S. "Elihu Palmer, Radical Deist, Radical Republican: A Reconsideration of American Freethought." *Studies in Eighteenth-Century Culture*. Vol. 8. Madison: U. of Wisconsin Press, 1979.

Gay, Peter. *Deism: An Anthology*. Princeton, N.J.: Van Nostrand, 1968.

Palmer, Elihu. *Extracts from an Oration, Delivered by Elihu Palmer, the 4th of July, 1793, in Political Miscellany*. New York: G. Forman, 1793.

———. *An Enquiry Relative to the Moral and Political Improvement of the Human Species. An Oration Delivered in the City of New York on the Fourth of July, Being the Twenty-first Anniversary of American Independence*. New York: 1797.

———. *The Political Happiness of Nations; an Oration. Delivered at the City of New York, on the Fourth of July, Twenty-fourth Anniversary of American Independence*. New York: 1800.

———. *Principles of Nature; or, A Development of the Moral Causes of Happiness and Misery Among the Human Species.* New York: 1801. 2nd enlarged edition incorporating five new chapters, New York, 1802. Eight editions published in U.S. by 1830, four London editions by 1826. Reprint of 1819 ed., New York: AMS Press, 1975.

RODERICK S. FRENCH

PARANORMAL, UNBELIEF IN THE. Belief in the paranormal has always been with us. For the most part, the developing sciences ignored paranormal claims from the 16th through the 18th centuries. The church was the only institution that concerned itself with documenting or testing such claims. But in the 19th century scientists began treating paranormal claims as empirical and testable hypotheses.

19th-Century Experimenters and Believers. One reason for this concern for the scientific status of supernatural possibilities is indicated by the title of F. M. Turner's book: *Between Science and Religion* (see Bibliography below). Turner supplies biographies of six Victorian scholars—scientists, philosophers, and humanists—each of whom had rejected Christianity as outmoded and incompatible with the new sciences. But these same scholars feared that the naturalism of the sciences was inadequate to fill the void left by discarded religion. In particular, they saw science as irrelevant to the important questions about the meaning of life. They sought something between science and religion to fill this gap. This "something" turned out to be psychical research, which today goes under the label of parapsychology.

Another development that contributed to the involvement of scientists with the paranormal was the rise of modern spiritualism, which emerged from the rappings produced by the teen-age sisters, Katherine and Margaret Fox, in 1848. The girls' mother claimed that the rappings were produced by discarnate spirits who were trying to communicate with their living relatives. Within months of this news, other mediums found that they too could provide communications from the dead.

Immediately a religion and philosophy grew up around this phenomenon produced by mediums. The new spiritualism, unlike traditional religions, claimed to be compatible with modern science. It did not demand blind faith. Rather, belief was to be based on empirical phenomena, which could be tested by scientific methods.

Michael Faraday, England's leading scientist, took time from his research on electricity to test the phenomenon of table tilting in the 1850s. This particular form of spiritualism had become very popular in the United States and Europe. A small group of people would sit with their hands resting on a table top. They would implore the spirits to indicate their presence by causing the table to rise or move in a certain direction. After a suitable preliminary period, the table would begin to sway or twirl in circles and carry the sitters along with it. Sometimes, the sitters would ask questions which the alleged spirit would answer by an appropriate number of taps with one of the table's legs. It was from this latter practice that the ouija board developed.

Faraday published the results of his research on table tilting as "Experimental Investigation of Table Turning" in *Atheneum* (July 1853). He had begun by finding individuals whose integrity he thought was beyond reproach. He found that his subjects could sit by themselves with hands resting upon a small table and induce the table to move in a specified direction at Faraday's request. His subjects insisted that the table was moving of its own accord. After preliminary tests, which indicated that neither electricity nor other known physical forces were involved, Faraday devised an ingenious setup to determine if the table moved alone or was pushed by the medium. The results clearly demonstrated that the medium, without realizing it, was pushing the table in the expected direction. When Faraday added an indicator that let the medium know if he or she was pushing the table, the phenomenon ceased.

The next major scientist to try to test a paranormal claim was the chemist Robert Hare of the University of Pennsylvania. Hare had read Faraday's report on table turning and wrote a letter to the *Philadelphia Inquirer* to point out how Faraday's findings demystified the claims of the spiritualists. When a reader challenged Hare to experience the phenomenon for himself, Hare did so and, as a result, became converted to spiritualism. He even became a medium himself and claimed to have direct communications from Thomas Jefferson and Jesus, among others.

Soon after Hare's startling conversion, England's physicist and chemist, William Crookes, the discoverer of thallium, began testing the medium

Daniel Home. In the 1860s Crookes carried out experiments with the medium Florence Cook and claimed that she had managed to materialize on several occasions the full form of a spirit.

Also, in the 1860s, Alfred Russel Wallace, who with Charles Darwin formulated the theory of evolution through natural selection, began his experiments with spiritualistic mediums. Wallace, like Crookes and Hare, became convinced that the mediums he tested could produce paranormal phenomena such as materializing flowers and spirit forms out of thin air.

Hare, Crookes, and Wallace began a tradition that persists to this day. An eminent scientist, with otherwise impeccable credentials in his special field, tests the claims of an alleged psychic and endorses them as paranormal. The scientist's colleagues are incredulous and refuse to listen to such endorsements. Following these early ventures, we find such eminent scientists as Lord Rayleigh, Sir Oliver Lodge, Charles Richet, Claude Flammarion, and others supporting the claims of alleged psychics. In recent years we find many physicists endorsing Uri Geller's claim that he can bend metal by the power of his mind.

Questions for the 20th Century. The fact that many eminent scientists, including Nobel prizewinners, have been converted to a belief in the paranormal by witnessing the feats of psychics raises important questions about science and rationality. Does training and expertise in one area of scientific inquiry, for example, carry over into other areas of inquiry? Whether or not there is a pattern of activity that can be identified as *the* scientific method, the evidence indicates that an individual scientist can often be trapped into serious intellectual blunders when he or she strays outside a specific area of expertise.

Scientists are especially vulnerable when confronted with alleged paranormal phenomena. One reason might be that scientists ordinarily investigate phenomena that involve forces that are impersonal and do not change their rules as the investigation proceeds. As a result, scientists are ill-prepared when the phenomena are being produced by an alleged psychic who changes his or her tactics depending upon the scientist's activities. (See Ray Hyman, "Scientists and Psychics," in George O. Abell and B. Singer, editors, *Science and the Paranormal.*)

Early Psychical "Research." The search for something between science and religion, the rise of modern spiritualism, and the testing of psychics by scientists prepared the ground for the formal establishment of psychical research as a systematic area of inquiry. In 1882 the Society for Psychical Research was founded in London by a group of scholars and spiritualists. The American Society for Psychical Research began a few years later. Societies were also formed in France and Germany.

The early societies tested spiritualistic mediums, carried out surveys of premonitory dreams and hauntings, and from time to time conducted relatively informal experiments on mental telepathy. The major objective of most of these early psychical researchers was to obtain scientific proof for the survival of the soul after death.

By the end of World War I, psychical research was still groping for a consensus about its subject matter, as well as a methodology. Those who controlled the societies still felt that the central topic for psychical research was survival after death. These same individuals also tended to look upon rigorous scientific testing with suspicion. They felt it was irrelevant to investigations of the paranormal. In fact, they believed that too much attention to experimental controls and quantification inhibited the appearance of paranormal phenomena.

But a small and intellectually eminent minority disagreed with the majority on both points. They felt that the attempts to scientifically investigate the soul's survival lay outside the rigorous standards of current scientific technology, and hence could only produce ambiguous—or suspicious—results. It would be better in their opinion to focus first upon establishing the reality of telepathy and clairvoyance. To do this they would use the most rigorous procedures known to science.

J. B. Rhine. The man who was the most effective in transforming the views of this minority into what is currently known as experimental parapsychology was the late Joseph Banks Rhine. His 1934 monograph *Extrasensory Perception* helped establish experimental research using controlled conditions and statistical tests as a paradigm for later research programs. It also served to bring the issues of psychical research before the scientific community in a format that was not as easy to ignore as the largely anecdotal accounts that characterized previous psychical research. A good account of the impact of Rhine's work upon both the scientific community and the direction of later parapsychology can be found in *The Elusive Science.*

The Subject Matter of Parapsychology. As

already indicated, psychical researchers disagree among themselves as to what constitutes the proper subject matter of their field. Some of this disagreement is over strategy, and not necessarily over concept. As a minimal requirement, paranormal phenomena must involve events or happenings that violate current scientific expectations. But this, in itself, is not sufficient. New particles, elements, and forces might still be found that have not been predicted by current scientific theory, yet which would not be considered "paranormal." Something more than unpredictability or unusualness is needed.

At this point, many parapsychologists would agree with the philosopher Broad that the unusual event must violate one or more of the "basic limiting principles" of science. These limiting principles include such things as causality and the inverse-square law. Telepathy and clairvoyance, for example, violate the inverse-square law if, as claimed, they are not affected by the spatial distance between sender and receiver. Precognition violates the causality principle because it implies that a future event can determine a present premonition.

But even parapsychologists recognize problems with the limiting-principles account. For one thing, no one can agree upon a unique set of such principles. And even Broad kept changing his list from time to time. Furthermore, we can imagine types of phenomena that might violate these principles without being otherwise deemed "paranormal." Before the discovery of the planet Neptune, for example, some scientists suggested that the peculiar behavior of Uranus might be due to the possibility that the inverse-square law does not hold in the outer reaches of the planetary system. In the ensuing debates, neither side treated this suggestion as involving anything "paranormal." And when particles were recently postulated that could exceed the speed of light, even the scoffers did not treat the claim as paranormal.

Accordingly, some parapsychologists would add that the event must not only violate fundamental scientific principles but it must also exhibit some sort of "intelligence" in doing so. It is this implied attribution of unknown intelligent forces and powers that can operate beyond the reaches of known physical principles that both attracts some proponents to parapsychology and, at the same time, stirs up the wrath of establishment scientists who see such claims as attempts to return us to pre-scientific concepts of demons, goblins, and gods.

To further complicate matters, a small minority of parapsychologists do not accept these ideas about psychic phenomena that violate basic limiting principles or imply intelligent powers. Instead, they claim that ESP and psychokinesis (mind-over-matter) are real phenomena that, when fully understood, will turn out to be consistent with scientific knowledge but which will enlarge our conception about the structure of that knowledge.

Clearly, no consensus nor clear conceptions exist as to what constitutes the subject matter of parapsychology. Nor is it clear just what is claimed to have been established, even if we accept that the parapsychologists have established something.

THE CASE FOR PARAPSYCHOLOGY

After a century of existence as an institutionalized form of inquiry, what has psychical research accomplished? If we take as our criterion being accepted as a legitimate form of inquiry by the established scientific bodies, then the results have been equivocal at best. Some degree of acceptance has been acquired by the admission of the Parapsychological Association into membership in the American Association for the Advancement of Science in 1969. And recent surveys of scientists and academics show signs of increasing tolerance of parapsychological research as a legitimate pursuit. But even parapsychologists themselves will admit that they still have a long way to go to convince scientists that they have the right to say they are doing science.

While parapsychologists readily admit that establishment science still does not accept them, they attribute such reluctance to prejudice and not to rational evaluation of their evidence. They argue that if critics would fairly assess the evidence that has accumulated over the past hundred years, they would be forced to agree that the reality of ESP and psychokinesis has been more than established.

What are the evidence and arguments they employ to make this claim? One of the earliest endeavors of the Society for Psychical Research was to collect stories of premonitory dreams, experiences of hauntings, and other spontaneous cases of apparent supernatural happenings. Even after making allowances for distortions of memory, inadequate documentation and deliberate fraud, the psychic researchers argued that a sufficient number of cases withstood skeptical tests to justify concluding they were proof of the paranormal.

Another sort of evidence was based on the

results of tests made upon spiritualistic mediums and various gifted psychics. When the Society for Psychical Research was established in 1882, the founders put forth as two of the most solid experimental proofs of telepathy the results of their tests upon the Creery sisters and a team of telepaths, Smith and Blackburn.

The Creery sisters, daughters of a clergyman, were brought to the attention of Professor William Barrett, one of the founders of the S.P.R., in 1881. They convinced Barrett and other members of the S.P.R., after a series of tests, that they possessed telepathic powers. During these tests, one of the women would be sent from the room. The remaining occupants would mutually agree upon an object or a playing card as the target. Then the recipient would come back into the room and attempt to guess the target. This particular experiment was based upon a parlor game that was highly popular at the time. Because the recipient could guess the target correctly more often than seemed possible on the basis of chance, Barrett and his colleagues pronounced the outcome as crucial support for the telepathic hypothesis.

Smith and Blackburn were two young men who also convinced the early founders they could communicate telepathically.

The early psychical researchers were especially interested in spiritualistic phenomena. They conducted tests on various mediums. Physical mediums brought about phenomena such as rappings, playing of musical instruments, materialization of flowers and human forms, and the levitation of objects. One of the most famous of such people was an Italian medium, Eusapia Palladino.

Mental mediums supplied messages supposedly communicated from the spirits of the dead. Perhaps the most famous medium was Leonore Piper, who was discovered by William James. Supposedly, when Mrs. Piper was in a trance, her hand wrote under the control of various spirits. The proof of this was taken to be the fact that some of the information she produced could not have been known to Mrs. Piper, yet was supposedly known by the alleged spirit.

Today parapsychologists would argue that their strongest evidence for psi—as they now refer to ESP and PK—comes from laboratory experiments that employ rigorous controls and sophisticated statistical methodology. The pattern for such experiments was set at Duke University in the 1930s and 1940s by Rhine's experiments with card guessing. In some of these experiments, subjects could guess the target at a rate that was too high to attribute to chance.

Card-guessing experiments are no longer in vogue. Today's parapsychologists point to three experimental paradigms that they feel have established the existence of ESP and PK.

1. In the *"remote viewing" paradigm*, a subject is closeted in a laboratory room with the experimenter. A team of senders then drives to a randomly selected location within 30 minutes of the lab. At a previously agreed-upon time, the subject is encouraged to describe, for 15 minutes, all his or her thoughts and images about what the senders might be doing or looking at, at the target site. After a number of such sessions, the descriptions supplied by the subject and the list of target sites are given to an independent judge who visits each site and ranks, for each site, the subject's descriptions according to how well they match. Statistical procedures are then used to calculate if the judge's matchings of targets against descriptions are better than might occur by chance.

The early reports on these experiments in the 1970s claimed outstanding success, and the authors argued that anyone could get the same results. Other experimenters have conducted such experiments, some obtaining positive results and some obtaining negative results. But the parapsychologists argue that the number of successes and the degree of matching clearly indicate that this paradigm has been successful in demonstrating psi.

2. In 1969 a physicist, Helmut Schmidt, built a *random-number generator* for use in parapsychological experiments. The generator has been used for tests of telepathy, clairvoyance, and precognition. But its most interesting application is in testing psychokinesis (PK). A typical experiment might go as follows. A subject sits before a small box, the random-number generator, which has a red and a green light. At any moment only one of the lights is on. The generator is so set that over the long run each light will be on 50 percent of the time. During the experimental sessions the subject tries to mentally induce one of the lights, say the red one, to come on more frequently.

In some experiments some subjects have reportedly been able to bias the chosen light to come on slightly more often than chance, usually on the order of 52 to 55 percent of the time. While this deviation from chance is very slight, the huge number of trials involved makes even such slight deviations from 50 percent very unlikely on the chance hypothesis. Again, not every experimenter has succeeded in getting such results. But some parapsychologists claim that about half the experiments in this paradigm have produced significant results.

3. Perhaps the contemporary experimental paradigm that has received most attention from parapsychologists is the *Ganzfeld/psi experiment*. The first published Ganzfeld/psi experiment was by Charles Honorton and Sharon Harper in 1974. Since then more than 50 replications have been reported from several different laboratories. Parapsychologists claim that more than half of these experiments have produced successful findings in favor of psi. Honorton feels confident that even skeptics will get positive results if they sincerely conduct the experiment according to suggested protocols.

Honorton and Harper chose the Ganzfeld situation as a relatively quick and harmless way to induce an altered state of consciousness. The idea was that ordinary sensory inputs produce a lot of noise and interference against which relatively weak ESP signals have to compete. If outside sensory input could be reduced and subjects put into the proper state, ESP signals would be easier to pick out.

The subject is prepared by taping one half of a ping-pong ball over each eye. When a bright light is then placed in front of the ping-pong balls, the subject, deprived of any landmarks and faced with a homogeneous visual field (the *Ganzfeld*), experiences the sensation of being in a fog. The subject is placed in a reclining chair and white noise is fed into his or her ears through earphones. After a half-hour of this preparation, which subjects apparently find quite pleasant, the subject is presumably in an optimal state to receive ESP signals.

While the subject is being placed into the Ganzfeld state, an agent and a second experimenter go to another room and randomly select a target from an existing pool. At the agreed-upon time, the agent concentrates on the target. Meanwhile, the subject is encouraged to free-associate and verbalize any impressions and thoughts that come to mind. When the session is over, the subject is shown four pictures or slides, one of which was the actual target. The subject is asked to rank the candidates from one to four in terms of how closely each agrees with his or her impressions during the Ganzfeld session. If the subject ranks the actual target as one, this is counted as a "direct hit."

The experiment was conducted with 30 subjects. If they were guessing when picking the target, they should have produced approximately 7.5 direct hits. Honorton and Harper found, instead, that their subjects produced 13 direct hits, which they take as strong evidence for the existence of psi.

The foregoing examples represent only a small, but representative, sample of the evidence that experimenters have accumulated for psi over the past one hundred years. A recent estimate indicates that there have been about 3,000 experimental studies on ESP and PK published.

THE CASE AGAINST PARAPSYCHOLOGY

From its inception, psychical research has encountered criticism, much of it hostile. Most of this criticism has been directed, not against specific evidence and arguments put forth by the psychical researchers but at the underlying premises of such an endeavor. Many critics have relied upon DAVID HUME's argument against miracles. (See MIRACLES AND UNBELIEF.) Such critics dismiss parapsychology and its claims on a priori grounds. To them, by definition, a miracle that violates the laws of nature is impossible.

Other critics have attributed positive findings to fraud, maintaining that either the investigator has been duped by clever subjects or the investigator is also a party to the duplicity. Unfortunately, some justification exists for such charges. The Creery sisters, in later tests, were discovered to be employing both visual and auditory codes. Blackburn, many years later, confessed that he and Smith had also employed a code to fool the S.P.R. investigators. Eusapia Palladino was caught cheating on several occasions. In fact, so many physical mediums have been caught cheating the many psychic investigators eventually gave up investigating such phenomena and concentrated instead upon mental mediums.

During the 1940s the experiments by the British mathematician S. G. Soal were considered by most parapsychologists as the strongest evidence for telepathy and precognition. It is now agreed even among parapsychologists that Soal faked his data. More recently, the parapsychologist Walter Levy was caught by his own colleagues falsely enhancing the number of hits in one experiment.

When Rhine's early card-guessing experiments were reported, critics quickly pointed out that the relatively lax conditions permitted either witting or unwitting sensory cuing between agents and percipients. In many cases the agent was in the same room as the percipient, allowing for the possibility of deliberate or unconscious movements, vocalizations, or other sensory cues. It was also demonstrated that many of the ESP cards were so printed that one could, under some conditions, determine the symbol from the back of the card.

Since then, despite attempts by parapsychologists to tighten their controls, critics have usually pointed to weaknesses in experimental designs that could permit sensory leakage or other methodological flaws. In this category, the early attempts to randomize the targets by hand-shuffling of cards were a frequent object of criticism. Later, critics also found that the table of random numbers used was often biased in ways that could artificially produce significant results. Similar criticisms have been raised about the randomness of targets generated by computer and mechanical randomizers.

Mauskopf and McVaugh treat in detail the debates that raged over the use of statistics in Rhine's experiments. Critics sometimes still object to the use of statistics by parapsychologists. The most frequent criticism is that many different tests are often employed upon the same data, thus enhancing the probability that a fluke result will turn up. While most parapsychologists are aware of this problem, it still is not unusual to come across a parapsychological study that has employed as many as 20 different statistical tests on the same set of data.

Probably the two most serious charges brought by critics against the parapsychologists involve the problem of replicability and the experimenter effect. The problem of replicability occurs in a number of ways. In its simplest form, subsequent investigators fail to repeat the successful results of an initially successful design. In a variant of this, a new paradigm such as the sheep-goats design will result initially in successful replications but subsequently no more successes are reported with that paradigm. Some parapsychologists argue that this happens to be one of the properties of psi—it can only be successfully generated in relatively novel paradigms. Other parapsychologists realize, however, that their only hope of convincing the rest of science of the reality of psi is to find a design that is replicable. Today, many parapsychologists believe that the Ganzfeld/psi experiment may be the hoped-for replicable paradigm.

The experimenter effect is a variant of the replicability problem. Many parapsychologists argue that the demonstration of psi depends critically upon unspecified properties of the experimenter. Some experimenters can obtain psi; others cannot.

This difference is not simply a matter of belief. Many parapsychologists are noted for being unable to obtain successful results. In the Ganzfeld/psi design, for example, one experimenter has had at least eight successful experiments, but three experimenters have failed in several attempts. If the experimenter effect is real, it creates special problems for the acceptance of psi by orthodox science. It is taken for granted that a scientific result is one that can be observed by skeptic or believer, if proper procedures have been followed. If, despite proper procedures, only a chosen few can ever witness psi phenomena, the likelihood of such phenomena being accepted as real is quite low.

Rebuttals Offered by the Parapsychologists. Parapsychologists have tried to respond to such criticisms. They have tried to develop safeguards against fraud on the part of both the experimenter and the subject. And they themselves have often been instrumental in detecting fraud in their own experiments. The Creery sisters and Soal were found fraudulent by the parapsychological community itself. But both the concern and the competence to detect fraud varies greatly among psychic investigators. Parapsychologists point out that it is unfair to demand completely fraud-proof experiments because, after the fact, it is always possible to imagine a way that cheating could have taken place.

But the possibility of designing fraud-proof experiments places even greater emphasis on the need for truly replicable experiments. If careful investigators in different laboratories can independently come up with the same results, the possibility of fraud becomes relatively remote.

Parapsychologists have benefited greatly from criticisms of possible sensory leakage and the lax controls of the early Rhine experiments. Most parapsychologists today are quite aware of the necessity of preventing sensory leakage, of maintaining strict controls, and of employing adequate procedures for randomizing stimulus materials. And, they assert, they adhere to such rigorous standards much more than critics give them credit for.

Unfortunately, adherence to these standards is not as complete and consistent as parapsychologists claim. I recently surveyed 42 reports of Ganzfeld/psi experiments carried out between 1974 and 1981. The possibility of sensory leakage was clearly present in 60 percent of the studies. These studies presented for ranking the same pictures that the agent had handled in making the target selection. In the Honorton and Harper study, for example, the target has been a slide reel that was projected upon a screen. Among other ways that this target might differ from the other reels presented to the subject could be heating and warping from the fact of having been in the projector for 15 minutes or so just prior to being given to the subject.

In 45 percent of the studies, either the target set or the actual target, or both, were selected by methods known to yield nonrandom choices (for example, having the agent shuffle four slides by hand). And in 64 percent of the studies the experimenters employed multiple tests of signficance in ways that artificially increased the chance of getting a positive result. Such obvious flaws in a series of contemporary ESP experiments, which are considered by many parapsychologists to be their strongest argument for psi, suggests that the parapsychologists still have a long way to go before they can defend themselves against the charge of inadequate experimental rigor. I also found a significant correlation between the number of flaws in a given study and the probability of getting a "significant" result.

The Ganzfeld/psi experiments are, as indicated, considered by many parapsychologists to be their best hope of having a replicable experiment that even skeptics can conduct with positive results. But the skeptics will probably not take up the gauntlet until the parapsychologists demonstrate that they can conduct these experiments according to the standards they themselves profess and still obtain significant results. So far, over its century of existence, psychical research has yet to achieve this objective.

In summary: Contemporary parapsychologists offer two basic types of evidence to support their argument that psi has been demonstrated. One type depends upon ad hoc tests of psychic superstars or gifted individuals such as Uri Geller. Despite the fact that Geller's psychic powers have been endorsed by many well-known physicists, including a Nobel prizewinner, not one reproducible or scientifically adequate experiment has been documented to support such claims. The problem with all such ad hoc tests is that the experiments and conditions have been uniquely developed for the specific claims of the superstar involved. No standardized instruments, procedures, or measures are involved. As a result we have no basis for evaluating the procedures or for comparing results.

The second type of evidence is based upon laboratory experiments with unselected subjects and employing standardized instruments, procedures, and statistical procedures. To the extent that such evidence is positive and meets acceptable standards of rigor, it must be taken seriously. But close examination reveals that the claims for adequate rigor are still premature. Until parapsychologists can come up with a scientific paradigm that gives reasonably consistent results from independent laboratories under acceptable and rigorous conditions, it must be judged that the case for the paranormal has not been proven.

Other article of interest: **Conjuring and Unbelief in the Supernatural.**

Bibliography

Abell, George O., and B. Singer, eds. *Science and the Paranormal.* New York: Scribner's, 1981.

Hansel, C. E. M. *ESP: A Scientific Evaluation.* New York: Scribner's, 1966.

Mauskopf, S. H., and M. R. McVaugh. *The Elusive Science.* Baltimore: Johns Hopkins U. Press, 1980.

Rhine, J. B. *Extrasensory Perception.* Boston: Bruce Humphries, 1934.

Turner, F. M. *Between Science and Religion.* New Haven, Conn.: Yale U. Press, 1974.

Wolman, B. B., ed. *Handbook of Parapsychology.* New York: Van Nostrand, 1977.

RAY HYMAN

PERIODICALS OF UNBELIEF. See **Appendix 5.**

PERIYAR, popular name of Erode V. Ramaswami (1879–1973), Indian atheist. Ramaswami was probably the most controversial of all the leaders of social reform and of ATHEISM in modern India. Three factors—Tamil nationalism, anti-North India extremism, and RATIONALISM—were intertwined during his complex career that lasted more than 50 years. While his influence was restricted to southern India, it was sufficiently strong to make a sizable impact on the socio-political institutions of the Tamil area.

Early Life. Ramaswami was born in the town of Erode on Sept. 17 into a well-to-do, non-Brahman trading family. He had little formal education, having left school at the age of ten when he started working for his father. A marriage was arranged for him at 13, but he adopted religious asceticism and at the age of 19 went on a pilgrimage to religious centers throughout India. The ritualism and the superstition of popular Hinduism started his mind on the rationalist path. He returned to his family's business in Erode and began to take part in local municipal politics. At the mature age of 41, he joined the Indian National Congress even though the organization was dominated by the upper castes and, especially in Madras state, by Brahmans.

Political Activity. The princely state of Travancore was a backwater of feudal Hinduism, imposing odd restrictions on the lower castes. Not only the temples but even the streets around them were closed to the lower castes. A campaign of demonstrations and civil disobedience was started in 1924, under the inspiration of Mahatma Gandhi, in the small town of Vaikom. Ramaswami participated in the struggle and was imprisoned twice. In Tamil-speaking areas he became known as the "Vaikom hero." The campaign ended in a poor compromise: the temples remained closed to the lower castes, with only the streets opened to them. This did not please Ramaswami. Further offense was given by the Brahmans, who participated in the freedom struggle but maintained Brahman taboos against eating with non-Brahmans.

Outside the Congress party was the Justice party, which championed the non-Brahman cause and campaigned for communal reservation of government jobs for the lower castes. Ramaswami was also a fervent supporter of this demand, and as the Congress party would not support it, he broke with that party in 1925. This breach, rather than Vaikom, may be considered the turning point of his career.

Ramaswami formed the Self-Respect movement in the same year. A powerful orator, he held his audiences spellbound for hours with his earthy Tamil. Not only did he champion the many reforms that social reformers like Gandhi advocated but he also delivered frontal attacks on the Hindu caste system, Brahman domination, the myths, rituals, and superstitions of Hinduism and finally the very concept of God. The vehemence of his attack on theism can be gauged by words that were placed as an epitaph on his memorial in Madras: "There is no God. There is no God. There is no God at all. He who invented God is a Fool. He who propagates God is a Scoundrel. He who worships God is a "Barbarian."

Ramaswami was strongly influenced by ROBERT GREEN INGERSOLL and had much of his writing translated into Tamil.

While Ramaswami took a radical and even a revolutionary stand on social and religious matters, his immediate influence on political matters may be judged by posterity as negative. The Justice party, in its early years, regarded British rule as preferable to Indian home rule, which was condemned as a disguise for Brahman rule. As late as 1938, when Ramaswami was elected president of the party, it had formally resolved that Tamilnad should be a separate state, loyal to the British Crown and directly under the secretary of state for India.

In 1939, Ramaswami organized the Dravid Nadu conference, which advocated a separate and independent Dravidasthan, comprising the area where the four Dravidian languages were spoken, namely, Tamil, Telugu, Kannada, and Malayalam. When the Muslim League passed a resolution demanding Pakistan, Ramaswami extended his full support to the demand and expected reciprocal support from the Muslim League. This was perhaps the lowest point in his blindness to the political realities in India, where the sentiment for a federal union was quite strong even in Tamilnad. It was also a strange spectacle to see a militant atheist seeking an alliance with militant Muslims, whose policy of dividing the country on the basis of religion was disastrous.

The massive anti-British struggle in India nearly swept the Justice party away as a political force, but Ramaswami reorganized it in 1944 as the Dravida Kazhagam. The movement spread widely in Tamilnad, preaching atheism, advocating intercaste marriages, performing self-respect marriages without the presence of a priest, and so on. It also aroused Tamil linguistic and cultural nationalism, and in its extremism, denounced the entire Brahman caste (from 2 to 3 percent of the population) as representatives of the Aryan North. Occasionally, Hindu idols were destroyed or taken into the streets with garlands of shoes as a deliberate provocation. On the political side, Ramaswami's extremism led him to denounce Indian independence as a betrayal by the British of the non-Brahman masses. He boycotted Independence Day celebrations on Aug. 15, 1947, and refused to honor the national flag and to recognize the Indian Constitution.

Opposition. A younger section of the Dravida

Kazhagam (D.K.), led by C. N. Annadurai (born 1908), was getting restless over Ramaswami's negative attitude, since its members saw independence as the achievement of the South as well as the North. Ramaswami had no use for democracy in his own organization, and there was a walkout from the Self-Respect movement's conference in 1948, as a protest against his autocracy.

In 1949, at the age of 70, Ramaswami married a young woman activist of about 28 and, since his party was opposed to unequal marriages, his prestige suffered a severe setback. The younger section took the opportunity to secede in large numbers and to form the Dravida Munnetra Kazhagam (D.M.K.), *munnetra* meaning "progressive." Later, the D.M.K. gave up the thoroughly unrealistic notion of secession and accepted the federal union, while jealously guarding the autonomy of Tamilnad and monitoring any attempt to impose the Hindi language. Anti-Brahmanism was a matter of condemning priestcraft but not the entire ethnic group. Unlike the leader-dominated D.K., the D.M.K became a democratic and popular party, obtaining increasing support in the general elections, until they were swept into office in 1967.

After the split, the D.K. carried on its militant campaigns but took no part in the elections as a political party. Ramaswami, however, threw his considerable weight in favor of whichever party or candidate appeared to him to be curbing Brahman domination and supporting the non-Brahman castes. In 1954, the Brahman domination of the Tamilnad branch of the Indian National Congress had come to an end and the organization was in the hands of Kamraj Nadar, a powerful lower-caste politician. Ramaswami therefore tended to support the Congress party rather than the secessionist D.M.K. By 1967, however, he had been sufficiently reconciled with his old disciples to support them in the general elections. The victory of the D.M.K. against the Congress party marked the beginning of a new era in Tamilnad.

Ramaswami's atheism was so organically linked with his anti-Aryan and anti-North attitudes that his brand of rationalism could have little appeal to people in areas speaking Sanskrit-based languages. In the non-Tamil, Dravidian-language areas, his influence was peripheral. Indeed, even in Tamilnad, the Tamil-speaking people have not gone all the way with him in demanding territorial secession from India or with his militant atheism. And yet, by his extremist attitudes and persistent activity, he pushed Tamilnad into a mold different from the rest of India, leaving an indelible stamp on the sociopolitical institutions of that state. The passage of time may show that he was fortunate to have had disciples who could supply the necessary corrective to his extremism. The name Periyar (great leader) was affectionately bestowed upon him by the people.

Periyar died on Dec. 24, 1973, at Vellore at the age of 94, actively campaigning to the last. His body was laid in state in Madras, where vast crowds gathered to pay homage. The normal Hindu custom of cremation was abandoned in favor of burial in a simple wooden coffin. Periyar's grave in Madras is now a monument to atheism and to Tamil aspiration.

Other articles of interest: **Hinduism and Unbelief. India, Unbelief in.**

Bibliography

Diehl, Anieta. *E. V. Ramaswami Naicker—Periyar.* Stockholm: Lund Studies in International History, Scandinavian University Books.

Hardgrave, Robert L., Jr. *The Dravidian Movement.* Bombay: Popular Prakashan.

———. *The Nadars of Tamilnad.* Berkeley: U. of California Press.

Irschick, Eugene. *Politics and Social Conflict South India.* Berkeley: U. of California Press.

The following booklets are all published by the Periyar Self-Respect Propaganda Institution, Madras: K. Veermani, *Periyar and His Ideologies;* A. Sattanathan, *Periyar—The Man and the Revolutionary;* K. M. Balasubramaniyam, *Periyar E. V. Ramaswami;* M. Dharmalingam, *Periyarana;* Periyar E. V. Ramaswami, *Ramayana—A True Reading;* and V. Anaimuttu, *The Thoughts of Periyar E. V. R.—Cintanaikal.*

GOVIND N. DEODHEKAR

PHILOSOPHES. See **Enlightenment, Unbelief During the.**

POSITIVISM is the name given by AUGUSTE COMTE to his ideology, perhaps the most comprehensive devised in the 19th century, offering as it did a scientific blueprint for a new social, political, intellectual, and religious order, complete with a philosophy and a theory of history to legitimize it. The term quickly gained a looser connotation, and *positivism* is now widely used to label any tendency to extend the methodology of the natural sciences into other disciplines. Here, however, the term will be confined to the doctrines of Comte and his followers.

Auguste Comte was a child of the Enlightenment and of the French Revolution. To the first his doctrines owed much, and he conscientiously acknowledged his intellectual debts to such *philosophes* as Etienne Bonnot de Condillac, the Marquis de Condorcet, Jean Le Rond d'Alembert, Anne Robert Jacques Turgot, the Baron de Montesquieu, and DENIS DIDEROT, all of whom contributed to the idea of a science of society. It fell to Comte to develop and systematize into the "true" science that which he was the first to call sociology.

To the French Revolution Comte's debt was more emotional or visceral—a profound sense of crisis, of social, political, and intellectual disorder, a sense of the power for good and ill of ideas, and a conviction that society must be reconstructed, reintegrated on a firm basis of consensual hierarchy. To do this, however, it was not enough simply to denounce the Revolution and wish it away, in the manner of reactionary thinkers like Joseph de Maistre or the Vicomte de Bonald, however sympathetic he was with their antilibertarian, antirationalist ideas. The Revolution witnessed the necessary birth pains of a new era; in the positivist calendar the year 1 would be 1789.

Comte's most direct debt was to the Comte de Saint-Simon, who attempted to come to grips with the great realities of the modern world—the French Revolution and the industrial revolution. However he regarded Saint-Simon's system as insufficiently scientific and premature. Comte's own system was to be much more elaborate, sophisticated, and rigorous, but their kinship is undeniable, however reluctant Comte (who was Saint-Simon's secretary in his formative years) was to admit it.

Comte divided his life into two phases—his "two careers"—and it is convenient to consider his system in two parts, without implying that they were separate or discrete. Though some of his contemporaries took this view, the evidence is quite convincing in support of Comte's claim that his doctrines formed a unity, one that he sketched in outline as early as 1822.

The Law of the Three Stages. The *Cours de Philosophie Positive* (1830–42), his first major

work and the one most respectfully alluded to today, presents the philosophical, historic, and scientific aspect of his system. In one sense it is a history of scientific knowledge and a theory of the development of that knowledge. Here Comte develops his two most enduring ideas: the law of the three stages and its corollary, the hierarchy of the sciences. According to Comte the structure of the human mind has so developed that mankind passes through three major stages that correspond with levels of comprehension of reality.

In the first or theological stage the mind resorts to fictions, which explains the world in terms of the will and deeds of supernatural beings. In the metaphysical stage—not so much a stage as an interval of disintegration of the first stage and preparation for the third—abstract forces such as "nature" or the "popular will" replace the gods as primary causes. Finally, in the positive stage the mind abandons its search for ultimate causes and rests content with knowing "how" things happen rather than "why." Accordingly, a sufficient "scientific explanation is one which describes interrelationships between observed phenomena in terms of general and invariable laws.

The transition from one stage to the next is not made all at once, however, but is gradual, coming earliest in the least general and least complex areas of knowledge and progressing upward to the most complex and dependent sciences. Comte's hierarchy of sciences established the order of this transition: mathematics, astronomy, physics, chemistry, biology, sociology. The arrival of this last science at the positive level marks the culmination of the progress of the human mind. It affords the certain knowledge of man and society that finally makes possible the realization of the ultimate, organic society.

At this point Comte shifts from the descriptive to the prescriptive function, and his system becomes much more controversial. Many who were impressed by his earlier work were repelled by his later work, thinking that he had abandoned true science for religion. Comte was in turn contemptuous of such "incomplete positivists" for their inability to recognize that the "positive polity," developed most fully in his work of that title (1851–54) was the necessary scientific consequence of the earlier work, true scientific knowledge being for him that which had a comprehensive, practical social outcome.

Positivism and Science. Sociology, like any natural science, entailed prediction, which in turn entailed action. For Comte scientific knowledge was not an end in itself but only a means to an end, the service of man in society. Nor did he shrink from the self-assigned duty of defining those ends and prescribing the means of achieving them. He was hardly a scientist by any common definition of the term. A mathematician by profession, he was, ironically, trained in the most rudimentary of the sciences according to his hierarchy. At the outset of his career he was fairly well informed on the current state of the sciences, and he effected his synthesis at perhaps the latest moment a single mind could pretend to such a claim.

Subsequently, of course, the growth of scientific knowledge continued to accelerate, but Comte, rather than try to keep up, which would have necessitated the perpetual postponement of synthesis, instead chose to practice "cerebral hygiene" —his term for systematic abstention from reading any current publications and, in a sense, making a virtue of ignorance. He felt that the increasing specialization of science was retrogressive—tending toward anarchy rather than order. He reconciled "Order and Progress" (positivism's motto) by defining as progress only that which tended to meet his definition of order.

The theory of evolution (because of its metaphysical preoccupation with origins), stellar astronomy (only the solar system was relevant to man's needs), and probability theory (statistical abstractions were unreal) were all denounced as retrograde. Comte unerringly identified and attempted to cauterize some of the major growth points of modern science. He did so in the name of the social responsibility of science, a concern we can appreciate all the more today. But the price would have been very high, and it is hardly surprising that Comte gained the adherence of no major research scientists. What credibility he had among natural scientists rested on his history of science, which generally seemed to ratify their ideology of progress.

Positivism and the Intellectuals. Comte's "complete" adherents—the true Comtists, as we might conveniently label them—were overwhelmingly from the class of intellectuals. Many of these were attracted by his scientific theory of history, a highly idealistic one in the sense that, according to Comte, ideas ruled the world and were the chief forces of historical change, as the French Revolution had lately and impressively demonstrated. Material forces were relatively insignificant: man is what he thinks—or rather, *how* he thinks. This

being so, societies were not to be changed by institutional or material means.

Comte was far from being the crude "materialist" that many who were ignorant of his work assumed him to be, just as he was far from being the champion of science, militant and triumphant, as was widely conceived. Comte's view of history put intellectuals at the center of events, rather than on the periphery, thereby offering them welcome recognition. Being so important, however, they had to be organized. As they had started out in history as a priesthood, so they would end. The metaphysical interval of independence for intellectuals—the *littérateurs*, lawyers, free-floating "men of ideas"—was an unfortunate but necessary historical phenomenon continuing into Comte's own time but which would soon end.

The "spiritual power" was Comte's term for the duly reconstituted intellectual estate. He regarded it as an authoritative body which, in the positive state, would be able to pronounce on social and political problems with the same confidence in the agreement of other experts and the same expectation of unquestioning assent from the nonexpert, as might a chemist pronouncing on some chemical reaction. Politics, in the usual sense of the word, would disappear; scientific administration would replace it. The positive priesthood would not do the administering however. They would only establish the principles for the practical administrators to follow, confining themselves to the theoretic level and above all to education which was, given Comte's idealist tendency, of vital importance for the creation and maintenance of the positive social order.

Positivism and Religion. The spiritual power was an essential feature of Comte's system from the start. Similarly, religion is a central feature of Comte's schematic history of mankind, religion being the surest index of mankind's intellectual development. His three stages had their corresponding religious manifestations—fetishism and polytheism, monotheism, and the religion of humanity. Here Comte's exposition shows most vividly his dislike of the metaphysical stage, which was nevertheless presented as a necessary development. An unbeliever from boyhood, his mature system necessarily excluded belief in God, since for Comte, God was by definition a metaphysical abstraction with no scientific existence.

Comte did not regard himself as an atheist, however, for he considered ATHEISM as futilely metaphysical in its preoccupations as monotheism is because atheism "tends to prolong the metaphysical state indefinitely by continually seeking new solutions of theoretical problems instead of ruling out all accessible research as inherently fruitless." Comte might be considered nearer to AGNOSTICISM, except that while that position tends to leave doors open, Comte resolutely shut them.

Comte believed religion to be necessary for mankind; it was only a question of having the appropriate one for society's stage of development. Intellectual recognition of this need was certainly strengthened by personal sentiment as he passed through the various emotional crises of his life, particularly his great passion for Clothilde de Vaux. This lent a certain spiritual dimension to his religious concerns, though one which was open to criticism, if not ridicule.

As he aged, Comte became increasingly aware of feelings that were unclassifiable in his system (he denied psychology any independent status as a science). Above all, he felt that religion was a social necessity, a vital mechanism for promoting morality and social harmony that were for him intimately connected, social harmony, altruism, and solidarity being the aims of morality. Comte frequently dwelt on the etymology of the word *religion* as that which "binds together"; the masses especially needed something that unites them publicly, that sacralizes life, that underwrites and enforces morality. (Comte believed that humanity was progressing ethically toward a greater altruism, but he did not believe that human selfishness could or would be abolished.)

The Religion of Humanity. The object of reverence was to be humanity itself, as represented by its greatest exemplars. There are certain obvious similarities between Comte's religion of humanity and the revolutionary cult of theophilanthropy sponsored by the French government in 1795, though Comte denied any connection, regarding the cult as part of the last wreckage of monotheism. Humanity was no abstraction in Comte's thinking. Comte argued that if anything was an abstraction it was the idea of the individual, for every person was so closely tied to society and shaped by society that the idea of there being any essential entity in a human being that was truly individual—completely independent of society—was a fiction. The ideology of individualism was of course part of the baneful legacy of the metaphysical era, which unfortunately lived on in such harmful pseudosciences as political economy.

The worship of humanity was in a sense a throwback to polytheism. This helps to explain Comte's notorious tenderness for Catholicism and his undisguised hostility to Protestantism, which, if anything, ran counter to the expected priorities of unbelief. Comte's strongest objection to Protestantism was to its individualism, the fatal mark of its metaphysical origins and nature. Not only did it emphasize the direct and unmediated relationship between God and the believer, which was fatally selfish, anarchistic, and even democratic in its tendencies, but the Protestant God was a peculiarly abstract entity.

The Catholic church, by contrast, remained much closer to the polytheistic phase, especially during its prime in the high Middle Ages, when the cult of saints and the Virgin rivaled the worship of God. THOMAS HENRY HUXLEY was quite accurate in his famous characterization of positivism as "Catholicism minus Christianity." Comte explicitly contrasted Catholicism and Christianity to the detriment of the latter.

Comte regarded Jesus (See JESUS, HISTORICITY OF) as an imposter and would not even give him a subordinate place in the eclectic positivist calendar, which honored such figures as Muhammed, Moses, and Confucius; he justified the exclusion with the scornful comment, "Since he ranked himself as God, let him so remain." St. Paul was for Comte the true founder and hero of Christianity, and all the greater for not claiming the title but modestly yielding to the pretensions of Jesus.

What Comte admired in Catholicism was its organization and its rituals. He transposed the Catholic sacraments into a key element in positivism. His social sacraments celebrated and sanctified the various stages of human life: Presentation (at birth), Initiation (at 14, commencement of public education, previously confined to the home), Admission (at 21, commencement of vocational training), Destination (at 28, entry into vocation; for women Admission and Destination are the same, their vocation being motherhood), Marriage (after 21 for women, 28 for men), Maturity (at 42, men only), Retirement (at 63), Transformation (at death), Incorporation (into humanity seven years after death if deemed worthy).

Comte also admired the hierarchical and authoritarian character of the Catholic church, especially as embodied in the Jesuit order (which he referred to as "Ignatians," such was his aversion to Jesus). He particularly hailed the Catholic church for first enunciating the doctrine of separation of powers: that spiritual or moral authority and temporal or political authority must be kept distinct, the church claiming only the first. This was to be the cardinal principle of the positivist order.

Comte had a horror of institutional vacuums—of anarchy. Being no revolutionary he was ready to make "provisional" accommodation with existing institutions, judging them by their proximity to the positivist ideal; he did not subscribe to the radical *politique du pire*—"the better is the enemy of the best." Hence Catholicism won his guarded approval for interim purposes. He was also inclined to hope that for religious reasons the Russians, thanks to the Russian Orthodox church, and the Turks, with their Muslim theocracy, might avoid the painful metaphysical stage altogether, and pass directly to the positive. The Hindus also were viewed as potential "stage skippers."

Another of Comte's favorite mottoes, "to destroy one must replace" (said to have been borrowed from Napoleon III, whom he admired), helps to explain the minuteness of detail with which Comte legislated his religion, even down to the wage scales for priests and to temple design. The result is a synthetic religion par excellence which, despite its pedantic architecture, revealed a shrewd appreciation of the spiritual landscape of the 19th-century middle class and of the linkage between religion and ethics.

When Comte died, the theoretical side of his work was largely complete—indeed his last writings were leading into rather vague, acrostic reveries over the triple cosmos of humanity, earth, and space, yet another transposition from Christianity. One suspects that he had lived longer, he might have further harmed the prospects of his cause. He died without even appointing his successor and without having established an actual church, apart from his own house, in which he worshiped the memory of Clothilde de Vaux.

Comte's Disciples and Successors. Comte left behind a small but able group of enthusiasts, their quality and numbers owing something to Comte's rigid standards for discipleship, which included intelligence as well as moral soundness and, most importantly, commitment (to himself). His disciples were most numerous in France and in Britain. This surprised him, since he felt Protestant Britain was deeply tainted by metaphysical patterns of thought. (Positivism in Latin America is dealt with separately. See LATIN AMERICA, PHILOSOPHICAL BASES FOR UNBELIEF IN.)

In France the scientific element was stronger,

doctors and engineers being prominent—the latter through Comte's Polytechnique connection, the former through Comte's specification that future positivist priests should have medical training, which epitomized socially useful science. In both cases their professional ideologies conformed closely with positivist values.

Pierre Laffitte (1823–1903), a mathematician, was chosen Comte's successor as "director of positivism." But even among the complete positivists there eventually recurred the divergence of opinion that had split the admirers of his "first career." Although his later adherents accepted the religion of humanity in principle, they differed over whether the time was yet ripe for institutionalizing it. To do so would be to invite dismissal as a bizarre sect and would perhaps jeopardize the broader intellectual appeal of Comte's writings. Like any movement in its early organizational phase, positivism had to choose between casting a wide or a narrow net. Comte had increasingly inclined to the latter course (as evidenced by his inability to find a worthy successor), though his published works had an independent existence and appeal.

Laffitte, like most of the French positivists, did not share Comte's faith in the imminence of the Comtean dispensation. Lafitte felt that he should emphasize the propagation of Comte's ideas on a fairly wide front. For this he was well suited; he was an excellent lecturer, capable of the lucidity that Comte badly lacked. He occupied the middle ground of the movement. On one side of him was Émile Littré (1801–1881), perhaps the most brilliant of Comte's French disciples. He had broken with Comte in 1852 but continued as a powerful intellectual presence, claiming to represent a "true" positivism purged of the authoritarian and sacerdotal excesses of Comte's "aberrant" later years. Littré rejected institutionalization in any form as premature.

On the other side were some "fundamentalists," who were for the immediate and full institutionalization of the religion of humanity in all details. In addition, there were some political fundamentalists, who were preoccupied with instituting Comte's rather authoritarian political order, especially after the collapse of the Second Empire in 1870; but these men were rather lukewarm toward the religious side of positivism, even to the extent of advocating an alliance with freethinkers. Laffitte managed, despite some intrigues and differences, to keep the movement together, though he made some concessions to the religious fundamentalists, such as adopting the title "high priest of humanity." His "broad" approach prevailed, and his prestige was unmatched, especially after he was appointed to the newly created chair of the history of science at the Collège de France in 1892, where he had been lecturing to large audiences since 1881. The disadvantage of Laffitte's approach was that it offered little incentive to join the official movement, which tended to become rather inbred and grew scarcely at all.

After Laffitte's death in 1903, there was a disputed succession and another divergence, in which certain more authoritarian Positivists inclined politically rightward and religiously toward Catholicism; some even joined the Action Française movement. Meanwhile the movement declined in numbers and quality until by World War II it was in effect dead in France, though it was resuscitated—or perhaps embalmed—after the war by some Brazilian disciples. Of course, the influence of Comte's ideas, unmediated by orthodoxy, continues unabated in the various mysterious ways that ideas have of surviving.

Positivism's English career is perhaps more remarkable, given its very improbability by strict positivist criteria. The central figure is Richard Congreve (1818-1899), a product of Thomas Arnold's Rugby School and Cardinal John Henry Newman's Oxford. Congreve was an intellectually unsettled Oxford tutor and Anglican priest who came to Comtism via a Carlylian route. He was attracted to Comte by his political and historical theories, but most of all by his religious ideas. Congreve's own powerful influence ultimately brought into positivism three of his most able students from Wadham College, Oxford—Frederic Harrison, E. S. Beesly, and J. H. Bridges. Religious factors were important for them too; all were of religious, particularly evangelical, background, had undergone crises of faith, and were drawn to the claims of positivism to provide a surrogate that was invulnerable to the science and scholarship that seemed to be eroding traditional Christian beliefs.

The scientific pretensions of positivism attracted classically trained gentlemen for whom science was a rather threatening mystery. Comte's masterful taming of science and his denigration of specialization were reassuring to generalists somewhat uncertain about their own continuing relevance in the age of Charles Darwin and Thomas Henry Huxley. Comte's whole system afforded particular security to the intellectual; it is significant that the intellec-

tuals who were drawn to the system were themselves of the establishment. This gave positivism an unusually privileged position in England.

Its exponents were articulate publicists—Harrison in particular—with access to some of the most prestigious channels of opinion, both journalistic and social. They made such a stir in the late 1860s that their opponents believed them far more numerous than they were, even counting such sympathizers as George Eliot. Harrison's particular forte was making positivism seem like quintessential English common sense. That he could do so reflected both his skills as an advocate (like many English positivists he was a barrister) and the considerable measure of "give" Comte had built into his system, which was not as rigid as some critics, like JOHN STUART MILL, claimed. Even some advanced, liberal Anglican clergymen gave positivism a respectful hearing.

Harrison dwelt especially on Comte's allowance for the provisional or transitional state of affairs preparatory to the full advent of positivism, a period of indefinite duration when it was important that things should not be allowed to develop in any direction contrary to positivism—for example, socialism. The doctrine of the provisional could come very close to a defense of the status quo.

The views of Harrison, Beesly, and Bridges were quite near those of Laffitte on the matter of positivist strategy, but they differed sharply from Congreve's. Although Congreve had resigned his Anglican orders, he remained a priest, relishing the sacerdotal aspect of the religion of humanity and rejoicing in positivism's most authoritarian features. He pushed for the institutionalization of the religion of humanity against his more reluctant Oxford followers, who wished to avoid the stigma of sectarianism. They also did not want to diminish their influence by revealing their actual numbers.

In 1878 a split occurred, and until reunion in 1916 there were two London congregations, Chapel Street and Newton Hall, the former ritualistic, the latter more moderate. Both gained some followers and a few affiliated provincial congregations, notably at Leicester, Liverpool, and Newcastle. However the initial nucleus of the movement, even split, was of such social position and so close knit as to be almost a coterie—complacent and reluctant to seek converts actively. Full adherents numbered perhaps 200 in nine congregations at the movement's zenith. Working-class membership was proportionately even smaller than in France.

Yet the English positivists were probably more successful than their French brethren as a movement, barring the independent influence of Comte's writings, which were of course more widely read in his own country (though the English translations are excellent and clearer than the turgid originals).

The *Positivist Review* (1893–1927) was a creditable journal of opinion published by the Newton Hall group, which perhaps attracted the more distinguished adherents, such as S. H. Swinny, F. S. Marvin, and Patrick Geddes.

Without identifying itself with the broader ethical-rationalist movement (perhaps partly for social reasons, the latter being somewhat déclassé), positivism did attract some of the movement's adherents, notably F. J. Gould and Philip Thomas. GEORGE JACOB HOLYOAKE had an early interest in Comte, even before the British positivist movement was organized, but he never became actively involved. Positivism also maintained an intellectual presence at the universities, especially Oxford, and a number of *fin de siècle* liberal-radicals, including some future Fabians such as Graham Wallas, Sydney Olivier, and Sydney Ball imbibed its doctrines there with possibly lasting consequences. Although the English movement managed a fairly successful transition of leadership from the founding to the second generation after the deaths and retirements of the Wadham group, it did not recruit sufficiently to maintain a "critical mass." It died out in the early 1930s.

Offshoots of the English movement were the very marginal United States movement, confined largely to the irregular person of Henry Edger, an English emigrant and disciple of Congreve, and a rather larger Indian movement introduced through a group of positivists in the Indian civil service and briefly taken up by a few prominent Hindu intellectuals. Elsewhere (apart from Latin America) organized positivism was virtually nonexistent.

Bibliography

Chadwick, Owen. *The Secularization of the European Mind in the Nineteenth Century.* Cambridge: Cambridge U. Press, 1975.

Charlton, D. G. *Positivist Thought in France during the Second Empire.* Oxford: Clarendon Press, 1959.

———. *Secular Religions in France, 1815–1870.* Oxford: Oxford U. Press, 1963.

Comte, Auguste. *A General View of Positivism.* 1848. London: Reeves & Turner, 1880.

DeLubac, Henri. *The Drama of Atheist Humanism.* Cleveland: World Publishing, 1963.

Kent, Christopher. *Brains and Numbers.* Toronto: U. of Toronto Press, 1978.

McGee, John E. *A Crusade for Humanity.* London: Watts, 1931.

Marvin, Frederick S. *Comte: Founder of Sociology.* London: Chapman and Hall, 1936.

Mill, John Stuart. *Auguste Comte and Positivism.* 1865. Ann Arbor: U. of Michigan Press, 1961.

Royle, Edward. *Victorian Infidels.* Manchester: Manchester U. Press, 1974.

Simon, Walter M. *European Positivism in the Nineteenth Century.* Ithaca: Cornell U. Press, 1963.

CHRISTOPHER KENT

PRESS, FREEDOM OF THE. See **Freedom of the Press and Unbelief.**

PREVALENCE OF UNBELIEF. There are many beliefs with which one can disagree, even after restricting the area of interest to religious belief and unbelief. The first task in discussing the prevalence of unbelief is to restrict the range of topics to which *unbelief* will apply. This involves advancing a definition of religion, and if one is to talk about differences in the prevalence of unbelief in religion across place and time, the definition must be applicable to many periods and societies.

Despite many efforts to expand the range of phenomena deemed religious, the most common definitional approach in the sociology of religion is probably one based on supernaturally oriented beliefs and practices. Like any other definition, this approach has no exclusive claim on truth and offers analytical advantages and disadvantages, depending on the topic to be studied. A supernaturally oriented definition is particularly useful for studying unbelief, in that it allows for the existence and relatively easy identification of unbelief. We can immediately specify, in fact, that unbelief is present in individuals who do not subscribe to supernatural beliefs, for example, a transcendent god, the continuance of a soul after physiological death, miracles, and so forth. These individuals can be identified simply by asking them relatively straightforward questions about their beliefs.

Many broader definitions, on the other hand, are often based on the functions religion performs

TABLE 1: Belief Items by Country
(in percentages)

	Belief in God "No" or uncertain	Belief in active God "No" or uncertain	Belief in afterlife "No" or uncertain
Japan	56	75	82
Scandinavia	35	72	65
West Germany	28	64	67
France	28	63	61
United Kingdom	24	66	57
Benelux	22	52	52
Australia	20	58	52
Italy	12	44	54
Canada	11	51	46
United States	6	32	31
Mexico	6	30	67
Africa (sub-Sahara)	5	14	31
India	2	6	24

SOURCE: Gallup International Research Institutes, 1974 and 1976.

Questions:—1. "Do you believe in God or a universal spirit?"
  —2. "Do you believe that this god or universal spirit observes your actions and rewards or punishes you for them? (asked of those who answered "yes" to belief-in-God question)
  —3. "Do you believe in life after death?"

rather than its substance, and they may implicitly define practically every person as religious or make religiosity so subjective that an outside observer cannot determine the presence or absence of it. These latter definitions allow for the exploration of new or subtle forms of religious expression, but are weak as far as analyzing the prevalence of unbelief is concerned.

The major disadvantage of the supernaturally oriented definition is that some world religions do not focus on the supernatural. BUDDHISM, for example, is often cited as a religion whose official doctrine does not incorporate a transcendent being. It seems that there is no definition by which unbelievers can be identified that would also be applicable to all societies. One consideration that alleviates the contribution of this problem to measurement error is that many adherents of religions that are relatively free of supernatural doctrinal elements actually do believe in transcendent beings and phenomena, as Melford E. Spiro and Leonard Glick have each pointed out (see Bibliography below).

It is somewhat easier to specify the mainstream

beliefs of supernatural religion than to define religion in the first place. Buddhism notwithstanding, the most central belief in the overwhelming majority of religions is in a god or transcendent being. A god is generally perceived as being some combination of omnipotent, omniscient, and/or omnipresent, and as having created the world and its inhabitants. Beliefs about the current role of a god or gods in the affairs of the world may vary to a greater degree, and those who do not believe in godly intervention on earth must be viewed as less supernaturally oriented than "interventionists." The most important criterion of unbelief, then, will be unbelief in the existence of God. (See GOD, EXISTENCE OF.)

The other major belief (or lack thereof) to be treated here is in the continuance of the soul after the death of the body—life after death. The form of continuance varies widely among world religions. It may involve some sort of nonearthly abode (e.g., heaven or hell, the Elysian Fields, etc.) or a return to earth in human or nonhuman form. This belief is by no means necessitated by a belief in a god, but it does seem to make belief and adher-

TABLE 2: Unbelief Items over Time

	Unbelief in God	Unbelief in life after death
1944	3	23
1947	6	32
1953	2	—
1954	2	—
1957	—	26
1960	—	26
1967	2	—
1968	—	27
1973	—	31
1975	6	33
1976	—	28
1978	—	30
1980	—	27

For the wording of questions and for survey numbers, see Bibliography below: Hastings and Southwick (1975). Figures from 1973 to 1980 are based on the National Opinion Research Center's General Social Survey (Davis, 1980).

ence to a divine order more reasonable and salient. Uncertainty about life after death is perhaps easier for many individuals to face than uncertainty about the existence of a god. (See IMMORTALITY, UNBELIEF IN.)

With these preliminary matters out of the way, the actual question of prevalence can now be addressed. Prevalence will be treated here as varying over time, place, and sociodemographic characteristics, although there is relatively little quantitative, empirical information available on temporal variations in belief in divine beings and life after death.

Unbelief in God—United States. The question of belief in God is not especially popular with survey researchers. Neither of the two best, continuing sources of survey data on religion—the Gallup Polls and the General Social Surveys of the National Opinion Research Center (N.O.R.C)—include the question. The probable reason for the omission is that in the United States the question exhibits remarkably little variance over time, place, or any other factor. Using data from a number of different survey organizations (see Hastings and Southwick), whose differences in surveying procedures alone might be expected to lead to some variation in prevalence, nonbelief in God ranged from 2 percent to 6 percent over a period of 30 years—1944 to 1975. Such remarkable consistency

over time is rare in any survey question, as is the degree of consensus. We might therefore wonder if there are factors which inhibit the discovery of unbelief in these surveys.

Although the U.S. is undoubtedly a very religious nation as a whole, there are reasons to believe that most survey questions on belief in God underestimate the prevalence of unbelievers. First of all, there is a normative pressure in the U.S. against unbelief that might discourage its expression in a survey interview. More importantly, the phrasing of the unbelief-in-God question seems to make the expression of doubt difficult. The simple "yes–no" format results in the recording of unbelieving responses for only the most hardened of atheists.

Demerath and Levinson have shown that unbelief among their sample of college students rose dramatically (as many as 45 percent chose atheistic or agnostic responses) when asked to state their specific beliefs about God. Findings from other surveys bear this out. Only 51 percent of a San Francisco Bay area sample expressed definite belief in God when presented with a wide range of alternatives (see Wuthnow for a description of the study). Some of the high incidence of unbelief is probably attributable to the Bay area sample, but relatively high levels of unbelief or doubt in God's existence can also be found in at least one national sample.

The National Opinion Research Center's Ultimate Beliefs Survey, conducted in 1972, allowed for five levels of agreement with several propositions about the existence of God (see McCready and Greeley for a description of this survey and a questionnaire). Only 68 percent of the sample agreed strongly that "I believe in the existence of God as I define Him." An even smaller majority, 62 percent, disagreed strongly with the assertion "There may be a God and there may not be." The in-between responses included "agree somewhat," "can't decide," and "disagree somewhat," and because responses were scattered throughout these options it is difficult to say where belief ends and unbelief begins.

It is obvious from these surveys that the true level of unbelief in God in the United States is substantially higher than the 2 to 6 percent figures mentioned earlier. When more surveys begin to include extended-response categories and as questions and response phrasings become more standardized, the change in the prevalence of unbelief in God among Americans can begin to be measured accurately.

Unbelief in God Outside the U.S. Although some of the same measurement difficulties with respect to unbelief in the existence of God are also present in comparative data, there is strong evidence that the U.S. population ranks relatively low in that variety of unbelief. A study conducted by the Gallup International Research Institutes in 1974 and 1976 included information on belief in God for 14 countries or areas; this information is found in Table 1. The percentage for each country includes both those who said they did not "believe in God or a universal spirit," as well as those who were uncertain. The percentages range from a high of 56 percent unbelievers in Japan to an almost nonexistent 2 percent in India. The U.S. has the lowest percentage of unbelief among industrialized nations, and the figure here agrees with those cited earlier for the simple "yes–no" belief-in-God question.

Also in Table 1 are figures for the percentage of respondents in each country or area who did not think that their god "observes your actions and rewards or punishes you for them." These percentages are much higher. Only in India and Africa do they approach the low levels of unbelief in the existence of God. These data indicate that while in most cases a majority of the populations of these areas profess belief in God (at least when they have

only two answers to choose from), many do not feel that their god plays a very active role in their lives.

Data on other countries are quite scarce, either because they are not industrialized enough to support survey-research organizations or because their governments do not encourage dissemination of information about religion. There is one source of data on the religious profiles of many nations (see Mol), but for only a few of these is there information specifically about unbelief in God. In Australia, for example, Mol reports that 57 percent of males and 45 percent of females in a 1969 national survey were unwilling to agree that "I know that God really exists and I have no doubts about it." These respondents did agree to statements with varying degrees of doubt in them, as was the case in extended-category questions in the U.S.

The remainder of the God-related, unbelief data in the volume edited by Mol is from Communist countries. The general conclusion that one reaches from these reports is that unbelief in these nations is at quite high levels. In Hungary, for example, Varga (in Mol) estimates that about 57 percent of the citizens are atheists and 26 percent undecided in terms of their beliefs about God. In Yugoslavia, although in the 1953 census only 12.6 percent of the respondents called themselves atheists, smaller surveys show much higher levels of unbelief. Among students at one university in 1957, 52 percent were atheistic and 42 percent were indifferent to belief in God. In surveys of workers and teachers, roughly half of both groups considered themselves atheistic.

Some comparisons of surveys over time in Czechoslovakia indicate that unbelief has risen sharply since the onset of the Communist regime. In 1946 a national survey found 36 percent unbelievers in God, whereas in 1963 belief had eroded to the point that 66 percent of the respondents in a survey of only Moravia did not believe in God. This decline may be less marked in strongly Catholic countries such as Poland, but even there secularized schooling and governmental hostility to religion have chipped away at belief. Although from the preceding statistics it would be difficult to identify the exact level of unbelief in God in any country, it is apparent that the levels in most industrialized countries are higher than those in the U.S. and quite high in general throughout the Communist world.

Unbelief in Life After Death—U.S. Just as the concept of God means many different things to different individuals, there are many possible meanings of life after death. An individual could be thinking of anything from continuance of influence and of genes to joining God in the heavens. The percentage of unbelievers, as with the belief-in-God question, will therefore be likely to vary with where and how the question is asked.

In the United States, when respondents are simply asked whether or not they believe there is a life after death, more unbelief is evident than for the belief-in-God question. In Table 2 are the figures for the time period 1944–80. (For survey numbers and exact wording, see Hastings and Southwick.) From 23 to 33 percent of Americans said they either did not believe in life after death or did not know what they believed. There is no discernible trend over time, and variations between surveys could easily reflect differences in wording questions or different sampling practices.

One might wonder why Americans are much more likely to be skeptical about the existence of an afterlife than about God. God would seem a much more salient being to people's lives if he or she guaranteed eternal life. But it is probably easier to abandon belief in life after death and still remain within a religious tradition than unbelief in God.

More detailed and sensitive questions, as usual, reveal much unbelief among Americans. In a national study of church members done in the early 1960s (Glock and Stark), only 41 percent of moderate Protestants, 48 percent of Catholics, and 59 percent of conservative Protestants said they were "absolutely sure there is a life after death." Inclusion of nonchurchgoers would undoubtedly increase the level of unbelief for this question. In another national study (McCready and Greeley) only a third of the 61 percent of the sample who agreed that "Man survives after death" were "very sure" of their believing response.

Finally, in the San Francisco Bay survey, there is a wide range of beliefs about the afterlife. In that sample 16 percent did not believe, 19 percent were unsure, 37 percent agreed that "I believe there must be something beyond death, but I have no idea what it may be like," and 21 percent thought that there is a life after this one, either with or without punishment and rewards. As with the issue of unbelief in God, the prevalence of unbelief in life after death clearly is dependent on the context and method of inquiry. It is also clear that at least a substantial minority—and perhaps even half—of the American population has at least strong doubts about the existence of life after death. This fact,

while generally unacknowledged in discussions of American religion, probably has major consequences for the behavior and world views of the unbelieving individuals.

Unbelief in Life After Death—Other Countries. We might expect the level of unbelief in an afterlife to be quite high in most industrialized nations, given their relatively high degree of unbelief in God. That is indeed the case, according to the previously mentioned Gallup study done between 1974 and 1976. In Table 1 are the figures for each country or area. The highest levels of definite unbelief are found in Western Europe, in Germany, France, Scandinavia, and the Benelux nations.

Uncertainty about the issue is quite high in many countries, reaching the remarkable level of 82 percent in Japan. Perhaps it is easier to remain undecided on this issue than on belief in God, just as it seems easier to disbelieve. As with the question of God's existence, the countries or areas with the lowest levels of unbelief in an afterlife are India, the U.S., and Africa. In many countries, respondents were almost twice as likely to express unbelief in life after death than in God. Although most religions offer the existence of God and eternal life as something of a packaged combination, it is obvious that the adherents of these religions may be quite selective in the doctrines they accept.

Demographic Factors and Unbelief. The prevalence of unbelief varies not only by country and time but also by the demographic characteristics of individuals within them. Data on the influence of these factors on unbelief is quite spotty and generally restricted to the population of the United States. In the following sections I will discuss demographic variations in unbelief in both God and an afterlife.

Sex Differences in Unbelief. The evidence on sex differences for all sorts of religious behavior points overwhelmingly toward greater religiousness on the part of females. (See Argyle and Beit-Hallahmi for a review of the sex-differences literature.) Information on actual differences in belief, however, is hard to come by. Two Gallup Polls—in 1960 and 1968—treat sex differences in belief in life after death and in God, respectively. In 1960, 22 percent of American females did not believe in an afterlife, while 32 percent of males were unbelievers. In 1968, when American adults were asked about belief in God, a much smaller difference—2 percent unbelief for women and 4 percent for men—was discovered. The latter question, however, was of the "yes–no" format which, as was argued earlier, tends to inhibit the expression of doubt or disbelief.

In a more recent 1972 survey, the N.O.R.C. Ultimate Beliefs study, where degrees of unbelief could be expressed, larger male-female differences in belief in God were found. To the statement, "I believe in the existence of God as I define Him," 36 percent of males did not "agree strongly" (they answered either "agree somewhat," "can't decide," "disagree somewhat," or "disagree strongly"), while 27 percent of women fell into those relatively unbelieving categories. In that same survey, women were 6 percent less likely—33 percent against 39 percent for men—to agree that "Man survives after death." It is likely that greater sex differences in afterlife beliefs would be discovered with more detailed response categories.

Racial Differences in Unbelief. The pattern of findings for the United States on racial differences in unbelief suggests that blacks and other nonwhites are generally more religious than whites (see Glenn and Gotard for an overview of these findings). Nonwhites, for example, were 14 percent more likely than whites to say that their religious beliefs were very important to them. Although information on racial differences in unbelief is probably available from the Gallup surveys cited above, I know of no published figures from them. I will therefore report only figures from the 1972 N.O.R.C. study.

Blacks are about 5 percent more likely to agree strongly when read a statement supporting the existence of God. About 27 percent of them put themselves into the relatively unbelieving categories, while 32 percent of whites are skeptical. The race difference for unbelief in an afterlife is three times that large, however: 15 percent fewer blacks (34 percent versus 49 percent) did not believe that man survives after death. The larger racial difference for afterlife belief follows the pattern established by sex differences; there are larger differentials for demographic variables when there is more overall disagreement on a question. This pattern also holds for age-related differences.

Age Differences in Unbelief. The great majority of age-related studies of religiosity have two undesirable characteristics for present purposes: (1) they involve measures of religious participation rather than belief; and (2) they are cross-sectional, so that it is impossible to determine whether the differences in religiosity between age groups related to aging, to being born at a certain time, or to

living in a particular period. Most cross-sectional studies of adults (see Argyle and Beit-Hallahmi) have revealed that religious activity decreases between the ages of 18 and 30, and remains generally stable thereafter. Religious belief, however, shows a general pattern of stability throughout the life cycle. Longitudinal studies of belief show either no change or period effects for the 18–30 range, and some increases in belief after age 30.

All that I will attempt to show here is that young people are more likely to be unbelievers than old, and leave the reader with the idea that there are several possible explanations of this fact. The 1972 N.O.R.C. data allow a direct look at the relationship between age and both unbelief in God and life after death. The trend is quite clear and shows that both types of unbelief decrease with age: 39 percent of the respondents age 18-30 had doubts about the existence of God; this percentage fell to 33 percent for the 31-45 group, 27 percent for those 46 to 60, and 23 percent for those over 60. For unbelief in an afterlife, the corresponding percentages are 42, 37, 33, and 28 percent. This pattern is in general agreement with other findings on the age-unbelief relationship; the reason for it, however, has yet to be clearly determined.

In summary: Although a study of the prevalence of unbelief leaves questions of definition, evidence, and the nature of change in prevalence over time, there are some clear findings that can be advanced. First of all, there are sizable differences in the prevalence of unbelief depending on the subject of the unbelief; most simply, people are more likely to disagree that there is a life after death than that God exists. Secondly, most statistics on the prevalence of unbelief seem to underestimate the true level, especially for unbelief in God. When relatively detailed questions on religious belief are used in survey research, they yield higher levels of unbelief.

Looking at unbelief across different contemporary societies, the United States appears to be among the lowest nations of the world in prevalence of unbelief—or at least of those that do much survey research. European nations have generally higher levels of unbelief, and Communist ones are among the highest of those where unbelief is measured systematically.

Finally, when differences in unbelief by demographic variables are analyzed, males, whites, and the young emerge as having relatively higher levels of unbelief. Although more exact determination of the prevalence of unbelief would require a greater commitment to the study of religious behavior among survey researchers, the preceding findings are well-established in the relevant literature and in empirical data analyzed for this article.

Other article of interest: **Geography of Unbelief, The.**

Bibliography

Argyle, Michael, and Benjamin Beit-Hallahmi. *The Social Psychology of Religion.* London: Routledge and Kegan Paul, 1975.

Davis, James A. "A National Data Program for the Social Sciences—General Social Surveys, 1972–1980." Chicago: National Opinion Research Center, 1980.

Demerath, N. J., and Richard Levinson. "Baiting the Dissident Hook: Some Effects of Bias in Religious Belief." *Sociometry* 34 (1971).

Gallup, George. *International Public Opinion Yearbook.* Wilmington, Del.: Scholarly Resources, Inc. 1979.

Glenn, Norval, and Erin Gotard. "The Religion of Blacks in the United States: Some Recent Trends and Current Characteristics." *American Journal of Sociology* 83 (1977).

Glick, Leonard. "The Anthropology of Religion: Malinowski and Beyond." *Beyond the Classics.* Charles Y. Glock and Philip Hammond, eds. New York: Harper & Row, 1973.

Glock, Charles Y., and Rodney Stark. *Christian Beliefs and Anti-Semitism.* New York: Harper & Row, 1966.

Hastings, Philip K., and Jessie Southwick. *Survey Data for Trend Analysis.* Williamstown, Mass.: Roper Public Opinion Research Center, 1975.

McCready, William, and Andrew Greeley. *The Ultimate Values of the American Population.* Beverly Hills, Calif.: Sage Publications, 1976.

Mol, Hans, ed. *Western Religion.* The Hague: Mouton, 1972.

Spiro, Melford E. "Religion: Problems of Definition and Explanation." *Anthropological Approaches to the Study of Religion.* M. Banton, ed. London: Tavistock, 1966.

Wuthnow, Robert. *The Consciousness Reformation.* Berkeley and Los Angeles: U. of California Press, 1976.

THOMAS H. DAVENPORT

PROPAGANDA, ANTIRELIGIOUS. This occurs primarily in settings where ATHEISM has a central political role. Although one may think of some types of antireligious propaganda emanating from one religious group in opposition to another, such interreligious propaganda is so varied as to have little general cogency as a topic and is often more a matter of historically determined cultural and class strife than of conflict over religion itself.

Clearcut programs of opposition to religion in general are, however, not infrequent in modern European history, and the thought of the Enlightenment period (see ENLIGHTENMENT, UNBELIEF DURING THE) gave a special impetus to movements supporting such programs. More recently, antireligious propaganda has become politically important in Communist nations, where it is the official policy of the state. It is in these nations, and particularly in the Soviet Union, that antireligious propaganda has been most highly developed in both theory and practice (see RUSSIA AND THE SOVIET UNION, UNBELIEF IN).

Although not widespread in present-day Western Europe, antireligious propaganda was a significant preoccupation of several groups of continental European socialists and rationalists (see AUGUSTE COMTE, DENIS DIDEROT, ENCYCLOPÉDIE, LUDWIG FEUERBACH, KARL MARX, RATIONALISM, and VOLTAIRE). The United Kingdom has also had a variety of movements that engaged in some form of antireligious propaganda (see ANNIE BESANT, CHARLES BRADLAUGH. NATIONAL REFORMER, NATIONAL SECULAR SOCIETY, and UNITED KINGDOM, UNBELIEF IN). While the environment has not been as conducive to antireligious movements in the United States as it has been in Europe, several American groups have put out agitational literature and engaged in other propaganda activities in their struggles against religion (see UNITED STATES, UNBELIEF IN).

The American Scene. One very active group in the U.S. was the American Association for the Advancement of Atheism. The "Four A's movement," as it was frequently called, was incorporated—after a court battle centering on the wording of its charter—in late 1926, and the organization remained active through 1933. The association's original charter described its task as "purely destructive." "Specializing as it does in mental reconstruction, the society shall contribute to the building of a better civilization by operating as a wrecking company, leaving to others the designing and establishing of the new order."

Although there was dissent, the association refrained from advocating any political platform or economic code. Instead, it concentrated upon challenging the validity of biblical interpretations of creation, of evangelistic claims about faith healing, of the efficacy of religion in deterring crime, and similar matters. The association's leader was arrested several times for violating a New York ordinance requiring that public religious meetings have a permit, though city officials eventually backed down on enforcement.

The association attempted to organize chapters at colleges and universities, and felt its special role was to remove religious influence from the activities of scientists and statesmen. With the support of the Washington Secular League, the Four A's unsuccessfully sued the U.S. government for the removal of chaplains in Congress and the military services from federal payrolls and employment, and the association also wanted to eliminate the motto, "In God We Trust," from coins. Having failed to obtain a broadcasting license for a radio station in 1928, the association continued to leaflet evangelistic services and to hold public meetings in support of atheism and against religion, the clergy, and the churches.

The association's president, CHARLES LEE SMITH, was active in issuing public statements discrediting various religious figures and challenging them to debates over the truthfulness of religion and the claims made in the name of religion. A writer for the TRUTH SEEKER, Smith was sometimes joined in his public statements by James I. Elliott, who was both the chairman of the association's board of directors and the president of the Anti-Bible Society.

As the Great Depression spread over America, the association, in a convention held in February 1931, urged President Herbert Hoover to proclaim a "Blame-Giving Day" instead of Thanksgiving, at which time people who were suffering from massive drought and unemployment could publicly express their grievances about "their lack of favors from Providence." At the same convention, the Four A's condemned the pope's stand on birth control, the system of tax exemptions for church property, and the removal of books on evolution from some libraries. Smith charged at the convention that the Catholic church had taken over the Democratic party, and he decried religious influence in politics. Finally, the association resolved to develop an outdoor campaign to teach the tenets of atheism. Ultimately, the Four A's died a natural death.

The Communist World. Although there are some antireligious propaganda activities in the U.S. and Europe, the issue is now of significance primarily in Communist nations. All of the European Communist nations, as well as China, Cuba, and other Marxist regimes, have established programs of antireligious propaganda, all of which more or less parallel the practice of the Soviet Union. Variations from nation to nation depend upon the following factors: (1) the relative strength of religious groups in the countries (for example, Poland's powerful Roman Catholic church is a much more formidable force than, say, the disunited religious groups of Czechoslovakia); (2) the type of religion that predominates (for example, a different approach is needed for attacking ancestor worship in China as against Islam in Soviet Central Asia or Lutheranism in East Germany); and (3) the strength of political and ideological commitment to an all-out struggle against religion (for example, it is exceedingly great in Albania but relatively weak in Yugoslavia).

While Albania probably has the world's most virulent antireligious policies at present, its antireligious propaganda is hardly subtle. The major theoretical underpinnings for sophisticated antireligious propaganda are found in prerevolutionary and postrevolutionary Russian Marxist ideology, and, with the longest history of any state atheist program, the activity itself is most highly developed in the U.S.S.R. Therefore, the remainder of this discussion will be based upon the Soviet case.

A Range of Approaches. Propaganda, as usually conceived in Western social-science literature, includes what theorists in the Soviet tradition have earlier considered as two types of organized influence upon people's attitudes, that is, propaganda per se and agitation. The distinction between these two types was made in the writings of a turn-of-the-century Russian Marxist, Georgi Plekhanov. For Plekhanov and the Leninists, who accepted his ideas in this area, agitation was a matter of presenting a few ideas simply and directly to many people at once, with the goal of arousing them to action. Conversely, propaganda was more complex and was aimed at one or a few individuals. It, too, was seen as a way to motivate action, but it was to provide a much more complete picture of the problem situation, and it was to involve many ideas coming together in the explanation. With the Soviet population having attained levels of literacy and education far higher than Russians of the early 20th century, the distinction between agitation and propaganda has become less central, and both together seem to be included under such rubrics as "political information," "political education," or "indoctrination."

Plekhanov viewed religion essentially as cognitive errors or "bad science." Hence, from his perspective, religion was to be attacked by means of the popularization of natural science, which allegedly contradicted religious notions. V. I. LENIN saw religion as the tool of the exploiting classes, and, taking a voluntaristic approach to overcoming religion, he saw the revolutionary task as including militant antireligious propaganda that discredited both the church as an institution (including the clergy) and religion as an idea. Also, more in the voluntaristic mold were the "God Builders," who argued early in this century for the development of a new religion that would replace contemporary forms. The new religion would be in awe of humankind's great potential and ultimate perfection in the utopian future. Although their theories were rejected by the Bolshevik party well before the Revolution of 1917, the tendency to make a religion out of socialism and Communist development has been manifested in various ways in the U.S.S.R. most clearly during the last two decades in the attempt to create and encourage "new socialist traditions" and atheist rites and ceremonies that exalt the promethean goals of communism.

Atheist Upbringing. While Lenin's militant stance is closest to what Westerners usually think of as antireligious propaganda, current Soviet thinking stresses a judicious mix of all the approaches just outlined in such a way as to create an environment that eliminates, or at least limits, religious influences in the lives of citizens. The overall task is called "atheist upbringing," and much of the research and writing within the field of "scientific atheism" is devoted to improving the means of atheist upbringing.

Atheist upbringing is the general program for socialization into atheism. It is part of the overall process of character transformation aimed at creating the "new Soviet person." When the transformation is finally completed, the result is to be "the new Communist person," a species fundamentally different from current human types in motivation and moral level. The program of the Communist party of the Soviet Union includes the "Moral Code of the Builder of Communism." This code indicates that the ideal new Soviet person should be collectivistic, disciplined, a lover of work, patriotic, a proletarian internationalist, and an atheist.

As a program of character education, atheist upbringing has ramifications in all parts of Soviet society. Reflecting the emphasis highlighted by Plekhanov, Lenin, and the God Builders, respectively, three major forms of antireligious propaganda make up atheist upbringing: (1) atheist propaganda, (2) antireligious propaganda per se, and (3) secular rites. Since all three are forms of organized mass persuasion aimed at the overcoming of religion, logically they may be considered together as varieties of antireligious propaganda.

Mass Media. Atheist and antireligious propaganda through the mass media is coordinated by a public organization called the Knowledge (*Znanie*) Society. Taking over the tasks of the former League of Militant Atheists, the Knowledge Society has, since its creation in 1947, broadened its scope to promote scientific and philosophical-ideological propaganda in all areas. Central to its role is the organizing of a vast number of public lectures on atheist and antireligious topics and the publication of many books and pamphlets consistent with its goals. Besides its popular-scientific journal, *Science and Life,* the society also publishes two major, popular antireligious and atheist journals, *Science and Religion* and *Man and the World,* in Ukrainian. Much scientific research of a sociological, psychological, ethnographic, or philosophical nature appears in *Znanie* pamphlets or books soon after it is formally reported in publications of the Academy of Science or various universities. There seems to be a constant difficulty in motivating members of the intelligentsia other than professional atheists to participate in the society's activities. (See YAROSLAVSKI, E. M.)

In addition to books, pamphlets, magazines, and journals devoted to atheist topics, antireligious and atheist propaganda appears in general-circulation newspapers and magazines, on television and radio, and on posters and other public displays. Most schools and factories have areas where propaganda is placed on bulletin boards. Atheism and antireligion is also a theme found in film and other art.

Education. Another major forum for atheist and antireligious propaganda is the schools. Formal education is especially important as a place at which the patterns of religious socialization centered in the family may be disrupted and counteracted. The approved curricula of the natural sciences, social sciences, and the humanities all include points at which atheist themes are to be emphasized. On the higher levels, required classes in the fundamentals of scientific atheism serve to propagandize antireligious and atheist ideas. In addition, many primary and secondary schools have atheist clubs, which attempt to stimulate enthusiasm about scientific atheistic activities among the pupils. Special activities of the Young Pioneers (similar to Scouts but with virtually all schoolchildren having membership) may center on antireligious or atheist themes. In higher education, the Young Communist League (*Komsomol*) is charged with antireligious functions. Both the Pioneers and the Komsomols may engage in personalized efforts to persuade religious classmates or classmates' parents (or other relatives) of the validity of the atheistic worldview. Teachers are charged with guiding students and stimulating their interest in such activities.

Also serving an educational purpose are the many museums of atheism, which are organized under the aegis of local, regional, and national authorities. The most important is the Museum of the History of Religion and Atheism in Leningrad, which has ties to the Soviet Academy of Sciences and the party's Academy of Social Sciences. This museum is housed in the former Kazan Cathedral, and the nearby St. Isaac's Cathedral has also been transformed into a museum, but one showing 19th-century religious art and architecture. Many of the churches in the Soviet Union have been similarly converted into museums of either atheism or of art and architecture.

Work and Leisure. Factories, offices, and other work sites are also supposed to fulfill atheist functions. Especially important in organizing activities are the cadres of Komsomol or the party. Activists, who find guidelines in the periodical *Agitator,* may help to establish atheist clubs or discussion groups at the workplace, and they may also organize "individual work" with believers. The latter is essentially intensive propaganda on a personal, one-to-one basis so as to convince believers of the falseness of religion and the validity of an atheistic worldview. Of particular significance is the attempt to keep believing adults from teaching their children religious beliefs, practices, and values.

All of the aspects of atheist upbringing are seen as means of character formation. Consistent with a strain of asceticism present in Russian Marxism, even leisure is supposed to be utilized for one or another form of self-improvement. Thus, atheistic activities are options for leisure. Attendance at atheist lectures, participation in atheist clubs, and excursions to museums, as well as study of atheist literature and art, can all be seen as the proper use of leisure. In addition, night classes in scientific atheistic topics are available in most cities in the Soviet Union.

Secular Rites. The final major aspect of the program of atheist upbringing is the series of secular rites and holidays that are now being vigorously promoted in the U.S.S.R. Some of these are made to displace religious rites directly, as, for example, the rite of the newborn, the secular wedding—which may now be carried out in solemn ritual in "palaces of weddings" in the cities—and the socialist funeral. In some areas, an elaborate set of socialist rites of passage has been instituted to commemorate all major stages in the life cycle from birth to death. Other than birth, marriage, and death, the most significant rites are those celebrating the first day of primary school, the receipt of the internal passport at age 16, the beginning of the first job, and the completion of major stages of education.

Expanding upon the individual secular rites are the collective holidays. Major occupations all enjoy one day of special honor each year, and the major events of Soviet and Marxist history are also remembered with greater or lesser vigor. Most important are the celebrations of the anniversary of the Revolution of 1917, Lenin's birthday, the First of May, International Women's Day, Constitution Day, and the like.

In summary: Antireligious propaganda can be built upon the disenfranchisement of religious groups and the persecution of believers. Where this occurs, mass persuasion is displaced by coercion and violence. Adoption of the persecutorial approach is probably strongly linked to cultural resistance against political change—as when the church becomes a bastion of counterrevolutionary sentiment and activities—and to deep-seated cultural ambiguity vis-à-vis the conflict of religion and atheism. The latter may lead to contradictory application of antireligious policies. Although it is unfortunately the case that the U.S.S.R., Albania, and some other communist nations have moved in the persecutorial direction, there appears to be no *necessary* link between antireligious propaganda and coercion or violence against religion. Just as some (but not all) religions seem to live in peace with nonbelievers while at the same time promoting religious propaganda through varied forms of "witness," similarly unbelief or atheism is capable of antireligious propaganda without coercion or violence.

Even if clearly violent or coercive persecution is avoided, proponents of antireligious propaganda —and indeed of religious propaganda as well—are increasingly open to the charge of influencing people in an undue manner. Sophisticated psychological and sociological knowledge about mass persuasion have provided new tools for more subtle and devious forms of persuasion. The limitations of a "just" program of propaganda are not self-evident.

One of the greatest points of struggle between state atheism and religion—or religious "vestiges" (psychological and institutional traces allegedly left over from the capitalist or precapitalist past)— is the sphere of morality. Viewing morality as relative to the stage of socioeconomic development, Marxists and Communists have argued that, with the establishment of a socialist order, a new morality comes to govern relations between people. Although many of its propositions may be similar to religious propositions, the Communists argue that its essence differs from religious morality because it emerges from fundamentally different sources. Hence, part of the antireligious task is to discredit religious claims that morality is rooted in religion.

The success of antireligious propaganda in atheist nations is extremely difficult to gauge. Since all of these nations are involved in rapid change in their social and economic structures, many causes of the reduction of religious activities and sentiments can clearly be located in the general processes of secularization, apart from antireligious propaganda. Furthermore, although antireligious efforts may appear to be similar, there seems to be a great deal of variation from country to country in outcome, depending upon the strength of the indigenous religious institutions and traditions. Even the apparently most secularized societies of this group—the U.S.S.R., Czechoslovakia, and East Germany, for example—have levels of religious participation comparable to other highly secularized European societies like Sweden or France. On the other hand, in the case of a society like the Soviet Union, which was largely agrarian and nonindustrialized at the beginning of this century, it would seem that the antireligious pressure of the Soviet period has pushed it along the path of secularization at a rate faster than otherwise would have occurred.

Although this century has witnessed a considerable amount of secularization everywhere, there seems no assurance that the process is one-directional or inevitable. While antireligious propaganda has a role in affecting religious beliefs and activities, the amount of effort and energy invested in it seems to be directly related to the degree of threat perceived to inhere in religion. Thus, antireligious propaganda is part of a complex equation of social forces influencing religion and unbelief during a period of secularization.

Bibliography

Bociurkiw, Bohdan R., and John W. Strong, eds. *Religion and Atheism in the USSR and Eastern Europe.* Toronto: U. of Toronto Press, 1975.

DeGeorge, Richard T. *Soviet Ethics and Morality.* Ann Arbor: U. of Michigan Press,1969.

Inkeles, Alex. *Public Opinion in Soviet Russia: A Study in Mass Persuasion.* Cambridge, Mass.: Harvard U. Press, 1967.

Lane, Christel. *The Rites of Rulers: Ritual in Industrial Society—The Soviet Case.* New York: Cambridge U. Press, 1981.

Mol, Hans, ed. *Western Religion: A Country by Country Sociological Inquiry.* The Hague: Mouton, 1972.

Powell, David E. *Antireligious Propaganda in the Soviet Union.* Cambridge: MIT Press, 1975.

JERRY G. PANKHURST

PROTESTANTISM. See **Christianity, Unbelief Within. Church, State, and Religious Freedom.**

PUBLISHERS OF UNBELIEF. See **Appendix 4.**

PUSHKIN, ALEXANDER (1799–1837), Russian author. See **Russian Literature, Unbelief in.**

PUTNAM, SAMUEL PORTER (1838–1896), American FREETHOUGHT lecturer and author. Putnam was born in Chichester, N.H., where his father was a Congregational minister. Samuel worked his way through Pembroke Academy and entered Dartmouth College in 1858. In 1861 he enlisted in the army. After two years of duty in Virginia, he was promoted to captain and served in Alabama, Texas, Mississippi, and Louisiana during the Civil War. In 1865 he decided to become a minister, entering the Chicago Theological Seminary to prepare himself for that occupation. He graduated after three years, was ordained, and preached in downstate Illinois for several years.

In 1871 Putnam decided that he could no longer subscribe to the orthodox creeds that he was preaching. He joined the Unitarian church and found that he was able to successfully reconcile his feelings with that denominational label until 1877. During that time, he preached in Ohio, Nebraska, Indiana, and Massachusetts. When Putnam thought that he could no longer support Unitarian doctrines either, he left the ministry entirely, taking a job in the Customs House in New York City. He became a materialist and freethinker at about this time, a philosophical outlook he maintained for the rest of his life.

Career in Freethought. Putnam began contributing articles to the various freethought journals, gradually becoming better known in the freethought movement. He was soon asked to run for office and was elected secretary of the American Secular Union in 1884. When in 1887 he was elected president of that union, he quit his customs job to devote full attention to the freethought movement.

In 1888 Putnam moved to San Francisco with George E. Macdonald, the brother of the man who was then editor of the TRUTH SEEKER, in order to found a new magazine called *Freethought*. While Macdonald ran the magazine most of the time, Putnam covered thousands of miles throughout the U.S. and Canada, delivering hundreds of lectures and organizing dozens of freethought groups. He estimated that he traveled more than 100,000 miles in the cause of freethought from 1887 until 1894.

The extensive notes Putnam took during his journeys provided a series of articles for *Freethought*, and later formed the basis for his huge book, *400 Years of Freethought*. The details of freethought organization that appear in that book are unique and firsthand.

After *Freethought* ceased publication in 1891, Putnam was elected president of the Freethought Federation of America (1892), whose aim was legislation for the separation of church and state.

One of the federation's accomplishments was to keep the World's Fair in Chicago (1893) open on Sunday. This was a difficult task, as the policy at that time was for all public "amusements" to be closed on Sunday. Putnam was also instrumental in organizing the International Congress of Freethinkers.

Putnam's other writings consist of several pamphlets, a novel (*Gottlieb: His Life*), poetry (*Waifs and Wanderings*), a partial, philosophical autobiography (*My Religious Experience*), as well as a large number of articles for the freethought press.

Putnam's death caused more of an outcry than anything he had been able to produce in freethought circles during his lifetime. That was due to the mysterious circumstances and hint of scandal that surrounded his death. On the night of Dec. 11, 1896, Putnam and a young freethought lecturer, May Collins, went to Boston. Putnam obtained a room for Miss Collins in the home of Josephine Tilton. He and Miss Collins went out to dinner and returned at about 8:00 P.M. They had been drinking to some extent, but the exact amount was unknown. Several other roomers in the house noted that the gas light in Miss Collins' room was on all night and some even noted a smell of gas. Because no sound was coming from her room and because the light was on, they assumed that all was well. In the morning, the smell of gas was more distinct, so the door to Miss Collins' room was forced. Both Miss Collins and Putnam were discovered on the floor, fully clothed but quite dead, evidently overcome by leaking gas.

While there was no evidence of any impropriety having occurred between Miss Collins and Putnam, it was brought out later in the freethought press that both had privately expressed sentiments in favor of "free love," and it became known that Putnam was a divorced man with two children, a fact he would not reveal publicly. A number of Putnam's enemies in the freethought movement had a field day with the circumstances of his death.

Putnam's contribution to unbelief lies in his organizing ability and his chronicling of the movement. Of his many publications issued separately, only *400 Years of Freethought* remains of significance; it is essential for understanding the history of organized unbelief.

Bibliography

Green, H. L., et al. *Free Thought Magazine* (Chicago) 15 (Jan. 1897). Obituary notices and articles about Putnam's death.

Putnam, S. P. "Samuel P. Putnam." *Freethinkers' Magazine* (Buffalo) 12 (Feb. 1894). Short autobiography.

———. *400 Years of Freethought.* New York: Truth Seeker Co., 1894.

———. *My Religious Experience.* New York: Truth Seeker Co., 1891.

GORDON STEIN

R

RAND, AYN (1905–1982), American writer. See **American Literature, Unbelief in.**

RATIONALISM. Etymologically derived from the Latin word for reason, the word *rationalism* has been used to refer to three logically independent movements of thought, each of which attaches some sort of preeminent place to reason as a basis for genuine knowledge. The three movements can be understood best if we consider three opposites of REASON.

First, we might oppose reason, which is characteristically concerned with inference and justification, with authority, as when certain opinions are put forward for acceptance simply because of the alleged standing of their alleged source. Second, we might oppose reason, our justification-seeking and critical faculty, with faith, superstition, and mysticism, which lead to the entrenchment of opinions in the absence of supporting evidence or argument, and even in the presence of weighty, indeed overwhelming, evidence to the contrary. Third, we might oppose reason, which is concerned with intellectual processing of data in accordance with sound principles of classification and inference, with sensory experience, which is concerned with the gathering of data about the external world through the five senses of sight, hearing, touch, taste, and smell, as well as through introspection, which gathers data concerning the content of consciousness.

Rationalism in the first sense is an intra-theological movement that plays up the human capacity to draw inferences in a way which, its supporters contend, leads ultimately and unequivocally to the deduction of the existence of God and to the demonstration of certain truths about God's nature and attributes. It plays down the importance of revelation as an authoritative and therefore accurate and compelling basis for belief in God. (Its extreme opposite within contemporary religious movements would be irrationalist fundamentalism.) This rationalist movement within theology was particularly significant among German theologians in the late 18th and early 19th centuries.

Although there is still a lively debate within theology as to the relative importance of reason as an actual or potential source of knowledge and comprehension of God, on the one hand, and authority (such as the authority of what is taken to be the revealed word of God) on the other, it is rare today for the proreason positions within theology to be described as forms of rationalism. The reason is simply the danger of confusion with the other two rationalist movements, for which the term has gained far wider currency.

Rationalism in the second sense is the name taken for a position adopted by many opponents of traditional religion in the late 19th and early 20th centuries. Like many who today would call themselves humanists, they held that all beliefs should be subjected to critical examination by exactly the same standards. In particular, they rejected the view that there were certain beliefs which it was improper, or even wicked, to put to the test. Rationalists in this sense objected strongly to the willingness of many religious apologists to accept certain doctrines (miracles, resurrection, life after death, and the efficacy of prayer) on the basis of levels of evidence far lower than would be demanded in other, nonreligious domains. They also observed that many people used these lower levels of evidence to support their preferred religion but not the often incompatible religions of others.

According to rationalists, the degree of attachment one should have to a belief should be proportional to the weight of the argument or evidence in its support. If the evidence and argument either way is feeble or if the support for the opposing positions is in balance, then one should adopt an agnostic attitude and refuse to either affirm or deny the belief. In respect to traditional religions, such as Christianity, some rationalists have adopted an agnostic attitude, while others, believing that the case against it is far more powerful than the case for it, embrace ATHEISM.

Rationalists in this sense have extended their thinking to the practical, as well as the theoretical, domain. In particular, they have followed the Socratic precept that the unexamined life is not worth living. This means not accepting automatically the established values of the culture to which one is heir. The values one adopts, the moral standards by which one lives and which one commends to others should be rationally justified. Rationalists have typically, but certainly not invariably, adopted some type of utilitarianism according to which practices are to be judged good or bad in terms of their likely consequences, and the consequences judged good or bad depending on the extent to which they contribute to the meeting of human needs (as opposed to alleged divine preferences) or the raising of general levels of well-being and happiness.

Critics of rationalism in this sense have charged that rationalists have a dogmatic faith in the validity and relevance of reason, which is surely just as objectionable as the blind faith and uncritical devotion to which they take exception in their religious opponents. The charge may be framed in the style of a dilemma. How would the rationalist answer the question "Why be rational?" Either he would give a reason for being rational, or he would not give a reason for being rational. But if the first option is taken, and a reason offered, the defense of the rational approach is circular (giving a reason in defense of the policy of having reasons for everything) and therefore irrational. If the second option is taken, and no reason, or something other than a reason, is appealed to, then the rationalist is conceding that there is something more fundamental than reason that can serve as the basis for one's belief-selection policy.

The best response the rationalist can make is to avoid the dilemma by clarifying his position. The 18th-century Scottish philosopher DAVID HUME observed that, in all spheres, reason not only is, but ought to be, "the slave of the passions." This is fairly obvious in the practical sphere, where one gives a reason for one's conduct when one demonstrates how the conduct in question furthers or brings nearer to fulfillment some desire, short-term or long-term, that one has. The same is true,

although less obviously so, in what has traditionally been called the theoretical sphere, the sphere concerned with a belief and knowledge. To give a reason for a belief is to point to something that enhances the probable truth of that belief. To put it generally and abstractly: something P is (to some extent, or to some degree) a reason for some belief Q, only if the probability of Q's being true, given P, is greater than it would have been had it not been the case that P.

What has this to do with "passion"? Unless one has a desire for—or in Hume's term—passion for the truth, there is no point in being rational about one's beliefs. Only a person who is concerned to hold only true beliefs will bother with reasons, for these are, by definition, pointers to the truth. Something earns its status as a reason precisely from this connection.

To dismiss or downgrade the policy of being rational in one's believing is to express contempt for truth, for it is to say that one prefers, in some cases at any rate, to give greater weight to factors other than probable connectedness with truth as the standard for what is worthy of belief. If the rationalist's opponent does not profess a passion for truth as the ultimate desire that shapes his or her beliefs, then the rationalist cannot rationally argue with that person, for argument only makes sense when there is a common desire for truth.

In sum, the rationalist meets the challenge posed by the dilemma by pointing to the conceptual connection between rationality in belief and truth. If the opponent wishes to assign a higher place to something other than truth in judging whether or not a belief is worthy of acceptance, he has placed himself necessarily in a position where it is impossible to prove that his policy is wrong. For there can be no argument with those who have, in any sphere and to any degree, the contempt for truth that is shown in making it subservient to any other standard as the basis for belief acquisition and retention.

Rationalism in the third sense is a philosophical movement that developed in the 17th century on the Continent (and is therefore commonly called continental rationalism). It is particularly associated with the French philosopher RENÉ DESCARTES, the Dutch philosopher BENEDICT SPINOZA, and the German philosopher Gottfried Leibniz. Unlike rationalists in our second sense, thinkers belonging to this tradition have generally believed in the existence of God and maintained that this belief is demonstrably true, but it is not this which is their distinguishing mark.

Rather, it is their conviction that reason is not merely a pointer or arbiter in relation to truth but is itself a positive source of substantial and important truths that cannot be derived from experience through the senses. Its antithesis as a movement is empiricism, often called British empiricism, a historically parallel development centered on the English philosopher JOHN LOCKE, the Irish philosopher George Berkeley, and Hume. Unlike rationalism, empiricism in some form or other has survived to the present. Unlike its first two architects, contemporary empiricists tend to be skeptical about religion.

For empiricists, sensory experience is the ultimate test of truth. For rationalists however, experience is only a legitimate test of truth if it can be validated by reason, here thought of as a faculty of innate ideas of certain application, eternally and necessarily true principles capable of a priori utilization in the construction of new systems of knowledge. Some rationalists held that rational principles permeated the physical world so that, according to the "principle of sufficient reason" of Leibniz, if something is so which could have been otherwise, then there must be some reason why it is so, and not otherwise.

Unfortunately, the principle of sufficient reason fails itself. It is not a logically necessary truth, nor is it capable of a priori demonstration. Today, few accept it, believing instead that the ultimate facts about the world are what have been called brute facts—facts which just happen to be, and are not the case because of any further facts. Of course we may not know which facts these are, and even if we do succeed in reaching them, we may not acknowledge them for what they are, for our inquiring natures are Leibnizian in that we insist on seeking explanations for whatever could have been different from what it in fact is. We know that the Leibnizian dream is unfulfillable, but we can never be sure we have reached the last point of explanation.

Like the principle of sufficient reason, the doctrine of innate ideas and the doctrine of innate principles are today rejected. Still, there is a willingness to acknowledge—particularly since the linguistic work of Noam Chomsky—that it may be necessary to postulate innate predispositions to respond to the stimuli associated with language acquisition, in order to explain the otherwise improbable patterns of responses young children develop in successful mastery of their mother tongue. It would be most misleading, however, to represent this as a substantial concession towards the innate ideas and principles of continental rationalism.

Other article of interest: **God, Existence of.**

Bibliography

Benn, Alfred W. *The History of English Rationalism in the Nineteenth Century.* 2 vols. New York: Russell & Russell, 1962.

Hampshire, Stuart, ed. *The Age of Reason: The Seventeenth Century Philosophers.* New York: Mentor Books, 1956.

Kekes, John. *A Justification of Rationality.* Albany: State U. of New York Press, 1976.

Scriven, Michael. *Primary Philosophy.* New York: McGraw-Hill, 1966.

Wilson, Bryan R., ed. *Rationality.* New York: Harper and Row, 1971.

LAUCHLAN CHIPMAN

REASON. Introduction. It is not unnatural to wonder if reason is wanton. Much talk of what is reasonable and what is rational is not itself very rational. People, not infrequently, use such talk as a club to beat down those they oppose. Even when there is sensitivity to such ideological employments of talk of rationality, it is still anything but evident that there are objective criteria of rationality of sufficient strength to enable impartial, well-informed people capable of exact reasoning to achieve a reflective consensus on the comparative rationality or irrationality of various social institutions and social practices—to say nothing of whole ways of life or societies. I am skeptical, though ambivalently skeptical, of this extensive skepticism about reason. I shall try here to give some of the grounds for my SKEPTICISM.

Often we are not able to make fine enough discriminations and, in such circumstances, we have no basis for rankings or judgments in terms of the rationality of the various practices, institutions, or ways of life we are reflecting upon. But in some other circumstances it is plain enough what should be said. Before we judge reason to be wanton, we should be careful not to assimilate certain difficult cases to the more general run of things where what the rational or reasonable thing to do is often not that problematic. That reason cannot always tell us what we ought to do does not mean that it never can or even that it cannot often give us guidance in important areas of our lives.

I shall first set out a characterization of what is ordinarily meant by *rationality,* followed by a characterization of criteria of rationality both instrumental and noninstrumental, followed in turn by some examination of the limits of our commitment to rationality. That will be followed in sections 8-11 by what might be taken as a crucial test case: namely, whether Jewish or Christian belief for an educated, 20th-century person is a reasonable option. I shall attempt to show something of what must be done to answer this question and I shall end with an examination of a Wittgensteinian challenge which claims that to attempt to make such global assessments of the rationality of whole belief systems is to give reason a rationalistic task that is not genuinely its own.

1. To understand rationality, we can start with a dictionary. If we look up *rational* and *reasonable* in the Oxford English Dictionary (OED), we find such things as the following. To be rational is to be endowed with reason to have the faculty of reasoning. It is also to exercise one's reason in a proper manner and to have sound judgment and to be sensible and sane. Rational beliefs or rational principles of action are those which pertain to or relate to reason or are based on or derived from reasoning. They are beliefs and principles which are "agreeable to reason" and thus are "reasonable, sensible, not foolish, absurd or extravagant."

If we turn to the closely related term *reasonable,* we are told that to be reasonable is to have sound judgment, to be sensible, sane. We are also told that it sometimes means, curiously enough, "not to ask for too much." And in former times, but now only rarely, when someone speaks of someone being reasonable, he means that this person is "endowed with reason." Moreover, something which is reasonable—say a consideration, claim, or argument—is something which is agreeable to reason, not irrational, absurd, or ridiculous. And there is in the OED, as well, the somewhat surprising claim that being reasonable is "not going beyond the limit assigned."

I think philosophers would be ill-advised to make sport of these notions. They give us a sense of the terrain we are concerned with, and we might indeed even be somewhat skeptical whether in such a specification we philosophers have done much better. But all the same, if we are perplexed about rationality, these dictionary definitions are

not going to do much to help us. We surely are going to be puzzled about this "faculty of reason" or about being "endowed with reason." And we are going to be suspicious about talk of "being agreeable to reason." What is this reason that we are or may be endowed with? If it is only the faculty of speech and the ability to think and argue that is being talked about, then it should be remarked that thoroughly irrational people have that ability too and thoroughly irrational claims have been expressed in nondeviant English, French, German, etc. Moreover, extravagant and irrational claims have had valid arguments as their vehicles. Validity is but a crucial necessary condition for sound and rational argumentation. So, if being "endowed with reason" or having the "faculty of reason" is only understood as being able to speak, to think, and to be able to form valid arguments, it will not be sufficient to give us an understanding of rationality.

Alternatively, we need to ask whether being endowed with reason or being agreeable to reason is simply its being the case that what is agreeable to reason is established or establishable by sound arguments, namely valid arguments with true premises. If it is, then we are at least on familiar terrain. The problem becomes that of determining when arguments are valid and of determining when statements are true or probably true. While this is surely part of the task of determining what is rationality, it is not all of it, for there are principles of action which are said to be rational and attitudes of which the same thing is said. Yet, concerning both such principles and such attitudes, it is not clear that the notions of truth or falsity have any determinate and/or unproblematic meaning. Moreover, we do not, in some instances at least, seem to be talking about knowledge claims here. But then why should the lack of that rule out rationality? Finally, in this context, and to make a quite different point, it is also the case that not everything that is reasonably believed is believed for a reason or (arguably) because it is known to be true or probably true. So, while reason is perhaps not wanton, it is, on such a characterization, still perplexing.

We are, if we are perplexed by rationality, also going to have trouble with the OED's characterizations of rationality in terms of "exercising one's reason in a *proper* manner" and "being *sensible, sane* and of *sound* judgment," "not *foolish, absurd, or extravagant.*" And having trouble with those, we are going to have still more trouble with such at least seemingly conservative ideological notions as "not asking for too much" or "not going beyond the limits assigned." The various notions cited only have a determinate meaning in a contextual and culture-specific environment. Some of them at least are definitely ideological; some of them are normative terms with a definite emotive force (*foolish, absurd, extravagant*); and *proper, sensible, sound*, if not characteristically emotive in their force are still normative and, as well or at least, are terms with criteria which are contestable and perhaps even essentially contestable.

Manifestly rational and reasonable human beings—or at least intelligent and well-informed human beings capable of cool judgment—disagree about their criteria and about who is or is not of sound judgment, sensible, reasonable, and the like. When Henry Kissinger announces that such and such is a reasonable policy or that the parties in question are not being reasonable, I suspect a rather ideological *persuasive* definition has been utilized; I realize that he and I do not, in some very important ways, agree about the criteria for rationality and reasonability. (Is that actually the right way of looking at it? Perhaps we do agree about *criteria* of rationality and reasonability but just very fundamentally and systematically disagree about *what* is rational or reasonable. Or is that, in this context, a distinction without a difference?) Whatever we might want to say about that parenthetical remark, the general thrust of the argument in these two paragraphs shows that the dictionary will not take us out of the woods, even if we use it sensibly.

2. Let us now look at some criteria that philosophers have set out for *rational belief* and *rational principles* of action to see if they are any improvement. Presumably a rational human being will have rational *principles of action* and *rational beliefs*. Moreover, to have rational attitudes is at least to have attitudes that square with these principles and beliefs, and to be irrational is—though this perhaps is not all that it is—to not act in accordance with these principles and beliefs. But what are they? And are they as essentially contested and as indeterminate as the conceptions expressed in the dictionary entries?

Rational beliefs are typically beliefs that can withstand the scrutiny of people who are critical of their beliefs: that is to say, they are beliefs that are typically held open to refutation or modification by experience and/or by reflective examination; rational beliefs—to spell out a little of what is involved in the notion of reflective examination—

are beliefs that must be capable of being held in such a way so as, *ceteris paribus* (other things being equal), not to block or resist reflective inspection, namely attempts to consider their assumptions, implications and relations to other beliefs. Rational beliefs also are typically beliefs for which there is good evidence or good reasons or at least they are, *ceteris paribus*, beliefs for which such evidence or reasons are conscientiously and intelligently sought, and evidence or reasons (when available and utilizable) will not be ignored by people who hold such beliefs. Finally, rational beliefs are, *ceteris paribus*, beliefs for which it is known or reliably believed that there are good grounds for believing that they do not involve inconsistencies, contradictions, or incoherencies. (The heavy reliance on *ceteris paribus* qualifications will no doubt cause unease. I will address that after I specify the rational principles of action.)

A rational person will also have rational principles of action, and it will be irrational of him not to act in accordance with these principles. The following are at least plausible candidates:

a. The most efficient and effective means are to be taken, *ceteris paribus*, to achieve one's ends.

b. If one has several compatible ends, one, *ceteris paribus*, should take the means which will, as far as one can ascertain, most likely enable one to realize the greatest number of one's ends.

c. Of two ends, equally desired and equal in all other relevant respects, one is, *ceteris paribus*, to choose the end with the higher probability of being achievable.

d. If there are the same probabilities in two plans of action, which secure entirely different ends, that plan of action is, *ceteris paribus*, to be chosen which secures ends at least one of which is preferred to one of those secured by the other plan.

e. If one is unclear about what one's ends are or what they involve or how they are to be achieved, then it is usually wise to postpone making a choice among plans of action to secure those ends.

f. Those ends which, from a dispassionate and informed point of view, a person values absolutely higher than his other ends, are the ends which, *ceteris paribus*, he should try to realize. A rational agent will, *ceteris paribus*, seek plans of action which will satisfy those ends; and plans to satisfy his other ends will be adopted only insofar as they are compatible with the satisfaction of those ends he or she values most highly.

A rational person will have rational beliefs, that is, beliefs that satisfy the preceding criteria of rationality, and rational principles of action; and he or she will in almost all circumstances act in accordance with them. (This does not mean a person will constantly be calculating what is the rational thing to do. To act rationally will be in accordance with those principles, but that does not mean one necessarily must be consciously following those principles.) However, with these principles of rationality, as with the dictionary definitions, there are areas of indeterminateness. Indeed they were quite self-consciously introduced in their statement. The *ceteris paribus* clause is essential, as well as such qualifiers as *typically* or *usually*, for without them the principles will surely fall to counterexamples: that is to say, there will be situations, real or plausibly imaginable, when it will be at least arguable that the reasonable thing to do in those situations will not be to act in accordance with one or another of those principles. In that way their function in guidance and "absoluteness" is closely analogous to the way in which prima facie duties work. I think to ask for anything more is unrealistic and perhaps even unreasonable.

However, even if something tighter is possible and is ultimately to be desired, a strong consideration for our discussion in favor of the principles of rationality I set out is that they are at least a good subset of the principles of rationality and that these principles, like prima facie duties, usually always hold. That is to say—so as to make clear that I am not unsaying what I say here—it is always the case that these principles, where applicable, usually hold in a way quite analogous to the way that for everyone all of the time it is the case that promises, generally speaking, are to be kept.

3. The preceding characterization of rationality is a rather minimal one that might plausibly be thought to be normatively neutral. Jürgen Habermas, developing a conception of rationality following in the tradition of the Frankfurt School, has given us a much richer but normatively freighted conception of rationality. (See Bibliography.) It would, no doubt, contain the principles of rationality specified and it, like those principles, goes beyond what is specified in the ordinary use of *rational* and *reasonable* and their German equivalences, but it is still, I believe, in the spirit of that use. At least it is plainly not in conflict with that use. It will be well, in trying to gain an understanding of rationality, to set alongside the principles of rationality I have articulated those conceptions of Habermas that are distinctively different. The ensemble should then be up for critical examination.

Habermas in a very considerable measure cashes out the concept of rationality in terms of an articulation of the concepts of enlightenment and emancipation. A fully rational human being will be an emancipated, enlightened human being. Such people will have critical insight and an enlightened consciousness, that is, a coherent total consciousness. They will have a firm sense of self-identity, have achieved adult autonomy, an understanding of human needs and a liberation from the various illusions and dogmatisms that fetter humankind. Rationality, of course, admits of degrees, and this conception is trying to capture that heuristic ideal—a fully rational man—but it is also an attempt to specify what we put into our conceptualization of and indeed our ideal of full rationality or, perhaps, more in accordance with ordinary usage, full reasonability. This full reasonability will be coextensive with what it is to be enlightened and emancipated. Where enlightened and emancipated conditions obtain, and thus fully rational conditions (reasonable circumstances) obtain, people will be informed, perceptive, liberated, autonomous, self-controlled agents committed to developing their own distinctive powers and capable of fairness, impartiality, and objectivity. They will be reflective about their ends, knowledgeable about the means for their efficient attainment, and they will be critical people not under the bondage of any ideology. Indeed, free from all self-imposed tutelage and indoctrination, they will see the world rightly. They will have identified the evils of the world, and they will understand the conditions for surcease or amelioration of these evils and for the achievement of human community, to the extent that that community can be achieved at all.

4. With both the specification in section 2 of a minimal conception of rationality—an instrumental conception of rationality—and in 3 of a more ramified, noninstrumental conception of rationality before us, consider now whether we are ever justified in living according to commitments which we have cogent grounds, or at least very plausible grounds, for believing involve the holding of irrational or thoroughly unreasonble beliefs. To get some purchase on this, let us examine one putative case. What we are looking for is whether there are any plausible examples of plainly irrational beliefs which are still beliefs, where the requisite self-deception is possible, which it would be reasonable to have. To show that there is such an example is to show that there can be justified irrational beliefs. To establish this, we need a paradigmatically irrational belief—a belief whose irrationality is un-questionable—which is also a belief that is the ground for a justified commitment or reasonable mode of acting. In other words, can we give an airtight case of an action A, which is something, everything considered, we ought to do, which in turn is based on an irrational belief B, where it is better that we believe B and do A than either not to believe B and do not-A or not believe B and not do or believe (B aside) anything about such matters at all?

Consider, for example, the case of a man with a terminal cancer, a plainly and unquestionably ter-minal cancer, whom the medical experts have given up and who knows they have given up on him. Moreover, he is also a man who knows that there is no reason at all to believe that in the two or three months he is expected to continue living that there will be a breakthrough in cancer research such that he can be cured. Yet, like most people, he wants very much to be cured; he does not want to go on suffering only to die in a couple of months.

Suppose, further, that there is a man in Para-guay hounded out of the medical profession and almost certainly a quack who claims—in the face of the considered views of the medical profession and with no good evidence of his own—that he can cure cancers of this type, but that it is essential for the working of that cure that the patient believe that he will most certainly get well. Suppose further that this "doctor's" treatment will not shorten our terminal patient's life or cause him or anyone close to him any more pain or distress than he or they would otherwise experience. Suppose the man goes to Paraguay, puts himself under the "doctor's" care and in some way deceives himself into believ-ing that he most certainly will get well.

This belief that he will get well is a paradig-matically irrational or at least unreasonable belief, yet the act—in effect, betting on a long shot where he has everything to gain and nothing to lose—is, under the circumstances, not an irrational act; but it is an act that requires a paradigmatically irra-tional or unreasonable belief about what is likely to happen. Yet it is at least arguable, to put it minimally, that the individual in question is justi-fied in so acting and—as *ex hypothesi* he must to so act—in believing that he will get well. (Remem-ber that *so acting* refers to the prescribed course of treatment and that it is part of the prescribed cure that he believe that he will get well.) That is to say, in terms of what, everything considered, he is *justified* in doing or at least can reasonably do, he

is justified in having a belief that is plainly irra-tional or unreasonable. In this instance, it is the belief that he will get well. (How such a belief in such a circumstance can be stamped in is another question.)

Such cases are no doubt exceptional and the context is odd, but they can occur. The lesson is that our very straining for such examples shows the close tie between justifiability and rationality and the exceptions show that, while the tie is very close, it is not so close that circumstances of a far-out sort cannot arise where we are justified in hoping that we will be able to deceive ourselves into having an irrational belief. We recognize that, if we can actually believe it, it would be a good thing if we could actually come to hold such an irrational belief.

What cases of this type show is that in certain circumstances we are justified, or at least not irrational, in acting in accordance with a particular irrational belief. Indeed, I think they even reveal something stronger, namely, that sometimes it is rational—in this context reasonable—deliberately to set ourselves on a course of action that will subsequently in certain very circumscribed situa-tions make it possible for us to act in accordance with a belief we *now* recognize to be irrational. (If, because of the power of the emotive force for *irrational* it seems too jarring to speak this way, substitute for *irrational* the phrase *utterly ground-less, utterly without warrant*, or *utterly without rational warrant*. Even with such substitutions, substantially the same point will be made.)

There is no paradox here if one reflects a moment, for it is, given the criteria and principles of rationality they jointly define, everything con-sidered, the rational thing to do to act in such circumstances on such irrational beliefs. That is to say, the weight of reasons, justified by the principles of rationality, justify our acting on such an ir-rational belief.

The most crucial thing to see about such cases is that in so acting a human being is not acting "against reason" or "acting irrationally." Indeed, in so acting one is, everything considered, being guided by reason, being reasonable, and is acting rationally—or at least one is not acting irration-ally.

5. So we can see that it is sometimes in accord with reason to act in certain circumstances, in accordance with an irrational or unreasonable belief. However, to say this is one thing, but it is another thing again to say that someone would be

justified, or even conceivably could be justified, in living according to a whole cluster of commitments that involve the holding of what she or he knows, or has very good grounds for believing, involve the holding of irrational or unreasonable beliefs. To make this clear, take a case at the most extreme. What would it be like to be justified in jettisoning all of the principles of rationality I have specified above? I shall argue that it is problematical whether this is even something that can be intelligibly done. To try to ascertain whether this is so, let us consider whether we can describe what it would be like to do it and to be justified in doing it.

Our person trying to reject rationality *tout court* would have to have beliefs that were not open to modification or refutation by experience. Thus, if he believed his lunch is in his briefcase but upon reaching for it he did not find it in his briefcase, he would still perfectly well go on believing that it is in his briefcase. But, as most beliefs at least are not voluntary matters, it is doubtful whether he could actually go on believing that his lunch is in his briefcase in such a circumstance. Somehow most of our beliefs—at least our mundane beliefs—get modified by experience. In that limited way we cannot avoid being critical. Moreover, and even more centrally, people could not negotiate with the world, get around in the world, and live with other human beings if their beliefs were not so modifiable by experience. If an agent had no concern with whether his beliefs involved inconsistencies, contradictions, or incoherencies and if he succeeded in being thoroughly incoherent and inconsistent, then there would come a point where he could not communicate with people and would not even understand himself so that he could believe what he tells himself and us he believes.

Suppose Wayland is such a chap and he tells us that he is not concerned to be constrained in his beliefs by considerations of consistency or coherence, but he believes—or so he proclaims—that he sleeps faster than Plumtree and yet at the same time, and in the same respect, Plumtree sleeps faster than he does. We point out to him, assuming first counterfactually that it is coherent, that his belief is contradictory—he believes p and not-p and that, now dropping that assumption, it is incoherent to boot, for it makes no sense to say, "x sleeps faster than y" or "x sleeps slower than y." He replies that—contradictory or not, coherent or not—he believes it all the same, for he is not constrained in his beliefs to what he at least takes to be that which is coherent and consistent. But

then the answer should be, in turn that though he *says* he believes these things, he cannot possibly actually believe them, for he, in uttering a contradiction, unsays what he *apparently* says and in uttering something that is genuinely incoherent it cannot be specified or stated *what* he believes: his utterance lacks propositional content. Indeed, even he cannot do it for himself. He does not understand *what* it is that he is to believe. But if there is no saying or in any way specifying what is believed, there is no belief. Wayland thinks he can believe such stark incoherencies and contradictions, but he cannot.

Moreover, just to have a disposition to act in a certain way is not enough to constitute a belief. So the man who sets out to have beliefs and commitments—things that involve beliefs but are not identical to them—cannot simply jettison rationality and still have beliefs and commitments. If a human being is to have any beliefs or commitments at all, there is no "rejecting rationality" in this *wholesale* manner, though this is not, of course, to show or claim that his beliefs and commitments must have all the earmarks of rational belief.

Where the attempt is not to put all the principles of rationality under the ax but only a few, *perhaps* some circumstances could arise in which someone might reasonably not act in accordance with some of them. But the closer one gets to anything like a wholesale or even extensive rejection of them, the closer what one does and says will be to a kind of utter incoherency. If we have a whole battery of diverse unreasonable beliefs, then our actions (if we try to act on those beliefs) will become utterly unreasonable. It is only in isolated, exceptional cases or perhaps (to be maximally liberal about possibilities here) closely interconnected cases where it even can be the case that the reasonable thing to do is to act on the unreasonable beliefs.

6. So in the above *crucial way* there is no *possible* alternative to rationality. Let us now ask as well if it is at least logically possible for a human being with rational beliefs simply to jettison rational principles of action in a similar wholesale way? Here it does, I believe, seem to be some kind of weak possibility, though hardly, and indeed by definition, a *rational* possibility. That is to say, we can, without vast tricks of the imagination, imagine situations in which we would understand what it would be like for an agent not to act on these principles. We are indeed *appalled* by such behavior, but we understand it: we can follow the descriptions describing what it would be like to so behave.

We can, I believe, understand a description of someone acting in such a way that he did not postpone acting on a matter which normally would be thought to be important and where there was no pressure to act immediately though he had no even tolerably clear idea of the consequences in that circumstance of choosing to act one way rather than another, where he had no concern for which of his ends would have the greater likelihood of being achieved, where he didn't care whether he satisfied a greater rather than a lesser number of his ends which were compatible, and where he did not even try to take the most effective means to achieve his ends. We might very well wonder just how all the compatible ends could be his ends when he was so indifferent about maximizing their achievement. But why should we not say that such perversity and irrationality are possible?

It is somewhat more questionable whether there really are alternatives to principles (d) and (f) stated in section 2. It might be thought that we could not choose to do, where this is a voluntary action, what we do not, everything considered, prefer most. But that is not so on a straightforward use of *prefer*. I might prefer Chopin, and indeed even at that moment prefer Chopin, and still perversely, for no reason all, listen to Brahms. In a similar vein—vis-à-vis (f)—it might be said that if an individual did not try to achieve something *p* or did *not* try to achieve it more than he tried to achieve *s, r* or *q*, we would not, *ceteris paribus*, say that he valued it more highly than those things. What one does not go after, one does not value unless there is some specific overriding reason for not going after it. This *may* be true. But it is not plainly and evidently true, and it seems at least to make nonsense out of what at least looks like the perceptive psychological remark that it is sometimes the case for some individuals that the good they would do they do not. It at most shows that with (f), alone of the various rational principles of action, it may be impossible not to act in accordance with it. If that were true, as I do not think it is, it would raise serious questions about the logical status of (f).

The upshot of these remarks is that while there is no possibility of rejecting at least certain of what I have called our criteria for rational belief, it does appear to be possible to reject the principles of rational action and to act quite irrationally and on a massive scale, though there is not a scintilla of a reason to believe that circumstances could arise in which those actions are justified. But, even if such circumstances could arise, if my above arguments are correct, there still is no way of rejecting reason en masse.

7. I have been concerned to show what rational beliefs are, what the principles of instrumental rationality are, and something of what noninstrumental conceptions of rationality come to. Together they give us some understanding of rationality, an understanding that goes beyond, yet is still compatible with, what can be garnered about rationality from an examination of the ordinary employments of the terms *rational* and *reasonable* in everyday contexts. I then try to show that even with such an understanding of reason there is a problem about coping with reason, namely, that our rationalistic expectations to the contrary notwithstanding, it may sometimes be the case that in the living of our lives it is, everything considered, reasonable to have unreasonable beliefs. But this fact, if it is indeed a fact, does not make reason wanton. It does not show that it is even possible, let alone justified, to reject reason, to abandon reason, to not live one's life largely in accordance with the unproblematic elements in the concept of reason that I have characterized.

Even the most psychotic people, where they can function at all, cannot quite pull off anything like that. It is indeed only by appealing to these principles of rationality that we can in some specific situation justify our having an unreasonable belief or not following one or another of the principles of rationality. More generally, there is no alternative to acting in accordance with the principles of rationality. In that general way, there is no sense to the question "Why be rational?" though this does not show, or give to understand, that "cold reason"—hard, careful thinking—can by itself, or coupled with knowledge of the facts, independently of our reflective sentiments or our deepest hopes, resolve for us how it is we ought to live or show us that, in all circumstances, maximally reliable information is a desideratum for all human beings, no matter how they may be placed.

8. Consider a specific religion such as Judaism or Christianity. Can we both understand it and believe it? Are our criteria of rationality and intelligibility such that it can be established that the core beliefs of Judaism or Christianity are irrational? Most fundamentally what we—or at least many of us—want to know is whether Jewish or Christian belief in God is a rational belief or at least not an irrational belief. Note that this is perfectly parallel to a question pursued by Evans-Pritchard, Winch, MacIntyre, Lukes, Hollis, and others: "Is the Zande belief in witches a rational belief?"

What we are trying to ask, both in the Zande case and in the Jewish or Christian case, is whether in terms of a common notion of rationality such as we have articulated in the previous sections such beliefs can and indeed should be said to be rational or at least not irrational. For now, we are assuming that it is *not* the case that one standard of rationality applies to the Azande and another to us or one standard of intelligibility applies to the Christian and another to the secularist. I will, that is, start by assuming a unitary conception of rationality and see where it leads us.

In asking about the rationality of the Jewish and Christian belief in God, as well as in asking about the rationality of Zande belief in witchcraft, it is wise, I believe, to break down the question in the following way. (I shall do it first for the Zande.) "Is the Zande belief in witches a rational belief?" can be taken as either (a) "Can we members of the 20th-century Western culture with the rather full information and learning available to an educated member of our culture rationally believe in witches as the Azande do?" or (b) "Are the Azande rational in believing in witches? Have they acted reasonably and not disregarded evidence, reasoning, and information readily available to them in believing in witches?"

In talking about the Azande it is plainly evident that it is important to distinguish between these questions because what we have learned from social anthropology concerning other cultures should make us extremely loath to claim that the average Azande or the average member of any other tribe is irrational. But, given the pervasiveness and centrality of Zande belief in witchcraft, this is exactly what we should conclude if we answer (b) by claiming that the Azande are irrational in believing as they do. Yet, on the other hand, we do not want, in acknowledging that the Azande are not behaving irrationally in believing in witches, to give to understand that if we Westerners do not believe in witches we are being irrational. Hence the importance of distinguishing between (a) and (b).

I will maintain that it is important to make a parallel distinction in talking about the rationality of Christian and Jewish belief in God. However, since in speaking of Christian and Jewish belief we are talking intraculturally and not cross-culturally

between radically different cultures, the importance of drawing that distinction is not so evident to us. (It may be perfectly evident to someone coming from another culture.)

Let me first draw this distinction with greater exactitude, and then I shall try to show the importance of drawing it. "Is the Judeo-Christian belief in God a rational belief?" can be understood as either (c) "Can we members of 20th-century Western culture with the rather full information and learning available to an educated member of our culture rationally believe in the God of the mainstream Jewish and Christian traditions?" or (d) "Are Christians and Jews rational in believing in God? Have they acted reasonably and not disregarded evidence, reasoning, and information readily available to them in believing in God?"

There is an important disanalogy between (a) and (b), on the one hand, and (c) and (d), on the other, that we should immediately note. There is no overlap in the class of persons referred to in (a) and (b), but there is in (c) and (d). There are plenty of Christians and Jews who are manifestly rational and are members of the class of 20th-century persons who are highly educated and reflective. This is a sociological fact that we should not allow any ideological or philosophical convictions to obscure or distort. If anyone is to answer (c) in the negative, as one presumably would answer (a) in the negative, one will need to make out a very good case for the claim that while there are some Christians and Jews who are reflective, well-educated and manifestly rational, that nonetheless their belief in God is irrational and that, in living in accordance with that belief, they—though perhaps understandably enough—are being irrational. (This, of course, does not mean that in other respects they are being irrational.)

This is a strong and indeed an embarrassing claim to make in our tolerant and (in many respects) liberal ethos. However, it is just the claim that anyone who consistently supports (c) must make and it is a claim, radical as it is, that I shall make. The important thing to see is whether it can be given a reasonable explication and a sound defense. There are many who believe that any such claim is thoroughly wrong-headed. T. M. Penelhum believes that while the claims of natural theology to give sound reasons for believing in God do not succeed, neither do the allegedly clinching arguments against religious belief, so that vis-à-vis Judaism and Christianity we are left in a stalemate. Reason—that is, human ratiocination and rationality—cannot, he and many others believe, settle the matter one way or another.

What we are asking (assuming we are members of the class of reasonably educated, 20th-century Westerners or are people who have gained a participant's understanding of that cultural background) is whether it is rational to believe in the God of the Jews and the Christians. We want to know whether such a belief is irrational for such people, that is, educated Westerners or people who have gained a firm participant's grasp of Western culture. Just as there are Azande who reasonably believe in witches, given what they can readily know, so there are plenty of Jews and Christians who are neither scientifically nor philosophically educated, who, given what they know and what is readily available to them, reasonably believe in God. This is not at all a patronizing remark, for we all stand—and unavoidably so—in that position vis-à-vis some beliefs.

Hegel is right in asserting that we cannot overlap history. (This note is not a form of relativism.) But unless a certain relativism about rationality is true (and indeed sufficiently coherent so that it could be true), there is no obvious reason, and perhaps no sound reason at all, for thinking that it could not correctly be claimed that reasonable people can have some irrational beliefs and indeed some very fundamental ones at that. In recognizing that we all are in the same boat, that we all may very well have some irrational beliefs, I show that I am not being patronizing to Jews or Christians. (It could not, of course, be the case that we could knowingly hold what we regarded—everything considered—as an irrational belief and still remain fully rational. Recall also that rationality admits of degrees.)

9. What synoptically should be said about the rationality/irrationality of beliefs is this: a belief (religious or otherwise) is in most circumstances irrational if the person holding it knows or has very good grounds for believing that it is either (a) inconsistent, (b) unintelligible (does not make sense), (c) incoherent, or (d) false or very probably false. It is also something which is irrational for him to believe if (e) it is held by that person in such a way that no attention is given to considerations of evidence that might be relevant (directly or indirectly) to the holding of that belief, (f) the person in question knowingly ignores relevant evidence or grounds for his belief, or (g) the belief is held in such a way that the holder of the belief will not countenance the reflective inspection of its

implications for other beliefs or practices.

Parenthetically, it is tricky to state (f) without saying something false or misleading. Where there are no equally good competing theories that can account for what for a given theory is recalcitrant evidence, such evidence can be rightly ignored. But that isn't ignoring evidence *full stop* but deliberately ignoring some of it under very determinate constraints. For this practice to even be understandable, there must be a standing presumption that evidence will not be ignored. But, like a prima facie obligation, that presumption can sometimes with reason be overridden.

A belief system which at a given time has many central beliefs that have achieved this status is a belief system which it is irrational for people at that time and place to subscribe to, if they have a reasonably good scientific and philosophical education.

Centrally in asking whether the Judeo-Christian belief in God is rational, or at least not irrational, we are asking: (a) Is belief in such a God free of inconsistencies or contradictions? (b) Is belief in such a God intelligible? (Does such a belief make sense?) (c) Is belief in such a God a belief in a coherent conception? (d) Is belief in such a God a belief in something which we have very good grounds to believe not to be the case?

If any of these four questions obtain, then belief in such a God is irrational for a man who recognizes any of these things or for a man who is in a position where he could, but for self-deception, recognize these things. We can say derivatively, if this is so, that the beliefs are irrational beliefs.

The first and fourth questions, at least on the surface, are fairly straightforward, and only careful examination of the appropriate strands of religious discourse would give us good grounds for answering one way or another. But (b) and (c) are more troublesome. What are we claiming when we claim that such a religious belief is unintelligible or incoherent? What counts as "being unintelligible" or "being incoherent" here, and how can we ascertain when this condition obtains? It would seem, from the above, that we are saying such beliefs are irrational because they are unintelligible or incoherent. But it has also been suggested that to say "a belief is irrational" is to say (among other things) that it is inconsistent, incoherent, or unintelligible. But then the *because* loses much of its force. Plainly, to make any headway here we must gain some clarity concerning what we are talking about when we claim that a religious belief is incoherent or unintelligible.

10. However, here, with the issues posed as they were in the previous section, as is certainly characteristic of the posing of most philosophical questions, there will be those who will feel that in posing them in that way we have already gone down the garden path: we have unwittingly steered things in the wrong direction. There are, some will claim, no substantive norms or principles of rationality or criteria of reasonableness that afford us an Archimedean point in accordance with which we can make such sweeping judgments. We need to take to heart Wittgenstein's penetrating and unsettling realization that there are just a diverse, incommensurable number of language-games and forms-of-life, with their attendant world-pictures with no possible objective ground, if that isn't a pleonasm, for ranking them or choosing between them. We simply are taught some world-picture; we are unreflectively and matter-of-coursely drilled in or indoctrinated in or, if you will, socialized into one such world-picture. With that we have a number of beliefs—indeed, a system of beliefs—that stand fast for us, that we, at least in our practice and actual judgments, feel certain of and assume in any genuine investigating, doubting, knowing, or rational believing that we engage in. They are, if you will, our *vor Wissen* that we take as a matter of course in our diverse activities. They are the grounds or at least the essential background for what we rationally believe but they themselves are ungrounded—and necessarily so.

Christians—say, of the Middle Ages—had one such world-picture with its related language-games and forms-of-life and Zande at the time Evans-Pritchard visited them and contemporary Western secularists (to take two very different cases) have other importantly dissimilar world-pictures. It is in accordance with these world-pictures that we can say what rational/irrational or reasonable/unreasonable beliefs, practices and institutions are. But we have no vantage point—and indeed can have no such vantage point—for making assessments of these diverse and incommensurable world-pictures themselves.

If this is so, then the questions I tried to ask—or so at least it seems—are in reality questions that cannot sensibly be asked. We have no possible way of answering them that would not involve the question-begging procedure of simply, in accordance with the norms of rationality of one world-picture, criticizing and judging the beliefs distinctive of an incommensurable world-picture. There

is no way of sensibly asking whether Christian belief is irrational because incoherent or inconsistent or whatever. This can no more be made out than it can be made out that English is inconsistent or German is incoherent or ordinary language is inconsistent. In all such talk the engine is idling.

So, at least some Wittgensteinians would say, we should not try straightforwardly to answer my questions, but we should first examine in this domain the adequacy of Wittgenstein's account—an account which, if correct, shows the senselessness or at least pointlessness of asking what I am trying to ask. However, it is also important to note that, whatever the results of that endeavor, Wittgenstein's account not only presents a challenge for arguments with a skeptical thrust such as my own but it is also a challenge for a variety of theistic accounts as well. If one argues, as has been argued, that (a) the ontological argument, if sound, provides a rational ground for worship, and (b) that the ontological argument is sound, one runs afoul of the preceding Wittgensteinian questions about "rational ground."

One faces a similar difficulty if one claims that we should believe in God because the theistic interpretation is the most rational explanation of human religious experience. And finally, if Wittgenstein's remarks about rationality and world-pictures are right, it is impossible to establish, in any significant way, that, as John Hick puts it, "faith-awareness of God is a mode of cognition which can properly be trusted and in terms of which it is rational to live." Even if we do not balk at "faith-awareness" and a "mode of cognition," whether it is rational to place our trust here and so live is trivially "answered," if we accept Wittgenstein's account, in terms of the world-picture we were taught. If you were brought up with a Christian, Jewish, or Islamic world-picture and the instruction and indoctrination took, it is rational for you to trust that "faith-awareness." If you were brought up with a secular or Buddhist or Zande world-picture, it is not. And that is the end of it. There is no superior vantage point of reason.

There is, in short, if Wittgenstein is right, no vantage point from which we could make progress with the "question" that many of us who have no taste for metaphysics at all, in certain moods at least, very much want answered: to wit, and most centrally, which vantage point or world-picture is "really rational" or even—coming down a bit—which vantage point or world-picture is the more reasonable to accept and to live in accordance with? These are not—and cannot be—genuine questions if Wittgenstein's account is on the mark.

11. We should, however, be cautious about drawing such severe relativistic conclusions. Language-games and forms-of-life are not compartmentalized. The criteria of rational appraisal I have described cut across them. Very basic things like asserting, inquiring, questioning, hoping, concluding, and remonstrating are distinct language-games, but these can be done in a rational and in a not so rational way. If we think of larger activities such as the particular forms that science, religion, and law take in a particular society of a given time, there is no reason to think they are *sui generis* and uncriticizable. At the very least, questions can be raised about how the various practices and forms-of-life of a society fit together. If elements of the law or of religion conflict with well-grounded scientific claims or with plain and careful empirical observations of what is the case, then, given these conflicts, there is plainly a need to make adjustments somewhere in the belief system of the society and, given the strong way in which the scientific claims in question and the common-sense empirical claims in question are warranted, there are good reasons in such a circumstance to abandon or radically modify at least certain elements of the religious or legal claims.

Similarly, since the language-games in a given culture are not insulated from each other (they are not self-contained units), there is good reason to believe that the criteria of what it makes sense to say and believe are not utterly idiosyncratic to a particular language-game. Our conceptions of consistency, coherence, and evidence are not utterly language-game dependent. *Not* does not function differently in religious, scientific, and legal discourse, though to what it will be applied may be in part domain-dependent.

Coherence criteria are more difficult but if, in one domain, we are forced to use conceptions that are very different from our other conceptions and that are conflicting or at least are apparently conflicting with conceptions in other domains of what it makes sense to say, conceptions we are indeed very confident of, we have good reason to be skeptical of the idiosyncratic conceptions. This is exactly the position that certain key religious conceptions appear at least to be heir to.

Jews and Christians, for example, must believe that there is an infinite individual (indeed a person) who is transcendent to the world yet standing in a personal relation of caring and loving to the world. Yet it is anything but evident that such talk makes any coherent sense at all. How can we give to understand that an individual is both transcendent to the world and at the very same time that very same individual stands in some personal relation to it? Here the theist surely seems at least to be unsaying what he has just said. It is only a thinly veiled way of saying that at time *t, S* has property *p* and property not-*p*. Furthermore, it is anything but evident that we can understand talk of "a being transcendent to the world." If we are honest with ourselves, we should be very skeptical about whether such a conception has any coherent sense at all. And it is doubly impossible for an individual to have such a characteristic. (If we say all these terms are used metaphysically, then we still must be able to say in nonmetaphysical terms what they are metaphors of.)

Considerations concerning evidence are also not *that* language-game or form-of-life eccentric. It is true that theories are underdetermined by the evidence or data. We know, for example, from the archeological evidence that agricultural tools of a certain sort spread gradually into Europe over a certain period of time. The theory that they arrived with new invading peoples who pushed out the hunters and gatherers and the opposing theory that the hunters and gatherers themselves, through cultural borrowing, gradually took up their use are both plausible and they are both equally compatible with the evidence. The evidence does not determine which, if either, theory to accept. We cannot simply read off our theories or overall accounts from the evidence. However, while this undetermination thesis is true, it is also true that rationally acceptable theories still do require evidence. When we have well-elaborated and systematically coherent theories for which there is a paucity of evidence and equally well-elaborated and systematically coherent theories for which there is evidence, the rational thing to do is to accept the theories for which there is evidence. (Stated in just the way I have, Galileo's theory is not a disconfirming instance.)

While there *may* be some groundless beliefs for which nothing like evidence is in order which are still rationally believed (for example, "Every event has a cause"), it is still the case that reasonable people will in almost all situations assume that if their beliefs are justified there is evidence for them and when their beliefs are not in accord with the evidence and others come up with a plausible set of beliefs that are in accord with the evidence, reasonable people will alter their beliefs in accordance with the evidence. Such remarks are not scientistic remarks reflecting the hegemony of "the scientific attitude" but cut across the various forms-of-life and, in that crucial sense, are language-game independent.

The upshot of this argument is to show that reason is not wanton. There are principles of rational belief and rational action that are universal and there are general ways in which we can appraise institutions, practices, and forms-of-life with respect to their rationality without falling into ethnocentrism or into some tendentious ideological stance. Judaism, Christianity, and Islam are such forms-of-life, and they can be so appraised in the light of reason and experience.

The consistency, coherence, and evidential warrant of Jewish, Christian, and Islamic belief systems are of a very low order indeed. In terms of the conception of rationality I have articulated (a reasonably unproblematic conception, I believe), such belief systems are not reasonably believed by a 20th-century person with a good grounding in Western scientific and philosophical culture. It is not reasonable for such a person to believe in Azande witchcraft, and it is not reasonable for such a person to believe in the belief systems of Judaism, Christianity, and Islam either.

Bibliography

Deardon, R. F., et al. *Education and the Development of Reason*. London: Routledge and Kegan Paul, 1972.

Geraets, Theodore, ed. *Rationality Today*. Ottawa: Ottawa U. Press, 1979.

Habermas, Jürgen. *Toward a Rational Society*. Boston: Beacon Press, 1970.

Nielsen, Kai. *Reason and Practice*. New York: Harper and Row, 1971.

Penelhum, Terence. *Religion and Rationality*. New York: Random House, 1971.

Richards, David A. *A Theory of Reasons for Action*. Oxford: Clarendon Press, 1971.

Wilson, Bryan R. *Rationality*. Oxford: Basil Blackwell, 1970.

KAI NIELSEN

REICH, WILHELM (1897–1957), Austrian psychiatrist with enormous influence on current therapeutic techniques, second perhaps only to that of SIGMUND FREUD and one of the most outspoken opponents of religion, especially its harmful effects on character and mental health. As a psychological rather than a philosophical critic of religion, Reich continued the work of FRIEDRICH NIETZSCHE and Freud, developing this critique more systematically and in greater detail than his predecessors.

Reich's Life. Reich obtained his medical degree from the University of Vienna in 1922. He then did postgraduate studies in psychiatry with Julius Wagner-Jauregg and Paul Schilder. Even before graduating he had begun to practice as a psychoanalyst and to publish clinical and theoretical articles. These articles, his books *Der Triebhafte Charakter* (The Impulsive Character, 1925) and *Die Funktion des Orgasmus* (The Function of the Orgasm, 1927), and his active involvement with socialist youth groups made him a controversial figure quite early in his career.

In 1930 Reich moved to Berlin, which was the center of radical movements at that time. Shortly after reaching Berlin, Reich joined the Communist party, but his various unorthodox positions led to collisions with the ideologists of the Communist movement. Reich maintained that neuroses were by no means the fads of middle-class women but were emotionally crippling illnesses of almost epidemic proportions. Contrary to the assertions of various Marxist writers, Reich argued that sexual repression, biological rigidity, and puritanism were ubiquitous and not confined to certain classes or groups of the population.

In 1933, shortly after Hitler's rise to power, Reich was expelled from the Communist party. In the same year he published in Copenhagen the first edition of *Charakteranalyse* (Character Analysis). This book contained ideas that were not acceptable to the more conservative psychoanalysts, and, at a tumultuous conference in Davos in 1934, Reich was expelled from the International Psychoanalytic Association. He was now completely on his own. He taught in the Psychology Institute of the University of Oslo for a number of years, and he also edited the *Zeitschrift für Politische Psychologie und Sexualökonomie,* which was published in Copenhagen between 1934 and 1939.

During Reich's stay in Scandinavia he published several articles and a monograph describing his studies of the muscular rigidities of neurotics—their "muscular armor"—and his ingenious technique for dissolving these rigidities. (The articles and reviews published in the *Zeitschrift* are on an extremely high level. There has perhaps never been a journal that published so many original psychiatric ideas in such a short span.)

Reich in the U.S. In 1939 Reich moved to New York, where he resumed his practice and trained numerous psychiatrists in the new technique he had developed during his stay in Scandinavia. He also lectured at the New School for Social Research from 1939 to 1941. Although Reich was reviled by orthodox analysts and by other branches of the psychiatric establishment, his new therapy had a wide appeal among professional people during the years after World War II. From about 1950 on, Reich showed little interest in psychiatry or in advancing the sexual revolution, one of whose leading spokesmen he had been during the preceding 25 years. Most of his energies from then on were devoted to his theory of orgone energy and the healing effects this energy was claimed to possess. Reich became notorious for this theory, and his claims were generally misreported. In 1954 the Food and Drug Administration obtained an injunction against Reich, which he openly defied. In 1956 he was tried for contempt of court and given the maximum sentence of two years' imprisonment. He died in Lewisburg Federal Penitentiary in 1957.

This is not the place to discuss the tragic last years of Reich's life or the F.D.A. injunction that led to the burning of Reich's books and periodicals. However, it should be mentioned that, according to all his most responsible biographers (Myron Sharaf, Ilse Ollendorff Reich, and Jerome Greenfield), Reich was suffering from serious paranoid delusions for several years before his death. Some of his fanatical followers deny this and shower intemperate and extremely vicious abuse on the biographers, but the evidence shows that the biographers have written the truth.

"Armoring." Writing in the emigré periodical *Das Neue Tagebuch* in 1937, the German poet Stephan Lackner expressed his outrage at the treatment meted out to Reich—this "contemporary heretic"—by leading figures in the psychoanalytic movement and the left-wing parties. "It was not enough," wrote Lackner, "to expel Reich from their organizations"; in the struggle against this man and his disturbing ideas, "every kind of slander and distortion is a permissible weapon." In this article we are primarily concerned with Reich's disturbing ideas concerning the causes and consequences of religious belief, but these ideas cannot

be adequately comprehended without a brief explanation of Reich's concept of "armoring."

To a greater or lesser degree almost everybody growing up in a repressive culture develops a set of defensive attitudes whose function it is to protect the individual against external injury, such as being hurt or rejected by other human beings, as well as against his own repressed emotions. This is particularly true of severe compulsion neurotics and of chronic depressives. The affective personality of such people acts like "an armor, a rigid shell on which the knocks from the outer world as well as the inner demands rebound." The armor does indeed make the person less sensitive to pain, but it also reduces his "libidinal and aggressive motility and with that, his capacity for pleasure and achievement."

In his Scandinavian publications Reich described how neurotic conflicts and traumatic experiences become "anchored" in the body. They do so by means of chronic muscular rigidities—in the forehead, in the eyes, around the mouth, in the chin, in the throat, the shoulders, the chest, the abdomen, the pelvis, the thighs, and in many other areas. The technique Reich then developed and which he called "character analytic vegeto-therapy" is no longer a purely verbal technique but prominently involves direct work on the muscular rigidities or what he came to call the "muscular armor." The goal of therapy is the dissolution of the armor, and, in retrospect, Reich admitted that prior to the discovery of the muscular armor and methods of dissolving it, analytic treatment could not achieve more than a very limited measure of success.

Mystical Longings and Sexual Repression. Religion, or what Reich preferred to call "mysticism," plays an extremely significant role in the emotional crippling of human beings. Armoring and neurosis are largely the result of the moralistic and authoritarian upbringing to which, until very recently, children were subjected all over the world. The preaching and antisexual moralism of the religious home stifle every vital impulse of the child. They produce human beings with a craving for authority, a fear of responsibility, mystical longings, impotent rebelliousness, and pathological drives of all kinds. The "morals" fostered in the conventional home and school and supported by the "guardians of the higher values" create "the very perverted sexual life which it presumes to regulate moralistically; and the elimination of these 'morals' is the prerequisite for elimination of that immorality which it tries in vain to fight." In *Beyond Good and Evil*, Nietzsche had said about Christianity that it "gave Eros poison to drink; he did not die of it but he degenerated into vice." This is essentially Reich's point, except that Reich would extend the indictment to all life-denying religions.

After religion, through the education and morality it fosters, has made people incapable of experiencing pleasure, particularly the joy of sex, it supplies them with a substitute gratification in the form of what Reich variously calls "religious excitations" or "mystical feelings." The religious individual is subject to states of sexual tension just like any other human being, but his sex-negating upbringing and his fear of punishment have made him incapable of release and satisfaction in normal sexuality. The result of this is that he suffers from a chronic state of *excessive* somatic excitation. The more thorough his religious education, the more it appears to him that happiness is not obtainable in this life and, in the long run, it does not even seem desirable any more. However, as a living organism, he cannot completely renounce the goals of "happiness, relaxation and satisfaction." In these circumstances all he can do is seek "the *illusory* happiness provided by the religious *forepleasure* excitations." His "somatic suffering" creates in him the need for consolation and for help from the outside, especially in the fight against "the evil instincts."

What the religious person calls his longing for "delivery from sin," is in fact longing for relief from sexual tension. Religious experiences may "transport" the individual, but they do not bring about genuine somatic gratification or relaxation. Reich concludes that, from the point of view of energy, mystical feelings *are* "sexual excitations which have changed their content and goal." The energy of these emotions is the energy of natural sexuality, which has become attached to mystical contents. Religious patients, upon establishing a satisfying sex life, invariably lose their God-fixation.

Religious people themselves, according to Reich, frequently have a good understanding of this condition, which exists side by side with their antisexual attitude. Like everybody else, they have both an official and a private personality. Officially they declaim against sex and sexual freedom in particular, but privately they know that they too are longing for sexual happiness and that their religious attachments are "substitute gratifications without which they could not exist." In spite of their professions and their perfectly genuine belief that sex is evil and degrading, they nevertheless have deep inferiority feelings and secretly envy and admire those who are (or whom they believe to be) sexually happy. This accounts for their characteristic appearance of insincerity, especially when engaged in activities like the "saving" of sinners. The people whom Reich was describing were presumably mostly Germans and Austrians, but their counterparts exist all over the world, and they often wield enormous power.

The Proreligious Psychologists. William James, who grew up in a deeply "spiritual" and puritanical family during the heyday of the Victorian period, not surprisingly did not look kindly at suggestions, already current early in the 20th century, that religious emotions are a form of perverted sexuality. He airily dismisses them in a footnote in his *Varieties of Religious Experience*, where he remarks that one might "almost as well interpret religion as a perversion of the respiratory function."

Reich would probably have commented that the early proponents of the "sexual" theory were on the right track, but that they did not have any clinical evidence to support their view. If mystical feelings and religious excitations were really something "primary" and not substitute gratifications, patients would not invariably lose their "God-fixation" on achieving sexual happiness. They usually do not lose their interest in music or in science. Reich would probably have dismissed in much the same way the contentions of proreligion psychologists like Viktor Frankl and Carl Jung that religious needs are part of the innate endowment of human beings and that neurosis is liable to result if they remain ungratified.

In one of his earliest books, *The Unconscious God*, Frankl develops the thesis that neurotic patients suppress their natural religiosity and that noticeable improvements in their condition are observed if they allow free rein to their religious impulses. Some patients even have dreams with a religious content after they have been reassured that there is nothing shameful about their religious longings. Freud, Frankl maintained, "abused the unconscious" by overlooking its "spiritual" qualities. Neurotic patients not only suppress their needs for divine protection; they equally suppress the true conscience, which is not identical with the superego but is the instrument of the "super-human Absolute," an "entity higher than ourselves," an "extra-human authority" to which all of us are responsible.

Jung, who was not as pious as Frankl and who never claimed that our conscience is an instrument of the "super-human Absolute," nevertheless shared Frankl's conviction that the suppression of religious impulses leads to neurosis. "It is safe to say," Jung wrote in *Modern Man in Search of a Soul*, referring to his patients above the age of 35, that "every one of them fell ill because he had lost that which the living religions of every age have given their followers." Later in the same book he remarks that he has seen thousands of such patients and that "all have been people whose problem in the last resort was that of finding a religious outlook on life."

Reich would not dispute some of the assertions of Frankl and Jung, but he would regard their analyses as extremely superficial. It may well be the case that the liberation of suppressed religious impulses will produce a symptomatic improvement, but this does not prove that the impulses are innate. The liberation of suppressed sadism and homosexuality may also be helpful, but this does not prove that sadism or homosexuality are innate. Similarly, it is entirely believable that Jung's patients felt the absence of religious belief as a loss, but this does not show that their neuroses were caused by the loss of their religious belief. People who are not severely armored can take pleasure in love and work, and they do not find life meaningless because they cannot accept the claims of religion. A person who is severely armored and who loses his religion or, for that matter, any other substitute gratification, is going to experience such a loss as painful. Moreover, it is much less embarrassing to one's self-image to ascribe the sources of one's unhappiness to cosmic or philosophical causes than to attend to one's own (often not very admirable) character traits and to the not so spiritual contents of one's repressed desires.

The Great Cultural Revolution. Near the end of *The Future of an Illusion*, a book Reich greatly admired, Freud remarked that "in the long run nothing can withstand reason and experience, and the contradiction religion offers to both is only too palpable." Reich disagreed with this judgment. He agreed that religious mysticism is likely to die out, but he did not share Freud's confidence in the psychological effectiveness of rational considerations. Intellectual arguments are no match for the "most powerful emotion" on which the mass-psychological influence of religious institutions is based: sexual anxiety and sexual repression. People who no longer believe in God and the various doctrines of the churches are frequently subject to mystical feelings. If they are intellectuals, they will be attracted to a metaphysical philosophy like that of G. W. F. Hegel or Martin Heidegger; if they are not intellectuals they are liable to be attracted by one of the many political pseudoreligions and direct their worship to the worthless leaders of these movements.

Mysticism can be effectively opposed only if one is guided by the realization that it stems from inhibited sexuality. "Mysticism having dominated humanity for thousands of years," Reich writes, "it can expect of us beginners that we do not underestimate it, that we comprehend it correctly and show ourselves better informed . . . than its representatives." Whatever temporary setbacks there may be, the power of religious mysticism will be broken; and this will happen not as the result of the admirable and logically compelling criticisms of religious doctrines by philosophers and scientists, but because of social changes that have become irreversible. Ever since the beginning of the 20th century there has been a "thorough disintegration of the moralistic ascetic forms of living" and this "objective loosening of the reactionary fetters on sexuality cannot be undone." The passage just quoted was written in 1933. Who could dispute its prophetic accuracy in the 1980s? Reich realized that the "great cultural revolution" would at first lead to rebellions taking various grotesque forms, but he had no "fear for the final outcome."

A year earlier, in a pamphlet entitled *The Sexual Struggle of Youth*, he had made the same point with a flourish worthy of KARL MARX or THOMAS PAINE: "Socialism will put an end to the power of those who gaze up towards heaven as they speak of love whilst they crush and destroy the sexuality of youth."

As yet, moved by obscure "oceanic feelings," human beings fail to master their existence. Instead they dream and "perish from these dreams." However, once they master their existence—when they become capable of giving and receiving love and when work will be a source of pleasure and not a burden—we shall witness the death of "all transcendental mysticism, of the 'absolute objective spirit,'" and of all the metaphysical and irrationalist philosophies that are "subsumed under mysticism in the . . . wider sense." A person who is sexually happy "does not need an inhibiting 'morality' or a supernatural religious experience."

In this article nothing has been said about any of Reich's publications after 1950, because they do not add anything of substance to the topics discussed. Moreover, during this period Reich began to believe all kinds of absurd things and to see Communist conspiracies everywhere. On the basis of no credible evidence he asserted the existence of UFOs, which were said to be driven by orgone motors. He even toyed with the idea that he himself was the son of a spaceman. These are just a few samples. Those eager to dismiss him as nothing but a crank were quick to seize on these wild notions. It cannot therefore be sufficiently emphasized that the importance of Reich's psychiatric discoveries and the profundity of his insights into the causes of human misery are in no way affected by the nonsense he came to believe during his last years.

Bibliography

The theories discussed in this article are presented in the following four books by Reich (dates are of the American editions, all published in New York): *The Function of the Orgasm* (1942), *The Sexual Revolution* (1945), *The Mass Psychology of Fascism* (1946), and *Character Analysis* (3rd ed., 1949).

The following publications deal with Reich's life or aspects of various of his theories or both: M. Hodann, *A History of Modern Morals* (London, 1937); Martin Gardner, *Fads and Fallacies in the Name of Science* (New York, 2nd ed., 1957); Paul Edwards, "Reich, Wilhelm," *The Encyclopedia of Philosophy,* vol. 7 (New York, 1967); Ilse Ollendorff Reich, *Wilhelm Reich—A Personal Biography* (New York, 1969); J. S. Turner (representing the Ralph Nader Study Group), *The Chemical Feast* (New York, 1970); D. Boadella, *Wilhelm Reich—The Evolution of His Work* (London, 1973); J. Greenfield, *Wilhelm Reich vs. USA* (New York, 1974); and Myron Sharaf, *Fury on Earth* (New York, 1983).

The following articles in the *Zeitschrift für Politische Psychologie and Sexualökonomie* deal with the relation between religion and sexuality: J. H. Leunbach, "Religion und Sexualität," vol. 1 (1934); K. Teschitz, "Grundlagen der Religion," vol. 2 (1935); and "Religiöse Ekstase als Ersatz der sexuellen Auslösung," vol. 4 (1937); and T. Hartwig, "Der Sinn der 'religiös-sittlichen' Erziehung," vol. 4 (1937).

PAUL EDWARDS

REIMARUS, HERMANN SAMUEL (1694–1768), German theologian and writer. See **Germany, Unbelief in. Lessing, Gotthold Ephraim.**

RELIGION VS. SCIENCE. Are religion and science compatible or incompatible? Before this question can be addressed rationally, it is essential that its meaning be understood. What meanings are to be attached to the key terms: *religion, science, compatible,* and *incompatible*? Although a definitive treatment of the conceptual issues involved is beyond the scope of this inquiry, some clarification is absolutely necessary to avoid confusion.

Our question is not a question about psychological possibilities or actualities. That is, we are not concerned with whether people can accept both religious and scientific perspectives. It is a well-known fact of human psychology that by means of various psychological mechanisms (such as compartmentalization) people are able to accept beliefs that are logically inconsistent. For the same reason our question is not concerned with whether a particular culture can have religious as well as scientific features. All such empirical associations are without any logical force—of interest no doubt to social and behavioral scientists but logically irrelevant to the issue that concerns us here. Our concern is much more fundamental. The question we shall explore concerns the *logical* relations among various ideal cognitive aspects of religion and science. We may therefore reformulate our question in this way: Are religion and science, considered in terms of some of their essential ideal cognitive aspects, logically compatible or incompatible?

However, even this reformulation of the original question is insufficient. The terms *religion* and *science* must also be clarified. Both *science* and *religion* are used to refer to a multitude of diverse and complex human concerns and activities. Even if we limit ourselves to the logical relationships among some of their cognitive aspects, conceptual confusion is still overwhelming unless further delimitation is effected. For this reason I propose to limit *religion,* for the purpose of the present investigation to supernaturalistic religions, that is, to religions in which belief in some reality allegedly above or beyond nature, together with special, privileged modes of apprehending and adapting to such supposed realities, predominates. Limited in this way, the subject matter involved is still extremely diverse and complex, but not as hopelessly confusing as is the total field of religious cognitive phenomena. And it has the further advantage of being applicable to some of the most significant aspects of those religious phenomena most familiar to those of us exposed primarily to the dominant Western religious traditions.

For the same reasons, by *science* I mean the methodological and related cognitive conditions that ideally guide the development, testing, and systematic incorporation of explanatory principles in those enterprises that are commonly acknowledged to be sciences (and, to the extent permitted by the complexities and vagaries of their subject matters, by the so-called behavioral and social sciences as well).

Understood in this way, the pursuit of knowledge in science and religion involve characteristic complexes of interrelated components—attitudinal, ideational, volitional, and behavioral. Our analysis and comparison of these two fields will touch on all of these interrelated aspects of religious and scientific cognition, but since some of them have far more importance for cognition than others, the amount of attention given to the various components will vary considerably. The amount of emphasis to be given is also of course determined to a large extent by the overall purposes of this investigation: (1) to demonstrate unequivocally that religion and science, delimited as indicated, are logically incompatible, that is, that they ideally presuppose and imply logically inconsistent epistemic positions; (2) to demonstrate that scientific modes of understanding reality, or at least certain of its significant aspects, are reliable, whereas those alleged ways of knowing reality ideally employed and espoused by religionists are untrustworthy; and (3) to demonstrate that (1) and (2) supply cogent reasons why any rational person should adopt a position of unbelief toward religiously based, supernatural knowledge claims.

We should briefly consider a common subterfuge used by supernaturalists to avoid the conclusion that science and religion are incompatible while admitting their epistemic inconsistencies. The tactic involves the claim that religion and science occupy different domains, have different concerns, ask different kinds of questions, and therefore that there is no reason why the two should have the same cognitive stance. The fact is, however, that scientists and religionists have always made some of their claims about the same subjects—for example, human nature, the origin of things, and the reason why things are as they are. So the attempt to sharply compartmentalize the concerns of the two fields is absurd.

Let us begin with the ideal attitudes encouraged, and to a large extent realized, in the two fields. By *attitude* I mean a particular affect together with an inclination to act or abstain from acting in particular ways as a result of certain beliefs and values. If one critically examines the activities and discourse of scientists and religionists, when they are confining themselves to these preoccupations, one can identify clusters of closely related attitudinal components promoted as ideally characteristic of scientists and religionists. Furthermore, when this is done, it becomes manifest that at least some of the components of the ideal scientific and religious attitudes are diametrically opposed to each other.

First we may mention that scientists manifest a desire to understand nature strictly in terms of natural laws and concepts. When they are functioning as scientists they avoid supernatural or supernormal "explanatory" principles. In contrast, religionists, when they are functioning as religionists, manifest a desire to understand everything as essentially related to a supernatural basis. For them, explanation, in the fullest sense of that word, requires supernatural or supernormal "explanatory" principles.

Scientists also manifest a desire to have beliefs that are justifiable exclusively by means of publicly factual evidence and rational operations that require nothing more than normal minds and senses trained in the use of tested scientific procedures. Religionists, in contrast, show a willingness, sometimes even a distinct preference, for beliefs supposedly justified by appeal to such ways of "knowing" as mystical trance, revelation, authority and faith, methods which, in the final analysis. involve private experiences incapable of meeting the rigorous objective standards involved in scientific intersubjectivity.

Scientists tend to be skeptical of unsupported personal feelings of assurance, that is, they are usually clearly aware of the fact that psychological certitude is not equivalent to either logical certainty or empirical probability. Religionists, in contrast, tend to accept psychological certitude (that is, an unquestioning feeling or conviction that something involving their religion is true) as being cognitively equivalent to logical certainty or at least to empirical probability. Indeed, faith becomes, for many religious people, the paramount criterion of truth.

Scientists tend to think of scientific explanations in provisional, probabilistic terms, that is, as justifiable only to the extent warranted by the evidence accumulated up to that point (as well as other rigorous cognitive requirements they have satisfied) but always open to possible revision or even rejection if further evidence warrants. Religionists tend to think in absolute dogmatic terms. Fundamental religious beliefs are thought to be immutable, eternal, absolute truths that no evidence could possibly undermine.

Scientists tend to be cognitively manipulative, that is, they tend to try to understand those aspects of reality that interest them by experimental manipulation; they connect theory to carefully controlled, objectivity-based experimental alterations. Religionists, in contrast, tend to cultivate a passive receptivity, an uncritical openness to supposed supernatural influences expected to "enlighten" them.

Scientists tend to prefer logical simplicity, that is, a preference for not making unnecessary assumptions in order to explain phenomena. Religionists prefer to assume whatever seems to support their favorite interpretations of the world, even when logically simpler explanations of the phenomena are possible.

Scientists prefer conceptual clarity, that is, clear, unambiguous terms with logical connections to theoretical systems and to the objective aspects of nature. Religionists manifest a willingness to use vague, ambiguous, even essentially mysterious terms (*spirit, God, truth,* and *soul*) that lack any clearcut, logically systematic connections or any unambiguous objective empirical references.

This brief presentation of some of the contrasting aspects of the ideal scientific and religious attitudes suggests where the really basic incompatibility between science and religion is to be found, namely, in the incompatible cognitive methods and requirements that scientists and religionists tend to advocate and employ. Scientists, in their roles as scientists, insist that ways of knowing are reliable only if they satisfy stringent logical requirements, requirements that tend to minimize subjective bias and other sources of cognitive distortion. It is easy to show that religious ways of "knowing"—appeals to so-called mystical experiences, alleged revelations from supernatural beings, authority, tradition, faith, and so forth—fail to satisfy comparably stringent requirements

and as a consequence are cognitively suspect.

It is not necessary to argue at length that scientific methods have as high degree of reliability as cognitive methods. The fact that these methods have produced an evolving, self-correcting, increasingly comprehensive and internally consistent conceptual framework yielding innumerable objectively testable predictions, as well as practical applications that work in the objective world (that is, not just in someone's mind), is sufficient to rationally justify confidence in their cognitive adequacy. Scientific methodology is constantly being refined, and conclusions reached by scientific methods are never more than highly probable, but the cognitive excellence of such methods is beyond any reasonable doubt. The fact that scientific conceptions are sometimes revised or even replaced does not in any way detract from the usual reliability of scientific methods; indeed, such revisions and replacements point to the real virtue of such methods.

When we carefully and honestly examine the ways religionists acquire knowledge, we are forced to a very different assessment. In addition to the conceptual confusions generated by the vagueness of many key terms used in their discourse (*mystical, religious experience, spirit, faith*), analysis reveals serious logical inadequacies inherent in all the alleged ways of knowing espoused by religionists.

Let's consider the nonrational methods first. By *nonrational methods* I mean those alleged cognitive methods—such as fideism and mysticism— that even religionists concede do not involve either rational demonstrations or the logically controlled empirical procedures of science. Many religionists view such nonrational methods as the final court of appeal, that is, as the ultimate source and justification for religious beliefs. The fact is, however, that when methods such as these, or the beliefs supposedly established by their use, are questioned, no logically adequate response to the challenge is possible.

Any attempt to justify the ultimacy of a challenged nonrational method leads to logical difficulties. Any attempt to justify its adequacy as an ultimate way of knowing simply by insisting that it is cognitively ultimate begs the question, committing the fallacy of circular reasoning. Any attempt to justify its ultimacy by appeal to other methods (for instance, trying to justify the claim that one's faith is a sure source and justification for some knowledge claim because it is endorsed by some supposed authority) is paradoxical because it treats whatever nonrational method is used to justify the challenged nonrational method as the ultimate method rather than the method which, at first, was supposed to be ultimate. In other words, it ends up by conceding that the supposedly ultimate method is really derivative. The sort of problems that arise can be illustrated by considering the consequences of challenges to one of the nonrational ways of "knowing." What applies in such a case applies, *mutatis mutandis,* to all nonrational ways of "knowing."

Consider the appeal to religious experience as an ultimate justification for some belief. The expression *religious experience* has been used to refer to diverse phenomena and frequently inconsistent conceptions. For the purpose of analysis, let us take it to mean any sort of powerful, self-transforming experience attributed to a supernatural encounter. This definition is of course too narrow, since it excludes many sorts of powerful, self-transforming experiences that are commonly accepted as religious even though they are not considered to be due to a supernatural agency (for instance, some of the experiences cultivated by Zen Buddhists). The definition is, however, consistent with the circumscribed meaning adopted for the term *religion*, a meaning that fits much of what passes for religious phenomena in the better-known supernaturalisms. And it will serve our purpose at least as well as a more comprehensive meaning would.

Now, although such experiences are psychologically persuasive, at least for the person undergoing the experience, it must be admitted that there are many logical reasons to be skeptical of their pretensions. Indeed, even those who accept some such experiences as ultimate sources and justification for certain beliefs generally acknowledge that some alleged religious experiences are not genuine. Some, they aver, are faked or due to mental aberrations or due to demonic influence, and so forth. Logical and scientific considerations, reflecting careful studies of such phenomena and their attendant circumstances, lead to cogent reasons for a much more profound SKEPTICISM. Here I shall not consider the relevant discoveries from such diverse fields as anthropology, psychology, and psychiatry, discoveries that make it quite clear that the causes of such experiences have natural rather than supernatural causes. Instead, I shall limit myself to some of the logical problems involved.

Suppose that an individual, A, claims that some belief must be true because it has been revealed to him or her during a powerful religious experience, one not allowing for the slightest doubt. Under these circumstances it is reasonable for a skeptic to pose certain questions to A, such as: (1) Is it possible for people to be mistaken about the source and significance of unusual and powerful experiences? (2) How can you be certain that you are not mistaken about the source and significance of your own experience? (3) On what basis do you feel justified in dismissing a purely psychological origin for your experience? (4) If you were confronted by a person holding a contradictory belief also allegedly based on a religious experience, could you establish the genuineness of your own experience and the spuriousness of the other person's experience?

There are only two alternatives, aside from violence or silence, open to A when he or she is challenged by questions such as these: (1) A can try to justify his or her conviction that the religious experience was a genuine supernatural experience, or (2) A can simply reaffirm his or her conviction that the experience was genuine.

The first alternative is self-defeating. The person began by appealing to religious experience as the ultimate justification for a religious belief and ends up conceding that the supposedly ultimate justification is itself in need of justification. And how can anyone try to defend the authenticity of a supposed religious experience anyway? There are only two ways to go—"rational" argumentation or some sort of appeal to other nonrational methods (appeal to authority, tradition, intuition, commonsense).

However, the use of *rational* demonstrations has been notoriously unsuccessful, leading to diverse and discordant conclusions, reflecting nothing more than the dubious assumptions of particular thinkers—that is one of the principal reasons why people have made appeals to religious experiences to ground their beliefs. But nonrational defenses are even less effective. If appeal is made to authority, intuition, and so forth to authenticate one's religious experience, the skeptic can raise questions analogous to those involved in critiquing the appeal to religious experience. And these questions, in turn, compel the religious person to choose one of the two alternatives—defense or reaffirmation—with the same sort of consequences if defense is attempted.

The second alternative is also self-defeating, but for a different reason. If the religious believer simply reaffirms his or her conviction that the religious experience is reliable, the skeptic can reasonably point out that this amounts to an arbitrary, circular position. It amounts to saying "*x* is dependable because I assume (claim) it is dependable," which is simply the fallacy of begging the question.

We are led to conclude, therefore, that although scientific modes of understanding aspects of reality generally tend to be reliable, the alleged ways of knowing reality ideally employed and promoted by religionists are untrustworthy (since they lead to inconsistent differences of opinion which the methods do not make it possible to adjudicate) and rationally indefensible (since any attempt to defend their adequacy as cognitive methods leads to either a logical paradox or commits a *petitio* fallacy).

In view of the unreliability and rational indefensibility of religious cognitive methods, how much confidence should a person who tries to be as rational and scientific as possible have that religious knowledge claims are true? I do not ask this question only in connection with those cases where religious knowledge claims concern matters also addresssed by scientists (such as claims about the nature of human beings, the origin of the earth, the origin of living things, human free will, the reason why pain and other forms of suffering occur in the world), but also in connection with knowledge claims about matters which scientists, *qua* specialized scientists, do not address (such as claims about the reality and nature of various sorts of alleged supernatural entities, dimensions, processes and forces).

Although the historical conflicts between scientific and religious accounts have made it much easier to be aware of the dubiousness and occasionally pernicious effects of claims of the former type, there are cogent reasons for considering claims of the latter kind with equal suspicion and with at least some degree of apprehension.

If by "a person who tries to be as rational and scientific as possible" is meant an individual who (1) always tries to reason correctly from carefully ascertained objective evidence (in order to reach logically justified conclusions about the world and other aspects of human experience) and who, furthermore, (2) refuses to give credence to any claim where evidence is insufficient or nonexistent, then the answer to the question posed is obvious. When such a person is presented with the untenable claims of religionists, that is, the claims based exclusively on their indefensible and unreliable ways of "knowing," logical consistency seems to demand that such a person's response be one of

unbelief, that is, a refusal to believe a claim "justified" by such means. At least this is true unless a rationally persuasive justification can be given for adopting a dual standard of truth and cognition.

Of course, those who prefer to believe that religious ways of knowing really are reliable, at least in connection with various theological questions, adopt certain defenses against charges of irrationality and intellectual dishonesty. Those whose theological positions have been deeply molded by St. Thomas, for instance, insist that there are two kinds of truths about divine matters—truths that reason can reach and revealed truths that exceed reason.

The trouble with this tactic, however, is that it rests on dubious assumptions. It assumes, for instance, that the existence of God can be, or has been, proven and can be known on the basis of genuine revelations that have occurred; but neither of these claims can meet the reasonable objections of skeptics. The commonest strategem, however, is some variant of the positions adopted by Sören Kierkegaard and William James, which amounts to suggesting, in one way or another, that if one adopts a skeptical, rational stance—of the sort appropriate in science—one may be closing the door to divine inspiration or revelation.

People who hold such a position suggest that an attitude of trust, openness, uncritical acceptance (or at least the willingness to relax our critical defenses) is, or may be, a necessary condition for divine knowledge. It is their contention that to insist that only scientifically rational, cognitive requirements are really justificatory is to impose conditions that may preclude real knowledge of divine matters. There is an obvious weakness in all such tactics, however. If one must relax critical safeguards in order to make divine inspiration possible, then it becomes impossible to prevent oneself from being fooled into confusing purely subjective fantasies for objective realities. In the requisite state, credulity, the operation of suggestion, imagination, data-selection biases, and so forth can hardly be avoided. How, then, can one who adopts such an attitude ever be assured that what he or she takes to be divine knowledge really is what it seems to be?

History makes it abundantly clear that the cultivation of various altered mental states (especially those in which passivity, trust, openness, and uncritical acceptance predominate) has led to the acceptance of a vast assortment of metaphysical notions (many so obscure that we are not entitled to call them conceptions), many of which must be delusional, since they contradict each other.

All such stratagems are dismal failures. It appears to be impossible to successfully pose as rational and at the same time accept doctrines "established" by the cognitive conditions ideally employed and espoused by religionists.

Unfortunately, intellectual dishonesty is not the only pernicious consequence of easy believing. The individual who tries to persuade himself that there is nothing dishonest or irrational or unscientific about accepting the dubious claims and cognitive methods of religion may suffer some personal difficulty (perhaps a vaguely nagging sense of cognitive dissonance), but in itself this is probably the least of the harmful consequences.

Scholars such as Andrew Dickson White (see Bibliography) have amply documented the horrendous social and intellectual consequences of dogmatic religious belief. The religious wars, the torture and other forms of persecution of heretics, the censorship of ideas (including the burning of books), the attempts made to impose narrow and ill-founded moral practices on others, and so forth, are well known concomitants of religious bigotry. And although this is more subdued in much of today's world, there are still plenty of indications of actual and potential mischief manifested in the utterances and actions of many religionists. Nor are the social and intellectual dangers limited to the crude fundamentalisms. There are all sorts of mystical, magical, and esoteric phenomena in the world today that prevent intellectual and social health.

In my own view, however, even more serious consequences are likely to result from the adoption of a dubious religious cognitive stance. The fact is that our attitudes and beliefs constitute the basis for our attempts to adapt ourselves (as individuals, social groups, and as a species) to the real world, to the total global ecosystem and its subsystems. So viewed, cognitive stances translate into adaptive mechanisms which, depending on their natures and the nature of the world, will tend to be more or less functional or disfunctional, tending to be either life-promoting or life-defeating.

Unrealistic and irrational modes of adaptation (such as the defense mechanisms of neurotic and psychotic individuals) may work up to a point, but they are not optimally effective (because they rest on mistaken presuppositions or half-truths). Usually, the more realistic and rational a mode of adaptation is, the more successful it will be, at least

in the long run. So the cognitive framework that forms the basis for adaptation to the natural world has tremendous practical significance. It follows, therefore, that the unreliable cognitive conditions cultivated in religion, in marked contrast to those cultivated in science, constitute a significant threat to the improved quality of human life and perhaps even to human survival.

These are cogent reasons why any rational person should adopt a position of unbelief toward religiously based, supernatural knowledge claims and encourage the development of a scientific humanism.

Other articles of interest: **God, Existence of. Miracles, Unbelief in. Rationalism. Reason. Revelation, Unbelief in.**

Bibliography

Angeles, Peter, ed. *Critiques of God.* Buffalo, N.Y.: Prometheus Books, 1976.

———. *The Problem of God.* Buffalo, N.Y.: Prometheus, 1980.

Asimov, Isaac. *In the Beginning.* New York: Crown, 1981.

Clements, Tad S. *Science and Man, The Philosophy of Scientific Humanism.* American Lecture Series in Philosophy, ed. Marvin Farber. Springfield, Ill.: Charles C. Thomas, 1968.

Flew, Antony, R. M. Hare, and Basil Mitchell. "Theology and Falsification." *Philosophy, the Basic Issues,* ed. E. D. Klemke, A. David Kline, and Robert Hollinger. New York: St. Martin's Press, 1982.

Johnson, B. C. *The Atheist Debater's Handbook.* Buffalo, N.Y.: Prometheus, 1981.

McCloskey, H. J. "God and Evil." *Philosophy, the Basic Issues,* ed. E. D. Klemke, et al. New York: St. Martin's Press, 1982.

Montagu, Ashley. *Ways of Knowing.* New York: Humanities Press, 1978.

Nagel, Ernest. *The Structure of Science, Problems in the Logic of Scientific Explanation.* New York: Harcourt, Brace, 1961.

Nielsen, Kai. *Reason and Practice.* New York: Harper & Row, 1971.

———. *Scepticism.* New York: St. Martin's Press, 1973.

Russell, Bertrand. *Religion and Science.* 1935. New York: Oxford U. Press, 1980.

———. *The Impact of Science on Society.* New York: Columbia U. Press, 1951.

Smith, George H. *Atheism, The Case Against*

God. Buffalo, N.Y.: Prometheus, 1979.

Stein, Gordon, ed. *An Anthology of Atheism and Rationalism.* Buffalo, N.Y.: Prometheus, 1980.

White, Andrew D. *A History of the Warfare of Science with Theology in Christendom.* New York: George Braziller, 1955.

TAD S. CLEMENTS

REVELATION, UNBELIEF IN. Apart from a few tentative inquiries by BENEDICT SPINOZA, the infallibility of literal revelation was not questioned by Christians, Jews, Muslims, or Zoroastrians until the 18th century, although there were some sects, such as the Islamic Mutazilites and Zoroastrian Mazdaks, who were rationalists in the Hellenic sense of holding pure reason to be the means of attaining absolute truth. In this respect, however, they were not very different from the Muslim, Jewish, and Christian Scholastics of medieval times, who subscribed to Aristotelian logic and constructed what they termed natural theologies on that basis. Natural theology is what can be known of the divine apart from revelation, the famous "proofs" for the existence of God by Thomas Aquinas and Anselm being cases in point. Averroës, Moses Maimonides, and Aquinas, the principal Muslim, Jewish, and Christian Scholastic philosophers respectively, all accepted the ultimate authority of revelation as recorded in the Bible or the Koran.

Major Monotheistic Religions. To Jews the fullest revelation, or divine self-disclosure, was in the Torah (Pentateuch), the first five books of the Bible, known to Jews as the Law of Moses, and, on the basis of tradition but not scripture itself, allegedly written by Moses and presumably dictated to him by Yahweh himself in the form of visions, oracles, and occasions such as the initial divine encounter in Sinai when Yahweh spoke to Moses in an audible voice from the burning bush that was not consumed. In Orthodox Judaism the Torah remains the cornerstone of revelation, with the rest of Jewish biblical literature considered divinely revealed but of lesser authority.

Canon, or the official corpus of revealed scripture, was determined by rabbinical councils such as the Council of the Great Synagogue during the 2nd century B.C. on the basis of consensus. While the Book of Daniel (probably composed around 168–165 B.C.) was held to be revelation, other contemporary texts such as First and Second Maccabees and the Books of Enoch were considered valuable and authoritative but not revelation. While literary excellence and apparent authenticity were taken into account, the principal reason for holding some texts to be worthy of canon and others consigned to Apocrypha and Pseudepigrypha is not easily determined. The reasoning seemed to be that a text was canonical if it was so regarded, consensus, therefore, being vital to the determination of revelation.

The Hebrew-Jewish model applied directly to both Christianity and Islam, and either influenced Zoroastrianism or coincided with it. All living Western religions are, as mentioned, based on revelation and stand or fall on the authority of canon, a concept foreign to Eastern religions.

Early Christians accepted the Jewish Bible as sacred scripture but, during the course of the first two centuries after the birth of Jesus, they treated the books called Gospels, as well as Revelations, as divinely inspired, and also the letters of apostles such as Paul, Peter, James, Timothy, and Jude. As late as the Reformation, there was disagreement about which of these writings should be regarded as revelation, with Luther particularly dubious about James. Again, consensus was the basis for decision, ratified, finally, by church councils and papal decrees. Because the period of canonization belongs to the early period of church history, for which data is generally lacking, it is not really known just how the New Testament came to be composed and canonized; it is only certain that by the end of the 3rd century it was in its present form and, along with what was now called the Old Testament, was considered to be divinely revealed scripture.

In medieval Catholic tradition, however, the Bible was the beginning of revelation, and the decisions of church councils, doctrinal formulations, and the rare ex-cathedra papal decrees were all treated as revelation. This became a major issue during the Reformation, with the Protestant reformers rejecting all texts except the Old and New Testaments. In consequence, while even conservative Catholics have few problems with the biological theory of evolution, for example, orthodox Protestants are threatened by the challenge to the literal version of the creation story since the infallible inerrancy of revealed scripture is basic to Protestant Christianity.

Like Judaism, Islam is a legalistic religion in which the *shari'a* (law) corresponds to the Talmud.

Most of the Koran is believed to have been written by Muhammed himself on the inspiration of oracles and visions. Unlike Christians and Jews, Muslims do not depend on the veracity of an oral tradition preceding the literary recording of texts. Orthodox Muslims consider the Arabic Koran to be the earthly correspondent of a heavenly archetype. Although there have been a few Muslim scholars, such as Muhammed Iqbal, who have applied critical techniques to Koranic study, the great Islamic centers of learning such as Al-Azhar University are fundamentalist. Every word of the Koran is as God revealed it, in the Muslim view.

In addition to the Koran there is also Hadith, or orally transmitted tradition, also considered to be revelation though of lesser authority than the Koran. Finally there is *ijma,* or consensus, also considered a less authoritative form of revelation. To Muslims, the sacred scriptures are the Old Testament plus the New Testament plus the Koran plus the Hadith plus *ijma.*

While considerable secularization has occurred in the Muslim world during the present century, unbelief is rarely encountered. Westernized Muslims sometimes drift away from their traditional religion but seldom challenge doctrine or scripture.

Both Sikhism and Baha'i are young religions of basically Islamic origin. Sikhism rose out of the syncretist tendencies of the India of the Mughal Empire as a blend of Hindu and Muslim elements as proclaimed by the poet-prophets Kabir and Nanak. Their utterances were recorded in the Granth, which, along with the Muslim scriptures and Hindu texts constitutes revelation in Sikh tradition. Baha'i, an Iranian movement that emerged from the Shi'ite sect of the Twelvers, is also syncretist, and, in addition to the Bible and Koran (and to some extent the Buddhist scriptures) holds the writings of the Bab, Baha'ullah, and Abdul Baha to be divinely revealed and authoritative. Most Baha'is are fundamentalists where scriptural authority is concerned; many Sikhs are secularists, Sikhism being chiefly an ethnic identity.

There is, finally, Zoroastrianism, preserved by the 125,000 Parsis of India and by a handful of Gabars in Iran. The Gathas, the oldest of the Zoroastrian texts, supposedly record the words of the prophet Zoroaster, based on oracles and visions. Actually the Gathas are probably later writings of followers. Subsequent sacred scriptures, the Avestas, survive only in fragmentary form, having been lost in the course of the persecutions

suffered by Zoroastrians in Iran and in their subsequent migration to India. Contrary to popular impressions, Zoroastrianism is a monotheistic religion with a theistic creed very similar to the basic creeds of Jews, Christians, and Muslims though, as far as is known, of independent origin.

In earlier times, orthodox Zoroastrians were scriptural literalists. Today, however, because of secularist tendencies that have reduced the number of practicing believers considerably, the tightly knit Parsi community may be regarded as a highly traditional society, exceptionally exclusive, but mainly composed of highly educated business and professional families who are secularist and for whom Zoroastrianism is chiefly an ethnic identity. There is, in brief, a great deal of unbelief in revelation among Zoroastrians though not, for the most part, based on any conscious philosophical deliberations.

The Higher Critics. Unbelief in revelation as a consequence of deliberate rational-empirical inquiry is overwhelmingly a product of Protestant scholarship of the last century with some 18th-century forerunners involved. The inerrancy and infallibility of the Bible was universally accepted until the end of the 17th century. Later, much influenced by the Enlightenment, scholars appeared, chiefly in Germany, who applied the comparatively young techniques of literary analysis and historiography to biblical literature. Thus, pioneer studies by Johann Gottfried Eichhorn (died 1827), the founder of modern Old Testament studies, preceded the efforts of Ferdinand Christian Baur who, as professor of theology at Tübingen in Germany from 1826 to 1860, founded the school of so-called higher criticism.

As opposed to what is sometimes called lower criticism, which concerns itself only with accuracy of translation, the higher critics attempted to distinguish the documentary origins of biblical texts on the basis of philological, linguistic, and stylistic considerations. They also took an interpretative point of view. For the most part, the higher critics confined themselves to technical problems of a highly specialized nature, but the implications of their work were highly significant as a challenge to revelation.

Scholars such as Julius Wellhausen (died 1918) found the Pentateuch to be composed of texts that showed such abrupt changes of style and vocabulary in their original Hebrew form as to be indubitably of varied origins. There was not one creation story but two in Genesis, for example, and, indeed, at least three distinct strands of literature could be identified. These were labeled J (Jahvist), E (Elohist), and P (Priestly). Because of these studies the alleged Mosaic origins of the first five books of the Bible could no longer be sustained.

While all of the Tübingen scholars were orthodox Lutherans, their investigations of necessity opened doubts concerning revelation itself. If, as seemed the case, the texts as they appear in the Bible were derived from separate sources gathered by redactors at a later period, and if these, as seemed to be the case, were, in turn, based on folk tales, oral traditions, Canaanite, Babylonian, Hurrian, and Egyptian precedents, at what point could it be said that this or that text was divinely revealed? Was it when the story first occurred as a folk tale among shepherds, say, or when J, E, or the priests wrote it down, or when the unknown redactors brought all three together, or when the Council of the Great Synagogue decided what was canonical and what was not? While the higher critics themselves did not dwell on such questions, and although their writings were chiefly confined to theological circles, such implications could not do anything but affect theological thinking.

Higher criticism was a major reason for the rise of the modernist school of Protestant theology at the turn of the century of which Albert Schweitzer (*Quest for the Historical Jesus*, 1907) was an important figure. The modernist or liberal scholars rejected literalism and held that divine revelation occurred through the vehicle of myth and symbol and that scientific and historical accuracy was not important. In this view, the myth is not a fanciful tale but a metaphorical means by which truth is expressed in poetic language. In the modernist view, what were called fundamentalists (from a conference of conservative Protestants at Niagara Falls, N.Y., in 1907) erred in their narrow literalism, which prevented them from seeing the deeper mythopoeic meaning of scriptural texts. Thus the main point is missed in the Jonah story if one becomes preoccupied with whether or not a man could survive in the belly of a great fish. The story, from the modernist view, is an allegory by which the message was communicated that God cares as much about your enemies as he does about you, since Jonah was unable to escape a divine call to preach to Israel's foes in Nineveh.

Beginnings of Skepticism. Inevitably, however, it occurred to some to wonder if the Bible was divinely revealed at all; since the texts of which it is composed are not remarkably different from writings that are not uncanonical and also very similar to the allegedly revealed texts of other religions, such as the Koran. If the Bible is revealed, why not the Koran as well? If the Koran is not revealed, is the Bible? Unthinking compliance to authority as such was not adequate for people with inquiring minds. As a consequence, and from the end of the 17th century, a skeptical tradition arose; it was composed of rationalists who were not willing to accept the authority of creeds and church and who demanded proof that would meet the test of rational-empirical inquiry.

Thus, accompanying the emergent school of Protestant higher criticism, and intimately associated with it, was the Enlightenment with its rationalist and skeptical strains. These included the latitudinarians, pioneer religious liberals, who were chiefly Unitarian and Anglican, and also the deists, who belonged to a more radical segment of the population. In various forms, latitudinarianism and DEISM won over most intellectuals during the Enlightenment. Fundamentalism has never recaptured more than a few members of the intelligentsia. Unbelief in revelation or, as in the case of the liberals, interpretation of revelation in rationalist terms has become characteristic even of neoorthodox theologians such as Reinhold Niebuhr, Emil Brunner, and Karl Barth, who speak of the truth of myth.

What is now called fundamentalism was called *enthusiasm* in the 18th century, a term meaning "fanatic." It survives today only among people of narrow educational background or persons who could be characterized as authoritarian personalities. Belief in literal revelation has tended to disappear among the great majority of Western Christians, both Protestant and Catholics, and survives only among the most orthodox of Jews. Although right-wing movements such as the Moral Majority have given fundamentalism some apparent strength during the late seventies and early eighties, most American conservatives, such as Barry Goldwater and Billy Graham, do not subscribe to the notions of the Moral Majority.

Contemporary attitudes toward revelation vary considerably, even within the Judeo-Christian tradition. As mentioned, the New Right, which includes the Moral Majority, have revived strict fundamentalism, an approach which had languished considerably since the twenties and the infamous "monkey" trial in Tennessee. (See CLARENCE DARROW.) Old-style fundamentalism, mainly confined to culturally and intellectually impoverished areas in the American South and Middle West advocates a naive literalism. Every word of the King James version of the Bible is accepted as written. Interpretation is confined to doctrinal positions accepted by various evangelical denominations and sects, these latter being the actual authority by which the Bible itself is authorized. There is, for example, no prohibition against alcoholic beverages in the Bible, but most fundamentalists of the older variety insist, nevertheless, that it is divinely prohibited. Proof texts, usually taken out of context, are employed to support doctrinal positions. An early Protestant precedent, which occurred among the Anabaptists, put direct revelation or the "inner light" ahead of scripture.

In these radical forms of Protestantism, God speaks directly to the mind of the sanctified Christian, through what some Great Awakening itinerant preachers called "impulses and impressions." All thoughts in the stream of consciousness, however random and absurd, are revelations, sometimes pointing to scriptural proof texts but just as often not. Thus, in this highly individualistic form of Protestantism, at one time much favored among Southern Baptists and other conservative sects, revelation is first and foremost personal experience. During the 17th century, the Friends or Quakers were distinguished by this sort of religious individualism but, since the 18th century, members of this denomination have tended to be distinguished for both RATIONALISM and liberalism, especially those of the Hicksite tradition, who are actually unitarian.

Emphasis on personal experience and the inner light have had the long-term effect of encouraging unbelief in scriptural revelation, the latter being held to be lacking in spiritual vitality. Intelligent fundamentalists usually retain their simplistic literalism only by compartmentalizing, in which case religious belief is carefully sealed off from other areas of thought so that, inconsistently, such individuals often entertain contradictory views concerning science, say, and avoid conflict by a stop-think process. Since such inner contradiction seldom endures much stress, it is by no means unusual for fundamentalists to become fierce unbelievers. As such, they are usually extremists. Most fundamentalists, however, are unreflective and, as mentioned, fit the pattern of the "authoritarian personality." (See T. W. Adorno, et al., *The Authoritarian Personality,* New York, Harper, 1950.)

Among fundamentalists, in effect, the divinely revealed authority is actually the preacher or elder who interprets scripture rather than scripture itself—or the community of believers in more democratic situations—so that, as in postexilic Judaism, primitive Christianity, and early Islam, consensus is the real authority. The divinely revealed word is not scripture alone or even primarily but rather what is held to be the will of God in the particular community. This, rather than textual problems, is the principal reason for contradictions and inconsistencies. Textual ambiguity is more often the reason for conflict rather than specific variance in the texts. Thus, while the classical inconsistency concerning Cain's wife is invariably glossed over by fundamentalists, they will often differ sharply among each other concerning adult baptism. This happens because proof texts are usually capable of more than one interpretation and because the doctrine was formulated and the proof text sought, rather than the other way around.

In the case of the New Right, neofundamentalism is entertained by a considerably larger segment of the population, many of whom have been exposed to higher education. By 1985, Jerry Falwell and other Moral Majority leaders seemed to be primarily interested in finding grounds for making conservative political, economic, and social attitudes into absolutes. The same technique of applying proof texts is used, but, to an even greater degree than among the older fundamentalists, those of the New Right assume prophetic roles. The Bible has little or nothing to say about capitalism or the kind of family patterns that have developed in America, nothing whatsoever about erotic art and literature, and very little about sexuality. Old Testament patriarchs who practiced polygamy, for example, must be glossed over or ignored. On the other hand, many neofundamentalists find no scriptural objections to the occasional cocktail. Quite clearly, the New Right, which includes a very large number of affluent and sophisticated people, is tolerant about the conventional vices of the middle class while, at the same time, harshly punitive toward deviant minorities such as marijuana users, another issue for which there is no appropriate proof text. In brief, the "word of God" is what Jerry Falwell says it is, and it is here that he differs sharply from other evangelicals such as Billy Graham.

Self-styled prophecy is a peculiarity of American Protestantism, the Church of Jesus Christ of Latter-day Saints (Mormons) and Christian Science being classical examples. Since no one but Joseph Smith saw the mysterious plates from which the text of the Book of Mormon was supposedly dictated, the real authority was not the text but Joseph Smith as prophet. Thus, belief in the authority of the Book of Mormon as revelation depends on acceptance of Smith, just as belief in the resurrection of Jesus ultimately depends on acceptance of the veracity and reliability of the apostolic witnesses. In the case of Christian Science, while *Science and Health* is known to have been adapted from the writings of a faith healer, its authority rests on the prophetic role of Mary Baker Eddy, so that for Scientists as for Mormons the textual origin of these special scriptures is irrelevant.

During the 19th century, doubts in some quarters about the historicity of Jesus raised problems that would be common to all revealed religions. Would it really matter if Jesus, for example, turned out to be a mythical figure like Krishna? While the vast majority of Christians resisted this possibility, a few like the Unitarian Theodore Parker suggested that even such an important and central figure as Jesus was of passing significance compared to the Gospels themselves and that his teachings rest on their own veracity rather than on the personal authority of Jesus. (See UNITARIANISM.) To be sure, this position was possible for a 19th-century Unitarian for whom Jesus was not the incarnation of deity but a spiritual and ethical teacher. Biblical scholarship, even in Parker's own day, did not support the uniqueness of the teachings of Jesus, since most of the sayings are easily traced to Old Testament sources.

By 1907, after a half century or more of debate, the question of the historical Jesus was dropped by most scholars, when Schweitzer's *Quest for the Historical Jesus* showed that the Gospels do not provide enough biographical material to reconstruct a life of Jesus and that his ethical teachings were of less importance than his theological role as redeemer, which must be accepted, if at all, on the testimony of the apostles.

Among most Christians—Protestant, Catholic, and Orthodox—the authority of revelation is accepted on traditionalist grounds and there is, as mentioned, little problem with higher criticism and biblical scholarship. It is generally conceded that the Bible is a highly complex library of books, very difficult to interpret, and that there is much ambiguity, especially where important doctrines such as the Trinity are involved. Officially or not, the authority of revelation rests with consensus, determined in Roman Catholicism by the College of Cardinals, by the patriarchate among the Eastern Orthodox, and usually by council and confer-

ence among Protestants. A like process occurs among contemporary Jews and Muslims. Both rely very heavily on tradition and consensus, which is determined by rabbinical councils in the case of Judaism and by the Ulema or doctors of theology in the case of Islam, the Ulema being a kind of supreme court.

Many unbelievers in revelation openly reject the interpretations of denominations, sects, and evangelists and are skeptical of scriptures. Some reject both. They represent the enduring tradition of dissent, which occurs in all religious traditions in a process by which the old dissenters, in time, often become the new orthodoxy. This is certainly true of the Peoples Republic of China and the Marxist-Leninists of the Soviet bloc, where unbelief itself became normative and supported by institutions such as the League of the Militant Godless in the Soviet Union during Stalinist times.

Also, a kind of humanist orthodoxy often occurs in Unitarian-Universalist churches and fellowships despite attempts at inclusiveness, and, to an even greater degree in rationalist associations, humanist associations, and in the ETHICAL CULTURE Society. While all of these reject supernaturalist revelation there is usually operant consensus. Thus, while Unitarian-Universalists stress individual freedom of belief, people of a conservative Protestant orientation are self-excluded and, indeed, the same processes of exclusion frequently occur when militant humanists, advocates of gay rights, or socialists attempt to advocate their beliefs in middle-class, family-oriented congregations where any sort of militancy is frowned upon.

Thus, while religious liberals and humanists usually stress the authority of reason rather than revelation, much the same processes often occur as in congregations that are based on such. In all traditions, while the psychology of religious experience, and of prophetic experience in particular, is often of interest to historians of religions, this is usually not the real source of revealed authority. Not Moses, Jesus, and Muhammed themselves but how they are regarded by the dominant elites among their followers determines what is revelation and what is not. It is also not the Bible or the Koran but the authoritative interpretation to which the religious elites adhere that determines scriptural authority. This is a dynamic process that applies to all creeds, doctrinal formulations, and religious law.

Other articles of interest: **Christianity, Unbelief Within. Enlightenment, Unbelief During** the. Islam, Unbelief Within. Jesus, Historicity of. Judaism, Unbelief Within.

R. W. BROCKWAY

RICKER, MARILLA (1840–1920), American freethinker and attorney. See **Women and Unbelief.**

ROALFE, MATILDA (1813–1880), English freethinking bookseller. See **Women and Unbelief.**

ROBERTSON, JOHN MACKINNON (1856–1933), British freethinker. He had perhaps the greatest knowledge of freethought of any freethinker who has ever lived. The author of about 115 books (the exact number is difficult to determine since he sometimes used pseudonyms), Robertson was born on the Scottish island of Arran. He left school at the age of 13 to help support his family.

Robertson was entirely self-educated, a fact that makes his later scholarly achievements only that much more amazing. After a series of jobs, he accepted a position as a writer on the Edinburgh *Evening News,* eventually rising to become assistant editor of that paper.

Career in Freethought. Robertson became a freethinker after hearing a lecture by CHARLES BRADLAUGH in 1878. He was an active member of the Edinburgh Secular Society in the early 1880s and was recruited in 1884 by ANNIE BESANT to work on Bradlaugh's NATIONAL REFORMER. His arrival in London to take the job marks his formal entrance into freethought leadership.

Robertson became assistant editor of the *National Reformer,* becoming editor when Bradlaugh died in 1891. Although the magazine did not last long under Robertson's editorship, that is more a tribute to the power of Bradlaugh's personality than attributable to a flaw in Robertson's ability.

Robertson kept his personal life to himself. He married Maud Mosher of Des Moines, Iowa, in 1893, and had a son and a daughter. Elected to Parliament in 1906 as a Liberal from Tynside, he was a success there, becoming parliamentary secretary to the Board of Trade in 1911 and a member of the Privy Council in 1915. That brought him the

title "The Right Honorable."

Robertson's literary output can be measured in earnest from the time he first arrived in London. Many of his articles were later expanded or revised as books. His crowning scholarly achievement was undoubtedly his *History of Freethought, Ancient and Modern, to the Period of the French Revolution* (2 vols.) and *History of Freethought in the Nineteenth Century* (2 vols.). These masterpieces are the fourth edition of a work that was originally published as *A Short History of Freethought* in 1899. Although these volumes are not easy reading because of Robertson's dense style, they are unlikely ever to be surpassed. His definition of FREETHOUGHT was broader than is commonly used; he used *freethought* almost as a synonym for progress in the liberalization of the philosophy of religion.

Another area of Robertson's expertise concerned the authorship of the plays of William Shakespeare and the sources from which Shakespeare drew his plots. Perhaps the most important work was *The Baconian Heresy,* in which he definitely disposes of the theory that Francis Bacon wrote the plays. Robertson also became the leading British authority on free trade and wrote a number of books on the subject. Another area in which he could be called a master was the history of religion.

The Jesus Issue. Robertson was perhaps the foremost exponent in his time of the myth theory of Jesus, which held that a figure named Jesus of Nazareth never existed (see JESUS, HISTORICITY OF). The five-volume series he wrote began as articles and were expanded, eventually including: *Christianity and Mythology, Pagan Christs, The Jesus of History, Jesus and Judas,* and *The Jesus Problem.*

Robertson's thesis was an entirely original one, although subsequent research has made some of his conclusions suspect. He held that portions of the Gospels were actually derived from morality plays and that this was forgotten with the passage of time. He cites a number of Bible passages where the action described is compressed in such a way that the passage makes sense only if it represents a play where one scene has ended and another begun, with the stage directions omitted.

After initially propounding his theory in the first two of his "Jesus" books, Robertson devoted most of the other three to answering his numerous critics. Almost no theologian liked his ideas about the existence of a lost morality play as the basis for the stories of Jesus in the Gospels. Few historians and other scholars agreed with his ideas either, although he attracted some support. Robertson's thesis has now been more or less discarded, but the theory that Jesus may never have been a historical person is an idea that is still viable.

Bibliography

Andreski, Stanislav. "A Forgotten Genius: John Mackinnon Robertson (1856–1933)." *Question,* no. 12 (1979).

Anonymous. "John Mackinnon Robertson. Born November 14, 1856; Died January 5, 1933." *The Literary Guide.* Feb. 1933. See also "Further Tributes to J. M. Robertson." *The Literary Guide.* March 1933.

Cook, W. Glanville. "John Mackinnon Robertson, 1856–1933." *The Rationalist* (Melbourne). May/June 1957.

Cutner, H. "John M. Robertson—1." *The Freethinker.* Nov. 9, 1956. See also "John M. Robertson—2." *The Freethinker.* Nov. 16, 1956.

Kaczkowski, Conrad. "John Mackinnon Robertson: A Freethinking Radical." Unpublished Ph.D. dissertation, St. Louis University, 1964.

Page, Martin. *Britain's Unknown Genius: The Life-Work of John M. Robertson.* London: South Place Ethical Society, 1984.

———. "J. M. Robertson—The Radical." *The Freethinker.* Sept. 28, 1968. See also Page's "J. M. Robertson the Literary Critic." *The Freethinker.* Nov. 9, 1968.

———. "The Paradoxical 'Genius' of J. M. Robertson." *The Ethical Record.* Sept. 1970.

GORDON STEIN

ROJAS, FERNANDO DE (about 1499). Spanish dramatist. See **Spanish Literature, Unbelief in.**

ROMAN WORLD. See **Ancient World, Unbelief in the.**

ROSE, ERNESTINE LOUISE (1810–1882), American freethinker, born E. L. Süsmond Potowsky in Poland, daughter of a Jewish rabbi. Her religious doubts seem to have been stimulated by her early travels in Europe. She was in Berlin in 1827 and in Paris during the revolution of 1830. Some years later she went to England and became a follower of ROBERT OWEN. She married William E. Rose, a man of liberal views, and in 1836 they went to the United States and became citizens.

Ernestine Rose traveled widely on the continent, lecturing on such subjects as ATHEISM, the social system, character formation, priestcraft, and the antislavery movement. She was also one of the earliest fighters in the struggle for women's rights, and in 1838 she presented the first petition to give married women the right to own land in their own names. Her pamphlet, *A Defense of Atheism,* published in Boston in 1851, constitutes her chief contribution to FREETHOUGHT.

Mrs. Rose described the year 1855 as "the busiest . . . of my life." She had by then been active in public life for 19 years, and her energy had been boundless. In the following year she and her husband visited Europe, where she renewed her contact with Robert Owen in England in addition to visiting France, Germany, and Italy. During a six-month vacation she had no speaking engagements, but upon her return to the U.S. she carried on her activities with renewed vigor. She was an abolitionist throughout the Civil War.

A lifetime spent in struggling for radical causes began, by the time the war ended, to take its toll on her. Though her spirit was undiminished, by 1865 her health had given way. At about the same time the radical movement was undergoing a period of of intense disagreements, which resulted in splits and personal quarrels. In 1869, nearly 60 years old and in bad health, though with her best work done, Ernestine Rose and her husband left America for another trip to Europe. After extensive traveling they decided to settle permanently in England, where they counted GEORGE JACOB HOLYOAKE and CHARLES BRADLAUGH among their friends.

Oddly enough, there appears to have been no obituary notice of Mrs. Rose in either the FREE-THINKER or the NATIONAL REFORMER. On the other hand, JOSEPH MAZZINI WHEELER, who thought highly of Mrs. Rose, did write a few lines about her in an article entitled "A Walk Through Highgate Cemetery," published in the *Freethinker* Nov. 21, 1897. He wrote: "My old friend Ernestine Louise Rose, who, loving America, her adopted country, yet stayed in England to be placed with her devoted husband in a grave hard by. This brave woman, who preached Freethought and Woman's emancipation in the pioneering days, had denounced slavery in the slave-holding States. I knew her only in age and infirmity. Yet how her kindly face lighted when she spoke of the past, and said, a little before her death, 'I have lived.'"

Other article of interest: **Women and Unbelief.**

Bibliography

The standard biography is Yuri Suhl, *Ernestine L. Rose and the Battle for Human Rights* (1959). It contains a full bibliography, including details of the six pamphlets she published, including *A Defense of Atheism, Being a Lecture Delivered in the Mercantile Hall, Boston, April 10, 1861.* See also Sara A. Underwood, *Heroines of Freethought* (1876) and *The Dictionary of American Biography,* Vol. 16 (1935).

VICTOR E. NEUBURG

ROSS, WILLIAM STEWART, pseudonym, Saladin (1844–1906), British freethinker, the son of a Scottish farm servant.

The career of Ross exemplifies the quarrels and divisions that were endemic among prominent freethinkers in the 19th century. The cogent and outspoken ATHEISM of CHARLES BRADLAUGH did not always find a ready response in the hearts and minds of all unbelievers of the period. There were those, including GEORGE JACOB HOLYOAKE, who preferred to describe themselves and their ideas as agnostic rather than atheistic. Inevitably, too, there were clashes of personality; in the case of Ross this took the form of a great hostility toward atheists in general and Bradlaugh in particular. So strong were his feelings in this respect that he was widely believed to be one of the authors of a scurrilous book, *Life of Charles Bradlaugh M.P.,* published in 1888 under the name of "Charles Mackay."

Still, Ross' contribution to FREETHOUGHT was a positive one. He studied for the church at Glasgow University, but he abandoned religion and became a writer. Ross moved to London, where he became editor of the *Secular Review* (founded by Holyoake in 1876), succeeding CHARLES WATTS. The precise dates of Ross' editorship are not known, but in 1889 he founded the *Agnostic Journal,* which replaced the *Secular Review.* At the same time he founded the publishing firm of W. Stewart & Company, which published the periodical and a number of his books.

His Writings. Unfortunately, none of his books is dated; they can be ascribed, however, to the 1890s, since it is sometimes possible to trace the first publication from advertisements in the *Agnostic Journal.* His most famous book, *Roses and Rue,* is described as being "just issued" in the number dated Jan. 24, 1891. Among others were *The Bottomless Pit, The Holy Lance,* and *The Book of Virgins.*

As a writer, Ross urged what might be called a kind of HUMANISM. His belief was qualified, and he fit the tradition of Holyoake rather than Bradlaugh. On these terms Ross became prominent in the secular movement at the close of the 19th century (see SECULARISM). Most of his work consisted of short essays, a form he handled with skill and often with considerable sensitivity.

In argument Ross was quietly persuasive; he totally lacked—indeed, he did not strive for—the tone of clamorous opposition to religion that characterized so much avowedly atheistic writing. He typified the more restrained, agnostic approach to freethinking. This quality is particularly apparent when one considers his editing of the *Agnostic Journal.* Over the years its contents were much more widely ranging than was usual in the FREETHINKER, for example. It is arguable that Ross was able to be less bellicose precisely because others had fought and won the battle for the right to publish freethought journals.

The agnostic approach is best illustrated by the obituary notice of Bradlaugh published in the *Journal* on April 4, 1891. Little more than half a column in length, it is almost entirely about the famous freethinker's parliamentary career, with his activities as an atheist scarcely mentioned. Although Ross was not the author, to read this obituary is to see just how deeply the divisions ran between the two kinds of freethinker in the 19th century. The *Agnostic Journal,* it should be remembered, had been started as a revolt against what might be called Bradlaughism.

Bibliography

Biographical material on Ross is sparse. A pamphlet by G. G. Flaws, *Sketch of the Life and Character of Saladin (W. Stewart Ross),* published in 1883, consists of 16 pages and includes a portrait on the front cover. The contents are chatty and impressionistic, lacking perception and depth, and there are no critical comments.

From a psychological point of view, a pamphlet by Ross himself, *From the Valley of the Shadow of Death* (1882), written and published after the tragic death of his infant son Bruno at the age of two years, is more revealing.

VICTOR E. NEUBURG

ROUSSEAU, JEAN JACQUES (1712–1778), French publisher and author. **See French Literature, Unbelief in.**

RUSSELL, BERTRAND (1872–1970), English philosopher, mathematician, and writer, born May 18, the younger son of Viscount Amberley and Kate Stanley. Russell was heir to his grandfather, Lord John Russell, in fact (upon the death of his brother Frank) and in spirit. Lord John, who was twice prime minister (1846–52 and 1865–66), was the author of the Reform Bill of 1832 and left a legacy of Liberal philosophy to his grandson.

Early Life. Russell's parents, who both died very early in life, were radical in their social thought and appointed two freethinkers as guardians for their sons. Amberley's parents nullified the guardianship, which resulted, from 1875, in Russell's being raised by his paternal grandparents at Pembroke Lodge in Richmond Park. His grandmother came from a staunch Presbyterian family and held strong moral and religious views, which brought a rift between young Bertrand and his grandmother. This added to the unhappy and lonely childhood that was his lot, since he was kept at home to be educated by governesses and tutors.

His brother Frank introduced him to the study of Euclid when Bertrand was only 11, but the lessons almost came to an abrupt end when the boy's skeptical mind objected to having to take the axioms on trust. When told that he had to in order for his studies to continue, his curiosity overcame his tendency to doubt, and he reluctantly set aside his unbelief. But one biographer notes that the doubts raised then in Russell's mind were to occupy him from that time until the writing of *Principia Mathematica*. The same biographer, Alan Wood (see Bibliography below), records that the next step in the young skeptic's path of unbelief was to question the arguments for the various religions. In short time, Bertrand rejected personal immortality, and after reading JOHN STUART MILL, abandoned the first-cause argument and with it all belief in God.

At 18, Russell went to Cambridge on a scholarship in mathematics, for which Alfred North Whitehead was the examiner. At the university he came to know G. E. Moore and the Hegelian J. E. McTaggert. The latter's influence dominated Russell until he and other rebels broke away from Hegelianism under the influence of Moore's common-sense realism.

His Writing. By the turn of the century, having published works on German social democracy and on G. W. Leibniz, Russell directed his interests and energies in the direction of his Cambridge fellowship thesis on the foundations of geometry. Following the publication of *The Principles of Mathematics* (1903), he collaborated with his friend and former tutor, Whitehead, on the monumental *Principia Mathematica*, which advanced the thesis that mathematics and logic are identical in nature.

Partly due to the terrible intellectual strain of writing *Principia* on top of *Principles*, and partly due to conflicts in his personal life, Russell's thought expressed a strain of pessimism and abandoned hopes ("A Free Man's Worship," 1903) in contrast to his espousal, in the spirit of his parentage, of various liberal, even radical, causes. Earlier he had followed Beatrice and Sidney Webb in their support of the Boer War, but, changing sides, he avowed pacifism, free trade, and women's suffrage. As the work on *Principia* came to a close, he tried, unsuccessfully, to stand for Parliament. His professed AGNOSTICISM was an impediment in this pursuit, as (so he thought) it was in his quest for a fellowship at Cambridge, which was also not to be his at this time.

While Russell continued to pioneer on the frontiers of logic and mathematics, the outbreak of the war in 1914 precipitated him from the realm of pure thought into the arena of political conflict. Working with the No Conscription Fellowship, he was tried in court, largely at his own insistence, and convicted for writing an antiwar pamphlet. Refusing to pay the fine, he prepared to accept the jail sentence. When word of this reached the Council of Trinity College, Cambridge, they voted unanimously to remove Russell from his lectureship. Later reinstated, he took leave and then resigned to avoid scandal and embarrassment for Trinity over his second marriage to Dora Black.

Russell the Radical. By 1921 Russell was well into a socially and politically radical phase of his career. He had earlier been sent to prison for six months, not for the pamphlet case (his friends had paid the fine he refused to acknowledge), but for an article critical of the American forces in England. The solitude of prison life had provided Russell the opportunity to write in the vein of his earlier work on mathematical philosophy, a calling he had not abandoned during the war years. (It is told that when the jailer asked Russell's religion, Russell replied, "agnostic." After asking how to spell that, the jailer avowed he had not heard of that one, but sighed, "I guess we all worship the same God.")

The early twenties found Russell traveling to Russia and then to China, where he almost died. Though he was critical of the Soviets, his radical political and moral stands are reflected in a notice, in a missionary journal, of his falsely reported death in China: "Missionaries may be pardoned for breathing a sigh of relief at the news of Mr. Bertrand Russell's death."

Upon returning to England, Russell married Dora Black, who had nursed him back to health in China. She had become pregnant with their first child, John Conrad, during the return trip. Finding public sensitivities to their moral and political stands a barrier to renting lodgings, Russell bought a place in Chelsea, and to accommodate John and his sister Kate, later bought in Cornwall.

Later Writing. In pursuit of both the abstract lines of his earlier thought, and also to express his dissident moral and religious views, from 1921 to 1929 Russell published such diverse works as *The Analysis of Mind* (1921) and *The Analysis of Matter* (1927), on the one hand, and controversial popular titles on religion, foreign affairs, and education. These latter include *Why I Am Not a Christian* (1927), *Skeptical Essays* (1928), and *Marriage and Morals* (1929), which advocated trial companionate marriage.

ALFRED JULES AYER, in his *Bertrand Russell*, says of the militant rationalist and humanist stance of these popular works at the end of this decade that they "were thought shocking at the time and were, indeed, to do their author harm because of their advocacy of a certain measure of sexual freedom," though now they seem outdated, in some measure because they were effective in changing the climate of opinion on such matters.

Included in the views expressed by Russell during this period were a refutation of the classic arguments for the existence of God, a denial of immortality, and an attack upon the idea that Jesus was the most perfect of men. He said, "I cannot myself feel that either in the matter of wisdom or in the matter of virtue Christ stands quite as high as some other people known to history. I think I should put Buddha and Socrates above Him in those respects" (*Why I Am Not a Christian*).

Russell's *The Conquest of Happiness* (1930), as well as his excursion into the practical field of running the Beacon Hill School, reflects his continued struggle to uproot and expose the remnants of Puritanism's emphasis upon guilt, sin, and moral condemnation. In the school, founded in 1927 with his wife Dora Russell, approximately 20 boys and girls, ages 4 to 11, were given a wide range of personal freedom within the context of regular compulsory lessons and the observance of rules of cleanliness and regular bedtimes. The children were allowed to go about in various states of undress, receiving no physical punishment, coming and going as they wished and bathing together freely. Russell strove to get the children to accept his guidance on the basis of its reasonableness rather than dogmatically imposing such in an authoritarian manner. Students were allowed to read whatever they chose, were given no religious instruction, and had their questions openly and freely answered.

Russell had earlier affirmed that "Religion is based . . . primarily and mainly upon fear . . . fear of the mysterious, fear of defeat, fear of death. Fear is the parent of cruelty, and therefore it is no wonder if cruelty and religion have gone hand in hand" (*Why I Am Not a Christian*). Here Russell is echoing the opening words in his *Has Religion Made Useful Contributions to Civilization?:* "My own view on religion is that of LUCRETIUS. I regard it as a disease born of fear and as a source of untold misery to the human race."

In 1932, Russell left his wife and partner, Dora, and ended his relationship with Beacon Hill School. But the thirties saw a flood of timely and provocative books flow from his pen. Detractors note that in inheriting the title upon his brother Frank's death, Russell also inherited significant debts on top of his own increasing financial obligations. So, argue these critics, Russell turned from pure philosophy toward popular subjects.

Russell himself lends credence to this interpretation, and yet with another world war looming on the horizon, what better application of his brilliant literary style than to expose the entrenched forces of conservatism, repression, and reaction? Thus he wrote *The Scientific Outlook* (1931), *Freedom and*

Organization, 1814–1914 (1934), and *Religion and Science* (1935). Here he consistently defended the values of science and liberalism against the forces of ignorance, dogmatism, superstition, parochialism, and orthodoxy. He proclaimed that what can be known, science can know, and what science cannot know, cannot be known.

Power, published in 1938 when Russell took his third wife, Patricia, and the three children to America, ironically reflects the very forces that in 1940 deprived him of his teaching post at the City College of New York. Though his lectures, previously given at the universities of Chicago and California, were of a largely technical nature on logic and the theory of knowledge, he had written among other things, "I say quite deliberately that the Christian religion, as organized in its churches, has been and still is the principal enemy of moral progress in the world" (*Why I Am Not a Christian*).

The reactionary forces closed ranks when an Episcopal bishop and the Roman Catholic hierarchy found Russell morally unfit to teach in a public university. His secular humanist writings on sex, marriage, and child rearing were used against him in a legal maneuver that left him for the moment stranded, financially and physically, in a war-bound foreign country.

By the fall of 1944, Russell had returned to Trinity and a mantle of respectability, which led to his receiving the Order of Merit in 1949, the year his marriage with Patricia ended. Three years later, he married Edith Finch, who survived him. However, the 18 years he shared with her were not ones of quiet retirement. While campaigning for nuclear disarmament, they were arrested for civil disobedience, only to be spared a two-month imprisonment due to their health, which fortunately served quite well for active political engagement until he died Feb. 2, 1970.

His biographer Alan Wood said of Russell, "He is certainly the leading questioner of our times. He started by asking questions about mathematics and religion and philosophy, and he went on to question accepted ideas about war and politics and sex and education, setting the minds of men on the march, so that the world could never be quite the same as if he had not lived."

Other articles of interest: **God, Existence of. Immortality, Unbelief in.**

Bibliography

Ayer, A. J. *Bertrand Russell.* New York: Viking Press, 1972.

Clark, Ronald W. *The Life of Bertrand Russell.* New York: Knopf, 1976.

Pears, D. F., ed. *Bertrand Russell: A Collection of Critical Essays.* New York: Doubleday, 1972.

Russell, Bertrand. *The Autobiography of Bertrand Russell.* 3 vols. London: Allen and Unwin, 1967–69.

———. *My Philosophical Development.* London: Allen and Unwin, 1959.

Schlipp, Paul Arthur. *The Philosophy of Bertrand Russell.* Evanston, Ill.: The Library of Living Philosophers, 1944.

Wood, Alan. *Bertrand Russell: The Passionate Skeptic.* New York: Simon & Schuster, 1958.

JOHN L. MCKENNEY

RUSSIA AND THE SOVIET UNION, UNBELIEF IN. Early Heresies. A close study reveals aspects of unbelief in the popular vitality of ancient Russian paganism, but organized freethinking did not arise until a dissenting movement appeared at the end of the 14th century. Coming about the same time that a major expansion of monastic life occurred in Russia, the so-called *strigol'niki* (shearers) were opposed to the orthodox church hierarchy and the sacraments, and they did not believe in the necessity of prayers for the dead. Although they taught a concept of earthly utopian heaven, they should be seen as pursuing perfectionist and evangelical Christian goals, rather than materialist ones.

The next two major movements of dissent from the church emerged almost simultaneously at the end of the 15th century. The Judaizers (*zhidovstvuiushchie*) and the Volga Hermits were both antiformalist and rationalist in their theology and ideology. The Volga Hermits were essentially anti-institutional monastics who adhered to a strict rule of poverty in the wilderness. The best-known was Nil Sorsky (1453–1508), who is now venerated as a saint. He believed in nonviolence and opposed state influence and control over the church.

The Judaizers rejected the Trinity, the religious hierarchy, ritual, monasticism, icons, and prayers for the dead, and they proclaimed the supremacy of reason over faith. They were aided in their growth by the failure of messianic-apocalyptic predictions made by some churchmen for the year 1492. As vocal opponents of these predictions (they pointed to a climactic date 1,747 years later), the Judaizers gained some adherents.

The Volga Hermits and the Judaizers were united in their opposition to the ecclesiastical estates that were such a central feature of the church's power. Because Ivan III (1462–1505) and then Vasili III (1505–1533) sympathized with the land secularization ideas of these dissenters—for the state would be the primary beneficiary—these two czars wavered and did not directly condemn the movement. The church, however, was anything but indecisive, using the Spanish Inquisition as the model for its attack. The Judaizers were imprisoned and executed, and then the leading Volga Hermits were imprisoned. Both movements had been dispatched by the middle of the 16th century. While they left no direct descendants, these dissenting movements reflected ongoing tensions within the Russian religious tradition, one that repeatedly contributed to the development of divergent perspectives and FREETHOUGHT, first in theistic, but later in atheistic forms.

In the middle of the 15th century, a doctrine had arisen in the Russian church that exalted Moscow as the "third Rome," that is, as the successor in the role of torchbearer of true Christianity after Rome itself and then Constantinople had fallen to alleged heresy and corruption. Kluchevsky has convincingly argued that this doctrine contributed to the congealing of the Russian church. Thereafter, the corrective evaluation of other Christian churches became irrelevant. Thus, the strict formalism of Ivan IV ("The Terrible," 1533–1584) was not only the preference of the monarch but the necessary pattern of observance for generations of Russians. While the general population was lax and largely indifferent to religious vicissitudes, under Czar Alexis (1645–1676) the characteristic Russian pattern of outward piety (ritual, crossings, genuflections, etc.) was imposed by the police.

The Protestant Reformation had a direct effect only upon the western regions of Russia, most of which were under Polish or Lithuanian control at the end of the 16th century. The Jesuit-led Counter-Reformation succeeded in erasing most vestiges of Protestantism from the Roman Catholic areas, and the creation of the Uniate church at Brest in 1596 fanned the flames of anti-Catholicism among the Orthodox Russians. The Russian church hierarchy then became devoted to two major goals: (1) encouraging the political struggle against Catholicism and Poland, and (2) ensuring that the state leaders were not seduced by the Protestant ideas that were being brought into Russia by the increasing number of Westerners and Western-educated Russians.

In response to a reform aimed at bringing the Russian church closer to the practices of the other Eastern Orthodox churches—and, thus, more "orthodox" in general—the largest schism in Russian history occurred as thousands of avid believers followed the Archpriest Avvakum and lesser leaders into fanatical preservation of the "old belief." Officially condemned by the church in council in 1667, the schism splintered the organic unity of the Russian church community and weakened the political voice of the church, allowing secular power greater freedom. Paradoxically, however, the schism fostered theological education and the acceptance of Western science. These were things which the Old Believers feared and damned, so the campaign against the schismatics naturally encouraged what they opposed.

Religious Experimentation Among the Aristocracy. While Poland was being contained politically, Latin learning was making giant strides in the theological schools of Russia. However, the political authorities were beginning to move toward church-state relations based upon the model of the Protestant establishments of Europe. During the reign of Peter I ("The Great," 1682–1725), the Russian church was shorn of its last major aspects of autonomy from the political authorities and given a Western form of subservience to the state through the replacement of the patriarchate with the Holy Synod. Henceforth, the church became essentially a department of government.

Peter himself was not constrained by traditional Orthodox religiosity. Although regularly observant, he nevertheless showed little interest in theology or dogma, and wasted no reverence upon the hierarchs of the church. Peter's drinking bouts were notorious for their iconoclasm, as they centered upon an elaborate ceremonial group of friends that was called the "Most Licentious Council of Buffoons and Drunkards." The group amused itself by parodying Orthodox and Roman Catholic prelates and their practices in grotesque and bizarre role-playing. This kind of freethinking at court presaged by half a century the flowering of ENLIGHTENMENT freethought and ATHEISM at court during the reign of Catherine II ("The Great," 1762–1796).

While the thrust of Peter's activities had reduced the level of power and prestige of the nobility and gentry, in succeeding reigns there was a gradual reinstatement of these groups. Under Catherine, the upper strata became a unique corporate entity, separating itself distinctly from the general population and experimenting with Western ideas and beliefs more than any previous group of Russians had. Sponsored by the empress, "Voltaireanism" became the infatuation of the aristocracy, and DENIS DIDEROT caused heads to turn. Since the nobility was separated from the populace by language and manners, these activities had little direct effect beyond the elite. While Catherine's reign witnessed the last great peasant revolt, led by Pugachev in 1773–74, it also marked the beginning of an era of elite intellectual ferment that was to culminate in the Revolution of 1917.

As the St. Petersburg aristocracy adopted Enlightenment ideas, a mystical and pietistic reaction against RATIONALISM began to grow. The turn away from Voltaireanism was evident in the growth of sectarianism among the upper strata and in the transformation of Russian Freemasonry, which had first appeared in the 1730s, from its original lower-order "English" forms to the higher-order "Scottish" variety, which was imported via Swedish and German connections. Lower-order Masonry stressed brotherhood and ceremony and was relatively acceptable at court, but the mystical and secretive patterns of higher-order Masonry, which in the 1780s assimilated Rosicrucianism from Prussia and additional occult tendencies, was under steady attack from 1785 until Catherine's death. The late-18th-century development of higher-order Masonry and the growth of pietistic sectarian groups like the Khlysty and the Skoptsy indicated that the pendulum had begun to swing away from the Russian Enlightenment.

The French Revolution fueled the trend away from rationalism and toward conservatism in politics and religion. The aristocracy, which had developed a modern identity during Catherine's reign, now showed signs of splitting into antagonistic groups, with reformers and radicals on one side and conservatives and reactionaries on the other. The right flirted first with Catholicism, then with Protestant Evangelical pietism, before anchoring itself once again in Russian Orthodoxy by the middle of the 19th century; the left moved from the uncertain reformist politics of Alexander I (1801–1825) through Saint-Simonian, then Comtean socialism, and on to Hegelian revolutionism.

The harsh regime of the "Iron Czar," Nicholas I (1825–1855), which began with the suppression of the liberal "Decembrist" revolt and adopted the slogan "orthodoxy, autocracy and nationality," was the backdrop for the great debate between the Westernizers and the Slavophiles. While the Slavophiles glorified family life, pietistic inner regeneration, and a new universal church, the Westernizers looked more toward Christian socialism in the Catholic mold so as to establish both order and national purpose in Russia. The latter movement became increasingly secular as it embraced socialism more than the church, through adoption of the views of Saint-Simon and AUGUSTE COMTE. Finally, the Slavophile-Westernizer debate became more polarized when the Westernizers turned to Hegelian philosophy and came to believe that revolution was possible and even inevitable.

Prerevolutionary Atheism. At about the time that KARL MARX was seeking to develop a philosophy of action that would link ideas with historical change, the intelligentsia of Russia was seeking to redefine the terms of its relationship with the people. Marx and the German theorists shared many intellectual sources with the Russian Westernizers, and Marx frequently engaged in lively and denunciatory debate with one of the great Russian thinkers of the era, the anarchist Mikhail Bakunin, who is frequently counted among the Westernizers. (Bakunin made the first Russian translation of the *Communist Manifesto* in 1863; it was published in Geneva by the press of Alexander Herzen's influential, Russian-expatriate periodical, *Kolokol* [The Bell].) In many ways, the development of Marx's thought was paralleled by the evolution of 19th-century Russian thought.

As the oppression of Nicholas I gave way to the early reformism of the reign of Alexander II (1855–1881), the left intelligentsia became more materialistic, antiauthoritarian and antitraditionalist. The 1860s were characterized by such "nihilists" as Nikolai Chernyshevski (1828–1889), who argued for the liberation of the masses through the development of agrarian socialism in such a way that the evils of capitalism could be avoided. In their elevation of science and their ascetic subordination of personal interests to those of the society, the nihilists evidenced an evolving theme that later came to characterize Russian Marxism as it approached the revolutionary era.

The next step in the development of the identity of the Russian intelligentsia was its rejection of the utopian tendencies of nihilism in favor of a more action-centered approach to the central problem of how to relate the upper classes to the "people." In the 1870s and 1880s, this rejection took the populist form of *narodnichestvo* (*narod*, common people). Whether from the point of view of the "social" or the "religious narodniks," the masses were viewed as having a special wisdom that the intelligentsia needed to tap. Although anticapitalist like the Marxists, the narodniks believed in the supremacy of the individual over the social, and thought of their duty as preparing the peasantry for the advent of socialism.

However, the people did not embrace the narodniks quickly, and frequently turned them away. By the mid-1870s the movement of *narodnichestvo* was breaking apart. Unable to motivate cooperation and interest on the part of the peasants, the intelligentsia split again, with some stressing gradual transformation under the general guidance of the elite and others advocating violence and revolution. When the peasants did not rise after the assassination of Alexander II in 1881, the more comprehensive and industrial-oriented theory of Marx became very attractive.

Over the course of the 19th century, a general revival of Russian theology and religious thinking was taking place, and it frequently tied into the activist *narodnichestvo*. However, the patterns of evolution in the political realm seemed to be leading many away from the church, and frequently all the way to atheism. Undoubtedly, one of the major sources of Russian unbelief was the disreputable state of the Orthodox parish clergy. During the previous century the parish clergy had become a closed caste, unable to survive on their state salaries and thrown to the mercy of a peasantry still somewhat skeptical of the demands of spirituality and resentful of burdensome payments for the religious services provided by the still largely illiterate priests. While the situation had begun to change in the 19th century, change came first and most deeply not for the parish clergy but rather for the monastic clergy and the hierarchy, which came only from the latter group. Without possibilities for advancement in the church, saddled with a system of support that degraded them, and experiencing the scorn of many a peasant, the parish clergy frequently reflected their deep alienation in excessive drinking, family strife, and general boorishness.

To the rapidly developing intelligentsia, the spectacle of illiterate clerics, mumbling the liturgical formulas without comprehension and in a drunken stupor, was reprehensible. However exaggerated such an image may have been, it was rooted in some real problems of the clergy. Furthermore, while the monastic clergy became more learned overall, the monasteries maintained great landholdings (increasing at the turn of the century), which were the focus of peasant unrest, even after the formal liberation of the serfs in 1861. Many members of the radical intelligentsia saw the ecclesiastical lands as evidence of the exploitation of the peasants by the church. Thus, anticlericalism grew steadily and fed the trend either toward sectarianism or toward AGNOSTICISM and revolutionary atheism.

The problems of the Russian Orthodox church often led to disillusionment, even as the church moved into a reformist era at the turn of the century. While Leo Tolstoi's thought turned toward a nontheistic, anarchistic ethicism which inspired a new sect, a significant portion of the left intelligentsia moved beyond the antiecclesiastical, humanistic SECULARISM of the Westernizers like Belinski and Herzen, beyond Bakunin's atheistic anarchism, beyond the sometimes simplistic materialism of Pisarev, Nikolai Dobrolyubov, Chernyshevski, and the other nihilists, beyond the sentimentalism of narodniks like Lavrov and Mikhailovski, and toward the class-based, hard-nosed, action-centered revolutionary theory of Marx.

The militant atheism of the Russian Marxists seems to have been a natural outgrowth of the Russian intensity and immoderation in social thought. Although related to the earlier forms of unbelief, the core of the theory of atheism was found in Marxist ideological writings. The primary Russian interpreters of Marxist atheism were Georgi Plekhanov and VLADIMIR ILYICH LENIN, with Maxim Gorki and A. V. Lunacharski playing an interesting role in the early 1900s as the so-called "God Builders."

The God Builders and Lenin. Gorki and Lunacharski, along with A. A. Bogdanov and V. A. Bazarev, combined elements of the Russian radical tradition with the philosophical anthropology of LUDWIG FEUERBACH and the *Übermensch* motif of FRIEDRICH NIETSZCHE to propound a doctrine that looked to the building of a new order of humankind far transcending the present one. The far-off perfect culture, made up of perfected individuals, was the "God" of the God Builders. With Nietzsche, the God Builders saw that future humanity as divine, or at least divine-like. It should be, they believed, the object of present worship and of the higher strivings of the people.

The God Builders' thinking was in stark contrast to that of Plekhanov, who saw religion primarily as superstition, intellectual errors, or simple tradition. While the God Builders credited religious feelings with some substance, Plekhanov discredited them altogether. Viewing religion largely as religious doctrine, he believed that all aspects of religion would "wither away" as people became fully conscious of their natural state and as the church was eliminated as an influence upon thinking and attitudes. Science, as the corrective for religious doctrine, was to overturn religion, Plekhanov thought, and this would happen, even without a Marxian social revolution. If there was anything of substance in religion, Plekhanov saw it in aesthetics; hence, religion could be replaced by art.

Lenin saw religion much more as a part of the general class struggle: it was a tool used by the bourgeoisie to exploit and oppress the people. While Plekhanov would counter religion with the popularization of natural science, Lenin required that a much more intense struggle be waged to wipe out the illusion that blinded people to the machinations of the class enemy. In order to overcome religion, it was necessary, in Lenin's view, to extirpate it by its socioeconomic roots. Thus, the struggle against religion was a central part of the revolutionary struggle. Only if believers were drawn into this struggle would they come to abandon the illusion.

Neither Plekhanov nor Lenin could accept the religious imagery and language of the God Builders. Although both held a utopian vision of ultimate social development to a much higher level than the present (Lenin more utopian than Plekhanov), they were neither so romantic nor so lofty in their rhetoric as Gorki and Lunacharski. As early as 1909, Lenin's critique of the God Builders was officially adopted by the Bolshevik Central Committee in its condemnation of this trend. Although its leading spokesmen no longer espoused the notion publicly, the tendency to build a religion around the utopian ideals of Marxism has persisted in the U.S.S.R. alongside the antireligious militancy of Leninism.

Postrevolutionary Atheism. Two major tendencies are apparent in the immediate postrevolutionary patterns of Soviet atheism. First is the militancy of the antireligious attack, which was always viewed as a part of the revolutionary struggle against exploitative social and economic relations. Since this militancy was subordinate to broader revolutionary goals, however, Lenin and the other Bolsheviks recognized the necessity not to alienate potential supporters and would-be proletarians by offense to their faith. Thus, the second tendency was to moderate antireligious militancy whenever it worked against the solidification of Bolshevik support or the development of proletarian culture.

Except for the brief period of "War Communism" (1917–21), which immediately followed the Revolution of 1917, the first tendency led to a general policy during the 1920s of direct intervention into the organizational life of the Russian Orthodox church so as to take away its political options and leave it incapable of counterrevolutionary activity. The church itself was split over how to operate under the new circumstances; the Bolsheviks aided the split by supporting nonestablished groups.

Patriarch Tikhon, who was elected at the time of the revolution as the first Russian patriarch since the era of Peter I, was harassed by the secret police and imprisoned more than once before he died in 1925. Potential successors were prevented from effectively administering the church until 1927, when Metropolitan Sergei reached a compromise with the government that abandoned all church hostility against Soviet rule. Even though he headed the church until his death in 1944, the authorities forbade Sergei's consecration as patriarch until World War II initiated a new period in church-state relations.

The moderation of militant atheism was manifested in two ways during the 1920s. First, there was an ongoing effort to draw believers *as individuals* into the party and state activities, with the dual aim of enlisting their efforts in rebuilding the society and helping them to overcome their religious attachments. This followed Lenin's lead, which had been further developed by such important atheist writers and party workers as V. D. Bonch-Bruevich, I. I. Skvortsov-Stepanov, P. A. Krasikov, and EMEL'YAN YAROSLAVSKI.

The second aspect of moderation was evidenced in the lenient attitude toward most sectarian groups. These groups were seen, first, as rivals of the more dangerous Orthodox church, and therefore, as means to further undermine the counterrevolutionary tendencies of Orthodoxy. On the other hand, however, many of them were thought to represent latent proletarian tendencies that could be developed toward socialist consciousness. In particular, the Western groups such as Baptists and Evangelical Christians were thought to represent rationalizing religious strains whose development would culminate, under the new circumstances, in the proletarianization of their adherents.

Well before the revolution, Bonch-Bruevich had tried to encourage cooperation between sectarians and revolutionaries, and the moderate stance of the party toward these groups during the 1920s extended this effort.

Whatever form they took, the tendencies to moderate a Leninist militant atheism were always seen as pragmatic and intermediate steps along the path to full "atheization," on the one hand, and full socialization of Soviet society, on the other. Antireligious propaganda was a constant feature of the era. The Eighth Party Congress in 1919 adopted a resolution requiring the organization of the "broadest scientific-educational and antireligious propaganda," and the Agitation-Propaganda Section (Agitprop) of the national and local party organs was to spearhead this task.

From 1921 through 1929, Agitprop's Antireligious Commission directed these efforts. In 1922, the newspaper *Bezbozhnik* (The Godless) was founded, and it became the most important, broad-based atheistic publication of the time. A less subtle approach to antireligious propaganda was taken by a competitor magazine, *Bezbozhnik u stanka* (The Godless at the Lathe), which a recent Soviet writer termed "vulgar" and "anarchist" in approach. Even more harshly condemned was an extremely crude magazine, *Vavilonskaia bashnia* (Tower of Babel), which the Leningrad district committee closed after only four issues. Besides differences of opinion over the approach to religious questions, the friction between these journals represented deep power struggles within the party.

League of the Militant Godless. The Antireligious Commission also directed the unification of various local atheist organizations and the national society of Friends of the Newspaper *Bezbozhnik* into a single League of the Godless in 1925 (the name became League of the Militant Godless in 1929). *Bezbozhnik* and the league became the major coordinating organizations for the antireligious effort in the U.S.S.R. From 1925, the central committee of the league published a magazine bearing the same name as the newspaper, and in 1932, *Bezbozhnik u stanka* was merged with the second *Bezbozhnik* into a single magazine. From 1926, the league central committee also published a journal, *Antireligioznik* (The Antireligionist), which was directed more to the development and dissemination of scientific methods of antireligious propaganda among activists.

The League of the Militant Godless was headed throughout its existence (from 1925 to 1941) by Yaroslavski. Constituent local groups were founded in industrial shops and factories, in *kolkhozes*, and in educational institutions. By the end of 1928, the league counted half a million members, and by 1932, at its peak, there were some five and one-half million members. Though it went into the doldrums for a period after its peak, it recovered somewhat between 1937 and 1941, when it terminated with some three and one-half million members. The league's slogan was: "The struggle against religion is a struggle for socialism." However, the league seems to have encountered considerable indifference in the provinces, and often stimulated strong reactions by its frequently simplistic and sometimes crude methods. Nevertheless, as an effort at mass mobilization, it cannot be ignored.

Variations in Antireligious Policy. Soviet religious policy took a sharp turn toward the militant atheist pattern in 1928–29, when a campaign of church closings and persecutions of the clergy began. This coincided with "forced collectivization," and represented the triumph of Stalinist politics. Though antireligious activity slackened off as a clear campaign after 1933, the remainder of the 1930s saw the religious leadership continue to disappear into the prison camps, along with most of the old Bolsheviks, and political and other dissenters of all types. As the purges eliminated religious activists, all church organizations were shut down. Nor did sectarians retain any special privileges. Although contemporary records indicate that the population continued to engage in most religious celebrations and to observe most religious holidays, there was little that one could desribe as "the church." Nevertheless, the ill-fated census of 1937, whose official results have never been made public, showed, according to Yaroslavski, Krupskaia and others, that a majority of the population still considered themselves "believers."

As war with Germany became more clearly imminent, a reevaluation began in party circles of the religious oppression of the 1930s. The Nazi invasion of the Soviet Union turned policy again toward pragmatic moderation, as the government sought allies in its struggle to save the homeland. By the end of the war, all the church organizations had been reestablished, with most of the new leadership having come from the camps. It was clear that a church leader was allowed to return if he would not oppose the government, although some who were asked refused this condition of their freedom. As a reward for those who accepted it, the major leaders became "junior partners" in the government, sharing many privileges of the elite. Having provided patriotic service during the war, the churches then experienced a period of relative calm through Stalin's death in 1953.

The period of Nikita Khrushchev's supremacy marked a new stage of antireligious militancy. Although he liberalized intellectual life in many ways and initiated some new and bold social and economic experimentation, Khrushchev's program of de-Stalinization was also characterized by a new antireligious campaign, equally as militant as the one of 1928–33. During the period 1958–64, half of the remaining churches were closed, as were many monasteries and some seminaries. Many of the clergy found themselves once again in prison camps or exile.

With the ouster of Khrushchev in 1964, the most repressive features of the antireligious campaign abated. However, the campaign had stimulated the development of a new religious activism that was characterized by organized dissent and the demand for religious rights on the part of significant segments of most religious groups. Although underground religion had been present since the beginning of the Soviet state, it took on varied forms and gained significant and influential foreign support in the late 1960s and 1970s. This provided the regime with significant challenges on the religious front; its general response has been to re-create a dual policy somewhat reminiscent of the late 1920s. Simply stated, this policy has involved limited support for the officially recognized religious organizations, coupled with strong police and propaganda pressure against unrecognized groups. All the while, general antireligious propaganda has become more and more complex and sophisticated.

Neither Stalin, Khrushchev, Brezhnev, nor any other major political leader since Lenin has developed the theory and ideology of atheism as he did. Although the leaders' personal predilections have been reflected in the policy of their regimes, the intellectual development of Soviet atheism has been left largely to professional ideologues, philosophers, and social scientists. Significant developments have so far been consistent with Leninism; they date from the early 1960s, when the question of religion began to be examined anew and given a new scholarly legitimacy.

Scientific Atheism. In the U.S.S.R., official scholarly studies of atheism have always been linked to the ideological tasks of Marxism-Leninism. During the 1920s and 1930s there were signifi-

cant historical, ethnographic, and sociological studies of sectarianism, animistic and tribal religions, and the religions of ancient Egypt and the Greco-Roman world, as well as of Russian Orthodoxy; these provided the basis for a general critique of religion. While this scholarship went into eclipse from the mid-1930s until the mid-1950s, when "scientific atheism" began to be reformulated as an academic area of specialization, these earlier studies provided a foundation for later work.

In 1932, the Museum of the History of Religion and Atheism was founded and housed in the former Kazan Cathedral in Leningrad. The *Yearbook* and other publications of the museum were major outlets for atheistic and antireligious scholarship until the early 1960s, and the museum continues to be a major center for such research. However, since the creation in 1964 of the Institute of Scientific Atheism as a part of the Academy of Social Sciences (which is under the direction of the Ideological Commission of the Central Committee of the Communist party of the Soviet Union), national coordination of the social scientific and philosophical study of religion and atheism has been carried out by this institute. The Institute of Scientific Atheism grants graduate degrees, and all major universities and the U.S.S.R. Academy of Sciences (especially its Institutes of History and Philosophy), as well as the academies of sciences in the various republics, provide graduate training and carry out research on atheist topics. Active research is now being pursued in the sociology, psychology, history, ethnography, and philosophy of atheism and free thought, and in the philosophical and ideological critique of religion, theology, and "bourgeois" atheism.

Also of importance is the pedagogical study of atheist education and the methods of atheist and antireligious propaganda. Courses on the fundamentals of scientific atheism are included in the required curricula of all institutions of higher and secondary education, and atheist topics are included in courses at all levels of education.

Most of the scientific atheist research and training is directed toward improving the "atheist upbringing" of the Soviet people. Local party and Komsomol activists are frequently given roles in research activities—for example, as interviewers in sociological studies—and much of the research seeks to develop better means to educate the population in atheism.

It is difficult to assess the level of atheism or religious faith in the Soviet population today, but the most reliable estimates from the U.S.S.R. indicate that from 15 to 20 percent of the population may be categorized as "religious" (10–15 percent of the urban population and 20–30 percent of the rural population). A significantly larger group probably retains at least sentimental or traditional attachments to religion. Between the religious population and the small, fully atheist group lies a large proportion of the Soviet people who, though not fully adopting an atheistic world view, are indifferent or uncertain about religion. This type of unbelief is probably characteristic of the largest segment of Russians.

In summary: Modern Soviet atheism and unbelief have evolved out of a long history of popular and elitist clashes over religion. From the original pitting of paganism against Orthodoxy, battle lines were later drawn between various sectarian movements and the Orthodox church. From the 18th century onward, the elite began to take an increasingly important part in developing varieties of unbelief, and this tendency culminated in the elaboration of the Marxist-Leninist form of revolutionary atheism that became supreme after the Revolution of 1917. Although there has now developed a large institution of scientific atheism in the Soviet Union, it is still true to its Leninist roots. The current population is probably broadly characterized as unbelievers, although in aesthetics and cultural traditions the church remains a central point of reference.

While it is unlikely that the state could, in the near future, abandon its atheistic commitments, within the Leninist tradition there is room for considerable variation in policy between militant atheists and pragmatic moderation of antireligious activity. Successions of leadership and the evolution of Soviet Marxism itself will determine where, along this continuum of possibilities, official policy will be found in the future.

Other articles of interest: **Propaganda, Antireligious. Russian Literature, Unbelief in.**

Bibliography

Academy of Sciences of the U.S.S.R. *Po etapam razvitiia ateizma v SSSR.* Leningrad: Nauka, 1967.

Academy of Social Sciences. *Voprosy nauchnogo ateizma.* Moscow: Mysl', series volumes since 1966.

Billington, James H. *The Icon and the Axe: An Interpretive History of Russian Culture.* New York: Knopf, 1966.

Bociurkiw, Bohdan R., and John W. Strong, eds. *Religion and Atheism in the U.S.S.R. and Eastern Europe.* Toronto: U. of Toronto Press, 1975.

DeGeorge, Richard T. *Patterns of Soviet Thought.* Ann Arbor: U. of Michigan Press, 1966.

Kline, George L. *Religious and Anti-Religious Thought in Russia.* Chicago: U. of Chicago Press, 1968.

Kobetski, V. D. *Izuchenie religioznosti i ateizma.* Leningrad: Leningrad U. Press, 1978.

Marshall, Richard H., Jr., ed. *Aspects of Religion in the Soviet Union, 1917–1967* Chicago: U. of Chicago Press, 1971.

Novikov, M. P., et al., eds. *Istoriia i teoriia ateizma.* Moscow: Mysl', 1974.

Treadgold, Donald W. *The West in Russia and China: Religious and Secular Thought in Modern Times, Vol. 1: Russia, 1472–1917.* New York: Cambridge U. Press, 1973.

JERRY G. PANKHURST

RUSSIAN LITERATURE, UNBELIEF IN. Introduction.

Tolerance of differences is always precarious in human societies; people feel more comfortable in the company of lookalikes and thinkalikes. But in Russia this universal yearning for uniformity appears stronger than elsewhere. An originally sparse population was dispersed over a huge territory, one almost entirely lacking in natural frontiers and exposed to enemies from all sides. The need for political unity was paramount, and the appeal for it has been a theme of Russian literature from the beginning. Unhappily, in most countries the need for political unity and the fact of linguistic and cultural community tend to become all-inclusive and coercive, leading to an insistence on total ideological, including religious, uniformity. Thus, rulers throughout history have equated uniformity of belief with political loyalty; the corollary of this proposition is that unbelief is equated with treason.

During most of recorded Russian history the religious conformity required of the population was belief in Orthodox Christianity. The rulers' thousand-year effort to impose belief in this faith was abruptly ended in 1917—only to become an even more intolerant effort to coerce belief in a new "religion"—Marxism-Leninism. Whatever the label, however, the Russian state, like many others, has consistently felt impelled to generate and maintain the unanimity regarded as essential to its own survival. Its means have been partly positive: to instill the faith in the hearts of the people by all available techniques of persuasion, among them literature. But negative means are not lacking, and often seem swifter and surer to state enforcers— namely, censorship, prisons, internal exile, and execution blocks.

Whether these efforts have actually resulted in greater uniformity of inner belief among Russians than elsewhere cannot be determined, but in any case the Russian state seems to have been unusually successful in maintaining at least a facade of uniformity, and especially in keeping dissidence out of legally published literature. The power of the censor has almost always stood between an unbelieving or dissident Russian writer and his potential public. Whatever the writer's private beliefs or unbeliefs, they were not likely to find their way into literature if they veered too far from prescribed orthodoxy.

Yet occasionally there have been leaks. Sometimes Russian writings are published abroad, beyond the reach of native censors. Sometimes writings are duplicated clandestinely and circulated privately at home. (In recent years the Russian word *samizdat* that denotes this practice has entered the international vocabulary.) Finally, from time to time there have been periods of relative relaxation of controls when some "unbelieving" utterances were published legally. The period from 1855 to 1918, and especially from 1905 to 1918, is the most notable of these eras of tolerance, when censorship was greatly weakened, almost to the vanishing point. It is with these leaks of unbelief that this literary history will be largely concerned.

The Middle Ages. In the year 988, according to the *Primary Chronicle*, Vladimir, prince of Kiev and senior Russian ruler, after examining the relative merits of Judaism, Islam, and Roman Catholicism, decided to embrace Christianity in its Greek Orthodox version, an act for which he was later canonized by that church, despite his decidedly unsaintly earlier life. Orthodoxy thus became the official Russian state religion, a position it was to enjoy for nearly ten centuries. It replaced an earlier Slavic paganism, about which we know comparatively little, partly because, as the mythology of a preliterate society, it left no texts and partly because the later custodians of both the nation's conscience and its records did everything they could to erase its

memory. For a time, however, at least in a secular milieu, pagan memories survived as poetic echoes of past glories, notably in the most celebrated monument of ancient Russian literature, the *Igor Tale* (end of the 12th century).

In the population at large the transition from paganism to Christianity was complex and prolonged: it was not a process accomplished by the mere stroke of a royal pen. For centuries there persisted a syncretism of Christianity and paganism known as *dvoeverie* (dual faith). Its camouflaged pagan survivals were denounced and fought by the official church, but the Russian people never quite assimilated a "correct" version of Christian theology (for instance, concerning the nature of the Trinity). The religious oral epics (*dikhovnye stikhi*), mostly recorded in the 19th century but of much earlier origin, seem to make no distinction at all between God the father and Jesus Christ, the king of heaven. Thus, anomalously if not incestuously, Jesus seems to be at once the son and the husband of Mary, the mother of God and queen of heaven.

Most of the written literature of the Russian Middle Ages, however, is an acceptably Orthodox Christian literature, composed by ecclesiastics with the express aim of indoctrinating the faithful with their religion's truths. Believing themselves possessed of the one true faith, Russians saw themselves surrounded by "godless" enemies. In the East they faced a succession of menacing Asian nomads, culminating in the Mongolo-Tatars, whom in 1240 "for our sins" God allowed to conquer the country and impose a "yoke" that lasted 240 years. In the West, the Russians confronted the almost equally abhorrent Roman Catholics, from whom the schism of the Orthodox had become final in 1053. Thus, all around the Russians were alien peoples profesing "false" religions, a circumstance that left a deep imprint on the national psyche.

The "godless" Tatars (though later converted to Islam) made no attempt to impose their religion on their Russian vassals. Yet, as edifying demonstrations of their power, they were not averse to occasional sacrilegious acts such as riding their horses into churches or slaughtering priests on Christian altars. In the period of greatest Tatar power it seemed the better part of Russian valor to offer ritual submission to them while fighting off Catholic invaders from the West, a strategy successfully employed by Alexander, grand prince of Vladimir (1220–1263). He was so successful that he was subsequently canonized by the Orthodox church as St. Alexander Nevsky (of the Neva), and much later reenshrined in the film by Sergei Eisenstein as a symbol of Russia's determination to defend her Western frontiers.

Little by little the Russians gathered the strength to reduce and finally throw off the Tatar yoke, in the process building a new center of political and religious authority in Moscow. The growth in Muscovite wealth and power seemed perfectly timed, in the 15th century, to enable the country to lay claim to the religious and political authority in the Orthodox Christian world formerly wielded by the emperors of Byzantium. When Constantinople fell to the Turks in 1453, the Russians saw the event as clear evidence of God's punishment inflicted on the Greeks for sullying the true Orthodox faith by their impious concord with the papacy at the Ferraro-Florentine congress of 1439. Isolated but pure, Moscow thus became the "third Rome," the one last undefiled repository of true Christianity, destined to stand until the end of time, according to an earlier 16th-century ideologue, Philotheus of Pskov.

Early Dissidence. Such, of course, was the "official" line. Unofficially, manifestations of heterodoxy, if not true "unbelief," occasionally appeared. Unfortunately, such "heresies" survive in literature only in the denunciations of their opponents, the heretics' own writings having been lost, probably destroyed. Notable among them are the dissidents mysteriously known as *strigol'niki* (shearers), who arose in Novgorod and Pskov in the late 14th century, and the *zhidovstvuiushchie,* or Judaizers, of about a century later. Both these heresies illustrate the danger to any official orthodoxy of dislodging even a single stone in a carefully constructed ecclesiastical edifice. The shearers began by denouncing as simony the exaction of a fee for the sacrament of ordination of clergy—a seemingly minor point of church economics. The logical consequences, however, were devastating. One could conclude that all ordinations obtained by simony were invalid; since all existing Orthodox clergy had been so ordained, the entire priesthood was therefore falsely constituted and all sacraments performed by them likewise invalid. No wonder the perpetrators of this heresy had to be tied up and cast into the Volkhov River.

Concerning the Judaizers, there is a long and acrimonious scholarly controversy, especially over the question of actual Jewish influence. Were Orthodox Christians in fact converted to Judaism, as their enemies charged, or were their doctrines rather a manifestation of the same sort of critical rationalism applied to Roman Christianity by reformers in the West? How important were contacts with Jews and Jewish writings in the genesis of these ideas? Scholars differ, but there is no doubt that the Judaizer heresy spread widely and had adherents in high places.

The questions the heresy raised were fundamental ones. Could the lot of souls in the next world be improved by masses said for them here? Were prayers said before icons more likely to reach God's ears than prayers said elsewhere? Was church tradition equal to scripture as a medium of revelation? In general, were sacraments necessary for salvation? And most dangerous of all, was Jesus the son of God in a sense different from that according to which we are all God's children? After a long struggle, the Judaizer heresy was formally condemned at the church council of 1504; its adherents were either burned or imprisoned, and their literary heritage was destroyed.

The Great Schism. Later Russian heresies, though far more widespread in society, are intellectually less interesting. The so-called Great Schism in the Russian church of the 17th century occurred over issues that seem to an outsider amazingly trivial: technicalities of ritual, the correct spelling of the name *Jesus*, the position of the fingers in making the sign of the cross. Nevertheless, the schism's literary echoes are impressive. One of the most vivid and moving monuments of early Russian literature, the autobiography of the Archpriest Avvakum (1620–1682), was written by a schismatic leader. But it certainly cannot in any sense be considered a manifestation of unbelief.

This schism itself was, to some degree, a conservative reaction among true believers against a major historical process that began in the 17th century—the westernization of Russia, a process rife with controversy and conflict and still far from complete. These momentous changes, though begun under Czar Alexis, were greatly accelerated by the forcefulness of his son, Peter the Great, who was desperately anxious to "catch up with and overtake" Western Europe (as a later Soviet slogan had it), especially in military technology. For this purpose he packed hundreds of young gentlemen off to study in the West and subjected countless others to secularized, if rudimentary, schooling in Russia.

One of the long-term consequences of this "cultural revolution," though not part of Peter's conscious plan, was to displace the clergy as the country's primary transmitters of culture. It is a striking fact that until about 1740 practically all of Russia's best writers, poets, dramatists, and historians were clergymen; after that date almost none of them were. The cultural torch had, for the time being, passed to the ever more westernized gentry, their ranks supplemented by other elements—upwardly mobile peasants and secularized priests' sons.

The Effects of the Enlightenment. In the 18th century a Western-style education meant some exposure not only to contemporary Western science and technology, but also to the complex of philosophical and political ideas known as the ENLIGHTENMENT. Even a measure of enlightenment was likely to engender a degree of unbelief in the whole system of Orthodox Christianity. In this way a gulf developed and increasingly widened between the old culture, adhered to by the peasants and the Orthodox clergy, and the new one of the educated nobility. The nobles, though recognizing the importance of Orthodoxy to the peasant masses, found less and less need for it themselves. From the other side, the traditional seminary education given the clergy in no way prepared them to cope with the ideas of the *philosophes* or to deal with westernized gentlemen on intellectually equal terms; moreover, they were almost always poor and dependent. As an ingrown, self-producing caste, the Russian clergy were thus far more isolated socially and more backward intellectually than their Catholic and Protestant colleagues in the West—a fact that had important consequences.

No Russian thinker seems to have gone as far in the direction of atheism as PAUL HENRI HOLBACH or JULIEN DE LA METTRIE, certainly not in print; but it is a remarkable fact that a Russian translation of DENIS DIDEROT's *La religieuse* was published in 1760; this happened even before the great encyclopedist had become an object of Catherine II's patronage. No doubt the fact that Diderot was satirizing Roman Catholic and not Orthodox monasticism helped its passage through Russian censorship. Despite this fluke, however, the ecclesiastical censors were still very much alive. The difficulties Russian writers had with them are illustrated by the fact that crucial lines from the original translation, by Nikolai Popovsky (1730–1760), of Alexander Pope's *Essay on Man* ("See worlds on worlds compose one universe") were expunged and rewritten by a priest on the grounds that it was impious to speak of a plurality of "worlds."

Several leading Russian writers of the 18th century went as far in their unbelief as the DEISM then fashionable in the West, acknowledging an impersonal God as the creator and infinitely ingenious author of the universe but silently rejecting most tenets of Christian dogma.

Prominent among these was the great scientist and poet Mikhail Lomonosov (1711–1765), who not only vigorously endorsed the Copernican heliocentric theory of the solar system, but whose studies of geology convinced him, long before such ideas were current even in the West, that the earth was a great deal older than the biblical creation legends allowed. Though he celebrated in resounding and eloquent verse the greatness of God as manifested in his creation, and though he was acutely aware of the historical importance of Christianity to Russian culture, Lomonosov was hardly an Orthodox believer. He found the clergy generally an impediment to the advancement of science and learning in Russia and composed an anticlerical satire in verse, "Hymn to the Beard," in 1757 (but it was only published much later).

The most radical of the Russian Enlightenment philosophers, Alexander Radishchev (1749–1802), in his famous *Journey from St. Petersburg to Moscow* (1790), explicitly univeralized his deism, shockingly equating Christianity with other religions and the Christian God with other gods: "Jehovah, Jupiter, Brahma; the God of Abraham, the God of Moses, the God of Confucius, the God of Socrates, the God of Marcus Aurelius, the God of the Christians, O my God, everywhere Thou art one." Such relativism was remarkable—and dangerous—for a Russian. Radishchev was duly arrested and exiled and his book confiscated, though to be sure more for its social and political opinions than for its religious ones.

Radishchev's follower, Ivan Pnin (1773–1805), though less radical in his social views, seems to have been more of an atheist than his master. At any rate he managed to publish in 1798 a translation of Holbach's *Système de la nature*, although the most irreligious passages had to be greatly toned down to pass the censor.

Alexander Pushkin (1799–1837). The aristocratic era in Russian literature reaches its apogee in the age of Pushkin, the most brilliant in a dazzling galaxy of poets. Russian literature now shed its last traces of derivativeness and provincialism, taking a prominent place among the great literatures of the world. Religious issues, for most bluebloods of this generation, were not of overriding concern; social, psychological, stylistic, and even linguistic issues loomed far larger. The attitude to religion of most writers of Pushkin's time, as of most Russian gentlemen throughout the 19th century, was rather casual: nominally Orthodox, they attended services only when they had to and concerned themselves little with religious matters.

Pushkin himself is more or less typical. Immersed in French books in his childhood, he adored VOLTAIRE ("the first among poets") and especially *La pucelle d'Orléans*, of which he attempted, at the age of 14, a sort of Russian version, "The Monk," taking as his theme a medieval legend about a monk who tricked a devil into carrying him to Jerusalem in a single night. The devil, however, took vengeance by leaving a deposit of tell-tale female garments in the monk's cell, with unfortunate consequences for the latter.

The same spirit of light-hearted anticlerical mockery pervades Pushkin's literarily much more mature poem, *The Gabrielad* or *Gavriliada* (1821). There, in verses of scintillating elegance, he tells of the successive seduction of the "Virgin" Mary by Satan, by the Archangel Gabriel, and only last by the Holy Ghost in the form of a dove. As a result of these salacious shenanigans the actual paternity of Jesus is very much in doubt: "God Almighty, as is meet, acknowledges as His own the Hebrew maiden's son; / But Gabriel (lucky one!) ceased not to visit her in secret . . ." Impotent old Joseph is rewarded with sainthood, much, as in Pushkin's experience, complacent husbands cuckolded by monarchs were rewarded with titles and estates. *The Gabrielad*, of course, could not be published in Russia until after the Revolution, but it circulated in countless handwritten copies. Indeed, to copy *The Gabrielad* became almost a rite for generations of Russian schoolboys.

Pushkin might have suffered serious consequences for writing this blasphemous poem, when in 1828 the government was obliged to take cognizance of it, but forgiveness of his youthful indiscretion was part of the special arrangement concluded between the poet and Czar Nicholas I. It should be noted, however, that earlier, in 1824, a letter of Pushkin's had been intercepted by the police; partly in consequence of it he was confined to his mother's estate near Pskov. "I am taking lessons in pure atheism," he wrote. "Here [in Odessa] there is an Englishman, a deaf philosopher, the only clever atheist I have ever met. He has covered with writing no less than a thousand pages to prove *qu'il ne peut exister d'être intélligent Créateur et régulateur*, in passing annihilating the weak proofs of the immortality of the soul. This

system is not as consoling as is usually thought, but unfortunately it is the most probable."

Whether Pushkin remained—or indeed ever was—a true atheist is a matter of much dispute. Protean in his ability to assume all sorts of literary and even philosophical stances, he is hard to pin down to any orthodoxy, even an atheistic one. One of his most beautiful late lyrics, "Desert fathers, immaculate women" (1836), is a paraphrase of a prayer of St. Ephrem the Syrian used in the Orthodox liturgy.

After the Pushkin era, Russian writers mainly produced prose masterpieces that have left a permanent mark on the literary consciousness of the world. From the point of view of belief and unbelief, each of the masters is a case unto himself; it is impossible to find a denominator common to them all.

Nikolai Gogol (1809–1852). The great humorist, Gogol, never seems to have questioned the Orthodoxy taught him in childhood. Ultimately, after a pilgrimage to Palestine failed to cleanse his soul, he starved himself to death in desperate penance for multiple sins of body and spirit, encouraged in his anguished self-castigation by a sadistic priest. Gogol's celebrated creature, the artful dodger Pavel Chichikov, was luckier; after making a successful getaway at the end of the first volume of *Dead Souls* he was scheduled by the author for penance and redemption in the second volume, a spiritual metamorphosis never completed because of the author's demise. In any case, especially in view of his book of philosophicoreligious essays, *Selected Passages from Correspondence with Friends* (1847), Gogol must be listed firmly on the side of belief.

Ivan Turgenev (1818–1883), however, is already the typical unbeliever of modern times. Much influenced in his philosophical thinking by ARTHUR SCHOPENHAUER, Turgenev gloomily perceived human beings as hapless denizens of an existential void, with each generation mostly doomed to repeat the crimes and follies of its predecessors: "The same credulity and the same cruelty, the same thirst for blood, gold, and dirt, the same cheap pleasures, the same senseless sufferings in the name—well, even in the name of the same nonsense ridiculed two thousand years ago by Aristophanes . . ." ("Enough," 1865).

"Nature is not a temple, but a workshop," proclaims Bazarov, the nihilist hero of *Fathers and Sons* (1862). But for Turgenev, man is himself a more or less fortuitous product of nature's own workshop, a product about which she cares little; he lives out a short interval between nothing and nothing. "Hard is it for man, the creature of a single day, born yesterday and already condemned to death today, hard is it for him to endure the cold gaze of the eternal Isis, directed at him without sympathy . . . . He feels his loneliness, his weakness, his fortuitousness—and with a hurried, secret fright he turns to the petty cares and labors of life" ("A Trip to the Polesye," 1857). In a late "poem in prose" (1879), the author imagines an actual dialogue with Mother Nature: "'Are we human beings not thy favorite children?' . . . . 'All creatures are my children,' she replied, 'and I care equally about all of them and equally destroy them.' 'But good reason, justice,' I stammered once again. 'Those are human words,' the iron voice resounded. 'I know neither good nor evil. Reason is no law unto me, and what is justice? I gave thee life—and I shall take it away and give it to others, worms or human begins, it is all the same to me.'" In such a pessimistic philosophy there was no room for traditional beliefs.

Fëdor Dostoevski (1821–1881), on the other hand, was engaged in a lifelong struggle for faith; the battle between belief and unbelief was relentlessly waged in his mind, his heart, and his novels. The utopian socialism of his early years was essentially atheistic in character, inspired by the great critic Vissarion Belinski (1811–1848). But the experience of undergoing a death sentence, commuted at the last moment to eight years of prison and army service in Siberia, brought Dostoevski to the conclusion that the rationalist and progressivist utopia of the socialists did not adequately account either for the dark irrationality of the human soul or explain man's tragic destiny.

Dostoevski longed for some evidence of cosmic purpose and cosmic reconciliation, some explanation for the prevalence of evil in the world, and some vision of a moral order in the universe, a supernatural foundation for ethics. He found his isolation not so much in the official Orthodox church (though he professed allegiance to it) as in the personality of Jesus, "the lustrous image of the God-man," "wonderfully, miraculously beautiful." Yet, like his creature Shatov in *The Devils*, Dostoevski's faith was more a wish to believe than belief itself. He wrote a friend in 1854 from his Siberian prison: "I am a child of the age, a child of nonbelief and doubt, up till now and even (I know it) until my coffin closes."

In novel after novel, Dostoevski dramatized the dilemma of modern man, caught between the longing for a faith that would establish a firm definition of right and wrong and give his life an ultimate meaning beyond time, and reason, which constantly demolishes the consoling structures erected by faith. "If there is no God, then all is permitted"—this equation of atheism with moral relativism and chaos terrified Dostoevski. In *Crime and Punishment* (1866) Raskolnikov commits murder to prove that he is one of the leaders of humanity, a Napoleon not bound by the moral laws imposed on ordinary mortals. The proof fails, at least for Raskolnikov, and with the help of the soulful prostitute Sonya Marmeladova he must find his way through suffering and Siberia to the Gospel.

In *The Idiot* (1868) a "positively good man," the Christlike Prince Myshkin, is immersed in the "world of darkness," a world of money-grubbers and thieves symbolically presided over, in the conception of the drunkard Lebedev, by the third horseman of the Apocalypse, the black one with a balance in his hand; it will be followed by the pale horse whose name is death. Man's loss of faith in Jesus, Dostoevski maintained, has caused the collapse of his moral universe; it can lead only to an orgy of murder, an orgy duly demonstrated in the novel's finale.

Finally, in *The Brothers Karamazov* (1879), atheism again leads inexorably to murder. The three brothers personify a Hegelian syllogism of the soul, the antithesis of heart and mind. The man of passion, Dmitri, only desires his father's death but does not cause it; he will ultimately be redeemed after years of penance and suffering. But the man of intellect, Ivan, the up-to-date "scientific" atheist, actually inspires his father's murder, though it is physically performed by their degenerate half-brother, Smerdyakov. Satanic in his intellectual pride, Ivan finds himself fully in the power of the Prince of Darkness, who actually appears to him in characteristic 19th-century guise. The devil is doubtless also the inspiration for Ivan's famous "poem," the "Legend of the Grand Inquisitor."

This text-within-a-text is preceded by a discussion between Ivan and the third brother, Alyosha, concerning the nature of evil. Citing several examples (many taken from contemporary newspapers) of appalling cruelties inflicted upon children, Ivan concludes that a moral order founded on the suffering of even one sinless child is unacceptable to him. Though he still claims to ackowledge God as the creator, he "most respectfully" returns to him his ticket of admission to such a flawed creation.

In the "Legend" itself, Jesus returns to earth in 16th-century Spain and is promptly arrested. The aged Grand Inquisitor, visiting him in prison, pours out what Dostoevski regarded as the true "theology" of Roman Catholicism, which he regarded as fundamentally identical with the atheistic "theology" of 19th-century socialism. The church, the Grand Inquisitor avers, has recognized that Jesus erred in rejecting the three temptations placed before him by Satan. Give men bread and rule them by mystery and unswerving authority, and they will be happy—in the same sort of antlike society envisioned by the socialists. Jesus, however, rejected these solutions, insisting on giving men the freedom to choose between good and evil. It was a cruel decision since few men can endure such freedom. Inspired by the "great spirit," Satan, the Grand Inquisitor concludes, the church has corrected Jesus' mistake. Men are too weak to be given such freedom. Using miracle, mystery, and authority, the church has hoodwinked men into happiness, to their eternal gratitude. Only a few unhappy rulers know the secret—that the religion officially called Christianity is actually the worship of Satan. The Grand Inquisitor condemns Jesus to be burned the next day "for coming to hinder us." Jesus does not reply in words, but he kisses the Inquisitor on the mouth. Imitating this gesture, Alyosha kisses Ivan after hearing the "poem."

Alyosha embodies the longed-for synthesis between Dmitri and Ivan, between passion and intellect. With the model before Alyosha of his beloved mentor, Father Zosima, Dostoevski intended that after much error and suffering he would find his way to salvation, in a continuation of the novel that remained unwritten. Meanwhile, in his publicist writings (*The Diary of a Writer*, 1873–81) and in his famous "Pushkin speech" (1880), Dostoevski, less profoundly and more bluntly, called for a Russian crusade, though not necessarily a military one, against all the emanations of Satan in the modern world—the Turkish Empire, Jews, Catholicism, and socialism. Russians, Dostoevski proclaimed, would finally reconcile all the contradictions of Europe, "show the way out of European anguish in their all-human and all-unifying Russian soul . . . and at last, perhaps, utter the final word of a great, universal harmony, a final fraternal consort of all tribes according to the evangelical law of Christ."

Tolstoi. Dostoevski's great contemporary,

Count Lev, or Leo, Nikolaevich Tolstoi (1828–1910), acts out another scenario of belief and unbelief, very different, yet with the common ingredient of a struggle for faith against the destructive power of reason. As early as 1855, at the age of 27, Tolstoi conceived the idea of providing the world with a "rationalized" Christianity. As he wrote in his diary, "A conversation about divinity and faith has suggested to me a great, stupendous idea, to the realization of which I feel capable of devoting my life. That idea is the founding of a new religion corresponding to the present state of mankind: the religion of Christ, but purged of dogmas and mysticism—a practical religion, not promising future bliss, but giving bliss on earth." It was an extraordinary, not to say hubristic, ambition, certainly, but even more extraordinary is the fact that it was actually carried out, though much later in Tolstoi's life. In the meantime, Tolstoi pursued what he termed a "secondary" career as a writer of fiction, one that soon catapulted him to the very summit of world literature.

As for belief and unbelief, the alter-ego characters in the great novels, Pierre Bezukhov and Andrei Bolkonski in *War and Peace* and Konstantin Lyovin in *Anna Karenina*, are forced to confront the same "accursed," existential questions that tormented their creator. Of these the most painful, the most obsessive for Tolstoi was the question of death—death both of the individual and of the race itself. He asked in essence: If I must die, then what is the use of anything—working, loving, writing novels, even eating breakfast? Why not just get a rope and put an end to it now? In addition, the human race is likewise doomed. Science tells us (one of the few scientific predictions Tolstoi seems to have accepted on faith) that the sun is cooling off. The earth will eventually become too cold to support life. Thus everything human is transitory, everything is finite. Human life fades into insignificance when projected against the infinity of the sky, as Andrei Bolkonski perceives while lying wounded on the battlefield at Austerlitz.

For two decades or so, in the 1860s and 1870s, Tolstoi found it possible to endure the thought of death by immersing himself in nature and biology. Man is an animal like any other, he decided, and his biological mission is simply to live, procreate, and die. Civilization, culture, the city, the pursuit of position, power, money, and fame—all this was the vanity of vanities. Only the farmer in the country, digging in the earth, raising food, breeding and rearing children with his woman was living the true life, a life in harmony with the rhythm of the universe.

But the "biological" life" was an unthinking life, and though he tried to live it, it could not for long satisfy Tolstoi the thinker. In the late 1870s he passed through the most profound and most celebrated of his many spiritual crises, after which he dedicated himself in earnest to the creation of a new religion, as he had planned 25 years earlier. After purging his soul with *A Confession* (1879–80), he proceeded to construct his new edifice. First the ground had to be cleared by a savage attack on the doctrines of the Orthodox church (*A Critique of Dogmatic Theology*, 1879–80). Then the Gospels themselves had to be unified and "sanitized," cleansed of any nonsense about miracles or the divinity of Jesus (*Union and Translation of the Four Gospels*, 1880–81). Following these came an explication of the basic tenets of the new faith (*What I Believe*, 1882–84) and its social and moral consequences (*What Then Must We Do?* 1882–86), especially with regard to sexual morality ("The Kreutzer Sonata," 1887–89, particularly its "Afterword," 1889–90). After these came the aesthetics (*What Is Art?* 1897–98) and a renewed attack on militarism and violence (*The Kingdom of God Is Within You*, 1890–93).

The cornerstone of Tolstoi's ethics is the crucial passage in the Sermon on the Mount (Matt. 5:39): "But I say unto you, that ye resist not evil; but whosoever shall smite thee on thy right cheek, turn to him the other also." From its stress on this formula, Tolstoi's ethical doctrine acquired the misleading label "non-resistance to evil," though he insisted that by *resist* Jesus had meant only resist by violence. Evil *should* be resisted, but by nonviolent means. In any event, the doctrine of nonviolence led Tolstoi to a sweeping repudiation of the state—any state—since its agencies, such as law courts and armies, are based on violence. He also, of course, renounced the official Orthodox church (and other official churches), charging them with gross distortion and falsification of the teachings of Jesus.

Tolstoi was too famous to persecute directly, but the Russian government energetically harassed his followers; and the Orthodox church in 1901 formally excommunicated him, partly in response to the harshly satirical representation of the divine liturgy in his last big novel, *Resurrection* (1889–99). As prophet and conscience of the world, Tolstoi courageously kept up the fight to the end. Somewhere deep down, however, there were persistent

doubts. As Maxim Gorki acutely perceived, there was part of the old Tolstoi that could not be contained within the image of "St. Leo." The complete Tolstoi was a complex, elusive, sly, contradictory, immensely creative personality, bigger and richer than his doctrines. His relations with his God, Gorki thought, were "very suspicious: they sometimes remind me of the relation of two bears in one den."

Anton Chekhov (1860–1904), the last of the 19th-century Russian giants, presents yet another, strikingly different scenario. Most notably, he speaks in a quieter voice, much less shrill, less insistent, less dogmatic than either Tolstoi or Dostoevski. As he himself put it, the task of the artist is to pose questions correctly, not to answer them. For this reason it is harder to identify an author's point of view, to read a moral in Chekhov's stories and plays. But the point of view is there all the same. In fact, in all Russian literature Chekhov's is the most consistent voice of understanding, breadth, and tolerance.

Born into the family of a poorly educated, provincial shopkeeper, Chekhov was given a severely Orthodox upbringing, forced to stand through long church services and sing in the choir. By the time he reached maturity, however, he was no longer a Christian believer, though he retained a lifelong appreciation of the beauties of the Orthodox liturgy and a remarkably sympathetic understanding of the actual life of the Russian clergy—something neither Dostoevski nor Tolstoi paid much attention to. This feeling for the religious life is manifested, for, example, in a wonderful late story, "The Bishop" (1902), and in the story Chekhov claimed as his own favorite, "The Student" (1894). The latter story evokes, in the most moving and eloquent way the anguish and weeping of Peter in the garden after his three denials of Jesus.

One of the most remarkable features of Chekhov's treatment of the clergy—and of religious experience generally—is its neutrality. There are good priests and bad priests; there are saints and stingy, cruel bigots. Religion may provide experiences of intense meaning and beauty, and it may also be used to cover the worst sort of meanness and poverty of spirit. The bishop, ironically, dies of typhus just before Easter, but he dies with dignity and courage. On the other hand, the mealy-mouthed, "pious" tradesman Matvei in "Peasant Women" recites scripture and delivers moral lectures to the mistress he heartlessly abandons. He even testifies against her and sees her convicted of the murder of her husband, which she probably did not commit.

Chekhov's philosophy—he would never have given it such a pompous label—was a by-product of his medical education. It is best expressed in a famous "credo" he included in a letter to the poet Alexei Pleshcheyev in 1888: I am neither liberal, nor conservative, nor gradualist, nor monk, nor indifferentist. I would like to be a free artist and nothing else, and I regret that God has not given me more strength to be one. I hate lies and violence in all of their forms. . . . I look upon tags and labels as prejudices. My holy of holies is the human body, health, intelligence, talent, inspiration, love, and the most absolute freedom imaginable, freedom from violence and lies, no matter what form the latter two take."

Death is a reality we must all face, but Chekhov saw no point in railing against it as Tolstoi did, shaking one's fist at the heavens and demanding that one's life have meaning for all eternity. Suffering is real too, all too real, even if not eternal, as Dr. Ragin in "Ward No. 6" (1892) learns from the brutal fist of the orderly and guard, Nikita. For years Ragin had neglected his official duties in the town hospital, on the "philosophical" grounds that disease and mortality will remain whether you treat people or not; so what's the use? "Everything in this world is nonsense and vanity of vanities"; "in time everything will rot and turn to clay." But when the doctor himself is confined to the ward for mental patients and beaten by Nikita, this "philosophy" is of little help. Life may be transitory, but the pain and the humiliation are real. One concludes that we must construct a human ethic on a human scale, ephemeral as it may be.

Our responsibility, according to Chekhov, is to try to gratify our own needs without hurting others and to leave the world a little better, a little richer than we found it, if only by planting trees instead of cutting them down. Chekhov himself, needless to say, was a great planter of trees—both real ones and the symbolic ones of his literary art, which are as immortal as any human artifact is likely to be.

Besides the great novelists and poets, the Russian 19th century also boasts among its literary luminaries a number of journalistic writers, most of whom were traditionally known as "critics." Their influence in Russia was in some ways stronger than that of the great novelists themselves; at any rate it is more homogeneous, less idiosyncratic and personal. The Russian "intelligentsia"—another word the Russians have bestowed on the world— was shaped far more by these ideologues than by novelists, let alone poets.

Alexander Herzen (1812–1870), the most talented and attractive of this group, was a novelist who abandoned belles lettres for political journalism when he emigrated permanently from Russia in 1847. Herzen's writings, thereafter, all published abroad and smuggled into Russia, were thus produced free of censorship, which gave added play to the bite of his keen satirical talent. Herzen's book of memoirs, *My Past and Thoughts* (1855–68), is one of the great masterpieces of the 19th century, a wonderfully rich, vivid, colorful account of a full life. As a political and social thinker Herzen was also enormously influential.

An implacable enemy of czarist absolutism and a proponent of liberal socialism, Herzen was also acutely sensitive to the illiberal and despotic tendencies endemic among socialists and revolutionaries both in Russia and the West, an attitude that set him at odds with KARL MARX and his followers, among others. Urbane, cultivated, humorous, and ironic, a genuine believer in freedom— freedom for everyone, not just those who agreed with him—Herzen is the most like Chekhov of all the 19th-century Russian social thinkers. It is therefore one of history's many ironies that this outspoken opponent of all tyrannies should have been canonized (largely because of a single pious article written about him by VLADIMIR ILYICH LENIN) as a spiritual godfather by the Soviet regime, which proved to be the very antithesis of everything Herzen stood for.

One of the consequences for Herzen of Soviet canonization is that he is taken seriously in present-day Russia as a "philosopher." In that capacity he is given great credit for having come in his philosophical development up to the very brink of dialectical materialism itself—that final Soviet truth at which all philosophical thought stops. In fact, Herzen was a lively but not very original thinker on philosophical questions. On the other hand, he was an extremely able popularizer, one of the transmission lines into Russia of the most advanced ideas then circulating in the West, especially Saint-Simonism and left-wing Hegelianism. As far as religion is concerned, he is of especial interest, though more as an illustrative case than as a generator of ideas.

Herzen's father, Ivan Yakovlev, was a typical Russian gentleman in 18th-century style—nominally Orthodox, but with little more than a pro forma interest in religion. His mother was a dutifully pious German Protestant, but she too seems to have made little effort to indoctrinate Herzen with her beliefs. Her precocious son thus emerged from childhood without any deep religious emotions or allegiances, essentially a skeptic and a relativist. He read VOLTAIRE and the Gospels at the same time, responding to the latter without hostility, indeed with sincere respect, which continued throughout his life.

When preparing for the examination in "God's law" required for admission to the university, Herzen surprised his priest-tutor with his detailed knowledge of the scripture, but the priest also noted that it was a knowledge of the head, not the heart. Later, under the influence of Saint-Simon's "New Christianity" and during his deep immersion in the mysteries of Hegelianism, Herzen for a time felt obliged to postulate a deity as the final link in the great chain of becoming, the ultimate manifestation of the absolute. But it was a very abstract and impersonal deity, and it did not long survive the assaults of reason. By the time he first read LUDWIG FEUERBACH's *Essence of Christianity* (about 1840), Herzen had already worked his way to a "left Hegelian" position similar to Feuerbach's, and he immediately recognized a kindred spirit. "After reading the first few pages I jumped for joy," he wrote to a friend. "Down with the masquerade attire, away with double-talk and allegory . . . . We do not need to clothe reality in myths." There is no God at all, he concluded, and man is alone in an impersonal universe. All values, purposes, and meanings are his own. This remained Herzen's position to the end.

Essentially an aristocrat in culture and style, Herzen was exceptional among the left-wing publicists of his time. Far more typical, and in the long run more influential, was the succession of "critics" who dominated Russian radical jouralism at home in the period after 1840. Leading this procession are Belinski, Nikolai Chernyshevski (1828–1889), and Nikolai Dobrolyubov (1836–1861); many more followed, but they added little, at least concerning the issue of belief and unbelief. On that issue, Belinski, Chernyshevski, Dobrolyubov, and their followers established a dominant tradition, a set of "unbelieving beliefs" that were eagerly and unquestioningly embraced by succeeding generations of left-wing Russian intellectuals. They eventually hardened into dogmas as rigid as any orthodoxy, ultimately becoming the established religion of the Soviet state: MATERIALISM,

ATHEISM, worship of science, belief in progress, social as well as scientific, the last—and not far distant—stage of which will be a "revolution" that will inaugurate a society of equality and justice.

Vissarion Belinski (1811–1848). The son of a poor provincial doctor, Belinski attended Moscow University, but was expelled without completing the course. After that, he supported himself entirely by journalism, churning out in his brief life a remarkable number of essays and reviews. Written with great verve and passion, these articles, despite their turgid style and the limitations imposed by censorship, for a whole generation represented the most vital voice within Russia of opposition to the tyrannical regime of Nicholas I. Belinski was even less a systematic philosopher than Herzen, but his ideological evolution was similar. He too, during a period of enthusiastic veneration of the philosophy of Hegel, enthroned the deity as an absolute idea immanent in creation: "The whole infinite, beautiful, divine word," he wrote, "is nothing but the breath of a single, eternal *idea* (the shape of a single, eternal God), manifesting itself in innumerable shapes as a great spectacle of absolute unity in infinite diversity."

However, before long Belinski too, not without assistance from Feuerbach, had found his way to atheism. As he wrote to Herzen in 1845, "In the words 'God' and 'religion' I see darkness, gloom, chains, and the knout, and my love for those two words is the same as for the four words that follow." But he complained that he could not say such things in print: "What is the use of truth if you can't popularize it?"

Not long before his death, however, Belinski did get a chance to "popularize" such truth free from the shackles of censorship. From a spa in Germany where he had gone for treatment of the tuberculosis that killed him a year later, he wrote his famous "Letter to Gogol," a smashing attack on the writer's just published *Selected Passages from Correspondence with Friends*. In its advocacy of humility, acceptance of the world as it is, and concentration on moral self-improvement, Gogol's book was the opposite of everything Belinski believed in passionately, and the disillusionment was especially bitter because the critic had quite mistakenly enshrined Gogol as the Russian exemplar of "realism," a ruthless satirist of social corruption. Belinski's "Letter" contains the most vehement atheistic and anticlerical pronouncements made by any Russian in the 19th century, though to be sure, like other radical prophets he tries to separate Jesus from the church.

"Proponent of the knout," Belinski hurls at Gogol, "apostle of ignorance, champion of obscurantism and Stygian darkness, panegyrist of Tatar morals—what are you about? . . . That you base such teaching on the Orthodox church I can understand: it has always served as the prop of the knout and the servant of despotism; but why have you mixed Christ up in it? What have you found in common between Him and any church, least of all the Orthodox church? He was the first to bring to people the teaching of freedom, equality, and brotherhood, and to set the seal of truth to that teaching by martyrdom. . . . The church, on the other hand, was a hierarchy, consequently a champion of inequality, a flatterer of authority, an enemy and persecutor of brotherhood among men— and so it has remained to this day . . . . A man like Voltaire who stamped out the fires of fanaticism and ignorance in Europe by ridicule is, of course, more the son of Christ, flesh of His flesh and bone of His bone, than all your priests, bishops, metropolitans, and patriarchs, Eastern or Western."

Though such resounding phrases could not, of course, be printed in Russia until after 1917, Belinski's letter to Gogol quickly became one of the sacred texts of the Russian left, transmitted piously from hand to hand, copied, read aloud, and recited. It was for such a reading that Dostoevski was arrested and originally sentenced to death.

Other "Critics." As shapers of the mentality of the typical Russian radical intellectual of the later 19th century, Chernyshevski and Dobrolyubov were perhaps more influential than the erratic and somewhat inconsistent Belinski. For, despite his insistence on harnessing literature to social ends, Belinski had a strongly developed aesthetic sense and a latent, unregenerate love for literature for its own sake. Chernyshevski and Dobrolyubov had no such "weaknesses." For them aesthetics was frivolous nonsense. The value of all art is only as a "reflection of reality"; literature can be, first, an instrument for cognition of the world and second, a means of inspiring readers with the will to change it. Chernyshevski provided the example himself, choosing the novel as the most unimpeded avenue into the young hearts he sought to galvanize. His *What Is to Be Done?* (1862), written while he was a prisoner in the Peter and Paul Fortress in St. Petersburg, despite its lack of literary merit, became yet another sacred text of the Russian left, a secular saint's life from which generations of young rebels derived their ideas.

As a "reflection of reality," literature provided the pretext for essays in "criticism"; and these, rather than fiction, were the principal media for both Chernyshevski and Dobrolyubov. These writings about literature pay scant attention to anything so trivial as questions of literary art, but focus entirely on the social issues "reflected" in the works discussed, treating literary characters as if they were real people.

Social issues loom much larger in such writings than religious or philosophical ones. Nevertheless, atheism, because of censorship more implied than openly stated, is a basic point of departure, a keystone of the radical edifice. For most latter-day radical intellectuals the emancipation from religion came easily, almost casually; but for both Chernyshevski and Dobrolyubov personally it was a much more drastic and traumatic break. Both were the sons of Orthodox priests. Both, like all sons of priests, were expected to become priests themselves and were educated accordingly. In their youth both were devout Christian believers. Yet by the age of 20 or so each had lost his faith and renounced the sacerdotal calling. For both men a sense of the isolation, intellectual stagnation, and social conservatism of the Russian clergy was undoubtedly a crucial ingredient in this decision, but the most powerful intellectual lever was Feuerbach's *Essence of Christianity*. This Bible of unbelief, with its "anthropological" discovery that God is but a projection and idealization of human qualities and human emotions, was received as revelation by both Chernyshevski and Dobrolyubov.

In Chernyshevski's novel Feuerbach's book is piously brought to the heroine by her tutor and future husband, with the aim of helping her outgrow her constricted and conventional background. Amusingly, her mother allows this anti-Gospel into the house in the conviction that its author is none other than King Louis XIV (since in Russian *Louis* and *Ludwig* are similar).

A similar scene, with a "tutor" sacramentally presenting his "pupil" with a sacred radical text, is treated ironically in Turgenev's *Fathers and Sons*, which was published in the same year as *What Is to Be Done?* There Arkady Kirsanov takes the beloved volume of Pushkin's poems out of his father's hands and replaces it with another radical bible by another Ludwig: LUDWIG BÜCHNER's *Kraft und Stoff* (1855). Incidentally, the transition from Feuerbach to Büchner can be taken as symbolic of a transition from "philosophy" to "science" as the foundation of Russian unbelief. Büchner had based his materialism on what he regarded as the necessary philosophical underpinnings of science, which was gathering prestige as fast as religion was losing it. As Chernyshevski put it, "Chemistry is the greatest glory of our age."

Pre-Revolution Literature. The creed of materialism, scientism, and progressivism promoted in Russia by the radical critics has remained the dominant ideology of the intelligentsia ever since. However, adherence to this creed was far from universal, especially among literary people; and in the last decades before the Revolution the range of belief and unbelief expressed in Russian literature expanded enormously. Beginning in the 1890s, the literati, especially the poets, began to revolt against what seemed to them the dry and sterile POSITIVISM of the intelligentsia tradition. A whole series of reversals took place, transformations of "beliefs" into "unbeliefs" and vice versa. Early symbolists or "decadents" like Konstantin Balmont (1867–1943) and Valery Bryusov (1873–1924) sought to liberate art from the shackles of social responsibility and the flesh from burdensome moral ones; they began waving such shocking *fin de siècle* flags as art for art's sake and pleasure for pleasure's sake.

Later, symbolists like Alexander Blok (1880–1921) and Andrei Belyi (1880–1934) pushed farther in the direction of a neoromantic mysticism, following the neo-Platonic philosopher and poet Vladimir Solovyov (1853–1900) as their prophet and guiding light. Still others like Dmitri Merezhkovski (1865–1941) and his wife, Zinaida Gippius (1869–1945), initiated a genuine intellectual dialogue with liberal-minded representatives of the Orthodox clergy—something almost unprecedented in the Russian context.

Thus in the immediate pre-Revolution years a very broad spectrum of philosophical and religious opinion developed among Russian writers. It was maintained more or less intact in the emigration that followed the Revolution, but in the Soviet Union it was truncated and largely suppressed by the enforcers of a new official orthodoxy. It included ex-Marxists turned Orthodox philosophers like Father Sergei Bulgakov (1871–1944) and Nikolai Berdyaev (1874–1948); converts to Catholicism like the symbolist poet Vyacheslav Ivanov (1866–1949); those like Andrei Belyi, who ranged even further afield in their search for ultimate truth (Belyi for a time espoused Rudolf Steiner's neo-Hinduism known as "anthroposophy").

Still others, like the great poet Osip Mandelstam (1891–1938, killed by Stalin), without joining any sect or embracing any specific package of beliefs, sought through religious—and particularly Christian—explorations a sense of continuity with the cultural history of mankind and some explanation of the meaning of human history. Of course the materialist, indifferentist tradition continued as well, but it is a curious fact that even such a stalwart Marxist fellow-traveler as Maxim Gorki (1868–1936) and the loyal Bolshevik Anatoly Lunacharski (1875–1933), later Soviet commissar of education, strayed off into a foggy territory known as "God-building," an effort to create a new Christianity out of Marxian socialism. For their pains they were severely rapped on the knuckles by the senior Marxist theoretician, Georgi Plekhanov, and by Lenin.

The Revolution. All this burgeoning heterodoxy was quickly stamped out, at least within the Soviet Union, after the October Revolution and the establishment of dialectical materialism as the new state religion. It is curious, however, how little inspiration Soviet writers have drawn from this faith, at least its atheist components. To be sure (though mostly in prerevolutionary days), the most talented of the pro-Soviet poets, Vladimir Mayakovski (1893–1930) made some poetic capital out of the loud—then, still shocking—assertions of atheism: "Listen, Mister God . . . . I thought you were the Almighty Godhead, / but you're just a wee little godlet, a school dropout. / Look, I'm bending over. / From inside my boot-leg / I get a pocket knife . . . . And you, all smelling of incense, I'll slice / From here to Alaska!" In fact, however, Mayakovski was a deeply religious man, even a mystic; though hardly a Christian, certainly not an Orthodox one, he clearly identified himself closely with Jesus, regarding himself as the new sacrificial victim whose death would redeem mankind from the slavery of time.

Of course, there were some compliant writers and poets willing to turn out propaganda pieces for the well-subsidized publications of the League of the Militant Godless. Here is a specimen of this genre by Demyan Bednyi (1833–1945): Out was kicked pope Anton. / Fat kulak curses his fate. / In the church now for quite a while / There's been a ComYouth Club, a movie theater / Where the kids raise hell." Some prose writers such as Alexander Serafimovich (1863–1949), now considered a Soviet classic, made similarly inspired contributions to the same cause. Serafimovich's short story "The Miracle" (1923), for example, describes how the clergy encourage some Cossack peasants to celebrate as a "miracle" the appearance of a pool of water in the middle of a hitherto dry and frozen field. The water is even believed to have curative powers. In the end the pool turns out to have been caused by a broken underground water main.

In general, however, the issue of religion and antireligion was relatively insignificant in post-revolutionary Russian literature. Whether or not it offers truth about the world, dialectical materialism is not likely to excite any writer's creative powers: it has no mythology, no story, no poetry, no deep symbolisms, no passion. Anticlericalism was equally sterile as a literary theme. Only the most fanatical converts to communism or the most callous cynics could stomach the brutal icon-smashing and church-wrecking of the early post-revolutionary years, along with the regime's crude mockery of the people's faith and its ruthless persecution of the priesthood. Likewise, the large, existential questions so prominent in Russian literature of the 19th century seemed to fade away in the Soviet period. It is to be presumed, apparently, that they are all satisfactorily answered in the textbooks—so why flog a dead horse?

As in centuries past, however, the life of Russian literature continues. It can never be wholly stifled or confined within official walls; it percolates beneath the surface, occasionally breaking out in leaks and eruptions—*samizdat*, books written or published abroad, works that somehow squeak past the official censorship. As for belief and unbelief, it seems that the signs have once again been reversed. If *belief* means belief in the official Communist ideology, very little of that seems to survive in the Soviet Union, however exhilarating it may be to intellectuals in the Third World. Among Russian intellectuals a general cynicism about Marxism-Leninism prevails. Writers' unbelief is expressed mainly in assiduous avoidance of the public themes that have been so loudly belabored in the past, of the "boy meets tractor" variety. The spiritually nonconforming writer concentrates on the private, the personal, the eternal themes of human emotion and human relationships.

In view of the sterility and lifelessness of the official ideology and the repressive horrors perpetrated by the regime, it would not be surprising that a dissident, "unbelieving" literature would look backward toward the older, traditional beliefs of the culture, especially Christianity. Open advocacy is of course impossible in books published in the Soviet Union, though occasionally through allusion and camouflage some evocations do manage to squeeze by the censors. One thinks of the retelling, as "obbligato" to the main narrative, of the story of the trial and execution of Jesus (called by his Aramaic name, Yeshua) in Mikhail Bulgakov's long-suppressed novel *The Master and Margarita* (1967); or the many echoes of the story of Jesus' death and resurrection in Boris Pasternak's *Doctor Zhivago* (1957; never, however, published in the Soviet Union).

Alexander Solzhenitsyn (born 1918). In considering all the living Russian writers, undoubtedly the most profound confrontation of belief and unbelief is to be found in the work of Solzhenitsyn, who represents yet another reversal in the tortuous history of belief in Russian literature. Belonging wholly to the Soviet period, Solzhenitsyn received in childhood the requisite indoctrination in official unbelief. During his youth he experienced some twinges of political, though apparently not religious, doubt, even daring to question the supreme wisdom of Stalin's conduct of the war against Germany—a doubt that earned him a sentence of eight years in the Gulag (a Soviet acronym that Solzhenitsyn's work has made an international word). Those eight years were a crucible for Solzhenitsyn's soul, and for all their misery they inspired him to deep and rewarding meditations on the nature of good and evil, both in the behavior of individuals and in the life of nations. He tried to confront in all its horror the fundamental truth about mankind, especially Russian mankind, in the 20th century: the efforts to realize the utopias conceived in the 19th century had led to orgies of cruelty and killing without precedent in human history. Whatever its nominal ideals and paper hopes, therefore, the regime that had created the Gulag was *evil*.

This was the first truth that Solzhenitsyn felt Russians—and the world—must face. His books, both the novels and *The Gulag Archipelago*, document the indictment in excruciating detail—and with the authority of one who has experienced that hell and survived with certain convictions. First of all, for the individual, spiritual (and even physical) survival depends on recognizing that there are higher values than life; there are things one will not do no matter what the cost. In the camps the religious prisoners, the Baptists even more than the Orthodox, were generally better able to endure than those without faith, since they perceived their lives in a larger context than a finite existence on this planet. Likewise, in the life of nations there are higher values than mere survival. For the Russian nation

(Solzhenitsyn does not presume to speak for the other nations in the Soviet sphere), it has been ruinous to break with the historical traditions of the culture and with the church that embodied its ideals. As a man and as a Russian, therefore, Solzhenitsyn has become an Orthodox Christian, though he is fully aware of, and makes no effort to gloss over, the many "sins" of that church, especially its supine capitulations to the Soviet state. Correspondingly, since his exile from the Soviet Union, Solzhenitsyn has perceived Western man as afflicted by the same disease he had observed in Russia, though in a different form. He sees only the shallowness, the materialism, the consumerism, the triviality of Western life, finding it in many ways more empty and "godless" than what he knew at home.

Solzhenitsyn, of course, is only one individual, and very far from typical at that. In any event, the evidence from contemporary Russian literature, as well as the testimony of numerous recent emigres, is that "belief" in the official Communist religion is dead. Hardly anyone takes it seriously any more, let alone finds it a source of spiritual uplift. Yet the yearning for faith is alive. Many people, perhaps the best people, still long to see their lives as something more than a meaningless biological march from birth through procreation to death, and to see death as something more than a descent into oblivion. In their disillusionment with the sterile official ideology, such people seek other values, other meanings. Some, like Solzhenitsyn, turn to Orthodox Christianity, some to Protestant sects, some to Judaism. Some even seek a purified dialectical materialism, either Leninism without Stalinism, or Marxism without Leninism. Some, perhaps the wisest, are left with only unbelief—either in the old gods or the new.

Other articles of interest: **Russia and the Soviet Union, Unbelief in. Propaganda, Antireligious.**

Bibliography

Berlin, Isaiah. *Russian Thinkers.* New York: 1978.

Brown, Edward J. *Russian Literature Since the Revolution.* 2nd ed. New York: 1969.

Brown, William Edward. *A History of Seventeenth-Century Russian Literature.* Ann Arbor: U. of Michigan Press, 1980.

———. *A History of Eighteenth-Century Russian Literature.* Ann Arbor: U. of Michigan Press, 1980.

Cizevskij, Dmitrij. *History of Russian Literature from the Eleventh Century to the End of the Baroque.* The Hague: 1960.

Mirsky, Dmitry S. *A History of Russian Literature.* Ed. Francis J. Whitfield. New York: 1949.

Mochulsky, Konstantin. *Dostoevsky: His Life and Work.* Princeton: Princeton U. Press, 1967.

Struve, Gleb. *Russian Literature Under Lenin and Stalin.* Norman: U. of Oklahoma Press, 1972.

HUGH MCLEAN

S

SANTAYANA, GEORGE (1863–1952), Spanish-born American philosopher. Santayana lived in Spain until 1872, when he came to the United States. He was educated at the Boston Latin School and Harvard College, where he received his Ph.D. in philosophy. He became a member of the faculty following the receipt of his degree and quickly established a reputation as one of America's foremost philosophers.

Religious Upbringing. Santayana's mother was a deist, his father an atheist. Although both regarded religion as sheer superstition, they thought it socially desirable to conform to all the outward requirements of the Catholic church. Hence, young Santayana was reared with extensive exposure to religious belief, sentiment, and behavior. He was then and all his life fascinated by religion. He became intimately acquainted with the major religions of the world and with the widest assortment of religious and theological writing, acquiring an extraordinary sympathy with and understanding of the religious life.

Santayana was, nevertheless, an atheist and materialist. Indeed, he evidently regarded the arguments for the existence of God or the immortality of the soul to be unworthy of attention, for, with one minor exception, he never addressed them explicitly in his work.

Santayana's earlier writings are distinguished by the profound influence of classical Greek philosophy. The fundamental idea informing the publications of this period is Aristotelian: All natural powers are capable of ideal fulfillment, and everything that is ideal is a fulfillment of natural processes. His philosophy, then, was naturalistic; but it was also humanistic, in that he was absorbed in the identification and elaboration of ideal values in human life. His greatest work of this period—indeed, the greatest of his life—is *The Life of Reason* (1905–06). Here he specifies his naturalistic assumptions and utilizes them to distinguish what is ideal in human life—in art and science, society and the moral life, and religion. Employing the Aristotelian principle, he not only illuminates the ideal but traces it to its natural origins. Whereas the supernatural or extranatural had been invoked in traditional interpretations, Santayana provides a thoroughly naturalistic analysis.

The aim of reason, Santayana says, is harmony: the various powers of human nature may be united and ordered in a whole. Through the disciplines of natural and social existence, human passions and instincts may reach their fulfillment in the ideal endeavors of human life. This achievement is not won at the expense of mutilating human nature. Unification and order may be achieved without the sacrifice of the passions, per se, as is required in asceticism; and there is no sacrifice of the intellect, as is required above all in mysticism.

According to Santayana, the rational life is embodied in various ideal forms, including religion. That religion may be an embodiment of reason is argued in Vol. 3 of *The Life of Reason* (*Reason in Religion*), and so it had been stated less systematically in an earlier work, *Interpretations of Poetry and Religion* (1900). The key to understanding religion as part of the rational life is to insist that it not be understood as being in any sense scientific, or superscientific. Rather, religion is poetry. This is not to trivialize religion, but to recognize how profoundly poetry may intervene in life. The greatest poetry, and hence religion, is an imaginative rendering of the ideal possibilities of life and a presentation of natural forces in dramatic guise. To take religious claims as literal truths is to make them preposterous. At the same time it is to miss their crucial value in distinguishing life's deep, elusive, inchoate promptings for ideal fulfillments. To literalize religion, then, is not only to make it incredible, but to obscure its moral lessons as well.

Santayana addresses, for example, the meaning of the dogma of eternal punishment. Taken literally, the dogma sanctifies the ultimate in moral barbarism. The poetic function, on the contrary, gives poignant expression to the inherent limitation of life. Life is final, irrevocable. Whatever trial we make of it is our epitaph for all eternity. Accordingly, one cannot conduct one's life as if no value for good or ill were sealed in it unalterably and forever. Taken poetically, the dogma teaches a lesson of human finitude, not of existence without end.

Santayana notes that liberal theologians are also fond of saying that religious claims are symbolic; but the liberals say such claims are symbolic of man's encounter with the supernatural, not the natural. Symbolism in this sense makes belief in the supernatural no less incredible. While it is an attempt to characterize divine behavior in a less repulsive form, it succeeds in losing the import of the original dogma. When theologians urge that eternal punishment is inconsistent with the divine nature and is therefore impossible, they vitiate that sense of the finality and fatefulness of mortal existence that is imparted poetically in the dogma.

The most conspicuous example of the moral barbarism consequent upon taking religion as a system of cognitive knowledge is in the notion of the divine governance of the world. When we conceive that there is one God who is at once providential and morally perfect, then we must regard both the hideous suffering and the moral governance of the world to be the authorship of one and the same will. We are confronted, that is, with the problem of evil, with its desperate and morally grotesque arguments—not the least consequence of which is to identify the glory of God with the damnation of man.

Poetically, polytheism is the most robust and complete religion. Gods are imaginative celebrations of ideal ends, or they are dramatizations of the primal forces of nature with which all human life must reckon. Accordingly, man may be naturally pious by respecting these forces, as they work for both good and ill; and his spirituality consists in devotion to ideal ends. The human condition is presented with crucial moral distinctions and with utmost force and clarity when piety and spirituality are not directed to the same object.

Santayana believed that pagan religions were spontaneously accepted by their adherents as imaginative expressions. The corruption of religion into cognitive doctrine is owing to the Jews, Christians, and Muslims. The Jews were the first, he says, to deny authenticity to all other religions; later Christians and Muslims perpetuated this intolerance and made it a virtue. If religion, then, can be the richest embodiment of reason, Santayana is quick to insist that it is more often a miscarriage.

With exceptional insight and sympathy, he addressed the full range of religious feeling, thought, and practice, displaying the grasp of life rendered therein. Not surprisingly, he finds that religions vary greatly in their capacity to do justice to the task of exhibiting the fundamental conditions and aspirations of mortal life. One may quarrel, of course, with many of the particulars of Santayana's interpretations and with the accuracy of some of his historical claims, but the essential lesson of his thought in this regard is that the abandonment of religion as a cognitive exercise makes it accessible to us as the wise and imaginative expression of human values in their natural setting.

Santayana occasionally referred to himself as disillusioned and as a pessimist, but he was by no means expressing despair with those terms. He meant *disillusioned* literally: one must be free of illusion if one is to have a clear conception of the ideal. He was pessimistic in a technical sense: to be pessimistic means to regard the universe as functioning according to laws that are indifferent to human interest and independent of human will. One of Santayana's heroes was BENEDICT SPINOZA, who was disillusioned and pessimistic in just these senses; and Spinoza regarded himself as having attained the highest happiness.

Indeed, Santayana is scornful of those who crave for meaning in eternal life. As natural and social beings we have intense attachments, loyalties, and joys; and when these are ordered in the life of reason, there is abundant justification for natural piety and celebration of the ideal. Religion, after all, is the poetic expression of the values of natural existence, not their denial; and morally earnest believers are simply mistaken in assuming that religion is the source rather than the result of human values.

Santayana's naturalism was not consistently elaborated, and it should be noted as well that his thought became less humanistic. Even in his earlier writings there is a noticeable interest in the detached and contemplative life, rather than a life actively devoted to ideal ends. This tendency intensified as his life went on, and he even came to characterize the spiritual life as a disengagement from values. The fact that his philosophy was not wholly systematic by no means works to the detriment of his characterization of religion as an embodiment of reason. Few philosophers have done so much to show how religion can become obscure and debased when it pretends to science; and no philosopher has argued so well that religion can be a poetic expression and celebration of temporal life.

Other article of interest: **Evil, Problem of.**

Bibliography

Munitz, Milton K. *The Moral Philosophy of Santayana.* New York: Columbia U. Press, 1939.

Santayana, George. "Brief History of My Opinions. *Contemporary American Philosophy.* Vol. 2. Ed. G. P. Adams and W. P. Montague. New York: Macmillan, 1930.

———. *Interpretations of Poetry and Religion.* New York: Scribner's, 1900.

———. *The Life of Reason.* 5 vols. New York: Scribner's, 1905–06.

———. "Ultimate Religion." *Obiter Scripta.* Ed. J. Buchler and B. Schwartz. New York: Scribner's, 1936.

JAMES GOUINLOCK

SARTRE, JEAN-PAUL (1905–1980), French philosopher and writer, was born in Paris on June 21. His full name was Jean-Paul Charles Aymard Sartre. He never knew his father, Jean-Baptiste, who died when his son was an infant. The adult Sartre attributed to his fatherless state his sense of being free from higher authority and his resistance to the temptation to wield power over others. His mother, Anne-Marie, was a Schweitzer from Alsace, and Sartre was first cousin to Albert Schweitzer. The careers of these two dominant personalities are almost polar opposites: the two had in common only a love of music and a commitment to improving the lot of humanity—though their views of human needs and possibilities differed greatly.

After the death of her husband, Anne-Marie took her son to live with her parents, first at Meudon and four years later in Paris. In his autobiography, *The Words,* Sartre has given a highly interpretive narration of his childhood. His account shows him to be something of a prodigy, a spoiled brat, and a bit of a showoff. He began to read and admire the French classics long before he could understand them, and he dreamed of becoming a great writer himself. Behind his grandfather's back he devoured adventure stories and at the age of seven was writing some of his own.

Sartre regularly used religious terms and imagery in his writing, even in contexts where his intention was avowedly atheistic. This practice seems to have been due partly to his recognition of the influence of Judeo-Christian culture on the thinking of any Westerner and partly to his desire to explain the psychological reality underlying experiences commonly held to be religious. He held that his own life had progressed through a series of conversions by means of which he simultaneously achieved a more comprehensive social vision, and he lived out the consequences of his ATHEISM to the end.

In *The Words* Sartre tells how one day when he was about 12, he decided to think about God. To his "polite surprise," the Almighty simply disappeared into the blue, and Sartre said, "He doesn't exist," settling for himself the question of God once and for all. But the matter was not quite so simple. Sartre's Protestant grandfather, Charles Schweitzer, allowed his Catholic wife and daughter to raise the boy as a Catholic, but at home he continually scoffed at the women's religious convictions. The result of all the religious argumentation, Sartre reports, was that he believed none of the supposed truths of either side.

Still, Sartre claimed a religious belief remained with him in the form of a mandate, the conviction that as a writer he was endowed with a mission to discover and reveal truth to the world. As he expressed it, God the Father had gone, but the Holy Ghost remained. While others have experienced the conflict between the longing to believe in something beyond the human and the rational conclusion that no supernatural force could be found, Sartre's inner struggle was waged between his love of imaginative literature and his increasing conviction that it was imperative to devote himself to political activism.

Up until the outbreak of World War II Sartre continued to put literature first. As a student at l'Ecole Normale Supérieure he studied philosophy and psychology. In his opinion, these disciplines did not conflict with literature. Indeed the stories, novels, and plays he wrote later served always as a platform for his philosophical ideas. The theoretical and literary works complemented each other.

In 1928 Sartre met Simone de Beauvoir. His

lifelong association with her has been to many a model of equality and good faith in personal human relations; only a few hostile critics have reproached the pair for their decision not to marry and to allow one another sexual freedom outside their relationship.

After receiving his degree (the *agrégation*) and doing his military service, Sartre taught at a lycée in Le Havre and later in Paris. In 1933 he studied phenomenology in Berlin, concentrating especially on the work of Edmund Husserl and Martin Heidegger. In his early and mid-thirties he published three works that acknowledged his debt to phenomenology, that broke decisively with both Husserl and SIGMUND FREUD, and that laid the groundwork for his own philosophy. These were *The Transcendence of the Ego* (1936), *The Emotions* (1939), and *Psychology of the Imagination* (1940).

Sartre's novel *Nausea* (1938), which was enthusiastically received, describes its hero's discovery of the meaningless contingency of all existents, human and nonhuman. Significantly, his attempt to escape from the consequences of this nauseating realization takes the form of deciding to achieve some kind of absolute being through art, by writing a novel. This solution had been Sartre's own, but he was soon to renounce it.

Refusing to become an officer, Sartre served as an ordinary soldier in the war and was imprisoned in a German stalag in 1940. He referred later to this experience as a conversion. In the early period of the war, Sartre had told Beauvoir that he decided it was wrong for him not to participate actively in the political arena. In the camp he learned the value of human solidarity. By means of a forged military discharge, he managed to get himself released.

Back in Paris, Sartre took part in resistance activities and continued to write *Being and Nothingness*. This book, which attracted little attention when it was published in 1943, was quickly recognized, after the war, as the central work of humanistic EXISTENTIALISM. It described the plight of the individual in a world without God or objective meaning. Radically free and therefore totally responsible for what they make of their lives, human beings must create their own values. Following the discussion of ontology was a presentation of the principles of existential psychoanalysis.

There were two results of Sartre's wartime conversion. First, he argued that literature must be committed to an effort to change the world. His

play *The Flies* (1943) called on his audience to recognize both the psychological and the political possibilities of human freedom. *No Exit* (1944) presented in dramatic form the view of human relations based on conflict that Sartre had developed in *Being and Nothingness*. For two decades he wrote novels and plays that dealt with contemporary problems.

Second, Sartre entered actively into political life. He was one of the founders of the Rassemblement Démocratique Révolutionnaire, an abortive attempt to form an effective working coalition of all leftist groups in France. He established and served as editor of *Les Temps modernes*, a monthly journal of literary, social, and political commentary. For the rest of his life, in articles and speeches and at conventions all over the world (except for the United States, which he refused to visit after 1949, in protest at what he considered to be a national policy of overt imperialism), he engaged in political controversy.

For a time Sartre worked closely with the Communists, but he never became a member of the party and frequently criticized it adversely on specific issues. He broke with it completely on the occasion of the Soviet action in Hungary in 1956. In France he took an active part in opposing the government's policy in Algeria. During the 1950s Sartre underwent another decisive conversion. Declaring that he had "dreamed his life" until then, he now decided that after all he had no mandate. The writer was not privileged, and literature was in no way a salvation. In his own words, he finally "nabbed the Holy Ghost in the cellar and threw it out" (*The Words*). Henceforth, Sartre felt that writing was not enough; he must act directly.

Sartre's social theory is most fully discussed in a major work, *The Critique of Dialectical Reason* (1960). This book offers a neo-Marxist analysis of sociological structures. Declaring that existentialism was a parasitic ideology on Marxism, the philosophy of our time, Sartre attempted to use his own version of existentialism as a leaven to revitalize Marxism by reinserting the individual project into history. The book was attacked by Communist critics, who accused Sartre of offering a revisionist form of Marxism, and by others who felt that his attempt to embrace Marxism was irreconcilable with his existentialism. Most critics subsequently have emphasized the continuity of his thought rather than seeing a divorce between the earlier and the later Sartre.

In 1964 Sartre refused the Nobel Prize for

literature, on two grounds—that the award of the prize had recently been politically motivated and that he did not wish to become canonized as a member of the cultural establishment. In 1966–67 he was one of the leaders at the BERTRAND RUSSELL tribunal, condemning the United States for its war in Vietnam. After initial reluctance and hesitation, he supported the formal charge that the U.S. was guilty of genocide.

If Sartre had, to some extent, retained one member of the Holy Trinity—the Messiah, in the guise of the teaching of Marx—he got rid of this, too, at the time of the student revolt in France in 1968, which he himself considered to be the occasion of his final and most radical conversion. Henceforth, he remained antiparty but issue-oriented, lending his support to all ultra-left groups that seemed to be keeping the idea of a social revolution open.

Although he now publicly reproached intellectuals who wrote on nonpolitical subjects, Sartre, openly admitting the inconsistency, finished a three-volume study of Flaubert, *The Family Idiot* (1971–72). In this work he combined his existential psychoanalysis with a Marxist sociology so as to understand the way in which an individual reacts to the conditioning of his family, his society, and the movements of history. The work explores the way in which a writer interacts with his own period, reflecting and influencing it, regardless of whether he deliberately engages himself, as Sartre did, or chooses "art for art's sake," like Flaubert.

Shortly before his 70th birthday Sartre's health began to deteriorate drastically, and he became almost totally blind. Unable to read or to write, he continued to develop his ideas in a series of interviews with close associates. He died on April 15, 1980. Although no public ceremonies had been planned, about 50,000 people came spontaneously to pay tribute at his funeral.

Bibliography

Anderson, Thomas C. *The Foundation and Structure of Sartrean Ethics.* Lawrence: The Regents Press of Kansas, 1979.

Barnes, Hazel E. *Sartre.* Philadelphia: Lippincott, 1973.

Beauvoir, Simone de. All of her autobiographical volumes contain an abundance of information about Sartre's life; especially valuable are the second and third: *The Prime of Life,* trans. Peter Green (New York: World, 1962); and *Force of Circumstance,* trans. Richard Howard (New York: Putnam, 1965).

Grene, Marjorie. *Sartre.* New York: New Viewpoints, 1973.

Hayim, Gila J. *The Existential Sociology of Jean-Paul Sartre.* Amherst: U. of Massachusetts Press, 1980.

McCall, Dorothy. *The Theatre of Jean-Paul Sartre.* New York: Columbia U. Press, 1969.

Morris, Phyllis Sutton. *Sartre's Concept of a Person: An Analytic Approach.* Amherst: U. of Masachusetts Press, 1976.

Sheridan, James F., Jr. *Sartre: The Radical Conversion.* Athens: Ohio U. Press, 1969.

Thody, Philip. *Sartre: A Biographical Introduction.* London: Studio Vista, 1971.

HAZEL E. BARNES

SCANDINAVIA, UNBELIEF IN.

SWEDEN

Beginnings of Unbelief. Ideas of nonbelief began to make headway, with difficulty, in the Sweden of 1880 but were to have little success in securing popular attention among members of the public. At that time social questions were prominent, and astute political leaders diverted the attention of the masses from antireligious preaching.

In 19th-century Sweden, one of the poorest countries of Europe, the struggle against religion was, in principle, limited to circles of a high cultural and economic level. Only Viktor Lennstrand, the country's first militant atheist, was heard by large groups of the proletariat. His preaching aroused the sympathy of this public; no true social reform, Lennstrand held, can come about if people "are blinded, weakened, imprisoned, and stupified by Christian doctrine," and consequently he proposed that social struggle be carried on along with a campaign of popular consciousness-raising about religion.

Christianity has always been powerful in Sweden, and the fight for nonbelief led to isolation, jail, and death. Up until 1879, and with few exceptions, religious criticism was set within the framework of Christian doctrine; so-called freethinkers were merely nonbelievers who engaged in polemics on various interpretations of biblical legends. Negation of the existence of a God or development of a non-Christian cultural concept was inconceivable at that time and continues to be so, to a greater or lesser degree, even today.

Early Intolerance. In the 19th century Sweden was not one of the more tolerant countries in the matter of religion (nor, obviously, had it been after the state church was established in 1593). Exile and the loss of inheritance rights had been established in 1604 as punishment for anyone denying the "pure evangelical doctrine." In 1619 Per de Grytnäs was hanged as a renegade, although not until 40 years later would intolerance be made legal; the death penalty was established for those promoting "useless polemics or polemics leading to error, divisions, etc." A ban on the importation of "heretical" books was written into law several years later.

The influence of these measures on keeping the Swedish people in a surprising cultural isolation and the absence of any national philosophical tradition have yet to be analyzed. (There is an extant document by King Charles XI in which "the freedom to investigate philosophy is permitted" but within the specific restriction that "no freedom to attack the Christian faith and doctrine shall be permitted.")

This stage of religious fanaticism culminated in the Ecclesiastical Law of 1686, which required all inhabitants of the Kingdom of Sweden and countries subject to it to profess the Christian faith. A religious oath was mandatory for all teachers in academies and schools, and such persons were forbidden to think and to disseminate "erroneous concepts." Anyone violating these regulations forfeited his property and estate.

In 1734 it was further provided that "whoever, by speech or in writing, with premeditation criticizes or offends against God, His holy word and sacrament, shall lose his life." While the enemy of religion was to lose his life, a person continuing to practice some kind of religion would suffer the gentler penalty of exile. The year 1766 saw enactment of the so-called Law of Freedom of the Press which, in the opinion of Ture Nerman, was "an offshoot of the Ecclesiastical Law of 1686." (See Bibliography.) This new edict granted the bishop's consistory the right to extend or withhold permission to publish any document related to Christian doctrine.

Introduced in 1812 was the "power of suppression," which could be exercised against anyone violating the law of 1766; it entailed discontinuation of the offending publication and, for its pub-lisher, a prohibition against the future publication of any other material. The power of suppression was abolished in 1845, but in 1866 the opportunity for circulating written materials was even more subtly restricted when the free sale of books was prohibited.

Hence, as late as 1880 the great majority of Swedes were kept "informed" by means of Sunday sermons, in which each pastor, in each parish, commented not only on passages from the Bible but also on events of public importance. RATIONALISM was thus checked and the Lutheran state church enjoyed several centuries of calm. The 19th century, however, stirred up the dark clouds of Swedish Protestantism.

After the French Revolution and its uncontainable anticlericalism, the medieval political and cultural age came to an end. In the 1850s the educated strata of Swedish society demanded the right to freedom of religion and elimination of the barbarous punishments imposed for "offense against religion." Other social groups joined the fight against religious oppression.

In 1861 the death penalty for blasphemy was abolished and replaced by forced labor. The countless burnings of "witches" had come to an end. Dissemination and study of the works of the great nonbelievers was begun, albeit limited to an intellectual elite, a phenomenon repeating itself today. The ideas of Charles Darwin, JOHN STUART MILL, CHARLES BRADLAUGH, Georg Brandes, and others were received with great interest. The timid religious criticism of the early part of the century gave way to a demand for elimination of the state church and, even more importantly, for abolition of the religious mentality.

The fight for nonbelief in Sweden, however, took place under difficult circumstances. At that time baptism, the payment of taxes to the church, religious instruction in the schools (parents were permitted to teach their children at home, but if the latter were not instructed in the catechism they could be removed from the home by the public authorities), religious marriage, confirmation, and the *kyrkotukt* or examination in catechism at home were all mandatory. The simple fact of being born a Swede made one a member of the Lutheran church, and the church might be left only by joining another Christian sect. The parish council could prohibit meetings and lectures spreading "false" doctrines or doctrines leading to religious disputes; this same council was empowered to prevent crimes against the "sanctity of religion and customs," being authorized to employ, for such purpose, the power of the state against any person residing in or passing through its parish. Schoolteachers and civil servants were required to belong to the state church, and the parish priest headed the school board, while education was in the hands of the Ministry of Ecclesiastical Affairs.

Nonbelievers in Sweden were confronted with a massive medieval and anticultural structure, certain aspects of which have survived to this day. Trials for offenses against religion were to continue; the last known one was instituted in 1965 against the writer Hannu Salama for his *Midsummer Dance.* Confiscation of writings and fines would be the order of the day, and figures such as the dramatist August Strindberg, the social reformer A. Danielsson, and the economist Knut Wicksell found themselves charged with "blasphemy and heresy." Danielsson and Wicksell, among many others, were jailed, although not so often and with such tragic results as in the case of Viktor Lennstrand.

Contemporary Swedes have forgotten almost all these early nonbelievers, and obscurantism has thus taken its silent revenge. Nevertheless, the Swedish people's debt to the nonbelievers of the 19th century is clear: the political, economic, social, and cultural reforms that have marked the country's progress are due, directly or indirectly, to the work of these early thinkers.

The Positivist Society and Anton Nyström. The physician, educator, and writer Nyström (1842–1931) began to introduce the ideas of AUGUSTE COMTE into Sweden in 1875. He gave lectures on POSITIVISM and devoted enormous efforts to raising the cultural level of the nation by means of dissertations on scientific subjects. In 1879 he founded the Positivist Society and the Reform Association and the next year the Workers' Institute of Stockholm. Active in this institute was Hjalmar Strömer, writer and lecturer, who died in poverty after devoting his short life to the dissemination of scientific principles and the destruction of theological and "mythological" values, as he called them. (On Strömer, see Nyström, *Christianity and Freethinking* in the Bibliography.)

Nyström also started the Progressive Union in 1881, later converted into a political party, the February Association (1882). Nyström was an active member of the Utilitarian Society and of the first Association for Freedom of Religion. He advocated the separation of church and state and the elimination of schools of theology on the ground

that this discipline lacked scientific standing.

The Positivist Society followed the model established by Comte in 1848. This was the first attempt to organize nonbelievers in Sweden, and it lasted 10 years. Its purposes were the diffusion of Comte's scientific and political teachings, the education of an intelligent, educated, and truly human public opinion, and the creation of a fraternal congregation of those thinking alike, without distinction of class or occupation. It proposed what it called "human religion," establishing as the commandments of positivism: "love as the basis, order as the foundation and progress as the purpose." Also preached were the effacement of egoism, the exercise of altruism, and the elimination of religious teaching in the schools.

The Verdandi Students' Association and Hjalmar Öhrwall. To stimulate the debate of ideas, the Verdandi Students' Association was founded in 1882 by a group of students at Uppsala University; they were headed by Karl Staaff, who later became prime minister. Among the earliest active members were Öhrwall (1851–1929) and O. von Zweigberg. The purpose of the association was to organize students around the principles of freethinking and to cooperate with other organizations in condemning the conservatism and taboos of the society of the time. Between 1888 and 1954 the association published more than 530 small tracts, preference being given to popular scientific works and polemic books. Among the titles were *The Atheist Manual,* a collection of antireligious essays published by Claes-Adam Wachtmeister; *Essays* by George Orwell; and *The Art of Scandalizing,* by Ingemar Hedenius. Although the Verdandi Association was not designed to combat religion, it cooperated for almost a century with nonbelievers' organizations such as the Utilitarian Society and the two Associations for Freedom of Religion.

Beginning in 1887, Verdandi organized public discussions that caused conservatives great discomfort, leading academic authorities to put obstacles in the way of their activities. The association's editor, from the date of its founding, was Öhrwall, a professor of physiology at Uppsala from 1899 to 1917. Influenced by Darwin, Mill, and HERBERT SPENCER, he worked for a new, empirical and realistic vision of society. While teaching at Uppsala, he was refused the doctorate because at Uppsala, he was considered a "malignant revolutionary" and a "dangerous corrupter of youth." He left a vast collection of writings on subjects such as psychiatry, anthropology, politics, and history, and he translated Mill, ERNST HAECKEL, and Brandes, among others.

The First Association for Freedom of Religion. As a result of the suit for blasphemy brought against Strindberg for his novel *Married*, Nyström decided to establish the Association for Freedom of Religion in 1884. On his board of directors were both atheists and believers, the latter being members of religious sects who wanted to limit the monopoly of the Lutheran church. Noted nonbelievers such as Wicksell appeared alongside pastors and Christian agitators. Although this association was gradually abandoned by many believers and never had more than 300 members, it became a relatively influential center for intellectuals. The purposes, according to the program adopted in 1885, were "to work for complete freedom of religion and complete separation of church and state." The association declared itself "neutral" in the matter of religion, although it wanted to eliminate the teaching of religion in the schools.

The association opened branches and held public meetings, all the while maintaining good relations with the Positivist Society and the Verdandi Students' Association. It distributed a petition calling for elimination of the teaching of religion in the schools and of mandatory religious marriage, and demanding the right to leave the state church without having to enter some other religious sect, as well as freedom from the payment of taxes to the church for those who were not members of it. Pamphlets against communion were also distributed and, in 1889, a manual explaining rights and duties vis-à-vis the state church.

By late 1890 the public had lost interest in the association, and under the chairmanship of a believer named J. Mankell its activities were almost nil. The last meeting of which anything is known was held Jan. 14, 1892.

The Utilitarian Society: Viktor Lennstrand and Knut Wicksell. The first and only atheist association of its time was founded in Stockholm on April 1, 1888. Its founder was a teacher named Viktor Lennstrand (1861–1895). At the age of 20 he entered Uppsala University. He was born a Christian, but his clear and penetrating mind and his acquaintance with rationalist literature led him to abandon his parents' faith. In 1884 he published *Of My Own World,* a work revealing the incipient humanist, but it was a lecture given at Uppsala in 1887 that marked the beginning of his fight against

religion. Because of this lecture he was obliged to leave the university, thereby becoming an outcast to his family.

This was but the beginning of a short and intense life devoted entirely to the ideal of nonbelief. Lennstrand was imprisoned, fined, and harassed for his lectures and writings, but only death put an end to his struggles. He left behind the example of a modest life devoted to freeing his fellow Swedes from ignorance and superstition, as is evident in his essays, translations, and debates. In 1889 he founded the organ of the Utilitarian Society, the *Freethinker,* which in the 1890s attained a circulation of 3,500 copies; a year later he began another publication, *Think for Yourself!* which continued until he was forced to give up all his activities in December 1894, because of the painful illness that was to take him to his grave. These periodicals are a good source of information on the activities of nonbelievers of the time, not only in Sweden but also in the United States, England, and France.

Lennstrand maintained contact with the principal representatives of nonbelief of the late 19th century: Charles Bradlaugh and the NATIONAL SECULAR SOCIETY of London, La Libre Pensée of France, and ROBERT GREEN INGERSOLL and the BOSTON INVESTIGATOR. Both of his journals published polished articles analyzing biblical legends, church activities, essays on freedom of thought, and news of scientific and historical research.

The program of the Utilitarian Society announced that its aim was "to fight unwaveringly against all Christian ideology and to combat all belief in the supernatural and every kind of theology, unreason and superstition, while seeking to disseminate culture and to found morality and customs on a rational basis." The society was popular from the start, and Lennstrand came to compete in fame with the leaders of incipient socialism, whose attitude toward the religious problem was ambiguous. The society eventually had 15 branches in various parts of the country, a chorus, sewing circles, and a Sunday school.

Lennstrand not only devoted himself to attacking the church and religion but spoke equally firmly against the death penalty, the monarchy, and war. His relentless preaching and the great reputation that he enjoyed among the working masses and in intellectual circles made him an embarrassment to the monarchy as well as to the social democracy then on the rise. In 1893 Lennstrand received an anonymous letter in which he was threatened with death, and in September of the same year he was hospitalized for a serious infectious disease (actinomycosis). He died on Nov. 1, 1895, after a series of painful operations.

Lennstrand left numerous essays and lectures: *What We Believe and What We Want* (1888), *Jehovah Is Dead* (1891), and *The Republic, the Popular Vote and Freethinking* (1891). The Utilitarian Society was reorganized, in the year of his death, by W. Åberg, G. Olsson, and others. In 1899 it became known as the Freedom Union, and between 1900 and 1903 it published the review *Free Word*.

Knut Wicksell (1851–1926), an inseparable friend and collaborator of Lennstrand's, replaced him as editor of the *Freethinker* and *Think for Yourself!* Wicksell was the first in Sweden to discuss the subject of birth control. He was a social reformer, lecturer, journalist, and professor of economics at the University of Lund. His works on national economy were translated into a variety of languages and his ideas influenced the economies of Germany and Austria. In 1908 he was accused of being a blasphemer and sentenced to two months in prison for his lecture, "The Throne, the Altar, the Sword and the Pocketbook." Wicksell is one of the intellectual bulwarks of Swedish nonbelief.

The Second Association for Freedom of Religion. Founded in 1951, with Ture Nerman as its first president, this was a smaller organization than the first but with similar, chiefly intellectual leanings. Its members were persons who had ceased to belong to the Lutheran state church and wanted to protect the interests of nonbelievers. Its progam was to work for the legal recognition of complete freedom of religion. The associaton declared itself politically independent and, in accordance with the United Nations' Declaration of Human Rights, it proposed to work for tolerance, freedom of conscience and expression and, by means of education, to combat the spiritual oppression and conventionalism of religious customs. The association functioned for some 20 years and collaborated with the Verdandi Students' Association. Its last president, the writer Per Anders Fögelstrom, later joined the Humanist and Ethical Union of Sweden.

The First International Exhibition of Literature for Nonbelievers. Beginning in early 1978 José M. F. Santana, a Spanish lawyer living in Sweden, contacted organizations and nonbelievers in different parts of the world, seeking assistance and material for an exhibit of antireligious literature at Stockholm University. This exhibition was held in September 1979, and then taken in October 1980 to the Munch Museum in Oslo. A total of 221 books, 43 magazines, and hundreds of leaflets, catalogs, newspapers, and pamphlets were shown, the first time that a large number of old and modern exponents of the philosophy of nonbelief had been gathered together in a common display.

The Humanist and Ethical Union of Sweden. In September 1979 Santana, together with other nonbelievers, established an association whose purpose would be "to combat and destroy the obstacles standing in the way of complete freedom of thought . . . to work for a true non-confessional education in the schools . . . to support and make known the right to a concept of life without faith in gods or religions . . . to estabish cultural contacts with nonbelievers of other countries." The union publishes a magazine, *HEF News*. It is not a member of the International Humanist and Ethical Union and is the only Swedish organization for nonbelievers.

Other Important Freethinkers. The following merit recognition as advocates of freethinking in Sweden:

Olof Von Dalin (1708–1763), poet, author of anticlerical satires and parodies, was influenced by VOLTAIRE, Racine, and Molière.

Johan Tobias Sergel (1740–1814), a painter, sculptor, and cartoonist, worked basically with non-Christian sources of inspiration and belonged to Bellman and Kellgren's circle. His cartoons are reminiscent of Goya's "Caprichos."

Carl Michael Bellman (1740–1795) was the author of poems, songs and parodies satirizing biblical legends and ridiculing the clergy. His works *Ahasverus Was So Powerful* and *Judith Was a Rich Widow* achieved great popularity and aroused strong protests in Christian circles. Up until 1980, the year in which it was prohibited, 30,000 persons celebrated a holiday in July in memory of Bellman.

Johan Henric Kellgren (1751–1795) was a poet and publicist, master of arts in 1772 and lecturer in Latin poetry in 1774 at the University of Turku (Finland); he became a member of the Swedish Academy in 1768. He promoted the ideas of JULIEN DE LA METTRIE, JOHN LOCKE, and the ENLIGHTENMENT and founded a brotherhood, Pro Senso Communi. Declared an enemy of Christianity, he wrote satires considered blasphemous.

F. W. C. Areschoug (1830–1908) was a botanist and admirer of Darwin, whose ideas he introduced at Lund University.

G. J. Leufstedt (1830–1901) was called "Lennstrand's predecessor" and "the Antichrist" for his lectures, first given in 1870.

Svante Arrhenius (1859–1927), recipient of the Nobel Prize in chemistry (1903), was a declared atheist and the author of *The Evolution of the Worlds* and other works on cosmic physics.

Hinke Berggren (1861–1936), agitator, journalist, author of dramatic plays, lecturer, was expelled from the Social Democratic party in 1908, accused of being an anarchist. His attacks were directed particularly against the church and the military. In 1910 he was sentenced to prison for giving a lecture advocating greater sex education, especially in methods of birth control.

Anna B. Wicksell (1862–1928), wife of Knut Wicksell, worked with Lennstrand. She was a pacifist, fighter for women's suffrage, and a member of a League of Nations' committee.

Allen Vannerus (1862–1946) disseminated atheism through such works as *Atheism Versus Theism* and *For a Critique of Religious Knowledge*. He developed a philosophical system in which the universe is considered an autonomous unit where there is no room for any god.

Henrik Petrini (1863–1957), professor of physics and mathematics, lecturer, and author of numerous works against the church and religion, such as *The Crime of Religion and Freedom of Expression* and *Christian Bankruptcy*.

Bengt Lidforss (1868–1913), botanist, writer, politician, disciple of Areschoug, and sympathizer with Nietzschean philosophy. His work, together with that of Anton Nyström, is important in Swedish nonbelief.

Hjalmar Söderberg (1869–1941), a novelist, shifted from almost neutral skepticism to open criticism of the Christian religion in *The Messiah Transformed* and *Restlessness of the Heart*.

Ingemar Hedenius (born 1908) became professor of philosophy at Uppsala University in 1947, emeritus in 1972. He has written many books on ethics and the philosophy of religion and aesthetics, criticizing modern theology from the standpoint of atheism. His most important ones are *Faith and Reason* and *To Choose One's View of Life*. A considerable influence on the general intellectual climate of Sweden, Hedenius was a supporter of the second Association for Freedom of Religion and is a member of the Humanist and Ethical Union of Sweden.

Attention should also be called to the publica-

tions *New Truth* (1895), which became *Free Thoughts* in 1897, *Godless* and *Yellow Peril*, periodicals of the early 20th century, and to organizations such as the Swedish Freethinkers' Union (1928) and the recently created Nordic Committee for Freedom of Thought, the first organization uniting Scandinavian nonbelievers in a common task.

FINLAND

The first association to discuss a philosophy of enlightenment was the Valhalla Association (1781–86). At that time, with Finland a part of Sweden, there was no freedom of religion. In 1809 Finland became a part of Russia, but the situation remained virtually the same, although Anders Chydenius and Robert Lagerborg wrote on freedom of religion in 1863.

Shortly afterward, Darwinism reached Finland, and Nils Nordenskiöld discussed the new theories in the *Literary Magazine*. The first attempt to acquaint the common people with Darwin's ideas occurred in 1889, in the city of Jyväskylä, where the Keski-Suomi newspaper published popular articles on Darwinism, written by well-known individuals such as Juhani Aho and Minna Canth.

The first nonbelievers' organization was the Association for Freedom of Religion and Tolerance, founded by Viktor Heikel and Mathilda Asp in 1887 but immediately suppressed by the Russian government. The first journal for nonbelievers, *Free Thoughts*, was published in 1889, but czarist censorship put an end to it. The Raketen Club (1896–1900) was a forum where the influence of Brandes' and Nietzsche's ideas was notable.

One member of this club was Rolf Lagerborg, a philosopher and author who fought the church on questions concerning morals and equality between men and women. He was the most rebellious of Edward Westermarck's disciples and his academic career was a thorny one. His two dissertations on moral philosophy were rejected in Finland, but their French version was subsequently (1903) approved at the Sorbonne. Lagerborg studied moral philosophy, epistemology, and psychology, and was the first exponent of behaviorism in Finland. His professional advancement was vehemently resisted by theologians because of his opinions and his participation in the Prometheus Association, and he failed to get a professorship. He was a contributor to the magazine *Euterpe* (1902–05), which promoted the ideas of separation of church and state and elimination of religion from the schools.

The student association Prometheus was established in 1905. Its chairman was Edward Westermarck (1862–1939), professor at the universities of London and Helsinki and the founder of Finnish sociology. His most important work is the gigantic *The Origin and Development of the Moral Ideas.* The school of social anthropology created by Westermarck was the best known in the world in the early 20th century. Westermarck's life was devoted to science and enlightened humanism. His naturalistic criticism of religion became a guiding influence, especially among academic youth. Westermarck headed the Prometheus Association during the entire period of its activity (1905–14).

Another member of the Prometheus Association was Rafael Karsten, who held the post of professor of practical philosophy at the University of Helsinki, 1922–48. Karsten wrote several books on anthropology and the science of religion, as well as many reports on his travels. The journal *Free Thought* was published by S. E. Kristiansson from 1909 until his disappearance during Finland's civil war. He was probably murdered. All atheistic thought of the time was reported in this publication. Kristiansson also wrote many books under the pseudonym "Asa Jalas" and spent time in jail for blasphemy.

The civil war of 1918 was a catastrophe for nonbelievers in Finland; most freethought leaders were murdered by the White Guard.

The first and last law providing for freedom of religion was enacted in 1922, but it was no more than a compromise between the church and political parties. Today there is no freedom from religion in Finland. Atheists' human rights are violated in the schools, and in some areas the situation is becoming worse.

The first freethinkers' association after the civil war was organized in 1927, but the oldest existing freethinkers' organization was established in the city of Kotka in 1929. The Union of Freethinkers' Assocations of Finland was founded in 1937. The latter was sharply attacked by the church, and Interior Minister Kekkonen (later president of Finland) tried to stop it. However, the union survived and became a member of the World Union of Freethinkers in 1946. About 30 associations numbering 4,000 members, are still in existence. The secretary general, Erkki Hartikainen, is seeking to develop the union in association with international organizations of nonbelievers. It publishes a magazine, *Free Thinker,* and maintains seven cemeteries, where secular burials take place. Today the Union of Freethinkers is very active in educational matters and has prepared a new curriculum, with proposals for teaching ethics and the history of religion and atheism. It receives financial support from the government of Finland.

An independent freethinkers' association, in the city of Pori, and the Humanist Association of Finland also exist.

NORWAY

The first public manifestation of nonbelief in Norway was probably the denouncement of Christianity by Bjørnstjerne Bjørnson (1832–1910) in 1877. Bjørnson was a poet and playwright. In 1877 he gave his lecture, "To Be with Truth," in which he accepted and joined the antireligious positions of Brandes, DAVID FRIEDRICH STRAUSS, and Darwin.

In 1892 Bjørnson attacked the Norwegian educational system in the article "Our Dishonest Teaching of Religion." He maintained cordial relations with Lennstrand, whom he admired. He was a member of the Rationalist Press Association of London from 1906 until his death. In 1903 he received the Nobel Prize for literature.

One of Norway's greatest novelists, Alexander Kielland (1849–1906), attacked Christianity in several of his works, particularly in *St. Hans Fest* (1887, "The Feast of St. John"). Influenced by Mill and Brandes, he attacked the hypocrisy of Christian morals.

In the following generation, Helge Krog (1889–1962), critic and playwright, and Arnulf Överland, an outstanding poet, must be mentioned. Överland's lecture to the Norwegian Student Society in 1933, "Christianity, the Tenth Scourge," resulted in a trial for blasphemy, of which Överland was acquitted. A man of great independence of thought, he was jailed and sentenced to a concentration camp during the Nazi occupation. At the end of the war, he took a position critical of communism. He was a member of the Rationalist Press Association of London.

Another Norwegian nonbeliever of international fame was Fridtjof Nansen (1861–1930), scientist and explorer, professor of zoology at Oslo University, and a diplomat. After World War I he worked with the League of Nations, and he was awarded the Nobel Peace Prize in 1923.

In the early 1950s, Kristian Horn (1903–1981), a

botanist, introduced so-called "civil confirmation" as an alternative for young nonbelievers who did not wish to participate in ecclesiastical confirmation. In 1956 Horn formed the Humanist and Ethical Union of Norway. However, Horn and his followers remained almost unknown to the younger generation. In 1974 the success of the "Children of God" and similar movements frightened a number of these young people and they formed the Norwegian Pagan Society, whose main object was to fight the power of the Norwegian state church.

The Humanist and Ethical Union has grown rapidly since 1976 and now numbers 10,000 members. The Pagan Society had a membership in June 1981 of some 500. The aim of the union is to secure civil and ceremonial rights and legal status for all nonbelievers. It publishes two magazines, *Human Ethics* and *Humanism,* and is a member of the International Humanist and Ethical Union of Amsterdam.

The Pagan Society takes a different approach. Its members are often out in the street on Saturday mornings, speaking to passers-by and starting discussions concerning the church and its teachings and religion in general. They sell their periodical, *Believe THAT?* and anti-Christian publications. They occasionally arrange open meetings to which members of the clergy or other believers are invited. Lively discussions usually take place at these meetings. The Pagan Society is hampered by a lack of funds. It receives none of the official financial support granted to the Humanist and Ethical Union. The founders of the Pagan Society were Erik and Dagfinn Eckhoff. Dagfinn (born 1947), Erik's son, has always been the driving force behind the initiatives taken by the organization. He is an architect and author of numerous articles and leaflets.

Another important figure in nonbelief in Norway is Andreas Edwien (born 1921). He is an investigator and critic of religion and theology. His publications, *Is Christianity a Danger to World Peace?* (1977) and *Jesus in Conflict with Human Rights* (1979) are excellent references for students of the subject.

DENMARK

Ideas of unbelief were disseminated in Denmark by only a few (but very important) people. Active between 1960 and 1975 was the Humanist Union, which periodically published a review attacking religion and inviting members to leave the state church. Its organizers were professors Erik Elten and Karsten Normann Larsen. Their publication continued the literary tradition of several brilliant predecessors, who were circulating antireligious ideas during the 19th-century Students' Association.

Frederik Dreier (1827–1853) wrote *Spiritual Belief and Freethinking* in 1852, in which he attacked metaphysics. He committed suicide at the age of 25. Rudolf Varberg, of Dreier's group of friends, distinguished himself by a violent attack on Christianity in 1851.

The *New Danish Monthly Review*, founded by Vilhelm Møller (1846–1904), was a radical organ that published the thought of Darwin, Paine, Mill, and German freethinkers.

Georg Brandes (1842–1927), writer and literary critic, was influenced by Feuerbach, Strauss, and Mill. He introduced Nietzsche to Scandinavia, and his lectures at the University of Copenhagen made him a noted defender of evolution and freethinking. In 1871 he applied to the university for a post as professor but, because of his atheism, was not awarded it until 30 years later. The author of voluminous works on Goethe, Voltaire, and Shakespeare, he continued to attack Judeo-Christian ideology until the end. Working with nonbelievers' organizations in other countries, Brandes made his influence felt beyond the borders of his country.

Jens Peter Jacobsen (1847–1885) was a poet and novelist, author of *Mogens* and *Nils Lyhne*, two novels that long influenced Nordic fiction. A confirmed atheist, he considered Christianity a mythology. In 1872 he founded a literary society, called by his opponents the Freethinking Society. He translated Darwin and disseminated his ideas. On a trip to Italy he fell ill of tuberculosis, which caused his death at the age of 38.

Johannes V. Jensen (1873–1950), a writer and journalist, was the author of *Madame D'Ora* and *Hjulet*, in which a homosexual preacher is given the name of Cancer. His writings also dealt with evolution. He won the 1944 Nobel Prize in literature.

Jeppe Aakjaer (1866–1930), a novelist, made his debut with *The Mission and Its Chief*, in which he calls the church and Christianity "powers inimical to life."

There is no nonbelievers' organization in Denmark at the present.

Other article of interest: **Scandinavian Literature, Unbelief in.**

Bibliography

Adamson, Einar. *Gallerkåserier*. Göteborg: Svenska Fritänkareförbundet, 1931.

———. *Prästlist*. Göteborg: Svenska Fritänkareförbundet, 1931.

Alexandersson, N. *Svensk Tryckfrihet*. Fanstal: Studentförening Verdandi, Prisma, 1966.

Austin, Paul Britten. *Carl Michael Bellman*. Malmö: Alhems, 1970.

Bodin, G., and Staffan Rylander. *Tryckfrihetsgränser*. Stockholm: Wahlström & Widstrand, 1974.

Bonniers Lexikon. Stockholm: Bonnier, 1965.

Hedenius, Ingemar. *Helvetes Läran*. Stockholm: Bonnier, 1972.

———. *Tro och Vetande*. Stockholm: Bonnier, 1949.

Lagerborg, R. *Uskonnonvapaustaistelun Historiaa*. Helsinki: Vapaa Ajattelija, 1948.

Lidforss, Bengt. *Kristendomen Förr och Nu*. Malmö: Framtiden, 1911.

———. *Modärna Apologeter*. Malmö: Framtiden, 1922.

———. *Onda Makter och Guda*. Malmö: Framtiden, 1909.

———. *Polemiska Inlägg*. Malmö: Framtiden, 1913.

———. *Urval av Axel Danielssons Skrifter*. Malmö: Framtiden, 1908.

Lindberg, Folke. *Växande Stad*. Stockholm: Liberförlag, 1980.

Nerman, Ture. *Hjalmar Branting, Fritänkaren*. Stockholm: Tiden, 1960.

———. *Ögonvittnen om Hjalmar Branting*. Stockholm: Wahlström & Widstrand, 1961.

Nyström, Anton. *Kristendomen och den Fria Tanken*. Stockholm: Björk & Borjesson, 1908.

Ruhe, Algot. *Kampen för Religionsfrihet*. Malmö: Socialdemokratiska Ungdomsförening, 1906.

———. *Töm Kyrkan!* Malmö: Framtiden, 1908.

Söderberg, Hjalmar. *El Doctor Glass*. Barcelona: Seix Barral, 1968.

———. *Makten, Visheten och Kvinnan*. Stockholm: Bonnier, 1946.

Stangerup, H., et al. *Dansk Litteratur Historie*. Copenhagen: Politiken, 1967.

Svensk Biografisktlexikon. Stockholm: Statens Arkivstyrelse, 1979.

Svensk Upplagsbok. Malmö: Nordens Boktryckeri, 1950.

Svenska Män och Kvinnor, Biografisk Upplagsbok. Stockholm: Bonnier, 1948.

Tribe, David. *100 Years of Freethought*. London: Elek Books, 1967.

Wachtmeister, Claes-Adam. *Ateistens Handbok*. Stockholm: Studentförening Verdandi, Prisma, 1964.

Westermarck, E. *Minnen ur Mitt Liv*. Helsinki: 1927.

JOSÉ M. F. SANTANA
HELEN HASSELRIIS, translator

SCANDINAVIAN LITERATURE, UNBELIEF IN.

The Scandinavian countries were Christianized roughly about the year 1000, but since the Nordic countries were sparsely populated and, in those days, seemingly immense, it was centuries before the new religion took firm root in the Scandinavian populace.

The Middle Ages—Sagas and Ballads. Unsurprisingly, the literature of the Middle Ages is both Christian and pagan. Old Nordic literature, although written down during a Christian age, can hardly be said to reflect Christian beliefs, but neither can it be said to reflect a deep-seated adherence to Norse mythology. In a sense, both mythologies are reduced—probably most explicitly in the Icelandic sagas—to mere trimmings for a belief in fate: each human being is allotted an inescapable destiny in this life, and it is often in part a product of that individual's nature. The sagas thus, at least implicitly, question belief in an afterlife, a belief that was heralded by both Old Norse mythology and Christianity.

The sagas are quite monistic: they focus on the human being's actions in this life; they do not define eternity metaphysically, but rather in terms of how the individual meets his fate and gains remembrance by subsequent generations. Even the gods were fated to die; therefore, the words of Odin, the All-Father and god of poetry, in the *Hávamál* ("Words of the High One") from *The Elder Edda* (composed between 800 and 1000 A.D.; see Taylor and Auden, Bibliography) are significant:

> Cattle die, kindred die,
> Every man is mortal:
> But the good name never dies
> Of one who has done well

In a sense, Nordic literature was a means of

creating a record of those who were to be remembered—but scarcely for their Christian virtues. Among those so remembered were *Gisla saga Súrssonar*'s noble outlaw, Gisle Sursson, who is tormented by anguished, paradoxical dreams over what his seemingly accursed fate and ultimate death will bring him, and *Hrafnkel saga Freysgoða*'s pagan priest of Freyr, Hrafnkel, who announces that he thinks it folly to believe in gods. Hrafnkel changes from a supercilious believer in Freyr to a mature and self-controlled religious skeptic. Both sagas belong to Iceland's anonymously composed "family sagas" of the 1100s to 1200s.

The Icelander Snorre Sturlasson (1179–1241) depicts three such skeptics in his *Olafssaga* about the Norwegian king St. Olav. This appears in his 17 *Sagas of Kings* (c. 1223–35), covering reigns from about 900 to 1177. The robbers Gauketore and Avrafaste are neither pagan nor Christian; they believe only in themselves, their strength and luck in battle, and that belief has been quite sufficient. At last they reluctantly allow themselves to be baptized, as the only means of being accepted by Olav among his troops. Arnljot Gjellinge, a giant of a man who believes in his own "power and strength," which have served him well, also accepts baptism in order to please and serve Olav. All three men fall with their king in the first onslaught at the Battle of Stiklestad in the year 1030.

Another major achievement of Scandinavian literature during the Middle Ages is that of the ballads (which were inspired by French and, possibly, German and English examples). Although this genre flourished in the late Middle Ages (1250–1500), like the sagas it pays little attention to Christian dogma. The fictional universe of the ballad is pagan, and the concept of fate is still quite pervasive in the ballads. Whenever the characters attempt to thwart the workings of fate by seeking aid in Christianity, which is often resorted to merely as a type of magic, it usually proves to be impotent against the forces of destiny.

The ballad *German Gladensvend* is a prime example of a man who, in spite of a Christian ritual like baptism, is fated before birth to fall victim to the forces of evil in the form of a vampiric sea troll. Although some ballads find glory in the reward of life with God in paradise, most focus on this life and merely state that death has occurred. In a few ballads the dead person simply rests in his grave, and no indication is given of an expectation of his resurrection. Even such a ballad as *Aage and Else*—in which Aage's spirit is called forth from his grave by Else's weeping— admonishes the living that the dead are better off forgotten than mourned.

The attitude of the ballad toward Christianity was perhaps an antidote to the clerical literature of the age. Although it seems apparent that the church attempted to use some of the popular genres of the day to get its own ideology across, it is difficult to know just how purposefully this was done. This battle of belief against SKEPTICISM perhaps comes out most clearly in the oral prose genres of tale, fabliau, and legend. In some of these short texts, first collected and published in the early 19th century, Christian heroes and heroines (for example, St. Olav and St. Birgitta of Sweden) are celebrated; but many of these texts are, both implicitly and explicitly, very critical of the Christian clergy and its message. Not only are clergymen often shown to be either foolish and corrupt or magicians of dubious ethics, but also a belief in ghosts—restless, often ill-willed, and dangerous— is emphasized. Both thematic tendencies cast serious doubt on belief in Christian dogma.

It is telling in Scandinavian literature of the period that magical beings, such as trolls, nixies, elves, huldre, etc.—all at once thought to be a part of the natural universe—exercise vast power over human lives, no matter what Christians may do to thwart them. It is even more telling that, in some texts, those magical beings—outlawed and demonized by Christianity (a strategy on the part of the church against native beliefs)—are sometimes accorded a good deal of narrative sympathy and that the church is the recipient of some hostility.

It is difficult, if not impossible, to date such oral-formulaic literature, since it was not collected until fairly recently. But the very fact that it survived to be an object of study for scholars during the past two centuries indicates that, among the common people, a skepticism existed not only against the institution of the church but also against its credo. Those people, who were mostly rural, were either sincerely or nominally Christian, for they were baptized, confirmed, married, and buried by the church. Whether they realized it or not, they also held other beliefs that in the eyes of the church questioned the Christian interpretation of existence. If such popular and long-lived texts can be trusted, Christianity was a veneer over old ideas about the structure of the natural world, ideas that formed the core of the narratives, which remained intrinsically skeptical of Christian dogma.

Lutheran Scandinavia. There can be little doubt that the advent of the Lutheran Reformation early in the 16th century strengthened Christianity's hold on the Scandinavian people, and for about two centuries the major authors were often fervent servants of the church. The major genre was that of the hymn. Curiously enough a few hymns, such as those by the Dane Thomas Kingo (1634–1703) and the Swede Lucidor (Lars Johansson, 1638–1674), testify to emotions that seem heretical. At times Kingo expresses a fear of death that is so devastating that the thought of possible salvation and an afterlife seems feeble. Lucidor goes even so far as to express terror at the thought of eternity.

Obviously there was little of the free Renaissance spirit in Lutheran Scandinavia, although the Swede Georg Stiernhelm (1598–1672) came close to the ideal of the Renaissance man, skilled in all fields. In his epic poem "Hercules" (1658), which was quite obviously written to prove that the Swedish language could compete in eloquence with those of southern European cultures, he picked a classical motif—that of a meeting at a crossroads—in order to test his hero and send the reader a moral message. At the crossroads Hercules meets two women, Lust and Virtue, and each in turn describes the kind of life the young hero would lead if he picked her particular route. As would be expected, the two women differ completely in outlook, but amazingly enough they agree about death. According to his poem, death is a place in which all ends in darkness. Although God is mentioned, the word seems to be used merely rhetorically, and no reference is made to Christian dogma or to an afterlife.

Skepticism and Deism in 18th-Century Scandinavia. Stiernhelm was a startling exception among his contemporaries, and it was to take more than a century before similar voices could be heard in Scandinavian literature. With the rise of RATIONALISM early in the 18th century, one would expect a rise in unbelief, but the most notable of the Scandinavian rationalists, the Dano-Norwegian historian, philosopher, satirist, poet, and playwright Ludvig Holberg (1684–1754), did not truly break with Christian tradition. Holberg has been called a Christian deist, for he contrasted belief with dogma, and he opposed Christian dogma that defied the senses and common sense and objected generally to orthodoxy, sectarianism, and fanaticism, as well as to ATHEISM (*Moralske Tanker*, 1774; *Epistler*, 1748–54).

DEISM usually permitted a focus on this life and prevented metaphysical ponderings about matters of philosophy, but there was no Scandinavian PIERRE BAYLE. Such skeptical minds as those of the Swedish feminist poet Hedwig C. Nordenflycht (1718–1763)—who was indirectly influenced by Bayle—the poet of the middle-class Anna Maria Lenngren (1754–1817), the Epicurean poet Gustav Philip Creutz (1731–1785), the often philosophically pessimistic moralist Gustaf Fredrik Gyllemborg (1731–1808), and that bohemian master of parody, the Norwegian Johan Herman Wessel (1742–1785) may have doubted religious doctrine, but if they did so, it is only their general lack of concern with theology that indirectly reveals it (even though Nordenflycht and Gyllemborg wrote a few religious poems).

It is obvious however that Scandinavian literature was quickly becoming much more secular, and that was perhaps most evident in the songs of the Swede Carl Michael Bellman (1740–1795). Bellman wrote not only hymns but also Bible parodies, but since literature of that age was scarcely personal—rather, dependent upon certain conventions—it is difficult to tell exactly what Bellman believed. In his darkly humorous drinking songs, death is nearly always waiting close at hand, and the human beings who frolic in the taverns of his verse do so because they are profoundly aware of their mortality. Bellman's texts advocate *carpe diem*, for death is on its way. Death is alluded to in terms of classical mythology's Charon, the ferryman of souls; Christian belief in resurrection is never expressed.

The first Scandinavian author who was to take an explicit anti-Christian stance was the Swedish poet, critic, and editor Johan Henric Kellgren (1751–1795); thus, late in the century we find a representative of radical rationalism. In his ode "En stadig man" ("A Dependable Man, 1777"), he developed the belief that certain men could partially determine their own destinies, and he asked what need there could be for gods when such men could look to themselves.

Romanticism. Early in the 19th century the romantic wave swept over Scandinavian culture, and gradually a vague romantic religiosity permeated literature. The romantic writers had often little use for the church or its dogma but saw Christianity as just another expression of the principle behind the universe. For the Swede Thomas Thorild (Thomas Thorén, 1759–1808), who was a transition figure between classicism and romanticism, God, poetry, nature, and the poet himself were pantheistically one. At times the romantic awareness that permitted the human being to feel a oneness with everything gave way to a sense of desperation, to a feeling of man's nothingness and meaninglessness. For men of that mind, a return to Christianity was scarcely possible; instead, they express, albeit sporadically and hesitatingly, an attitude that seems close to nihilism. One major example of this is a famous poem by Esaias Tegnér (1782–1846), "Mjältsjukan" ("Ode to Melancholy," 1825), in which the melancholy mind longs for extinction; but in the very last line of the text the poet expresses the hope that his present dark vision is an illusion and that he may meet his father beyond the sun.

Existential anguish (see EXISTENTIALISM AND UNBELIEF) was, it seems, often intolerable to an age not accustomed to facing the void. In the poem "Till forruttnelsen" ("To Putrefaction," 1824–26), Tegnér's contemporary and countryman, Erik Johan Stagnelius (1793–1823), who was torn obsessively between eroticism and asceticism, the poet accepts that nihilistic view. The first-person speaker in the poem, as if parodying pietistic imagery and belief, asks Death, his bride, to hasten to their bridal bed, so that his body may be devoured by worms. The Christian hope of an afterlife seems to have been rejected.

Although the Danes Hans Christian Andersen (1805–1875) and Steen Steensen Blicher (1782–1848) have written stories that seem deeply influenced by Christianity, they both—and particularly the latter—have also composed stories that seem quite nihilistic, for example, Andersen's "Skyggen" ("The Shadow," 1849) and Blicher's "Sildig Opvågnen" ("Tardy Awakening," 1828). The Swede Abraham Viktor Rydberg (1828–1895) advocated religious freedom, and in *Bibelns lära om Kristus* ("The Teachings of the Bible About Christ," 1862) he shocked his contemporaries by questioning the dogmas of the Trinity and Jesus' simultaneously divine-and-human nature.

The industrial revolution in Scandinavia in the latter part of the 19th century brought about a philosophical and aesthetic reorientation toward POSITIVISM and realism/naturalism. The catalyst for this change was the Danish-Jewish critic Georg Brandes (1842–1927), who was seen as a dangerous atheist by his opponents. Many of Brandes' followers were definitely atheists, and Jens Peter Jacobsen's (1847–1885) famous novel, *Ni ls Lyhne* (1880), was read by many as the ultimate atheistic document. Although the novel had been planned as a testimony to the liberating effect of atheism, it

recorded the loneliness of a human being in a godless world. Many other authors of those decades show that belief in a transcendental order is an illusion and that the church is a bourgeois machination, but very few works show feelings of joy and liberation through unbelief.

Both the great dramatists of the Scandinavian theater, the Norwegian Henrik Ibsen (1828–1906) and the Swede August Strindberg (1849–1912), wrote moving plays about men of God—respectively, *Brand* (1866) and *Mäster Olof* (1872–78)—but rather than attempting to perpetuate Christianity, the playwrights were exploring the inhuman nature of idealism. Their tormented protagonists meet their fates, not because those fates are ordained by God, but because they are the result of human instinct and cultural ideologies.

In 1883 the Norwegian playwright Bjørnstjerne Bjørnson (1832–1910), who had broken with the church in 1880 and composed the psalm "Aerer det evige forår i livet" ("Honor Life's Eternal Spring") in behalf of his belief in evolution, also added his pastor, Adolph Sang, to the growing gallery of those who destroy and are destroyed by misplaced and unrealistic faith. His fellow countryman, Alexander Kielland (1849–1906), widened his attacks on social institutions to include the church. In the novel *Sne* ("Snow," 1886) two High Churchmen, father and son, are finally defeated in their efforts to break the spirit of the freethinking heiress to whom the son has become engaged, and in *Sankt Hans Fest* ("The Feast of St. John," 1887) a minister of the Low Church spreads a reign of terror that paralyzes all those who would hold other opinions than his own. A fourth Norwegian, Arne Garborg (1851–1924), in the novel *Ein fritaenker* ("A Freethinker," 1878), treated the disintegration of the life of a doubter and a fighter against religious oppression. In a later novel, *Traette Maend* ("Tired Men," 1891), Garborg illustrated the possible fates of three modern dogmatic atheists—pessimism, materialism, or religious conversion.

Both Ibsen and Strindberg wrote about individuals whose fates were determined either by genetic inheritance (Ibsen's *Ghosts*, 1891) or by the struggle involved in the survival of the fittest (Strindberg's *Miss Julie*, 1888). The Norwegian author Amalie Skram (1846–1905), in the novel tetrology *Hellemyrsfolket* ("The People of Hellemyr," 1887–98) depicts the curse of "bad blood" in several generations, a curse that is based in the social milieu and that religious devotion cannot lift. Although her countryman Hans Jaeger (1854–1910) had described men made decadent or impotent by society's moral restrictions, in *Fra Christiania-Bohémen* ("From Christiania's Bohemia," 1885), the Dane Herman Bang (1857–1912) had treated genetic degeneration within the family in *Håbløse Slaegter* ("Hopeless Generations," 1880). It was a theme that his countryman Gustav Wied (1858–1914) was to carry to an extreme.

A wave of religiosity again made itself felt in the 1890s, and some authors—among them, Strindberg—once again explained chaotic life in terms of a divine power. The majority of authors, however, left Christian belief for good and many—like the Danish poet Viggo Stuckenberg (1863–1905), the Swedes Gustaf Fröding (1860–1911) and Ola Hansson (1860–1925), and the Norwegian Knut Hamsun (1859–1952)—proudly began to sing Nietzschean hymns to the "I." Representative of the mood of this time was the fervently antireligious Swedish novelist Hjalmar Söderberg (1869–1941), in whose *Dr. Glas* (1905) the futility of life is brilliantly rendered in a nihilistic tour de force. This same holds true for what is possibly Scandinavia's greatest novel, Johannes V. Jensen's (1873–1950) chilling Danish masterpiece, *The Fall of the King* (1900–01), in which all human aspirations seem ridiculous in view of the very brevity of human life. A human being's fate, as shown through the symbol of grinding millstones, is simply to be smashed to bits—into nothingness.

20th-Century Currents. It was nevertheless Jensen who, early in the 20th century, was to formulate a more positive atheistic outlook. In the short myth "Fusijama" (from *Myter og Jagter*, 1907) he marvels at the beauty of the volcano, and in it he finds eternity. In the splendid poem "At Memphis Station" (from *Digte*, 1906) he rejects the typical human impatience that has always forced a person to demand more than can be expected from everyday life—such as is to be found, for example, in the seemingly trivial city of Memphis, Tennessee. That impatience has been the source of all the dreams of a higher reality. Jensen admonished his readers to accept this life in all its beautiful banality, for that is all there is. Jensen jubilantly tried to depict that beauty by describing our millenium-long cultural evolution in *Den lange rejse* ("The Long Journey," 1908–21). Jensen thus rejected not only Christian belief but also that melancholy atheism that turns people into fatalists or nihilists. He denounced FRIEDRICH NIETZSCHE, as well, for being a grand and dangerous

seducer who distracts the human mind from this very real world of facts.

Jensen's optimism was rarely shared by others. The Swedo-Finnish poet and dramatist Ernst Runar Schildt (1888–1925) was an intellectual skeptic who continued to write in the *fin de siècle* spirit of destined doom. His countryman Mikael Lybeck (1864–1925) was a skeptic and fatalist of the same era, who in 1900 wrote *Den starkara* ("The Stronger") that contrasted FREETHOUGHT and religious scare stories. The Norwegian novelist and short-story writer Hans Ernst Kienck (1865–1926), who treats the national degeneration of spirit, and the poet Sigbjørn Obstfelder (1866–1900), who turns to a melancholy pantheism, also belong to that era.

The Swedish novelist Sigfred Siwertz (1882–1970) expressed his pessimistic determinism through characters made weak or egoistic by their childhood milieu (*Selambs*, 1920). Siwertz advocated "strength of will" as the means of turning misfortune into good fortune. The Swedo-Finnish poet Edith Södergran (1892–1923) turned to a Nietzschean, anti-Christian view of life in *Septemberlyran* ("September's Lyre," 1918) and *Rosenaltaret* ("The Rose Altar," 1919), a view that like others eventually gave way. The posthumously published collection of her poetry, *Landet som icke är* ("The Country That Is Not There," 1925), bears a telling title. The Danish poet, critic, and novelist Tom Kristensen (1893–1974) in the novel *Haervaerk* ("Havoc," 1930), treats the crisis of a man who has no set of views on life and whose anguished restlessness leads him to seek those truths in the depths of his own being through self-destructive acts. He finds there only primitive instincts. The following lines of poetry are from the novel: "Asiatically vast is anguish / I have longed for shipwrecks / For destruction and sudden death."

The Swedo-Finnish author Elmer Diktonius (1896–1961) wrote in 1932 the novella "Janne Kubik: A Woodcut in Words" about a man who similarly finds nothing to believe in and nothing within himself. The Dane Karen Blixen (1885–1962), who wrote under the pen name "Isak Dinesen," declared in *Out of Africa* (1937) that God and Satan—or the good and evil in life—are equally glorious and equally eternal. The human being must have the courage to accept his fate and live dutifully in pride and honor. Her countryman Martin A. Hansen (1909–1955), in the novel *Løgneren* ("The Liar," 1950), similarly finds that when the world consists only of the warring forces of good and evil, it is one's "duty" to believe even if one is a skeptic who cannot truly do so. He called that attitude "ethical pessimism." Finally, the Swede Harry Martinson (1904–1978), in his epic poem *Aniara* (1956), treats man's venture from the earth into science's cold timelessness: the vast reaches of outer space in which a ship is lost with 8,000 people aboard. There, the earth has become a myth, and religious cults, one after the other, are turned to for consolation.

Not to be overlooked are the proletarian authors who appeared on the Scandinavian scene in the early years of the 20th century. They rarely express an interest in Christian belief for its own sake but either criticize its oppressive influence or tend to hope that its religious fervor might be generally manifested in support of their conviction that MATERIALISM should be man's guiding light. This is especially true of the socially critical Dane Martin Andersen Nexφ, whose widely translated, many-volumed works such as *Pelle the Conqueror* (1906–10) and *Ditte, Child of Man* (1917–21) express a belief in the essential dignity and value of the human being.

Having similar interests are the Swedes Ivar Lo-Johansson (born 1901), who has written extensively about the lives of farm laborers, and the individualist Vilhelm Moberg (1898–1973), who has not only treated rural life in Sweden but, in the first of his four novels about Swedish emigration to the United States, has described the economic and political-religious oppression from which the emigrants fled (*The Immigrants*, 1949). The Finnish novelist Väinö Linna (born 1920) wrote first of the ambitions of a working-class youth and later of the psychological, social, and political pressures that culminated during the Finnish Civil War of 1918 (*Tuntematon sotilas*, "The Unknown Soldier," 1954).

The noted Icelandic novelist and social critic Halldór Laxness (born 1902), a Catholic who became a Communist, described the everyday strivings in the lives of Icelandic fishermen and farmers. Two of his most famous works were translated by F. H. Lyon in 1936 as *Salka Valka*. The works of the Dane Hans Kirk (1898–1962) are founded on a Marxist understanding of the necessity for socialism to use literature as a weapon to reform society. Kirk's novel, *Vredens søn* ("Son of Wrath," 1950), poses Jesus as a revolutionary theorist who would free the poor and downtrodden of his time from both their own priests and foreign rule and who would create a "propertyless" state in which all people live as brothers and sisters.

Feminist Writers. Another group of writers who are primarily critical of society, but who find the basis of its oppression in the Judeo-Christian tradition, as it has been interpreted by the churches, are the feminists. Such writers dwell little on the religious background for sexual roles but tend rather to deal with the long-lived myths about women that have been its outgrowth. The Dane Lone Fatum (born 1941) wrote in 1975 about both in an article called "Jesus, the Women—and the Christian Double Standard." From a division of women characters into Marias, Marthas, and Magdalenes (mothers, housekeepers, and mistresses), the woman in much 20th-century literature has been made to comprise all three and has become the strong and tender earth-mother who serves as a savior—the cosmically ordained biological connection between life and nonlife. The poet and essayist Lise Sørensen (born 1926) discussed the latter tendency in the works of some 20th-century male authors.

Elsa Gress' (born 1919) *The Undiscovered Sex*, which in 1964 advocated a harmonious balance between the sexes and a freedom from stereotypes in thought and act, was answered in 1973 by a third Dane, Suzanne Brøgger (born 1944) in her book, *Free Us from Love*, in which woman's new "duty" of self-love is seen as a frightening "sentence" to a condition of freedom. She must meet it without any points of reference upon which to rely, for not only history but also her own feelings, ideals, and conscience are products of a system that is past. Woman must be a *tabula rasa* and must now make her first appearance as the "unknown sex"—as Mogens Brøndsted (born 1918) pointed out in 1974 in his article "Features of the Danish Debate on Sexual Roles Since 1920."

Finally, it can be suggested that, even though it would be folly to try to enumerate more unbelievers in the Scandinavian literatures of the 1900s, the author who seems closest to taking a stand as an unbeliever is one whose works ring with existential echoes. The Swede Pär Lagerkvist (1891–1974) is an unbeliever preoccupied with the plight of the unbeliever. He often turns a reassuring myth around to show the ludicrousness of its promise. The novel *Barabbas* (1950) may be, in fact, the ultimate characterization of the unbeliever who cannot transcend his own belief. In Denmark, Peter Seeberg (born 1925) in the novel *Fugls Føde* ("Bird Seed," 1963) has captured the strength, pitiful and sordid as it seems to be, of that unbeliever who could not care less about the ongoing debate concerning belief or unbelief.

Other article of interest: **Scandinavia, Unbelief in.**

Bibliography

Beyer, Harald. *Norsk litteraturhistorie.* Oslo: H. Aschehoug, 1963.

Brønsted, Mogens, and Sven Møller Kristensen. *Fra oldtiden til 1870,* Vol. I, and *Fra 1870 til nutiden,* Vol. II of *Danmarks litteratur.* Copenhagen: Gyldendal, 1963.

Downs, Brian W. *Modern Norwegian Literature: 1860-1918.* Cambridge: Cambridge U. Press, 1966.

Fonsmark, Henning, ed. *Litteraturen i Danmark— og de øvrige nordiske lande.* Copenhagen: Politikens Forlag, 1954.

Gustafson, Alrik. *A History of Swedish Literature.* Minneapolis: American-Scandinavian Foundation, 1961.

Hertel, Hans, ed. *Kønsroller i litteraturen. En antologi.* Copenhagen: Forfatterne og Informations Forlag, 1975.

Johnston, George, trans. *The Saga of Gisli.* London: J. M. Dent, 1963.

Jones, Gwyn. *Eirik the Red—And Other Icelandic Sagas.* London: Oxford U. Press, 1961.

Mitchell, P. M. *A History of Danish Literature.* New York: American-Scandinavian Foundation, 1971.

Sturlasson, Snorre. *Kongesagaer.* Trans. Anne Hallsmark and Didrik Arup Seip. Oslo: Gyldendal, 1959.

Svenskt litteraturlexikon. Lund: C. W. K. Gleerup Bokförlag, 1964.

Taylor, Paul B., and W. H. Auden, trans. *The Elder Edda: A Selection.* New York: Random House, Vintage Books, 1970.

Thomsen, Ejnar. *Dansk litteratur efter 1870. Med sideblik til det øvrige norden.* Copenhagen: Rosenkilde og Bagger, 1962.

Tigerstedt, E. N. *Svensk litteraturhistoria.* Stockholm: Natur och Kultur, 1967.

FAITH INGWERSEN

SCHLEIERMACHER, FRIEDRICH ERNST DANIEL (1768-1834), German philosopher and

theologian. See **German Literature, Unbelief in Modern.**

SCHOPENHAUER, ARTHUR (1788-1860),
German philosopher of pessimism, who regarded will as the fundamental reality.

Life, Works, and Character. Schopenhauer was born on Feb. 22 in the free city of Danzig, son of a successful businessman who moved his family to Hamburg when Prussia annexed Danzig in 1793. He afforded his son the privilege of early education and travels in France, England, and Germany. Two years after his father's death in 1805 (probably by suicide), Schopenhauer followed his mother to Weimar, where she had moved earlier to advance her aspirations as a novelist. After further training in the classics there, he received a substantial inheritance upon coming of age in 1809, affording him financial independence for the rest of his life. Subsequently, he studied at Göttingen (where Plato and IMMANUEL KANT first made a lasting impression on him) and at Berlin; he received his doctorate from the University of Jena in 1813. His dissertation, *On the Fourfold Root of the Principle of Sufficient Reason* (1813), shows Kant's strong influence.

The next four years Schopenhauer spent in Dresden studying Indian philosophy (the third main influence on his thought) and writing his chief work, *The World as Will and Idea.* He was deeply disappointed when it made no impact after it was published in 1818. But it enabled him to obtain the position of *Privatdozent* at the University of Berlin in 1819, where he foolishly scheduled his lectures at the same time as the famous Hegel, whose views he opposed. When he failed to attract students, he gave up his only attempt at an academic career, and from then on withdrew into a rather solitary life as a bachelor. He left Berlin after cholera broke out there in 1813, and eventually settled in 1833 in Frankfurt, where he stayed the remainder of his life.

Schopenhauer continued to write, producing a number of works that were, in essence, attempts to confirm, clarify, and elaborate the theories put forth in his main work. After publishing three essays, *On the Will in Nature* (1836), *On the Freedom of the Will* (1839), and *On the Basis of Morality* (1840), he issued a second edition of *The World as Will and Idea* (1844), adding a volume of important supplementary commentaries to the original text. In 1851 he published his last work, *Parerga and Paralipomena,* a two-volume collection of essays and aphorisms on such popular topics as women, suicide, worldly prudence, and literary style. It finally bought him, during the last decade of his life, some measure of the recognition and personal adulation he had always longed for. He died on Sept. 21, 1860.

The possible influence of temperament and experience on philosophical thought is perhaps nowhere more evident than in Schopenhauer's writings. He led an unhappy life, feeling at odds with the world around him. The bitter and acrimonious relationship with his mother, a woman with little affection for her son, led to complete estrangement after 1813. This undoubtedly contributed to his low opinion of women and his inability to form relationships beyond occasional amours, into which he is said to have been driven by strong sensual impulses and about which he felt ashamed afterwards.

Schopenhauer's personality added to his loneliness and misery, as he was egocentric, moody, abrasive, and arrogant. (He knew he was altogether unsuccessful in attaining his own ideals of compassion and ascetic self-denial.) Contemptuous and critical of others, he could not tolerate criticism himself. He was susceptible to irrational fears and obsessively concerned with his health. Suspicious and cynical toward people, he preferred to spend most of his affection on animals, especially his poodles. From early on he disliked academicians and the academic life, and he was deeply resentful of the long neglect and lack of recognition of his philosophical theories. Though Schopenhauer frequently could take pleasure in music, the theater, good food, and travel, his life was basically one of disappointment and frustration. Whatever the intrinsic merit of his theories, there can be little doubt that the circumstances of his life and personality had a profound effect on the development of some of the central themes of his philosophy, in particular, his wretched estimation of people and the human condition in general, and the pessimistic form of his voluntarism.

The World as Idea. The dominant philosophical influence on Schopenhauer, especially his epistemology, was Kant, whom he admired as the greatest modern philosopher. He despised his own "Idealist" contemporaries (Fichte, Schelling, and Hegel), speaking of them as sophists and charlatans, who acted as though they had special access to supernatural reality. He wanted philosophy returned to Kant's concept of it as the "critical"

investigation of human cognition and the limits of human knowledge. Within the proper boundaries, speculation about the ultimate nature of the universe, and man's place and significance in it, is then legitimate.

Though Schopenhauer was critical of some aspects of Kant's theory of knowledge (which eventually led him to a metaphysical theory very different from Kant's), he agreed with its basic features. Our perceptions of the world are not mirror-like reflections on an (ontologically) objective reality by a passive mind, but they are mediated in every aspect by the nature of our senses and intellect. Moreover, all experience and knowledge of the external world (perceptual reality) is *necessarily* determined by a priori conditions the mind imposes (as shaping and organizing principles) on the raw materials of sensation. These conditions, which also form the basis for the validity of the sciences, are twofold: the intuitions of space and time; and causality, the sole category of the understanding (to which Schopenhauer reduced the twelve Kantian categories). Thus, since both the content and the form of our perceptions are determined by the nature of the mind, the world as it appears in perception is only subjectively real. As Schopenhauer declared at the beginning of *The World as Will and Idea,* "The world is my idea."

The World as Will. But the world is not merely idea. Following Kant again, Schopenhauer not only denied the ultimate reality of the *phenomenal* realm (the world as it appears), and hence MATERIALISM, but he also affirmed (in sharp disagreement with Hegel) the existence of a transcendent, *noumenal* realm (things in themselves) out of which the phenomenal sphere arises. And with Kant he further held that it is impossible to know utlimate reality through the employment of non-logical, formative principles (such as causality), nor through a priori conceptual analysis and deductive reasoning—as found in the writings of some earlier rationalist metaphysicians. (In particular, this meant that theoretical proofs for the existence of God had to be rejected.

Schopenhauer carefully analyzed and dismissed the ontological argument (especially as found in RENÉ DESCARTES and BENEDICT SPINOZA), as well as the causal version of the cosmological. His position also entailed a sharp distinction between religion and philosophy, reiterated throughout his writings. He considered religion a kind of popular metaphysics, springing from the same source as does philosophy—a deep metaphysical urge (rooted in our awareness of suffering and death) to give an interpretation of the world as a whole and the meaning of human existence within it. Man is an *animalum metaphysicum*.

As one way of satisfying this metaphysical urge, therefore, religion (especially the doctrines of immortality and eternal justice) may well serve a useful purpose for the individual and society. But religious doctrines, Schopenhauer stressed, taking their evidence mainly from authority and revelation, can at best be interpreted in an "allegorical" sense (for example, as lofty embodiments and reinforcements of our moral and social beliefs). To interpret them in a literal sense (*sensu proprio*). would lead to nonsense and contradictions. Philosophy, by contrast, must aim at knowledge *sensu proprio*, arrived at in a lucid and intelligible manner, and based only on what is, or can be, given in experience.

Yet—and herein lies Schopenhauer's main departure from Kant, and one of the crucial theses of his whole philosophical system—Schopenhauer did not consider noumenal reality completely beyond the limits of human knowledge. For while we do experience ourselves as phenomena, as objects among other objects, we are also aware of ourselves from within—and not just as experiencing subjects but as agents driven by impulse and desire, as a striving force. It is when *immediately* and *intuitively* aware of ourselves in this manner that we know ourselves as noumena, as what we ultimately and essentially are, which Schopenhauer called "will." The body and its perceptible behavior are simply the "objectification" of will, as is, in fact, the rest of the phenomenal realm. (Yet will and the phenomenal realm are not causally related; they are one and the same, simply seen under two different aspects.)

Ultimate reality is will—one unitary will. It manifests itself in every aspect of the natural world and on every level, from the simplest to the most complex, animate and nonanimate, human and nonhuman. Each thing, furthermore, is an instance or reflection, to a greater or lesser degree, of timeless "Platonic" essences (*Ideen*) which themselves are expressions of the will.

With this conception of ultimate reality, Schopenhauer felt he had (perhaps inconsistent with his own and Kant's epistemological stance, as some critics have charged) significantly extended the Kantian conception of the universe, while not being subject to the objections against rationalist-dogmatic metaphysics.

Antirationalism, Atheism, Pessimism.

Schopenhauer's view of ultimate reality as essentially will not only opposed the Hegelian identification of the real with the rational, but it also differed radically from conceptions of will in basically rational and ethical terms, as found in Descartes, Kant, Fichte, and others. Schopenhauer's own temperament, experience, and observations led him to an entirely different view on the nature of will. Will is a blind, nonrational striving force, whose workings are in the end without plan or purpose. Inasmuch as the phenomenal realm is an objectification of this will, nature—on and between all levels of reality (corresponding to the hierarchy of Platonic ideas)—is a never-ending, and ultimately meaningless, competitive struggle for existence, with stress and suffering the inevitable consequence. From the perspective of man's desires and aspirations, the cosmic will is an evil and malignant force, which at every turn is a source of fear and anxiety, conflict and tension, frustration and misery. When the will in any of its various manifestations *is* satisfied, the result is but a brief relief from pain, only to be replaced by ten other unfulfilled desires, or by boredom, in an endless cycle.

Schopenhauer's voluntarism led him, specifically, to a highly original and important conception of human nature and behavior. Since ultimate reality is blind, nonrational will, of which the whole realm of nature is a manifestation, the will of each person is not—as philosophers like Descartes and Kant had supposed—a tool or aspect of our rational faculty. On the contrary, reason is derivative from will; it is merely one of its many evolutionary expressions. Far from controlling the will and being the true source of human action, reason is no more than the will's servant, and a frequently troublesome and ineffective one at that.

Much of the true motivation of human behavior, moreover, lies in the unconscious, and hence not within rational control. This vision of man, as the product and victim of urges he can neither understand nor control—clearly anticipatory of much that became central in SIGMUND FREUD and modern psychological theory in general—constitutes a devastating assault on the longstanding and cherished Western (especially Greek and ENLIGHTENMENT) conception of reason as the essential and most notable aspect or faculty of man, to whose guidance all human behavior can and should be subject.

In addition, and also based in large part on his theory of will, Schopenhauer came to deny explicitly the existence of God and immortality—though his argumentation here is not always clear. Thus, while he had indeed extended the Kantian conception of reality, he significantly reduced it at the same time, rejecting both Kant's theoretical AGNOSTICISM, as well as his arguments for God and immortality. One reason why the existence of a perfect, personal God seemingly has to be denied is that the concept of such a being, as usually defined, involves unintelligible notions. "*First cause* is, just like *self-caused cause*, a *contradiction in terms*," he wrote.

Moreover, the attempt to infer God's existence on the basis of the *nature* of the world (along the lines of the *teleological* argument) not only would appear unwarranted on epistemological grounds, but in view of the horror of the world, well-nigh preposterous. "Nothing stands so much in the way of a correct insight into Nature and into the essence of things as this view, by which they are looked upon as having been made according to a preconceived plan." Conceptions of the natural world as expressions of an ultimately rational and moral reality (hence usually in optimistic or melioristic terms) are fundamentally amiss. Finally, if it is (then) positively argued, as did Schopenhauer, that ultimate reality is but blind will, the existence of God would, of necessity, appear to be ruled out.

The survival of the personal self or ego after the death of the body appears equally impossible and unintelligible. For one, "*individual consciousness*, thus consciousness as such, cannot be thought of in a *noncorporeal being*." Furthermore, our sense of ourselves as individuals is tied to our perception of ourselves as part of the phenomenal realm. But space and time, the "principle of individuation," do not pertain in the noumenal sphere. Hence the notion of individual immortality is devoid of meaning (the reality of the phenomenal self, in fact, being an illusion to begin with).

Among the major religions, he felt the strongest affinity to HINDUISM and BUDDHISM, with their belief in the transmigration of the soul (metempsychosis) and its eventual release from earthly bondage and final dissolution. Yet even this doctrine, he held, must not be interpreted in a literal sense (as this would lead to "absurdities"), but only allegorically. As such, however, he felt it can plausibly be understood as an expression of a view close to the nature of things. According to the latter, as he saw it, individual selves do not survive bodily death; only the species survives and the indestructible cosmic will, of which all individual selves are manifestations and with which they are all essentially and ultimately one. Only in this sense, therefore, is it meaningful to speak of immortality at all.

Schopenhauer's views resulted in perhaps the most unrelenting pessimism ever expounded, including as its main components unbelief in God and immortality, the primacy and supreme value of reason, the perfectibility of human nature and society, the ultimate value and meaning of human endeavor and existence, and above all, the possibility of achieving lasting happiness and fulfillment in life.

Deliverance Through Art, Morality, Asceticism. Since suffering, in Schopenhauer's view, permeates our whole existence, it is not surprising that the central concern of his philosophy of life was the alleviation of suffering. He rejected suicide as a means of escape, since it constitutes a final affirmation of the will, hence leaving unscathed the single noumenal will that is at the root of all human evil and misery. But he did consider three possible paths of relief which, unlike suicide, *are* directed at negating the varied and ceaseless strivings of the will itself.

The first of these lies in aesthetic contemplation. It brings about a suspension of the ordinary mode of perception in which everything is considered from the point of view of serving our needs and desires, of satisfying the demands of the will. During aesthetic contemplation we become disinterested in the practical affairs of the world, free from the "penal servitude of willing." This is the result of the unique objects of aesthetic experience (except in music, which expresses the will directly), namely, the unchanging Platonic ideas, of which all particular objects of experience are but imperfect imitations. When man is lost in the contemplation of these timeless ideas, he forgets his individuality, and his will ceases to struggle. He becomes a "*pure will-less, painless, timeless subject of knowledge.*"

Aesthetic experience, however, is only temporary, for the mind is soon brought back to the world of striving and frustration. For a more permanent relief from suffering man must turn to the practice of morality and the development of moral character. To Schopenhauer this meant abandoning behavior motivated by self-centeredness and egoism, the main source of all human strife and misery, and to replace it with actions springing from the only other possible motive, altruism or compassion (*Mitleid*). This—and not the Kantian moral imperative, which is but the Mosaic Decalogue in disguise and is thus "based on concealed theological hypotheses"—is the true source of all morality, and is itself an expression of the intuitive realization, found in the wisdom of India and the experience of all mystics, that ultimate reality is one, and that hence the distinctness and separateness of individual wills is but an illusion (*maya*). Genuine morality, therefore, by giving up the particularity of our striving will, by "abolishing the barrier between ego and nonego," hence enabling us to feel another's pain "as [our] own," will lead to a more permanent quieting of the individual will, and thus to the alleviation of much suffering.

However, though love and compassion can greatly reduce human misery, they cannot eliminate *all* of it. For even the compassionate person is not totally "will-less." Complete release from the insatiable demands of the cosmic will, and hence from all suffering, can come only when all attachment to worldly things ceases, when every impulse to be involved in the world is annihilated, when the will to life is negated altogether by "denying itself" through mystic asceticism. Then the blessed state which the ancient Hindus and Buddhists called *nirvana* is reached.

Importance and Influence. Critics of Schopenhauer have pointed to many inconsistencies in his philosophy, and undoubtedly some of these exist. Yet, while few have accepted Schopenhauer's metaphysical voluntarism, his theories have exercised considerable influence. His theory of art affected novelists and composers of note, such as Thomas Mann and Richard Wagner, and his critical estimate of the value and power of the human intellect has had a profound and lasting effect on modern psychological conceptions of man.

Schopenhauer's voluntarism became a link between Kant and such later thinkers as FRIEDRICH NIETZSCHE and Henri Bergson. His then novel conception of philosophy as centrally concerned with understanding the meaning and place of human existence in the context of the rest of the universe, left its mark on the development of many themes in EXISTENTIALISM. But his main significance lies in his original conception of reality and in his compellingly argued and terrifying bleak and pessimistic vision of human existence as a meaningless, unceasing, and futile struggle, full of torment and suffering, in a hostile and godless universe. This vision still stands as a disturbing and powerful challenge to anyone of a more optimistic persuasion.

Other articles of interest: **German Literature, Unbelief in Modern. God, Existence of. Immortality, Unbelief in.**

Bibliography

All of Schopenhauer's chief works have been translated into English. Only *On the Will in Nature* (London: Bell & Sons, 1897; trans. K. Hillebrand) is out of print.

Caldwell, William. *Schopenhauer's System in Its Philosophical Significance.* Edinburgh: Blackwood, 1896.
Copleston, Frederick. *Arthur Schopenhauer, Philosopher of Pessimism.* London: Burns, Oates & Washbourne, 1946.
Fox, Michael, ed. *Schopenhauer, His Philosophical Achievement.* Totowa, N.J.: Barnes & Noble, 1980.
Gardiner, Patrick. *Schopenhauer.* Harmondsworth: Penguin, 1963.
Hamlyn, D. W. *Schopenhauer.* London: Routledge & Kegan Paul, 1980.
Taylor, Richard. In *A Critical History of Western Philosophy.* Ed. D. J. O'Connor. New York: Free Press, 1964.
Wallace, William. *Life of Schopenhauer.* London: 1890; reprinted, St. Clair Shores, Mich.: Scholarly Press, 1970.
Zimmern, Helen. *Arthur Schopenhauer: His Life and Philosophy.* London: Longmans Green, rev. ed., 1932.

RUDOLF ZUCKERSTÄTTER

SCHROEDER, THEODORE (1864–1953), American libertarian crusader and publicist, was born on a farm near Horicon, Wis., on Sept. 17. The son of German immigrants, Schroeder grew up in the liberal environment of exiles who fled Germany after the revolution of 1848. His father, a miller, came from a Lutheran family, his mother from a Roman Catholic one. Both had been disowned by their parents for marrying outside their faiths. His father became an agnostic who openly scoffed at religion; his mother joined an evangelical Protestant sect. Thus, from early childhood Theodore was aware of religious conflict.

Early Life. At the age of 15 Theodore left home, and for the next 10 years he traveled throughout the country, particularly in the West, taking such odd jobs as dishwashing and surveying but seldom staying in one location for more than a few months. His wanderlust brought him in contact with persons in all walks of life—teachers, engineers, preachers, ranchers, hobos, prostitutes, and gamblers. In 1882 he enrolled at the University of Wisconsin, and for the next seven years, between his travels and temporary jobs, he studied engineering and law. In addition to his formal education and the insight gained from travel, Schroeder was greatly influenced by his reading, particularly in philosophy and religion. He became an admirer of the lives and works of THOMAS PAINE and ROBERT GREEN INGERSOLL, and was especially influenced by reading LUDWIG FEUERBACH's *The Essence of Christianity*.

On receiving his law degree in 1889, Schroeder moved to Salt Lake City, where he opened a law office and conducted a successful and lucrative practice for 10 years. In 1891 he married Mary Parkinson, daughter of a University of Wisconsin professor, but she died five years later, leaving a young daughter, who died in childhood.

Schroeder developed an early sympathy for the Mormons, whom he saw as a persecuted people, but within a short time his views changed radically when he began to perceive the Mormon theocracy as a threat to the separation of church and state. He expressed his anti-Mormon views, including criticism of polygamy, which he called "sanctified lust," in numerous articles, pamphlets, and letters to the editor. While Schroeder campaigned for Utah's statehood, his concern over church-state conflict led him to prosecute Congressman-elect Brigham H. Roberts, resulting in Roberts' exclusion from Congress. Schroeder feared that Roberts' commitment to the authority of the church would take precedence over his political obligations, a view he later expressed during Al Smith's campaign for the presidency.

A lifelong crusade for intellectual freedom began in 1900, when Schroeder gave up his law practice in Salt Lake City and moved to New York. Over the years he associated with most of the nation's leaders of liberal and radical reforms, although he never became part of an organized movement. In 1902 he joined Leonard Abbott, Lincoln Steffens, and other liberals in forming the Free Speech League, which provided leadership in civil liberties until it was superseded in 1920 by the American Civil Liberties Union. Schroeder served as secretary of the League, writing most of its publications and providing legal aid to persons in various parts of the country whose speaking and writing were threatened.

In 1908 he married Nancy Sankey-Jones, an ardent feminist and fellow libertarian, and they moved to Cos Cob, Conn., which became their permanent home.

In the early years of the century, Schroeder became a leading opponent of Anthony Comstock, self-appointed arbiter about public expression of sexual matters. He defended numerous clients (generally without a fee) who had been charged with violating the obscenity laws. It was during these years that Schroeder developed his unorthodox views on obscenity, which he expounded in *"Obscene" Literature and Constitutional Law: A Forensic Defense of Freedom of the Press* (1911). He maintained that all obscenity statutes were unconstitutional, violating both the First and Fourteenth (due process) amendments; that obscenity existed only in the mind of the reader or beholder; and that suppression of so-called obscene works contributed to ignorance, which, in turn, produced emotional disorders.

During the decade before World War I Schroeder figured in a number of cases involving suppression of political ideas, including the San Diego and Denver trials of anarchist EMMA GOLDMAN, a longtime friend, and free-speech fights in Chicago and Patterson, N.J. After the A.C.L.U. was founded, Schroeder left the defense of political causes largely to that organization, concerning himself with blasphemy and obscenity cases. In 1911 he defended William Lloyd Clark, an anti-Catholic editor, charged with obscenity for publishing a book alleging vice and corruption in the Catholic church.

Over a period of years, beginning in 1916, he defended a freethinking Lithuanian minister, Michael X. Mockus, charged with blasphemous utterances. Schroeder argued that blasphemy could not be a crime under the Constitution, which specifically prohibited the establishment of religion and the enactment of laws abridging freedom of speech and the press. He used the Mockus case as a springboard for what became his major work on the subject, *Constitutional Free Speech Defined and Defended in an Unfinished Argument in a Case of Blasphemy* (1919). In an imaginary statement of how an enlightened Christian judge might charge the jury in a blasphemy case, Schroeder wrote: "The freethinker has the same right to discredit the beliefs of Christians that the Orthodox Christians enjoy in destroying reverence, respect, and confidence in Mohammedanism, Mormonism, Christian Science, or Atheism."

Over a period of several years in the 1920s

Schroeder was involved in the defense of Episcopal Bishop William Montgomery Brown, brought before the House of Bishops on charges of heresy. Bishop Brown had publicly denied the divinity of Jesus and the doctrine of the Trinity and had espoused communism in his book, *Communism and Christianity; Analyzed and Contrasted from the Marxian and Darwinian Point of View* (1920), a work that had caused heated controversy between modernists and fundamentalists. Brown was eventually found guilty of heresy and expelled from his church.

The psychology of religion became, as early as 1901, a field of study. Schroeder was pursuing an interest that began during his youth and was fed by his experience among the Mormons. He developed an erotogenetic theory of religion, tracing its origin to primitive man's mystification and exaltation over sex. He cited numerous examples of psychic correlation between sexual ecstasy and religious emotion, both in primitive phallic worship and in modern sects. His radical and dogmatic views appeared in numerous medical, psychology, and theological journals, eliciting strong response, largely negative. William James refuted Schroeder's theory as being simplistic and absurd, but CHAPMAN COHEN and Havelock Ellis came to his defense. Schroeder's attacks on religion grew so vitriolic in later years that he termed religion "the most pernicious single influence in human society; without one redeeming feature." However, he distinguished between religion and theology, which he considered a worthy intellectual pursuit; and he consistently defended a person's right to hold and expound religious beliefs.

Schroeder underwent psychoanalysis with Dr. William Alanson White, superintendent of St. Elizabeth's Hospital in Washington, D.C., during 1914–15, in order to develop a better understanding of himself and the nature of intellectual freedom. During the remainder of his career, Schroeder practiced as a "maverick psychologist," applying psychoanalytic methods to such issues as religious bigotry, crime, divorce, judicial decision-making, and education. Believing that psychoanalysis was the key to solving the great problems afflicting society, he became an exponent of evolutionary psychology, writing and speaking on the need for emotional maturity, unhampered by myth and prejudice. The emotional maturity of the individual, he contended, was as important as constitutional guarantees in establishing intellectual freedom.

In the last years of his life, Schroeder was plagued by fading eyesight, by the illness of his wife to whom he was devoted, and by dwindling financial resources. He died at his home on Feb. 10, 1953.

In summary: In each area of his interest—religion, sex, and psychology—Schroeder wrote with dogmatic conviction and the passion of a revivalist, a combination that led his friend, Hutchins Hapgood, to describe him as "a cold enthusiast." He published his books at his own expense, and many of his articles appeared in obscure journals. During his entire career Schroeder was frustrated by the inability to get his ideas accepted, and rejection even followed his death. Schroeder's will, providing for the publication of his collected works, was invalidated by the Connecticut Supreme Court, which found his writings obscene, offensive to religion, and of no social value.

Schroeder's seminal, if dogmatic, views never became part of the intellectual mainstream, although his advanced ideas on obscenity are widely accepted by today's liberals. In a marginal way, he contributed to the advancement of rational thought and tolerance, and is important for his lifelong defense of the persecuted and the dissident. In an introduction to the 1971 reprint of *"Obscenity" and Constitutional Law,* Jerold Auerbach observed the paradox in Schroeder's career: "His was an intolerant crusade for tolerance, an authoritarian struggle for liberty, an emotional pursuit of reasoned truth."

Other articles of interest: **Blasphemy Laws. Church, State, and Religious Freedom.**

Bibliography

Brodnoy, David B. "Liberty's Bugler: The Seven Ages of Theodore Schroeder." Ph.D. dissertation, Brandeis University, 1971.

Domayer, Dennis L. "Theodore Schroeder: A Biographical Sketch." In Ralph E. McCoy, *Theodore Schroeder, A Cold Enthusiast: A Bibliography.* Carbondale, Ill.: Southern Illinois U. Library, 1973.

Ishill, Joseph. *A New Concept of Liberty.* Berkeley Heights, N.J.: Oriole Press, 1940.

Maddaloni, Arnold. "Theodore Schroeder: Personal Impressions." In Ralph E. McCoy, *Theodore Schroeder, A Cold Enthusiast: A Bibliography.* Carbondale, Ill.: Southern Illinois U. Library, 1973. Maddaloni was Schroeder's companion in the crusader's later years and remains a disciple of his evolutionary psychology.

RALPH E. MCCOY

SCIENTIST AS UNBELIEVER, THE. If we are to think of a scientist as a possible "unbeliever," then we must assume that there is something he does not "believe." What might that be?

In the context of this Encyclopedia, that which a scientist is to believe or not believe are the tenets of religion, in particular those of the Judeo-Christian belief-system. (There is some question in my mind as to whether it would not be appropriate, as the world shrinks and the Middle East gains in importance, to speak of the Judeo-Christian-Muslim belief-system, but such a change would not affect the line of argument.)

Judeo-Christian religious beliefs are heterogeneous in nature. Jews and Christians are separated by the unbridgeable gulf of Jesus Christ. For 2,000 years, Jews have refused to accept Jesus as the Messiah, savior, and son of God, while Christians tend to make the acceptance of Jesus central to salvation.

If we restrict ourselves to Christians, then there is an unbridgeable gulf, in the form of the papacy, between Catholics and Protestants. Catholics accept the pope as the vicar of Christ and the head of the universal church, while Protestants do not. Within the realms of Judaism, Catholicism, and Protestantism there are other divisions, large and small, over matters of doctrine, which at some periods of history (such as our own) are glossed over, and which at other periods have led to fiery and explosive disputes—as fiery as the stake and as explosive as gunpowder. For over a century, from 1522 to 1648, Europe suffered from wars of religion, which were bloodier and more merciless than anything prior to our own century.

Naturally, then, it makes no sense to ask if scientists believe in (or do not believe in) baptism by total immersion, in the use of incense during church services, in the inspiration of Joseph Smith, or even in the divinity of Jesus, since many non-scientists and many sincerely and totally religious people devoutly believe or disbelieve these points or any of a thousand others.

The Bible. We must find something that all segments of Western Judeo-Christianity agree upon. It is not very difficult to decide that the fundamental belief-system rests in the Bible—the Old Testament for Jews and Christians alike, and the New Testament for Christians alone.

No matter how the various sects and divisions within Judaism and Christianity differ in doctrine, all agree in taking the Bible seriously. Different people may be worlds apart in their interpretations of the Bible and the deductions they make from it, but all "believe" the Bible, more or less.

In considering the Bible, it is important to realize that it is not all of a piece. It is not written by one person, so it is not presented from a single point of view. Those who "believe" the Bible are apt to consider it the inspired word of God, so that whether one person or many persons held the pen (or pens) that wrote the words, only one "mind" was behind it. However, if we look at the Bible *as though* it were purely a human book, it would *seem* to be a heterogeneous mass of material.

The Old Testament consists of solid history in the two books of Samuel and the two of Kings. It also contains legendary material in Genesis and Exodus, liturgical directions in Exodus, Leviticus, Numbers and Deuteronomy, comments on (then) current affairs, poetry, philosophy, visions of the future and so on. The New Testament consists of four short biographies of Jesus, historical material in Acts, a series of letters on doctrinal matters, and an elaborate vision of the future in Revelation.

For much of this the question of unbelief does not arise. The histories of the kings of Israel and Judah might conceivably be wrong in detail, but so might a particular history of the presidents of the United States. No one seriously questions that the historical sections of the Bible are correct in essence. Nor can anyone quarrel with the liturgical material, which are authentic by definition, just as the ritual of a Masonic society might be; or with the poetry, which is widely recognized as among the most glorious in the world.

Where in the Bible, then, does the question of belief arise. To answer that question, let us shift to a consideration of science. Science, properly speaking, is not a noun but a verb, not a thing but a process, not a specific set of conclusions but a way of looking at the universe.

Science is based on certain assumptions, as all things must be. It assumes that the universe "makes sense," that it can be reasoned about, that the rules of logic hold. It assumes that by reasoning from sense impressions one can work out the general rules ("laws of nature") that seem to govern the behavior of the universe, that these general rules can be grasped by the human mind, and that they can be tested by experiment.

Under these circumstances, science deals with those aspects of the universe that can be observed by the senses, that can be measured by instruments in a reproducible manner with results that do not deviate erratically from time to time or place to place or experimenter to experimenter. The *scientific universe* is by no means coterminous (at least, not yet) with the *total universe*.

Naturally, science is a cumulative process. As more and more observations are made, and more and more experiments are conducted, a broader, deeper, and more useful understanding of the scientific universe is obtained. It follows that we understand many aspects of the universe far more thoroughly than our predecessors did 25 centuries ago, or one century ago, or, in some ways, ten years ago.

Scientists accept contemporary conclusions, not blindly, not without understanding that they are possibly temporary as well as contemporary, and not without considerable discussion and dispute, but it is a rare scientist indeed who does not accept the fact that the conclusions of today are in general more nearly correct and useful than those of a century ago, and certainly more nearly so than those of 25 centuries ago.

I choose the period "25 centuries ago" deliberately since much of the Bible (although in part based on older material) received more or less its present form at the time of the Babylonian captivity of the Jews in the 6th century B.C. It follows, therefore, that the Bible contains some sections that detail matters concerning the scientific universe as they were understood 25 centuries ago.

There is nothing essentially wrong with this. It was the best that the compilers of the Bible could do. The first chapter of the Book of Genesis, for instance, which describes the manner of the creation of the universe, accepts the cosmogony worked out by the Babylonians, which at the time was the most advanced in the world. The biblical version improved on the Babylonians, eliminating polytheistic notions, and introducing a lofty abstraction that is much more attuned to modern feelings. It might be maintained in all fairness that the biblical tale of the creation is the most reasonable to have been produced by the human mind before the rise of modern science.

Nevertheless science has advanced in 25 centuries, and scientists do not, in general, accept the version of the creation presented in Genesis 1. Nor

do they accept many of the other aspects of the picture of the scientific universe presented in the Bible.

To present a few examples: there is no convincing evidence of a worldwide flood (as distinct from local flooding of the Tigris-Euphrates valley) in the third millennium B.C. There is no convincing evidence that humanity spoke a single language in that same millennium, or that that language was Hebrew. Again, there is no real evidence, outside the Bible, that such individuals as Adam, Eve, Cain, Abel, Nimrod—and perhaps even, Abraham, Isaac and Jacob—ever lived. The various "miracles" of the Old and New Testaments, in which divine intervention suspended or subverted the operation of the laws of nature, are not acceptable as part of the scientific universe, and there is no evidence outside the Bible that any of them actually took place.

If we subtract all these things from the Bible, if we subtract such things as talking serpents and talking asses, the Red Sea parting and the sun standing still, the spirit of the dead Samuel being raised by the witch of Endor, angelic messages and demonic possession, there yet remains a great deal of prose and poetry concerning which there is no possibility of conflict with science.

To Believe or Not to Believe. It is therefore possible for the most rigid scientist to accept the Bible, almost all of it, without reservation. He can accept the history, the poetry, the ethical teachings. In fact, he can even accept those portions that do not fit the scheme of the scientific universe, if he is willing to accept them as allegorical or figurative statements. There is no great difficulty in feeling that God's initial command, "Let there be light," symbolizes the initial existence of energy, out of which all else followed. Indeed, it is possible to see an equation between that command and the initiation of the "big bang," which is the current view of the origin of the universe. With a little ingenuity almost any of the miracles can be given poetic or allegoric meaning.

In this way, any scientist can, if he wishes, find no conflict between religion and science. He can work in his laboratory through the week and go to church on Sunday and experience no difficulty in doing so. It is possible for priests, ministers, and rabbis to fulfill all their religious duties and, when those are done, turn to scientific labors without a qualm.

It is not surprising, then, that many first-rank scientists have been sincerely and honestly religious as well: Edward Morley of the Michelson-Morley experiment, Robert Millikan, Abbé Georges Lemaître, Teilhard du Chardin, and many others.

The catch is this, however. No matter how religious a scientist may be, he cannot abandon the scientific view in his day-to-day work and explain some puzzling observation by supposing divine intervention. No scientist of any standing has ever done this, nor is one likely to. Again, when a literal reading of the Bible is apt to promote a view incompatible with the scientific universe, any scientist, however religious, is bound to accept that view in some allegorical fashion.

It is not much of a catch. Not only do scientists, generally, find no difficulty in living up to this requirement, but large numbers of religious leaders and followers, who are not themselves scientists, have no difficulty in accepting the scientific universe and the current scientific conclusions concerning it. Specifically, they find it easy to accept a universe that is billions of years old in which our earth and its load of life (including *Homo sapiens*) developed by extremely slow stages.

The Fundamentalist View. We can, however, begin from the other end. Suppose we assume that the Bible is divinely inspired, that every word represents ultimate truth and is inerrant. This is the fundamentalist view. In that case, the Bible represents, once and for all, a view of the universe that cannot be changed. The only function science can have in such a fundamentalist universe is to uncover evidence that supports that universe or, at the very least, does not conflict with it. What happens if science uncovers evidence that does conflict with the literal word of the Bible? Then it follows, to the fundamentalist, that the evidence is wrong or is, at the very least, misleading.

In the fundamentalist view, then, the universe was created some six (or possibly ten) thousand years ago in a period of six days—all of it. The earth was created first, then the sun and moon and stars. Plant life was created before the sun was and every species of plant and animals was created separately so that there was no change from one to another.

The firmly established scientific view that the universe is probably 15 billion years old, that it began in a gigantic explosion out of which the galaxies slowly formed, that the sun and its attendant planets were formed perhaps 10 billion years *after* the universe generally was born, that earth is nearly five billion years old, that humanlike beings slowly developed out of previous nonhuman forms of life a few million years ago, with *Homo sapiens* established on earth for some hundreds of thousands of years—all this is entirely rejected by the fundamentalists.

There are many other places where the fundamentalist universe and the scientific universe are totally at odds, but nothing new would be added by listing them all. The actual quarrel today is over manner of origin. Was it long ago (scientific) or recently (fundamentalist)? Did the universe develop slowly through evolutionary processes (scientific) or suddenly through divine creation (fundamentalist)?

No compromise would seem possible. Scientists cannot give up the results of scientific observation and experiment or the laws of logic and remain scientists. And fundamentalists cannot give up the literal interpretation of every word in the Bible and remain fundamentalists.

The scientific view is that fundamentalism is a form of religion that clings to Babylonian science of 25 centuries ago and by modern standards is nothing but superstition. Fundamentalists, on the other hand, wish to appropriate the respect given to science, and wish to have their views taught in the public schools as "science." This cannot constitutionally be done if their views are backed only by biblical evidence and nothing more, since that would violate the principle of separation of church and state. Therefore, they present their fundamentalist views without mention of the Bible, surround it with a potpourri of undigested scientific terminology, and call it "scientific creationism." However, calling a horse a golden-haired princess doesn't make it any the less a horse, and "scientific creationism" is merely fundamentalism.

Now, then, if by religion, we mean fundamentalism (but please note that *only* fundamentalists make that equation), and if a "believer" is defined as one who accepts fundamentalism while an "unbeliever" is one who rejects it—then every scientist is, by definition, an unbeliever. No one who accepts the scientific universe can possibly accept the fundamentalist universe; the two are incompatible right down to their basic assumptions.

To be sure, it is possible for people to call themselves scientists, to own pieces of paper that give them the legal right to put initials after their name, and yet to profess a belief in the fundamentalist universe. But then, anyone can *call* himself a scientist but it takes more than a piece of paper to make one.

Other articles of interest: **Evolution and Unbe-**

lief. Life, Origin of, and Unbelief. Miracles, Unbelief in. Religion vs. Science. Universe, Origin of the.

Bibliography

Asimov, Isaac. *In The Beginning: Science Faces God in the Book of Genesis.* New York: Crown, 1981.

Draper, John William. *History of the Conflict Between Religion and Science.* New York: Appleton, 1874.

Eldredge, Niles. *The Monkey Business: A Scientist Looks at Creationism.* New York: Washington Square Press, 1982.

Russell, Bertrand. *Religion and Science.* New York: Oxford U. Press, 1961.

White, Andrew Dickson. *A History of the Warfare of Science with Theology in Christendom.* 2 vols. New York: Appleton, 1896.

ISAAC ASIMOV

SEAVER, HORACE (1810–1889), American freethinker and editor. See **Boston Investigator.**

SECULAR HUMANISM. See **Humanism.**

SECULARISM. The term *secularism* was coined by GEORGE JACOB HOLYOAKE in 1841. The word at present, however, is used in rather a different way from what he originally meant it to mean. In fact, the word now has several different meanings, none of which is identical to that intended by Holyoake. Holyoake's original meaning was "the extension of FREETHOUGHT to ethics." Although Holyoake thought that secularism had nothing to do with either ATHEISM or theism, it is hard to reconcile his definition with that belief. In 1870, Holyoake had a long public debate with CHARLES BRADLAUGH on the subject of whether secularism had anything to do with atheism. Holyoake took the position that it did not, while Bradlaugh held that atheism was a necessary presupposition to secularism.

The usual definition of secularism, as it is used today, is "indifference to or rejection or exclusion of religion and religious considerations" (*Webster's Seventh New Collegiate Dictionary*). However, even this definition is incomplete and confusing. It does not say from what religion is excluded, rejected, or treated indifferently. Perhaps a better definition is that given by Virgilius Ferm in his *Encyclopedia of Religion.* He says that it is "a variety of utilitarian social ethic which seeks human improvement without reference to religion and exclusively by means of human reason, science and social organization. It has developed into a positive and widely adopted outlook which aims to direct all activities and institutions by a non-religious concern for the goods of the present life and for social well-being." Holyoake would probably have approved of this definition, while Bradlaugh would not.

Another meaning that *secularism* has today is the attitude that religion (of any sort) and government (of any sort) should not be mixed. It underlies the concept of separation of church and state. A secularist would be, by this definition, one whose philosophy demanded an absolute separation of church and state.

Still another, although related, meaning of *secularism* applies to the beliefs that the members of such organizations as the NATIONAL SECULAR SOCIETY hold. This definition is more closely related to the idea that a secularist is a supporter of absolute separation of church and state. In the case of members of the National Secular Society, however, most of the members would be likely to call themselves either atheists or agnostics. This would *not* be the case when we consider the religious beliefs of the members of the largest group supporting separation of church and state in the United States, namely Americans United. This group is overwhelmingly made up of religious Protestants, often Baptists, although by no means exclusively so. This suggests that Holyoake's position that secularism does not require atheism or theism may be correct in the sense that not all secularists are atheists, but almost all atheists are secularists.

To return to the debate held in 1870 between Holyoake and Bradlaugh, we can briefly examine the arguments of the disputants to see whether we can draw any conclusions about the necessity of atheism to secularism. In his speeches, Holyoake quotes approvingly from a pamphlet of CHARLES WATTS entitled *The Philosophy of Secularism:* "Atheism includes Secularism, but Secularism does not exact Atheistical profession as the basis of co-operation; it is not considered necessary that a man should advance as far as Atheism to become a Secularist." However, as Holyoake admits in the next part of the same paragraph, Watts subsequently changed his mind and adopted Bradlaugh's position that atheism was a necessary part of secularism.

The use of the word *secularism* in the context of the National Secular Society is explained in that article, while secularism in general in the United Kingdom is treated in UNITED KINGDOM, UNBELIEF IN, plus the biographical articles on Bradlaugh, ANNIE BESANT, and GEORGE WILLIAM FOOTE.

We can close with a brief statement defining secularism as Holyoake used the term in his old age. In 1896 he said: "Secularism is a code of duty pertaining to this life, founded on considerations purely human, and intended mainly for those who find theology indefinite or inadequate, unreliable or unbelievable. Its essential principles are three: (1) The improvement of this life by *material* means. (2) That science is the available Providence of man. (3) That it is good to do good. Whether there be other good or not, the good of the present life is good, and it is good to seek that good" (*English Secularism*). That is about as succinct a statement as I have encountered, and it avoids the theism issue entirely.

Other articles of interest: **Agnosticism. Church, State, and Religious Freedom.**

Bibliography

Holyoake, George J. *English Secularism: A Confession of Belief.* Chicago: Open Court, 1896.
——. *The Trial of Theism, Accused of Obstructing the Secular Life.* London: Trübner, 1877.
Holyoake, G. J., and Charles Bradlaugh. *Secularism, Scepticism and Atheism* (a two-night public debate). London: Austin, 1870.
Royle, Edward. *Radicals, Secularists and Republicans: Popular Freethought in Britain, 1866–1915.* Manchester: Manchester U. Press, 1980.
——. *Victorian Infidels: The Origins of the British Secularist Movement, 1791–1866.* Manchester: Manchester U. Press, 1974.

GORDON STEIN

SEMPLE, ETTA DONALDSON (1855–1914), American freethinker. See **Women and Unbelief.**

SEXUAL VALUES, IMPACT OF UNBELIEF UPON. The study of sexuality documents just how difficult it is to separate religious attitudes about sex from societal ones. This is because sex, until fairly recently, has not been subjected to the kind of critical analysis that so many other aspects of our belief-system have been. Thus the unbeliever, unless he or she was personally unable to conform, tended to accept the norms of society as set forth by the Christian church.

Christianity and Sexual Ethics. The Christian view, which is primarily the view of Augustine (A.D. 354–430), was a combination of neo-Platonic, neo-Pythagorean, Gnostic, and Manichaean dualistic views of sex. Augustine held that sex was a weakness of the flesh and that continence was the most desirable lifestyle. He was particularly offended by the act of coitus, which he held brought the manly "mind down from the heights." He was disturbed that propagation of the human species could not be accomplished without what he felt were bestial movements and violent lustful desires. Sexual lust was, for him, the inevitable result of the expulsion of Adam and Eve from the Garden of Eden.

Though Augustine recognized that the Bible commanded humanity to be fruitful and multiply, and he had to accept this as a Christian, he was unhappy about it. He compromised enough to allow the justification of sexual intercourse—providing that it led to reproduction. Marriage, he held, transformed coitus from a mere satisfaction of lust to a necessary duty, but it was the employment of the sex act for human generation that ultimately allowed it to shed some of its inherent sinfulness. Augustine condemned all sexual activity between the unmarried, and sex within marriage was only to be engaged in for the purpose of procreation and then only in certain positions, the male-superior position. Though Christians found these teachings about sex difficult to accept in practice, the teachings were reinforced by a series of other doctors of the church, including Thomas Aquinas (1225–1274). The result undoubtedly was to cause those people who strayed from the teachings to feel guilty.

Though Protestants in general objected to the imposition of celibacy as a law, they continued to regard it as an ideal, although unattainable by most. Sex, however, was still to be limited to those who were married, and Martin Luther (1483–1546) even ended up condoning bigamy in order to keep sex within marriage. The most positive of the religious reformers in the area of sex was John Calvin (1509–1564), who held that coitus was undefiled, honorable, and holy because it was an institution of God, although Calvin also remained uneasy about the pleasurable aspect. Calvin also accepted the traditional Christian limitations on sex in marriage and on the variations of sexual activities.

Enter the Unbelievers. Though a significant portion of the Christian population failed to live up to the Christian ideal—and even Augustine had accepted prostitution as a necessary evil—it was not until the 17th and 18th centuries that a challenge was raised to some of the basic Christian assumptions. Several factors led to this growing "unbelief." In England, one of the main factors was a reaction by those segments of the population who opposed Puritan attempts to enforce Puritan ideals upon them. In Europe as a whole there was a recognition that other cultures had quite different sexual customs and ideas. Travelers, explorers, and settlers reported on the way things were done in India, China, and the Americas, and this led to an examination of some of the traditional beliefs. The secular state was also reluctant to turn over controls of morals and beliefs to organized religion and was demanding more and more control over such matters. The new scientific discoveries of Galileo and Newton had also given a different view of the way nature worked.

The result was a growing feeling that men and women should follow their natural instincts, and not just do what church authorities told them. Nature, it was believed, prescribed a reason and place for everything, and this could be determined by reason and observation. The most prominent advocates of change were the French *philosophes*, who attempted to apply reason to every phase of life, even sexuality, in order to undermine superstitious religious beliefs. DENIS DIDEROT in the 18th century, for example, complained that "religious institutions have attached the labels 'vice' and 'virtue' to actions that are completely independent of morality." He called for a return to the natural man.

The difficulty with such challenges to traditional religious beliefs about sexuality is that they had no evidence to disprove such traditions except logical thinking. They could question traditional sexual attitudes, but they were not sure what should replace them.

VOLTAIRE (1694–1778), in his *Philosophical Dictionary* (1764), questioned traditional ideas about "Socratic Love": "How can it be that a vice, one which would destroy the human race if it became general, an infamous assault upon nature, can nevertheless be so natural? It looks like the last degree of thought out corruption, and at the same time, it is the usual possession of those who haven't had the time to be corrupted yet. It has entered hearts still new, that haven't known either ambition, nor fraud, nor the thirst of riches; it is a blind youth that, by a poorly straightened-out instinct, throws itself in the confusions upon leaving childhood."

Though Voltaire wound up opposed to laws against morals, the *philosophes* were very much people of their time. Jean Jacques Rousseau, in his *Confessions* (1781–1788) indicated that he masturbated but that the guilt feelings were not entirely eliminated. "Even after the marriageable age, this odd taste, always increasing, carried even to depravity, even to folly, preserved my morals good, the very reverse of what might have been expected."

Still the critics had their influence, most notably in the Napoleonic Code, which removed many sexual activities from the criminal category.

The 18th-century attack on Christian sexual beliefs led primarily by unbvelievers was soon undermined by a counterattack led by believers, who claimed scientific backing for their more restrictive stance. Though these new traditionalists were not scientific investigators themselves, but rather were religious moralists, they looked to such "scientific" writers as Herman Boerhaave, George Ernst Stahl, Frederick Hoffman, and John Brown for proofs of traditional Christian values.

Tissot and His Influence. The key formulator and popularizer of this new theory of "scientific morals" was S. A. D. Tissot, a Swiss physician and devoted Catholic who was concerned with the "rising tide" of sexual immorality around him. In a monograph on masturbation written in 1758, Tissot incorporated some of the ideas of Boerhaave and his successors, to attempt to prove that physical bodies suffer a continual waste, a wastage that ultimately results in death. In fact, death could be speeded up or slowed down by an individual's ability to control this wastage. Tissot wrote that some of the loss was replaced by eating, but even with an adequate diet the body inevitably wasted away through diarrhea, loss of blood, perspiration, and sexual activities. Since seminal emission in males or orgasm in women was normally not involuntary but could be controlled through sexual abstinence, Tissot's argument was seized upon to reinforce traditional religious morality.

The critics of Tissot were hard put to disprove his arguments. Observation, in fact, tended to confirm them. This is because Tissot wrote in the period before third-stage syphilis was recognized as a disease, and so the horrors of that phase of syphilis such as paralysis, mental deterioration, skin ulcers, and others, were regarded by him and other people as evidence of the actual effect of an active sex life upon the individual. Tissot also observed that people in institutional settings, such as the mentally ill, often masturbated, and he believed that this was the cause of their illness rather than a consequence of their boredom. In addition Tissot remarked on the lassitude that seemed to affect people in the aftermath of an orgasm. From these observations he concluded that all of these horrible afflictions came from an overactive sex life, which so weakened the body that it would be subject to all these horrors. Frequent intercourse in itself was dangerous, but, like Augustine, Tissot held that at least it could be risked in order to procreate. Any sex not potentially leading to procreation, however, was so dangerous to one's health that it should be avoided. Disease and early death could easily be interpreted as God's punishment to those who did not obey his rules.

Dr. Tissot held that a waste of semen (or its equivalent in women) would lead to (1) cloudiness of ideas, and sometimes even madness; (2) a decay of bodily powers, resulting in coughs, fevers, and consumption; (3) acute pains in the head, rheumatic pains, and an aching numbness; (4) pimples on the face, suppurating blisters on the nose, breast, and thighs, and painful itchings; (5) eventual weakness of the power of generation as demonstrated by such things as impotence, premature ejaculation, gonorrhea, priapism, and tumors in the bladders; and (6) disordering of the intestines, resulting in constipation, hemorrhoids, and other ailments.

Though Tissot observed enough to know that not everyone with an active sex life suffered these "punishments," he felt it was a precipitating cause, and that masturbation in particular made individuals subject to such afflictions. Females were even more harmed than males by sexual activities, since in addition to all the ills suffered by the male they were subject to hysterical fits, incurable jaundice, violent cramps in the stomach, ulceration of the cervix, and uterine tremors. The result of the widespread acceptance of Tissot's notions was that the earlier assault of unbelievers upon religious assumptions about sex had been beaten back in the name of science.

Pseudoscience in the 19th Century. Some of the 19th-century pseudoscientists went so far as to claim that women had been created by God as asexual creatures whose only function in marriage (and interest in sex) was to endure the lustful desires of their husbands in order to have children. In fact those women who enjoyed sex were not good and true women, but bad women who were prostitutes at heart. Good women, by their disdain of things sexual, in fact were helping to save their more lustful husbands' lives by preventing them from having sex as often as they wanted. Inevitably, the challenge to traditional religious mores made by BENJAMIN FRANKLIN, Charles Brockden Brown, and other writers of the same period was soon undermined in the United States by the new "scientific" morality.

The height of this new religious and scientific morality was reached in the last part of the 19th-century when surgery was performed on children and others to prevent them from touching their genitals. Chastity became the mark of female gentility. Many women accepted this variety of religious morality in part because the idea that they were made of finer stuff gave them one of the few weapons they had in dealing with the male-dominated world. Being regarded as of higher morality gave them the clout to get some of their programs on child welfare and family protection through the legislative process, or even to get their way with their husbands. Those women who might have objected to the status quo were forced by fashion to conform, since the tight corset, trailing skirts, and confining clothing made it difficult if not impossible for them to participate in the more vigorous world of men. The ultimate was reached when some of the "scientific" writers on sex went so far as to "document" that women's brains were inferior to men's since women had been designed by God to bear children; thus all the nervous energy that might have gone into developing brain power was needed to develop the womb and "maternal organs."

With both science and religion arguing for traditional morality, those opposed to the dictates of religion on sexuality had a difficult time challenging it. Ultimately, it was the very ludicrousness of extreme views during the last part of the 19th century that helped defeat them. Science, which had seemed so supportive of religious ideology, proved not to be. The major breakthroughs came in discovering and describing third-stage syphilis, and then by isolating the gonococcus that caused gonorrhea and the spirochete that brought on syphilis. Once these were isolated, cures were also developed by Paul Ehrlich and others. The unbeliever could argue that God or nature might well punish individuals for active sex lives, but the punishment could be avoided in the earthly life by using effective prophylactics or cured by treating the disease.

Modern Sex Research. Scientists also began to investigate sexual behavior itself, and while those who did so were sometimes adherents of organized religion, they had to have the courage to challenge traditional religious attitudes and the self-esteem to investigate a stigmatized field. At first this work, by such individuals as the English physician Havelock Ellis (1859–1939), was designed to raise the same kind of questions Voltaire and Diderot had asked in the 18th century. Ellis was supported by skeptical groups such as the socialists, who wanted to challenge traditional religious ideas of morality. Going further than Ellis were individuals such as Magnus Hirschfeld and SIGMUND FREUD. Hirschfeld compiled numerous sex histories and propagandized for a change, while Freud demonstrated some of the consequences of traditional inhibitions. Though only some of these researchers were unbelievers, the effect of their work was to give information and data to those who wanted to challenge the ideas of organized religious groups.

Much of the sex research in the United States between 1912 and 1952 was sponsored by the Baptist-oriented Rockefeller family, who believed that before dealing with a "problem" it was essential to know the dimensions, causes, and effects. They were not concerned so much with sex but with prostitution, venereal disease, family life, and overpopulation. Because sex research was so delicate a topic, supporters of research tended to avoid giving support to a person who was too controversial; instead they supported "safe" researchers, such as Dr. Alfred C. Kinsey, a zoologist located in a traditional American community, Bloomington, Ind. There was also a desire to support the "true" scientist rather than a social scientist who might be more unorthodox. Such policies were designed to prevent the boat from rocking too hard. Still, the culmination was the Kinsey reports.

Unbelievers proved a receptive audience for

these challenges to traditional morality, but so did many religious people. The Society of Friends (Quakers), as early as the 1940s, was advocating change, and after the Kinsey report appeared, Unitarians, Episcopalians, Congregationalists, and others modified their traditional stance. The major area where the unbelievers both as a group and as individuals broke new ground was in promulgating new findings about sex, in openly challenging the religious beliefs and customs already being undermined by the new science. In England, for example, the atheists CHARLES BRADLAUGH and ANNIE BESANT had been campaigning for dissemination of contraceptive information since the last decades of the 19th century. They were tried and convicted for promulgating obscene literature, but the decision was overturned on appeal.

Not all FREETHOUGHT groups were happy over the actions of Bradlaugh and Besant, and some people mounted a campaign against them. Most freethinkers, however, supported Bradlaugh and Besant. The campaign against them serves to emphasize just how deeply influenced individual freethinkers were by the belief-system of the time. Still it was a freethought publisher who first published Havelock Ellis in English. Carrying on the tradition in the United States was Margaret Sanger (1883–1966), a nurse who became a leader in the campaign for widespread dissemination of contraceptives. EMANUEL HALDEMAN-JULIUS, (1889–1951), publisher of the Little Blue Books provided the main source of sex information for vast numbers of Americans in the 1920s, 1930s, and 1940s; later such humanists as Lester Kirkendall pioneered in introducing sex education into the schools.

Increasingly, however, Sanger and her supporters allowed their religious skepticism to be played down, and as some of the religious objections to change weakened, the majority of teachers and therapists seemed to see their mission as one of reconciling the old and traditional ideas about sex with the new, a movement which is still under way. Though some churches remain hostile to information about sex and the dissemination of contraceptives, as the Catholic church does, the mainline churches' religious teaching and doctrine on such issues have been effectively undermined, not so much by unbelievers but by believers who simply do not follow their religion on such issues. Among Catholic countries, for example, only Ireland remains opposed to both contraception and abortion, although that is changing.

Similar trends existed in other areas of the world where religions had incorporated traditional sexual beliefs and made them part of their religious value system. Adherents to Buddhism, Taoism, Hinduism, and Islam all had different ideas about sex and sexuality from those of western Christians, but increasingly they also have accepted the western scientific ideas first promulgated by "unbelievers" in their way of life, and these ideas are now promulgated by believers. In terms of sex, in fact, it seems that the role of the unbeliever is to be skeptical of traditional assumptions, to challenge them, and to seize upon and disseminate findings contrary to traditional moral values. Some unbelievers did research disproving these traditional values, but mostly they were the advocates and proselytizers of the new findings. As their success grew, others from within traditional religious groups picked up the torch and continued to agitate for change; some groups have changed faster than others, but ultimately all seem to undergo some kind of reevaluation—if only to affirm traditional values, even though these values lack scientific validity. There is a continuous and ongoing agitation for change; at least, such a challenge is still going on within western Christianity as more and more Christians adopt the sexual mores of the society in which they live, and proclaim them as their own.

Once the challenges to traditional ideas had been made, whether by believers or nonbelievers, the nonbelievers were more active in promulgating the new ideas and information. In the post-Kinsey period, among the most receptive audience for new ideas about sexuality were the readers of the *Humanist*, edited by Edwin Wilson and later Paul Kurtz. In fact it was, in part, American HUMANISM's interest in changes and the magazine's popularization of the new that, in the late 1970s and early 1980s, led the Moral Majority and its allies to look upon secular humanism as the causal factor in changing American morals. Nonbelievers, however, were never alone in their efforts, and they were often joined by individuals and groups representing organized religion.

Bibliography

Bullough, Vern L. *Sex, Society and History*. New York: Neale Watson, Science History Publications, 1976.

———. *Sexual Variance in Society and History.* New York: Wiley Interscience, 1978; Chicago: University of Chicago Press, 1980.

Bullough, Vern L., and James Brundage. *Sexual Practices and the Medieval Catholic Church*. Buffalo: Prometheus Books, 1982.

Bullough, Vern L., and Bonnie Bullough. *Sin, Sickness, and Sanity*. New York: Garland Publishers and New American Library, 1977.

Bullough, Vern L., Dorr Legg, Barrie Elcano, and James Kepner. *A Bibliography of Homosexuality*. 2 vols. New York: Garland, 1976.

VERN L. BULLOUGH

SHAFTESBURY, LORD (1621–1683). ANTHONY ASHLEY COOPER, 1ST EARL OF SHAFTESBURY, English statesman. See **Deism**.

SHAW, GEORGE BERNARD (1856–1950), Anglo-Irish playwright, was born in Dublin on July 26. His parents were Irish Protestants, and he was duly baptized into the National Church of Ireland. His father, George Carr Shaw, was in partnership as a wholesale grain dealer. His mother, Lucinda Elizabeth Gurly, had some pretensions of gentility and was a gifted amateur singer. There were two older sisters, Lucinda Frances (Lucy) and Elinor Agnes. The latter died of tuberculosis when she was 20.

Early Life. By all accounts, the Synge Street household was glum. Shaw's mother, though not uncaring, lacked any display of affection. Whether as cause or result, his father had taken to drink, until he swore off and became a silent and bitter teetotaler. The atmosphere was occasionally enlivened by visits from a maternal uncle with a humorous taste for blasphemy, and, eventually, by the presence of Lucinda Elizabeth's voice teacher, who moved in to make a *ménage à trois*. George John Vandeleur Lee was a charismatic musical conductor and teacher who became a second father to young Sonny Shaw—a relationship later alluded to in some of his plays, notably, *Misalliance*.

Irish Protestantism, as Shaw later explained, was not so much a religion as a mark of social caste, which placed the Shaws a step above the common workers and shopkeepers who were Roman Catholic. However, the Shaw income was not sufficient to keep up such pretensions, and

Shaw claimed that he grew up in a state of "genteel poverty" in some ways more debilitating than "abject poverty."

But religion, except for its social status, was taken lightly in the Shaw household. There was some attempt to see that Sonny Shaw was taken to church, but even this stopped by the time he was 10. His nurses were invariably Roman Catholic. He learned his bedtime prayers under their tutelage, and made no objection to being sprinkled with holy water. In his preface to *Immaturity,* one of his more extended autobiographical revelations, he recalls that he composed prayers on an aesthetic rather than a theological basis. "I remember that it was in three movements, like a sonata, and in the best Church of Ireland style . . . I did not care whether my prayers were answered or not. They were a literary performance for the entertainment and propitiation of the Almighty."

At 15 Shaw left school and went to work as clerk in a land agent's office, where he eventually became a cashier. In 1866 the Shaw family, through Lee, secured Torca Cottage as a summer home. Located just outside Dublin, at Dalkey, overlooking Dublin Bay, it was Shaw's first escape from the sordidness of the city. All his life he looked back on the time when his mother told him of it as the one ecstatic moment of happiness in his childhood.

But Lee himself had found Ireland too small to hold his genius, and he crossed the channel in a vain attempt to make his fortune in London. In 1874 Lucinda and Lucy followed (Elinor having been placed in a sanatorium), leaving George with his father in Dublin. By this time the young Shaw had set himself higher sights. He wanted to be a painter, or perhaps a musician.

Interestingly, Shaw's first published work, at the age of 19, was a letter to the editor of *Public Opinion* on the occasion of the visit to Dublin of the famous revivalist team of Moody and Sankey. The letter, signed "S," objected to an earlier correspondent's assessment of the evangelical revival. The revival was crowded, "S" maintained, because it was free entertainment and because Mr. Moody had "the gift of gab." The effect of the revival was to make individuals "highly objectionable members of society," and caused their "unconverted friends to desire a speedy reaction."

Move to London. The next year, 1876, Shaw resigned his position with Uniacke Townshend Co., and with a formal letter of recommendation in his pocket, joined his mother and sister in London. He had been in the process of writing a play—a "passion play"—called "The Household of Joseph." The 49 pages of handwritten manuscript were in verse; it was unfinished and not published until 20 years after Shaw's death. There is little doubt that the household in this piece of juvenilia is that of George Carr Shaw, and that the writer had cast himself in the central role.

In his early London years Shaw boldly proclaimed himself "like Shelley, a socialist, an atheist, and a vegetarian." For nine years he contributed little financial support to his family's London establishment. His mother continued to give voice lessons and had a small annuity. But these were the years of Shaw's maturation and self-education. He spent many of his days in the great reading room of the British Museum and his nights at various debating societies, struggling to overcome his natural shyness and learning to speak in public.

During these years, too, Shaw discovered socialism, first through KARL MARX's *Capital,* which he read in a French translation before it was available in English. In the meantime he began to write novels. He wrote five of them and began a sixth. They attracted little attention, though all but the first (*Immaturity*) were published in some form or other.

In 1884 Shaw joined the newly formed Fabian Society, which gave his life a direction and a purpose. He became, with Sidney and Beatrice Webb, a guiding spirit of that body and its leading spokesman both on the lecture platform and as a pamphleteer. Shortly thereafter he was launched on a career in journalism. He wrote literary, musical, and theatrical reviews, principally for the *Star* and *the Pall Mall Gazette*, from 1888 to 1898. Through these pieces he established himself as a commentator on social and political issues as well as on the arts.

Though obviously attractive to women and attracted to them, Shaw remained aloof from sexual relationships until his 29th birthday, when he was seduced by a widow in her forties, a voice student of his mother. This initiation began a series of philanderings that continued until his marriage to Charlotte Payne-Townshend in 1898 at the age of 42. But sex was always a secondary interest for Shaw. He never gave up an opportunity to lecture on socialism in order to spend a romantic evening.

When CHARLES BRADLAUGH died in 1891, leaving the NATIONAL SECULAR SOCIETY leaderless, the secularists at the Hall of Science kept casting about for a new leader, inviting various speakers to their gatherings much as a church group might try out possible new ministers. At length they got round to Shaw, who had been vocal in his support of Bradlaugh's right to a seat in Parliament. Years later Shaw recalled how he had shocked the secularists by his rejection of MATERI- ALISM as a way of life and by his reliance on purely mystical assumptions. He called them the funda- mentalists of the secularist movement. They did not offer to make him Bradlaugh's successor.

Shaw's playwriting career began inauspi- ciously in 1892 with *Widowers' Houses*. By the turn of the century he had written 10 plays, but he was still not widely known as a dramatist in spite of the fact that these included plays that have since become standard repertory items: *Candida, Arms and the Man, The Devil's Disciple, and Caesar and Cleopatra*. By this time he was doing reason- ably well financially. However, he was overwork- ing, was generally run down, and developed an infection of the left foot, which turned out to be necrosis of the bone and kept him on crutches for a year and a half. To take care of him, his fellow Fabian, Charlotte Payne-Townshend, returned from a vacation in Italy. They were married in a civil ceremony on June 1, 1898. The marriage was a compassionate one in which, apparently, sex had no part, but it was a turning point in Shaw's life. Charlotte brought a sense of order to his life as well as a sizable independent income.

The marriage, along with enforced vacations and sea travel that Charlotte kept arranging, was accompanied by a spiritual change. What had been a general sense of mysticism now became centered in the idea of a specific "Life Force"—a spirit that directs all of life in its evolutionary climb. It made its first official appearance as the motivating force in *Man and Superman*—often regarded as Shaw's most brilliant comedy. The nature of the Life Force was further explicated in the long preface to the play.

From this point forward socialism and the Life Force became the twin forces necessary for the world's salvation. Beginning about 1906, Shaw began making speeches that can only be described as "Life Force sermons." Many of them were delivered to liberal religious congregations. There were times when he equated the Life Force to the concept of God, or spoke of it as "divine Provi- dence." All of his 20th-century plays reflect the power of the Life Force and in some of them it is a central element: *John Bull's Other Island, Major Barbara, The Shewing-Up of Blanco Posnet, An- drocles and the Lion, Saint Joan, Too True to Be Good, The Simpleton of the Unexpected Isles*. But it is in *Back to Methuselah* (1920) that he offers a complete five-part mythology to support his new religion; the unusually long preface to that work is the most complete statement of his credo.

Shaw had many careers—playwright, critic, journalist, platform spellbinder, protestor against censorship, unpopular critic of Britain's war poli- cies, producer and director of many of his own plays, champion of the rights of women. In addi- tion to his 54 plays and his more than 20 volumes of nondramatic writings, Shaw was probably the most indefatigable correspondent of modern times. Of his published letters it is appropriate to note his 25-year exchange with the enclosed nun, Dame Laurentia McLachlan of Stanbrook Abbey. This correspondence contains vigorous efforts by the nun to convert Shaw to Catholicism and Shaw's equally vigorous attempts to lure the reverend mother away from orthodox theology. Both, of course, failed. And Dame Laurentia could never forgive Shaw for his blasphemous picture of Jesus as "the conjuror" in his fable *The Adventures of the Black Girl in Her Search for God* (1932). Nevertheless the correspondence continued until the end of Shaw's life. He died at his home in Ayot St. Lawrence on Nov. 2, 1950, at the age of 94.

Shaw would never allow himself to be called a Christian. Yet he can be classed as an unbeliever only in the sense that there was, as he said at the end of his life, no church in the world that would receive him, or any in which he could consent to be received.

Bibliography

Abbott, Anthony S. *Shaw and Christianity*. New York: Seabury, 1965.

Bentley, Eric. *Bernard Shaw, 1856–1950*. Amended edition. New York: New Directions, 1957.

Chesterton, G. K. *George Bernard Shaw*. New York: Hill and Wang, 1958.

Ervine, St. John. *Bernard Shaw: His Life, Work, and Friends*. New York: Morrow, 1956.

Pearson, Hesketh. *Bernard Shaw: His Life and Personality*. London: Collins, 1942.

Shaw, Bernard. *An Autobiography*. 2 vols. Se- lected from his writings by Stanley Weintraub. New York: Weybright and Talley, 1969, 1970.

———. *Collected Letters*. 2 vols. Ed. Dan H. Laurence. New York: Dodd Mead, 1965, 1972.

———. *Collected Plays with Their Prefaces*. 7 vols. Ed. Dan H. Laurence. New York: Dodd Mead,

1970–1974.

"Shaw and Religion." Entire issue of the journal *Shaw, the Annual of Bernard Shaw Studies* 1 (1981).

Smith, Warren Sylvester, ed. *Shaw on Religion.* New York: Dodd Mead, 1967.

———. *The Religious Speeches of Bernard Shaw.* University Park: Penn State U. Press, 1963.

WARREN SYLVESTER SMITH

SHELLEY, PERCY BYSSHE (1792–1822), one of the luminaries of English romantic poetry, lived briefly but intensely. His exuberant poetry, radical and uncompromising in its ideas, has not been received as entirely to the taste of either the 19th or the 20th centuries. But the careful student can have no doubt of the genius of Shelley's lyricism, allied to a profound and idealistic faith in the eternal principles of liberty and beauty.

Shelley's life was one of generosity, integrity, and sorrow. Though buffeted by the constraints and complexities of convention and human nature, Shelley was driven throughout by his principles and his high ideals. Born into an aristocratic and well-to-do family on Aug. 4, 1792, Shelley was educated at Eton where, characteristically out of step with his peers, he came to be known as "mad Shelley." At Oxford, he thought and read deeply and unconventionally, and with his friend Thomas Jefferson Hogg produced a pamphlet, *The Necessity of Atheism* (1811). Their refusal to bow to college authority and repudiate the pamphlet, which they had sent to a number of bishops, led to their removal from college.

As an 18-year-old idealist, Shelley eloped with and married Harriet Westbrook, the 16-year-old daughter of a retired tavern keeper, in part to rescue her from parental oppression. Together, in 1812 they agitated politically in Ireland, distributing an *Address to the Irish People.* Ever an advocate of the individual's rights and a fierce opponent of all forms of tyranny, Shelley, in his warmth of feeling, could sometimes misapprehend character. Certainly his alliance with Harriet turned out to be an intellectual mismatch. Though the couple had two children, Shelley found himself, as he often did throughout his life, drawn to an ideal outside the domestic circle. From his youth an admirer of the radical tenets of WILLIAM GODWIN, Shelley fell in love with Godwin's daughter by Mary Wollstonecraft—Mary Wollstonecraft Godwin. Godwin's principles influenced both *A Refutation of Deism* (1814) and Shelley's elopement with Mary the same year. With Mary's half-sister, Claire Clairmont, Shelley and Mary toured the continent until the lack of funds forced them home.

With the death in 1815 of his grandfather, Shelley came into a handsome income, which he often put at the disposal of those who he thought needed it more than he did. This included the improvident Godwin, who had been disappointed at his daughter's putting into practice his own disregard for the convention of marriage. In 1816 Shelley again visited the continent, and wrote perhaps the most quintessential of his poems, the "Hymn to Intellectual Beauty," with its understated linking of freedom and Platonic idealism. In late 1816, Harriet drowned herself. Within the month Shelley married Mary, already the mother of their first child. During 1816 Shelley published his *Proposal for Putting Reform to the Vote,* as well as the narrative poem *Laon and Cythna,* which was withdrawn and, with its allusions to God's agency and to incest tempered, republished as *The Revolt of Islam.*

During this time Shelley developed his friendships with the journalist Leigh Hunt and the satirist Thomas Love Peacock. In early 1818, continuing what had become a peripatetic life, and followed later by Mary and their two children (both soon to die), Shelley left England once again, bitter at having been denied custody of his children by Harriet because of his beliefs and style of life. Shelley never returned to England; he moved about Italy and settled finally, and happily, among friends in Pisa. He wrote such central works as his visionary drama of political, social, and psychological liberation, *Prometheus Unbound*; his play on political and parental tyranny, *The Cenci*; the lyrical "Ode to Liberty" and "To a Skylark," as well as more occasional poems like "The Mask of Anarchy," "England in 1819," and "A Song: To the Men of England," a rousing challenge to the laboring classes of England.

During his last years, Shelley's output was prodigious, including such major works as "Epipsychidion" (1821), a record of his infatuation with Teresa Vivian, imprisoned by her father, with its famous exaltation of free love and poetic autobiography; "A Defence of Poetry" (1821; published 1840), a central statement of romanticism's expectations of poetry; and perhaps the finest elegy in

English, "Adonais" (1821), written on the death of John Keats. "Adonais" is an exemplary statement of Shelley's highest principles of idealism and the depths of his unhappiness with life. Indeed, the glorious anticipation of death at the end of the poem seemed to bear fruit, a year later, in July 1822, when Shelley sailed to his death, drowned in the capsizing of his boat while returning from a visit to Byron and Hunt. Shelley's body was cremated and his ashes buried in Rome in the cemetery evoked in "Adonais."

Shelley's poetry is his claim to immortality. His early novels, written at Eton (*Zastrozzi* and *St. Irvyne*) are juvenile in both senses of the word; his philosophical prose, though compelling in its fervor, is ultimately interesting for hermeneutic reasons; and his plays largely the same. But his poetry burns with immortal passion and melody, from the iconoclastic visions of the early *Queen Mab* (1813) to the richly evolving complexity of "The Triumph of Life," which he was working on at the time of his death. In all that he did and wrote, Shelley was a fearless critic of convention, and an irrepressible visionary of what could and would be.

Religious Views. Shelley never abated in his opposition to Christianity. He had nothing but disdain for "the impudent contradictions and stupendously absurd assertions which the teachers of the Christian religion pretend to deduce from the Old and New Testament" ("On Miracles and Christian Doctrine"). Shelley's antipathy largely derived from Christianity's oppressive constraint of human nature and its union with tyrannical monarchy in politically subordinating and morally perverting the great masses of men. The passion of *Queen Mab* never left Shelley: "Kings, priests, and statesmen, blast the human flower / Even in its tender bud; their influence darts / Like subtle poison through the bloodless veins / Of desolate society."

Whereas, for Shelley, classical Greece had seen the highest fulfillment of man as a free being, the introduction of Christianity withered man's spirit and constrained his estimate of himself. In "Hellas," Shelley, typically, keeps the growth of Christianity separate from Jesus (like Shelley himself a martyr for his high ideals), whom he viewed as a "Promethean conqueror" treading the "thorns of death and shame." With Christianity, "Hell, Sin, and Slavery" prey on man like ravening bloodhounds, and tight-lipped evangelicalism destroys paganism's more fulfilling mythologies: "The powers of earth and air / Fled from the folding star

of Bethlehem; / Apollo, Pan, and Love / And even Olympian Jove / Grew weak, for killing Truth had glared on them."

In the "Hymn to Intellectual Beauty," Shelley's sensitivity to the numinous experience he thought religion should be (as in the "Defence of Poetry," "the partial apprehension of the agencies of the invisible world") deepens his denunciation of "the name of God and ghosts and Heaven," which are the "poisonous names with which our youth is fed."

Bibliography

Cameron, Kenneth Neil. *The Young Shelley: Genesis of a Radical.* New York: Macmillan, 1950.

―――. *Shelley: The Golden Years.* Cambridge: Harvard U. Press, 1974.

Dawson, P. M. S. *The Unacknowledged Legislator: Shelley and Politics.* Oxford: Clarendon, 1980.

Foot, Paul. *Red Shelley.* London: Sidgewick and Jackson, 1980.

Wasserman, Earl R. *Shelley: A Critical Reading.* Baltimore: Johns Hopkins U. Press, 1971.

Webb, Timothy. *Shelley: A Voice Not Understood.* Atlantic Highlands, N.J.: Humanities Press, 1977.

TERRY L. MEYERS

SHINTOISM. See **Japan, Unbelief in.**

SHRINES AND MONUMENTS OF UNBELIEF. A Catholic thinks of a shrine as a place to worship God or to reflect upon the important events that befell some person of esteem to the church at that spot. The unbeliever, too, has shrines and monuments that are important to him, although he does not worship there. Rather, there are a number of statues, graves, and buildings where an important event in the history of unbelief occurred, or which are memorials to heroes of unbelief. The purpose of this article is to locate and examine the most important of these sites.

We can start with the obvious: sites associated with THOMAS PAINE. The birthplace of Paine (Thetford, Norfolk, England) has a statue of him, erected by JOSEPH LEWIS. The site of Paine's birthplace is marked with a plaque, courtesy of the Thomas Paine Society, while the Thetford Public Library has a large collection of Paine items. Paine is also commemorated by a statue in New Rochelle, N.Y., where he lived for many years, and by the presence of the cottage where he lived, which has been turned into a museum. Next to the cottage is the Huguenot Historical Society, which incorporates the collection of the defunct Thomas Paine Historical Association. These are largely printed materials relating to Paine. There is also a statue of him in Morristown, N.J., in Burnham Park, donated by Joseph Lewis. Lewis also donated a statue of Paine to France; it is located at Montsouris Park in Paris. The site of the house where Paine died in New York City is located in Greenwich Village and is marked by a plaque. He was originally buried in New Rochelle, but William Cobbett disinterred the body and moved it to England in 1819, hoping to have a worthy memorial erected there. His plans ran into trouble, and nothing was done. The body has disappeared. There is also a bust of Paine in the Hall of Fame at New York University, New York City.

There are a number of monuments to ROBERT G. INGERSOLL. His birthplace in Dresden, N.Y., still stands, and at various times has been a small museum dedicated to Ingersoll. There is a statue of him in Glen Oak Park in Peoria, Ill. It was erected in the 1920s with funds raised by an appeal. Ingersoll's grave is number 1620 in Arlington National Cemetery in Virginia. There is a rectangular stone with the name "Ingersoll" and an inscription from Ingersoll's writings on the other side. Ingersoll's ashes and his wife are buried at the site, which overlooks the Tomb of the Unknown Soldier from a hillside. There used to be a plaque on the wall of the Gramercy Park Hotel in New York City, announcing it to be the site of one of Ingersoll's houses (he lived there in the 1890s). The house where Ingersoll died still stands. It was his son-in-law's house in Dobbs Ferry, N.Y., which he called "Walston." The house, a stone, castle-like building, sits on top of the highest hill in Dobbs Ferry. Ingersoll's period in Peoria is marked by several plaques on buildings. Among them is the site of Ingersoll's home in Peoria, now marked by a plaque in a parking lot where the house stood.

DEROBIGNE MORTIMER BENNETT is buried in Greenwood Cemetery in Brooklyn. His gravestone is a large obelisk, with copper plates on all four sides, containing a picture of Bennett and extracts from his writings. The monument was donated by "one thousand friends." It is just off Greenwood Avenue, near the intersection of Sylvan Road and Ossier Path.

EMANUEL HALDEMAN-JULIUS is a man without a gravesite. His ashes were scattered over the grave of his wife Marcet in the small cemetery in Cedarville, Ill. No stone was ever erected on the spot. ABNER KNEELAND was buried on his farmstead in what was then called Salubria, Iowa. A number of years later (1881) the grave was moved to a cemetery in nearby Farmington, where it is still located. FRANCES WRIGHT was buried in Cincinnati, Ohio, at the Spring Grove Cemetery.

The ashes of MONCURE D. CONWAY are interred in Kensico Cemetery, Kensico, N.Y. The grave monument of Joseph Coveny, erected as a large Freethought Memorial, can be found in the Buchanan, Mich., City Cemetery, on Front Street. There is a freethinkers' cemetery called Thomas Cemetery near Fergus Falls, Minn. It is off County Route 4, near Vergas, Minn. The graves are mostly of German-American freethinkers.

The graves of many British freethinkers can easily be visited. RICHARD CARLILE and HENRY HETHERINGTON are buried in Kensal Green Cemetery, London. The former's grave is poorly marked, however. GEORGE JACOB HOLYOAKE, AUSTIN HOLYOAKE, KARL MARX, WILLIAM KINGDON CLIFFORD, CHARLES WATTS, and a number of lesser freethinkers are buried in Highgate Cemetery, London. The graves of CHARLES BRADLAUGH and WILLIAM STEWART ROSS are in the Nonconformists' section of the Brookwood Necropolis, in Brookwood, southwest of London. THOMAS HENRY HUXLEY is buried in Marylebone Cemetery, Finchley.

A number of sites in the United Kingdom have historic associations with unbelief. For example, in London, a site on Fleet Street at the West Corner with Bouverie Street (now a Wimpy's hamburger restaurant) was the location of Carlile's shop for many years. It was here that he printed and sold the books and magazines that led to his various arrests. On the site of the Rotunda, where Carlile and ROBERT TAYLOR lectured, there is a new building. It is on Blackfriars Road at the corner of Stamford Street. Johnson's Court was for many years the site of the Rationalist Press Association offices. This is a small street which runs from Fleet Street, back into the site of Samuel Johnson's house. There is now a modern office building on the site.

GEORGE WILLIAM FOOTE's Progressive Publishing Company, and the place where the FREE-THINKER magazine had its birth, was at 28 Stonecutter Street, another tiny street off Fleet. A modern office building also occupies this site. JOSEPH MAZZINI WHEELER's home for many years was at 27 Enkel Street. This small street, off Holloway Road, is located right behind a large Woolworth's store. This site is not far from Holloway Gaol, where Foote served a year for blasphemy. The prison still stands. The Giltspur Street Compter (jail), where Carlile spent a number of years, has been demolished. It stood at the junction of Giltspur and Newgate Streets. The site is marked by a plaque.

A site associated with both Carlile and Charles Bradlaugh can be found on Warner Street, off Hackney Road. At 1 Warner Street was the home of Carlile's widow, where Bradlaugh took refuge, while at 13 Warner Place was one of Bradlaugh's boyhood homes. In the public square of Northampton, is located a life-size statue of Bradlaugh, who represented Northampton in Parliament for many years. There is also a marble bust of Bradlaugh in the Shoreditch Public Library.

One of the famous freethought societies is still in existence in its own building. This is the LEICESTER SECULAR SOCIETY, located at Humberstone Gate in Leicester. The Hall of Science, at 142 Old Street, London, is no longer standing. The earlier Hall of Science, at 58 City Road, is also gone. D. M. Bennett named his first publishing building the "Hall of Science." It was at 141 Eighth Street in New York. There was also an earlier Hall of Science, built by Frances Wright and ROBERT DALE OWEN in New York in 1829, but no trace of it remains.

One of the most famous buildings in London associated with the freethought movement was Conway Hall in Red Lion Square. This was built in 1929, to replace the South Place Chapel. This building was demolished, except for the facade, which was attached to the outside of the new building placed on the site.

The Rationalist Press Association moved from its two sites in Johnson's Court to its own building at 88 Islington High Street. The building is still occupied by the R.P.A. The NATIONAL SECULAR SOCIETY occupied a series of rented premises, starting with the old Hall of Science building on City Road. Among the locations were Stonecutter Street, Drury Lane, Farringdon Street, and two locations on Holloway Road. The offices are presently at 702 Holloway Road.

There are a number of sites in Australia and New Zealand that relate to freethought history. In Auckland, N.Z., there is Rationalist House in Symonds Street. It is the headquarters of the New Zealand Rationalist Society. Nearby, in Symonds Street Cemetery, is the grave of CHARLES SOUTHWELL. In Dunedin, N.Z., is the building which served as a Freethought Hall for many years, although it is no longer used for that purpose. In Melbourne one can still see the facade and remodeled interior of JOSEPH SYMES' Hall of Science, which now forms part of St. Vincent's Hospital.

Miscellaneous sites throughout the United Kingdom associated with unbelief include the following. In Brighton, the building called Eastern Lodge, the place where Holyoake spent his last years, still stands. In Wales is the site of New Lanark, ROBERT OWEN's utopian colony. In Edinburgh is the site of the bookstore from which Thomas Paterson and Matilda Roalfe sold freethought books; it was at 102 Nicholson Street. Near Corby in Northamptonshire is Oakham Gaol, in which Robert Taylor spent a year following his blasphemy conviction. His two-year term after a second blasphemy trial was spent in Horsemonger Lane Gaol, London, but it is no longer standing. In Bristol, in Narrow Wine Street, is the location of the publishing offices of Charles Southwell's *Oracle of Reason*, the first openly atheistic magazine in English, and of his bookstore. Both were located there in 1842–43. In Manchester is the headquarters of the Cooperative Union. Holyoake was one of the founders of this movement, and his papers, as well as those of Robert Owen, are housed in the library there.

There are portraits of Carlile, HERBERT SPENCER, PERCY BYSSHE SHELLEY, Huxley, JOHN STUART MILL, W. K. Clifford, and Paine in the National Portrait Gallery in London.

Here is a grab bag of miscellaneous sites in the United States that are associated with FREE-THOUGHT and unbelief. In Sauk Center, Wis., is the old FREIE GEMEINDE hall, now used as a Unitarian meeting house. In Milwaukee, on Jefferson Avenue, is the Freie Gemeinde hall of Milwaukee, but it is no longer used for freethought purposes. In Silverton, Ore., was the site of the Liberal University, the first freethought school. In San Diego, the office of the Truth Seeker Company was located. It has been moved several times since being located there in 1964; the first site became part of a college campus. In October 1981, a house that served as the office of the Truth Seeker Company was firebombed by an arsonist and totally destroyed.

In Vijayawada, India, is the Atheist Centre run by the family of GORA. In Rome, at the Piazza del Flora, is a statue of GIORDANO BRUNO, who was burned at the stake near this spot in 1600. In Leningrad, in the U.S.S.R., the former Kazan Cathedral has been turned into the Museum of the History of Religion and Atheism. The octagonal boyhood home of CLARENCE DARROW still stands in Kinsman, Ohio.

Bibliography

Gaylor, Anne. "Joseph Coveny." *Freedom from Religion Foundation Newsletter,* Sept. 1982.

Kent, William. *London for Heretics.* London: Watts, 1932.

Macdonald, G. M. *Fifty Years of Freethought.* 2 vols. New York: Truth Seeker, 1929.

GORDON STEIN

SINCLAIR, UPTON (1878–1965), American writer. See **American Literature, Unbelief in.**

SKEPTICISM

DEFINITION

Skepticism, in general, is the questioning of beliefs, dogmas, or claims to knowledge. The term derives from the Greek *skepticos,* meaning inquirer. The term was broadened to include questioning and doubting as well, so that a skeptic asks whether various views are true, are based on adequate evidence, or should be accepted or believed.

Politically everyone is skeptical about some claims. We doubt the assertions of advertisers, of salesmen, of politicians, of storytellers, and so on. As we become more aware of when and why we doubt certain kinds of news, we organize our doubts into a more general kind of skepticism.

In philosophy skepticism is the questioning of any knowledge claims. One form of this is to deny that any unquestionable knowledge can be discovered. A more extreme form is to question this denial as well. In either case, philosophical skepti-

cism involves a series of doubts about kinds of knowledge. Sense information has been questioned by pointing out that our senses vary according to internal and external conditions. Can we be sure that what we see with eyeglasses is correct? Can we be sure that what we see at twilight is correct? Can we be sure that what we see when we have consumed several glasses of wine is correct? In order to tell what sense information is reliable, we require some standard or criterion of correct vision, hearing, and so forth. But how do we tell what is the correct criterion? Just because optometrists say 20/20 vision is correct does not guarantee that it is an accurate view of the world.

The skeptic questions the standards and their applicability to reality. Skepticism, in its general philosophical form, has raised epistemological problems—that is, questions about knowledge, how it is gained, and when it is reliable. These epistemological queries have been raised about sense information in general, about generalizations from such information, about rational procedures and inferences, and about any conclusions about the world. So, skeptics have challenged scientific claims about various aspects of nature, metaphysical claims about the nature of reality, ethical claims about the content of moral rules, and so forth.

Skepticism Applied to Religion. In questioning accepted beliefs, one of the most challenging forms of skepticism has been the one applied to religious beliefs. In ancient times this took the form of casting doubt on traditional mythologies. As religions developed, so did the skeptical questioning of them. This has involved, in the Judeo-Christian tradition, the application of certain kinds of philosophical skepticism to the basic claims of Judaism and Christianity—questioning the evidence concerning the existence and nature of God, and the evidence that scripture contains special information about man's relation to God and about the nature and destiny of man.

Skeptics have contended that there is insufficient evidence from sense experience that there is a God. Can he/she be seen? Can we trust the reports of those who claim to have seen him/her, and so on? As theology became more refined, it based its claims about God's existence and nature on certain sophisticated arguments, such as (1) the ontological argument, claiming that from the very definition of God it follows that he/she necessarily exists; (2) the cosmological argument claiming that there must be an ultimate first cause of the universe;

and (3) the argument from design, claiming that it can be inferred from the order that is observed in the world that there must be a designer. Skeptics have sought to cast doubt on these arguments and to show that either the arguments are invalid or inconclusive. DAVID HUME and IMMANUEL KANT presented definitive criticisms of these arguments. Even some of the greatest theologians accepted this kind of skepticism, and insisted that religion was based on faith, not rational or scientific evidence, and that the content of this faith was revealed in the Bible. (See GOD, EXISTENCE OF.)

The challenge to the Bible has engendered another kind of skepticism, doubts concerning the content of Judeo-Christianity. This kind of skepticism has developed since the Renaissance, and has centered on two kinds of questions: (1) those concerning the status of the Bible; and (2) those concerning the truth of its content. After Europe became Christian, the Bible was accepted as the statement of what the world is like, how it came to be, and what man's role is in it. The Bible does not purport to prove the existence of God. It just begins with the announcement "In the beginning God created heaven and earth," and then proceeds to describe God's actions, man's interactions with God, God's direction of human history, and a forecast of what will be the culmination of our history. It was traditionally accepted that the account in the first books of the Bible was written by Moses, who received the information contained in these books by divine revelation.

Modern religious skepticism has involved questioning the claims about the Mosaic authorship, about the revelatory status of the Bible, and about the truth of the contents of the Bible. Biblical criticism since the 17th century has raised doubts about whether the Pentateuch had just one author and about whether it was written at one time or over many centuries. In questioning the Mosaic authorship, doubts were then raised about the accuracy of the text (has it changed over the years in the course of so much copying and recopying?) and, more important, about the special status of the text. If several people wrote the text and if it was altered and changed over the years, can we be sure that it contains superhumanly revealed information? Can we determine if it is in reality different from mythology, or if it is early Jewish history written from a one-sided perspective? What evidence is there that it is a revealed document, and not just a human product? The traditional assurances by the Catholic church were questioned, leaving the revelatory character of the text in doubt.

A deepening religious skepticism resulted from questioning the accuracy of the content of scripture. The Bible had been accepted by Jews and Christians as the history of the human race from its beginnings with Adam's creation. Evidence of the existence of people in America, the South Sea Islands, Greenland, and so forth raised the possibility that not everybody was a descendent of Adam and a survivor of the Flood. Information about the age of the earth, of flora and fauna, and of human groups has cast doubt on the literal accuracy of the account in Genesis. Modern science does not support the story of a universal flooding of the whole planet. Examination of archaeological remains in the Middle East raise questions about whether the Bible encompasses all of the histories of human societies in the area, or just the history of a rather small group, the ancient Hebrews.

Skeptics like PIERRE BAYLE questioned the message of the scriptures. Bayle sought to show that the moral character of the leading figures in the Old Testament and of Christian leaders from early days to the present is hardly defensible. Far better moral models are to be found in the character of a professed atheist like BENEDICT SPINOZA. VOLTAIRE followed out this line of skepticism to question whether the Bible did in fact contain a moral message, or rather represented a nasty kind of immorality.

The skeptics who have pressed their doubts against the Judeo-Christian tradition have marshaled evidence from modern science to challenge various religious beliefs. From Galileo onward, the findings and theories of modern science have raised questions about whether supernatural claims were compatible with the best results in physics and chemistry. Charles Darwin and modern biologists have presented the theory of evolution that questions the religious claims about the separate creation of man. (See EVOLUTION AND UNBELIEF.) More recent theories in psychology and the social sciences have questioned whether religion is more than a way humans look at the world and whether religion contains objective truths about the world. The so-called warfare between science and theology, especially over the last two centuries, has provided increasing ammunition for the religious skeptic.

As a result of applying skepticism to traditional beliefs, many religious thinkers have modified their claims, either in terms of what evidence they contend is available, or in terms of what beliefs can still be accepted. On the one hand, liberal theologians have reinterpreted religious claims so that they do not conflict with the best available scientific theories and data. They have stressed the positive moral teachings, while demythologizing the supernatural claims. On the other hand, some staunch believers have accepted the full consequences of the application of skepticism to religion, namely, that there is insufficient evidence to support any religious belief, while insisting that beliefs are to be accepted on faith. From Blaise Pascal and Sören Kierkegaard to 20th-century neoorthodox theologians, passionate believers have asserted their faith, regardless of the rational or scientific evidence.

Another skeptical motif that has been raised against religious belief as far back as the Book of Job is whether God can be believed to be allpowerful and good and just in view of what happens in the world. If God controls everything, then why is there evil? If he/she cannot prevent it, then is he/she really a deity? Religious skepticism arising from a consideration of the problem of evil has recurred throughout the centuries. More recently there has been a resurgence of discussion of this issue as a result of the horrors of the Nazi-directed Holocaust. Can one believe there is a just God who could permit millions of innocent people to be slain? Some thinkers, examining the question, have questioned whether any God still exists. Out of this has emerged what is called the death-of-God theology, in which belief in any supernatural being is denied. (See EVIL, PROBLEM OF.)

During the last three to four hundred years religious skepticism has eroded much of the confidence in traditional religious beliefs for many people. The application of skeptical questions to basic claims of the Jewish and Christian traditions has weakened the acceptance of these religious views, and has led to the development of secular ideologies. Now these ideologies are being submitted to similar skeptical bombardments leading to a crisis about what is believable. Much current literature and philosophy reflects the prevalence of skepticism over firm beliefs in most areas of human concern. (See CHRISTIANITY, UNBELIEF WITHIN. JUDAISM, UNBELIEF WITHIN.)

HISTORY

The history of skepticism, as an organized intellec-

tual questioning of accepted beliefs, begins in ancient Greece. In the Hellenistic period, the skeptical observations of earlier thinkers were developed into groups of arguments to show either (1) that nothing can be known, or (2) that as yet there is inadequate evidence to determine if any knowledge is possible. In either case people should suspend judgment concerning all knowledge claims. The first of these views is called Academic skepticism, the second Pyrrhonian skepticism.

Academic skepticism traced its origins to a saying of Socrates. When the Delphic oracle told Socrates that he was the wisest of the Athenians, he realized he was the wisest because he alone was aware that he knew nothing. Teachers in Plato's Academy Arcesilaus (c. 315–241 B.C.) to Carneades (c. 213–129 B.C.) worked out a theoretical formulation of this view, in terms of a forceful series of arguments to show that nothing can be known by our senses or our reason. These arguments appear in writings by Cicero and Diogenes Laertius, and in the attempted refutation of skepticism by St. Augustine.

Arcesilaus and Carneades sought to establish that there was no way to distinguish true or real perceptions from illusory ones. No certain criterion was known. Therefore, they contended, one had to suspend judgment on all knowledge claims about any reality beyond our immediate experience. Instead, all that we possess is reasonable or probable information that may or may not actually be true. Acting on probabilities is sufficient to guide us through life.

The views of Academic skeptics dominated the teachings in Plato's Academy from the 3rd century until the 1st century, when Cicero studied there. Cicero discussed the teachings in his *De Academia* and *De Natura Deorum* ("Of the Nature of the Gods"). In the latter work, arguments were presented to show that there are no adequate proofs of the existence or nature of God. However, the Academics claimed they accepted traditional religion since it seemed to be the most reasonable thing to do. They did not challenge the religion of their society as the Stoic or Epicurean philosophers did.

The Pyrrhonian skeptics derive their name from a somewhat legendary figure, Pyrrho of Elis (c. 360–c. 270), who was supposed to have lived as a skeptic or doubter about everything. We are told he suspended judgment about all claims about the nature of reality, while living according to the way things appeared to him. He is supposed to have said that this way he attained happiness, or at least peace of mind or tranquility.

Pyrrho's attitude was developed into a systematic attack on all kinds of dogmatic teachings by Aenesidemus in Alexandria in the 1st century B.C. A school developed among some medical doctors, and its arguments were organized and written down by one of its last known leaders, the Greek Sextus Empiricus (probably lived about A.D. 200), in his *Outlines of Pyrrhonism* and his treatises against the dogmatists.

Sextus Empiricus. Beginning with the ten tropes (ways of skeptical argumentation leading to suspense of judgment about what is not evident) attributed to Aenesidemus, Sextus developed an attack on knowledge claims based on sense information, on custom, and on reasoning. Sextus raised questions about criteria that could be employed to judge when our sensory or rational faculties were operating correctly. He showed how our moral beliefs are relative to the customs of our society. The result of all of this was not to deny that any knowledge is possible but to lead the seeker after knowledge to suspend judgment on all non-evident questions. By so doing, people will achieve *ataxaria*, a state of being unperturbed, and they can then live undogmatically following the dictates of nature and custom and acting on how things appear to be. Sextus said that Pyrrhonians were doctors treating a disease called "rashness" or dogmatism, which led to great mental distress. The cure was to suspend judgment, at which point one was no longer disturbed about whether various beliefs were true or false. If the opponent asked whether Pyrrhonism itself was a set of true beliefs, Sextus said it was like a purge that eliminates everything including itself.

Sextus pointed out that the Pyrrhonians were the least dangerous philosophic sect with regard to political, social, or religious beliefs. They suspended judgment about whether any of these were true or false but accepted the ones prevailing in their society undogmatically. Hence the Pyrrhonians were not revolutionaries, or opponents of traditional religion.

In contrast to the sort of neutrality or undogmatic acceptance of prevailing religious beliefs, criticism of Greek and Roman mythology developed among both the Stoics and the Epicureans. The former claimed that there was a universal reason pervading the universe. Therefore the capricious picture of the activities of the deities could not be taken as true. The Epicureans accepted only

sensory and material beings and insisted everything could be explained in terms of the acting of material atoms. So, there was no need to believe in supernatural forces or Providence. (See ANCIENT WORLD, UNBELIEF IN THE.)

Some of the critical views of late Greek thought seem to have been raised within ancient Judaism. The term used in the Talmud for a religious skeptic or a person who doubts any of the claims of Judaism is an *Aipikuros,* derived from Epicurus' name. No organized form of this kind of questioning has come down to us, but Jewish works from the Talmud onward indicate the need to answer various doubters.

The school of philosophical skepticism disappeared in the Roman world as the empire became Christianized. The last major indication of skeptical influence appears in St. Augustine's early work, *Contra Academicos,* in which he tried to overcome the doubts he learned from Cicero's writing. Augustine became a believing Christian by accepting revealed truths as the answer to skepticism. "I believe in order to know," he declared. Then faith can seek understanding.

Jewish and Muslim Skeptics. During the Christian Middle Ages, little of Greek skepticism was known or considered beyond what was presented by Augustine. Even the term *skeptic* was not used in medieval writings. However, in the Islamic world there is more indication of skeptical views. The Muslim and Jewish philosophers and theologians in Islamic Spain and in the Near East had more direct access to classical writings. They also lived and wrote in a world in which there were competing claims to religious knowledge amongst Jews, Christians, Muslims, and many kinds of pagans. Attempts to justify religious positions led to two quite opposite kinds of skepticism, one as a road to faith and the other as a way of making philosophy independent of religion.

The Jewish writer Judah Halevi and the Muslim writer Al-Ghazzali propounded the first kind of view. Halevi wrote a dialogue, *The Kuzari,* which tells how a Jew, a Christian, and a Muslim try to convince the king of the Khazars (a medieval kingdom in southern Russia) of the truth of their religion. The Jew wins. In the course of developing his case, Halevi attacked the possibility of gaining true religious knowledge through science and philosophy and insisted on the primacy of revelation.

Al-Ghazzali went further than Halevi did, attacking the basic tenets of the prevailing Aristotelian philosophy and theology of his contemporaries. In his *Auto Destruction of the Philosophers* he argued that no rational knowledge about the world is possible. God is omnipotent and can do and cause anything at any time. Therefore, no state of affairs can be necessary unless God so wills. Any science or philosophy is an attempt to limit what God can do (by stating fixed laws or conditions of the world) and is blasphemous. Only through mysticism can one become aware of God's will. Al-Ghazzali was a Sufi; his views led to the condemnation and expulsion of Muslim philosophers from Spain.

Averroës and Moses Maimonides. The greatest opponent of Al-Ghazzali was the last great Islamic philosopher, Averroës, who wrote the *Destruction of the Destruction,* as well as a series of commentaries on Aristotle trying to justify Aristotle's rational philosophy. To avoid the conflict Al-Ghazzali posed between philosophy and theology, Averroës (1126–1198) sought to show that each dealt with a different way of gaining truth. The rational scientific person pursued one course, through Aristotelian science and philosophy. Other methods were used by theologians, by religious people, and so forth. Averroës did not say that the philosopher-scientist had the best or the better way, but his orthodox opponents attacked him on these grounds. Averroës also stressed that Aristotle's philosophy denied the creation of the world and personal immortality. If one accepted the philosopher's way to truth, this seemed to deny basic religious claims.

This problem was central in the attempt by Averroës' Jewish contemporary and fellow Cordoban, Rabbi Moses ben Maimonides (1135–1204), in his *Guide for the Perplexed.* Maimonides was a thoroughgoing Aristotelian. However, he contended that when rational science and philosophy came in conflict with faith, this showed that reason could not resolve the issue, and one ought to accept revelation as the guide. So, Maimonides showed that reason could not determine if the world is eternal or was created in time, or whether the individual soul dies with the body or is immortal. But scripture gives us answers that are beyond rational justification, he maintained. Maimonides was attacked by orthodox rabbis because they feared that he was casting doubt on various basic claims of Judaism by asserting that they cannot be justified by reason. His works were banned or censored.

The writings of Averroës and Maimonides were translated into Latin and became available to Christian thinkers in the 13th century. This seems to have created a crisis, leading to various condemnations of Aristotelian and Averroëan ideas. The so-called Latin Averroists stressed the rigorous, logical conclusion of Aristotle's views, showing that they came into direct conflict with articles of faith. These thinkers were accused of denying the ultimate truth of religion and of holding that something can be true in philosophy and science and false in theology, and vice-versa (the doctrine of the double truth).

Most scholars, however, doubt that any Latin Averroist from the 13th to the 17th century said quite that. The texts we possess almost all contain the formula that though by reason (following Aristotle and Averroës) we reach such and such a conclusion, nevertheless faith and truth tell us otherwise, and we accept the articles of religion on faith. So, for instance, Pomponazzi at the beginning of the 16th century showed how Aristotle's philosophy—especially when studied in Greek and not in the medieval Latin translations—leads to the conclusion that the individual human soul is mortal. However, since we are told otherwise by scripture and by the church, we therefore should accept the doctrine of the immortality of the soul on faith. Critics of the Averroists suspected that these philosophers did not have much faith, and that their fideistic conclusion was just camouflage. If this were the case, then various of the Latin (and Jewish) Averroists and Maimonideans may have been advancing a form of religious skepticism in the guise of expounding Aristotelian science and philosophy. The actual nature of the beliefs of these thinkers is still being seriously debated by modern scholars.

Classical philosophical skepticism reenters the European intellectual world in the 16th century. At the same time that great changes were occurring in the conception of the world through the voyages of exploration, through the revival of Greek and Roman ideas, through the development of science beyond Aristotle and Ptolemy, and through the conflicts over the bases of religion, the ancient skeptical texts of Sextus Empiricus and Cicero were rediscovered. Erasmus had presented an ironic skepticism against many practices and beliefs of the church, and in his *In Praise of Folly* had said he found the Academic skeptics the least surly of the philosophers. When he argued against Martin Luther about whether we have free will, he insisted that the question was basically unanswerable and that one ought to suspend judgment about it and accept the church's teachings undogmatically. Luther fought back, insisting that the Holy Ghost is not a skeptic and that one had to find true beliefs.

The texts of Sextus Empiricus were published in Latin in 1562 and 1569, after several Greek manuscripts had been brought to Italy during the Renaissance. The translator of Sextus' *Against the Dogmatists*, Gentian Hervet, immediately saw the value of Pyrrhonian skepticism in the religious debates of the time. Hervet was the secretary of the cardinal of Lorraine and had been active against the Protestants at the Council of Trent. He wrote in the preface of his edition of Sextus that if nothing can be known, then Calvinism cannot be known. Various 16th-century authors such as Gianfrancesco Pico and Cornelius Agrippa von Nettesheim had been attacking all kinds of knowledge claims of the Scholastics, the Renaissance humanists and scientists, and various kinds of theologians. They stressed the vanity of human knowledge-claims and the need to turn to faith. Gianfrancesco used much material from Sextus in advancing his case. Hervet contended that human reason is incapable of opposing or resisting arguments that can be raised against it. Only revelation provides certainty. John Calvin claimed to have found new religious knowledge. But all such claims are dubious. So, people should learn from Sextus that all human attempts to understand the universe are vain. Then people will become humble and will realize that God can be known only by faith, and not by the reasoning of reformers like Calvin. Hervet's use of skepticism against Calvinism was soon to become "a machine of war" used by leading Counter-Reformationists.

Montaigne. The full impact of the revival of ancient skepticism appeared in two 16th-century authors, Michel de Montaigne (1533–1592) and his distant cousin, Francisco Sanches. The former, in his "Apology for Raimond Sebond," and the latter, in his *Quod Nihil Scitur* ("Why Nothing Can Be Known"), surveyed the wreckage made by applying skepticism to various human knowledge-claims.

Sanches, a professor of philosophy and medicine at the University of Toulouse, presented a devastating skeptical attack against Aristotelian science. He marshaled the best skeptical arguments of antiquity to show that no necessary science of nature was possible. Instead, all we could do is compile individual facts and make probable generalizations from them, to be tested by later ex-

perience. Sanches, like many of the skeptics after him, exempted religion from his doubts, and asserted that he accepted the Christian religion on faith. (Both he and Montaigne were from Spanish-Jewish families that had been forcibly converted to Catholicism, having fled to France to escape the Spanish Inquisition.)

Montaigne had studied the Latin translations of Sextus Empiricus and in his longest essay, "Apology for Raimond Sebond," presented the fruits of his skeptical musings. This work was to have great influence on all subsequent skeptics. Montaigne had earlier published a French translation of *Natural Theology,* by the rational Catholic theologian, Sebond, who claimed that all the doctrines of Christianity could be proven by rational scientific means. People had objected to Sebond's rationalism, and Montaigne offered as a defense that Sebond was no worse than any other philosopher, scientist, or theologian, because nothing could be established by human reasoning. The "Apology" is a long rambling presentation of various levels of doubt developed by the ancient skeptics and put in modern dress by Montaigne. The variability of human sense experience and its frequent unreliability require us to find a criterion for judging when it is accurate. But, how do we judge the reliability of a criterion? By another criterion, and so on to infinity? Or by itself?

When we examine how people judge, we find that human judgments are influenced by cutural and psychological factors. In no area can we find adequate rational bases for our judgments. The best we can do, Montaigne said, was to suspend judgment, and follow the classical Pyrrhonian advice of living according to nature and the customs of society. In this state, Montaigne averred, our minds would be blank and ready to receive whatever truths God wished to reveal to us. These should be accepted on faith.

Thus, for Montaigne, the stated resolution of the skeptical crisis induced by questioning everything is a fideistic one. And, Montaigne insisted, the complete skeptic would not become a Protestant since he would be purged of all doubtful beliefs and would have only those principles that God gave him. If he received no revelation, by the customs of his society he should accept the prevailing doctrines, which for most Europeans of that day would be Catholic ones.

What Montaigne actually believed we do not know. He has been interpreted as everything from a secret atheist to an ardent Catholic. His writings never make clear *what* had been revealed to him, and his religious practices were pretty minimal. He was a political adviser to the Protestant leader, Henri of Navarre. When Henri converted to Catholicism and became Henri IV, king of France, he apparently enacted Montaigne's advice in the form of the Edict of Nantes, granting toleration to both Catholics and Protestants.

Pierre Charron. Montaigne's skeptical "defense" of Christianity, and especially of its Catholic form, was popularized by his official heir, Father Charron (1541–1603). His first work, *Les Trois Veritez* ("The Three Truths") was a backwards defense of the Catholic religion; he first cast doubt on the atheist's claim that God does not exist, then on the non-Christian's claim that Jesus is not the Messiah, and lastly on the Calvinist's claim that the Church of Rome is not the true church. This negative approach was supplemented by Charron's more popular work, *De la Sagesse* ("On Wisdom"). This work put Montaigne's skepticism into organized form and again urged suspending judgment until God reveals truths to us. Father Charron insisted that a skeptic cannot be a heretic since, by having no views, he cannot have the wrong ones. Until one receives a revelation, one should live according to nature. Charron is credited with being the first modern European thinker to develop an ethics for natural living apart from any religious considerations, basing his morality on the views of the ancient Stoics.

The skepticism of Montaigne and Charron permeated 17th-century thought. Some of the forms it took were (1) a polemical defense of Catholicism, (2) a complete doubt of all philosophical and scientific views, (3) a mitigated skepticism that could be joined to the new science, and (4) a basis for questioning traditional views. Some of these strands joined together in the middle of the 18th century to become the critical skepticism of the Enlightenment.

As previously indicated, the revival of ancient skepticism was quickly seen as useful in combating religious opponents. Especially in Counter-Reformation debates, the new skepticism was turned into a machine of war to challenge the claims of Protestants. If the Protestants based their religion on the Bible, how did they know what book is the Bible, how did they know what it said or what it meant? How did they know what was the right text, or even if there were a text and not just a lot of ink spots on paper? Catholic polemicists like François Veron, the official arguer for the king of France, tried to reduce Protestant opponents to complete doubt since the Protestants claimed the Bible was the basis of their faith. When the Protestants tried to turn the attack around, Father Veron insisted his own views were based on faith, and so not open to such a skeptical barrage.

Some Protestants then developed a skepticism against Catholicism. If Catholics base their faith on what the pope declares, how do they tell who is the pope? Views on this are based on hearsay, sense evidence, and so forth, all of which can be deceptive. One Protestant, Jean La Placette, claimed that all Catholics, with the possible exception of the pope, ought to be complete Pyrrhonists, since they cannot be sure of what to believe.

As theologians used skepticism as ammunition against each other, some philosophers sought to determine the effects of questioning all the accepted bases of knowledge. Some, like François La Mothe le Vayer, contended that all knowledge-claims in philosophy and science were now seen to be dubious. Others, like Fathers Marin Mersenne and Pierre Gassendi, saw that skeptical arguments undermined confidence in the Aristotelian science and philosophy taught in the universities, and in the new metaphysical theories of the alchemists, the astrologers, the numerologists, the Cabalists, and so forth. But, though Mersenne and Gassendi admitted they could not overcome the skeptical challenge, they could at least partially ignore it by using the findings of the new mechanical science of people like Galileo to supply adequate answers to problems. This mitigated or constructive skepticism dropped the search for complete certainty, and accepted the hypothetical and tentative findings of modern science instead. Gassendi, the more skeptical of the two, developed the ancient atomic materialism of Epicurus as a model for a scientific explanation and to provide a guide for living. Both Mersenne and Gassendi were Catholic priests and insisted that they accepted the views of the Catholic church on faith.

Their great contemporary, RENÉ DESCARTES, tried to overcome the new skepticism by finding an absolutely certain basis for the new science. To do this, Descartes attempted to doubt all previous beliefs in order to find certainty. His method of doubt, and his purported discovery of truths that could be the basis of all knowledge, became the center of the philosophical struggles from the middle of the 17th century onward, some skeptics trying to show that he had failed and some that he had just set up new, unjustified dogmas.

Descartes carefully refrained from applying his method of doubt to religious beliefs and asserted that he accepted the teachings of the Catholic church. However, others used his skeptical method to question the authenticity of the Bible, and its truth concerning the history of mankind. Isaac La Peyrère, in his *Men Before Adam,* questioned whether Moses wrote the Bible, whether the Bible is the history of all mankind or just of the ancient Jews, whether human history began with Adam, and even whether we possess an accurate text of the Bible. Spinoza developed these sorts of questions into a full-fledged skepticism about religion. Starting with Descartes' criterion of youth, Spinoza found wanting the claims of scripture to special religious knowledge.

Uriel da Costa and Spinoza raised the possibility that the Bible was just a human document giving the opinions of some ancient thinkers. Bayle, and later Voltaire, questioned the value of these opinions, suggesting they were often highly immoral. Various English deists pressed these kinds of doubts and questioned most of the basic claims of Judaism and Christianity. Perhaps the culmination of these kinds of religious skepticism was the notorious anonymous work, *The Three Impostors: Moses, Jesus and Mohammed.* It is still not clear exactly when this was written. It apparently went through several stages, the final one using a Spinozistic outlook to deny the historical truth of Judaism, Christianity, and Islam. A social and political theory of the origin of these religions was offered instead. During the 18th century this work ciruclated secretly and was published several times.

Philosophical skepticism from Montaigne to Bayle claimed to be a challenge to dogmatic philosophy and science but not to religion, which was to be accepted on faith. Bayle's development of the complete irrationality of faith made this kind of fideism hard to accept. The Scottish philosopher David Hume developed Bayle's skeptical themes and challenged the bases for any evidence of the truth of religion, or of knowledge of the existence and nature of God. Hume's critique of all kinds of knowledge claims has constituted the culmination of modern skepticism. This, coupled with the skeptical effects of applying modern critical criteria to religious evidence, from La Peyrère and Spinoza, through the English deists, the French Enlightenment materialists, the so-called German "Higher Critics" of the Bible, had led to modern AGNOSTICISM. The skeptical doubts concerning what we can know, what the world may be like, and what we ought to believe about it have been fused during the last 200 years into a general doubt or disbelief in traditional religion and metaphysics. The term *skeptic* now more often means a doubter about religious beliefs, rather than a philosophical skeptic about the certainty of human knowledge. The development of scientific explanations in biology and psychology for matters that were previously explained in religious terms has increased these doubts.

The last 200 years have seen an expansion of this skepticism about religion and religious evidence. Darwinism, the nihilism of FRIEDRICH NIETZSCHE, and the theories of KARL MARX and SIGMUND FREUD have all contributed to intensifying doubts about the religious traditions. In our century, it is perhaps BERTRAND RUSSELL who most typified the scientifically minded agnostic, the modern skeptic. His *Skeptical Essays, Science and Religion,* and *Human Knowledge, Its Scope and Limitations* express the various facets of this skepticism.

On the other hand, a skeptical "defense" of religion has also appeared and flourished. Going back to Pascal in the 17th century, thinkers have suggested that a realization of the inability of human reason to find a satisfactory basis for accepting beliefs has been offered as the road to faith. This was proposed by Hamann as the way to deal with Hume's skepticism and developed by Kierkegaard as the answer to 19th-century, liberal religious views. From Kierkegaard onward, fideistic theologies, using skepticism as the road to faith, have been offered among Jewish, Protestant, and Orthodox theologians.

After a period in the first half of this century in which philosophers like the logical positivists thought that philosophical and theological problems could be either dismissed as nonsense or reduced to scientific questions, a new era of skepticism seems to be emerging. The prevalent philosophies and theologies are being attacked more and more as traditional skeptical doubts are applied to the latest intellectual panaceas. The classical skeptical arguments are being reapplied to all branches of human knowledge. After all of the scientific achievements of the last four centuries, skeptical thinkers are questioning whether we have actually found out any more about reality than our predecessors thought they knew. The various ideologies, secular and religious, have come under critical questioning and attack. Each month new skeptical problems are raised in the philosophical journals.

We may have come full circle in the intellectual journey from the Renaissance to the present and be back in the sea of doubts of Montaigne. If so, this journey has involved the questioning and undermining of most of our traditional beliefs in all areas of human concern.

Other articles of interest: **Deism. Enlightenment, Unbelief During the. Logical Positivism and Unbelief.**

Bibliography

Cicero, Marcus Tullius. *De Academica* and *De Natura Deorum*. Trans. H. Rackham. Cambridge, Mass.: Loeb Classical Library, 1956.

Naess, Arne. *Scepticism*. London: 1969.

Popkin, Richard H. "Bible Criticism and Social Science in the 17th Century." *Boston Studies in the Philosophy of Science* 14.

———. *The High Road to Pyrrhonism*. San Diego: 1980.

———. *The History of Scepticism from Erasmus to Spinoza*. Berkeley and Los Angeles: 1979.

———. "Scepticism, Theology and the Scientific Revolution in the 17th Century." *Problems in the Philosophy of Science*. Ed. I. Lakatos and A. Musgrave. Amsterdam: 1968.

———. "Skepticism." *Encyclopedia of Philosophy*. New York: Macmillan, 1967.

Sextus Empiricus. *Outlines of Pyrrhonism* and *Against the Dogmatists*. Vols. 1–4. Cambridge, Mass.: Loeb Classical Library, 1933–60.

Stough, Charlotte. *Greek Skepticism*. Berkeley: 1969.

RICHARD H. POPKIN

SLENKER, ELIZABETH DRAKE (1827–1908), American writer. See **American Literature, Unbelief in.**

SMITH, CHARLES LEE (1887–1964), one of the foremost American atheist leaders of the 20th century, yet virtually nothing has been written about him. He never revealed much about his personal life, although he wrote widely on FREETHOUGHT subjects for the TRUTH SEEKER and other publications.

Early Life. Smith was born in Sebastian County, Ark., near Ft. Smith. He lived in Missouri for a short time but spent most of his boyhood in Indian Territory (now Oklahoma). His parents sent him to Epworth University's preparatory school. This was a Methodist school, and Smith had considered becoming a minister. He spent several years as a law clerk in Guthrie, Okla., and then passed the Oklahoma Bar exam. He also attended the University of Oklahoma, later transferring to Harvard. However, his funds ran out, and he withdrew from Harvard in his junior year.

Smith had discovered THOMAS JEFFERSON's book of extracts from the New Testament about Jesus in the Oklahoma State Library about 1912. Reading it made him realize that Jefferson was an infidel, and started his interest in freethought literature, eventually culminating in his conversion to ATHEISM. After leaving Harvard, Smith traveled around the United States for about three years, doing odd jobs. When World War I began, he enlisted in the army and spent much of the war in Vladivostok, Russia, at an isolated outpost. After the war he returned to New York and began writing for and selling the *Truth Seeker*.

Protests in Arkansas. In 1928 Smith went to Little Rock, Ark., after he heard that there was to be a referendum about the adoption of an antievolution law in that state. He attempted to lobby in the state legislature, but he got off on the wrong foot by objecting to a hymn that several legislators were singing in the statehouse. As a result, a resolution was passed in the house instructing the sergeant-at-arms to keep "a certain atheist" out of the chambers. Smith had been preceded to Arkansas by the reputation he had left during his last visit the previous October, when he was scheduled to debate evolution with T. T. Martin. Martin had failed to appear, and the state legislator who agreed to fill in for him also backed out at the last minute. This time Smith rented a storefront and advertised that the store was an "atheistic headquarters," where evolution tracts and antireligious literature would be given away.

Since Smith was not selling any of his publications, he did not need a permit or license. In the window of his store, he placed a large sign which read "Evolution Is True. The Bible's a Lie. God's a Ghost." Among the leaflets he distributed were *The Bible in the Balance, Godless Evolution,* and *The Ape Ancestry of Man*. It was the sign that finally got Smith into trouble, even though many of the leaflets went like hotcakes.

The first sign of trouble occurred on the fifth

day, when two policemen came at the orders of the police chief (a brother of the legislator who was to have debated Smith and who was one of the prime movers in the antievolution legislation then pending in the legislature). The police arrested Smith, ostensibly for not having a permit to sell literature. His protests that he wasn't *selling* it were to no avail. He was released on his own recognizance, to appear in court the next morning. At court, a city ordinance that prohibited the use of the name of the deity except "in veneration and worship" was invoked. The police chief testified, but when Smith was called, he asked to affirm, not swear, to tell the truth. When the judge learned that Smith was an atheist, he ruled that Smith could not testify. Nevertheless, the judge dismissed the original charge, and changed it to distributing obscene, slanderous, or scurrilous literature. Smith was found guilty and fined $25 and costs. At first, no one would furnish bail for Smith, which had been set at $100. When someone willing to do so was finally found and Smith was released, he called the police chief and asked that his bond be nullified and that he be allowed to work off his fine at $1 a day in jail by serving 26 days. He then reported to jail and began a hunger strike.

Smith sent telegrams to the mayors of all the cities in Arkansas, asking if he would be welcome to distribute literature about evolution and anti-religion. The answer was a unanimous "No." Even with this discouraging news, Smith continued his hunger strike until he was so weak that he was taken to the hospital.

By now, the authorities in Little Rock had had enough of Smith. Part of their desire to be rid of him stemmed from the large amount of publicity newspapers had given to the situation, most of it painting Arkansas as some sort of a primitive backwater. The state requested that the case against Smith be dismissed, and it was. Smith requested that the truckload of literature that had been confiscated by the police be returned to him. When the judge asked him if he intended to reopen his storefront, Smith said yes, and the judge denied him the return of his literature.

True to his word, Smith reopened the store with the same sign in the window. That sign was confiscated by the police and another arrest threatened. No arrest occurred that day or the next, although his store was broken into during the night and vandalized by religious forces (apparent from the note that was left). Although Smith had been warned to get out of town for his own safety, he refused, and again reopened the store. It was only a little while before the police arrived and arrested him. This time Smith was charged with blasphemy. He was tried and convicted, with the judge refusing to allow him to testify in his own behalf, and also refusing to say why he would not let him do so.

Smith was sentenced to 90 days in jail and a fine of $100. He was released on $1000 bail. Throughout all of this, Smith insisted that his real aim was to "nullify the anti-atheist laws of this country." He was referring to the law in Arkansas (and several other states) that forbade the holding of public office by anyone who does not swear to a belief in God. Smith's actions were in vain on the antievolution law, which passed the Arkansas legislature. The blasphemy charge dragged on for several years of appeals and stalling before it was finally dismissed.

The 4As. In 1925, while in New York City, Charles Smith and his friend Freeman Hopwood founded the infamous American Association for the Advancement of Atheism. The "4As," as it was commonly called, was at first denied the right to incorporate in New York state. The grounds for the denial were that it was "against the public interest." However, the second attempt at obtaining the incorporation was successful. The 4As immediately began a campaign that struck terror into the hearts of many believers. It was a program that was largely symbolic and in many ways mostly bluff, but it did garner a large amount of publicity and soon had over 3,000 members. The 4As was quick to reap publicity from the fact that it had founded chapters on the campuses of 20 colleges and universities. While these groups appear to have done little and usually expired with the graduation of the founders, they had colorful names. There were the Damned Souls at the University of Rochester, the Sons of Satan at the Oklahoma City University, and the Legion of the Damned at the University of North Dakota, among others. Another branch was the Junior Atheist League, run by a young woman from Pennsylvania, with the help of another in California. They attempted to appeal to those of high-school age and under.

Other activities of the 4As consisted of holding a series of lectures, called the Ingersoll Forum, at which different speakers talked about an aspect of science, religion, or philosophy. There was a small admission charge, and this money helped fund the 4As. There was also an annual meeting of the 4As, at which accomplishments and plans were discussed. An annual report was also issued. At one point the Ingersoll Forum rented a hall just three doors from the church at which John Roach Straton was minister. Straton was one of the most popular fundamentalist antievolutionists of the period. Smith's comment was that there was no malice intended in the move, but that if Straton didn't like the fact that the atheists were so close to his church, he could always move.

Straton supposedly accepted an invitation to speak to the Ingersoll Forum. In turn, some atheists would attend a service at his church. Straton later denied that he had ever agreed to these terms, and left town on the day he was supposed to speak at the forum. The next thing Smith knew, he was being sued by Straton for "annoyance by mail" for having sent several tracts and a few marked issues of the *Truth Seeker* to Straton. The case came to trial, and Smith was convicted and fined $100. Most of Straton's annoyance with the 4As had come from the fact that Smith was threatening to notify the child-labor authorities that the child evangelist, Undine Utley, did not have proper working papers. Straton got out of that by noting that Undine was not being paid, but only "offerings" were collected.

Although the 4As brought suit to stop such things as the employment of chaplains in Congress, the reading of the Ten Commandments in schools, etc., its suits were usually not successful at lower court levels. Although it always threatened to appeal, most of the time it could not raise the necessary money. The Depression seems to have finally finished off the 4As. After 1933, annual reports do not seem to have been issued, and the organization disappears from the pages of the newspapers. Although it continued to exist on paper, for all intents and purposes it was dead.

Smith told his friends for years that he was working on an important book. The work finally appeared in two volumes in 1956. It was called *Sensism: The Philosophy of the West*. It hardly sold at all, and much of the edition was destroyed in a fire at the publishers in 1981. The work is a collection of comments on the writings of various philosophers, tied together with Smith's incomprehensible world view. His friends could not figure out what Smith was trying to say, and cannot explain what his intentions in this book were.

Smith purchased the *Truth Seeker* and its associated company in 1930. He converted the magazine from a folio-sized weekly to a smaller monthly. Although Smith's antipathy to Jews and Blacks was not obvious in his prior activity, around 1950 (perhaps due to the influence of his assistant editor, Woolsey Teller) antisemitic, racist attitudes began to become obvious in the *Truth Seeker*. This brought forth vigorous protests from many of the readers, along with many cancellations of subscriptions. As the circulation of the magazine shrank, Smith's enthusiasm for it waned. When James Hervey Johnson offered to buy the magazine in 1964 and to let Smith remain as editor, he agreed. Smith moved to San Diego, along with all the Truth Seeker Company files and stock, in early 1964. San Diego was Johnson's home base, and the location from which Johnson had run his freethought publishing and bookselling operations previously. Smith continued to edit the magazine from there for six months. On Oct. 26 Smith was walking along the street when he suffered a fatal heart attack. His body was cremated.

In summary: Smith had a good mind and a daring spirit, but he often produced only a frustrating result—or none at all. It is hard to identify any real lasting contribution Smith made but, if so, it wasn't for lack of trying. He certainly was one of the bravest public atheists this country has ever seen. It is tempting to compare him with CHARLES BRADLAUGH of England in this respect. In a sense, Smith was born at the wrong time in history. He would have done much better if he had lived as an adult during the last half of the 19th century, when freethought was in its Golden Age. Yet, Charles Smith deserves better treatment than history has given him. He is all but forgotten now.

Other article of interest: **Blasphemy Laws.**

Bibliography

Much of the material on Smith comes from personal interviews with people who knew him, plus a few articles in the non-freethought press that were highly critical of his activities, especially when those activities concerned the American Association for the Advancement of Atheism.

Croy, Homer. "Atheism Rampant in Our Schools." *The World's Work* 54 (1927).

Haldeman-Julius, Marcet. "Is Arkansas Civilized?" *The Debunker* 9, no. 1 (Dec. 1928).

———. "Arkansas Defends Its God." *The Debunker* 9, no. 2 (Jan. 1929).

Johnson, James Hervey. "Charles Smith: 1887–1964." *The Truth Seeker* 91, no. 11 (Nov. 1964).

Smith, Charles. "In Darkest Arkansas." *Third Annual Report of the American Association for the Advancement of Atheism.* New York: AAAA, 1928.

Smith, Charles, and W. L. Oliphant. *A Debate Between W. L. Oliphant . . . and Charles Smith . . . Shawnee, Oklahoma, August 15 and 16, 1929.* Nashville, Tenn.: Gospel Advocate Co., 1952.

Smith, Charles. *Sensism: The Philosophy of the West.* 2 vols. New York: Truth Seeker Co., 1956.

GORDON STEIN

SOLZHENITSYN, ALEXANDER (1918–   ), Russian writer. See **Russian Literature, Unbelief in.**

SOPHISTS, THE. See **Ancient World, Unbelief in the.**

SOUL, IMMORTALITY OF THE. See **Immortality, Unbelief in.**

SOUTHWELL, CHARLES (1814–1860), a maverick British FREETHOUGHT leader, born in London, the youngest of 33 children. Raised in poverty, he became a discipline problem at school and ceased formal education at the age of 12. Reading Timothy Dwight's sermons at the request of a religious coworker in the piano factory where he was employed led Southwell to begin a serious examination of theology.

London and Bristol Activities. He became a bookseller in London in 1830, then joined a lecturing group. Upon being asked to give one of the lectures, Southwell discovered that he had a natural oratorical ability. After serving in Spain in the "Spanish Legion," a group of mercenary soldiers, he returned to London. He was soon asked to lecture regularly, becoming one of ROBERT OWEN's "socialist missionaries." His argumentative nature soon brought him into disagreement with Owen, and he left the Owenites in 1841.

Southwell then opened a freethought bookstore in Bristol in the latter part of 1841, in partnership with a local printer named William Chilton. In November 1841, they published the first issue of the *Oracle of Reason,* the first openly atheistic magazine ever published in English (and perhaps in any language). Word soon reached Southwell that the authorities in Bristol were not pleased with the existence of his journal. This inflamed him, and soon the contents of the magazine became more daring and openly hostile to Christianity. The fourth issue of the magazine contained an article about the Bible, entitled "The Jew Book." This was too much for the authorities, and a warrant for Southwell's arrest on a charge of blasphemy was sworn out. He was arrested on Nov. 27, 1841, and forced to spend 17 days in jail while the authorities kept turning down people who had offered to guarantee his bail. The original people were finally accepted as guarantors.

Southwell went to London after his release on bail. While he was gone from Bristol, Chilton printed up some copies of the warrant charging Southwell with blasphemy. Of course, the text contained the text of the passages from the *Oracle* that had been found offensive. When Southwell returned to Bristol, he found that the authorities were about to charge him with a second count of blasphemy for having reprinted the warrant. He fled to London, where he remained, as editor of the *Oracle* until his trial in Jan. 1842.

At his trial for blasphemy, Southwell defended himself. He talked for several hours, quoting a long list of authorities, claiming that he could not be guilty of blasphemous libel (as the offense was called), because what he published was true. The jury returned after ten minutes of deliberation, with a verdict of guilty. Southwell was sentenced to a twelve-month imprisonment and a fine of 100 pounds. He served his time, but when he was released, he realized that the *Oracle* (which had continued to publish under four different editors, each being sent to prison for various offenses), was in severe financial trouble. Hence, he started his own new journal, called the *Investigator.* This lasted seven months, although it was later revived by others.

Southwell next went on a lecturing trip, and supported himself also by acting in various Shakespearean plays. He received good reviews for his performances. His next publishing enterprise was a magazine called the *Lancashire Beacon.* It lasted less than one year.

Emigration. In 1855, Southwell left rather

suddenly for Australia. He had thought of emigrating to America, but this period of his life is extremely confused. It is quite possible that his disgust at having been removed as the beneficiary in the will of a wealthy man might have been the last straw for Southwell, especially since his long-standing distaste for GEORGE JACOB HOLYOAKE's tactics seems to have played a role in his being disinherited.

When Southwell arrived in Melbourne in July 1855, the area was in the midst of a gold rush. He tried to earn his living as a lecturer on nonreligious topics. In fact, he did fairly well at first, since his reputation as an atheist had not accompanied him. But when Southwell tried to run for the Legislative Council of Victoria, someone spread the word that he was the same man who had been a public atheist and convicted blasphemer in England. Southwell lost the election. He became a Shakespearean actor again, joining a touring group. The troupe performed in Auckland, New Zealand, in January 1856, and Southwell appears to have decided to settle in New Zealand at this point.

In Auckland, Southwell began the final phase of his life. He started an iconoclastic newspaper called the *Auckland Examiner*. The paper was fearless in exposing corruption in all quarters. It seems to have been a one-man operation, continuing for over three years with Southwell as the only employee. Southwell's health was starting to deteriorate. He seems to have suffered from tuberculosis, although this is not certain. In July 1860, Southwell was forced by poor health to shut down the *Examiner*. Two weeks later, he died and was buried in the Symonds Street cemetery in Auckland.

In summary: Southwell's importance was largely as a publisher. He was responsible for reviving the wave of blasphemy prosecutions that occurred during the early 1840s, and his conduct in publishing the *Oracle of Reason* was largely responsible for moving the freethought movement into a more open and defiant atheistic phase.

Other article of interest: **Blasphemy Laws.**

Bibliography

Pearce, Harry Hastings. "Charles Southwell in Australia and N.Z." *New Zealand Rationalist* 18, no. 8 through 19, no. 12 (May 1957–Sept. 1958).

Southwell, Charles. *Confessions of a Freethinker.* London?: about 1845.

———, ed. *The Oracle of Reason.* Bristol: 1841–42, 104 issues as a weekly.

Standring, George. "Charles Southwell." *Our Corner* 11 (London, 1888).

Watts, John, and "Iconoclast" (Charles Bradlaugh). "Charles Southwell." In *Half Hours with Freethinkers.* 2nd Series, no. 24 (Feb. 9, 1865). Published in one volume by Austin & Co., London, 1865.

GORDON STEIN

SPAIN, UNBELIEF IN. Disbelief in, and more often hostility to, the Catholic church generally comprises most of the unbelief found in Spain. There is no notable Spanish philosophical movement based on AGNOSTICISM or ATHEISM. (Even Spanish anarchism, the strongest opponent of the church, should properly be regarded as a rival religious force). Furthermore, Spanish disbelief is a question as much of political intent as of religious attitude. For many centuries, the church held a preponderant role in Spanish life; the identification of church and state has continued to the present. Even in the Middle Ages—if we accept Americo Castro's theory—Christian Spaniards, living in a land in which Muslims possessed political power and Jews controlled the intellectual professions, defined themselves not by nation but by religion.

From the Middle Ages to the present, a common Spanish attitude has been to suppress vigorously all religious dissent as unpatriotic. At times, medieval Spaniards adopted an attitude of "holy war" against their Islamic neighbors. The Inquisition, founded in 1480, received great popular support in its tasks of extirpating heresy or signs of backsliding into Judaism or Islam. The reaction of those persecuted was correspondingly violent and long-lasting. Julio Caro Baroja (see Bibliography below) has argued in his panoramic account of anticlericalism that the wave of church burnings which accompanied the rising of the *moriscos* (descendants of converted Moors) between 1567 and 1571 reflects the enduring hatred of those converted by force to an alien religion. In modern times, struggles for political power have often provided the motivating force of Spanish anticlericals; attempts at national reform have involved massive attacks on the church, the reputed obstacle in the path of progress and change.

Spanish anticlericalism is also in large part the psychological reaction of individuals against the all-embracing role of the church in Spanish life. For centuries, the church controlled sexual mores, diet, dress, reading matter, diversions, conversations (through the spies of the Inquisition), charitable institutions, the educational system, baptisms, marriages, and burial rites. The pressure to conform to the views of the church was intense. Thought control was maintained by external forces (social pressure, the educational system, the Inquisition, censorship, the confessional) and internally, from within the conscience. (A sensitive young Spaniard, Joseph Blanco White has given an account of those pressures in his *Letters from Spain*.)

The reaction to these pressures was multifaceted and considerable. Priests and friars are the butt of many Spanish jokes. Priestly control of education gives an anticlerical tinge to attacks on educators; one can note the resentment of the statesman Manuel Azaña (1840–1940) at his Augustinian teachers and the bitterness with which the novelist Ramón Pérez de Ayala (1881–1962) attacks his Jesuit educators in *A.M.D.G.* (1910). Catholic restrictions on sexual conduct provoke strong reactions; thus, the novelist Vicente Blasco Ibáñez (1867–1928) assails both Catholic Puritanism and priestly sexual license. Cynicism and scandal also result from attempts at avoiding church discipline. (For example, 18th-century entrepreneurs obtained and sold certificates of confession, without which Spaniards could not fulfill their obligatory Easter duties.)

Salvador de Madariaga (*Spain*, 1942) has justly remarked on the intellectual weakness and negative stance of Spanish anticlericalism, which, with its persecutory zeal, is often little more than a mirror image of the Inquisitorial system it claims to replace. For the last three centuries, Spanish anticlericalism has been a powerful factor in Spanish political life. In the 18th century, quarrels between religious orders, the impact of French philosophical ideas, and attempts by the state to enforce royal authority weakened the political power of the church. Throughout the 19th century, liberal politicians persistently attacked the Catholic church as obscurantist; the support that influential members of the church gave to such a reactionary and authoritarian cause as Carlism further alienated many members of the urban middle and laboring classes. In the 20th century, the alleged economic power of the church (the Jesuits, according to popular rumor controlled one-third of the wealth of Spain) provided the excuse for attacks on the church.

Spanish anticlericalism has geographical and sexual, as well as political, components. Spanish Catholicism is traditionally strong in the north of Spain, in the Basque country, and in Navarre. Anticlericalism has deep roots in the south of Spain and in large cities. Church attendance is a female rather than a male activity. By 1910, the majority of Spaniards attended church services only for baptisms, marriages, and deaths. By 1931, only 1 percent of Andalusian men and only 5 percent of villagers in central Spain attended mass. Furthermore, the working-class attitude to the church was one of fanatical hatred, rather than indifference.

Signs of anticlericalism are found in Spain from the Middle Ages onward. Attacks on clerical figures are frequent in Spanish medieval and Renaissance literature. Anticlerical satires leave Christian doctrine untouched but assail the failure of priests and friars to live Christian lives. Popular proverbs portray friars as avaricious, immoral, idle, and gluttonous; priests are denounced as ambitious and warlike. With the stricter clerical discipline of the Counter-Reformation and the pervasive thought control exercised by the Inquisition, examples of overt anticlericalism are rarer in the 16th and 17th centuries.

In the eighteenth century, although the great mass of Spaniards adhered to traditional beliefs, signs of religious dissent appear. Such representative figures of the new critical and experimental spirit as the Benedictine Benito Feijóo (1675–1764) and the statesman Gaspar Melchor de Jovellanos (1744–1815), although orthodox Catholics, attack superstition and abuse of religion. Despite the efforts of the Inquisition, the ruling classes had access to the works of the French ENLIGHTENMENT, and at times they advocated a philanthropy based on DEISM and RATIONALISM.

Major conflicts arose not from rival beliefs but from church-state relations. The pious but reforming monarch Charles III (1759–1788) established increased royal power over the church. Papal documents could not be circulated in Spain without royal permission; the Inquisition and clergy were subjected to royal control; attempts were made to reduce the financial immunities of the church; and, in 1767, the Jesuits (accused of complicity in the bread riots of 1766) were expelled from Spain and its dominions. A rational, even anticlerical, spirit is often evident.

José de Cadalso (1741–1782), in the *Cartas*

marruecas, omits the clergy from a list of desirable professions and casts doubts on miracles; the dramatist Leandro Fernández de Moratín (1760–1828) attacks convent education; the artist Francisco de Goya (1746–1828) often satirizes the clergy. Other figures of the anticlerical Enlightenment are: the abbot José Marchena (1768–1821), an ardent supporter of VOLTAIRE and the French Revolution; the priest Juan Antonio Llorente (1756–1823), a freemason who published in France a *History of the Inquisition* (1817–18); Bartolomé Gallardo (1776–1852), a liberal pamphleteer; and José María Blanco y Crespo, known as "Blanco White" (1775–1841), a cultured Catholic priest who fled to England and became first an Anglican and later a Unitarian minister.

Nineteenth-century anticlericalism is deep-rooted, intimately connected with the century-long political struggle between progressives and reactionaries. The savage war against the French (the War of Independence, 1808–14) shattered the social structure of the *ancien régime,* leaving a legacy of violence and a power vacuum in which the restored monarchy would depend, after 1814, on the fickle loyalties of the army and the mob rather than on traditional respect for the divine right of kings. Many members of the clergy found a patriotic role, which they were subsequently loath to renounce, as leaders of *guerrillero* bands in the "crusade" against the French. Political battle lines were drawn between reformers ("liberals") and traditionalists during the Cortes of Cadiz (1810–12), which gave Spain her first, short-lived constitution. Although members of the clergy belonged to both political groups, the higher clergy tended to support reactionary policies; throughout the century, liberal priests found little ecclesiastical preferment. Furthermore, the Cortes of Cadiz, with its abolition of the Inquisition and timid steps at ecclesiastical disentailment, brought the liberal state, like its royal predecessors of the previous century, into conflict with the temporal claims of the church.

In 1814, the Catholic church enjoyed almost total popular support; rural priests shared the same values as their parishioners and only 6 percent of the population were literate and thus susceptible to the ideas of liberal reformers. Throughout the century, however, the working classes of the cities and of the south and southeast ("hungry Spain") became alienated from and violently hostile to the church. Nineteenth-century anticlericalism was political and emotional, not philosophical.

Regional and reactionary interests defended the Carlist cause, with its slogan of "God, fatherland, and king." The three Carlist Wars (1833–40, 1846–48, 1872–76) pitted rural regions of the north and east, under priestly leadership, against the cities and progressive regions of the south. Liberal propagandists caricatured the clergy as ill-educated, brutal, and sanguinary, the natural enemies of all progress. The middle classes, moreover, were shocked by the superstitions and sexual and financial irregularities of Queen Isabel II (reigned 1833–68); by the nun Sor Patrocinio, who, by manifesting the stigmata of Christ, sought to manipulate politics; and by the insane priest Martín Merino, whose attempted regicide in 1852 provided grist for progressive propaganda mills. Furthermore, after the restoration of the Bourbon monarchy in 1874, the impoverished but spiritually resurgent church allied itself with the ruling classes (the monarchy, the army, and vested economic interests). By the end of the century, except in the Basque country and Navarre, the church, with its doctrine of charity in the rich and resignation in the poor, was identified by left-wing politicians as the enemy of the downtrodden and the ally of the wealthy.

The strength of hostility in the church in 19th-century Spain is evident in the numerous anticlerical measures enacted by liberal legislatures (and rapidly annulled by subsequent conservative governments) and in the almost ritualistic mob attacks on churches and priests—often with the connivance of the authorities—in moments of revolutionary fervor.

Certain manifestations of anticlericalism formed part of the mythology of Catholic and anticlerical alike: the expulsion of the Jesuits and the requirement in 1820 that parish clergy preach in support of the constitution of 1812; the assassination in 1821 of the imprisoned royal chaplain Matías Vinuesa by a Madrid mob; the murder by another mob in Madrid of 75 friars falsely accused of poisoning wells with cholera, as well as the destruction of numerous churches, in 1834; numerous church burnings and killings of priests in the south and east of Spain in 1835; the shattering of the temporal power of the church by the prime minister, Juan Alvarez y Mendizábal (1790–1853), who suppressed most convents, monasteries, and religious institutions, appropriating their property for the state, in 1836; the attempt by the regent Espartero to appoint bishops in defiance of Rome (1840–43); the breaking of diplomatic relations with Rome in 1855; massive attacks on churches following the revolution of 1868; declaration of freedom of worship in the Constitution of 1869; and establishment of civil marriage and divorce during the First Republic (1873).

Ideological hostility to the church in 19th-century Spain took various forms. Popular romanticism, inspired by such French authors as Marie Joseph Sue and Victor Hugo, interpreted religion as love and charity while simultaneously rejecting the authoritarianism of the church. The popular mind sought new objects of devotion to replace the church and its beliefs; these were romantic symbols that took on a religious rather than a purely secular import: the constitution of 1812; the young María Cristina, who became queen regent in 1833; General Espartero, the "progressive hero" (1792–1879); and the notions of progress, democracy, and the federal republic.

On a more philosophical level, *krausismo* (named after its originator, the obscure German philosopher Karl Krause, 1781–1832) was introduced into Spain by Julián Sanz del Río (1814–1869). It prevailed in the University of Madrid in the late 1860s and early 1870s. *Krausismo* (or "harmonic rationalism") was a panentheistic system that held that the individual could reach God directly without the mediation of the church. The *krausistas,* with their obscure jargon, strict morality, and austere dress, seemed almost to be the priests of a new cult. Agnostic POSITIVISM, which ignored the claims of religion and considered God to be unknowable, was known in intellectual circles in the 1870s. In the same period, the teachings of Charles Darwin, John Tyndall, THOMAS HENRY HUXLEY, Ernest Renan, and DAVID FRIEDRICH STRAUSS were expounded in the Spanish press.

Hegelian dialectic flourished in the thought of Emilio Castelar (1832–1899) and Francisco Pi y Margall (1823–1901), both presidents of the short-lived republic of 1873. Castelar denied any absolute principle, save that of the continual metamorphosis and progress of ideas. Pi y Margall claimed that faith had produced as antithesis doubt; the new synthesis was philosophy; religions therefore should be destroyed as unscientific remnants of the past. Anticlerical novelists such as Benito Pérez Galdós (1843–1920), Armando Palacio Valdés (1853–1938), Vicente Blasco Ibáñez (1867–1928), and Pío Baroja (1872–1956) enjoyed a wide readership for their fictional portrayals of the harmful effects of Spanish religious practices on the individual and on the family.

The various Republican political parties that flourished at the turn of the century were united only in their hostility to the established church. Fernando Lozano ("Demófilo") founded the journal of FREETHOUGHT, *Las Dominicales*, in 1883; later, he organized an International Congress of Freethought in Madrid, which was attended by the prominent Portuguese Republicans Bernardino Machado and Magalhaes Lima. José Nakens (1841–1926) published for many years the violently clerophobic *El Motín*. More conservative Republicans, such as Melquiades Alvarez (1864–1936), the founder of the Reformist party, recognized the right of the church to exist but sought the secularization of the Spanish state.

Spanish Anarchism. The major challenge to the church came in anarchism. Anarchistic doctrines were brought to Spain by Mikhail Bakunin's emissary, Giuseppe Fanelli, in 1868. Falling on already fertile soil, anarchism readily gained adherents among the landless peasantry of Andalusia and the proletariat of Barcelona. Spanish anarchism declared itself to be atheistic. Its enemy, religion, would be replaced by science. Catholicism, with its teaching of resignation to suffering, was the enemy of revolution, the accomplice of the exploiting classes. With its strong moral content, its mystical belief in human brotherhood and the future paradise, its demands on its followers for sacrifice and even martyrdom, and its use of Christian terminology (Jesus is hailed as the first anarchist; anarchist propagandists are "redeemers," or "apostles"), anarchism became a subsitute religion, filling the spiritual void left in the souls of many who had abandoned, or considered themselves abandoned by, Catholicism.

In the 20th century, anarchism lost much of its appeal for intellectuals, who now sought the rational reorganization of society along socialist lines, rather than in the pseudoreligious fervor of the anarchist believer. Anarchism continued to gain ground, however, among the unsophisticated; in the 1930s, over three million Spaniards supported anarchist unions and political programs.

The religious problem became much exacerbated in the first decade of the 20th century. Anarchist bomb attacks, including one on the Corpus Christi procession in Barcelona in 1896, were frequent. Priests and friars returning after the Spanish-American War of 1898 were held responsible for the rising in the Philippines against Spanish rule. And the flight to Spain of members of French religious orders following the Combes legislation aroused the fears of such prominent anticlericals as Luis Morote, the author of an anticlerical treatment of the religious problem (see Bibliography). In late 1900, Liberals and Republicans, in part to distract attention from their obvious inability to develop any program for fundamental change in Spain, began a violent campaign against "clerical reaction."

In 1901 (the "anticlerical year"), anticlerical riots accompanied performances of Galdós' drama *Electra* (with its thesis of the destructive influence of the clergy on family life), the wedding of Princess Mercedes, and the trial in the Supreme Court of the Adelaida Ubao case. In the same year, the government required religious schools to be subjected to the same standards as state schools, taxed products manufactured by religious orders, and required religious orders to register with the state (the "law of associations"). In 1904, anticlericals campaigned against the appointment to the diocese of Valencia of the former archbishop of Manila, who was accused of complicity in the surrender of Manila to the United States. In 1906, the Liberal government exempted couples contracting a civil marriage from any religious declaration and proposed a new "law of associations." The failure to enact such a law prompted the prominent novelist Benito Pérez Galdós to affiliate himself with the anticlerical Republican party in early 1907.

In July of 1909, a protest in Barcelona against the sending of reservists to Morocco turned almost immediately into seven days of anticlerical violence, during which 34 convents, 22 churches, and numerous Catholic charitable and educational institutions were destroyed. This period has been called the "Tragic Week." The rioters had the support of the rabidly anticlerical Radical Republican party, and the army did not intervene to protect church property. The subsequent execution of the anarchist FRANCISCO FERRER (1859–1909) led to left-wing protests throughout much of Western Europe, although there were few repercussions in Spain.

Attempts at anticlerical legislation were revived by José Canalejas (1854–1912), prime minister from 1910 to 1912. Religious orders were required to register with the state; non-Catholic religious organizations were permitted external manifestations of their cult; and new religious orders were not allowed to enter Spain (the "padlock law"). Despite the hysterical hatred which Canalejas, a devout Catholic, aroused in right-wing circles, his measures were more apparent than effective. He

negotiated in secret with the Vatican, and historians have argued that his anticlerical legislation was symbolic and merely preserved the status quo.

With the formation of the Second Republic (1931–39), fanatical opponents of religion controlled the Spanish government. The first cabinet of the republic was dominated by anticlericals and atheists. Its leading member, Manuel Azaña (1880–1940), declared, to the alarm of Catholics, that Spain had ceased to be a Catholic nation. A wave of church burnings by anarchists in Madrid and Andalusia in May of 1931 met with no official interference; indeed, Azaña announced that he would rather every church in Spain burn than that a single republican be harmed. The constitution of 1931 was strongly anticlerical. Church and state were declared separate, the Jesuits were banished, and religious orders were closely controlled. Any "public manifestation of religion," such as a religious procession, would need prior government approval. Divorce and civil marriage were permitted. Priestly salaries, a charge on the state since Mendizábal's seizure of church lands, were no longer paid. Crucifixes were removed from the classrooms of state schools.

Furthermore, legislation—never enforced because the Azaña government fell in November 1933—was passed ordering all schools controlled by religious orders (the greater part of the Spanish educational system) to close by the end of 1933. A fresh resurgence of anticlerical violence occurred in October of 1934, when churches were burned during the short-lived socialist republic in Asturias. Left-wing Republican hatred of Catholicism was again apparent when the Popular Front government took power in 1936; 160 churches were destroyed during the first four months of Popular Front rule.

The Spanish Civil War (1936–39) brought with it a hideous persecution of the church. With the exception of the Basque republic (Catholic, bourgeois, and nationalistic), the various anarchist, socialist, and Communist factions controlling different regions of republican Spain sought to destroy any sign of religion: 7,937 priests and members of religious orders (including 12 bishops) were murdered, often after torture; many nuns were violated; 150 churches were totally destroyed and 4,850 were damaged, often heavily. In Barcelona, every church (save for the cathedral, which was protected by the state) was destroyed. Even such a traditional greeting as *adiós*, with its religious connotation ("Go with God"), could not be employed in republican Spain.

In part as a reaction to republican clericophobia, and at times out of genuine belief, many members of the Catholic hierarchy, as well as individual parish priests, supported Francisco Franco, with his strident Catholic nationalism. Franco, however, *used* rather than served the cause of religion. The reading of the encyclical *Mit Brennender Sorge* was prohibited in Spain. Priests who protested summary executions by Franco's tribunals were ordered not to interfere in state matters. When the Catholic Basque republic fell to Franco's forces, numerous Basque priests were deported and 16 were executed. In 1938, Cardinal Segura, the archbishop of Seville, denounced as "irreligious" the Falange, a party of fascistic tendencies and the only political organization tolerated by the Franco regime. Furthermore, Cardinal Gomá of Toledo criticized, in a barely veiled attack on Franco's ideology, "exaggerated nationalism."

As Franco successfully consolidated his rule (1939–75), religion was all but annexed by the state. Catholicism, again the official state religion, was declared the "essence of Spanish history." Religious teaching was obligatory in all schools, and Franco's propagandists vociferously linked Catholic faith and the nationalistic ideology of the regime.

Perhaps the most fundamental form of unbelief in Spain has been not that of the anticlericals but rather that of those Catholics who, from the time of the Inquisition to the rule of Franco, have implicitly denied spiritual values by relying on force to achieve their goals. Certainly, there is evidence that the church feared too close an identification with Franco. By the 1960s, the Spanish clergy—the youngest priesthood in Europe—were spearheading movements to prepare Spain for a more democratic structure. By the late 1960s and the 1970s, however, Spain, no longer an underdeveloped nation, was sharing the same ills as the rest of Western European society. The rabid anticlericalism of an earlier age had now disappeared. In its place emerged a more insidious form of unbelief, the unthinking embrace of a materialistic consumer society and indifference to religious and spiritual questions.

Other article of interest: **Spanish Literature, Unbelief in.**

Bibliography

Blanco White, Joseph ("Leocadio Doblado"). *Letters from Spain*. London: 1822. Rev. 2nd ed., 1825.

Brenan, Gerald. *The Spanish Labyrinth*. Cambridge: 1960.

Caro Baroja, Julio. *Introducción a una historia contemporánea del anticlericalismo español*. Madrid: 1980.

Dendle, Brian J. *The Spanish Novel of Religious Thesis, 1876–1936*. Madrid: 1968.

Fraser, Ronald. *Blood of Spain*. New York: 1979.

Gallego, José Andrés. *La política religiosa en España, 1889–1913*. Madrid: 1975.

Longares Alonso, Jesús. *La ideología religiosa del liberalismo español (1808–1843)*. Cordoba: 1979.

Madariaga, Salvador de. *Spain*. London: 1942.

Morote, Luis. *Los frailes en España*. Madrid: 1904.

Thomas, Hugh. *The Spanish Civil War*. New York: 1961.

Ullman, Joan Connelly. *The Tragic Week*. Cambridge, Mass.: Harvard U. Press, 1968.

BRIAN J. DENDLE

SPANISH LITERATURE, UNBELIEF IN. The phenomenon of unbelief in Spanish literature is somewhat different from that found in other Western traditions. One must bear in mind that Spain is often called—not without some element of truth—"the most Catholic country in the world." Concomitant with this is the proverbial saying that the Spaniard almost always leaves *un rincón de Dios* (a corner for God).

Introduction. Some general theological questions must be asked immediately: Unbelief in what form? Lack of belief in a Supreme Being, such as the God of the Old Testament or of Islam? Or, do we mean the DEISM of the ENLIGHTENMENT? In this last system, the universe was thought to have been created by a Supreme Being, but theological thinking made little effort to discover his attributes or presence in creation.

From another point of view, by *unbelief* do we mean lack of belief in God, the creator and sustainer of all being, and in Jesus, who founded and abides in the Catholic church? It should be emphasized at this point that the mainstream of Catholic theology long ago relinquished the restricted notion that salvation is reserved only for people in communion with Rome.

Continuing our pursuit of a definition of unbelief, do we mean the acceptance of God and Jesus but prefer some less dogmatic, Protestant concept of the church? This frequently seemed to be the case with the complex Miguel de Unamuno in volume 2 of *Mi Religión y Otros Ensayos*. (See Bibliography below.)

Again, by *unbelief* do we mean complete ATHEISM? Or, do we mean not knowing one way or the other—AGNOSTICISM? Let us remember also that history has proved that people of great feeling and intelligence can believe in a Supreme Being but prefer not to become adherents of any specific church or religion. There are many nonprofessing believers who feel that truth emerges from all great religions. Professing people, while preferring their own formulas, are also increasingly inclined to believe that all religions contain some truth.

The intricate problem of Oriental religions must be raised briefly. Spain, because of the long impact of Islam, is the most Oriental of Western cultures. Spain has a long tradition of mysticism that flowered brilliantly in the 16th century and was unquestionably influenced by the Muslims, especially the Sufis. When mysticism is encountered, one is not too far from Oriental concepts of deity. By this, we mean the almost mind-shattering awareness that God's transcendence cannot begin to be comprehended. Consequently, in comparison, the things of this world—beautiful though they sometimes may be—are ultimately shadows. In Spain this is found especially in the neo-Platonic mysticism of the 16th century. Many Spanish mystics suffered persecution from the Inquisition and their coreligionists, because the flight of the mind to God implied a supposed lack of mediation by the institutional church. In other words, the Inquisition suspected that the mystics might be tending toward some form of Protestantism or lack of orthodoxy—in short, unbelief.

Although all these positions can be found in Spanish literature, unbelief most frequently implies acceptance of Jesus the Redeemer, combined with some sort of rejection of the Catholic church. This rejection can be complete or partial. Most often it is simply a rejection of the people who represent the church—the clergy. This is known as anticlericalism, and Spanish literature is full of it. It is, paradoxically, possible for a person to be a fully believing Catholic and anticlerical at the same time. A distinction is made between the evangelical and institutional sides of the church.

Anticlericalism in Spanish literature began long before the Reformation. Before the Renaissance it was directed chiefly against clerical hypocrisy and ignorance. During the Renaissance the base was broadened, and it took on a political tone with the rise of the Inquisition. In the 19th and 20th centuries anticlericalism was directed against the clergy for unreasonable intrusion into people's private lives, as well as for trying to impose clerically manufactured formulas upon every aspect of politics and national life. Thus, anticlericalism is often proportional to a lack of credibility in the institutional church and its spokesmen.

A tremendous threat to Catholic Spain arrived with the Muslim invasion of 711. Before the last Islamic *taifa* (province), Granada, was defeated in 1492, Islamic culture and belief had mingled with the Germano-Roman. Coexistence, interspersed with violent fighting, had lasted for 781 years. Ultimately, it produced many beautiful cultural blendings. Islamic art is fanciful, ethereal, and romantic; the Islamic religion, especially in its mysticism, is moving and profound. Islamic culture influenced every aspect of Spanish life. Naturally there were doctrinal differences in the heresies of the *mohametizantes*. Marcelino Menéndez y Pelayo has documented these thoroughly in *Historia de los Heterodoxos Españoles* (Book 3, Epílogo; see Bibliography). He also includes the *judaizantes* because many Jews had entered Spain during the Muslim conquest and had made their own profound impact on orthodox Roman Catholic belief.

After Ferdinand and Isabella conquered the province of Granada, Spain was a united nation on the threshold of the modern world. They wanted to achieve purity of blood and belief; accordingly, they decreed the expulsion or conversion of all Jews in 1492 and all Muslims in 1502. Their majesties were unquestionably listening to their advisor, the terrible Cardinal Ximénez Cisneros.

The Inquisition was founded in Spain in 1478, and by 1538 there were 19 tribunals. It survived in Spain, in some form, until 1833. Actually, the Inquisition was a handing over of papal power to a national state. Thus, historians are unjust to no one when they speak of a distinctly Spanish Inquisition. Books were burned and thousands of accused persons were tried and put to death for heresy and various kinds of witchcraft. Of particular interest to the Inquisitors were the *conversos,* the Muslims and Jews and their descendants who chose to remain in Spain and convert. Of course, the Inquisition was, in the words of the Catholic historian Joseph Lortz, "a dreadful institution." It is difficult to understand it and it is insane to try to defend it. An inquisitional mentality survived even after 1833. It frequently provided the ultra-right-wing backdrop and lack of credibility against which the anticlericals fought.

Spanish literature begins around the 12th century. It consisted largely of lyrical court and popular poetry in both the Castilian and the Gallego-Portuguese dialect. The *Crónicas* of King Alfonso X and the heroic epics of which the *Cantar de Mio Cid* is the greatest example, are considered the first monuments of Spanish literature.

Juan Ruiz. It is in the second monument, however, that a sort of anticlericalism and unbelieving treatment of Catholic practices emerge. This is *El Libro de Buen Amor* ("The Book of Good Love"), written about 1335 by Juan Ruiz, the archpriest of Hita. Finding himself in jail, the archpriest decided to continue his ministry by teaching and instructing. He says in effect: I want to teach you about good love, the love of God, and holy things. But before I can do this, I must tell you all about *loco amor*, crazy sensual love, that leads to sexual profligacy, gluttony, and all sorts of sin. As a matter of fact I am a good example of the latter, even though *es umanal cosa el pecar* (sin is a human thing).

Thus, Father Juan fashioned a thick volume of mono-rhymed quatrains. They present a loosely picaresque story of Juan Ruiz, the womanizer. He had little success until he found a good go-between. This person was the skilled Doña Urraca, known as the *trotaconventos*, a word which has entered the Spanish language. It means one who trots from convent to convent to find the ripest virgins. She is the archetype of a surviving breed in Spanish literature also known as *celestinas*. Interspersed among the archpriest's quatrains are obviously sincere and lovely songs, in other meters, to the Virgin, and snippet-sized fables that indicate a thorough knowledge of sources. The book is bawdy, irreverent, and hilarious.

Juan Ruiz' chief verse form was the *mester de clerecía* (meter of the clergy). It had been deliberately created by the clergy to lure poets away from the raw, strong, blood-curdling, freely assonated rhythms of the epic, known as the *mester de juglaría* (meter of the troubadours). Thus, a new and more gentle meter was thought fit and proper for relating pious stories, such as the lives of the saints. It is a curious paradox, indeed a humorous literary-historical joke, that Juan Ruiz emerged in

all his rollicking irreverence as the greatest master of the pious meter.

In what way can Juan Ruiz be called anticlerical or related to unbelief? Simply because he is critical of clerical abuses and hypocrisy. By implication he is critical of the institutional church with regard to celibacy and other clerical standards. It was not so much that Juan Ruiz did not believe *in* celibacy; he simply did not believe it.

Fernando de Rojas. Unbelief, on a much more profound level, emerges in the third monument of Spanish literature. Commonly known as *La Celestina,* it was published at a surprisingly early date, 1499, in the form of a dialogued novel of 16 acts. Some critics rate it as the greatest work of world literature between Dante's *Divine Comedy* and the rise of Tudor drama. It is a hauntingly beautiful work; at the same time it is filled with frightening and realistic violence and the basest of human passions. *La Celestina* also presents problems for which there are only educated guesses. The author, Fernando de Rojas, a *converso*, revealed his identity in some acrostic introductory verses in the second edition of 1501. He also claimed that he *found* the long first act and completed the 15 additional acts during a two-week vacation at the university. It is hard to believe that a youth in his twenties could have completed a superb, dazzling work in so short a time.

In the edition of 1501 five more acts were added along with interpolations throughout most of the original text. Problems: Did Rojas write the first act? Did he make the interpolations? These questions are discussed in my study of *La Celestina*. Despite the problems, the work survives miraculously as a unified work with a strong element of unbelief as its principal message. Menéndez y Pelayo, who expresses his belief in the unity of the work, is supported by all critics.

La Celestina deals with the noble lovers, Calisto and Melibea and their contact with the Celestina and other picaresque denizens of the lower-class part of the city. At first rebuffed by Melibea, Calisto calls upon his servants, Sempronio and Parmeno, to enlist the aid of the Celestina. The latter is a bisexual, reluctantly retired whore, who makes her living by running a bawdy house and pimping. By calling upon the aid of all the powers of darkness and casting a spell upon a cord worn by Calisto, the bawd causes Melibea to fall hopelessly in love with Calisto. Sempronio and Parmeno kill the Celestina in a fight over booty and lose their own lives. Calisto falls from a ladder after one of his sexual encounters with Melibea. The girl runs to a tower and leaps to join her lover in death. Her father, Pleberio, concludes the work with a tragic lament.

The love of Calisto and Melibea is, of course, in the courtly tradition. Rojas, unquestionably aware that he was on dangerous ground, carefully planted hedges of medieval moralizing by means of his introductory summary and other devices. He claims he wishes to advise people who turn the object of their passions into God. Furthermore, the traditional medieval formula was fulfilled by the punishment of death. Since all had sinned, all had to die. Thus, by condemning courtly love, Rojas was safely within belief and escaped the condemnation of the Inquisition.

The problem of unbelief in *La Celestina*, however, is much deeper than this. In the prologue, the author heavily stresses a section from Heraclitus, the Greek philosopher who insisted that everything in life takes place as a battle and that the predatory nature of life extends even to the act of love.

Calisto, at the first sight of Melibea, sees in her the "glory of God," a not uncommon cliché in the language of the so-called pagan side of the Renaissance neo-Platonic revival. When Sempronio asks if he believes in God, Calisto proclaims he is "a Melibean." He believes in Melibea, indeed worships and adores Melibea.

All conversation between Calisto and Melibea is couched in the language of courtly love. No Christian principles are active, even though Melibea's ambiance is presented as the *cristiano viejo* (old Christian) tradition. We would expect Calisto to be a truly well-bred knight. He goes to church—but only to pray for Celestina's success in seducing Melibea. When Melibea is about to fling herself to the courtyard, she appears proud, beautiful, unrepentant, and fully liberated. There are no nagging doubts about the Christian God, no fear of punishment, no recourse to divine compassion or mercy. What she has done and is about to do she does freely, with only a vague glimmer of a vague reunion with her lover in a vague neo-Platonic heaven. Pleberio's immortal lament is not a religious or Christian statement. Rather, it is a philosophical discourse based on deep knowledge of the ancients. He sees the entire tragedy as a result of the human condition, and his thought is cast largely in the mold of the Stoics. His anguish is overpowering, but he must bow his aging head and accept.

Calisto and Melibea are well-born, noble, and beautiful. They speak in an elevated and flowing, romantic Renaissance vocabulary. The Celestina and her *picaros* are base and deceitful, lewd and totally without principles. Their state in life is also reflected in their language, which is coarse, vulgar, blasphemous, and hammered into rhythmic, almost overpowering explicitness. Yet Rojas does not always maintain a strict separation of the two levels. At times the author allows the strands to intertwine. Thus, when Calisto first bemoans his unrequited love, he sounds like a simpleton. One of the prostitutes claims to have seen Melibea naked, and her description is the opposite of Botticelli's neo-Platonic depiction in his painting *Birth of Venus*. In many examples, Rojas is saying: Strip away wealth, breeding, status, and lofty language, and Calisto and Melibea will appear no different from the lowest dregs, driven helplessly by their loins. The basic philosophic structure of the world of Heraclitus is everywhere apparent. Rojas was also challenging the double standard of his day when lovers pretended to be solid Christians but practiced courtly love.

Rojas saved himself from the Inquisition by his neat medieval moralizing. He left an immortal Renaissance masterpiece, which, however, also leaves a hollow feeling of awe and fright.

Cervantes. We now turn to the problem of unbelief in the fourth monument of Spanish literature, *Don Quijote de la Mancha,* by Miguel de Cervantes y Saavedra (Part 1, 1605; Part 2, 1615). Awareness of the work's multifaceted nature has developed slowly. On the most obvious level, it was a parody of the books of chivalry, intended to put that genre to rest forever. It did just that. Cervantes also succeeded in making it a tombstone for the heroic Golden Age of the reconquest of Spain and the conquest of the New World.

Cervantes used his vast technique to elicit tremendous multiplicity within a solid unity. The work is, after all, a product of the Baroque era. It is not difficult to see that the author was using his knight to elucidate many aspects of man. Don Quijote is not merely a gentle old man who went crazy over the ideals of chivalry. He is also a typical Spaniard, whose days of glory were several generations past; he is Spain, he is Everyman. At the end he realizes that the only reasonable route to follow is to confess his sins and make a good death.

The possibility of unbelief in the *Quijote* is a modern concept most forcefully proposed by the renowned Américo Castro, in *El Pensamiento de Cervantes* (see Bibliography). The book is a profound study of the cultural times and formative influences on Cervantes. From it a thesis emerges: Because of the Inquisition, writers had to disguise their message; basically Cervantes was heterodox. The author is constantly tampering with reality and posing the question as to what reality is. Thus, Cervantes is supposedly attacking the ultimate foundations of belief. For example, the knight fell upon the poor traveling barber and snatched his basin from his head. The Don was convinced that the basin was Mambrino's helmet. Quijote's companions discussed the matter at the inn and split the difference: from one point of view it was obviously a barber's basin; from another it was Mambrino's helmet.

The scholastic "principle of contradiction" states: What is, is; what is not, is not; what is, is not what is not. Once this principle is abandoned, the floodgates for multiple SKEPTICISM are open. The foundations of society are undermined and the ordered Thomistic logic of the Catholic church and its teachings are exposed to grave doubt. In later years Castro backed off somewhat from this position about Cervantes, but the question remains open. Without a doubt, Cervantes did play with reality and presented all sorts of ambiguities to entertain his readers and make them think. (Was the Don a hero or fool or both?) On balance, however, few critics feel that Cervantes was working to demolish Western civilization.

Between the dates of *La Celestina* and *Don Quijote* the Protestant Reformation arrived, and the Inquisitors had their hands full. In Spain, the controversy became centered in a cluster of problems known as *erasmismo*. The *erasmistas* were followers of Desiderius Erasmus of Rotterdam (1466–1536). To be a follower of this towering humanist meant that one must certainly be a heretic, a Lutheran, or some sort of crypto-Protestant.

It is not an exaggeration to say that in the 16th century practically every great Spanish writer, mystic, poet, or teacher had the hounds of the Inquisition snapping at his heels. The Inquisition's treatment of the 16th century's mystics has already been mentioned. St. Teresa of Avila was questioned, and one of her books was proscribed; St. John of the Cross was jailed and harassed. Fray Luis de León was dismissed from his teaching post at Salamanca and jailed for five years. He was from a partly *converso* family and made no secret of it. After he was reinstated, he is said to have begun his lecture with the words: "As we were saying yesterday . . ." Whether true or apocryphal, Fray Luis'

attitude was typical. There was little bitterness on the part of the persecuted.

It was natural that the humanists felt that reform of the church was long overdue. They all suffered for their efforts. To name but a few: Francisco de Vergara and his brother Juan were imprisoned. Juan de Mal Lara and the famous grammarian Antonio de Nebrija were similarly treated. Alfonso de Virues was imprisoned for translating eleven *Coloquies* of Erasmus. Francisco Sánchez was dismissed from the University of Salamanca. He had a bad habit of making fun of the Inquisitors from his lectern. Alfonso de Valdés made the mistake of letting his writing fall into the hands of the papal nuncio, Baldassare Castiglione, who wrote *The Courtier* (1528). The nuncio replied in a denunciation unparalleled in its savagery. He seemed to dance with glee as he contemplated the burning of Valdés in an auto-da-fé. But Valdés escaped when he joined the retinue of Charles V at the Diet of Augsburg.

The histories of these important figures are filled with human interest. (They can be found in Devlin's *Spanish Anticlericalism*.) Many felt that the Lutheran break might never have happened if the institutional church had reformed itself from within. The humanists rightly considered the sale of offices, benefices, *bulas*, indulgences, dispensations, and the like to be a scandal to the Christian faith. They were particularly scandalized by false relics and the linking of money with the sacraments. They called for greater emphasis on the spiritual life. To a great extent, these people were persecuted for supposed unbelief; the paradox is that most were highly orthodox.

As Spanish literature entered a new period, humorous depictions of clerics continued. The clergy, however, were considered regular members of society. They were not accorded the "hands-off," special status characteristic of recent American experience. Orthodoxy was the only thing that mattered. There was a fair amount of fun-poking in the theater before Lope de Vega.

The picaresque novel emerged as a genre with the publication of *Lazarillo de Tormes* (1554). This anonymous work was satirical and bitterly critical of priestly abuses. One edition was forbidden by the Inquisition in 1559. Yet it must be noted that the vices exhibited by unsavory priests were precisely those that prompted laws for reform in the Council of Trent. Mateo Aleman's *Guzmán de Alfarache* (1599) and Francisco Quevedo's *Buscón* (1626) are the next high points of the picaresque. Quevedo, a statesman and a towering artist in many literary forms, is particularly interesting. *Buscón* and other works exhibit profound disillusion with the Spain whose faults and decline he clearly saw. He also was a theologian of high idealism. Thus, the two strands of Spanish literature, realism and idealism, are united in the person of one author: Quevedo believed in God; his card-sharping priest in the *Buscón* believed in his own self-indulgence.

The supreme giants of the Golden Age of Spanish literature are the dramatists Lope de Vega (1562–1635) and Calderón de la Barca (1600–1681), but they are closely associated with the soldified concept of Spanish "theocracy."

Calderón's death is often used as a convenient signpost for the passing of the Golden Age. The overriding intellectual and literary trends now shifted to France and the galaxy of writers associated with the startlingly new ideas of the ENCYCLOPÉDIE and the Enlightenment. Under this influence, Spaniards experienced a secular spirit in the realm of the mind. Benito Feijóo, a Benedictine monk (1676–1774), was deeply influenced by the French tradition and produced his own encyclopedic *Teatro Crítico Universal* ("Critical Essays on Universal Topics"). He was, of course, subjected to heavy criticism; Menéndez y Pelayo damns him with faint praise.

The Inquisition continued with the autos-da-fé in an effort to rid Spain of heterodox impurity. But, as Gerald Brenan notes in *The Spanish Labyrinth*, the Inquisition had "ceased to inspire terror but exerted great political power." The people who were now being burned were relatively unknown recalcitrants and the crime of unbelief was usually connected with "philosophism," that is, circulation of French ideas. The naturalist José Clavigo y Fajardo and the mathematician Benito Bails were harassed. The best-known writers of the century involved in the inquisitorial process were the poets Tomás de Iriarte and Samaniego. Guilty of "philosophism," they made satirical anticlerical statements.

Because of incredible royal mismanagement and the accidents of history, a period of tears and violence characterizes the 19th century. Affairs went from bad to worse until the last remnant of dignity was shattered in the Spanish-American War of 1898. The list of disasters begins with Charles IV and Ferdinand VII and their quite bewildering abdications, which ended with Joseph Bonaparte as king of Spain. Immediately, popular uprisings against the French spilled Spanish blood in the wars for independence. Ferdinand returned

to claim the throne in 1814. He was "El Deseado" (the longed-for). He had promised to be a constitutional monarch and uphold the liberal tenets of the Cortes de Cádiz, but instead he revived the Inquisition and reigned as one of the most corrupt, cruel, and repressive leaders the peninsula had ever seen. Before he died in 1833, he had the law of succession changed. Thus, his brother Charles was denied the throne in favor of his daughter Isabel. His mother, Cristina, acted as regent. As a result, four Carlist Wars, with intermittent bloody uprisings, shook Spain. Agrarian reform and emerging industrial problems added to the confusion, but they were practically ignored. The *carlistas* symbolized attempts to apply medieval solutions to modern problems; unfortunately their spirit is not dead, even in the late 20th century.

As the 19th century progressed, the divisions between liberals and conservatives became much more intense and the anticlerical controversies more sharply delineated. Despite extreme antagonisms, unbelief does not emerge strongly until quite late in the century. One strong exception, however, is found in the romantic era. José de Espronceda (1808–1842) produced a masterful treatment of the Don Juan theme in *El Estudiante de Salamanca* ("The Student of Salamanca," 1836). In its linguistic structure the poem is the quintessence of romanticism. But the hero, Don Felix de Montemar, is a realist. Like Ahab in *Moby Dick*, he wants to know the nature of the reality behind reality. Failing, he shouts out his despair and defiance of God.

One would imagine that French naturalism and concomitant problems would have influenced Spain's 19th century. It did—but almost never in a deterministic way. Spaniards had absorbed too much orthodoxy—even subliminally—to follow that path.

Late in the century the philosophy of a German, Karl Krause (1781–1832), crept in. Krause's teaching consisted of a benign and attractive panentheism. Many writers, such as Benito Pérez Galdós and José Ortega y Gasset, were considered *krausistas* and accordingly came under heavy clerical fire. Francisco Giner de los Ríos (1839–1915) was of this persuasion. He founded the famous Institución Libre de Enseñanza. A neutral school and a refreshing challenge to the monopoly of the church in educational matters, it produced some of the greatest minds of Spain's late 19th and 20th centuries. It also became the object of lasting clerical attacks. Thus, anticlericalism became more focused as a reaction by liberal thinkers to attempts to impose an exclusive Catholic formula on all areas of life.

Emilio Castelar (1832–1899) struggled bravely in this area. The brief First Republic (1873–74) tried to limit clerical pressure; by so doing it contributed to its own downfall. Pedro Antonio de Alarcón (1833–1891), before switching to traditionalism, edited the caustically anticlerical newspaper *El Látigo.* José Echegaray addressed the problems of religious intolerance. Both Armando Palacio Valdés (1853–1938) and Juan Valera (1827–1905) objected to the rigorous asceticism that some clerics tried to impose on the laity. Valera was also a forerunner of the future storms against the Jesuits in his essay "Los Jesuitas de Puertas Adentro."

Leopoldo Alas (1852–1901), better known as "Clarín," in his novel *La Regenta* (1885) presented a priest who is insincere in his belief, falls into carnal love, and abuses his power over consciences. Clarín considered himself a Spanish Catholic—and a traditional one. He also insisted that he was a *krausista.* He was attracted to the doctrine's emphasis on the goodness of God, the idea that somehow all men are pieces of him, united in tolerance and an eager search for him. Of course, the ultraconservative clergy, in their long battle against *krausismo,* could never accept such syncretism. But a careful examination of Clarín's essays shows that he simply absorbed *krausismo* into the traditional concept of God's immanence. He was attacked but fought back strongly against the enormous usurpations of power by the church. Clarín's syncretism prefigured late-20th-century ecumenism. In his own time, he and his close friend Castelar made a truly significant contribution.

With the coming of the 20th century the anticlerical issue burst into the open. Unbelief and anticlericalism became interwoven in vital areas in need of reform. Established writers such as Benito Pérez Galdós (1843–1920) and Vicente Blasco Ibáñez (1867–1928) attacked the narrow positions of the institutional church. Pérez Galdós has been called "the Spanish Dickens." He was much beloved by Spaniards everywhere and is considered by most critics to be the greatest writer after Cervantes. A gentle person, he hated to see religious bigotry divide mankind. He felt religion should be a unifying force, and he probably would be at home in today's ecumenism. Although both sympathetic and critical portraits of priests abound in his *oeuvre,* in his first period he produced three thoroughly anticlerical novels: *Dõna Perfecta*

(1876), *Gloria* (1877), and *La Familia de León Roch* (1879). The first is a condemnation of a certain Spanish female, the *beata,* who considers herself holy but is not; Perfecta murders her scientist nephew to preserve family orthodoxy. Gloria's life is rent by her love for an English Jew; the families of both are intransigent. León Roch was a freethinker; his marriage was ruined when the Jesuits took over the direction of his wife's life.

Pérez Galdós belonged esthetically to the 19th century. So too did the fiery Blasco Ibáñez. As a young man he was known as a brilliant Valencian regionalist, but in his second period he wrote against the traditionalism that was impeding Spain's modernization. In *La Catedral* (1903), set in the archepiscopal surroundings of Toledo, he hit the clergy and the church unmercifully. In *El Entruso* (1904) he took up the by-now familiar topic of the power of the Jesuits and their influence on rich penitents. It closes with a terrible clash between leftist workers and Catholic traditionalists. The author foresaw that lines were being drawn that would lead to civil war. Blasco Ibáñez' late period was devoted to potboilers in which he dredged up scandals of the Renaissance church. It is difficult to consider him a believer, yet he returned to the church on his deathbed.

The authors whose work exhibits unbelief during the period up to the Republic of 1931–36 and the Civil War (1936–39) are Manuel Linares Rivas (1878–1938), Pérez de Ayala (1881–1962), Pío Baroja Nessi (1872–1956), José Ortega y Gasset (1883–1956), and Miguel de Unamuno.

Linares Rivas wrote against clerical interference in private lives in the matter of divorce, producing two plays, *Aire de Fuera* (1903) and *La Garra* (1914); the latter is considered his masterpiece. His thesis was that the Spanish church's implacable position on divorce was a scandal and the cause of much suffering and tragedy. Paradoxically, Linares Rivas always claimed that he was conservative and Catholic.

Pérez de Ayala mocked the church's traditional puritanical ideas on sex and sex education in his *Luna de Miel, Luna de Hiel* (1923). In *AMDG* (1910) he used the initials for the Latin motto of the Jesuits: *Ad Majorem Dei Gloriam* (to the greater glory of God). Powerfully written, the novel is unsympathetic to the Jesuits, their ideas on education, and the type of men who constitute their membership. The description of a Jesuit retreat for boys rivals the one found in Joyce's *Portrait of the Artist as a Young Man.*

Pío Baroja claims that AGNOSTICISM is the only decent path a man can take in life. In his large number of essays and novels he peppers his pages with every imaginable type of anticlericalism, with the Jesuits receiving special treatment. He also exhibits himself as one of Spain's most infamous anti-Semites. The great thinker Ortega y Gasset does not seem much concerned with the problem of God. A follower of Krause, he was also, at least indirectly, critical of the church's monopoly of power.

Miguel de Unamuno (1864–1936) presents a special problem. He was continually preoccupied with the problem of God and immortality. He wanted desperately to believe. He also felt that RATIONALISM had threatened belief. By the same token he said that the Catholic rational theologians proved nothing. If we are to know God it is through Christ, the Gospels, and the way of the heart. Some critics have said that Unamuno was like a pendulum swinging constantly between doubt and belief. This assessment is not quite true. It is more a question of believing and not believing at the same time. Unamuno developed this point in many works, the most famous being *Del Sentimiento Trágico de la Vida, en los Hombres y los Pueblos* (1912). He explains that life is an agony, a continual wrestling with this problem. If it is not, then it is not worth living. The condition of man in the modern world, Unamuno adds, is conducive to this struggle.

The most thoughtful people find it difficult to follow Unamuno all the way. The unbeliever wonders why, if he did not believe, he spent so much of his life writing superb Christian poetry that has been ranked with the works of the mystics. The believer will shrug his shoulders and answer that any healthy belief should always be challenged by doubt. Unamuno's metaphysics is open to criticism. Most theistic systems posit God first and immortality second. Unamuno's equation demands that God should exist because we desperately want immortality.

Unamuno liked to picture himself as Don Quijote, the eternal seeker. He also sometimes assumed the garb of a Protestant clergyman. He was anticlerical in practically every sense of the word; he was also antimonarchical. But, it should be noted, his wrath was mostly directed against Spanish problems. Spaniards, he claimed, were totally asleep. It was his mission to wake up these souls. If they searched carefully they would find that the problem of God was not neatly wrapped up.

The elections of 1931 brought the Second Republic. Ortega y Gasset was one of its founders. The new state was doomed to failure. This was in part the result of vindictive anticlerical clauses in the constitution. Among them was the call for the expulsion of the Jesuits. Spaniards simply could not forgive and forget, and reform went nowhere. The elections of 1936 split the vote almost equally between conservatives and liberals, and the Civil War ensued.

The greatest representatives of some form of unbelief in recent times are Rafael Alberti (born 1902), Arturo Barea (1902–1957), and Ramón Sender (1902–1981). Alberti was the declared Communist poet of the era and a man who advocated complete unbelief. Although age and the passage of time mellowed him, especially in the formulation of his politics, he appears not to have changed substantially.

Arturo Barea is noted chiefly for his monumental biography, *La Forja de un Rebelde* (1946), which was translated as *The Forging of a Rebel* by his wife, Ilsa. This magnificent work gives a vivid account of Spain's turmoils in the 20th century up until 1939. Barea is anticlerical, yet says that he never bothered to change his Catholic label. He never became a fully convinced Communist either. He longed for God and a clergy of true compassion. As far as unbelief is concerned, the only thing that can be said of him is that he was an embittered, lapsed Catholic.

Ramón Sender fought briefly in the Civil War. The truth and violence in his novels (dealing with the time immediately before, during, and after the war) make a shattering reading experience. *Siete Domingos Rojos* (1932) is probably the most powerful; it is also frequently blasphemous. One must remember, however, that Sender always states that he is merely recording the states of mind of the various revolutionary sectors of Spanish society. Sender's philosophy of life and God is found in *La Esfera* (1947). It is a murky melange of such pessimistic philosophers as ARTHUR SCHOPENHAUER and FRIEDRICH NIETZSCHE. The only strand that seems to emerge is that individual immortality can exist for man only to the extent that he participates in *hombria* (all mankind). It is a sort of closed-off, circular pantheism.

Before concluding, a word of caution is necessary. The Spanish republic was not a godless Communist state. It was a liberal, secular state sprung from the people and charged with its hopes, very similar to mid-20th-century European democracies. Many intellectual Catholics participated in its formation and tried to serve it. On the other hand the republic did not receive much support from the church hierarchy.

Similarly, the Civil War was not a war to rid Spain of communism, despite the fact that the Loyalists were called and are still called "the Reds" and despite the fact, also, that at the war's end Pope Pius XII congratulated Francisco Franco on his "Catholic victory." Conservative Catholic spokesmen and others did not try to understand or failed to understand the centuries-long battle between the Spanish liberals and conservatives. During the last several weeks of the collapse of the Loyalist armies in 1939, the government had its only Communist leader, Negrín.

This investigation has come full circle back to *un rincón de Dios*. As far as unbelief in the absolute sense is concerned, there is little in Spanish literature. By "absolute unbelief," atheism is implied, or, in a slightly different sense, the feeling that God is somehow absent. Unbelief *is* found, but largely in varying forms of anticlericalism, a phenomenon that dates from the Renaissance to the end of Franco's regime. Spanish writers failed to believe in the clergy because the latter resisted and condemned just about all the legitimate aspirations of modernity. This results in a paradox. Spain, a country that has been called the most Catholic in the world, is also the most anticlerical. There are hopeful signs, however, that changes are coming during the last decades of the 20th century as a result of the Second Vatican Council.

Other article of interest: **Spain: Unbelief in.**

Bibliography

Bernanos, Georges. *Les Grands Cimetières Sous la Lune.* Paris: 1958.

Bonacina, Conrad. "The Catholic Church and Modern Democracy." *Cross Currents.* Fall 1951.

Brenan, Gerald. *The Spanish Labyrinth.* 2nd ed. London: Cambridge U. Press, 1950.

Castro, Américo. *El Pensamiento de Cervantes.* Princeton, N.J.: Princeton U. Press, 1925.

Clancy, William P. "The Area of Catholic Freedom." *Commonweal* 61 (Nov. 5, 1954).

Denziger, Henricus. *Enchiridion Symbolorum: Definitionum et Declarationum de Rebus Fidei et Morum.* Herder, Typog. Editores Pontificii, 1937.

Devlin, John. *La Celestina: A Parody of Courtly Love. Toward a Realistic Interpretation of "La Tragicomedia de Calisto y Melibea."* New York: Las Americas, 1971.

———. *Spanish Anticlericalism: A Study in Modern Alienation.* New York: Las Americas, 1966.

Lea, Henry Charles. *The Inquisition in Spain.* New York: 1906.

Lortz, Joseph. *History of the Church.* Trans. Edwin Kaiser. Milwaukee: 1939.

Mendizábal, Alfred. *The Martyrdom of Spain.* Introduction by Jacques Maritain. Trans. from the French edition by Charles H. Lumley. London: 1938.

Menéndez y Pelayo, Marcelino. *Historia de los Heterodoxos Españoles.* 2 vols. Madrid: 1956.

———. *Origenes de la Novela.* Madrid: 1940.

Murray, John Courtney. "Contemporary Orientations of Catholic Thought in the Light of History." *Cross Currents.* Fall 1951.

Unamuno, Miguel de. *Mi Religión y Otros Ensayos.* Madrid: 1951.

JOHN DEVLIN

SPENCER, HERBERT (1820–1903), English philosopher, psychologist, and sociologist, born at Derby.

His Writings. Spencer's first book, *Social Statics* (1851), was a treatise on political philosophy which suggested the nationalization of land. His second book, *The Principles of Psychology* (1855), was an explanation of association psychology. He gained recognition in Europe, America, and Asia as a philosopher following the publication of *First Principles* (1862), which was the first volume of *A System of Synthetic Philosophy.* His system incorporated an expanded version of *The Principles of Psychology* (2 vols., 1872, 1873) and included *The Principles of Biology* (2 vols., 1864, 1867), *The Principles of Sociology* (3 vols., 1876, 1882, 1896) and *The Principles of Ethics* (2 vols., 1892, 1893).

Outside the framework of his *Synthetic Philosophy,* Spencer wrote many essays and several books; three of the latter had a wide readership. These were *Education, The Study of Sociology,* and *The Man 'versus' the State. Education* (1861) expounded the liberal educational views of George Spencer (his father). These encouraged the natural development of a child's intelligence. *The Study of Sociology* (1873) was a student's introduction to sociology and the first important English book on the subject. *The Man 'versus' the State* (1884) was a libertarian tract protesting the growth of socialism and state intervention.

The Man. Spencer, though often regarded as self-educated, was very carefully guided by his father, George, and his uncle, Thomas, both of whom included schoolteaching among their various interests. George Spencer, who was secretary of the Derby Philosophical Society (one of the many provincial groups that kept the sciences and arts alive in the new industrial towns) held views similar to those of some 20th-century radical educators, namely, that a child's learning was improved only by encouragement to study those subjects he liked. Subjects they did not like were ignored. Herbert received this "free school" type of education from his father and later from his uncle, Thomas. Although Thomas was an Anglican clergyman who kept a small school for coaching children in the classics, the nephew received no religious education nor any grounding in the classics, though he pursued mathematics and science with vigor. The only mark left on Herbert by Thomas Spencer was Herbert's adoption of radical politics. Both held extreme Chartist views on the reform of English politics, and both believed in the repeal of the Corn Laws. For the rest, the young Herbert was trained to trust his own judgment and to disregard authority.

At the age of 17, Herbert joined the staff of a railway and rapidly showed much ability at bridge design and construction, first with the London and Birmingham Company and then with the Gloucester and Birmingham Company. However, his rebellious temperament caused him to be dismissed from the latter at the age of 21. For the next few years, 1841–48, Spencer largely abandoned engineering, and occupied himself with writing articles and pamphlets. In 1848 he secured the position of subeditor of the *Economist,* a London newspaper and the leading anti-Corn-Law journal.

London in the 1840s and 1850s was a place of intellectual ferment, and Spencer soon enjoyed the friendship of other young writers and scientists, such as G. H. Lewes and George Eliot, THOMAS HENRY HUXLEY and John Tyndall. Editorial work for the *Economist* was supplemented by articles for journals such as the *Westminster Review,* and, from 1848 until 1860, he lived the exhilarating, exhausting and penurious life of a London journalist, while at the same time writing books on philosophy. This period of excessive activity damaged his health, and, as a result, he was often ill and weak in later years.

In 1860 he conceived the idea of publishing further work by subscription. With the help of his friends he obtained between three and four hundred subscribers to *A System of Synthetic Philosophy*. This financial aid, together with some small inheritances, meant that he was able to give up journalism for philosophy, though financial worries plagued him for another decade.

From 1860 until the end of his life Spencer was harried by writing deadlines. Since he was a bachelor, he had no family life to distract him from his work. His egalitarian and rather stern principles prevented him from taking part in society life, which was still dominated by the landed gentry of whose customs and titles he disapproved. In later years, he was lionized but always refused distinctions and honors.

Spencer never lost the independence he had gained during his schooling. This sense of independence would sometimes make him quarrelsome and overly concerned about his originality. He was also incapable of bending his views to suit his audience. On his only visit to the United States, in 1882, he was not tactful to the assembled business community of New York; instead of a speech praising energy and initiative he told them that the worst feature of the modern world was overwork. His dislike of authority was not confined to a rejection of government, but included a dislike of big business.

Spencer's philosophy was part of a 19th-century movement that rejected philosophical and theological extremism in favor of a common-sense philosophy which placed the mind on the same level as matter. Following the work of Sir William Hamilton and Henry Longueville Mansel, Spencer rejected RATIONALISM (or crude empiricism) and its subspecies, POSITIVISM. He also adopted their practice of leaving a philosophical niche for the unexplainable, which he called the "Unknown." *A System of Synthetic Philosophy* was intended to point out the various directions in which science led to the same conclusions as common-sense philosophy. Together, philosophy and science suggested belief in an Absolute that transcended human knowledge, and even human conception. The synthetic philosophy was, to Spencer, the only possible reconciliation of science and religion.

The basis of Spencer's version of the philosophy of common sense was a "universal postulate" (his essay on this appeared in 1853, and after 1860 it became part of his *Synthetic Philosophy*). He declared as axiomatic that there was a basic intuition or belief that would establish "facts" (that is, truths) about the real world. The constant presence of a belief was the only warrant for every truth of immediate consciousness, and further, for every low-level generalization based on these truths. Logical necessity had no more certainty than anything else, and one could not use reason to transcend ordinary knowledge. Certainty did not come through reason but through "belief," in the form Spencer allowed in his "universal postulate."

About this, he stated that "a belief which is proved, by the inconceivableness of its negation to invariably exist, is true." This allowed the immediate test of the truth of a belief, without going through a chain of deductions, each step of which would lead to less certainty. The establishment of certainty in beliefs was Spencer's main concern, and the "universal postulate" was intended as a trumpet blast against DAVID HUME and SKEPTICISM (though some orthodox clergy, who were not concerned with reconciling science with religion and who were more frightened of science than of Hume, charged Spencer with ATHEISM).

Spencer's philosophy was subject to severe criticism during his lifetime, and this, together with his fearless adoption of empirical and experimental findings, led to various inconsistencies and strains in his thought. The most important difficulty occurred in his notion of "truth." In *First Principles* (1862) *truth* had become "simply the accurate correspondence of subjective to objective relations; while *error*, leading to failure and therefore towards death, is the absence of such accurate correspondence." Even more radical was Spencer's subsequent statement that implied that this truth did not matter. Objective facts did not have to correspond to subjective states. A mysterious force called "Life" ensured that the correspondence between them would always be the same. Spencer concluded this analysis by explicitly denying one of the fundamental canons of realism and common-sense philosophy. He stated that "things in themselves cannot be known to us."

It would be convenient and satisfying at this point to state that Spencer ceased to be a common-sense philosopher in 1862 and adopted a semi-mystical evolutionary doctrine guided by an unknown Life-force. But this was not the case. Spencer kept elements of the universal postulate and common sense in his thought after *First Principles*, though their meaning became increasingly obscure. From 1862, Spencer's philosophy contained basic inconsistencies.

The Impact of Spencer's Philosophy. With the publication of *First Principles*, Spencer's thought took on a religious significance to his contemporaries, which overshadowed his more technical work on biology, sociology, and ethics. Mid-Victorians, unlike their 20th-century descendants, did not find metaphysics unpalatable, and they grasped at whatever hints Spencer gave as to the meaning of life and the significance of the scientific universe.

Those who took Spencer seriously regarded him as a prophet of a new religion, and it was as a prophet that Spencer aroused interest and emulation. He attracted his early followers, such as Huxley, Tyndall, and Alfred Russel Wallace, because he expressed scientific ideas in a form that allowed a role for the human spirit. His "spiritualism" suggested that religious truth could be discovered by man's soul, and his philosophy offered the hope that truth could be intuited through man's faculties. Both of these features gave the mind an active role in the discovery of truth, and promised the forging of a new harmony between man and the universe.

Spencerian philosophical and religious beliefs are not easily labeled; terms such as *agnostic, atheist, materialist, empiricist, rationalist, pantheist, spiritualist*, and *deist*, are wrong or misleading. Spencer offered philosophical certainty, which agnosticism excluded. Atheism, MATERIALISM, empiricism, and rationalism all denied that there was a link between the human mind or spirit and the universe; while pantheism, spiritualism, and DEISM, which seem more applicable, have misleading connotations of nature worship, spirits and ghosts, and of rationalism. Spencerian philosophy was distinct from these other doctrines, and served a different function. He was a philosopher who offered the Victorians both metaphysical and moral certainty, and an explanation of the place of religion in a scientific world.

Bibliography

Spencer's longer works are widely available in the many printings of *A System of Synthetic Philosophy*. Most of his important essays were republished as *Essays: Scientific, Political and Speculative* (London: Williams and Norgate, 1868–74, 3 vols.).

The most extensive and important works about Spencer are *An Autobiography* (London: Williams and Norgate, 1904, 2 vols.), and David Duncan, *The Life and Letters of Herbert Spencer* (London:

Methuen, 1908). These works have to be treated with care, however, because, though they were published posthumously, Spencer himself had carefully arranged and edited the material to overstress his independence, originality, and consistency.

Of recent monographs on Spencer, the most thoroughly researched is J. D. Y. Peel's *Herbert Spencer: The Evolution of a Sociologist* (London: Heinemann, 1971). However, since this is an examination of one of sociology's "founding fathers," it is not very illuminating about Spencer's philosophy.

Unfortunately, there is no recent work on his philosophy, and general works on Victorian intellectual history have tended to be hostile and unfair to Spencer. For example, See J. B. Schneewind's *Sidgewick's Ethics and Victorian Moral Philosophy* (Oxford: Clarendon Press, 1977) and J. R. Moore, *The Post-Darwinian Controversies* (Cambridge University Press, 1979).

The best article on Spencer's social theory is Robert G. Perrin, "Herbert Spencer's Four Theories of Social Evolution," *American Journal of Sociology* 81, no. 6 (May 1976). For Spencer's political theory, see Mark Francis, "Herbert Spencer and the Myth of Laissez-Faire," *Journal of the History of Ideas* 29, no. 2 (April-June 1979), and David Wiltshire, *The Social and Political Thought of Herbert Spencer* (Oxford University Press, 1978).

MARK FRANCIS

SPINOZA, BARUCH or BENEDICT (1632–1677), Dutch-Jewish philosopher, born Nov. 24, in Amsterdam in a community of Portuguese Jews. Spinoza has been called the "God-intoxicated Jew," and the intellectual love of God forms the core of his *Ethics.* Thus, there is a certain Pickwickian element in speaking of his unbelief, for to some he was regarded as a person obsessed with God, a pantheist who interpreted every natural phenomenon as a revelation of God. But to others he was a harsh materialist and determinist who attempted to destroy morality and religion, and in his own time, it was politically inexpedient to be identified as his friend, such was his notoriety as an atheist.

His Education and Early Iconoclasm. Early in life, Spinoza found the rabbinical education in the synagogue unsatisfactory and undertook the study of Latin to satisfy his desire to know secular philosophy and science. Thus RENÉ DESCARTES

and GIORDANO BRUNO were available for his thirsty mind. He pursued Latin with Francis van den Ende, a known freethinker. Even while a student at the synagogue, Spinoza's heterodox views could not be suppressed, for on one occasion he voiced thoughts on God's nature unacceptable to his teachers. The elders of the synagogue first tried to bribe the 24-year-old youth into silence by offering him an annuity and, failing in this, threatened him with excommunication. When Spinoza did not yield, he was duly excommunicated in 1656.

Spinoza's attack upon orthodox religious belief was focused in two of his principal works, the *Tractatus Theologico-Politicus* (published anonymously in 1677) and the posthumously published *Ethics.* In the former, Spinoza furthered his aim of destroying the power of theological prejudice to the end that philosophy might be unimpeded. He demanded a purely secular state, indifferent to matters of religious doctrine and free from ecclesiastical interference. He defended personal religious opinion as a human right, along with freedom of thought and conscience, while following THOMAS HOBBES in holding that in the interest of order and domestic tranquility, the public expression of religion be fixed by the sovereign.

In the *Tractatus Theologico-Politicus* Spinoza demonstrated that religion has no claim on theoretical truth, that its proper domain is in the disposition of the will and the formation of morals. This view reinforced his conviction that the state has no basis or justification for concerning itself with the doctrinal orthodoxy of its citizens, but rather should use its authority to prevent the churches from constraining freedom of conscience.

Spinoza asserted that religious writings, specifically the Bible, must be subject to the same thorough scholarly scrutiny of historical method as any other literature. To this end he argued persuasively that Moses did not write the Pentateuch and concluded that biblical miracles are contrary to the eternal, immutable nature of God. Spinoza did not accept the divinity of Jesus, but regarded him as the highest expression of humanity. He believed that, were the improbable stories surrounding Jesus' life and the unbelievable dogmas about his nature withdrawn, Jews could regard him as the highest and noblest of the prophets. He made no sharp division between the Old and New Testaments, treating Christianity and Judaism as one religion.

In the Ethics, one finds four clear expressions of unbelief in prevailing theological opinions. For

Spinoza (1) God is not personal, conscious, or purposive; (2) there is no freedom of the will; (3) there is nothing in Nature that is either good or bad, the latter concepts being applicable only to sentient beings' desires, strivings, fulfillments, and frustrations; (4) there is no personal immortality.

Spinoza conceives of substance (literally that which "stands beneath" and supports) as that which immutably and eternally is, that upon which everything else depends and which itself depends on nothing. There can by definition, then, be only one such substance, God or Nature, which necessarily exists and is its own cause. Everything else is but an attribute or mode of this single substance. God is not a creator distinct from the creation. Spinoza writes in Epistle 21: "I take a totally different view of God and Nature from that which the later Christians usually entertain, for I hold that God is the immanent, and not the extraneous, cause of all things. I say, All is in God; all lives and moves in God."

From God's nature, all things follow with logical necessity, just as it follows from the nature of a triangle that the sum of its interior angles equals 180°. Since the will of God (so to speak, for "neither intellect nor will pertains to the nature of God," *Ethics* I.17 note) and the laws of nature are one and identical, the order of the material world follows with necessity. This is a world of DETERMINISM, in which humanity has no free will. Humans think themselves free because they are conscious of their desires and volitions, but they are unaware of the causes which inevitably produce such. The only possible freedom from bondage to the passions is through the action of the intellect. We are free only when through reason we stand above the fragmentary and futile realm of uninformed desire.

In the Tractatus-Politicus (posthumously published, 1677, along with the *Ethics*) this latter thought is related to the third point regarding the extent to which Spinoza expressed unbelief in the prevailing teachings of his and of our own day. He writes, "As for the terms *good* and *bad*, they indicate nothing positive considered in themselves. . . ." (*Ethics*, IV, preface). *Good* and *bad* are subjective and personal terms reflecting our idiosyncratic demands that the universe satisfy our desires, but not standing for anything in God's eternal nature.

Our greatest good is to see things "under the aspect of eternity," to merge our own desires with the universal order of things, to become an indistinguishable part of nature. The more we achieve this end, the more eternal become our thoughts. But unlike much Christian teaching, and like the older biblical Judaism, Spinoza neither affirms personal survival, nor does he hold out for heavenly rewards.

"The human mind cannot be absolutely destroyed with the human body, but there is some part of it which remains eternal," Spinoza says in the *Ethics* (V.23). But that eternal part is not an immortal soul, but is the mind, which is filled with eternal thoughts of God or Nature, eternal and immutable substance. Such a mind is conscious of God and the order of things by a certain eternal necessity.

While his philosophy denies a person whatever comfort is to be found in a belief in personal immortality, Spinoza's own unbelief in such brought him no apparent discomfort, when at the age of 44 he died on Feb. 21, 1677, quietly of consumption, having previously locked the manuscript of his *Ethics* in a small desk with instructions that it be conveyed to an Amsterdam publisher. This man's brave act of posthumously publishing the philosopher's works assured Spinoza of the only true immortality he ever desired.

Bibliography

Feuer, Lewis Samuel. *Spinoza and the Rise of Liberalism.* Boston: Beacon Press, 1958.

Hampshire, Stuart. *Spinoza.* Baltimore: Penguin Books, 1951.

Kayser, Rudolph. *Spinoza: Portrait of a Spiritual Hero.* New York: Greenwood Press, 1968.

Strauss, Leo. *Spinoza's Critique of Religion.* New York: Schocken Books, 1965.

The reader desiring guidance to standard works and commentaries, such as Frederick Pollock's *Spinoza: His Life and Philosophy* (London: Duckworth, 1880) and H. A. Wolfson, *The Philosophy of Spinoza* (Cambridge, Mass.: Harvard U. Press, 1934), will find an extensive bibliography in Kayser and a select listing in Hampshire.

JOHN L. MCKENNEY

STOUT, ROBERT (1844–1930), was one of New Zealand's leading public figures of the late 19th and early 20th centuries. Indeed, in the history of this small country he still has few rivals as regards the range of his contributions to public life. He gained eminence in the political, legal, and educational spheres: as prime minister, 1884–1887, chief justice, 1899–1926, and chancellor of the University of New Zealand, 1903–1923.

Stout's political career was brief and stormy, and it was interrupted by retirements from Parliament to concentrate on his legal business. In the 1890s he was defeated in a struggle with R. J. Seddon for the leadership of the Liberal party. He retired finally from politics in 1898. He is a rare example of a New Zealand intellectual in politics. He was interested in political theories, as few other New Zealand politicians have been, and he frequently lectured and published pamphlets on political topics (see the Bibliography below). In many ways he was a typical 19th-century radical, believing in the necessity of state action against land monopoly but otherwise strongly favoring laissez-faire capitalism. However, in the 1890s he modified this latter stance when he saw certain Old World evils, such as "sweated labor," appearing in the New World. He was also for a time the parliamentary leader of the prohibitionist movement. Stout was a keen debater and loved to get involved in controversies. Supremely confident of the validity of his own ideas, he sometimes irritated opponents by the arrogant manner in which he responded to their attempts to present a different side of an argument.

Stout was born at Lerwick in the Shetland Islands; his father was a merchant and landowner. He was educated locally and worked for a time as a student teacher before migrating to New Zealand at the age of 19 in 1863. He settled in Dunedin, commercial capital of the province of Otago. Free Church Presbyterians from Scotland had founded the Otago settlement in 1848, and it retained a strongly Presbyterian character. But, when Stout arrived, Otago was in the throes of the gold rushes, and the character of the community was being transformed by the influx of large numbers of gold-seekers and traders, who had no respect for the ecclesiastical aspirations and moral principles of the founding fathers. Dunedin was then New Zealand's wealthiest and liveliest community. The wealth generated by the gold rushes fostered the growth of a sizable middle class, and many cultural societies were founded. Stout plunged delightedly into this new world of theological and political controversy.

Influences on His Attitude Toward Reli-

gion. Stout's attitude to religion had been shaped during his boyhood in Lerwick. An important part of social life there was discussion about politics, theology, and international affairs. His uncle William was keenly interested in geology, and from 1859 Darwin's *Origin of Species* was one of the main interests in family discussion groups. Stout said, in an autobiographical note held in the Victoria University of Wellington library's Stout collection, that William was "orthodox" in religion and "especially attentive to his religious duties," but he also "accepted evolution when it was being denounced from every pulpit." The influence on Stout of his uncle's attitude toward the relationship of scientific truth to religion is obvious. Stout remembered him saying: "It is not for us to discuss the effect of Evolution on religion; the question is: 'Is it true?' If it is true we must say so, whatever may be the effect on our views of the universe." Like Stout in later life, William denied that "the world was so constituted that the truth could harm humanity."

Stout also attended Bible class, where the doctrines and histories of the various churches were explained, and he became fascinated by those matters. "We lads," he wrote in the same autobiographical note, "often used to discuss these positions, some taking one side and some another. I have seen half a dozen or more of us sitting under the shelter of a rock talking on these subjects for an hour or more at a time. We knew the various passages in the Bible that were used as 'proofs' of each particular doctrine and could refer to them. Theological disputation was part of our social life. . . . We had no football matches to talk about, for our football was a game—an amusement—and we took little note of who won. Horse racing and gambling we knew nothing of." It is clear that from these experiences Stout derived an intense interest in, and intellectual contempt for, the divisions within Christianity.

Stout also recalled the influence of his uncle James, "especially broad in his religious views" (although a staunch member of the Free Church), and of one of his cousins, a theist, who introduced Stout to 19th-century English and American literature (including Ralph Waldo Emerson and George Eliot). The various Stout households took most of the leading English and Scottish reviews (such as the *Spectator, Blackwood's,* and *Fraser's*), and Stout became widely read in and knowledgeable about the latest trends in theological, political, social, and economic thought.

Freethought Activity in Dunedin. When he reached maturity in Dunedin, Stout tried to carry on this way of life as far as possible. Although his interests were many and varied, he became best known—or most notorious—for his work as an aggressive propagandist on behalf of FREE-THOUGHT principles. Stout loved debate and controversy, and in Dunedin, because of the ecclesiastical character of its founding and the continuing influence of the Presbyterian church in community life, the major areas of controversy were theological and moral. Stout played a prominent role in the Dunedin Free Thought Association. He frequently lectured on topics connected with freethought, science, and humanistic morality, and in 1880–1883 edited a freethought journal, the *Echo*. Its interests were not, however, narrowly theological; radical policies were also canvassed in its pages. For example, it was the *Echo* that first published important articles by JOHN BALLANCE on "A National Land Policy," which formed the basis for the land reforms of Ballance's Liberal government of the early 1890s.

In the early 1880s Stout's freethought activity reached its peak. He had entered Parliament in 1875 and became a cabinet minister in the government of 1877–1879. An American visitor to Dunedin in 1881, Daniel E. Bandmann, left this impression on him in *An Actor's Tour or Seventy Thousand Miles with Shakespeare* (New York: Brentano, 1886): "As extremes generally meet, so Dunedin is the centre of free-religious thought and of episcopal orthodoxy in the Australasias. The head and front of the former is represented in a Mr. Stout, who is considered one of the ablest lawyers in the country, and who, with others earnest in modern religious liberalism, gives, every Sunday evening, lectures to crowded audiences in the Lyceum, and encourages the people in their love of intellectual and religious freedom, science, art, and the drama. . ." (pp. 34-35).

Stout returned to politics in 1884 after a five-year absence and was thereafter less active in freethought circles. In the early 1890s he moved to the capital, Wellington, where he spent the rest of his life.

Views on Religion and Education. Stout was not antagonistic to religion but he deeply disliked sectarianism. His attitude was that there is some good in *every* religion and in every branch of the Christian religion. This was because religion was an aspect of humanity. In this most basic respect, religion was best understood as morality and was instinctive in all human beings. He felt that churches and priests had warped and cramped its expression, substituting hatred and division for what ought to unite all humanity.

Perhaps Stout's main concern was to defend and strengthen New Zealand's system of secular education, established by the Education Act of 1877. For many years he was one of the most outspoken opponents of the Bible-in-schools movement, which sought to make religious instruction part of the school curriculum. Stout sought to exclude ecclesiastical influence from all levels of education. For instance, he tried to end the awarding of divinity degrees by universities, and he campaigned against continuing Presbyterian influence in appointments at the University of Otago in Dunedin. He even believed at one time that history, dealing as it must with the quarrels of churches, ought not to be taught in schools. In the late 19th century New Zealand could not afford to establish a system of free, compulsory secondary education out of tax revenue. Stout was afraid that this created a vacuum the churches would fill, and so, as minister of education, he had land reserves set aside as an endowment to help finance secondary schools.

Stout devoted much effort to proving that "Godless" schools were not immoral schools. He claimed that morality could and should be inculcated through the ordinary classroom activities and subjects. Thrift, for example, could be taught via mathematics. Another way in which Stout sought to demonstrate that religion in the school curriculum was not necessary for the fostering of morality in society was the publication of analyses and statistics indicating the low incidence of crime and vice in countries with secular education. Denying that secular education was associated with an increase in juvenile crime, he became obsessed with producing statistics that proved the opposite.

Stout believed that education should promote social cohesion. A major objection to sectarian schools and sectarian influence in schools was that they intensified division and disharmony in society. This view must be related to his New Zealand nationalism. He believed that a very young country such as New Zealand is seriously lacking in social cohesion. In such circumstances the education of the young—the first generation of native-born New Zealanders—became a vital means of fostering of nationhood and a sense of community. Stout identified sectarianism in religion as a major Old World evil, one of the evils that migrants such as himself had left Europe to escape.

To Stout the essence of freethought was the constant readiness to ask questions, to demand proof, to reject dogma, to take nothing for granted; without a strong freethinking element in society there would be no progress. But Stout refused to adopt a dogmatic position on religion; his viewpoint was that of the agnostic. The aspects of Stout's lectures that provoked the most controversy were those in which he expressed skeptical views concerning the Bible, especially stories of miracles. He also had doubts about the divinity of Jesus. Still, he was fascinated by some aspects of church life. His published account of a tour of the British Isles and Europe in 1910 contains many descriptions of visits to churches and sermons he heard. His own speeches and lectures often resembled sermons in their style and his emphasis on moral conduct. In later life Stout was closely associated with the Unitarian church and frequently spoke at Unitarian meetings (see UNITARIANISM). At the end of his long life his attitude toward organized religion mellowed considerably.

Other article of interest: **New Zealand, Unbelief in.**

Bibliography

Dunn, Waldo Hilary, and Ivor L. M. Richardson. *Sir Robert Stout: A Biography*. Wellington: A. H. & A. W. Reed, 1961.

Stout, Robert. *Can Morals Be Taught in Secular Schools?* Dunedin: 1878.

————. *Impressions of a Visit to Europe*. Auckland: J. W. Kealy, 1910.

————. *Inspiration*. Dunedin: 1880.

————. *A Lecture on Evolution and Theism*. Christchurch: 1881.

————. *Religion and the State*. Alexandra: 1914.

————. *The Resurrection of Christ*. Dunedin: 1881.

————. *What Is Freethought?* Dunedin: 1882.

D. A. HAMER

STRAUSS, DAVID FRIEDRICH (1808–1874), German skeptical writer and biblical scholar. Strauss' *Life of Jesus, Critically Examined* (1835) led to his dismissal from a theological teaching post at the University of Tübingen. In this book he compares and contrasts the accounts in different Gospels of each alleged incident in Jesus' life with exemplary lucidity and scientific detachment and exposes the frequent contradictions between the narratives. His predecessors (for example, Samuel Reimarus and Paulus) had mostly merely set aside the Gospel miracles, and had explained them as misunderstandings on the part of Jesus' entourage.

Strauss likewise rejected the miracles, saying that in his day, natural causation was accepted as applicable everywhere except to events portrayed in the Bible, and that, if its miracle stories are nevertheless to be accepted, they must be both well attested and internally coherent—neither of which condition, he showed, is actually fulfilled. But he went much further in that he challenged his predecessors' assumption that the Gospels are eyewitness reports. Thus he pointed to their anonymous character; their titles, for instance, where alone their authors are named, are not part of the original documents but later additions. They also contain literary "doublets," that is, two separate accounts in the same Gospel of incidents that are very similar (for example, miraculous feedings, first of 5,000 then 4,000, told partly in identical words). Such doublets are best explained, he argued, as deriving from two slightly different preexisting written forms of a single underlying tradition (for example, about a feeding on one occasion); and the evangelist incorporated both forms because he supposed them to refer to different incidents, a supposition impossible for an eyewitness of the alleged incident.

Strauss' principal thesis is that most New Testament stories (including those where miracle is not involved) are the outcome of Old Testament expectations. The evangelists made Jesus say and do what they expected—from their knowledge of the Old Testament—that the Messiah would say and do; and many passages that in fact make no reference to the Messiah were nevertheless taken as messianic prophecies. Thus, "then shall the eyes of the blind be opened" (Isa. 35) expresses the joy of Jewish exiles in Babylon at the prospect of release from captivity, but was understood by the evangelists as prophesying that the Messiah would cure blindness, which they accordingly make Jesus do.

Put in its most general terms, Strauss' thesis is this: written descriptions (in any old and respected document) of some event (historical or imaginary) may be read by persons who know nothing of the real subject represented, and who may freshly interpret the document in accordance with their own knowledge. In this way they may take the writing to refer to people and events entirely unknown to the actual writers. The truth of this principle (strikingly illustrated in the Qumran discoveries) and its relevance to the interpretation of the Gospels are no longer seriously disputed today.

Strauss gives the Old Testament parallels to incident after incident in Jesus' life, but does not explain the crucifixion and resurrection on this basis. He accepts the crucifixion as historical fact, attested by Tacitus. He shows that no stories could be full of more discrepancies than the Gospel resurrection narratives, but he does not explain how belief in Jesus' resurrection arose. In a final chapter he reinstates Jesus' virgin birth, miracles, resurrection, and ascension as "eternal truths," although not historical fact—the kind of double-think popular in theology today.

Strauss' second *Life of Jesus* (1864) written "for the German people," that is, for the laity, abandons all doublethink and tries to explain belief in Jesus' resurrection as originating from (1) his own assurances to his disciples that he would return, coupled with (2) their musing, after his death, on such "scriptures" as Psalm 16 ("Thou wilt not suffer thine holy one to see corruption").

In his final work, *The Old Faith and the New* (1872), Strauss declares he is no longer a Christian, and that the New Testament is, for modern man, an alien work that he declines to salvage by symbolic interpretation. He also argues against immortality, insisting on the physical basis of mind, and does not find it humiliating to be related to the gorilla. Many modern theologians write of him with bitterness because of his steadfast refusal to compromise or to allow that, somehow and in some sense, the New Testament can still be our guide.

Other articles of interest: **Jesus, Historicity of. Miracles, Unbelief in.**

Bibliography

George Eliot's 1846 translation of Strauss' first *Life of Jesus* (4th ed.) has been edited with an introduction by P. C. Hodgson. London: 1972.

Harris, Horton. *Strauss and His Theology.* Cambridge U. Press, 1973.

Wells, G. A. "Strauss, a Centenary Appraisal." *Publications of the English Goethe Society* 55 (1975).

G. A. WELLS

SWINBURNE, ALGERNON CHARLES

(1837–1909), English Victorian poet, dramatist, and critic who guided his life, as he did his literary work, with a thorough disdain for the conventions and pieties of Victorian belief and custom. He was an iconoclast in virtually all he undertook.

Early Life. Born in London on April 5, 1837, to a well-off and aristocratic family, Swinburne was raised between family homes in the Isle of Wight and Northumberland, the latter setting helping to inspire and sustain his fierce admiration for Mary, Queen of Scots. Though Swinburne's father retired from the Navy as an admiral, Swinburne was brought up largely by his mother, whose gentility and love of languages helped form Swinburne's own manners and his adeptnesss in languages.

Educated at Eton, Swinburne there manifested a dedication to independent studies, spending much time in that library, as well as in his grandfather's, where he read beyond his years. Because he came of age in the atmosphere of Eton's traditional obsession with canings, Swinburne's algolagnia came to permeate his works as well as his life. Even as a youth, Swinburne's literary enthusiasms set him off from his age: PERCY BYSSHE SHELLEY, the Jacobean playwrights, Walter Savage Landor, Victor Hugo, and, slightly later, Robert Browning (before he became popular), Charles Baudelaire, Walt Whitman, and the Marquis de Sade.

After four years at Balliol College, Oxford, ended in a suspension (presumably for alcoholic dissipation) that Swinburne liked to imagine as Shelleyan, he joined his acquaintances Dante Gabriel Rossetti, Edward Burne-Jones, and William Morris in London to make his literary career.

Poetic and Critical Work. Swinburne's first widely regarded work, *Atalanta in Calydon* (1865), a tragedy modeled somewhat too exuberantly along Greek lines, was highly praised, though some readers were disturbed by its antitheistic tone and tendencies. Christina Rossetti pasted a slip over the lines denouncing "the supreme evil, God." *Poems and Ballads* (1866) led to England's greatest eruption of literary squeamishness since the days of Byron and Shelley. Swinburne's aggressive hedonism and SKEPTICISM, expressed there in mesmerizing melody, profoundly disturbed most reviewers, though it also ignited generations of younger readers. The book was withdrawn by one publisher, then reissued by another, John Camden Hotten.

The year 1868 saw the publication by Swinburne of his first extended work of criticism—*William*

Blake: A Critical Study. His praise of Blake was predicated in part on Blake's supposed dedication to the same aesthetic principles he held, but Swinburne was the first critic willing to take seriously and attempt an exploration of the more obscure of Blake's prophetic books.

From an early age Swinburne had been a fervent proponent of political freedom. Though the 1860s saw Swinburne form his dedication to the doctrine of art for art's sake, in 1867, in part because of his idolization of the Italian patriot, Giuseppe Mazzini, he modified his belief that art ought to be divorced from social, ethical, or political ends. He rededicated himself to the cause of Italian liberty, which led to *A Song of Italy* (1867) and more impressively, to *Songs Before Sunrise* (1871), both inculcating a high scorn for tyranny and a deep faith in humanity. This faith in the divinity of man endured throughout Swinburne's life, as did his scorn for monarchies and tyrannies everywhere. His antipathy for the Russian czar was partly responsible for his not being considered for the poet-laureateship after Alfred Tennyson died.

A prolific writer of plays, primarily historical and chronicle plays often revolving around complexly erotic relationships as well as a critic who loved dispute, Swinburne in the 1870s continued to write poetry. Deeply disappointed in love in the early 1860s and constitutionally unable to handle alcohol, Swinburne lived in circumstances in London that provided little check and some encouragement to his destructive tendencies. A number of times he had to be taken to his parents' home for periods of recuperation.

In 1879, a friend of Rossetti, Theodore Watts, rescued Swinburne from a life accelerating toward death and domesticated him in a suburban menage in Putney, a 30-year arrangement that did not end until Swinburne died. In biographical terms, these years hold little interest, for the domestic life centered around daily walks and serious literary work. Nevertheless, even during this time, though tamed, Swinburne was a critical force to be reckoned with. And his spirited unconventionality is apparent even in the poems written about babies; their sentimentality makes an insistent use of imagery drawn from religion to counter the theological doctrines of original sin and man's depravity.

Perhaps the last work to show Swinburne at the top of his form, able to outrage many of his contemporaries, was the complexly erotic "Tristram of Lyonesse" (1882), though a number of Swinburne's later works have their interest. Swin-

burne's dedication to the pagan gods and goddesses, for example, informs not only his early *Poems and Ballads,* but, in a more restrained way, such a late poem as "A Nympholept."

Though often still misunderstood and approached without sympathy, Swinburne has a place in English literature that is likely to grow, not only for his own accomplishments but also for his part in enlarging the concerns of modern literature. The distance from Swinburne to Thomas Hardy and on to D. H. Lawrence and the 20th century is less than their distance from most Victorians.

Swinburne's fierce antitheism is wedded to his deep faith in the immense potential and necessary self-sufficiency of man. His beliefs lie most accessible in "Hertha," which Swinburne described as the one of his "mystic atheistic democratic anthropologic" poems that contained "the most in it of my deliberate thought and personal feeling or faith" (letters of Oct. 26, 1869, and Jan. 15, 1870). As "Hertha" portrays the complex division and unity of all things, God is presented as a conception entirely of man's making, made use of by religions and governments to cripple man in his otherwise inevitable growth toward freedom. Hertha, conceived of as a kind of earth spirit or vital principle of matter, proclaims that man wrongly debases and separates himself in "Looking Godward, to cry / 'I am I, thou art thou, / I am low, thou art high'" and that the God man has fashioned for himself must die. God's "twilight," Hertha reveals to man, "is come on him": "Thought made him and breaks him, / Truth slays and forgives; / But to you, as time takes him, / This new thing it gives, / Even love, the beloved Republic, that feeds upon freedom and lives."

The intensity of this testament rings throughout Swinburne's work. "The Hymn of Man" declares that "God, if a God there be, is the substance of men which is man. / Our lives are as pulses or pores of his manifold body and breath," and in "Thalassius," Swinburne's spiritual and poetic autobiography, the poet learns a "hate of all / That brings or holds in thrall / Of spirit or flesh, freeborn ere God began, / The holy body and sacred soul of man."

Swinburne's contempt for theism also repudiates the asceticism of Christianity. "The Hymn to Proserpine" laments the forbidden pagan pleasures, "The laurel, the palms and the paean, the breasts of the nymphs in the brake": "Thou has conquered, O pale Galilean; the world has grown grey from thy breath." To Our Lady of Pain in

"Dolores," the speaker complains of his Victorian and Christian age that "We shift and bedeck and bedrape us, / Thou are noble and nude and antique." In "Faustine" the age is one of "famished hours, / Maimed loves and mean / This ghastly thin-faced time of ours."

Bibliography

Chew, Samuel C. *Swinburne*. Boston: Little, Brown, 1929.

Connolly, Thomas E. *Swinburne's Theory of Poetry*. State U. of New York, 1964.

Henderson, Philip. *Swinburne: Portrait of a Poet*. New York: Macmillan, 1974.

Hyder, Clyde K. *Swinburne's Literary Career and Fame*. Durham, N.C.: Duke U. Press, 1933.

McGann, Jerome J. *Swinburne: An Experiment in Criticism*. Chicago: U. of Chicago Press, 1972.

Rosenberg, John D. "Swinburne." *Victorian Studies* 11 (1967).

TERRY L. MEYERS

SYMES, JOSEPH (1841–1906), Anglo-Australian freethinker and publisher. The son of a stonemason, Symes was born at Portland, Dorset, England, on Jan. 29, a birthday he was proud to share with THOMAS PAINE. He joined the Wesleyan church in 1858, became a local preacher, and, encouraged by his devout mother, in 1864 entered the Wesleyan College at Richmond-upon-Thames.

Early Life. Symes lost his Christian faith gradually. The reasons for this included exposure to Unitarian opinions, news of the Franco-Prussian War, proclamation of papal infallibility, and his church's attitude to illegitimacy. He refused ordination in 1872 and became a mechanics' institute lecturer and a journalist in Newcastle-upon-Tyne. In 1876 he became an out-and-out freethinker and started contributing to CHARLES BRADLAUGH's NATIONAL REFORMER. (He should not be confused with another contributor, the Rev. J. E. Symes.)

The following year Symes supported Bradlaugh, ANNIE BESANT, and the neo-Malthusian wing of the NATIONAL SECULAR SOCIETY in the dispute that followed Bradlaugh and Besant's republication of CHARLES KNOWLTON's birth-control pamphlet, *Fruits of Philosophy*. Symes was duly elected a vice-president of the N.S.S., a post he occupied until his death. He later became active in secularist circles in Leeds and Birmingham, running a secular school in the latter city in about 1882, and he toured the country giving lectures.

Symes was also one of a group of propagandists within the N.S.S. who were instrumental in launching the FREETHINKER in London, with GEORGE WILLIAM FOOTE as its first editor, in 1881. When Foote was imprisoned for blasphemy in 1883 Symes expected to be appointed acting editor, but was thwarted in this ambition by EDWARD AVELING.

Australian Life. In 1883 the Australasian Secular Association, founded in Melbourne in July 1882 by Thomas Walker, H. K. Rusden, and others, wrote to Bradlaugh asking for a reliable secularist lecturer to be sent to them. Symes was approached, agreed to go, left England in Dec. 1883 and arrived in Melbourne, Victoria, on Feb. 10, 1884. He was soon a public speaker of considerable, if notorious, reputation. In June 1884 he was given funds and a plant to start his own Melbourne paper, the LIBERATOR. In Sept. 1884 he was elected president of the Australasian Freethought Congress, held in Sydney. He later went on lecturing tours of Queensland and New South Wales.

In addition to lecturing and editing the *Liberator*, Symes wrote many pamphlets that were published in both Britain and Australia. The most celebrated of these was perhaps *Ancient and Modern Phallic or Sex-Worship* (Melbourne, 1887). A militant atheist and birth-control advocate, he also campaigned against monarchy, colonialism, sabbatarianism, racism, and anarchism. In 1889 he made an attempt to enter the Victorian parliament but lost.

In 1888 the Australasian Secular Association split between Symes and his followers on the one hand and various factions on the other who either disapproved of his propagandist style (contraception, ridiculing Christianity) or who were much more extreme politically than he was (e.g., anarchists). The Symes faction of the A.S.A. lost control of the Hall of Science, which he had opened in 1889, and after depleting their funds by legal actions both factions of the association collapsed as a result of the Australian trade depression of the eary 1890s. Undaunted, Symes went on a lecture tour of the South Island of New Zealand in 1893–94. In 1895, during one of the many legal cases, he was briefly imprisoned for contempt of court.

In 1897, with the aid of a doctor friend, Symes gained use of the Hall of Science, which was renamed Freethought Hall. He lectured there, and his family even lived in the building for a while, until he retired in 1904 to a small farm outside the city. He eventually became restless and decided to return to Britain, where he arrived in Aug. 1906. He was warmly received by Foote, now president of the N.S.S., was given a formal reception in London, and proceeded on a speaking tour of secular society branches. In December, in Newcastle-upon-Tyne, Symes celebrated the 30th anniversary of his first FREETHOUGHT lecture (in that same city). But he contracted bronchitis, which led to pneumonia, of which he died Dec. 29. He was cremated at Golders Green, London, on Jan. 4, 1907.

Symes married twice. His first wife, Matilda Wilson, née Weir, a widow about seven years his senior, married him at Kilmarnock, Scotland, in 1870. Matilda accompanied him to Australia, but her health declined in Melbourne and she died in 1892. In 1893 Symes married Agnes Taylor Wilson, allegedly an orphan who, with her sister, had been brought up by Matilda. Although nearly 20 years younger than Joseph Symes, Agnes played an important role as publisher (A. T. Wilson) of his Australian pamphlets; she also imported or reprinted freethought and birth-control literature. After Joseph's death in England, Agnes returned to Australia with their only daughter, Stella Bradlaugh Symes (1894–1935), who became a gynecologist and venereologist.

Joseph Symes was a stubborn, self-willed workaholic with a large martyr complex. He made enormous demands on his immediate family and was often politically naive and insensitive to intrigue. He was incorruptible, fearless, devoid of guile or treachery, and was touchingly loyal to both Bradlaugh and Foote. He made major contributions to secularism on two continents, and his views on sex were a century ahead of their time.

Bibliography

Sinnott, Nigel H. *Joseph Symes, the "Flower of Atheism."* Lidcombe, N.S.W.: Atheist Society of Australia, 1977.

———. "Joseph Symes in New Zealand." *N. Z. Rationalist and Humanist* 39, no. 1 (May 1979).

———. *Matilde, Agnes and Stella Symes: Biographical Notes on the Women in the Life of Joseph Symes.* Lidcombe, N.S.W.: Atheist Society of Australia, 1978.

———. "Notes on the Symes Family and Joseph Skurrie." *Atheist Journal* (N.S.W.), 6, no. 5 (June 1978). Supplement.

Smith, F. Barrymore. "Joseph Symes and the Australasian Secular Association." *Labour History* (Canberra), no. 5 (1963).

———. "Religion and Freethought in Melbourne, 1870–1890." M. A. Thesis, U. of Melbourne, 1960.

Symes, Joseph. *From the Wesleyan Pulpit to the Secularist Platform; or, the Life and Death of My Religion.* Melbourne: Liberator Printing and Publishing Co., 1884.

———. "My Twenty Years' Fight in Australia." *Freethinker* 26 (Sept./Nov. 1906).

NIGEL H. SINNOTT

T

TAOISM, UNBELIEF WITHIN. Context of Taoist Skepticism. In Chinese thought there was, strictly speaking, neither a concept of belief nor unbelief. The issue of SKEPTICISM was never stated in terms of the contrast of belief versus knowledge. In this central respect, the conceptual structure of the disputes in classical Chinese philosophy was radically different from that in Western philosophy. "Knowledge" in the context of Chinese philosophical disputes was not descriptive but prescriptive—not knowing-that but knowing-how or knowing-to. The issue was not what the world was like, but how we should act. This exposition will focus on four central terms in the conceptual structure that constituted "knowledge": (1) *shih*—this:right:agree; (2) *fei*—not-this:wrong: dissent; (3) *tao*—way:doctrine:speak; (4) *li*—ritual:convention.

Confucian philosophy, the dogmatic position in the Chinese tradition, spoke of knowledge as the mastery of a detailed traditional text—the *li*. The Confucian *tao* lay in allowing that text to shape one's behavior. A person had to be able to interpret the text in order to act in accord with it, and that required an authority or teacher to "rectify" the "names" in the text—that is, to show how they guided action. One had to follow traditional or contemporary "exemplars" to know what was *shih* or *fei*.

Taoists, who confronted Confucianism as the skeptics of the Chinese philosophical tradition, rather than doubting that we have knowledge, talked instead of abandoning knowledge. Shen Tao, one of the earliest Taoist philosophers, advocated that one "abandon knowledge and discard self." The only *tao* that counted was the actual course of events, and since no one could fail to do what was natural, it required neither teachers nor texts. Knowledge of traditional codes was viewed as interfering with spontaneous, natural action. Shen Tao represents the primitive Taoist school—arguing that we do not need to acquire knowledge of how to act. To do so is to struggle against nature.

The Tao Te Ching. The *Tao Te Ching* of Lao-tse works out a theoretical expression of this primitive Taoist philosophy. Lao-tse, according to legend, wrote the book under some duress—preferring, we must suppose, to remain silent and avoid contributing to "knowledge." His analysis in favor of abandoning knowledge focused on the Confucian view of names. As Confucius assumed, learning names does indeed constrain our action. When we acquire a name, we divide stuff into two—what the name applies to and what it does not. Thus all contrasting names come in pairs. To have a term in one's language is to have its opposite as well. To know what is *shih* (this) is to know what is *fei* (not-this).

When we have been trained by our teachers, parents, or peers to make some distinction and to use a pair of names, we also develop desires for one or the other of the opposites. Thus, when we learn from art "experts" to distinguish "balance" or from wine "experts" to discriminate "bouquet," we acquire more specific desires. This linkage of terms to favorable and unfavorable attitudes is reflected in the philosopher's use of *shih*. *Shih*, depending on context, may be interpreted as "this," "right," or "approve." The desires created by our learning to make distinctions lead us to actions that are departures from the "natural" or constant *tao*. Any *tao* (way) which can be *tao* (spoken) is not a constant *tao* (way). Any name that can be learned is not a constant name.

Thus Lao-tse, entreated to write a *tao* (way), offers a rationalization of Shen Tao's view as an illustration of how the evaluative force of conventional dichotomies can be reversed. Abandoning knowledge means abandoning names, abandoning distinctions, abandoning desires, and ultimately abandoning action—any behavior generated by such conventional, traditional means. Instead of learning, we should be forgetting. Instead of making us clever, rulers should return us to our blissful ignorance. Instead of building great civilizations, we should continue the natural life of small, peaceful agricultural villages. Learning and civilization bring unnatural desires and competitive, aggressive, destructive, violent behavior. It also distorts and dulls our natural appreciation of nature by making us categorize and classify it. Nature is a continuum and cannot be reduced to five colors.

There are problems with Lao-tse's view. If, instead of treating it as an illustration of how opposites can be reversed, it is interpreted as an absolutist assertion of primitivism, then two difficulties emerge. First Lao-tse's view of how language affects our behavior is surely the description of a natural process. Language, ritual, and civilization are natural social phenomena just as much as are nomads, farmers, cowboys, and warriors. Second, the advocacy of primitivist "forgetting" is itself a bit of prescriptive knowledge—taking the distinction between "nature" and "convention" as "constant" and as having implications for desire and action. "Abandon knowledge" is the prescriptive equivalent of "this sentence is false"—a self-forbidding imperative.

The first problem allowed Mencius to slip through with a defense of Confucianism. Mencius held that the *shih-fei* judgments of tradition were expressions of innate feeling structures in the heart. Behavior in accord with the Confucian *tao* is natural in the same sense that our taste for beef is natural. The second problem was clearly formulated by the neo-Mohist dialecticians who argued that any utterance that all language was perverse was itself perverse. The Mohists asserted a predication version of the law of the excluded middle to argue that some prescriptive utterances must be correct.

Chuang-tzu, sensitive to both problems, constructed a more sophisticated version of Taoism. Rather than suggesting that utterance was unnatural, he insisted that all of it was natural. Humans, with all their disputing voices and schools, are the "pipes of heaven." Mencius, with his sagelike intelligence, is no more "natural" than the drooling fool, the profligate no less natural than the moral gentleman. There may be a natural ruler but there is nothing special about him. Mencius' defense of Confucianism leaves him unable to *fei* (criticize anyone). All *shih* (agreement)–*fei* (disagreement) is from within one of the perspectives that nature contains. Our languages are not fixed to reality but

encode "perspectives"—all our classifications are like *shih* (this) and *fei* (not-this) in being a way of talking from a situational point of view.

Chuang-tzu recognizes that his own doctrine prevents him from making absolute claims about any metaphysical *tao*—any talk about the way the world is. We cannot say the world is one because that is to take a perspective on the world as a whole and thus to stand, linguistically, outside it. *One* and *the saying* make two, and with two one can generate infinities. The primitive Taoist claims are dogmatic and incoherent. We cannot say all language distorts reality or nature. Chuang-tzu recognizes that his doctrine is compatible with doing and saying the ordinary things. We can be a butcher, farmer, logician, or mechanic. All that his relativism can assert is that there are infinitely many ways to direct our lives. We can adopt a pattern from a tradition or a teacher, but in achieving perfection we go beyond anything taught, beyond skill. We can achieve the secret of life in perfecting our activities—whatever they may be.

Of course, some ways are more conducive to life than others. Chuang-tzu need not reject such pragmatic arguments, but he does insist that the valuing of human life is itself a perspective—one we can expect other animals might not take and certainly not the perspective of the universe. Once we have adopted a human perspective in favor of life, we can condemn the manufacturer of nuclear bombs but we cannot deny that those who made them were behaving naturally.

So Taoist or classical Chinese skepticism is skepticism of absolutism in value-theory, not skepticism of our senses or our factual beliefs. Chuang-tzu, like some Western skeptics, reflected on the problem of distinguishing dreams from reality. However, the point was not that we ought to wonder if we are dreaming when we seem to be awake, but that we ought to wonder how many other ways there could be of dividing up our event-consciousness and the ways we allow it to influence and direct our actions.

CHAD HANSEN

TAYLOR, ROBERT (1784–1844), English clergyman, surgeon, and freethinker, was one of the strangest of the important converts to unbelief. He was born at Edmonton into a fairly well-to-do family. His brilliance was recognized early, and he was sent to private schools. Taylor eventually became a pupil of Samuel Partridge, house surgeon at the Birmingham General Hospital. While engaging in his surgical studies, Taylor continued his classical education with a private tutor.

During his last year of surgical training, Taylor "got religion." Although he continued his medical studies, becoming a member of the Royal College of Surgeons, he decided to enter Cambridge University in 1809 to become a clergyman. Always a brilliant student, he earned his B.A. in 1813, was ordained an Anglican priest, and took his first curacy at Midhurst.

During Taylor's four years there (1814–18), he became friendly with a man named Henry Ayling, who had inherited a large sum of money from his former employers, and who, through voluminous reading, became an infidel in religion. Taylor spent a large amount of time reading in Ayling's fine library and discussing religion with Ayling, with the result that Taylor became a deist. For an ordained clergyman to profess DEISM, which Taylor did publicly in 1818, was considered by many to be a crime worse than murder.

Ostracized by everyone at Midhurst but Ayling, Taylor wrote to his superior, acknowledging his errors and asking for forgiveness. He was persuaded to relinquish his curate's license, but was promised that after he left Midhurst the bishop would give him the first available vicarage. This was a double cross, since without a license and without an actual commitment from the bishop, Taylor was unlikely to receive any future appointments. In addition, Taylor's public profession of deism had made his pious mother severely ill. In an attempt to help her, he placed an advertisement in the *Times* of London announcing his repentance.

On the strength of his reputation as a powerful pulpit speaker, Taylor continued to receive invitations to preach until word of his infidelity reached even the smallest churches. His career in the ministry finished, he left in 1820 for the Isle of Man, attempting to support himself by giving a series of lectures. Since there was little money to be made in that way, he wound up, almost penniless, in Dublin, where he managed to obtain a teaching position and even preached at a few churches until his reputation caught up with him.

Blasphemy Trial. In Nov. 1824, Taylor, now in London, held the first meeting of a group he called the Christian Evidence Society. He had founded this group (which is *not* the same as the one now bearing the name) for the purpose of critically

examining the evidence for Christianity. Meetings consisted of a reading from a standard Christian author (such as William Paley), followed by a lecture by Taylor, who analyzed the reading, and discussion involving the audience. Taylor had conducted 95 such programs before their growing popularity made the authorities determined to put a stop to them. Early in 1827 he was arrested for blasphemy. At his trial held the following October, Taylor defended himself eloquently and at length, dressed in the flowing robes of a clergyman. The jury took half an hour to return a verdict of guilty, and he was sentenced to a year in Oakham jail.

The time spent at Oakham was among the most productive in Taylor's life. He wrote two books, *Syntagma of the Evidences of the Christian Religion* (1828) and *The Diegesis* (1829), both published in London by his friend RICHARD CARLILE. The *Syntagma* was a reply to an attack made by the Rev. John Pye Smith upon the principles of the Christian Evidence Society. In effect, Taylor defended the printed Manifesto of the Christian Evidence Society against Smith's charges. The Manifesto had stated the following propositions: (1) the scriptures of the New Testament were not written by the persons whose names they bear; (2) they did not appear in the times to which they refer; (3) the persons of whom they treat never existed; and (4) the events they relate never happened. *The Diegesis*, a work of over 500 pages, attempted to examine all the writings extant from the first two centuries of the Christian era for information on the origins of Christianity. The many quotations in the book were all made by Taylor from memory, since he had few reference books available in prison. Although there are occasional errors in the book, it is a remarkable piece of scholarship, given the conditions under which it was written.

The Carlile Days. Shortly after his release in 1829, Taylor joined Carlile on an "infidel mission" to the north of England. The trip was not very successful, as few clergymen would debate them. Back in London, Taylor and Carlile opened a lecture hall called the Rotunda. After more than a year of his weekly lectures (published by Carlile in weekly numbers, 1829–30, under the title *The Devil's Pulpit*), Taylor was again charged with blasphemy for some remarks made in his Good Friday and Easter Sunday "sermons." Again Taylor defended himself (1831), and this time the jury took only seven minutes to reach its verdict. He was sentenced to two years in the Horsemonger Lane jail.

This jail experience was very unpleasant for Taylor. Although there is no real record of what happened, it is known that he was not allowed books or writing materials and that visitors could not come closer to him than six feet. Taylor emerged from prison a changed and shattered man and broke with his friend Carlile. Sued for breach of promise by a lady, Taylor married an older woman of wealth and left England for France, probably to avoid paying the 250-pound judgment awarded the plaintiff in the suit. He practiced as a surgeon at Tours, where he died in 1844. He never published another word about unbelief.

In summary: Robert Taylor was one of the first well-educated and scholarly men to write and lecture for unbelief. As such, he brought a new respectability and prestige to the field. People were no longer ashamed to be seen attending an "infidel" lecture. His writings are no longer read much, but they form an interesting chapter in the discussion of the historicity of Jesus. Taylor had claimed in many of his Rotunda lectures that Jesus' life was an allegory of the sun in its passage through the sky. He was among the first to propound this "astronomical myth" or "solar myth" theory of the origins of Jesus. His views are best stated in *The Devil's Pulpit*.

Other articles of interest: **Blasphemy Laws. Jesus, Historicity of.**

Bibliography

Aldred, Guy A. *The Devil's Chaplain: The Story of the Rev. Robert Taylor, M.A.* [sic], *M.R.C.S. (1784-1834)* [sic]. Glasgow: Strickland Press, n.d. (c. 1945).

Carlile, Richard, ed. and publisher. *The Lion.* London: 1828-29.

Cutner, Herbert. *Robert Taylor.* London: Pioneer Press, n.d. (c. 1950).

Gordon, A. "Robert Taylor." *Dictionary of National Biography.* London: Smith Elder, 1885-1901.

Smith, John Pye. *An Answer to a Printed Paper Entitled "Manifesto of the Christian Evidence Society."* 2nd ed. London: Holdsworth & Hall, 1830.

Trial of the Reverend Robert Taylor, A.B. M.R.C.S. Upon a Charge of Blasphemy . . . . on Wednesday, October 24, 1827. London: R. Carlile, 1828.

GORDON STEIN

TEILHARD DE CHARDIN, PIERRE (1881-1955), French geopaleontologist and Jesuit priest. See **Evolution and Unbelief.**

TINDAL, MATTHEW (1657-1733), English deist writer. Tindal, who came from a High Church background, attended Lincoln College, Oxford, where he studied under George Hickes, who was to become one of his most hostile opponents. Moving to Exeter College, where he received his B.A. in 1676, Tindal became a law fellow of All Souls in 1678 and a doctor of law in 1685. The lawyer's approach is apparent in his writings, and he retained his law fellowship for the rest of his long and uneventful life.

One major event was Tindal's conversion to Roman Catholicism. This was brought about, around 1685, by a "popish emissary" employed by James II at Oxford. Tindal's detractors have accused him of opportunism—he hoped, it was said, to become head of his college—but this seems unlikely since he publicly renounced Catholicism in 1687 or early in 1688, while James was still in power. His conversion to, and away from, Catholicism was no doubt a factor in his move to FREE-THOUGHT. Another, more general, factor was the social disorders of the time, for which religious intolerance was largely responsible.

Early Freethought. Opposition to religious intolerance and sympathy for freethought and for social order are evident in Tindal's two anti-Trinitarian pamphlets, *A Letter to the Reverend the Clergy of Both Universities* (1694) and *Reflections on the Trinity* (1695), as well as in his *Essay Concerning the Power of the Magistrate, and the Rights of Mankind, in Matters of Religion* (1697), which was approved by JOHN LOCKE and advocated toleration along Lockean lines. Tindal also wrote *A Letter to a Member of Parliament, Shewing That a Restraint of the Press Is Inconsistent with the Protestant Religion, and Dangerous to the Liberties of the Nation* (1698), which was republished in shortened form six years later as *Reasons Against Restraining the Press.*

In 1706 Tindal issued his first major work, *The Rights of the Christian Church Asserted, Against the Romish and All Other Priests Who Claim an Independent Power over It,* which, he is supposed to have said, would make the clergy "mad." It did, provoking about two dozen replies and drawing strong criticism from Jonathan Swift and George

Berkeley, among others. A more accurate, but less strategic title, would have been "The Rights of the Christian Laity," for the book defends liberty of conscience and worship against clerical claims to authority in these areas. The clergy, Tindal argues, can have no powers independent of the civil authority, which is obliged to protect the religious freedom of the laity, "so long as they do nothing prejudicial to the Civil Society." Tindal issued a *Defence of the Rights* in 1707, which, together with the *Rights,* was burned in 1710 by the common hangman by order of the House of Commons.

Between 1708 and 1713 Tindal published pamphlets relating to the *Rights* and the Sacheverell controversy. The most entertaining is *A New Catechism* (1710) and the most substantial is *The Nation Vindicated,* Part 2 (1712); here he vindicated previous freethinking works and lashed out at such enemies as Jonathan Swift, "this Reverend Buffoon"; Henry Dodwell, "this muddy-headed Irishman"; and his old teacher, "the Godly Dr. Hickes." Like ANTHONY COLLINS, Charles Blount, JOHN TOLAND, John Trenchard, and PETER ANNET, he defended DETERMINISM—a position, according to Leslie Stephen and Ernest Mossner, which English freethinkers were supposed to oppose.

From 1713 to 1729 Tindal wrote 15 more pamphlets, almost all of them on political topics. His next freethought work, *An Address to the Inhabitants of London and Westminster; In Relation to a Pastoral Letter . . . by the Bishop of London, Occasion'd by Some Late Writings in Favour of Infidelity* (1729), is also a defense of fellow freethinkers, notably Collins and THOMAS WOOLSTON.

The Deist's Bible. The "grand work," upon which Tindal's fame mainly rests, was issued in 1730 when he was more than 72 years old. This is *Christianity as Old as Creation: or, the Gospel, a Republication of the Religion of Nature,* the classic statement of constructive DEISM, often described as "the deist's Bible." The last part of his title was borrowed from a sermon by Bishop Sherlock, a practice that nicely illustrates his exploitation of the liberal or unguarded pronouncements of clergymen. Tindal drew out and synthesized the tendency toward natural and moral religion among Latitudinarian and Low Church writers such as Tillotson and Clarke. The book made the clergy even angrier than his first major work, eliciting well over a hundred replies. Although separated by almost 25 years, Tindal's two major works are closely connected. As the *Rights* opposed the clergy's having power independent of civil authority,

so *Christianity as Old as Creation* denies to revealed religion any authority independent of reason; and as the first pretension leads to social and religious disorder, so, Tindal argued, the second will "weaken the force of the Religion of Reason and Nature, strike at all religion; and [he adds] there can't be Two Independent Rules for the Government of human Actions."

As with the *Rights,* Tindal intended to issue a second volume of *Christianity.* However, none appeared, although he published a *Second Address* (1730), which contains a defense of *Christianity* against an attack by Daniel Waterland; in the British Library there is a fragment of the introduction to volume two, which contains answers to "Mr. Jackson, Mr. Foster, and Dr. Conybeare; the First a Low Churchman, the other a Dissenter, and the Third a High Churchman." It is often said that Edmund Gibson, bishop of London, suppressed the second volume, but there is good reason to doubt this.

Tindal was accused of being an immoral man, "a noted Debauchee and a man of very pernicious Principles," as Thomas Hearne put it. No doubt criticism of his moral character was designed partly to bring his principles into disrepute; showing that the man who virtually reduced religion to morality was himself immoral would certainly help the enemies of deism. However, there is probably some truth in the accusations, for in a private memoir of Collins, Lord Egmont says that Collins "used to say my friend Tyndal [sic] is a rogue and a disgrace to us, for he is not honest or virtuous . . ." (British Library, Add. MS. 47119).

Deist or Atheist? Even more difficult is the question of Tindal's actual theoretical position. Was he a deist, as most commentators hold, or an atheist, as some of his critics claimed? Although there is little suggestion of ATHEISM in his writings, we have two similar but apparently independent stories about how Tindal argued against the existence of God: one is in the *Religious, Rational and Moral Conduct of Matthew Tindal* (1735), and the other, more circumstantial account is given by Lord Egmont in his diary (Nov. 1735). In brief, Tindal argued "that space was infinite and eternal, and these were attributes commonly given to God; either therefore space is the Christian's God, or there are two Gods infinite and eternal, which at the bottom is as good as to say there is no God at all."

Tindal's assertion appears to be a garbled and materialistic version of the (Spinozistic) argument for pantheistic monism, which, in short, is this:

there can be only one, most perfect, necessary being; for if there were two, they would cancel each other's perfection and necessity. Hence the one perfect and necessary being must embrace everything within itself, including extension. It is likely that Collins and Tindal—and perhaps also Toland's pantheistic societies—grounded their pantheistic MATERIALISM in this way. As the writer of the *Religious . . . Conduct of Tindal* put it: "Their God is at last the Universe; or, as they sometime express themselves, one only extended or material Substance differently modified." However, without additional evidence, it is difficult to decide whether Tindal accepted this atheistic line of argument (a line of argument that contains resonances of his opposition to two independent powers in the *Rights* and *Christianity*).

Tindal died on Aug. 16, 1733, uttering blasphemies "scarce fit to be repeated," according to a witness, and "as proud of dying hard as ever he was to be reputed a Top Free Thinker."

Other article of interest: **God, Existence of.**

Bibliography

Berman, David, and Stephen Lalor. "The Suppression of Tindal's *Christianity as Old as Creation*, Volume 2." *Notes and Queries* 229 (March 1984).

Gawlick, Günter. "Introduction" to his edition of *Christianity as Old as Creation*. Stuttgart: 1967.

Lalor, Stephen. "Matthew Tindal and the Eighteenth-Century Assault on Religion." Dublin: Trinity College, unpublished thesis, 1979.

Stephen, Leslie. *History of English Thought in the Eighteenth Century*. 2 vols. London: 1876; r.p. New York: Harcourt Brace, 1962. Chapter 3.

"Tindal, Matthew." *Biographia Britannica*. London: 1766.

DAVID BERMAN

TOLAND, JOHN (1670–1722), British freethinker, originally named Janus Junius Toland. He was born in County Donegal, in the North of Ireland. "Educated from the cradle in the grossest superstition and idolatry," he says in his *Apology* (1697), he threw off Roman Catholicism at 15 by "his own reason and such as made use of theirs." From his conversion in 1685—a most imprudent time, given the known religious predilections of James II—Toland's life is marked by considerable traveling and intellectual development.

Education. Toland attended the University of Glasgow from 1687 to 1690, and aligned himself with the Presbyterians. His original conversion was probably to Presbyterianism, and not to Anglicanism as some claim, since in his *Apology* he speaks of "the Dissenter's worship [gaining] extraordinarily upon his affections, just as he was newly delivered from [popery]." From Glasgow he went to Edinburgh, and received an M.A. in 1690. He then moved to London, where he so impressed the Dissenters that they sent him to the University of Leyden to "perfect his education," as his biographer Pierre Desmaizeaux puts it (see Bibliography). In Holland he studied under Spanheim and Leclerc and became a Latitudinarian.

Benjamin Furley, JOHN LOCKE's Dutch correspondent, described Toland in 1693 as "a freespirited, ingenious man." This characteristic freespiritedness brought with it the besetting practical problem of his life; for, continues Furley, "having cast off the yoke of spiritual authority . . . has rendered it somewhat difficult for him to find a way of subsistence in the world." Having neither family fortune, as had Lord Shaftesbury and ANTHONY COLLINS, nor an Oxford fellowship, as MATTHEW TINDAL had, Toland was thrown upon the generosity of aristocratic patrons, such as the Duke of Newcastle, Prince Eugene of Savoy, Lords Shaftesbury and Molesworth, and the Earl of Oxford, who employed him as an editor, political pamphleteer, biographer, and probably a "general" spy. As his background was obscure, his prospects were generally uncertain, and he was forced to live by his pen. That he was an incessant writer and controversialist is amply shown in Giancarlo Carabelli's two-volume bibliography of his writings and replies to them; it runs to over 500 pages, and lists nearly 200 works by or attributed to him.

Toland is perhaps the first professional freethinker. Eliminating prejudice and religious intolerance was, by his own account, one of the main aims of his life. Most of his writings, and the best of them, are directed against established religion—not, of course, that he ever avowed this. Officially, he claimed, as in *Vindicius Liberius* (1702), to be a loyal member of the Church of England, anxious only to eliminate abuses of religion. However, critics such as Samuel Clarke saw him, rightly, as one of Christianity's most powerful enemies.

Christianity Not Mysterious. After leaving Holland Toland spent some time in Oxford, using its library facilities. From there he moved to London, where early in 1696 he published his most important work, *Christianity Not Mysterious*. This short and forceful book made him notorious; it also began the so-called deist debate. (See DEISM.) Like nearly all of Toland's books, its subtitle is informative: *A Treatise Shewing, That There Is Nothing in the Gospel Contrary to Reason, Nor Above It: and That No Christian Doctrine Can Be Properly Called a Mystery.* Drawing especially on Locke's theories of meaning and nominal essence, Toland argued that, since mysteries such as the Holy Trinity do not stand for clear ideas, Christianity must either employ meaningless doctrines, or else be nonmysterious; for assenting to doctrines of which we have no clear ideas is like trying to believe in *Blictri*, a traditional nonsense word.

Early in 1697 Toland revisited Ireland, where in a short time he had "raised against him the clamour of all parties," as we are told by Locke's Dublin friend, William Molyneux; the clergy, especially, were "alarmed to a mighty degree against him." *Christinaity Not Mysterious* was burnt by the common hangman, and it was even moved by one member of the Irish House of Commons "that Mr. Toland himself should be burnt." Yet for all that, his book initiated the one great flowering of Irish philosophy, drawing creative replies from Peter Browne (whom Toland claimed to have made a bishop), Edward Synge, William King, and George Berkeley.

It is not clear why Toland returned to Ireland. There is some evidence that he expected a political appointment. Possibly he also wished (notwithstanding his protests in the *Apology*) to encourage a return to the tolerant religion of the ancient Irish, the "Western Latitudinarians," as he described them in *Nazarenus* (1718). He boasted, according to Browne, that he would become "the head of a sect." In any case, he was forced to flee to England, where he published the *Apology*, which deals with his reception in Dublin and contains most of the meager information we have on his early life.

Toland's concern for civil liberty, another professed aim, begins to appear in his editions of John Milton (1698), James Harrington (1700), and in his *Anglia Libera* (1701), a book that encouraged the British government to send him with a delegation to Hanover, where he is said to have gained the esteem of the future ruling family of England. In 1702 he revisited Hanover and also traveled to Berlin, where he engaged in philosophical discussions with the queen of Prussia, to whom he addressed his *Letters to Serena* (1704).

The RATIONALISM of *Christianity Not Mysterious* is continued in the *Letters*; but whereas the first may be described as deistic, the *Letters* are pantheistic. Once again this is not Toland's avowed view. In fact, in the penultimate section of Letter 5, "Motion Essential to Matter," he expressly repudiates Spinoza's pantheism and affirms that there is an immaterial, presiding intelligence, which is responsible for the formation of plants and animals. But, as F. A. Lange has suggested, this caveat should be seen as an application of the esoteric/exoteric distinction, a subject Toland discusses at length in *Tetradymas* (1720), where he claims that the distinction is "as much now in use as ever; tho' the distinction is not so openly and professedly approved as among the Ancients."

That Toland was a pantheist in 1704—and hence that the penultimate section was designed for exoteric use—is borne out by the following considerations: (1) In *Socinianism Truly Stated*, a pamphlet printed in 1704, Toland signs himself "a Pantheist" (the first recorded use of the term). (2) The logical tendency of Letter 5 is toward pantheistic materialism, since allowing motion to be essential to matter undermines the most compelling reason for positing a transcendent cause of the world. (3) In the exuberant poem *Clito*, first printed in 1700, Toland explicitly develops and takes seriously a pantheistic theory. Moreover, his statements on key doctrines in the *Letters to Serena* are basically the same as those in the poem and in his *Pantheisticon* (1720; Eng. trans. 1751).

Letter 3 is a "History of the Soul's Immortality," in which Toland argues that the doctrine was invented by Egyptian priests for their own selfish interests. The drift of the letter is clearly irreligious, but once again in the penultimate section Toland issues a religious caveat. His strategy here bears comparing with that of DAVID HUME, who, in the final paragraph of his essays "The Immortality of the Soul" and "Of Miracles" issues a similarly crude religious caveat. A "Bouncing compliment," as Toland observes in *Tetradymas*, "saves all."

In 1707–09 Toland visited Prague and then the Hague, where he published his *Adeisidaemon* (directed against superstition) and *Origines Judaicae*, in which he suggests that Strabo was a sounder historian of the Jews than Moses. Leibniz commented critically on these works in letters to Toland, later to be printed in volume two of *A Collection of Several Pieces of Toland* (1726). In addition to writing numerous political pamphlets, such as *Reasons for Naturalizing the Jews* (1714) and *Political Anatomy of Great Britain* (1717), which continue his plea for religious toleration, Toland projected a number of "grand works." Among them was a history of the Druids, which appeared in a modest form in his posthumous *Collection*.

Later Work. *Nazarenus* is Toland's most significant contribution to biblical scholarship. It looks back to a controversy started by his *Life of Milton* (1698), where he defended Milton's view that *Eikon Basilike* was not written by Charles I, as claimed, but was a pious fraud composed by Gauden. Toland then suggested that this recent forgery helped to explain the acceptance in earlier times of "suppositious pieces under the name of Christ and his apostles," a thesis he defended in *Amyntor* (1699), in which he lists over 70 spurious Gospels, Epistles, Acts, etc. Toland said that he was not calling into question the canon of the New Testament; but few, if any, took this seriously. In *Nazarenus* he anticipates the so-called "higher criticism" in placing early Christianity firmly in a Jewish context. He argues that the first Christians—the Nazarenes, Ebionites or, as he calls them, Jewish Christians—were obliged to keep the Levitical law, and that although true Christianity was perverted by the heathenism of the Gentile Christians (who were not meant to keep the law), it can be extensively reconstructed from the Gospel of Barnabas.

In 1720 Toland had *Pantheisticon*, his most exotic work, printed. It contains an explicit statement of pantheism and a liturgy that was taken to be a burlesque of the Christian liturgy. Whether there were pantheistic societies that used this liturgy, as he suggests, is not known. It is generally agreed that his pantheism is closer to that of GIORDANO BRUNO (whose works he translated), than to that of BENEDICT SPINOZA, who is criticized in the fourth essay in the *Letters to Serena*. In 1720 Toland also published *Tetradymas*, which, apart from the study of the esoteric/exoteric distinction, contains an essay on the murder of Hypatia, a naturalistic account of the pillar of cloud and fire mentioned in Exodus, and a defense of *Nazarenus*.

Toland's impact on his generation was widespread and varied: few prominent writers of the time were not goaded by him. Many of his contemporaries affected a condescending attitude toward him, which has been continued, unjustly, by Leslie Stephen in the influential *History of English Thought in the Eighteenth Century*. Other commentators rightly feel that, given Toland's un-

doubted powers, his intellectual contribution might have been more solid and sustained than it is. There is something swashbuckling about Toland's work: he is, as it were, an Irish adventurer in scholarship. His last years were bedeviled by financial worries; he lost money in the South Sea scheme, whose secret history he helped write. Yet he died on March 11, 1722, Desmaizeaux says, "without the least perturbation of mind," having a few days earlier written an epitaph that concludes: "If you would know more of him Search his Writings."

Bibliography

Berman, David. "Enlightenment and Counter-Enlightenment in Irish Philosophy." *Archiv für Geschichte der Philosophie* 64 (1982).

Carabelli, Giancarlo. *Tolandiana: Materiali bibliografici per lo studio dell'opera a della fortuna di John Toland (1670–1722)*. 1975. *Errata, Addenda e Indici*. 1978.

Heinemann, F. H. "John Toland and the Age of Enlightenment." *Review of English Studies* 20 (1944).

Lange, F. A. *The History of Materialism*. 3 vols. Boston: James Osgood, 1877–81.

Nicholl, H. F. "John Toland: Religion Without Mystery." *Hermathena* 100 (1965).

———. "The Life and Work of John Toland," Dublin: Trinity College, unpublished thesis.

Simms, J. G. "John Toland (1670–1722), a Donegal Heretic." *Irish Historical Studies* 16 (1969).

Stephen, Leslie. *History of English Thought in the Eighteenth Century*. 2 vols. London: 1876; New York: Harcourt Brace. 1962. Chapter 3.

Sullivan, Robert E. *John Toland and the Deist Controversy*. Cambridge, Mass.: Harvard U. Press, 1982.

Toland, John. *A Collection of Several Pieces of Mr. John Toland, with Some Memoirs* [by Pierre Desmaizeaux] *of his Life and Writings*. 2 vols. 1726.

DAVID BERMAN

TOLSTOI, LEV NIKOLAEVICH (1828–1910), Russian novelist and mystic. See **Russian Literature, Unbelief in.**

TRUTH SEEKER, THE. In 1872, DEROBIGNE MORTIMER BENNETT, a seed merchant and sometime pharmacist, living in Paris, Ill., got into a dispute with several clergymen in the area about prayer. The clergymen wrote letters to the local newspaper about the matter, and they were published, while the newspaper refused to publish any of Bennett's letters critical of prayer. Bennett was so incensed by this unfair treatment that he decided to start his own publication. He printed several thousand copies of an eight-page issue (undated) of a magazine called the *Truth Seeker*, and sent them free to every person whose address he could obtain. The response was encouraging enough that Bennett felt he could successfully continue publishing the magazine, even though all of the articles and letters in the first issue had been written by Bennett himself, using several pseudonyms.

After the third issue, in early 1873, Bennett moved to New York City. The atmosphere there was much more favorable to a FREETHOUGHT publication, and the new magazine was soon a 16-page weekly. Bennett recognized the importance of making freethought books available to his readers, as well as the fact that there were difficulties in getting them published and distributed. As a result, he soon was running a book distribution and sales service and then his own publishing company. This was to become the largest American freethought publisher of the late 19th and early 20th century and was known as the Truth Seeker Company.

Although the circulation of the *Truth Seeker* was never more than about 6,000, it had a unifying influence on the freethought movement that far exceeded the importance of its modest circulation. Speeches and original articles by the leading freethought orators and writers were published there first, then often reissued as pamphlets or books.

The list of freethought notables who wrote for the *Truth Seeker* was exhaustive. Included were ROBERT G. INGERSOLL, BENJAMIN FRANKLIN UNDERWOOD, SAMUEL PORTER PUTNAM, C. B. Reynolds, John Remsburg, GEORGE JACOB HOLYOAKE, GEORGE WILLIAM FOOTE, CHARLES BRADLAUGH, and ANNIE BESANT. Even THOMAS PAINE was resurrected and published.

For the first ten years of publication, Bennett was the editor of the *Truth Seeker*. After Bennett's death in 1882, Eugene M. Macdonald, the compositor, became editor, serving until his death in 1909, upon which his brother, George E. Macdonald, became the editor. He remained until 1937. CHARLES LEE SMITH became editor and served until his death in 1964. At that time, the magazine moved to San Diego, and James Hervey Johnson became editor and publisher.

In 1930 the magazine went from a weekly to a monthly. At that point, its heyday was probably past. During the 1950s, under Smith, an anti-Semitic element began to appear in its pages, and by the time Johnson took over, it was anti-Jewish, anti-Catholic, anti-Black, and atheistic. This was probably the first time these particular elements of editorial outlook were all present at the same time in the same publication. As a result, most of the original audience was alienated, and deserted the magazine. In 1981 there was a circulation of only about 300 copies.

There was a fiftieth anniversary issue (Sept. 1923) and a one hundredth anniversary issue (Sept. 1973), both of which (especially the fiftieth) contain much about the history of the magazine. The fiftieth anniversary issue also reprints the entire first issue of the magazine in facsimile.

Bibliography

Brown, Marshall G., and Gordon Stein. *Freethought in the United States.* Westport, Conn.: Greenwood, 1978.

Macdonald, George E. *Fifty Years of Freethought, Being the Story of The Truth Seeker, With the Natural History of Its Third Editor.* 2 vols. New York: Truth Seeker Co., 1929.

Putnam, Samuel P. *400 Years of Freethought.* New York: Truth Seeker Co., 1894.

Warren, Sidney. *American Freethought, 1860–1914.* New York: Columbia U. Press, 1943.

GORDON STEIN

TWAIN, MARK (1835–1910), American author, pseudonym of Samuel Langhorne Clemens. See **American Literature, Unbelief in.**

U

UNAMUNO, MIGUEL DE (1864–1936), Spanish philosopher and writer. See **Spanish Literature, Unbelief in.**

UNBELIEF AS A WAY OF LIFE. Unbelievers do not find God or the gods to be necessary or even desirable as the wellspring of ethical behavior (see (ETHICS AND UNBELIEF), nor a satisfying and comforting source of consolation. The sources of this attitude vary, to be sure, but a major reason for rejection of theistic plans of salvation is usually the character of the persons who claim to have been twice born. Most unbelievers are unimpressed by these models and often prefer the same individuals in their allegedly once-born state to what seems to happen to them as a result of conversion. Thus, from the negative point of view, unbelief as a way of life involves both the absence of any supernatural support for human values and lack of admiration for the character of those who claim to have been saved.

Eastern Religions. "Way of life" in the context of religion is *soteriology* or salvation, how one can best conduct one's life so as to be worthy. In some contexts this might imply future rewards and punishments after death but by no means necessarily. In some religions, such as Theravada BUDDHISM, *samsara,* or sentient existence, does not necessarily imply survival of personality in the course of reincarnation, so that to all intents and purposes death means annihilation. Indeed, there is virtually no doctrine of personal survival at all in JUDAISM, while many forms of Christianity, both orthodox and liberal, regard life after death as a kind of bonus and focus entirely on the qualities of life in terms of the human situation as we know it. Even in the federal theology of New England Puritanism, primary emphasis was placed on the life of holiness rather than the afterlife, life being regarded as a journey from unregeneracy to conver-

sion to sanctification. As some critics of old orthodoxy pointed out during the 18th-century Great Awakening, there was more than a little resemblance between this Protestant sacramentalism and the formal sacraments of Roman Catholicism.

In virtually all religions there are stages of life. Thus, in orthodox HINDUISM, the individual is expected to follow the *margas* or "ways" by which, through various stages, the person matures and develops morally, psychologically, and spiritually. Thus, there are rituals surrounding birth, the attaining of maturity, marriage, the life of the householder, and, finally, retirement from the world as a *sadhu*, or holy man. Like most religions, Hinduism is male-oriented and, although there are rites for women as well, these seldom include the last stage of spiritual perfection. Women hope to be reborn as men. The *margas* are rites of passage and are intended to prepare the individual for a higher reincarnation, ultimately for *moksa*, or release, during which the ego dissolves in Brahm-Atman, the universal soul.

In Confucian China life was externally regulated by *hsiao* or ritual, the goal being to attain *jen*, or superiority as a human being, with only the vaguest notions of destiny beyond death. An alternate route in Chinese tradition was TAOISM, which, in its philosophical forms, was a way of attaining inner detachment and peace by a more intuitive process. Indeed, one could say that in most religions, if not all, there are usually choices among approved ways of life, some highly legalistic and sacramental and others intuitive and mystical.

In Judaism, while the normative tradition is highly legalistic, religion being chiefly a matter of observances, there are coincidental emotional and intuitive forms such as Hassidism and Kaballah. Much the same occurs in ISLAM, which closely resembles Judaism in terms of practice. The devout Muslim observes dietary laws, dress codes, regulations concerning recreation and the disposal of property, as well as moral strictures and, above all, the Five Pillars of Islam, which include strict monotheistic belief, the observance of Ramadan, the pilgrimage to Mecca, prayer five times a day, and the giving of alms. There are also the mystical and intuitive forms of Islam, however, such as Sufism, in which *tasawuf*, or ecstatic communion with the divine, is the basis for all else in life.

The great antiquity of rites of passage are indicated by Neanderthal burial sites, by Upper Palaeolithic sites such as Tuc d'Audoubert in Provence, where small heel prints, presumably of boys, have been found deep in the recesses of the cavern, in a chamber accessible only by a perilous journey. In other contemporary or near contemporary religions of early peoples, rites of passage are invariably encountered, initiation and death ceremonies being almost universal. For a practicing Dakota Sioux, for example, initiation after instruction by the elders may involve physical ordeals in the sweat lodge and at later, higher stages of spiritual development the ordeal of the Sun Dance.

Rise of Secularism in the West. According to historians such as Arnold Toynbee (*An Historian's View of Religion*) and William McNeill (*Rise of the West*), the humanistic movement of the Renaissance led to the scientific and philosophical revolutions of the 17th century, which, in turn, produced SECULARISM. Until the 17th century, everyone throughout the world was guided by religious tradition so that variant ways of life usually involved some form of supernaturalism. In Holland bourgeois city dwellers gradually broke from tradition in a secularizing process that involved a fading of orthodoxy in some quarters. The same secular spirit penetrated England after the Restoration in 1660 and also France during the reign of Louis XIV. Secularism gathered considerable momentum during the 18th century, during which time most educated people in Western Europe ceased to be orthodox Christians. The turmoil of the French Revolution and the Napoleonic era occasioned a Christian reaction during the romantic period, but from about 1850 on secularism gained strength once more; also, because of the expansion of Europe, secularism had some effect on non-Western cultures.

During the present century, secularism has become normative in Europe, North America, and the British dominions, with periodic revivals of orthodoxy. The Soviet bloc and China have become almost completely secular, though important religious minorities such as the Muslims flourish, and in both the Islamic world and India the Western-educated ruling elites tend to be secularists who pay some lip service to tradition. This situation has recently altered in the Islamic world with the revival of Islamic fundamentalism in Iran, Egypt, and Saudi Arabia.

As Marshall McLuhan observed, today's world is a "global village" in which the globe-circling traveler finds much similarity in the urban centers even where, as in India, older traditions survive in the villages. The primary concerns of most urban moderns seem to be careerist and economic, the quality of life being interpreted without much direct reference either to life after death or to supernaturalist considerations of any kind. Thus, while most Western people will, if asked, acknowledge the existence of God, they are apt to conduct themselves as if he did not exist. Conscious rationalists, humanists, and unbelievers are rare; people wholly or almost wholly caught up in their secular preoccupations are the norm. In spite of some spectacular revivals in progress, especially in the United States and Iran, these may prove to be ephemeral. If not, there could be some reason to see the late 20th century as a period of return to a theist tradition and a reversal of the trends in progress since the 17th century. Still, this is unlikely.

Secularism in North America. If secularism and unbelief could, for the moment, be equated, is there anything that might correspond to rites of passage and also to a way of life in the traditional sense of a journey of the soul? As has been pointed out by sociologists such as Will Herberg (*Catholic Protestant Jew*), intrinsic values of religious derivation can be detected on the part of even the most secular of persons in the United States. Thus, in a sense, skeptical, agnostic, and even atheistic people will identify themselves as Protestants, Catholics, or Jews in the sense that, at the least, they feel themselves to be vaguely affiliated with one or the other of these categories. As yet, there is no recognized category that could be labeled "humanist" although, by branding opponents as such, conservative Christians like the Moral Majority might indeed create such a category by their persecutions. What are encountered are nonpracticing, nonbelieving Catholics, Protestants, and Jews, who are such because of family background and ethnic customs. Even the most secular of Jews is likely to have a bar mitzvah for his son, and even the most humanistic of Christians is certain to keep Christmas.

In the secular society, however, and with the traditional religious background still significant, rites of passage of a social and economic nature have appeared which can be said to mark the stages of an unbeliever's way of life. There is the baby shower, the first day at school, first driver's license (draft registry, first legal six-pack), first job, first sexual encounter, first girlfriend or boyfriend, marriage or live-together, first child, promotion, retirement, funeral. Nowadays, most urban Europeans and North Americans, especially the middle-class people described in stories by John Updike and John Cheever, experience variations of this secular life. There are, as has been recognized by such psychologists as Eric Erikson, certain stages or phases of life for which there are more or less appropriate expectations and behaviors. While all of these stages tend to correspond to those of the traditional religions, there are perhaps more of them now, if only because people live longer and because there is apparently more complexity in modern life. Thus, the midlife crisis has become almost a rite of passage while the later stages of life, including old age, are being subdivided. More than anything else, this probably represents increased longevity. As recently as 1900, the average American male lived to be 45, married, and had three children, of whom one died. By 1981 the longevity had increased by almost 30 years, there are apt to be serial marriages and relationships, and the death of a child has become uncommon. Thus, while the traditional rites of passage usually included several stages in early life, adult life after marriage or holy orders was conceived to be a fairly short span followed by an early death and some form of extreme unction. The very brevity of life left most people with a strong sense of unfinished business and hence immediate reasons for believing in continuance on another plane of existence.

As Emile Durkheim pointed out in *The Elementary Forms of Religious Life*, God is actually society itself manifest in totemic symbolism. While his theories of totemism have not survived anthropological scrutiny, it is possible to say that his sociological idea of religion has some relevance to the secular society. In modern secular societies the old deities appear to have been displaced by other ultimate concerns—to use Paul Tillich's term—namely, the nationalism of the parochial state, the corporation, the party, and technology, among others. While traditional religion may have become peripheral to the unbeliever, his or her status as such is because he or she no longer finds reality in

Yahweh and Jesus rather than because of the absence of belief altogether. Many highly ambitious men and women pursue their careerist quest for affluence and power with monastic devotion, and most people have strong transpersonal concerns such as family and community. Indeed, the rewards of wealth and status do not really account for the enormous energy and commitment many active people put into their careers. Whether articulated or not, it is evident that careerism implies purpose, self-fulfillment, and growth, and that the pursuit of a career is a kind of spiritual quest, frequently involving sacrifices and austerities, discipline, and meditation techniques. A young junior executive in a major corporation will, in William Whyte's terms, strive to be a good organization man, in which case his entire life as well as that of every member of his family will be focused on his commitment. There is faith and perseverance, even sanctification in this. Careerism itself is a way of salvation, a soteriology.

While careerism, domesticity, and the arts of leisure have become the essential ingredients of the secularist life, much more is involved among those with conscious commitments as humanists, rationalists, Ethical Culturalists, and adherents of nontheistic ideologies such as Marxism-Leninism. These are not believers but rather devotees to alternatives other than the traditional religions or modern forms of supernaturalism such as the occult. Although there are many forms of naturalism or humanism, all share certain basic characteristics, most of which are negative. There is disbelief in the supernatural, including God (or any gods), an immortal soul, and a discarnate mind—although there is sometimes a grey area or two. Thus, unbelief in God, for example, may mean disbelief in Yahweh, the God of Judeo-Christian-Islamic piety, but not necessarily rejection of the concept of First Cause, the Oversoul, the *mysterium tremendum*, or Ground of Being, that is, ultimate reality which is not conceived in anthropomorphic or personal terms but as a philosophical principle. Intellectual entertainment of the possibility of metaphysical absolutes, however, is very different from experiential belief in a redemptive power, and it is this latter that humanists and naturalists reject.

The naturalist/humanist conducts his life without hope of intercession by a redeemer but nonetheless often resorts to soterial rituals. The inner child in most people sometimes cries out for help in times of distress, and, at such times, even an atheist might repeat prayers learned in childhood, invoke the name of deities, or reach for the comfort of amulet or rosary. Yet, at the very time he or she does so, the person will be fully conscious that such actions are security blankets, forms of magic in which he or she does not truly believe but which nonetheless soothe and calm the frightened inner child. In this way, unbelievers sometimes make use of what they rationally hold to be superstitious ideas and devices for the same psychological reasons that most people carry lucky coins or repeat lucky phrases before embarking on some sort of enterprise in which there are the possibilities of gain or loss. At the same time, this person does not expect anything to operate except the laws of chance (if there are any), and his real confidence will rest with the pilot of the airplane, the surgeon and his skills, or the person's own problem-solving abilities. He or she may have some faith in these but none whatsoever in the power that "passeth all understanding," even if that power is invoked.

There are some very austere, mature, and self-disciplined persons of humanistic persuasion who are in such control of the inner child that they meet all perils and terrors with the serene self-confidence of the fully matured adult. Still, they are very rare. Since the humanist/naturalist is just as prone to anxiety, fear, inner insecurity, and regressive tendencies, it is meaningful to speak of the terror-stricken Jesus in the Garden of Gethsemane rather than the serene Socrates about to drink the hemlock. The wide appeal of Jesus probably lies with the Gospel record of his occasional outbursts of impatience and rage, as well as moments of terror and despair, rather than with the alleged perfection attributed to him by devotees. The attraction of many humanists to Jesus lies mainly in these areas of vulnerability that were met and overcome with considerable personal effort and cost. Thus while humanist philosophers, such as Max Otto, advocated rather austere doctrines during the 1930s, most humanist philosophers of the post–World War II era have tended to be oriented toward psychology and to be more realistic in that regard. Recent humanists, unlike the logical positivists, are personologists alert to psychological problems and coping devices, to personality growth and personal effectiveness.

Psychotherapy. From the late 1950s through the late 1970s, there was a remarkable outpouring of popular psychological literature in the form of paperbacks, much of it originating with prominent psychotherapists based in California. All were naturalistic or humanistic in the sense that they did not take supernaturalism into account (save as a problem). While their principal concern was their work with disturbed persons, the paperbacks and lectures were usually addresssed to people without acute disturbance, the so-called "normals." The experience gained from psychotherapy with neurotics and people with personality disorder was applied to people in general on the basis of humanistic premises: how to live effectively without supernatural redemption. From the context of the history of religion, however, such psychotherapists must be regarded as prophets and reformers of sorts, who preach salvation, especially where their soterial techniques were concerned.

The meditation and therapy groups that became popular during the 1960s and 1970s, the use of relaxation techniques, and the adaptations from psychoanalysis all bore comparison with the means to salvation employed in traditional religions. Indeed, a religious technique from an Eastern religion—for example, yoga—was often taught, though without religious content. Finally, patients who consulted psychotherapists or joined group-therapy sessions were usually secular people who did not anticipate divine intercession even if they held some vestigial religious beliefs. It is perhaps significant that some psychotherapists such as Rollo May have become Christian therapists and that there is now a growing school of psychotherapy that takes religious salvation seriously.

Psychotherapists are usually eclectic but tend to be within either the psychoanalytic (Freudian) or behaviorist (learning theory) traditions. A small minority take the label *humanist* and are thereby distinguished for their emphasis on interpersonal relationships. In the religious or philosophical sense, all psychoanalysts and virtually all learning-theory adherents are humanists, being, generally speaking, agnostic, atheist, or, at the very least, highly skeptical. Their psychotherapies and life-coping teachings are also humanistic in character. Since psychotherapy is a phenomenon that began with SIGMUND FREUD, there is also a certain vague aspect of Jewish mysticism about the tradition, a point explored by Bakan (*Freud and Jewish Mysticism*), who traces the talking cure to the spontaneity of Hassidism, which he claims had some influence from Freud's personal background. While Freud vigorously rejected orthodox Talmudic Judaism and theism, he was very proud of his Jewish identity, and much that is intrinsically derived from Judaism found its way into psychoanalysis.

Indeed, in view of the large number of Jewish practitioners of psychoanalysis, it is possible to see this therapy as a secular manifestation of Judaism.

A number of post-Freudian psychotherapies have developed which, in view of the philosophical considerations involved, are humanistic denominations and sects. Of these, the rational-emotive school of Albert Ellis, the nondirective counseling of Carl Rogers, the transactional analysis of Eric Berne, and the gestalt therapy of Fritz Perls have been particularly important. Each is based on a theory of personality development and structure, or personology, and each emphasizes specific problem-solving techniques. Each recommends a way of life (or alternate ways of life) in which the goal is effectiveness, appropriate behavior, and psychological growth. In general, these ways of life are very much like a plan of salvation even though they do not depend on divine help.

People who do not believe in God or anticipate immortality confront life with courage or the lack of it depending on the individual's personal character. There is no notable absence of fear where death is concerned on the part of the devout even though their faith may instruct them to trust in God or anticipate glory to come. All human beings have to cope with joy and grief, confront the awesome specter of death, and, in the interim between birth and death, attempt to be more or less useful and effective. If anything is striking, it is how irrelevant religion is where these larger concerns are involved, how little difference religion seems to make—or, for that matter, the absence of it. It is the rare individual who really seems to derive much consolation from religion in times of grief. Rather, it seems that the traditional religions are aspects of culture that function mainly to control behavior in ways beneficial to elites. The ways of life of religious persons and of unbelievers may be said to differ chiefly in the ways that individuals differ from each other according to the peculiarities of their own personalities and life histories.

The social dimensions of unbelief are where the most positive commitments are made. While many, if not most, psychotherapists tend to be conservative in economics and political persuasion, other humanists, such as BERTRAND RUSSELL, have been distinguished for social radicalism. Whether the cause is peace, social democracy, ecology, or minority rights, the humanist is motivated by the conviction that if human beings do not work out their own problems no one will do it for them. Although historically Judaism and Christianity have been the wellsprings of various social-action movements, there is an essential humanism involved, and a concept of man that is at sharp variance with the despair of apocalyptic sects.

Certainly, unbelievers of all kinds have been distinguished for their activism in protest movements and revolutionary campaigns, as well as through established systems of political participation. As such, they are most likely to be in liberal and progressive parties, to be advocates of social change and amelioration, rather than conservative defenders of the status quo. Unbelievers are more likely to be opposed to elites, including religious elites, rather than members of such elites. They characteristically belong to the democratic tradition of the left, some as Marxists, others as democratic socialists, still others as liberals. They are seldom to be found among fascists, just as comparatively few humanists are to be found in mental hospitals and prisons (except as political prisoners). Thus, from the social point of view, as well as from the personal, an outstanding distinguishing feature of the unbeliever is his or her inner self-reliance and self-direction coupled with lively social responsibility. While religious unbelief seldom guarantees virtuous behavior, it tends to be characteristic of those comparatively rare persons with the courage to stand alone and take the consequences of their actions. Unbelievers lean neither on Jesus or a church but on themselves. They are, to use David Riesmann's term, inner-directed persons.

Other articles of interest: **God, Existence of. Humanism. Immortality, Unbelief in.**

R. W. BROCKWAY

UNDERWOOD, BENJAMIN FRANKLIN

(1839–1914), American author, lecturer, and newspaper editor. Born in New York City on July 6, B. F. Underwood attached the name of one of the most distinguished families in the northeastern United States to the concurrent thrusts of MATERIALISM and Darwinian evolution in 19th-century FREETHOUGHT.

Early Life. Benjamin was the second of seven children born to Raymond and Harriet Underwood, who moved their family to Westerly, R.I. His father, a granite cutter, could scarcely afford the formal education of his brood. Benjamin attended grammar school and completed studies at Westerly Academy. Beyond classroom tutelage he was self-educated and firmly grounded, by his voracious and eclectic reading habits, in philosophy, science, and literature. His first occupation as a young man is unclear; however, he distinguished himself during the Civil War.

On July 12, 1861, at the age of 22, Underwood enlisted in the 15th Massachusetts Volunteer Infantry. His company saw action in the battle of Ball's Bluff, Va., where he was wounded in the right leg. Confederate soldiers captured him on Oct. 21. For nearly ten months he was held at Libby Prison in Richmond, but was released through a prisoner exchange in August of 1862 and discharged two months later because of his disabled leg. By that time he had married Sara A. Francis, who remained his wife until her death in 1911. They had no children.

On Dec. 16, 1862, Underwood reenlisted at Providence and served with the 5th Rhode Island Volunteer Heavy Artillery for the duration of the war. He saw combat in North Carolina, was rapidly promoted from corporal to first lieutenant, was honorably discharged at the end of the war, having been commended for bravery in action.

Underwood's career as a journalist began during his active service. He was a war correspondent for the Newport, R.I., *Daily News*, 1863–65. When hostilities ceased he was appointed president of the Pawcatuck Library Association in Westerly, and held this post for two years. In ensuing decades he seems to have made his living as an essayist, lecturer, and, presumably, in some limited practice of medicine. It is known that Underwood was a surgeon with the John Wood Post, Department of Illinois, Grand Army of the Republic. He authored at least one medical book, *The Diseases of Childhood, With Therapeutic Indications* (1882).

From the early 1870s, Underwood distinguished himself as a debater and pamphleteer of powerful and impeccable logic, championing a materialistic philosophy and Darwin's theory of evolution. He challenged the Christian clergy of the eastern U.S. to face him in an open forum on the questions of evolution and the necessity of belief in God. Underwood eschewed the milder AGNOSTICISM of his contemporaries, ROBERT G. INGERSOLL and HERBERT SPENCER, and the DEISM of his 18th-century idol, THOMAS PAINE, in favor of a scientific explanation for reality, one that excluded any notion of God. In a short time, he was a known quantity on the public platform and a fearsome opponent to churchmen with intellectual reputations.

His Beliefs. Underwood's reasoning, in the direction of skepticism and outright unbelief, was clearly apparent in his debating style. He was adept at both inductive and deductive logic on the platform and in the press, but in every case his freethought was profoundly reductive but not pessimistic. In point of fact, he identified his reversal of Christianity's historical merits (in his first book, *The Influence of Christianity on Civilization*, 1871) as the perennial tendency of churches to arrest the progress of the sciences—and, therefore, human progress. Moreover, he sought to demonstrate that belief in dogmatic systems has no connection to morality.

Underwood likened his ATHEISM to that of CHARLES BRADLAUGH. Both men would shrug off what is unproven and deny what is demonstrably false. Such was his approach to the debate in July 1875 with Toronto's Rev. John Marples. The topic was the existence of a Supreme Being and the unbegotten origin of all creation. Underwood argued that the idea of a personal God is inconsistent with infinity and that to attribute intelligence and objective form to such an ideal being renders that being "finite, limited, imperfect, and, *as a God*, therefore impossible." Drawing upon the writings of THOMAS HENRY HUXLEY and the Irish physicist John Tyndall, Underwood sought to demolish the so-called "design argument" based on the alleged "order, harmony and adaptation" in the universe. He argued that the creation of a universe by an intelligence characterized by such traits was inconsistent with notions of eternity and infinity and said, "Adaptation must exist as the adjustment of objects to their environments." This adjustment, he asserted, can be explained by the findings of Charles Darwin; the dynamics of "survival of the fittest" have no basis in the concept of design, divine or otherwise.

Among his most famous debates was one in Boston in 1873, when he took on the eminent Harvard professor Asa Gray, a protégé of Darwin who professed theism and adherence to the Nicene Creed.

Underwood found a happy publishing arrangement for his lectures and tracts with DEROBIGNE MORTIMER BENNETT, founder and publisher of the TRUTH SEEKER. Their relationship began in 1874 with the appearance of Underwood's second book, *Essays and Lectures*. In 1875, when Underwood took his evolutionist and anticlerical oratory on a tour extending from major eastern cities far into the Midwest, Bennett printed such notable

Underwood texts as *Darwinism: What It Is and the Proofs in Favor of It, Evolution,* and *Address Delivered at the Paine Hall Dedication, Boston, Mass., January 29, 1875.* The following year, Bennett issued Underwood's *Twelve Tracts,* and, in 1877, his *The Crimes and Cruelties of Christianity* and *Christianity and Materialism.* Although his writings were also offered by other publishers, his association with the Truth Seeker Company lasted for more than three decades.

The high visibility of Underwood the debater, and his brilliance as a rationalist author, earned him the recognition of Boston's Free Religious Association. In 1880 that organization of freethinkers appointed him coeditor, with William J. Potter, of the *Index,* a weekly founded by the Unitarian Francis Abbot. In 1887 he moved to Chicago and served as editor and manager of *Open Court,* a distinctive and long-lived freethought journal. An internal power struggle among the magazine's staff triggered the resignation of Underwood and others, ending his connection in less than 12 months. Remaining in Chicago, he became editor of the *Illustrated Graphic News* in 1888.

Commenting on the turn of Underwood's mind, Ernest Bates wrote: "In spite of his penchant for debate, he was of a genial, kindly disposition, and during his later life he became much more reserved in the expression of his antireligious views and seems to have modified them to a considerable extent." This understates the record and indeed mollifies the arcane tangent upon which Underwood strayed from his once-trenchant materialism. He became affiliated with Chicago's Psychical Science Congress as its secretary, and was an editorial writer for its organ, *Philosophical Journal* (1893–95). Coincident with this activity, Underwood chaired the Congress of Evolution at the Columbian Exposition during the Chicago World's Fair in 1893, and edited a publication called *New Occasions* (1892–93).

His wife was an ardent women's suffragist and freethinker. She wrote *Heroines of Freethought* (1876) and involved her husband in the cause of women's rights. On May 6, 1877, B. F. Underwood addressed the Woman Suffrage Association in Denver. This lecture was published as *Woman: Her Past and Present, Her Rights and Wrongs,* and it was kept in print through the 1890s by the Truth Seeker Company. In the meantime the Underwoods produced a spiritualist work, *Automatic or Spirit Writing, With Other Psychic Experiences* (1896). In 1897, Underwood moved to Quincy, Ill.,

to work for the *Quincy Daily Journal.* He began as an editorial writer and soon took over the editorship, retaining that position until 1913. He retired to his home town, Westerly, R.I., where he died on Nov. 10, 1914.

Bibliography

Bates, Ernest Sutherland. "Underwood, Benjamin Franklin." *Dictionary of American Biography.* New York: Scribner's, 1936.

"Underwood, Benjamin Franklin." *Who Was Who in America.* Chicago: A. N. Marquis, 1942.

Underwood, Lucien Marcus. *The Underwood Families of America.* Vol. 2. Ed. Howard J. Banker. Lancaster, Pa.: Press of the New Era Printing Co., 1913.

WILLIAM F. RYAN

UNITARIANISM. The history of Unitarianism is the story of a way in which a religion began by asserting as true, doctrines considered heretical by Roman Catholics and Protestants, and developed into a religion committed to the principles of freedom, reason, and tolerance. Positively speaking, Unitarianism affirms the freedom and ability of individuals to be their own supreme authority in matters of religious or philosophical belief; negatively, it is a collection of some ancient heresies that have plagued the Christian church since its inception.

Historical Perspective. The word *Unitarian* first came into existence as early as 1568 in Transylvania, now in central Romania, when the Protestant Reformation was about 50 years old. However, the ideas that inspired Unitarianism are much older. When first used, the word *Unitarian* meant a belief in one God rather than the triune God of Christianity. At the time of the Reformation, Christian doctrine, as accepted by both Roman Catholics and Protestants, was centered in the concept of the Trinity: God the Father, God the Son, and God the Holy Ghost constituted a being who was one but also three separate persons. As a result, Jesus was viewed as both God and man. Unitarians, however, found no clear scriptural warrant for the Trinity; instead, they thought of God as a single person. Thus, Jesus was not God, not divine for Unitarians in the same way that he was for the majority of Christians.

Because all Roman Catholics and most Protestants accepted the doctrine of the Trinity, Unitarians were persecuted for several centuries by both groups. Today, the word *Unitarian* has lost its original theological meaning for Unitarians in North America and stands, instead, for freedom in individual belief, an insistence that reason must guide religious thought and action, and the conviction that tolerance and the exchange of different opinions are to be valued.

Unitarianism's historical origins are old and complex; however, they can best be described by following two major threads of Western history. On the one hand, Unitarianism developed directly from Jewish and Christian roots. Not only did key Jewish and Christian principles enter Unitarianism, but Jewish and Christian heresies became its lifeblood. On the other hand, Unitarianism has incorporated much of the emerging SECULARISM of the Western world. More than any other religion, Unitarianism accommodated itself to the scientific world view and the democratic process as these forces emerged in the 18th, 19th, and 20th centuries. Today, a majority of Unitarians no longer call themselves Christian; instead, their thought and inspiration are drawn from the best of the human heritage and worked into a perspective more secular than sacred.

The early Unitarians claimed that their perspective was as old as the Bible, for the Unitarian concept of God is much closer to the Jewish concept than it is to that of traditional Christianity. Jesus himself seems to have looked at God as the 16th-century Unitarians looked at him and not as the early church did: "Why callest thou me good, God alone is good," he is reported to have said. Whatever views Jesus held, it seems fairly certain that as a Jew he would have abhorred the idea of a triune Godhead; thus, his views on God were probably more in accord with those of the early Unitarians.

No scholar has demonstrated a satisfactory way of separating the genuine sayings of Jesus in the New Testament from the apologetic concerns of the early church, which wrote the Gospels without benefit of eyewitness accounts. However, when we turn from the beliefs of Jesus the Jew to the beliefs of doctrinal Christianity, we enter a world that would have been incomprehensible to Jesus. In A.D. 325 the Council of Nicaea, convened by Constantine, emperor of the Eastern Roman Empire, rejected as heretical a doctrine of Arius, a Christian leader, and banished him. Arius taught that Jesus was not the same substance as God the father: God was uncreated and had no beginning,

while Jesus came later from the Father; hence, Jesus had a beginning and was a created being. From the time of the Council of Nicaea and continuing throughout the course of Western history, Arianism was the name given to any heresy that viewed Jesus as a being who was, in any sense, less than God and more human than the orthodox view of him. Unitarianism, when it arose, was often labeled a form of Arianism because it tended to stress the human side of Jesus, rather than the divine.

The next Christian heresy to serve as a source for Unitarian beliefs occurred in 416, when St. Augustine had a controversy with the British monk Pelagius. Pelagius believed in the freedom of the human will, denying that original sin made man incapable of self-reform. Human nature was not, in other words, incorrigibly corrupt. Augustine won the battle against Pelagius and, ever since, Christianity has taught that human nature is corrupt and dependent upon God for salvation. However, the Pelagian heresy has arisen repeatedly in Western history and foreshadowed the Unitarian belief in human freedom and the positive qualities of human nature.

With the rise of the Protestant Reformation in the early 1500s Luther and Calvin attempted to reform some of the corrupt practices of the Roman church while retaining all historic Christian doctrines. Substituting the authority of the Bible for the authority of the church, they were often as narrow-minded and intolerant toward those who differed with them as the Roman Catholic church was toward others. Intolerant Protestants burned heretics and witches at the stake as readily as did the Catholic Inquisition. The anti-Trinitarian Michael Servetus (1511–1553) was hounded by the Roman Inquisition until he fell into the hands of John Calvin, who burned him at the stake.

Servetus' RATIONALISM, which made him a harsh controversialist, exemplified another Unitarian tendency in religion: interest in the natural sciences. He was the first to publish an account of how the blood circulates in the body. Interest in science has often gone hand in hand with heresy. When Servetus was burnt at the stake, one man in Europe spoke up for religious tolerance. In *Concerning Heretics* Gebastian Castellio castigated Calvin for his persecution of Servetus. Castellio asserted that the burning of men for their opinions was both wrong and ineffectual: wrong because it betrayed the ideal of Christian forgiveness; ineffectual because it removed heresy from the lips while confirming it in the heart.

These three heresies that led to Unitarianism echo down the brutal pages of Christian history: Arianism, thinking of Jesus as anything less than God; Pelagianism, believing in the power of human will and the potential for good in human nature; and anti-Trinitarianism, the denial of the triune Godhead. When these three heresies were linked together with a commitment to reason and tolerance, Unitarianism was born. Thus, from its inception Unitarianism has represented the right to reject the traditional doctrines and creeds of orthodoxy; from the beginning it was a system of unbelief. Where might such a religious program be given institutional embodiment? There was more chance for such a religion in countries far from the center of European power where people had been exposed to religious diversity. Poland, whose people lived between Roman Catholic Europe and Orthodox Russia and where Protestants and Catholics coexisted, provided one site for the rise of Unitarianism. The other site was Transylvania, whose people lived between the Islamic Ottoman Empire and Christian Europe and where, again, Catholics and Protestants lived side by side.

Unitarianism in Poland and Transylvania. In 1558 an Italian doctor named Giorgio Biandrata sought refuge in Poland because of his heretical religious opinions. The Polish nobility accepted his beliefs, and in 1565 Biandrata organized the first anti-Trinitarian church. His work and that of other reformers led to the founding of the Minor Reformed church, which was Unitarian in outlook and gained the allegiance of a significant portion of the Polish nobility.

Another Italian who taught religion in Poland was Faustus Socinus (1539–1604), who wrote a book on Jesus in which he said that "Jesus saved men not by dying for them, but by setting an example for them to follow." Under his leadership the city of Kraków became an intellectual and printing center of religious liberalism which had a profound impact on the rest of Europe, especially on the intellectual development of the Dutch. Not long after his death, Socinus' followers published the Racovian Catechism, a systematic exposition of Socinianism which greatly influenced the development of liberal religious thought in Europe. This fourth heresy linked to the development of Unitarianism is Socinianism. In fact, Faustus Socinus and his uncle Laelius Socinus, along with Biandrata, were the first to advocate the point of view that characterized early Unitarianism.

Not satisfied with starting a protounitarian movement in Poland, Dr. Biandrata left that country to become the court physician to King John Sigismund of Transylvania. In 1566 Biandrata urged the king to appoint as his court preacher a man named Francis David (1510–1579). David had tried all of the religions of his day: educated as a priest, he became a Lutheran, then a Calvinist, and finally an anti-Trinitarian. He is reported to have made the statement: "There is no greater piece of folly than to try to exercise power over conscience and soul, both of which are subject only to their Creator."

In 1568, at the Diet of Torda called by John Sigismund, David spoke in favor of religious toleration for *all* religious groups. Under his influence John Sigismund had already become a Unitarian, the label that was beginning to be used to describe the new religious movement in his kingdom. John Sigismund was the first and only Unitarian king in world history. Following the Diet of Torda and in response to David's plea for tolerance, King Sigismund issued the first edict of religious toleration in modern Western history. It read, in part: "Preachers shall be allowed to preach the Gospel everywhere, each according to his own understanding of it. If the community wish to accept such preaching, well and good; if not they shall not be compelled. . . . No one shall be made to suffer on account of his religion, since faith is the gift of God." At a time when most European countries were persecuting men and women for their religious opinions, there was in Transylvania an island of religious freedom. A Unitarian church still exists in Romania, although it is much diminished from its original size because of the great persecutions it has suffered over the past four centuries. Almost eradicated by the combined efforts of intolerant Roman Catholics and Protestants, today it struggles against a Communist government that actively opposes the practice of any religion other than communism.

The Socinian movement in Poland, also called the Minor church, did not survive. After Socinus had been in Poland for a number of years, the vast majority of the Polish nobility adopted his views. However, the Jesuits of the Catholic Counter-Reformation, whom the too-tolerant Poles allowed to found schools, eradicated Polish Socinianism by persuasion and force. Socinian writings and a few leaders of the Minor church made their way to Holland, an emerging center of religious freedom, and thus Socinian ideas became a liberalizing influence on the Dutch and on visiting Englishmen. One

Dutchman so influenced was Jacobus Arminius, a critic of Calvinism. While not a Socinian, his views were often denounced as such. Arminianism rejected the dogmatism of Calvinism and stressed Christianity's moral effort.

Unitarianism's Spread to the English-Speaking World. In the 17th century JOHN LOCKE, the English philosopher, fled to Holland because of his religious and political views, and he may have been influenced by Socinian writings, either while there or at an earlier date when some Socinian books were illegally circulated in England. In 1685 he wrote *A Letter Concerning Toleration*, an effective plea for the tolerance of diversity of opinion. Originally written in Latin for scholars, Locke's letter was translated and distributed by a London merchant, William Popple, who was a Unitarian. Later, in 1697, Locke wrote *The Reasonableness of Christianity*, which was widely denounced as a Socinian heresy. Locke's attempt to make Christianity rational was incorporated and amplified many times in the Unitarian tradition that emerged in England and America.

Two of the greatest Englishmen of the 17th century, John Milton and Sir Isaac Newton, held anti-Trinitarian views, and both were keenly interested in science. Milton, as a young man, visited the aging Galileo and left Italy with a lasting hatred of all forms of tyranny. His essay, *Areopagitica*, is the first defense of freedom of speech and press in the English language, while Newton almost single-handedly codified the emerging modern scientific view of the universe. With Locke and Newton religious interest shifted away from biblical investigations and doctrinal arguments and toward a religious perspective more accommodating of secularism and the scientific world view.

In 1774 the clergyman Theophilus Lindsey withdrew from the state Church of England, which required all clerics to subscribe to its Thirty-Nine Articles of belief and opened the first English Unitarian chapel on Essex Street in London. Two hundred people attended the first meeting; among those attending was Dr. Joseph Priestley, the discoverer of oxygen, who later became one of the noted Unitarian ministers of his day. Another person in attendance was BENJAMIN FRANKLIN, the deist, then in London representing the American colonies. Since Franklin was the first American to achieve international recognition, his presence was significant. Out of that first Unitarian meeting grew a movement that gradually spread to many of the major population centers in England, but it was not until 1825 that a national association of English Unitarian churches was formed.

During this same period in America a rather different course led to the development of Unitarianism. The Pilgrims and Puritans immigrated to America in the 1600s, coming as Calvinists committed to the practice of radical congregational polity, which permitted separate congregations a great deal of latitude. Congregational polity, originally conceived as a way of purifying the Anglican church while eluding the control of the government and bishops, evolved in the new world into a polity that allowed individual churches and preachers to drift in what was later perceived as heretical directions. Over the course of the first 200 years of the Pilgrim-Puritan experiment, the liberal and heretical tendency of many churches became increasingly apparent; Calvinist visitors from England were shocked and returned with reports that the New England Calvinist churches were riddled with the heresies of Arianism, Socinianism, and Arminianism. The reports were true: the Congregational churches in America were ripe for schism.

At Harvard University, which was originally founded to educate the New England clergy, a controversy erupted in 1805 over control of the appointment of the professorship of divinity: Would the liberals or the conservatives name the person to fill the recently vacated post, the possessor of which trained ministerial candidates. When the Board of Overseers chose Henry Ware, a liberal, the conservatives withdrew from Harvard and founded the conservative seminary, Andover. During the next 20 years, much to the dismay of the liberals who sought an inclusive church, the New England Congregational establishment split asunder. The liberals accepted the Unitarian label, which was hurled at them as a term of opprobrium. By 1825, 125 of the oldest churches in New England had become Unitarian, and on May 26, 1825, the American Unitarian Association was founded. By pure coincidence, this date was the same on which the English Unitarian Association was founded.

Impact of Unitarianism in the U.S. American Unitarianism has made a greater impact on American thought and history than English Unitarianism has on its national consciousness. English Unitarians had to struggle against a state church which, while imposing civil disabilities on dissenters, became increasingly inclusive and therefore attractive to liberals, while, in America, Unitarianism was in reality the established church in New England. Five American presidents, numerous thinkers, reformers, and scientists have identified themselves as Unitarians. Famous Unitarian reformers, to mention only a few, include Dorothea Dix, Joseph Tuckerman, Samuel Gridly Howe, Henry Bergh, Susan B. Anthony, Horace Mann, and Charles W. Eliot.

In the 19th century the intellectual currents that swept America were often initiated in Unitarian circles. The five greatest poets of the early period of American history were all Unitarians—William Cullen Bryant, John Greenleaf Whittier, Henry Wadsworth Longfellow, Robert Lowell, and Oliver Wendell Holmes—as were the historians Jared Sparks, William H. Prescott, and Francis Parkman. Two key architects of American democracy and also leaders of opposing political parties, THOMAS JEFFERSON and John Adams, were Unitarians. A. Powell Davies was correct when, in *America's Real Religion*, he claimed that the forces that brought the United States into existence were also the forces that created Unitarianism. American Unitarianism had yet another advantage over Unitarianism in England; its strong tradition of congregational polity continued to function, incorporating new heresies and leading Unitarians in America beyond Christian boundaries. In England, however, RATIONALISM, FREETHOUGHT, and HUMANISM were, for the most part, excluded from Unitarian churches, which retained a Christian orientation. Thus, the vitality of an ever more rational perspective was denied to English Unitarianism, while in the U.S. such thought enriched and vitalized the Unitarian tradition.

The process by which the Calvinism of the Pilgrims and Puritans broadened into Unitarianism, and the theological drift of autonomous congregations continued with greater force once the Unitarian churches separated from the Congregational ones. In 1819, William Ellery Channing (1780–1842) replied to the attacks of conservative Congregationalists in a sermon titled "Unitarian Christianity." It was widely disseminated and expressed the beliefs of most Unitarians of the period. He taught a rational approach to the Bible, accepting, however, the miracles in the New Testament as proof of the uniqueness of Christianity. Central to Channing's thought was what he called his "one sublime idea," the dignity and potential goodness of every individual human being. But in a few years his theology seemed old-fashioned to many younger Unitarians.

In 1838 Channing's younger colleague, Ralph Waldo Emerson (1803–1882), shocked the Unitarian establishment with his "Divinity School Address" before the Harvard Divinity School students. Emerson, approaching religion and God intuitively, cast doubt upon the miracles of the New Testament and preached a transcendental view of God, which represented him, not as a person, but as best known through human intuition. Many of the Harvard faculty were scandalized, and Andrews Norton, a noted Unitarian theologian, attacked Emerson's views as "the latest form of infidelity." But Unitarianism had no way of excluding trancendentalist views from its pulpits or pews, and within 30 years trancendentalism was widely accepted in Unitarian circles. Unitarianism was increasingly becoming a religion best defined by its refusal to espouse or insist on adherence to a particular creed or doctrine as a condition of worship. Many trancendentalists, almost without realizing it, strayed beyond the traditional boundaries of the Judeo-Christian tradition.

Theodore Parker (1810–1860), Emerson's colleague, carried Emerson's iconoclasm one step further. Not only did he deny the miracles, but he also introduced Unitarians to the new German scientific criticism of the Bible and was an early example of the preacher who used his pulpit as a platform for constantly urging social reform. Shunned by many of his ministerial colleagues, Parker ultimately had a profound impact upon Unitarian thinking and preached to the largest congregation of his day. Despite the discomfort he caused conservative Unitarians, there was no way to silence him as long as the congregations he served (first in Roxbury and then in Boston) were satisfied with his ministry. Still, the noncreedal principle was not widely proclaimed or agreed upon.

By 1865 the Unitarian movement was large enough to hold a national conference, or annual gathering of key laymen and clergy. Henry Bellows, the clergyman who founded the conference, helped pass a resolution at the first meeting that would have confined Unitarianism to the Christian tradition. The "radicals," as they were called, many of them followers of Emerson, insisted that Unitarianism or any modern religion must view religion from a more inclusive perspective. Their response to the perceived restrictive creed of the national conference was to found in 1866 the Free Religious Association, which proclaimed that, while "Christianity is limited by the Christian Confession . . . the Fellowship of Free Religion is universal and free; it proclaims the great brotherhood of man without limit or bound."

Emerson was the first to sign the document creating the new organization, and over the next 25 years the Free Religious Association gradually won acceptance of its views among a majority of Unitarians. Finally, in 1887, the National Association of Unitarian Churches adopted a noncreedal stance. Since that time, despite occasional controversies, Unitarians have been committed to a way in religion based on theological and philosophical inclusiveness. The Free Religious Association had an even more far-reaching impact on Unitarian and American religious thought: members like Francis Abbot and Octavius Frothingham led in refashioning religion to accord with the emerging scientific world view and the theory and practice of democracy. These men and others in the Free Religious Association created a religious perspective that was comfortable with the best of secular thought. The key elements of what is called the "humanist" stance in religion were stressed in their speaking and writing.

John H. Dietrich, the Unitarian minister in Spokane, Washington, from 1911 to 1916, was the first to refer to his way in religion as "humanistic." Echoing elements of the Greek enlightenment and of the Renaissance, Dietrich's humanism recalled THOMAS PAINE's "religion of humanity" and the ideas of thinkers as diverse as LUDWIG FEUERBACH, George Eliot, AUGUSTE COMTE, and ROBERT G. INGERSOLL. Dietrich moved from liberal theism to a "naturalistic humanism" beyond the usual theological boundaries of the Unitarianism in his day. Called to the First Unitarian Society of Minneapolis in 1916, he built it into a major Unitarian church, one composed mainly of humanists. Dietrich was an effective proponent of religious humanism, and his efforts were furthered by his friend Curtis Reese, another Unitarian clergyman, who first called his religious perspective "the religion of democracy" and then adopted the label "humanist." Reese encouraged the organization of Unitarian churches and the acceptance of humanism from his post as executive director of the Western Conference Office (Unitarian) located in Chicago.

Humanism, as an individual's religious or philosophical point of view, rapidly gained adherents among Unitarians, more so among the laity than the clergy, and especially in the Midwest. While some efforts were made to resist its spread, radical congregational polity made that impossible. Consequently, Unitarianism reaffirmed its commitment to the noncreedal principle as humanism became one of the accepted theological positions found in Unitarian churches. In 1933 Roy Wood Sellers, JOHN DEWEY, and a number of other intellectuals signed the first *Humanist Manifesto*, which publicized humanism as a religious option. Of the 34 original signers, 14 were Unitarian ministers, by far the largest religious group represented and indicative of how visible and widespread humanism had become in Unitarian circles.

Recent Developments. The merger of the American Unitarian Association and the Universalist Church of America in 1961 created a strengthened national organization for two groups who had previously had minimal national bureaucracies. (See UNIVERSALISM.) Both groups were committed to the principles of congregational polity and noncreedal religion. At the time of merger there were 150,000 Unitarians and 50,000 Universalists; Unitarians doubled their membership in a 10-year period following World War II, while Universalism was declining in membership.

In the 20 years following merger the combined organization, called the Unitarian-Universalist Association (U.U.A.), lost a significant number of members. No scientific study has established whether this loss of over 60,000 members was the result of a national trend in mainline churches or if some other causal factor was involved. It has been suggested that the social activism of Unitarian-Universalists in the 1960s (when they, for the first time took action on many social and political issues at national meetings) was a factor. Then, too, some of the loss may have been a continued decline of population in small towns where many Universalist churches were located. In 1982 membership in Unitarian-Universalist churches and fellowships was 137,000, with signs that membership was beginning to increase slightly.

Since merger, the U.U.A. has been rocked a number of times by debates over social and political issues. Not only were there differences between social advocates who offered conflicting remedies for particular social evils, but there was also a conflict between those Unitarian-Universalists who did not want to take institutional social-action stands and those who did. Advocates of institutional action view it as ethically essential and as an inevitable continuation of the prophetic tradition of the Judeo-Christian tradition and the historical interest of *individual* Unitarians and Universalists. Opponents of such an approach see the U.U.A.

primarily as an inclusive educational community and insist that the social action of historic Unitarianism and Universalism was done by *individuals* working through specialized voluntary associations in the wider community who did not try to make their churches organs of political activity.

To date, the weight of opinion at Unitarian-Universalist national gatherings has fallen heavily on the side of those who, in accord with the Hebrew prophets, the Roman Catholic pontiff, and Calvinist theologians, require the church to take social and political stands. By contrast, on the congregational level, most Unitarian-Universalists still want their local churches and fellowships to be religiously and politically inclusive. It is not yet apparent how this crucial difference of opinion will be resolved—whether the Unitarian-Universalist churches will gradually adopt the form of a theologically open church committed to a particular political program, or whether they will remain noncreedal and inclusive in political as well as religious beliefs.

Bibliography

Lyttle, Charles H. *Freedom Moves West: A History of the Western Unitarian Conference (1852–1952).* Boston: Beacon Press, 1952.

Olds, Mason. *Religious Humanism in America: Dietrich, Reese, and Potter.* Washington, D.C.: University Press of America, 1977.

Park, David B. *The Epic of Unitarianism.* Boston: Beacon Press, 1957.

Persons, Stow. *Free Religion.* Boston: Beacon Press, 1963.

Wilber, Earl Morse. *A History of Unitarianism: Socinianism and Its Antecedents.* Vol. 1. Boston: Beacon Press, 1945.

———. *A History of Unitarianism in Transylvania, England, and America.* Vol. 2. Boston: Beacon Press, 1945.

Wright, Conrad. *The Beginnings of Unitarianism in America.* Boston: Beacon Press, 1955.

PAUL H. BEATTIE

UNITED KINGDOM, UNBELIEF IN THE.

BEFORE 1915

The 17th and 18th Centuries. Unbelief in the central doctrines of the Christian religion—as opposed to mere heterodoxy or heresy—became common in Britain only in the late 17th century. The generation after that which had been torn apart by civil and religious strife in the mid-century seems to have settled for the relative quiet of philosophical skepticism, under the rationalistic influence of JOHN LOCKE. DEISM remained the dominant intellectual position among unbelievers in Britain throughout the 18th century; unlike the situation in France, outright atheistic materialism was rare in Britain and made its impact only in the early decades of the 19th century.

With the reception of ENLIGHTENMENT views among the more plebeian unbelievers in the years of the French Revolution, and with the development of scientific knowledge about the history of the earth and man, ATHEISM then became widely discussed for the first time. Even so, its open advocacy long continued to be legally suspect (see BLASPHEMY LAWS), and the British mind proved unusually impervious to the spread of rational theology and liberal biblical scholarship from Germany.

Organized unbelief differed in practice from deism and atheism in that it added to the philosophical position a social dimension. Its distinguishing characteristic and its "offense" lay in its appeal to the lesser people in society—small masters, artisan journeymen, and all those excluded from the civil and religious nation by law or by custom. Thus, although the first modern unbeliever in the British Isles might be JOHN TOLAND (1670–1722) and the first freethinker in the modern sense might be ANTHONY COLLINS (1676–1729), the first "infidel" (to use the contemporary pejorative for one who rejected the Christian faith) was probably THOMAS CHUBB (1679–1747), a chandler from Salisbury. In 1741 he joined the deists' debate with a pamphlet entitled *Discourse on Miracles*, in which he attacked the central foundation of Christian argument. Chubb belonged to a provincial debating society, and this, the pamphlet, and the public lecture were in 18th-century Britain the principal means of disseminating unorthodox religious and political views. Another such workingman, Jacob Ilive (1705–1768), a printer, lectured in London and was pilloried and imprisoned in 1753 for writing a pamphlet against divine revelation. His fate was shared by PETER ANNET (1693–1769), the most celebrated of the 18th-century plebeian unbelievers.

A great transformation in British unbelief came

with the French Revolution, the propagation of subversive French views among the artisans of Britain, and the publications of THOMAS PAINE (1737–1809), in particular *The Age of Reason* (1794–95). Unbelief now entered the radical political societies, including the London Corresponding Society, which was by far the most influential. During the dark days of government repression after 1799 the flame was kept alive by publishers of Paine's works, men like Daniel Isaac Eaton, who was pilloried in 1812. After the end of the Napoleonic Wars in 1815, this tradition of resolute publishing was continued by RICHARD CARLILE (1790–1843).

The 19th Century. Carlile made three important contributions to the development of organized unbelief in 19th-century Britain. First, by example, he led a concerted defiance of the law that limited the freedom to express views hostile to established religious and political beliefs and practices. Second, he began in the early 1820s to advocate an outright atheistic materialism that marked a significant break with past views, including those of Paine. Third, he encouraged his followers to band themselves together in Free Enquiry or Zetetic societies, which were the first such organized bodies of plebeian unbelief in Britain. Though most Zetetic societies, like Carlile's own materialism, lasted only a few years, they were to prove a lasting influence on later groups of radicals.

In the first half of the 19th century unbelief was widespread only in the loosest possible sense. Despite Carlile's efforts, it was never coordinated. The popular mood should more properly be described as anticlerical rather than unbelieving, for despite laments among the upper classes about widespread "infidelity" the actual number of avowed unbelievers was probably very small. Among the upper classes it was even smaller, for, since the easygoing days of 18th-century deism, the Evangelical revival had touched all sections of respectable society, and the French Revolution had brought home to the propertied classes the political dangers that were apparently inherent in unbelief.

Most important in running counter to this religious trend was the small group of men who, to varying degrees, came under the influence of JEREMY BENTHAM. Notable among these philosophic radicals was the young liberal philosopher and economist JOHN STUART MILL. Though "honest doubt" and AGNOSTICISM were later to become hallmarks of the Victorian intellectual consciousness, openly organized unbelief was to be associated in the 19th century largely with radicals—philosophic and plebeian.

The plebeian radicals, who from the 1830s were of the working and lower-middle classes, in many cases became followers of ROBERT OWEN, whose attacks on Christianity in 1817 had brought him a certain amount of notoriety. Owenism in the 1830s, however, was more extensive than Owen's own doctrines and practice. Where he was a paternalist, many Owenites were democratic radicals, and it is among them that a new organization to promote unbelief was conceived. Owen began his Association of All Classes of All Nations in 1835 as a propagandist agency, but by 1837 it had been taken over by the democratic radicals, many of whom showed a greater readiness to promote unbelief through its branch organizations than to spread Owen's communitarian socialism. As Owen attempted to reimpose control in 1841 a number of anti-Christian dissidents, led by CHARLES SOUTHWELL, broke away to start their own agitation.

Southwell began a periodical, the *Oracle of Reason*, in November of 1841, to advocate the sort of materialistic atheism Carlile had championed in the 1820s. After only a month Southwell was charged with blasphemy, an incident which drew into the fray GEORGE JACOB HOLYOAKE, another discontented Owenite lecturer. He too was arrested on a blasphemy charge in 1842, and his friends set up the Anti-Persecution Union to fight for the cause of free speech. During the next few years a separate freethought movement grew up within Owenism until, with the collapse of the latter in 1845, Holyoake was able to lead the unbelieving remnants into a new and explicitly "infidel" organization. Through his periodicals, the *Movement* (1843–45), the *Circular of the Anti-Persecution Union* (1845), and the *Reasoner* (1846–61), Holyoake rallied provincial Owenites and their branch societies, and in the early 1850s he gave to the new movement the name of SECULARISM.

Secularism. Holyoake himself saw secularism as an extension of the Owenite creed of RATIONALISM, modified to suit changing circumstances. His aim was to promote reforms in all walks of life without raising questions of either belief or unbelief, but this neutral attitude was almost impossible to maintain. Many unbelievers came to regard Holyoake's secularism as too mild and his leadership as too ready for compromise with Christianity. Their discontent was voiced by another former Owenite lecturer, Robert Cooper (1819–1868) of

Manchester, who in 1854 began a periodical entitled the *London Investigator* after the celebrated BOSTON INVESTIGATOR. By 1857, when the paper became the *Investigator* under the editorship of William Harral Johnson (born 1834), there was an open breach in the ranks of the unbelievers between Holyoake-type secularists and militant atheists who saw themselves as continuing the tradition of Carlile.

Holyoake's moderation at this time was in part a response to the development of unbelief among an intellectual minority of the upper classes, some of whom gave financial as well as philosophical aid to his work. Chief among these influences were J. S. Mill and George Henry Lewes, the associate of George Eliot (who in 1845 had translated DAVID FRIEDRICH STRAUSS' *Life of Jesus* into English); Harriet Martineau, sister of the liberal Unitarian theologian James Martineau, and her friend Henry G. Atkinson; Sophia Dobson Collet and William Johnson Fox of the South Place Chapel in London; and Francis William Newman, Unitarian and brother of the famous cardinal, John Henry Newman. A number of these people were closely connected in the 1850s with the *Leader*, a weekly periodical of enlightened liberalism edited by Holyoake's friend, Thornton Hunt, son of the radical poet Leigh Hunt. Through Atkinson, Lewes, and Mill, Holyoake also became acquainted with the ideas of AUGUSTE COMTE, whose POSITIVISM began to have an important modifying influence on sections of British unbelief.

Despite Holyoake, however, secularism was not allowed to merge with "honest doubt" at this time, and in the late 1850s those freethinkers who wished to lay renewed emphasis on the militancy of their unbelief found a ready champion in CHARLES BRADLAUGH, whose NATIONAL REFORMER, begun in 1860, rapidly replaced Holyoake's *Reasoner* as the principal organ of unbelief in Victorian Britain. In 1866 Bradlaugh cut short the various attempts that had been made to unite local freethought groups into a single national body by announcing the formation of the NATIONAL SECULAR SOCIETY (N.S.S.) with himself as president and CHARLES WATTS as secretary. Though Holyoake retained a measure of support, Bradlaugh, his paper, and his organization were to be the embodiment, in the public mind and in reality, of organized unbelief in the late 19th century.

Freethought in the 19th Century. CHAPMAN COHEN later characterized FREETHOUGHT under Bradlaugh as being political; under the next president of the N.S.S., GEORGE WILLIAM FOOTE, as biblical; and under himself, the third president, as materialistic. Broadly speaking, these three phases and emphases are accurate.

Bradlaugh was a campaigning radical, a republican, an advocate of birth control, and an unbeliever. His movement grew in response to all these aspects of his life and work, but never more so than in the early 1880s, when he was fighting to be accepted as a member of Parliament. The freethought movement reached its peak in these years with over one hundred N.S.S. branches. The actual number of unbelievers at the time is hard to ascertain. The Census of Religious Worship, held in England, Wales, and Scotland in 1851, does not help. The Irish religious census of 1861 reveals only 69 people willing to describe themselves in some broad sense as unbelievers, but in Ireland there was little room for unbelief between the Scylla of Protestantism and the Charybdis of Catholicism. Even in Great Britain, though, the sales of the *Reasoner* reached a maximum of only 5,000 in the 1850s, and the *National Reformer* in Bradlaugh's heyday probably did not sell twice that figure. Foote's FREETHINKER did sell over 10,000 copies when he was prosecuted for blasphemy in the early 1880s, but this peak was not maintained for long. The maximum, paid-up membership of the N.S.S. was under 4,000. Yet tens of thousands of people were attracted to lectures on unbelief, particularly when Bradlaugh and ANNIE BESANT were packing halls across the country, and unbelief was felt by many sincere Christians to be a very real threat to society.

As political radicalism occupied more and more of Bradlaugh's time, Foote began to play an increasingly important part in the organization of the movement, especially after his *Freethinker*, begun in 1881, had incurred a couple of prosecutions, for which Foote went to jail for a year. As the N.S.S. began to decline in the late 1880s, Foote took more of the organizational duties and in 1890 succeeded the ailing Bradlaugh as president. Foote was unable, however, to prevent the long slide into obscurity. The number of members dwindled to under a thousand, and many branches disappeared completely. When Foote died in 1915, the rational optimism of his generation and the once powerfully organized forces of unbelief were alike in eclipse.

Throughout these years, though, an alternative tradition of freethought continued. Associated with the name of Holyoake, it gained renewed strength after 1877, when Bradlaugh alienated some of his support by championing the cause of Malthusian birth-control propaganda in his defense of Dr. CHARLES KNOWLTON's work, *The Fruits of Philosophy*. The resulting quarrel between Bradlaugh and Watts, who had hitherto been his closest associate, marked the ascendancy of Annie Besant and the adhesion of Watts to the oppositionists. The latter formed the British Secular Union (B.S.U.) in 1878, and concentrated their journalistic efforts on the *Secular Review*, a paper begun by Holyoake in 1876 and edited by Watts from 1877 until 1884.

The bitterness of the *Secular Review* group deepened in 1882, when WILLIAM STEWART ROSS gained editorial influence on the paper. He mercilessly attacked Bradlaugh and Besant for their dictatorial manner and advocacy of "Knowltonian filth." The theological views of the two sides were not, however, very far apart though Ross was less of a dogmatic atheist than Bradlaugh. In 1885 Ross renamed the *Secular Review* the *Agnostic Journal*.

The freethinkers of the B.S.U. prided themselves on a more intellectual approach to unbelief than that practiced by supporters of the N.S.S. It would be more accurate to say that Ross in particular was more in touch with the changing intellectual fashions of the late 19th century, including the new morality of Grant Allen and Edward Carpenter. Among the *Agnostic Journal*'s patrons were Lady Florence Dixie and her brother, the Marquis of Queensberry, a one-time president of the B.S.U. Unbelief had become very avant-garde.

Another sign of the changing times, and the final vindication of the Holyoake approach, came in the 1890s with the formation of what was to become in 1899 the Rationalist Press Association (R.P.A.). Holyoake was president, but the leading figure was Charles Watts' son, the publisher and printer Charles Albert Watts. As the N.S.S. declined the R.P.A. rose, appealing to a new audience of state-educated, lower-middle-class people who did not necessarily share either the political views of Bradlaugh or the antibiblical rhetoric of Foote.

By the first decade of the 20th century the nature and scope of freethought and unbelief in Britain had changed dramatically from that of a century earlier. First, it had become respectable not merely to doubt but to disbelieve in Christianity. Evolutionary biology and nonliteral interpretations of scripture were widely accepted by Christian thinkers, and the intellectual grounds of unbelief were appreciated even by those who were not thereby led into unbelief. The course of this intellectual shift

can be charted by changing interpretations of the law on blasphemy, from the acknowledgement by a legal authority, *Starkie*, in 1830 that moderately expressed unbelief might not be illegal, through Lord Chief Justice John Coleridge's summing-up to this effect in Foote's case in 1883, to the final recognition of this state of affairs in the Bowman case, heard by the House of Lords in 1917.

Prominent unbelievers were now to be found in all walks of life: the distinguished sons of the Clapham Sect Evangelical, Sir James Stephen— Sir Leslie Stephen and Sir James Fitzjames Stephen, a judge and legal authority; the novelist Thomas Hardy; the dramatist GEORGE BERNARD SHAW; the poet ALGERNON CHARLES SWINBURNE; the mathematician WILLIAM KINGDON CLIFFORD; the scientist, THOMAS HENRY HUXLEY; and the Cambridge philosopher BERTRAND RUSSELL. The gap between popular and respectable unbelief was also narrowing, with JOHN M. ROBERTSON spanning in his career *National Reformer* journalism, scholarly unbelief, and success in politics, following in the steps of another unbeliever, John Morley.

Paradoxically, as the prevalence of unbelief in the society at large increased, so the power of organized unbelief diminished, with the exception of the publishing work of the R.P.A. Unbelief depended on the strength of belief for its relevance; apathy and indifference were the enemies of both. As the churches were edged from the center of the nation's life with the increasing secularization of institutions and, from the Edwardian years, with the marked decline in the custom of regular religious observance, militant unbelief of the kind that had flourished in Bradlaugh's day ceased to have any meaning for most people.

Politically, too, the old style of unbelief in alliance with radicalism and republicanism had become a thing of the past. Ever since the days of Paine and Carlile, unbelief in Britain had been associated with the political "left," but with the rise of a native socialist movement from the 1880s this ceased to be true. The secularist leadership in the main remained true to liberalism, and many socialists left to join the Fabian Society, the Social Democratic Federation, or even the Independent Labor party. It was an untypical minority who followed J. W. GOTT into both militant socialism and militant unbelief in the early 20th century. For most people the political arguments of socialism replaced the theological arguments of secularism as the basis of a program for radical change. Organized unbelief would continue after 1915 either as a pressure group to secure the complete secularization of the state or as an educational agency to counter the theological and philosophical arguments still being advanced to support the cause of Christian belief.

AFTER 1915

After World War I unbelief in Britain faced a very different religious and intellectual milieu from that which had prevailed in Victorian times. Organized religion and religious belief alike had begun to show signs of decline before the war, but most people were quite unprepared for the corrosion of orthodoxy that occurred with increased rapidity as the 20th century progressed. Though the horrors of war deepened the religious faith of some, the general effect of war, social dislocation, and rapid social change would undermine traditional beliefs and attitudes associated with religious practice. Though periodic revivals were experienced, by 1981 only about 10 percent of the total British population was counted among regular churchgoers. Practical secularism had become the principal characteristic of the popular outlook.

Organized unbelief in the National Secular Society, the Rationalist Press Association, and ETHICAL CULTURE experienced a similar pattern of decline and made few significant gains in membership over the levels achieved in the decades before the outbreak of the war. The number of N.S.S. branches dwindled and they were increasingly forced by lack of funds to hold their meetings out of doors. The R.P.A., which had been expanding before 1914, experienced financial difficulties and contracting sales in the 1920s until, in 1929, the highly successful Thinker's Library brought a welcome new look to the R.P.A.'s lists. Nevertheless, many idealistic young people were drawn more to communism than to RATIONALISM in the 1930s, and the Left Book Club rapidly outstripped the R.P.A. in membership. The Ethical Culture movement also struggled after the war, and by 1939 there were only a little over one hundred members and only eight branches, all of them in London. Not among these was the South Place Ethical Society, which moved from its famous chapel to new premises in Conway Hall, in west central London, in the summer of 1929.

A major problem for organized unbelief between the two world wars was its isolation from the mainstream of progressive thought and in particular its ambiguous attitude toward Marxism.

The ideological conflict of communism and fascism in the 1930s left little room for older issues. Economic and social questions came to the fore during the Great Depression, and some rationalists began to question the relevance of the old theological debate. The old certainties were being swept away. In psychology and anthropology the works of William James and SIGMUND FREUD raised new questions about the origin and nature of religious experience that challenged older religious and rationalist concepts alike.

The assumed relationship between science, reason, and morality was also changing with the rise of "scientific humanism." Julian Huxley, in particular, bewildered many older rationalists with his assertion in *What Dare I Think* (1931): "The vices of the scientific mind are intellectualism and lack of appreciation of the value of other kinds of experience." As the older generation of rationalists, led by men as diverse as J. M. Robertson and JOSEPH MCCABE, gradually died out, so the newer thinking of men like Huxley, Bertrand Russell, and J. B. S. Haldane began to reshape the concepts of unbelief for the later 20th century.

After World War II the social, intellectual, and religious context of unbelief was again transformed, but this time the rationalists were better placed to take advantage of developments. The 1950s saw an expansion in both religious and freethinking organizations, and in the mid-1950s the term HUMANISM emerged to describe the new mood and new ideas. First the Ethical Union and then the R.P.A. and N.S.S. responded to this development, and in 1963 the first two collaborated to form the British Humanist Association (B.H.A.). In that year there were 33 humanist groups in Britain; by 1967, when the R.P.A. left the B.H.A. to avoid threats to its charitable status, the number had risen to 91. The N.S.S., which was never a party to the B.H.A. despite some common aims and membership, summed up its own change of fortune and the ethos of the 1960s in the title of its 1965 annual report—"A Year of Expansion."

The 1970s, however, brought the end of this growth for both churches and freethinkers. A sign of this came in 1973, when the *Freethinker*, after 90 years of weekly publication, reverted to a monthly format. The decade also saw the R.P.A. lose its charitable status, despite its emphasis on humanist education in its publications.

If the societies of organized unbelief did not benefit from the supposed arrival of a post-Christian age, in a number of respects orthodoxy received additional and influential support. Extreme sects, such as Pentecostalists, maintained their earlier advances, and such new cults as Scientology arrived from the United States. The Education Act of 1944 went further than any previous act since 1870 in imposing compulsory religious observance and religious instruction in state schools.

In 1977, for the first time since 1922 the blasphemy laws were successfully applied in the *Gay News* case. There emerged a militantly evangelical organization, the National Festival of Light, which was closely allied with the National Viewers' and Listeners' Association, a puritanical pressure group led by Mary Whitehouse. The latter was formed partly in response to the gradual diminution of Christian moral values within the British Broadcasting Corporation (B.B.C.), which had been formed in 1922.

The first director of the B.B.C., Sir John Reith, was a stern Scots puritan who intended his organization to maintain traditional Christian standards. Only gradually did the voice of unbelief make itself heard in broadcasting. Well-known humanists who were also respected academics, such as Julian Huxley, Gilbert Murray, Bertrand Russell, and C. E. Joad, became household names on the radio, but when Margaret Knight of Aberdeen University made a series of broadcasts in 1955 on "Morals Without Religion," she generated a storm of outrage in the press and within the British establishment.

Nevertheless unbelief was making steady progress in academic circles, and theologians were being forced to express their beliefs in radically new terms. The "new theology" was not particularly new in the closed world of academic scholarship by the 1960s, but public opinion was taken by surprise in 1963 when Dr. John Robinson, bishop of Woolwich, published a slim paperback entitled *Honest to God*, a book that convinced many of its opponents that unbelief had penetrated the heart of the Church of England. In the same year a group of Cambridge theologians from the same school of thought published a frank examination, *Objections to Christian Belief*, which prompted a companion *Objections to Humanism*, edited by H. J. Blackham of the B.H.A.

The resurgence of popular Christian fundamentalism and continuing examples of prejudice experienced by unbelievers reinforced the determination of one section of organized unbelief, led by the N.S.S., to maintain existing propagandist work against religion and especially against the Roman Catholic church. Within the B.H.A., however, the emphasis was on particular social and political objectives derived from humanist values. This approach lost the B.H.A. its charitable status in 1965 and resulted in the R.P.A. leaving the B.H.A. two years later. Issues such as disarmament, censorship, population control, abortion and civil liberties were seen as central to humanist concern, and the considerable degree of cross-membership between the N.S.S., the R.P.A. and the B.H.A. makes it possible to conclude that this was the broad platform for most unbelievers in the latter half of the 20th century. The problem, however, for unbelief remained one of making sufficient impact on contemporary society. For the majority of people in Britain, a preoccupation with increasing material comforts had displaced any recognizable idealism—humanist or otherwise.

Other articles of interest: **English Literature, Unbelief in. Women and Unbelief.**

Bibliography

The two fullest outline histories of unbelief, both by unbelievers, are Leslie Stephen, *History of English Thought in the Eighteenth Century*, 2 vols. (London: 1876), and J. M. Robertson, *A History of Freethought in the Nineteenth Century* (London: 1929). The freethought movement has more recently been the subject of Susan Budd's *Varieties of Unbelief: Atheists and Agnostics in English Society 1850–1960* (London: Heinemann Publications, 1977) and Edward Royle's *Victorian Infidels: The Origins of the British Secularist Movement 1791–1866* (Manchester and Totowa, N.J.: Manchester U. Press and Rowman and Littlefield, 1974) and *Radicals, Secularists and Republicans: Popular Freethought in Britain, 1866–1915* (Manchester and Totowa, N.J.: Manchester U. Press and Rowman and Littlefield, 1980).

"Honest doubt" is described by Basil Willey, *More Nineteenth Century Studies: A Group of Honest Doubters* (London: 1956) and A. O. J. Cockshut, *The Unbelievers: English Agnostic Thought 1840–1890* (London: 1964). The changing religious climate is summarized in H. G. Wood, *Belief and Unbelief Since 1850* (Cambridge: Cambridge U. Press, 1955).

See also F. B. Smith, *"The Atheist Mission, 1840–1900"* in R. Robson, ed., *Ideas and Institutions of Victorian Britain* (London: Bell, 1967); W. S. Smith, *The London Heretics, 1870–1914* (London: 1967); David Tribe, *100 Years of Freethought*

(London: Elek, 1967); H. R. Murphy, "The Ethical Revolt Against Christian Orthodoxy in Early Victorian England," *American Historical Review* 60 (1955); and Gordon Stein, *Freethought in the United Kingdom and the Commonwealth* (Westport, Conn.: Greenwood Press, 1981).

For more specialized aspects of British freethought, see:

Campbell, C. B. "Humanism in Britain." *A Sociological Year Book of Religion in Britain* 2 (1969).

———. *Toward a Sociology of Irreligion* (London: Macmillan, 1971).

Nelson, W. D. "British Rational Secularism: Unbelief from Bradlaugh to the Mid-Twentieth Century," Ph.D. dissertation, University of Washington, 1963.

Ratcliffe, S. K. *The Story of South Place*. London: Watts, 1955.

Spiller, G. *The Ethical Movement in Great Britain: A Documentary History*. London: Farleigh Press, 1934.

Whyte, A. G. *The Story of the R.P.A., 1899–1949*. London: Watts, 1949.

EDWARD ROYLE

UNITED STATES, UNBELIEF IN THE.

Although it has been fairly well concealed from the average American, there is a long and fairly diverse history of unbelief in the United States. A number of books have presented this history in great detail. (See APPENDIX 1: BIBLIOGRAPHY OF UNBELIEF). This article will attempt to highlight some of the more interesting or important events in the history of FREETHOUGHT and unbelief in the United States.

Many of the founding fathers were deists of one sort or another. (See DEISM). While this does not mean that they were atheists (they weren't), it does mean that they were unbelievers in Christianity and Judaism. Among the founding fathers who have been positively identified as deists we can name THOMAS JEFFERSON, George Washington, John Adams, THOMAS PAINE, BENJAMIN FRANKLIN, and James Madison.

Although deism had no real pattern of organization—in spite of the fact that there were deist societies in the late 1790s and early 1800s—there was a large body of deist writings, mostly produced

in England. In the U.S., deism flourished considerably later than it did in England or the rest of Europe.

By 1787 the first openly anti-Christian book published in North America was issued in Bennington, Vt. This was ETHAN ALLEN's *Reason the Only Oracle of Man*. A fire in the publisher's offices destroyed a great part of the edition, and copies of the original edition are scarce. It has, of course, been reprinted several times, although Allen's rambling discourse is quite difficult to read all the way through.

The peak of the deist movement in the United States can be traced to the publication of Paine's *The Age of Reason* (1794–95). The first U.S. edition, published about a year after the first British edition, was in 1795. With the influence of Paine at its height between 1795 and 1810, ELIHU PALMER (1764–1806), a blind lawyer turned deist preacher, initiated organized unbelief in the U.S. Palmer founded a deistic society in New York in 1796 and wrote for two deistic magazines. He also wrote a book called *Principles of Nature*. (Some of the deistic societies are listed in APPENDIX 3: ORGANIZATIONS OF UNBELIEF.)

A few deistic magazines were being published at this time. Among them were the *Temple of Reason* (New York/Philadelphia), the *Mirror* (Newburgh, N.Y.), and the *Theophilanthropist* (New York). (Further data about these magazines can be found in the APPENDIX 5: PERIODICALS OF UNBELIEF.)

Organizations. After the death of Paine and Palmer, there was a gap in freethought activity in the U.S. until the mid-1820s. The revival of organized unbelief can be traced to the first Thomas Paine birthday celebration, held in New York on Jan. 29, 1825. These Paine admirers soon formed the Free Press Association, instituted weekly lectures, and aided the magazine the *Correspondent*. The Free Enquirers organization was started in New York City in February 1828. There was also the Moral Philanthropists (1829–39) and its successor, the Society of Free Enquirers, which began in 1842. All of these groups were lectured to or led by FRANCES WRIGHT, ROBERT DALE OWEN, George Houston, or Benjamin Offen, who were the most prominent British imports to the U.S. freethought movement during this period.

Another important figure was ABNER KNEELAND (1774–1844), a self-taught Universalist minister, who soon outgrew that creed. He went to Boston in 1830, where he started a rationalist and atheist newspaper, the BOSTON INVESTIGATOR.

He was prosecuted for blasphemy in a series of trials lasting from 1834 to 1836. (See BLASPHEMY LAWS.) Kneeland originally went to Boston to lecture to the First Society of Free Enquirers, which existed there from 1830 to 1840.

In the 1830s the first attempt at a national organization was made. In August 1836 a convention was held at Saratoga Springs, N.Y. Here Kneeland and Benjamin Offen urged such an organization, and in response the United Moral and Philosophical Society for the Diffusion of Useful Knowledge was formed. In spite of its unwieldy name, this group lasted from 1836 until 1841. It held annual conventions, and had members in many of the eastern states.

In 1845 another attempt at organizing was held in New York. The proceedings of this meeting were published as *Meteor of Light* (Boston: J. P. Mendum, 1845). The new group called itself the Infidel Society for the Promotion of Mental Liberty. It lasted three years.

The Hartford Bible Convention was the name given to a freethought meeting held in Hartford, Conn., in 1854. In 1857 another attempt at national organization was made when the Infidel Association of the United States met in Philadelphia. The report of this meeting was published as *Minutes of the Infidel Convention Held in the City of Philadelphia* (Philadelphia: The Central Committee, 1858).

Earlier, ROBERT OWEN had tried to start a cooperative colony in New Harmony, Ind. The community succeeded socially and intellectually, but foundered economically from the start, failing completely in 1827. Many of the buildings of the colony are still standing.

The period of greatest freethought activity in the U.S. was from 1860 to 1900. This has been called the Golden Age of freethought; it corresponded to a similar peak in freethought activity in the United Kingdom. The major personalities during this period in the United States were BENJAMIN FRANKLIN UNDERWOOD, ROBERT G. INGERSOLL, DeROBIGNE MORTIMER BENNETT, SAMUEL PORTER PUTNAM, H. L. Green, C. B. Reynolds, John E. Remsburg, Thaddeus Burr Wakeman and E. M. Macdonald. It was the age of the traveling lecturer. Among those lecturers for freethought were Ingersoll, Reynolds, Underwood, Putnam, and Remsburg. As there was little money in freethought lecturing, many of the lecturers did it only part time, and even then often worked for a small fee (based upon receipts) and for room and board at a friendly house in the area.

The greatest American freethinker, and without a doubt the most popular figure that has ever spoken out publicly against organized religion, was Ingersoll. He was the most popular American orator at a time when orators were popular. From 1875 to 1895 he was at his oratorical peak. During this period, Ingersoll often lectured to crowds of 3,000 people, who sat at attention for two or three hours. Although he may have used an outline for the first attempt at a speech on a given subject, Ingersoll almost never used notes or a text when he spoke. Ingersoll's popularity was a major factor in the increased popularity of the entire freethought movement during this Golden Age.

The Golden Age was also characterized by a greatly expanded number of freethought publications and organizations. Among the important publishers were Peter Eckler and the Truth Seeker Company. Among the magazines were the TRUTH SEEKER, *Freethought,* the *Iron Clad Age* and the *Boston Investigator,* still in existence from the previous period. The *Truth Seeker* was founded by Bennett in 1873. After one year in Paris, Ill., he moved the magazine to New York. There he rapidly expanded its circulation until he was able to publish it as a weekly. Bennett achieved some notoriety as a writer of freethought books and especially for his arrests and jailing at the behest of Anthony Comstock. When he died unexpectedly in 1882, the editorship of his magazine passed to Eugene Macdonald and then (in 1909) to his brother, George E. Macdonald. The latter was editor until 1937, when he was succeeded by CHARLES LEE SMITH. Its current editor is James Hervey Johnson. The magazine underwent a number of changes since the editorship of Smith. It has become anti-Black, anti-Jewish, and anti-Catholic, while remaining atheistic.

Other important freethought magazines of the 19th century were the *Freethinker's Magazine* (later called *Freethought Magazine,* published in Buffalo and then Chicago), the *Index* (Toledo and then Boston), and the *Blue Grass Blade* (Lexington, Ky., and then Cincinnati).

Some important freethought publishers have already been mentioned. The Truth Seeker Company was probably the largest publisher of pamphlets and books during the 19th century. A close second was J. P. Mendum of Boston. Originally founded by Kneeland as the Office of the Investigator (that is, the *Boston Investigator*), it was taken over by Josiah P. Mendum and Horace Seaver after Kneeland went to Iowa to live in a utopian colony. Mendum was succeeded by his son Ernest, and Seaver, by Lemuel K. Washburn. The Peter Eckler company was founded by Eckler in the 1840s; it existed until about 1920, publishing a great number of freethought books and pamphlets, as well as doing the printing for many other free-thought publishers. Among these was C. P. Farrell, Ingersoll's brother-in-law and official publisher. The Freidenker Publishing Company of Milwaukee published a number of items of a freethought nature in German for the large German-American freethought community.

There were a good number of freethought organizations in the U.S. during the last part of the 19th century. Among the most important were the National Liberal League (1876–1902); the American Secular Union, which merged with the Free-thought Federation of America in 1894, lasting as a combined group until the 1920s; and the New York Freethinkers' Association (1877–late 1880s).

Several notable contributors to American progress who were freethinkers (although not active in organized freethought) were Thomas Alva Edison, Andrew Carnegie, Stephen Girard, Luther Burbank, and Charles Steinmetz.

Women in Freethought. Susan B. Anthony (1820–1906) was a reformer who crusaded for woman's suffrage. She was born in Adams, Mass., into a Quaker family. Immediately before the Civil War, she was prominent in the antislavery and temperance movements. After 1854, she devoted her energies almost entirely to the woman's suffrage movement. She was fined one hundred dollars for casting a vote in the presidential election of 1872. In collaboration with Matilda Joslyn Gage, Elizabeth Cady Stanton, and Ida H. Harper, she authored *The History of Woman Suffrage* (4 vols.). A less well-known fact about Susan B. Anthony is that she was an agnostic. Along with Stanton, Gage, and Amy Post, she was associated with various liberal religious causes, and was a friend of Robert G. Ingersoll. All of these women were agnostics.

The suffrage leader who was most actively involved with the freethought cause was Elizabeth Cady Stanton (1815–1902). Stanton was the president of the National Woman Suffrage Association from 1865 to 1893. The daughter of a judge, she successfully pleaded the case for property rights for married women before the New York state legislature in 1848, causing a new law to be passed. For many years she was a member of the American Secular Union, a freethought group. One of Stan-

ton's best-known works was *The Woman's Bible*, an attempt to explain biblical texts from a non-sexist, non-denigrating-to-women position. It aroused a storm of protest when it was first published. Stanton's attempt to justify her position on women's issues by interpreting sections of the Bible as she saw fit was not welcome to traditionalists. She also wrote articles on her views for the *Truth Seeker*.

Matilda Joslyn Gage (1826–1898) was the daughter of an abolitionist and grew up in the reform movement. She was an associate of Anthony and Stanton in the suffrage movement. As the author of *Woman, Church and State* (1893), she traced the history of the oppression of women by religion, especially Christianity.

In the 20th century, the leading names in American freethought and unbelief have been CLARENCE DARROW, Marshall Gauvin, JOSEPH LEWIS, MADALYN MURRAY O'HAIR, Charles L. Smith, Franklin Steiner, and EMANUEL HALDEMAN-JULIUS. Darrow is well-known for his activities as an attorney, but he was also an outspoken atheist and supporter of and contributor to the freethought movement. Lewis was the president of the Freethinkers of America from 1925 until his death in 1968. He instituted many lawsuits on church-state matters and was a frequent guest on radio and television shows, presenting the atheist viewpoint. Lewis also wrote a number of books on atheist topics and edited a magazine called, among other things, the *Age of Reason*. Smith was the editor of the *Truth Seeker* from 1937 until his death in 1964. Prior to that he cofounded and led the American Association for the Advancement of Atheism (1926 to about 1932). Gauvin was a Canadian who led the Minneapolis and Pittsburgh Rationalist societies for many years, finally returning to Winnipeg, where he led the local Rationalist society and lectured widely. He wrote a number of pamphlets and many magazine articles before dying in 1978, at the age of 97.

Emanuel Haldeman-Julius was a publisher and newspaperman with a flair for publicity. He turned a small newspaper he had bought in Girard, Kans., into a large publishing company with his Little Blue Books and Big Blue Books. Starting in 1919, and until his death in 1951, Haldeman-Julius was responsible for selling more than 300 million books. Many of them were on freethought topics, including some by Ingersoll, JOSEPH MCCABE, Darrow, and Haldeman-Julius himself.

Madalyn Murray O'Hair was a party to the historic lawsuit, joined with that of Ed Schemp, in which the Supreme Court ruled that Bible readings were illegal in American public schools. She founded a magazine called *American Atheist* and an organization of the same name devoted to legal battles on church-state issues and to defending the rights of atheists.

Among the leading freethought publications in the 20th century were Haldeman-Julius' *American Freeman, Progressive World* (published from 1947 to 1982 by the United Secularists of America), the AMERICAN RATIONALIST (founded in 1956), *American Atheist,* the *Liberal* (published by the Friendship Liberal League), Lewis' *Age of Reason,* and the previously mentioned *Truth Seeker.* A recent addition was *Free Inquiry* (founded in 1979 by Paul Kurtz).

Organizations that played a role in 20th-century American freethought were the American Rationalist Federation, the American Secular Union, the American Association for the Advancement of Atheism, American Atheists, a different National Liberal League (1945 to the mid-1950s), and the United Secularists of America. The most important publishers were the Truth Seeker Company, Joseph Lewis' Freethought Press Association, and E. Haldeman-Julius.

The humanist movement, along with ETHICAL CULTURE, grew in the 20th century. HUMANISM, often called secular humanism, was felt by many fundamentalists to be a danger to society. However, the limited membership of these groups, plus their meager finances, would seem to preclude any significant influence.

Other articles of interest: **American Literature, Unbelief in. Women and Unbelief.**

Bibliography

Brown, Marshall G., and Gordon Stein. *Freethought in the United States.* Westport, Conn.: Greenwood Press, 1978.

Koch, G. Adolph. *Republican Religion: The American Revolution and the Cult of Reason.* New York: Henry Holt, 1933.

Macdonald, George E. *Fifty Years of Freethought.* 2 vols. New York: Truth Seeker Co., 1929.

Morais, Herbert M. *Deism in Eighteenth Century America.* New York: Columbia U. Press, 1934.

Post, Albert. *Popular Freethought in America, 1825–1850.* New York: Columbia U. Press, 1943.

Putnam, Samuel P. *400 Years of Freethought.* New York: Truth Seeker Co., 1894.

Warren, Sidney. *American Freethought, 1860–1914.* New York: Columbia U. Press, 1943.

GORDON STEIN

UNIVERSALISM. To understand the impulse behind universalism one must remember the powerful impact that the imagery of hell once held in Western civilization. Countless men and women have lain awake for seemingly endless nights in fear of final judgment and eternal damnation. How many people suffered tormenting fear on their deathbeds, repenting actions that would not even seem wrong to moderns! For centuries thousands of priests grew corpulent on the sale of indulgences. Universalism, an ancient theological heresy, sought to free men and women from the fear of hell by asserting that, in his loving goodness, God will eventually save all human beings.

Background. The early Greeks and Hebrews did not have a concept of hell or a doctrine of eternal torment. Each group believed in some kind of shadowy existence after death—Hades or Sheol—but the underworld was neither a full existence nor a place of punishment. Hades and Sheol were insubstantial, dreamlike places where only shadows or images of people flitted about. But in the 6th century B.C. Zoroastrianism taught that there was to be a final, ultimate conflict between the powers of light and darkness. By the time of Jesus this doctrine had influenced Judaism, with many Jews accepting a belief in an afterlife and in a fiery punishment for the wicked at the end of time. Jesus himself talks about casting people into a fire that cannot be quenched (Mark 9:43).

To realize the sort of fear that hell invoked in the human imagination, it is only necessary to ponder the productions of two creative artists who lived at the end of the Christian Middle Ages: Dante's *Divine Comedy* (about 1307–21) describes grotesque and bizarre punishments in the Inferno that last for eternity; or, for sadomasochism, one should examine the paintings of Hieronymus Bosch (1450–1511). Such Christian leaders as St. Jerome, St. Augustine, and Martin Luther betrayed almost a pathological fear of hell and often suffered hallucinatory visitations from the Devil. (See also DEVIL, UNBELIEF IN THE CONCEPT OF THE.)

In 18th-century America, when the best minds of Europe had turned to rational religion in the form of DEISM, the colonies produced one of the great apologists for hell, the Rev. Jonathan Edwards, who did much to revive the ancient fear. Many groaned, others fainted when they heard him proclaim in his famous sermon "Sinners in the Hands of an Angry God": "Sinner: consider the fearful danger you are in. 'Tis a great furnace of wrath, a wide and bottomless pit, full of the fire of wrath, that you are held over in the hand of a God whose wrath is provoked and incensed as much against you as against many of the damned in hell. You hang by a slender thread, with the flames of divine wrath flashing about it, ready every moment to . . . burn asunder."

How long ago and far away such a belief seems. Although this is still the official doctrine of the Roman Catholic church and many fundamentalists preach fiery damnation, few in the modern world believe in preachments about hell. One suspects that humor, as much as anything, has helped to weaken the power of hell on the human imagination. When someone claimed that Ralph Waldo Emerson was doomed to go to hell, the Methodist Father Taylor remarked that, if Emerson went to hell, he would change the climate there and turn migration in that direction. Many have also suggested that, if there is a hell, any sane person would prefer it to the boring descriptions usually given of heaven. At least in hell there would be some interesting and cheerful people.

As increasing scientific evidence indicates that the mind and body are one, it is ever more doubtful that there can be personal existence or consciousness beyond the grave. Although there can be no absolute proof on such a question, the best scientific guess is that, when we die, our conscious mind ceases to exist. (See IMMORTALITY, UNBELIEF IN.) As a result, in the modern age there is ever less reason to take hell seriously. Recent claims about deathbed experiences prove nothing except that human beings can have those kinds of psychological experiences; like dreams, deathbed visions prove nothing about the nature of existence beyond the grave but only that human beings can dream. However, it is only fair to say that hell was not weakened in the popular mind just by humor and the march of science. The battle, carried to the North American religious world, was fought and largely won by Universalists, who rebelled at the horrendous idea that a loving, father God could torture for eternity the children of his creation.

Universalism or universal salvation, the doctrine that God will eventually save all people, is a Christian heresy of ancient vintage. In the first 500 years of Christian history some of the leading Christian thinkers were universalists. For example, Clement of Alexandria (about 155–220) and Origen (185–254) both believed in universal salvation. Origen was one of the truly brilliant church fathers and brought a badly needed ratiocination to Christian thought that was unequaled until Erasmus began to publish during the Renaissance. The whole Eastern half of the early church, what later became Byzantine Christianity, was tainted with the universalist heresy.

However, in 544, the Emperor Justinian of the Eastern Roman Empire declared a belief in universal salvation to be heretical, not just in his own time but retroactively and in the future. Thus, many of the outstanding early church fathers, men like Clement, Origen, Diodorus, the bishop of Tarsus, and Theodore, the bishop of Mopsuestia, were branded long after their deaths as heretics. Universalism was suppressed whenever it arose, and many men and women lost their lives for asserting the infallible love of God. Yet, despite the threat of death, the idea of universal salvation kept reappearing in the minds of sincere Christians. Because persecution was so harsh, however, it was only in the United States that universalism was able to become the central tenet of a large, organized religious group.

The strands of history that helped make universalism known in colonial America are many and varied. The doctrine was brought to the New World by individual religionists and mystics, as well as by some religious groups seeking religious freedom in America. A group of Dunkers who migrated to Pennsylvania in 1719 were universalist; so were a group of Moravians who arrived in Georgia and then went to Bethlehem, Pa. Occasionally, there have even been Episcopalians who preached the universalist doctrine, as did some of the early Congregationalists.

George de Benneville, one of the most important of the early solitary universalists, was of Huguenot extraction but was raised in England. When he became a preacher of universalism in France during the reign of Louis XV, he was arrested and sentenced to death. Even in the 18th century, the age of ENLIGHTENMENT, extreme persecution for unconventional religious beliefs was not uncommon. De Benneville received a last-minute pardon because he could claim noble parentage, though some of those arrested with him were executed. Leaving France, de Benneville continued to preach in continental Europe until he migrated to North America and took up residence in the Philadelphia area. He did much to popularize universalism in his region of the country. He was a neighbor and friend of BENJAMIN FRANKLIN. His sons fought in the Revolutionary War, and he served the Continental Army as a physician during the Battle of Germantown, although at the time he was 75 years old. Typical of some of the independent thinkers and mystics who came to America with the message of universalism in their hearts and on their lips, he and other religious pioneers for universalism did not, however, found churches based on the universalist principle.

John Murray. The first to found a Universalist church in America was John Murray (died 1815), who arrived from England in 1770. Persecuted in England for his views, Murray had vowed to abandon his universalist preaching. However, when his ship was becalmed off the coast of New Jersey, he came ashore to find a farmer named Thomas Potter, who was hungry for every doctrine Murray had preached. The Calvinist doctrine dominating American religion at that time insisted that just a tiny elite would be saved by God, while the vast majority of human beings would be eternally damned. Because that doctrine did not satisfy him, Potter built a church on his own land, which he allowed any preacher to use, all the while hoping that one would come who believed as he, "that all mankind are equally dear to Almighty God . . ." To Potter it seemed that Providence had answered his prayers by sending Murray to the New Jersey coast; to Murray it seemed as if God had called him to take up the ministry he had resolved to abandon. So, in September of 1770, John Murray preached to a group gathered in Potter's church, and, in a sense, that date was the beginning of his unceasing missionary effort to develop a Universalist church in America.

Murray often faced persecution in the form of rotten eggs, and even rocks, when he preached. Once, when addressing a group in Boston, he was almost hit on the head by a large stone. Picking it up and displaying it to the audience, he said, "This argument is solid and weighty, but it is neither rational nor convincing." Murray found a small group of enthusiastic universalists in Gloucester, Mass., and settled there. In 1779 the Gloucester universalists founded the first organized Universalist church in America.

At the time the Gloucester church was founded, all citizens living in Massachusetts were taxed to support the Congregational church in their area. Some members of Murray's church refused to pay such taxes, desiring instead to support their own church. They claimed that the Bill of Rights in the federal Constitution protected them from involuntary religious taxation. Eventually, in a landmark case they established their right to support the church of their choice. Thus, Universalists helped to move American society away from enforced religious obligations. Murray ministered in Gloucester for 20 years and then moved to Boston to serve the First Universalist Church there. By the time of his death in 1815 Universalism had become an organized force in American religion.

The early Universalists were rationalists of a sort quite different from the deists and Unitarians of their day. (See UNITARIANISM.) The Universalists, more biblically oriented, wanted scriptural proof that God never intended eternal punishment. Their arguments and those of their opponents were often quite tortured. Although they held their own, there are passages in the New Testament (Matt. 25:31–46 and Luke 16:19–31) that seem to support a belief in the existence of some kind of fiery punishment at the end of time.

The most important aspect of early Universalist preaching was its appeal to the common man. The artisans, the farmers, the shopkeepers across the United States were little touched by the beliefs of the Unitarians, who remained primarily a New England phenomenon for the first 50 years of their existence.

Universalism reached a wider spectrum of people. It was a "called out" church. A Universalist preacher would visit a town and gather a group of sympathetic listeners; then, if there was enough interest, a church would be formed. By 1840, just 70 years after John Murray had landed in America, there were 800,000 adherents of the new faith: Universalism had become a mass movement. By the middle of the 19th century the lives of hundreds of thousands of people had been freed from the fear of hell. An even larger number of people who were not members of Universalist churches were also freed from the fear of hell by Universalist preaching. Religious liberalism in many denominations was furthered by the missionary efforts of the early Universalists. They quenched the fires of hell, or, at least, dampened them considerably.

Hosea Ballou. John Murray was the great organizer of the new movement in America, but Hosea Ballou (1771–1852), the New Hampshire-born son of a Baptist minister, became its greatest preacher. Ordained at a Universalist meeting in 1794, Ballou spent the rest of his life in the service of his religion. Eventually he inherited the mantle of leadership from Murray, even though they held many opposing theological views. A noted debater, Ballou was not dogmatic: "If we agree in brotherly love," he said, "there is no disagreement that can do us injury, but if we do not, no other agreement can do us any good." He had a light touch which was delightful at times. Once, when his doctrine of universal salvation was questioned from the audience with these words, "What would you do with a man who died reeking in sin and crime?" he replied, "I think it would be a good plan to bury him." Largely self-educated, his preaching and writing style were simple and direct, going straight to the hearts of the common folk. Because there was a wider gap between the educated and the uneducated at that time than there exists in the U.S. today, men like Ballou helped to bridge the gap between the literate classes and the general public.

Hosea Ballou printed many sermons, but his best-known publication was a book titled *A Treatise on Atonement* (1805). Penned on the cover of one copy of that scripturally oriented analysis of universal salvation are the touching words of a Universalist of the time: "This precious book cannot be read too often, nor studied too much." The treatise, little read today, was at that time the most complete arsenal of arguments against eternal punishment which the new movement possessed, and it was a blessing to those who were tormented by a fear of hellfire.

Ballou is significant for an additional reason. By 1805 his theology had become unitarian; that is, he no longer believed in the doctrine of the Trinity, which stated that God was three persons in one. He said that the Trinity represented "the amazing sum of infinity, multiplied by three." The Trinity was irrational and nonbiblical. He eventually persuaded most Universalists to become non-Trinitarian, an additional reason why Unitarianism and Universalism became parallel movements—and why a merger of the two churches was eventually possible. Just as Ballou led Universalists to become unitarian in their theology, so some of the proto-unitarians had been leading their followers to accept the idea of universal salvation. A precursor of Unitarianism, the Congregational divine Jonathan Mayhew was theologically a universalist. So was Charles Chauncy, who in 1762 had written a pamphlet titled *Salvation for All Men*, in which he

took a universalist stance. Despite the many affinities between both groups, the more class-conscious Unitarians had little to do with their country cousins, the Universalists.

John Murray, the father of American Universalism, and Hosea Ballou, its greatest preacher, knew each other and were friends despite their many differences. Once, when Ballou was filling Murray's pulpit while the older man was away, a bit of controversy arose. In the course of his biblical exposition Hosea took a wrong turn—at least it was a wrong turn as seen from Mrs. Murray's pew. She sent a hurried note to the choir loft, and at the end of the service a voice boomed out from the choir, "I wish to give notice that the doctrine which has been preached here this afternoon is not the doctrine which is usually preached in this house." Ballou had the presence of mind to respond, "The audience will please take notice of what our brother has said." That evening a committee from the congregation made a formal apology to Ballou for Mrs. Murray's rudeness.

An actual conversation between Murray and Ballou gives an impression of the rather strained biblical exegesis that interested the early Universalists. While Ballou was visiting Murray, the two of them fell into a conversation about the sheep and the goats (Matt. 25:31–46), with Ballou contending that the sheep represented believers in Jesus while the goats represented unbelievers. Murray, trying to persuade him that the goats were not unbelievers but instead devils who would go into everlasting punishment, was obviously concerned to show that only devils—and not human beings—experienced the everlasting punishment mentioned in the New Testament story. (By this time Murray, the revered leader of the Universalists, was called "Father" Murray.) Ballou listened patiently to the older man's argument, but finally he said quietly: "Father Murray, those who were on the left of the throne were accused of not having visited the sick. Do you think it is so desirable a thing to have *devils* visit the sick, and that they will be condemned to everlasting punishment for having neglected that duty [paraphrased in modern idiom]?"

Differing Theological Positions. Murray and Ballou were also on opposite sides of the greatest theological controversy to embroil the Universalists, a controversy that came close to splitting the new movement. Ballou, and those who agreed with him, believed that when a person died, God freed that person *instantly*, so to speak, from his sin so that he was ready to enter eternal blessedness. In addition, Ballou insisted that punishment for sin occurred in this life, not in the next. The evil person, even if he does not appear to suffer, actually pays the price for his evildoing in this earthly life. Hence, suffering after death is unnecessary.

The opposing view, held by Murray and those who supprted him, was that after death there would be a period of suffering during which individuals would be *gradually* purified from their sins so that they could eventually enjoy eternal life. They were called "restorationists" because suffering after death would *restore* human beings to purity in God's eyes. Ballou's doctrine had the advantage of emphasizing the absolute and unfathomable goodness of God, while Murray's restorationism had the advantage of inculcating virtue because good behavior in this life averted a long and unpleasant purging in the next. The restorationist controversy was never settled, although by the time of Ballou's death in 1852 it looked as if he had carried the day; however, later Universalists reverted to Murray's doctrine that some kind of purification following death was needed in order to restore a person to God's grace.

The debate over restorationism is an example of the bickering characteristic of Universalists at their worst. Unlike the Unitarians, who arose out of an existing established church by trusting the process of radical congregational polity, the Universalists tried again and again to conceptualize what a church meant to them and to give it embodiment in a written document. All sorts of shades of theological meaning impeded their organizational efforts; at regional and national meetings they were forever trying to write statements affirming what the church was and what Universalism was.

Fortunately, Universalists also developed a tradition of appending a "liberty clause" to all such statements which guaranteed that no doctrinal statement could be used as a creedal test to exclude those who differed, so long as those differing were in general sympathy with the statement. In time, the principle of the "liberty clause" became more and more important to Universalists, although individual freedom of belief never became as important in Universalist circles as it was to some Unitarians. In fact, there was at least one Universalist heresy trial, after which a person was excluded from the movement because of his beliefs; and more than one Universalist minister was forced out of the movement for theological reasons. The state conventions sometimes limited theological freedom. Universalists resisted pantheism and

other forms of impersonal theism favored by many Unitarians and espoused instead the traditional idea of a personal God.

In 1846 and 1847 the Massachusetts Universalist Association, one of the most influential in the country, passed a resolution that effectively silenced or drove out of its ranks adherents of the new "German philosophy." This was none other than the idealism of IMMANUEL KANT, which helped to stimulate the development of American transcendentalism and many other liberal intellectual currents that moved Unitarians like Ralph Waldo Emerson and Theodore Parker. The Universalist espousal of the naive personalism of the Bible slowed the intellectual development of the movement. They also resisted the Unitarian drift away from scriptural authority and toward a scientific biblical criticism. Until the 20th century Universalists did not adopt the free-mind principle as completely as the Unitarians. Even in the early part of the 20th century there is no doubt that HUMANISM, when it arose as a religious option around 1914, found it more difficult to make headway in Universalist churches than in Unitarian.

The Universalist church of America eventually espoused the noncreedal principle that each individual must be responsible for his own system of beliefs. In 1935 Universalists wrote a statement of faith that avowed a trust "in the authority of truth, known or to be known"; and in 1942 the charter of the Universalist church of America was rewritten so that its purpose was "to promote harmony among the adherents of all religious faiths, whether Christian or otherwise." As a result, merger of the Unitarians and Universalists in 1961 was based on a common agreement that religion had to be noncreedal and that there must be no theological test for membership in a free religion.

At the time of merger with Unitarianism, membership growth in the two movements had dramatically reversed itself from that of earlier days. The Unitarians, who had always been a small, elite movement, had in the 1950s experienced a dramatic doubling of their membership, and by 1961 they had reached a total of 150,000 adult members. By contrast, the Universalists were in a state of decline. A mass movement of 800,000 strong in 1840, they had dwindled to just 50,000 members—and perhaps less—by 1961. What had gone wrong? How had such a large movement shrunk to just 50,000 adherents? The Universalist decline was partly a result of their success. They were so effective in quenching the fires of hell that they undermined the need for their message. As early as 1911 one respected religious encyclopedia had predicted that "the course of [the Universalist] church as a separate body is nearly run." Another reason for their decline was the movement in American society from the country to the city. Primarily successful in the small town and in the country, Universalism was less effective in the large city, although a few individual churches proved the exception. As Americans became urbanized, the lifeblood of Universalism ebbed away as the small-town craftsmen and tradesmen joined the urban mainstream without taking their Universalist churches with them to the cities.

Furthermore, because Universalists were so given to the writing of regional and national statements that were supposed to represent their faith, statements which caused controversy and lasting bitterness, some members were alienated. This process also restricted the flow of new ideas in Universalist theology, ideas that might have revitalized it. By contrast, each local Unitarian church was entirely independent from all other Unitarian churches and groups, and so there was less organized pressure to conform to commonly agreed upon statements or even to write them; as a result, the Unitarian world view changed its perspective rather quickly, as, for example, from the rational Christianity of William Ellery Channing to the transcendentalism of Emerson. If the Universalists had not hardened their original theological purposes into organizational forms larger than the local church, they might have more quickly outgrown their bibliolatry and then attracted more people from the various FREETHOUGHT movements in America.

Finally, the Universalists declined because they did not set up rigorous standards for an educated ministry. In the Universalist church lay preachers could function without ever receiving a university degree; whereas, in the same crucial 40-year period (1820–60), most Unitarian ministers had graduated from Harvard College and then done further work at the Harvard Divinity School. The severe intellectuality of the Unitarian minister, of men like Emerson and Andrews Norton, insured that, even if Unitarians were at time abstract and pedantic, they were at least capable of dealing with modern intellectual developments. Although there were people in the Universalist ministry and laity who were both brilliant and well-educated, the standards for an educated ministry were not developed and encouraged rigorously enough, even though Uni-

versalists founded many institutions of higher learning. The lack of an adequately educated ministry meant that even when a situation was ripe for a modern Universalist church to flourish, leadership to help develop such a church was often lacking.

The sermons of Hosea Ballou seem outdated and unreadable today in a way that the sermons of Channing do not, and it would be hard to find Universalist clergymen of the mid-19th century who could write with the clarity and power of an Emerson or a Parker. The Universalist divines, as authors, did not have the talent of the Unitarians. The same is true with regard to the writing of hymns. The Unitarians made a lasting and still-usable contribution to American hymnology; many Unitarian hymns written in the 1800s are still used in the hymnbooks of different denominations. A Unitarian minister, Henry Wilder Foote, wrote the classic work on hymnody entitled *Three Centuries of American Hymnody*. The Universalists published hymnbooks and wrote numerous hymns, but most did not last. Ballou wrote 193 hymns, but today they are unsingable curiosities. As his biographer put it, his hymns "have not . . . stood the test of time." In the final analysis, the decline of Universalism was due to its failure to recognize the rigorous intellectual demands imposed upon any attempt to liberalize religion in the 19th and 20th centuries.

The 20th century has seen a number of attempts to redefine the meaning of the word *universalism*. Clarence Skinner attempted to make the word mean a religion of universals that transcend all narrow interests. That meaning, however, did not gain common usage. A more successful redefinition came from those who chose to think of Universalism as a religion open to all religious traditions. They believed that moderns should be able to learn from, and use elements of, the traditions of BUDDHISM, Confucianism, HINDUISM, TAOISM, and so forth. Many 19th- and 20th-century Unitarians held a similar point of view, and it is safe to assert that today the vast majority of Unitarians and Universalists are sympathetic to attempts to incorporate insights from other religious traditions into their own.

Contributions of Kenneth Patton. Beginning in 1949, under the auspices of the Massachusetts Universalist Convention, Kenneth Patton, an avowed humanist, carried on an interesting liturgical experiment. He attempted in his small Universalist church to blend all religious traditions in the life of a single congregation. At the Charles

Street Meeting House in Boston a worship center was developed that utilized elements from many religious traditions; the unifying factor was not theology, but, instead, the aesthetic and poetic awareness of Patton and his congregation. The Charles Street Meeting House was a church in the round with movable pews and lecterns; its flexibility facilitated dance and many other worship or celebration experiences. One wall of the room was covered by a giant mural of the Milky Way, symbolizing the cosmic awareness of religion; the opposite wall housed a bookcase containing the scriptures of all major religions. The room was decorated on all sides with art objects from many different cultures and religions. A wide range of sound and lighting effects were possible for use in services of celebration.

Patton's attempt to blend many religious traditions in the life of one congregation was summarized in his book *A Religion for One World*. His contribution to the new meaning of the word *universalism* as being a religion that draws from all religions must be counted as one of the most important experiments in American liberal religious thought and practice in the 20th century. Like many ministers, Patton held fellowship both in the Unitarian and the Universalist movements and served both kinds of congregations. Early in his ministry he was minister of the Unitarian church in Madison, Wis., when it built its lovely Frank Lloyd Wright building.

By the middle of the 20th century a number of local churches had merged with their Unitarian or Universalist neighbors. When the national merger came, not only did most Unitarians and Universalists believe in the noncreedal, free-mind principle but they also had knowledge of congregations in which Unitarians and Universalists had been working together for a long time.

Ethical Concerns. One further aspect of Universalism needs to be mentioned; like Unitarians, they had strong ethical concerns. There was, however, in the early days, a political difference between the two groups. The majority of Unitarians were from New England, were politically conservative, and were members of the Federalist political party; whereas, the majority of Universalists were anti-Federalist or Jeffersonians. While there were political liberals and conservatives in both groups, each group tended to have its own political tone. In the 19th century neither Unitarians nor Universalists took institutional action that could be identified as political. Most of their ethical or moral action for social justice was achieved through the work of individual reformers. Through the actions of their members Universalists had a significant impact in humanizing American life.

Dr. Benjamin Rush, medical reformer and signer of the Declaration of Independence, was a Universalist. The Rev. Charles Spear, ordained a Universalist minister in 1830, devoted much of his life to prison reform and for several years edited the *Prisoner's Friend*, a monthly journal devoted to prison reform and the improvement of people convicted of crimes. George Quimby, a Universalist minister in Maine, wrote a book titled *The Gallows, the Prison, and the Poor House* (1856), which became a stimulus for reform. He and his wife, Cordelia Quimby, worked for many years to abolish a state law in Maine that allowed capital punishment. Another Universalist prison reformer and penologist was Thomas Mott Osborn, the warden of Sing Sing Prison, who, despite bitter political opposition, succeeded in improving the lot of prisoners in New York.

The record of Universalist women is also impressive. In 1870 the first annual meeting of the Women's Centenary Aid Association was held. In its first year of existence $200,000 was raised for the extension of Universalism. This meeting has been called the first national organization of churchwomen to be founded in the United States. The Universalists were also more ready to open their ranks to female preachers than were the Unitarians or any other religious group. A statement in 1870 from the *Christian Register*, a Unitarian publication, reads: "The Universalists have a number of female ministers and most of them . . . [prove] themselves the peers of their brethren . . . in the pulpit . . ."

The talented Olympia Brown was the first woman to be ordained for the Universalist ministry, in 1863, and by the late 1800s and early 1900s Universalism had the largest proportion of women ministers of any denomination. However, as the movement declined in the 20th century, the decline occurred not only in terms of absolute numbers but also in terms of the percentage of Universalist pulpits served by women. Many women activists identified with Universalism. Mary Livermore, reformer, lecturer, and editor-in-chief of the Boston *Women's Journal*, was an effective advocate of women's rights. Clara Barton, founder of the American Red Cross, was also a Universalist. (Later, in honor of Barton, Universalists founded the Clara Barton Camp for Diabetic Girls, an institution still in existence.)

Thousands of Universalist men and women were active reformers and public-spirited citizens during the heyday of Universalism. Many of them did not achieve lasting national prominence, but their civilizing impact on 19th-century America was important. Though not as visible as their Unitarian counterparts, they were more numerous and their impact was more widespread. In their civic-mindedness, Universalists founded some four dozen universities and colleges, including Tufts University, the University of Akron, St. Lawrence University, Goddard College, and the California Institute of Technology. Meadville/Lombard Theological School, a seminary in Chicago that trains large numbers of Unitarian-Universalist clergy, is the result of an amalgam of Meadville Theological School (Unitarian) and Lombard College (Universalist).

At its best, Universalism has had a warmth and a loving compassion characteristic of religion at its best. It believed in a loving God and the cherishing of persons without class distinctions. A Universalist church was often an intelligent, warm, caring community; more than Unitarianism, it was a religion of familylike love. Thomas Starr King, raised as a Universalist but mininster to a Unitarian church, once characterized the difference between the two churches this way: "The Universalists," he said, "think that God is too good to damn them, while the Unitarians think they are too good to be damned."

King's oft-repeated comment is true both in terms of a theological and a sociological analysis of the two religions. Unitarian theology has tended to stress the idea of man's potential goodness and his ability to use reason to work out his own salvation, while the Universalist theology has sought to strip away false notions of God so that men and women could know his inexhaustible love. The Unitarians exalted human nature while the Universalists exalted God's goodness. Sociologically speaking, King's quip exposes the good-breeding and high-society bias of the early Unitarians. Boston Brahmin to the core, the Unitarian elite often lacked full compassion for the common man. Emerson, who in his best moments was eloquent about democracy, also epitomized the socially conditioned distance from humanity all too typical of the upper-class Unitarians of the mid-19th century when he said: "I love man but not men." For a long time, even though they held beliefs similar to those of many Universalists, Unitarians tended to stay aloof from contact with Universalists.

In modern times Unitarians and Universalists have lost the class distinctions that separated them and also their original theological distinctiveness. Today, Unitarian-Universalists tend to be middle or upper middle class (seldom upper class), with little interest in the theological questions that once moved them—the unity of God or belief in universal salvation. They still have a strong commitment to reason in religion and to social justice. Christians, theists, humanists who are agnostic or atheistic can be found on the membership books of most local societies. The central agreement that unites modern Unitarian-Universalists is their agreement not to have a creed, along with a tendency to cherish the use of reason, the democratic process, and the scientific method as crucial elements for the living of life. Thus Unitarian-Universalism is a religion that welcomes into its membership people who have rejected many of the traditional Jewish and Christian beliefs; it is a system of unbelief that opens the way to better beliefs for individuals who have cast off the trappings of traditional religion.

Bibliography

Cassara, Ernest. *Hosea Ballou: The Challenge to Orthodoxy*. Boston: Beacon Press, 1961.

———. *Universalism in America: A Documentary History*. Boston: Beacon Press, 1971.

Cheetham, Harry H. *Unitarian and Universalism: An Illustrated History*. Boston: Beacon Press, 1962.

Marshall, George N. *Challenge of the Liberal Faith*. Boston: Pyramid Publications for the Unitarian Universalist Association, 1966.

Miller, Russel E. *The Larger Hope: The First Century of the Universalist Church in America (1770–1870)*. Boston: Unitarian Universalist Association, 1979.

Patton, Kenneth L. *A Religion for One World: Art and Symbols for a Universal Religion*. Boston: Beacon Press, 1964.

Scott, Clinton Lee. *The Universalist Church of America: A Short History*. Boston: Universalist Historical Society, 1957.

Williams, George Huntston. *Journal of the Universalist Historical Society* 9 (1971).

PAUL H. BEATTIE

UNIVERSE, ORIGIN OF THE, AND UNBELIEF.

Despite wide publicity and vocal support, creation scientists represent a relatively minor religious group. Since the Roman Catholic church's bout with Galileo in 1632, the overwhelming majority of modern religious denominations have adapted their metaphysical dogmas to those findings that have become generally accepted by the scientific community.

Such was certainly true in Sir Isaac Newton's time, when his contemporary, the Rev. Richard Bentley, chaplain to the bishop of Worcester, was chosen to deliver eight sermons "in fulfillment of a bequest of no less than fifty pounds, in proof of the Christian religion against notorious infidels." Bentley, aware of Newton's law of gravitation, which describes a force of attraction between all objects in the universe, wondered if divine intervention were not required to prevent the universe from collapsing of its own gravity. Thus he wrote Newton to ask his opinion on the matter. In the correspondence that followed, Newton expressed the opinion that an infinite uniform universe could be stable, for then matter, extending equally far in all directions, would exert as much gravitational attraction in one direction as another, and all the forces would balance one another.

These thoughts of Newton's may have been the first serious speculation on what is now called the *cosmological principle*—the assumption that at least on the large scale the universe is the same everywhere. At that time there was really no empirical evidence to support the cosmological principle. Indeed, the first quantitative investigation of the distribution of stars around us, by William Herschel late in the 18th century, led to the opposite conclusion. Herschel showed that the sun is one of many stars (at least a few hundred thousand million, we know today) that make up a gigantic system—our galaxy. Modern estimates put the diameter of our wheel-shaped galaxy at more than 100,000 light-years (a *light-year*, nearly 6 million million miles, is the distance light travels in one year). Until the early 1920s, the weight of astronomical opinion was that our galaxy is the entire universe, which could thus hardly be infinite and homogeneous.

By 1925, however, Mount Wilson astronomer Edwin Hubble had shown that the thousands of faint patches of light discovered in telescopic surveys of the sky are in reality other galaxies, more or less similar to our own, but of course tremendously far away. The number of galaxies potentially observable with our present telescopes is certainly more than a thousand million. The galaxies are not distributed randomly, however, but bunch up into groups and clusters. Moreover, the groups and clusters of galaxies are parts of larger aggregates called *superclusters*. Typical superclusters are hundreds of millions of light-years across, and they are separated from each other by comparable distances. Superclusters, though, are the end of the hierarchy; on scales much larger than sizes of superclusters, the universe appears to be much the same everywhere, consistent with the cosmological principle.

The lack of empirical evidence (until relatively recently) for the cosmological principle was never an impediment to theoreticians, including Albert Einstein, who in 1919 first applied his new general theory of relativity to the universe as a whole. Unlike Newton's gravitational theory, relativity does not permit a static universe, even if it is infinite and homogeneous. In order that his theory could be made compatible with a static universe, Einstein actually doctored the relativistic field equations, which describe the curvature of space-time, with the introduction of a new parameter, called the *cosmological constant*. This parameter represents a long-range force of repulsion that can balance gravitation and provide a stable, static universe.

It seemed a shame, however, to bowdlerize an otherwise elegant and beautiful theory to save a static universe. Consequently other investigators looked anew at relativity theory to see if there were not a way out. They found that indeed there was—if the universe is *expanding*. Among the most famous of the early proponents of an expanding universe were the Russian mathematician Alexandre Friedmann, in 1922, and independently the Belgian priest and cosmologist Abbé Georges Lemaître, in 1927.

Lemaître, in particular, pointed out that in a uniformly expanding universe all observers should observe all objects surrounding them to be receding, and at speeds that are greater in proportion to their distances. He further noted that the spectra of galaxies that had been measured by V. M. Slipher at the Lowell Observatory in Arizona indicated those galaxies to be rushing rapidly away from us, and suggested that their speeds should be compared with their distances. By 1929, Hubble had found ways to estimate the distances to the galaxies whose spectra had been observed by Slipher, and found that indeed there is a correlation between their velocities of recession and their distances.

That conclusion was greatly strengthened by 1931, with many additional velocities of far more distant galaxies that had been measured by Milton Humason at Mount Wilson. It does not, of course, imply that we are at the center, for in a uniform expansion all observers, no matter where they are, must see the same effect. With this final realization that the universe is expanding, the need for a cosmological constant disappeared, and Einstein is said to have later remarked that its introduction was the "biggest blunder" of his life! The observational confirmation of the expanding universe was the first major triumph of 20th-century cosmology.

But that is only the beginning of the story. If a (perhaps) infinite universe is expanding into greater infinities, it must be thinning out in time; in the past, matter must have been packed densely together. It was, again, Lemaître who first gave serious thought to what that early dense universe might have been like. He postulated that in the beginning all matter was compressed to an incredible density into what he called the *primeval atom*. He envisioned the universe to have begun its expansion with a gigantic fission of the primeval atom. In the process, the mass broke into countless smaller masses, and each of them split up further, and so on, until we are left with the various atoms observed in the present universe. By the mid-20th century far more was known about nuclear physics, and it was then clear that Lemaître's hypothesis of a primeval atom could not be correct in detail. Nevertheless, his idea that the universe had an explosive beginning turned out to be prophetic.

In the late 1940s the American physicist George Gamow, and his associates, looked anew at the problem of the early universe, and advanced the idea that the universe was, in its beginning, extremely hot as well as dense. Under those conditions, neutral atoms could not exist; nor could atomic nuclei, other than the single protons that are the nuclei of hydrogen. There were only the most simple subatomic particles—protons, neutrons, electrons, neutrinos, and the like—in equilibrium with photons of radiation, the material particles constantly turning into radiation and vice versa. As the universe expanded from this hot, dense state, for the first few minutes some atomic particles could fuse into atomic nuclei; this is how Gamow and his coworkers imagined the atoms of the present universe to arise. Gamow dubbed the explosive beginning of the universe, the "big bang."

More recent calculations, based on the best modern nuclear-physics theory, show that only hydrogen and helium survived the big bang in appreciable abundance. The earliest stars must have been essentially pure hydrogen and helium. Today, however, about 1 to 2 percent of the mass of most stars is in the form of heavier elements: oxygen, nitrogen, carbon, silicon, iron, and others, which also happen to make up nearly all of the mass of small planets like the earth. In our modern picture, the sun (with its planets and other objects of the solar system) must be a later-generation star, formed in part of material synthesized by nuclear fusion in the centers of certain earlier-generation stars, where matter was once heated to very high temperatures, this time at densities where those heavier elements could fuse from helium. Old stars, so enriched in the heavy elements, often spew large parts of their matter back into interstellar space, as novae, planetary nebulae, and supernovae (exploding stars), from which matter newer-generation stars, like the sun, are still forming today.

But irrespective of the details of nucleogenesis of the heavy elements of the universe, the best theory today indicates that the material that survived the big bang should be mostly hydrogen and helium, and of that, three-quarters, by weight, should be hydrogen. The present-day universe is observed to be at least 98 percent hydrogen and helium, of which about three-quarters, by weight, is hydrogen! Chalk up a victory for the predictions of the physics of the big bang, and a second triumph for modern cosmology.

There is yet another consequence of a hot, dense early universe. It was first pointed out in 1948 by two of Gamow's associates, Ralph Alpher and Robert Herman, in a paper in *Nature*. Early in the big bang, matter was radiating energy with high efficiency, but that radiant energy was immediately absorbed by other matter, to be reradiated at once. In other words, radiant energy was passed rapidly back and forth between the particles in the fireball. But as the universe cooled, eventually the atomic nuclei (essentially all of hydrogen and helium) captured electrons and became neutral. From that time on (roughly a million years after the big bang), matter no longer absorbed or interacted with radiation. But what happened to that radiation? At the time the matter became transparent (and no longer absorbed the radiation), the universe was as hot as a star, and the radiation was in the form of visible light. Today, however, the universe has expanded enormously, and that original light, never absorbed by matter since the big bang thousands of millions of years ago, must still be floating around, but shifted in frequency, by the expansion of the universe, to that of radio waves.

Thus Alpher and Herman predicted that the universe should be bathed in a faint glow of radio waves. In 1948 there was no way to observe such radiation, and their paper was scarcely noticed. In the middle 1960s, Princeton University physicist Robert Dicke independently thought of the same thing. He, P. J. E. Peebles, P. G. Roll, and D. Wilkinson solved the problem afresh, and arrived at essentially the same conclusion as had Alpher and Herman. By that time radio astronomy was in full bloom, and the Princeton physicists actually built a special radio telescope to search for this primeval radiation from the early universe.

They were nearly ready to start their observations when they were scooped by the accidental discovery of a uniform glow of microwave radio radiation from all directions in space by Bell Telephone Laboratory physicists Arno Penzias and Robert Wilson, at the Bell station in Holmdel, N.J., about 30 miles from Princeton. That radiation has now been well confirmed, and is generally interpreted as the relic glow of the big bang. Another success for the big-bang theory! Penzias and Wilson received the Nobel Prize for their discovery.

The details of the astronomical observations, and especially of the physical theory involved, are highly technical, and enormously more complex than indicated here; nevertheless, the foregoing is the essence of the evidence in favor of the big-bang theory for the origin of the universe.

Science does not deal with certainties or absolute truths. All any of us can really be certain of is that he or she exists; the rest of the universe *could* exist only in the imagination. But most scientists adopt, as a working hypothesis, that there *is* a physical reality, that the earth, sun, planets, and their observed motions are real entities. Given that there is a physical reality, science attempts to describe the universe with models that account for its observed behavior.

Technically, we cannot assert even that the earth revolves about the sun with the positive authority of absolute truth. But the earth's revolution is the only model that is consistent with Newtonian gravitational theory, which has been so thoroughly documented (except in certain extreme circumstances where the refinements of relativity are required). The disputes over whether the earth rotates and revolves about the sun, which were at the frontier of science a few hundred years ago,

have long since been resolved. The orbital motion and rotation of the earth are examples of "scientific facts" about which there is no question in the scientific community today.

Such is *not* the case for the big bang. There are alternate cosmological theories, although none has been widely entertained as yet. Other possibilities, not yet conceived, must certainly exist. There are unanswered questions about the big bang, and implications of the theory that have not been resolved. Still, it is the best overall model proposed so far that is consistent with all observations and with the best gravitational theory yet advanced—general relativity. Moreover, it has survived three crucial tests: (1) the universe is observed to be expanding; (2) the hydrogen-to-helium ratio is as predicted by the theory; and (3) we have observed the faint glow of radio radiation that must surely be present if the big bang occurred. Perhaps the model is wrong, but any theory that replaces it must satisfy all of the tests the big bang has passed, and have superior predictive value as well.

The big bang, then, is the correct favored model of cosmology. That is not to say that cosmologists "believe" it is right, in the sense that fundamentalists "believe" in the literal interpretation of Genesis. To be sure, sometimes scientists, being human, tend to forget, in everyday life, the tentativeness of their current ideas, and speak of them as though they were "sure" or as though they "believed" them, but these are human reactions, not objective scientific judgments. Science does not "know" anything; it will give a very high priority to the motion of the earth, but to the big bang only a grade of "promising idea that so far has passed all the tests."

Recently some writers have tried to make the case that the favored position of the big-bang model of cosmology has brought modern science close to the religious idea of the creation set forth in Genesis. Nothing could be farther from the case.

Each of us has wondered about his or her origins. Every other culture has invented its gods to explain the unexplained mysteries. It is never explained where "God" came from, of course, any more than is explained by the four elephants that, in one early culture were supposed to have supported the earth on their backs, nor of the turtle on whose back the elephants stood.

Given that God, or various gods, somehow made the earth and heavens, it is then natural to ask whether he/she or they did it at one time, over a long time, or whether it was always so. It is extremely difficult for anyone (modern cosmologists included) to imagine infinities or eternities; hence it is natural to postulate a finite beginning at some discrete time in the past. This may leave unanswered the question of the origin of the gods, or of time, but at least by blaming it all on God we have consolidated the mysteries into one unexplainable—and that one is just assumed as a postulate, or to be accepted on faith, whatever that entails. In any case, if one assumes that the universe began at one moment, it might seem that the unique (in time) big bang might well be interpreted as that moment.

There is nothing wrong, I suppose, with believing that the universe began with a "bang" at the command of God. But, as I have said, it has nothing whatever to do with the scientific theory of the big bang. The Genesis (or any other) account of the origin of the universe that comes from religious dogma and is meant to be accepted on faith as absolute truth, was, in fact, invented by man to help him cope with the profound and perplexing questions of his origin. Such ideas were invented in terms of scenarios that were consistent with what was known of the universe at the time the scenarios were conceived. They were *not* derived from empirical laws or data.

It might be argued that the scientific hypothesis of the big bang does not explain the ultimate origin of matter any more than Genesis explains the origin of God. (For example, where did the matter and energy come from in the first place, how did it get so dense, and what started its expansion?) The point is that science does not attempt to "explain" ultimate origins. Science concerns itself only with hypotheses that can be tested, and, if wrong, proved wrong. That is, a scientific hypothesis must be *falsifiable*. Disciplines that offer no testable (or falsifiable) hypotheses are not part of science. Of course, science has its limitations, but science has no trouble at all with saying, "I don't know."

Thus despite the singularity of the "beginning" in both the Genesis and the big-bang accounts of the early universe, the two are actually entirely different. The Genesis account was *invented* to provide a credible (at the time) explanation of our origins. The big-bang model has been derived entirely from empirical evidence. Let us, very briefly, review the steps leading to the big bang.

Gravitation is discovered. It leads to a collapse unless the universe is infinite. A better theory of gravitation (relativity) shows that even an infinite

universe cannot be stable, without doctoring the theory of relativity in a nonaesthetic manner. It is then seen that relativity can be correct after all, without such doctoring, if the universe is expanding. It is observed that galaxies recede from us with velocities that are proportional to their distances, which indicates just such an expansion. If we then extrapolate the expansion backward in time, it leads to a very dense universe in the past. Theory says that at such densities the universe should be hot, and predicts that mainly hydrogen and helium should survive and dominate the universe, and that there should be (by mass) three times as much hydrogen as helium. Within observational uncertainty, that ratio is observed in the present universe. Theory says, further, that such a hot universe would be filled with radiation, but also be highly opaque. It is transparent today. When did it become so? When matter and radiation ceased to interact. Calculations show that this should have occurred when the universe, in its expansion, had thinned by a certain amount (at an age of nearly one million years). From that time on, the radiation should flow freely throughout the universe. Calculations show that it should be observed today as low-energy radio waves. Such radiation has now been discovered, coming from all directions in space.

The preceding line of reasoning reads not at all like the Book of Genesis. No one can prove or disprove that there is a God and that God created the universe, with all of its laws and properties we observe. The God-hypothesis has no tests; it is not falsifiable. It may be correct, but it is not part of science.

I do not mean to imply that speculation has no place in science. Some of the great inspirations in science have resulted from consideration of the consequences of highly speculative ideas. Speculation is acceptable as a means to finding a good idea, but the idea itself becomes a part of the scientific method only when it is developed to a hypothesis that can account for observed phenomena at least as well as existing hypotheses, and also make testable predictions of the results of new experiments or observations.

There is little doubt that entirely new and presently unimagined laws of nature will become part of the science of tomorrow. These new developments, however, will not mean that contemporary science is all wrong. The familiar foreground, well inside the scientific frontier, is extremely well tested and verified. New adjustments will be *at* the frontier—and will expand our understanding to new realms.

Perhaps, someday, science will extend beyond the big bang—that is, back to yet earlier epochs. In some present cosmological speculation that is already the case: for example, in the *oscillating model*, whereby the present expansion is envisioned as part of alternating expansion and contracting modes.

The oscillating universe has, at present, no theoretical basis. It is merely a speculative extension of one of the possible variations of the standard big-bang model that are consistent with general relativity. Whether the present expansion of the universe will continue forever or someday give way to contraction depends on the average, smoothed-out density of matter in space. If that density is high, the universe has enough gravitation at every point to eventually stop the expansion; if the density is low, on the other hand, although always slowing the expansion will never cease. In this sense, the expansion of the universe is analogous to a missile fired from the surface of the earth. If the missile has a launch-speed greater than the speed of escape from the earth (about 11 km/s), it will move out forever; if not, gravity wins out and the missile falls back to the ground. Present-day observations (very uncertain) suggest that the density and gravitation in the universe are too low, and that the universe will continue expanding and thinning forever. In the words of astronomer Allan Sandage, at the Mount Wilson and Las Companas Observatories, it would mean that "the universe happened only once."

On the other hand, if the universe *does* one day fall back on itself, it should collapse again to a state of extreme density—a situation sometimes whimsically called the "big crunch." If, under these conditions, another big bang could occur, we could imagine that the universe could be infinitely old, with no beginning and no end, oscillating between expansion and contraction. The idea has a certain romantic appeal, because it may seem analogous to the perpetuation of life, new forms emerging as old ones die, or to the cycles of night and day, or of the rebirth of each new spring. Science at present, unfortunately, can offer no support for this notion, because there is no known way the universe could ever get out of the "crunch"; it would literally have fallen back into its own black hole. On the other hand, it must be admitted that science can offer no explanation for the original big bang either. Anyway, the oscillating universe is a speculation, not a scientific theory.

There are other models of an infinitely old universe. The most famous is the *steady-state*, or *continuous-creation* theory of Thomas Gold, Hermann Bondi, and Fred Hoyle. In this, the universe is infinite and eternal, never changing on the large scale. Indeed, it is based on a single idea: the extension of the cosmological principle to the *perfect cosmological principle*, which asserts that the universe is not only the same (on the large scale) everywhere but for all time. The steady-state universe expands, but rather than thinning out, new matter is continuously being created to keep the overall density the same. The concept was a noble one with great philosophical appeal. Moreover, it was scientific, for it made specific predictions and was eminently falsifiable. Today the steady state has had to be rejected. There are several reasons. One is that *quasars* (evidently luminous regions in the centers of remote galaxies) appear to be far more common at great distances—where they are seen far in the past, as they were when light left them thousands of millions of years ago—than nearby, where we see them as they were in the recent past. The dying out of quasars in recent times shows that the universe is evolving, contrary to the perfect cosmological principle. Moreover, the steady-state theory does not predict the observed hydrogen-to-helium ratio. The biggest blow to it was the discovery of the cosmic background radiation, now interpreted as the fading glow of the big bang.

Of many other theories of cosmology, some with a finite beginning and some with eternal lifetimes, none has received wide interest, because the big bang is simpler, and follows directly from the best laws of physics presently known. That is not to say that in the future new observations will not show that the whole idea of the big bang will have to be abandoned. In any case, we must distinguish between scientific cosmological hypotheses—which are consistent with known theory and observations and which make testable predictions—and purely speculative ideas, which have no observational or theoretical bases and are not part of science.

Science is quite limited—it deals only with testable and falsifiable hypotheses. Science, as such, has no quarrel with the concept of God. It can neither prove nor disprove that God exists—or many gods, or none at all for that matter. We understand a certain amount about nature—tremendously more than we did a century ago—but still have only a tiny glimpse of its totality. So God, and a divine origin, are neither ruled out by nor are incompatible with science. They are simply irrelevant to it. There is no conflict between science and religion as long as science keeps to what can be tested and religion does not claim to be science.

Religion offers values that science cannot: fellowship, for example, inspiration, and ethical or moral principles. Such values can be of great importance to society. Even though they may never provide answers to the grand questions of nature that are satisfying to the scientist, they could well provide a guide to a more comfortable and orderly life.

There is thus no reason why science and religion cannot coexist to the benefit of mankind. But science must recognize that what it can say about moral or inspirational values is limited to the practical results of specific actions, and religion must understand that divine revelation has nothing to do with scientific "truth."

Bibliography

Couderc, Paul. *The Expansion of the Universe.* London: Faber and Faber, 1952.

Ferris, Timothy. *The Red Limit.* New York: William Morrow, 1977.

Hodge, P. W. *Galaxies and Cosmology.* New York: McGraw-Hill, 1966.

Hubble, Edwin. *The Realm of the Nebulae.* New Haven, Conn.: Yale U. Press, 1936; also, New York: Dover, 1958.

Peebles, P. J. E. *The Large-Scale Structure of the Universe.* Princeton, N.J.: Princeton U. Press, 1980.

————. *Physical Cosmology.* Princeton, N.J.: Princeton U. Press, 1971.

Sandage, A. R. *The Hubble Atlas of Galaxies.* Washington, D.C.: Carnegie Institution, 1961.

Sciama, Dennis W. *Modern Cosmology.* London: Cambridge U. Press, 1971.

————. *The Unity of the Universe.* New York: Doubleday, 1959.

Shapley, Harlow. *Galaxies.* Cambridge, Mass.: Harvard U. Press, 1972.

Shipman, H. L. *Black Holes, Quasars, and the Universe.* 2nd ed. Boston: Houghton Mifflin, 1980.

Silk, Joseph. *The Big Bang.* San Francisco: Freeman, 1980.

Verschuur, G. L. *The Invisible Universe.* New York: Springer-Verlag, 1974.

Weinberg, Stephen. *The First Three Minutes.* New York: Basic Books, 1977.

GEORGE O. ABELL

V

VALE, GILBERT (1788–1866), Anglo–American freethinker, was a prominent member of a contingent of British-born, radical émigrés who settled in New York in the 1820s, including George Houston, William Carver, George Henry Evans, and Benjamin Offen. They were among those who settled in the United States following the Panic and Peterloo Massacre of 1819 and an intensified English-government crackdown on religious radicalism.

His Career. In light of Vale's prolific literary activities and his key role in the FREETHOUGHT movement, the surviving biographical data is surprisingly sketchy. His education is obscure, beyond the fact that he started to prepare for a career in the Church of England. On his arrival in New York in 1827 or 1829 his training was sufficiently good to enable him to support himself by teaching mathematics, navigation, and "the modern system of bookkeeping."

Vale's principal educational writings were *Cometarium, or the Astronomy of Comets* (16 pp.; 1832) and *Elements of Astronomy: An Illustration of G. Vale's Geographical and Astronomical Card* (24 pp.; 1846). As a coordinated teaching aid he patented a "combined terrestrial globe and celestial sphere." This instrument sold for prices ranging from $12 to $150 depending upon its scale and the number of optional elements. It was recommended and used by two professors at Yale College as well as in the schools of New York, Boston, and Philadelphia. Vale's teaching establishment, which he called a "Nautical and Mathematical Academy" subsidized his career as a freethinking publisher, lecturer, and organizer.

The principles of traditional Anglo-American DEISM supplied the motivation for and set the limits to Vale's radicalism. He seems never to have moved beyond natural religion into outright unbelief. His animus was directed against that psychologically and socially destructive fanaticism that he believed to be the fruit of the so-called revealed religions. In *Fanaticism: Its Source and Influence* (1835), Vale wrote a meticulously detailed reconstruction of a notorious case in the greater New York area, with the didactic intent of exposing the destructive consequences for individuals who came under the influence of deluded religious figures.

The achievements of the natural sciences were the warrant for Vale's confidence that systematic rational analysis of the principles of government and economics would lead to comparable gains in human affairs. The declaration of editorial principles for one of his many periodicals contains the essence of this position. "The principles of the *Diamond* will coincide with the established works on Government as a science, and Political Economy. The *Diamond* will therefore be Radical in its character, supporting Equal Rights and the greatest happiness to the greatest number, and of course opposed to privileges and monopolies; and in support of the largest Education to the people, as a means of preventing crime and sustaining liberty. The *Diamond* will be a Reformer while abuses exist, and an independent supporter of good government and the Constitution" (*The Diamond*, no. 1 [May 1840]).

Among those particular abuses Vale set out to reform were privilege, the subordination of women, and legal quackery. The *Diamond*, for example, was "addressed to the mass of the people," and it sold for three cents a copy, 12 numbers for 25 cents. (Vale often asserted that he was not against *honest* acquisition of wealth; however, neither individuals nor countries should prosper at the expense of others or through fraud.) And Vale would "attempt to interest the female part of the community in some of the ramifications of these sciences" because there was "no reason why a lady should not understand the system which makes marketable articles dear." Law and lawyers were to be weighed "in the balance of reason."

Dedication to Paine. It was no doubt Vale's quintessential deism that accounts for his total

709

dedication to the rehabilitation of THOMAS PAINE in the minds and hearts of Americans. Vale regarded his efforts to counter Paine's detractors as the most important contribution of his own career. He provided the English-speaking world with the best sympathetic treatment of Paine until MONCURE DANIEL CONWAY's biography appeared in 1892. In 1837 Vale got out *A Compendium of the Life of Thomas Paine*. As he acknowledged, his work depended largely on W. Sherwin's 1819 London memoir, but he added new material on Paine's last years in New York.

In 1841 Vale published his expanded *Life of Thomas Paine*, which remained the standard biography among freethinkers for half a century, in spite of the refusal of many booksellers to carry it. There were at least seven editions printed in New York in the first dozen years following its publication. The BOSTON INVESTIGATOR kept the book in circulation during the second half of the century by issuing new editions every five or six years. In 1850 Vale published a small volume entitled *The Poetry of Thomas Paine*. (The Rare Book Room of the Library of Congress holds Conway's personal copy of Vale's *Life*, along with an interesting letter from Vale to L. L. Taylor dated Aug. 20, 1860.)

Vale raised over a thousand dollars to pay for the monument that was placed at Paine's gravesite in November of 1839. The monument was done without charge by a freethinking sculptor, John Frazee. Moreover, Vale raised another $1,500 in the late 1840s for the down-payment on what had been Paine's 60-acre farm in New Rochelle, N.Y. Vale's idea was that this farm could serve as a home for elderly, indigent freethinkers.

Although Vale seems not to have had the aptitude for steady organizational work, his intelligence was respected by other freethinkers and he was one of their more effective lecturers. In 1831 he began lecturing at FRANCES WRIGHT's Hall of Science on perspective drawing, as well as on the English language and grammar. Later in that decade he was a frequent lecturer to Benjamin Offen's group, the Moral Philanthropists, who met in Tammany Hall. Vale was often the spokesman for freethought in those curious marathon debates with Christian clerygmen which both sides seemed to relish in that era. In one such debate, in New York in 1836, he spoke for six straight evenings. In 1840 he did a "missionary" tour of the Midwest and a similar circuit in upstate New York and Ohio the following year.

However, it is unquestionable that Vale's greatest contribution to the American freethought movement was as a tireless publisher and editor. Given the ephemeral nature of radical papers and the marginal social status of most subscribers, it is impossible to reconstruct a definitive checklist of Vale's periodicals and pamphlets. He claimed, for example, to have published the first commercial Sunday newspaper in America. (This may have been either the *Citizen of the World* or the *Sunday Reporter*. His most distinguished achievement was the *Beacon*, an eight-page weekly he took over shortly after its founding by the U.S. Moral and Philosophical Society in 1836. He sustained the *Beacon* for ten years. There also were occasional and longer bimonthly or quarterly versions of the *Beacon*, but neither found a sufficient paying readership. Vale's weekly probably reached a high point of one thousand subscribers in 1838.

In summary: Vale was not a creative thinker in a philosophical sense, but he expounded his version of rational religion and rational republicanism with clarity and vigor.

Bibliography

Bennett, D. M. *World's Sages, Infidels and Thinkers*. New York: D. M. Bennett, 1878.

Brown, Marshall G., and Gordon Stein. *Freethought in the United States*. Westport, Conn.: Greenwood Press, 1978.

Post, Albert. *Popular Freethought in America, 1825–1850*. New York: Columbia U. Press, 1943.

RODERICK S. FRENCH

VANINI, GIULIO CESARE (1585–1619), Italian FREETHOUGHT martyr. Vanini was born in Taurisano, a small village in southern Italy. He spent his childhood in his native village and then moved to Naples to study jurisprudence. On his father's death, being the second of a family which though not poor was by no means rich, he found himself in difficult financial circumstances and thus was obliged to choose the monastic life, a tradition of the time. In 1603 he began his notiviate with the name Fra' Gabriele, in a branch of the Carmelite Order that followed the old rule. Once he had taken up residence in the monastery of Santa Teresa, he was able to complete his studies, and on June 1,

1606, he obtained a degree *in utroque jure*. Later, to perfect his studies in theology at the Stadium Generale of the Carmelites, he moved from Naples to the monastery of Santa Maria del Carmine at Padua. Here, however, he did not limit himself to ecclesiastical circles; on the contrary, it became clear that he was intolerant of monastic discipline.

During his stay at Padua, Vanini's life took a decisive turn. While studying philosophy, he had used the texts of John of Baconthorp, an English Carmelite of the 14th century who was influenced by Averroism. Perhaps it was from this source that Vanini had received encouragement to go beyond the strictness of the religious orthodoxy of the Counter-Reformation. Now, in Padua, he was in contact with a philosophical culture that was firmly connected to the exuberant tradition of Renaissance thinkers—that is, a philosophical culture encompassing heterodox Aristotelianism, a collection of doctrines based on natural reason that excluded all interference of faith in interpreting the phenomena of the natural world and the social structures of the human world. The remarkable speculative wealth of this current of thought, so impressive with all the force of its lay knowledge, caused Vanini to reconsider Catholic dogma with great care. He became increasingly familiar with philosophers divorced from problems of a religious nature, such as Pietro Pomponazzi, N. Machiavelli, G. Cardano, G. C. Scaligero, G. Fracastoro, as well as with the most eminent authors of the school of Padua, including Vanini's contemporary C. Cremonini. All of these men opened up to him the horizons of a coherent, rigorous, and systematic naturalism.

Moreover, Vanini did not fail to play an active and public role in the intellectual circles of the republic of Venice, which were in favor of the enlightened jurisdictionalism of Fra' Paolo Sarpi, the great theologian and canonist of Venice, and which supported his work of bringing about the reunification of all Christians, especially against the religious intolerance of the Roman Catholic church. Vanini's adherence to the ideals of Christian ecumenicalism compromised him with the Carmelites. Consequently, in order to avoid the serious sanctions that the superior had already adopted against him, he tried to leave Italy to seek refuge in a Protestant country. With the help of the English ambassador in Venice he succeeded, together with his brother monk Giovan Battista Maria Genocchi, in reaching England in secret. There, during a solemn ceremony held in London

on June 29, 1612, in the presence of Francis Bacon, Vanini embraced the Anglican faith.

It was not, however, a sincere conversion, since Vanini remained bound to the program of Christian Latitudinarianism, according to Sarpi's model. Therefore, the Anglican church appeared to him fully as intransigent and hostile as the Roman Catholic church. In England, moreover, he was placed under severe control by ecclesiastical authorities, who mistrusted Vanini and Genocchi. In fact, Vanini was prevented from holding any office, was isolated, and reduced to poverty. In this negative situation, bereft of hopes of creating a new life and making himself the emissary of religious renewal, he intensified his contacts, which had never been completely broken, with Catholic circles and decided to return to the Continent.

In 1613, together with Genocchi, Vanini contacted the Roman Curia asking forgiveness from Pope Paul V. He also asked to be released from his monastic vows, promising, however, to remain a secular priest. His offer to return to the church, formalized by Cardinal Roberto Ubaldini, the apostolic nuncio in Paris, and accompanied by payment of a hundred crowns, was promptly accepted, so obvious was the propaganda benefit to the Catholic church from the publicity attending a case of apostasy spontaneously repudiated. However, his plans were discovered by the English archbishop, George Abbott, who ordered the two Italians' arrest. The Roman Catholic diplomats and chaplains of the London embassies of Venice and Spain came to Vanini's assistance. In March of 1614, they helped him escape from prison and get out of England, as they had already helped Genocchi to do.

Vanini first visited the papal nuncio for Flanders, Guido Bentivoglio, in Brussels and afterwards went to Paris, where he stayed for several months at the house of Cardinal Ubaldini. There he completed an *Apologia del Concilio Tridentino*, which did not receive an imprimatur, remained unpublished, and may now be considered a lost work. With orders to return to Italy, he went to Genoa, but, suspecting that the "pardon" of the Roman Curia might not guarantee him immunity from inquisition and condemnation, he took the first opportunity of returning to the French capital. He felt much safer in Paris since he was able to rely on the protection offered him by the widespread, underground movement known as the *libertins érudits*.

With this movement, which supported religious

skepticism as an essential condition for the development of the critical activity of the reason, Vanini had in fact begun to unify on the basis of the radical change that had come about in his religious beliefs. Not even his "reconversion" to Catholicism, though more scandalous and apparently more sincere than his "conversion" to Anglicanism, had had any real effect on his soul; on the contrary, even his previous fervor for Latitudinarianism had completely disappeared. He had now reached a stage of complete unbelief, believing that no profession of faith on the part of men of culture could be supported by a valid awareness of the truth. His own experience had shown him that, apart from the degree of sincerity to be found in the naive beliefs of the popular classes condemned to ignorance, religious sentiment was always polluted by political calculation and used to hide and protect both unjust privileges and ambition for power.

Vanini was able to say that he was convinced of the duty of all *érudits* to safeguard their freedom of thought so that it might never be overcome by the fear of the supernatural. However, unlike almost all the other *libertins* of that age, he was not only a *déniaisé*, in the sense that he did not limit himself to enjoying his spiritual crisis interpreted as a sign of maturity, nor to scoffing unconcern for every ideal of life, nor to aristocratic isolation in his attitude toward the community. In fact, his attempt to obtain his individual emancipation as an *esprit fort* by means of overcoming every dogmatic and doctrinal subjection induced him to investigate speculative argumentation in favor of ATHEISM but also, and in particular, to commit himself actively to spreading his new convictions, to which, though in a very utopian way, he attributed the capacity of promoting a total renewal of man and the social order.

With this in mind, Vanini published at Lyons the *Amphitheatrum aeternae Providentiae* (June 1615) and then in Paris the dialogues *De admirandis Naturae Arcanis* (Sept. 1616; hereinafter known as *Secrets*). Both books are aimed at combating every form of acceptance of traditional metaphysics and theological justification for institutions that support public authority. The proofs of the existence of God and the norms of ecclesiastic morality based on the recognition of the action of providence are systematically ridiculed. Vanini claimed that God and providence are irreconcilable with the undeniable and prevailing presence of evil in the world. The historicity of every religion is affirmed, and hence the inevitable end of Christianity

is also foreseen. The thesis that faith is always an *instrumentum regni*—that is, the fruit of priestly imposture originally promoted by politicians in support of their autocracy—is once more taken up. The possibility of miracles is denied and they are considered to be unusual phenomena still not explained or mere products of the imagination. Similarly, witchcraft, astrology, prophetic divination, and so on are denounced as unacceptable superstitions. In short, man is conceived as an exclusively natural being without any immortality but capable of becoming the master of the world relying on the forces of his own reason.

Thus, the *pars destruens* of the *Amphitheatrum* and the *Secrets*, particularly influenced by libertine philosophic culture, is harmoniously united with the *pars construens*, which is derived directly from Renaissance Aristotelian naturalism. It is important to note that just as *libertinisme érudit* is the link between the Renaissance and ENLIGHTENMENT, so the works of Vanini are the link between the Renaissance and *libertinisme érudit*—that is, the means by which the "heterodox" Aristotelianism of the school of Padua was able to spread even in France and become part of the European circulation of modern thought. It must be remembered that two-thirds of Vanini's two works consist of whole passages taken from the texts of Aristotelian authors of the 16th century. They have been judged to be large-scale plagiarism. I reject this opinion, since the "plagiarized" passages acquire a completely new meaning in the theme of the *Amphitheatrum* and the *Secrets*, where they not only constitute the sources but also support a plan that is globally subversive of every tradition.

Obviously Vanini could not express his thought freely. Thus in his writings he used a language that was often ambiguous and involved. He trusted to the intelligence of his readers, having recourse to the device (typically "libertine") of the so-called "protective contexts." This consisted in secretly presenting one's own theses as if dealing with errors being refuted. He succeeded in deceiving his censors, but not for long.

In October of 1616, after a resolute intervention on the part of the Sorbonne, Vanini was compelled to flee from Paris to escape arrest. He wandered through various parts of France, finding protection in libertine circles, until he decided to settle in Toulouse, then a stronghold of French Catholicism. He hid under the pseudonym "Pompeo Ugilio" and dedicated himself at first to the practice of empirical medicine and the teaching of languages. Eventually, however, with indescribable courage he continued to spread his ideas and gather proselytes around him. It was inevitable that he should arouse suspicion, should be the object of informers, and should be discovered. It was precisely this unfailing tenacity in asserting and propagating his convictions that has made him not only a founder but also a martyr of freethought.

In August of 1618 the town parliament of Toulouse, informed of Vanini's atheistic commitments, had him imprisoned and tried. He defended himself with great skill as long as he was able to exploit the reticence of the witnesses who were afraid of endangering themselves. But, finally, after a violent address by the prosecutor, he was found guilty of the crimes of atheism, blasphemy, and profanity and condemned to death. The sentence was carried out immediately, on Feb. 9, 1619, in Salin Square. The executioner tore out his tongue, strangled him, and burned his body at the stake, afterwards scattering his ashes to the wind. An attempt had been made to force him to beg God, the king, and the judicial body for pardon, but Vanini had strongly objected, convinced that he had committed no crime and insisting that he believed neither in God nor in the devil. The only desire he had expressed was to have a doctor at hand to witness that he died *en philosophe*, that is, without showing any fear. It was this strength of mind at the moment of death, apart from the cruelty of the execution, which gave rise to many legends about the 33-year-old Vanini. He was described by both Catholic and Protestant writers as the Antichrist, the disciple of Satan, while his real name, which was not discovered during the trial, began to be associated with "Ugilio" (hence *Lucilio* or *Luciolo*), under which he had gone to the scaffold.

Other articles of interest: **Evil, Problem of. God. Existence of.**

Bibliography

Corsano, A. "Per la storia del pensiero del tardo Rinascimento. II. G. C. Vanini." *Giornale critico della filosofia Italiana* 37 (1958).

Corvaglia, L. *Le opere di Giulio Cesare Vanini e le loro fonti.* 2 vols. Milan: 1933–34.

Hegel, G. W. F. *Werke zweite Auflage. Vorlesungen über die Geschichte der Philosophie.* Vol. 15. Ed. C. L. Michelet. Berlin: 1844.

Namer, É. *Documents sur la vie de Jules-César Vanini de Taurisano.* Bari: 1965.

———. *La vie et l'oeuvre de J.-C. Vanini, Prince des Libertins, mort à Toulouse sur le bûcher en 1619.* Paris: 1980.

Papuli, G. "La fortuna del Vanini." *Le interpretazioni di G. C. Vanini.* Galatina: 1975.

———. "Pensiero e vita del Vanini: verso una nuova consapevolezza filosofica e una nuova prospettiva d'azione sociale." *Bollettino di Storia della filosofia dell'Università degli Studi di Lecce* 5 (1977).

Porzio, G. *Le opere di Giulio Cesare Vanini tradotte per la prima volta in italiano, con prefazioni del traduttore.* 2 vols. Lecce: 1912.

Spini, G. "Vel Deus vel Vaninus." *Ricera dei libertini. La teoria dell'impostura delle religioni nel Seicento italiano.* Rome: 1950.

Vanini, Giulio Cesare. *Amphitheatrum aeternae Providentiae divino-magicum. Christiano-physicum, nec non astrologo-catholicum. Adversus veteres Philosophos, Atheos, Epicureos, Peripateticos, et Stoicos.* 1615. New Italian trans. edited by F. P. Raimondi and L. Crudo. Galatina: Congedo, 1979.

———. *De admirandis Naturae Reginae Deaeque Mortalium Arcanis.* 1616. New Italian trans. edited by F. P. Raimondi and L. Crudo. Galatina: Congedo, 1983.

Vasoli, C. "Riflessioni sul 'problema' Vanini." *Il libertinismo in Europa.* Milan and Naples: 1980.

GIOVANNI PAPULI

VERIFIABILITY PRINCIPLE. See Logical Positivism and Unbelief.

VOLTAIRE, FRANÇOIS-MARIE AROUET DE

(1694–1778), French poet, playwright, novelist, historian, essayist, popularizer of science, philosopher, social reformer, and undoubtedly the most influential figure of the ENLIGHTENMENT.

VOLTAIRE'S FIRST SIXTY-SIX YEARS

Voltaire was born François-Marie Arouet in Paris to a prosperous notary. He was sent to the Jesuit school of Louis le Grand, where he received an excellent classical education. He was extremely precocious, and at the age of 12 he wrote polished verses that delighted his teachers. To the chagrin of his family, he abandoned the study of law for literary pursuits, in which he was spectacularly successful almost from the start.

In 1718 Voltaire's first tragedy, *Oedipe,* was performed with great success, and his plays dominated the French stage for the rest of the 18th century. His epic poem, *La Henriade,* which appeared in 1723, celebrated Henri IV, the last liberal French king. Although the poem was banned because of its undisguised hostility to Christianity, *La Henriade* had a vast circulation and was hailed by critics as the greatest epic in the French language. Voltaire's unorthodox opinions did not prevent his being a favorite at the court. The queen was said to have wept over his plays, and she gave him an allowance of 1,500 livres from her purse. This relatively serene period came to an end when a young nobleman, the Chevalier de Rohan, stung by some of Voltaire's derisive remarks, had him beaten up. Voltaire not only failed to obtain justice but, because of the influence of the well-connected Rohan family, ended up in the Bastille. The episode left an indelible impression on his mind and made him an unrelenting enemy of judicial arbitrariness and cruelty.

Voltaire was released from the Bastille only after promising to go to England, where he spent more than two years (1726–1729). He mastered the language and diligently studied the works of the English philosophers, scientists, and social reformers. On returning to France he wrote the *Lettres philosophiques,* which appeared first in London in 1733 in English translation as *Letters Concerning the English Nation,* and a year later in Paris. This slim volume was aptly described by Voltaire's biographer, Gustave Lanson, as the first bomb hurled against the *ancien régime* and became the inspiration of liberal reformers throughout the European continent for the rest of the century. Voltaire was in England when an exceptionally liberal government was in power, and he therefore tended to exaggerate the prevailing degree of freedom and toleration. In the *Lettres,* he praised English institutions and, by implication, condemned conditions in France—the wealth, intolerance, and immense power of the church, the despotism of the king, and the privileges of the aristocracy. He recommended equal status for merchants and nobles, a fair distribution of taxes, and toleration for all religions. England, he wrote, is a land of sects and "an Englishman, like a free man, goes to heaven by whatever route he chooses."

The *Lettres* also contain an exposition and defense of the empiricism of JOHN LOCKE and the methods and achievements of Isaac Newton, accompanied by satires of the theories of Aristotle and RENÉ DESCARTES. The French edition contained an additional "letter" on Blaise Pascal, whose gloomy fideism is vigorously opposed. Pascal's notorious "wager," as well as his appeal to the heart, were anathema to Voltaire, who thought that our opinions in all fields should be based on evidence. "The interest I have in believing a thing," Voltaire wrote, "is not a proof of the existence of that thing." As if to confirm his strictures, the authorities at once moved to suppress the *Lettres.* The publisher was sent to the Bastille, Voltaire had to flee from Paris, and the courts condemned the book to be "torn and burned in the Palace courtyard . . . by the common executioner, as being scandalous, contrary to religion, good morals, and the respect due to the ruling powers."

Most of the 15 years following the publication of the *Lettres* was spent by Voltaire in the company of his learned mistress, Madame du Châtelet, at Cirey in Lorraine. This was one of the most peaceful periods of his life. In 1734 he wrote the *Traité de métaphysique,* which is the most systematic and closely argued of his philosophical works. It was "written for" and dedicated to Mme. du Châtelet. It was also undoubtedly written for the world at large, but Voltaire made no effort to get it published during his lifetime. It finally appeared in Volume 40 of the first collected edition of Voltaire's works, prepared between 1785 and 1789. It seems that Voltaire wrote more candidly here about the touchiest questions, namely God and immortality, than in any of the books and pamphlets published while he was alive. He accepted the argument from design but stated the case against belief in God much more forcefully than elsewhere, and he totally rejected any kind of belief in life after death. In 1738, he published *The Elements of the Newtonian Philosophy,* in which he demonstrated the superiority of Newton's mechanics and cosmology to those of Descartes, whose views were still widely preferred by French scientists. The censorship in France was so severe that even this relatively harmless book had to be published in Holland, without mention of the author's name.

During this period, Voltaire also composed numerous plays—the incomparable philosophical tales, of which *Zadig* and *Micromegas* are the most famous—and several huge histories. Because of their glittering style and streams of amusing anecdotes, these histories make delightful reading, even after more than two centuries, but the significance of Voltaire's historical works transcends their literary merits. Explanations in terms of divine providence that fill the volumes of earlier historians, including Voltaire's illustrious predecessor, Jacques Bossuet, are not allowed and, perhaps more important, history is treated as the story of peoples rather than of rulers and military leaders, with special emphasis on progress in the arts and sciences and their impact on society.

During this time Voltaire also achieved, for the only time in his life, official recognition from the French court and the government. Through the influence of his friend Mme. de Pompadour, he was appointed royal historiographer in 1745, and the next year, after a most disingenuous display of piety, he was elected to the French Academy. Mme. du Châtelet died in 1749, and in 1750 Voltaire accepted an invitation from Frederick the Great to become "philosopher-poet" in residence at Potsdam. Here he spent three disagreeable and largely unproductive years, ending in an entirely predictable quarrel with the king. Neither of the two behaved admirably, but the king showed much greater forbearance. Among other things, Voltaire could not resist the temptation of ridiculing the king's French poetry. He also engaged in financial dealings that bordered on criminality and were most unbecoming in a distinguished member of the court. The break, when it came, was violent, but some years later all was forgiven, and the two resumed their amicable correspondence. In one of his letters, Frederick wrote with much justice: "Would that Heaven, which gave you so much wit, had given you judgment proportionately!"

Voltaire's extensive and often unscrupulous financial speculations had made him enormously rich by this time and, after traveling for a year, he bought a chateau in Geneva that he named "Les Delices." During his stay in Geneva, he published the first edition of his universal history, *Essai sur les moeurs* (1756), a multivolume work that introduced Western readers to the history of Arabic and Chinese civilizations. In Geneva he also wrote *Candide* (1759). On the front page it bore the inscription "Translated from the German of Dr. Ralph." Voltaire vigorously denied authorship of *Candide,* but he was not displeased by the book's enormous popularity.

The Calvinists of Geneva were by no means pleased with Voltaire's presence in their city. They objected to the theatrical performances at his chateau and they were particularly displeased by certain statements in the article "Genève," written for DENIS DIDEROT's ENCYCLOPÉDIE by Jean d'Alembert at Voltaire's suggestion. In 1759, he purchased a magnificent estate at Ferney, a few miles over the French border, where he lived unmolested by French, German, or Swiss authorities until shortly before his death.

L'HOMME AUX CALAS

When Voltaire settled in Ferney he was 66, immensely famous, and immensely rich. He was to live another 18 years, and this final period became the most rewarding and productive of his life. He waged two campaigns that shook Europe like nothing since Luther's break with the Church of Rome. The two campaigns were intertwined, but only the first was the result of deliberate planning.

It is not clear when Voltaire lost what little belief in Christianity he may ever have entertained. What is certain is that he opposed Christianity throughout his adult life and came to regard it as a major aberration of the human mind, as well as a terrible disaster for the human race. He believed Christianity had to be destroyed before one could achieve a rational and humane society. Christianity, he wrote to Frederick the Great, "is the most ridiculous, the most absurd, and bloody religion that has ever infected the world." Voltaire did not openly write against Christianity until the 1760s. From then until his death he waged an unrelenting campaign against "the infamous thing," as he called it. During the Ferney years, letters to his friends always concluded with the slogan "Ecrasez l'infâme," and "l'infâme" was not, as some squeamish historians have alleged, fanaticism in general but the Christian religion.

The first of Voltaire's major anti-Christian publications, *The Sermon of the Fifty,* was published in 1762, but it had been written several years earlier, possibly during his last years at Cirey. This pamphlet reads like a declaration of war on Christianity, and it is written in a deliberately inflammatory style. It attacks Christian mysteries like transubstantiation as absurd; Christian miracles as incredible; the Bible as full of contradictions; the Jews, whose religion had led to Christianity, as an ignorant and mendacious people; and the God of Christianity as a cruel and hateful tyrant. The true God, the sermon concluded, "surely cannot have been born of a girl, nor died on the gibbet, nor be eaten in a piece of dough." Nor could he have inspired "books, filled with contradictions, madness, and horror." May the true God "have pity on the sect of Christians that blasphemes him!"

As another installment in the war against Christianity, Voltaire published in Holland, also in 1762, extracts from the *Testament of the Abbé Meslier.* According to Voltaire's unsigned introduction, JEAN MESLIER was a country priest who, while living an outward life of conformity, had composed a powerful defense of atheism, democracy, and revolution. Voltaire professed to deplore the "melancholy spectacle" of a priest, with a fine sense of justice and a highly developed intellect, condemning Christianity in such harsh tones. Meslier's *Testament* became one of the great documents of the French Enlightenment, and its publication caused a tremendous stir. The fact that Voltaire did not share the more extreme of Meslier's incendiary views did little to mollify his clerical enemies.

Unquestionably, the most powerful and also the most delightful of Voltaire's missiles against Christianity was the *Philosophical Dictionary,* which is widely regarded as his true masterpiece. This melange of witty reflections on a vast variety of topics attempts to demolish the enemy by laughing him out of existence. Voltaire wrote the first articles in Potsdam as early as 1752. He kept jotting down ideas for a number of years, but he did not resume serious work on the *Philosophical Dictionary* until late in 1762. The first edition, then one small volume, appeared in Geneva in June of 1764 with a false London imprint and without Voltaire's name on the cover. As usual, Voltaire strenuously denied his authorship, but nobody took the denial seriously. The first edition sold out immediately. The Geneva government condemned the book to be burnt in September 1764; liberal Holland followed suit in December, and in Paris it was publicly burned in March 1765. In July of that year, it was put on the Index by the Holy Office.

In spite of these condemnations, new and enlarged editions appeared year after year. In the final form given to it by Voltaire, the work was published in 1769 in two large volumes. It was reprinted in this form several times during the remaining years of Voltaire's life. Even larger editions, incorporating material from other of Voltaire's writings and some running to eight volumes, were brought out in later years. These later editions have been a nightmare for bibliographers, but they contain many glorious riches that might not otherwise have been available to readers of later generations. It goes without saying that the *Philosophical Dictionary* outraged Voltaire's clerical enemies. Some started compiling "anti-philosophical" dictionaries that, as Voltaire would have put it, "regrettably" did not remotely rival the original work in popularity. From this time on, Voltaire came to be regarded by Catholic apologists as the Antichrist. Almost half a century later, Joseph de Maistre still proclaimed that hell had put "its entire power into the hands of Voltaire." Voltaire did not at all mind being called the Antichrist. In fact, he often referred to himself as "Beelzebub's theologian," and he knew that the hatred he provoked proved the enormous effectiveness of his campaign.

Voltaire's second campaign was against judicial barbarism, and it led to the writing of two of his best and most constructive books, *Commentary on Beccaria's "Of Crimes and Punishments"* (1766) and *Prix de la Justice et de l'humanité* (1777). This campaign, which did a great deal to prepare France for revolutionary change, was precipitated by the judicial murder of Jean Calas, a Huguenot trader in cotton goods, who, on the basis of malicious rumors, had been arrested for murdering his son. The rumors had it that the son, Marc Antoine, was planning a conversion to Catholicism and that, to prevent this, his father and the other members of the family had strangled him. Marc Antoine had not had the slightest interest in a conversion and had committed suicide in a fit of depression. The accusation leveled at the Calas family was unsupported by anything that would pass as evidence in a civilized court and was clearly inconsistent with common sense and all the known facts. The family was nevertheless tried and found guilty by the judges of Toulouse. The family property was confiscated, and Jean Calas was condemned to be broken at the wheel and then burned at the stake. The other members of the family were banished from France.

The sentence against Jean Calas was carried out with unspeakable brutality on March 10, 1762. When Voltaire heard about the execution he resolved to rehabilitate the wronged family. He mobilized all his influential acquaintances at the court of Versailles, including Mme. de Pompadour and the Duke of Richelieu, and his powerful friends elsewhere, especially Frederick the Great and the Empress of Russia. He published pamphlet after pamphlet, in several languages, exposing the judges of Toulouse. The Toulouse authorities would not make the court documents available, and at first the king and the government refused to overrule them. Eventually the public clamor became so great that a new trial was ordered. On March 9, 1765, 40 Paris judges, in a unanimous decision, declared Jean Calas to have been innocent. The Calas property was restored and the king granted 36,000 livres as compensation to the widow. There were festivities in Paris. Crowds gathered to applaud the widow and the judges. Voltaire, who always referred to this case as "mon meilleur ouvrage" (my best work), was from then on known as "the savior of the Calas."

Another case from the same part of France in which Voltaire intervened concerned Pierre Paul Sirven, a well-to-do Protestant, and his wife, who had been sentenced to be hanged for the murder of their daughter. Here, too, it was charged that the daughter had been planning to become a Catholic, and again the evidence against the accused was incredibly flimsy and at variance with all the known facts. Fortunately, the Sirvens fled to Switzerland before their trial. It took Voltaire nearly nine years to establish their innocence and to have their fortune restored. The Sirven case, Voltaire wryly remarked in a letter, lacked "the éclat of the Calas case" because "nobody was broken on the wheel."

Unfortunately the same could not be said about the beheading of the 19-year-old Chevalier de La Barre for blasphemy. La Barre and his young companion Gaillard d'Etallonde were accused of mutilating a wooden crucifix, making blasphemous remarks about the Virgin, and singing blasphemous songs. D'Etallonde escaped before the trial, and La Barre, pleading guilty to the other charges, steadfastly denied mutilating the crucifix. He was tried and found guilty of all charges by a court in Abbeville, near Amiens, on Feb. 28, 1766. He was condemned to have his tongue cut out, his right hand cut off, and to be burned at the stake. The verdict was appealed to the parliament of Paris. Voltaire and most observers expected that the sentence of the Abbeville court would not be upheld and that La Barre would get off with a prison sentence. However, chiefly because of the ravings of the Paris clergy about the dangerous spread of infidelity, the parliament ratified the original conviction. It spared La Barre from having his tongue and right hand severed, but the death sentence was confirmed, substituting decapitation for burning at the stake. To extract a further confession, La Barre was to be tortured before his execution. This incredible sentence was carried out on July 1, 1766. After his beheading, his corpse was burnt along with a copy of the *Philosophical Dictionary*.

Voltaire was powerless to save La Barre, but he obtained a position for d'Etallonde in the Prussian army and tirelessly worked for his rehabilitation,

which was not granted until 1788, ten years after Voltaire's death. No case infuriated Voltaire more, and none contributed more to his determination to change the French legal code and its administration. "The atrocity of this act," he wrote to d'Alembert, "seizes me with horror and anger," and eight years later he told Condorcet that rage came into his heart and tears into his eyes every time he thought about this horror, which he described as "a hundred times more hellish than the assassination of Calas."

There were a great many other cases. Voltaire succeeded in freeing Claud Chaumont, who was on the galley bench because he had attended a Protestant service. He also succeeded in freeing Jean Pierre Espinas, who had spent 23 years in the galleys because he had given lodging to a Protestant clergyman for one night. Not all cases involved religious bigotry. One of the most celebrated concerned General Lally, the French royal commissioner in India, who had been defeated by the English and was executed on unproven charges of disloyalty. Voltaire pursued his efforts to vindicate the general's name for ten years and received the news of his rehabilitation as he lay dying in Paris in May 1778. It roused him to write the last letter of his life. "The dying man revives upon hearing this great news," he wrote to the general's son, ". . . he will die content."

In 1778, Voltaire's latest play, *Irène,* was to be performed in Paris, and he expressed a wish to attend its premiere. He had been banished from Paris during the lifetime of Louis XV, but with the accession of Louis XVI and a new ministry that included his friend the Encyclopedist Turgot, Paris was once again open to him.

Voltaire was recognized and hailed by crowds at every step of the journey from Ferney. In Paris, there were tremendous ovations in the streets, and everywhere he was hailed as "l'homme aux Calas." Voltaire did not lose his head. "What crowds to greet you," somebody said to him. "Alas!" he answered, "there would be just as many to see me on the scaffold." The royal family ignored his presence, but he was feted at the Comedie Française and the Academy, where only the clerical members refused to attend. At the Hôtel de Villette, where he was staying, he received visitors eager to pay their respects. The callers included BENJAMIN FRANKLIN and Diderot, with whose writings and activities he was familiar, but neither of whom he had met. Franklin brought his grandson and asked Voltaire's blessing for him. Voltaire stretched out his hand and simply said, "God and liberty." Diderot was so eager to impress him with his wit and eloquence that Voltaire had to accept the unaccustomed role of passive listener. After their meeting, Diderot is reported to have described Voltaire as a fairy castle, fallen in ruins, but still inhabited by an old sorcerer. When asked his opinion of Diderot, the "old sorcerer" remarked that there could be no doubt about the man's brilliance, adding that unfortunately "nature has denied him one essential gift, that of dialogue."

In May of 1778, Voltaire was seized by a fever. The doctor diagnosed cancer of the prostate, and he died on May 30. There were the usual rumors of agonized shrieks and deathbed confessions. The Marquise de Villette, who was with him when he died, denied all such assertions. "To the very last moment," she said, "everything showed the goodness and benevolence of his character, everything bespoke tranquility, peace and resignation."

Refused a Christian burial in Paris, Voltaire was buried surreptitiously outside the city. In 1792 his remains were moved to the Pantheon, but they were once again dispersed at the onset of the Restoration. The Nazis, quite fittingly, melted down his statue during their occupation of Paris. The best epitaph for Voltaire was perhaps written by Thomas Macaulay. "Voltaire possessed a voice," Macaulay wrote, "which made itself heard from Moscow to Cádiz, and which sentenced the unjust judges to the contempt and detestation of all Europe. . . . Bigots and tyrants, who had never been moved by the wailing and cursing of millions, turned pale at his name."

GOD AND MATTER

It has been maintained by some reputable scholars that, regardless of his numerous public and private statements to the contrary, Voltaire was an atheist. However, the great majority of commentators agree that he was a sincere and ardent believer in God. It is true that, in one or two places, Voltaire discussed the subject without reaching a definite conclusion. Thus, in a late article entitled "On the Existence of God," he simply set out the arguments in favor of God's existence and those against it and did not declare that he sided with either. There are also passages in his correspondence that dismiss belief in God as absurd. Against this, it must be emphasized that in literally hundreds of books, articles, and letters he insists, with almost compulsive repetitiveness, that the order of nature and the teleological character of biological systems requires us to infer the existence of a "supreme intelligence." Moreover, Voltaire wrote extensively against the atheism of some of his fellow-Encyclopedists and of BENEDICT SPINOZA, whom he always regarded as an atheist. Voltaire not only rejected atheism as false, but also believed that, if it became widely accepted, it would cause vast harm to the human race. It seems on balance more reasonable to assume that, like many other believers, Voltaire occasionally wavered and had spells of doubt and disbelief than that he engaged in a lifelong, deliberate charade, deceiving not only the religious world but also his fellow-philosophers, many of whom he loved and admired.

Voltaire called himself a theist, but in fact the position he advocated is more commonly described as "deism." This means that he believed in the existence of God while opposing revealed religion—miracles, dogmas, and any kind of priesthood. He always made a careful distinction between "true religion" and "superstition," and he argued that, unlike superstitious religions, especially Christianity, the kind of religion he championed could only do good. He once wrote: "The sole religion is to worship God and to be an honorable man. This pure and everlasting religion cannot possibly produce harm." "Superstition," he wrote in the *Treatise on Toleration,* "is to religion what astrology is to astronomy—the mad daughter of a wise mother. These daughters have too long dominated the earth."

In several places Voltaire tells us both what we can and what we cannot know about God. The lists of divine attributes supplied in different books are not entirely consistent. In the article "Theist" in the *Philosophical Dictionary,* the theist, i.e., the Voltairean believer, is said to be "a man firmly convinced of the existence of a Supreme Being, as good as it is powerful, which has created all the extended, vegetating, feeling, and reflecting beings, which perpetuate their species." To this he characteristically adds that the theist's religion "consists neither in the opinions of an unintelligible metaphysics nor in vain display, but in worship and in justice. To do good—that is his worship; to submit to God—that is his doctrine." It should be noted that the Supreme Being is described as good but not as perfectly good, and as powerful but not omnipotent. In his very late essay "We Must Take Sides," which deals exclusively with the existence and nature of God, goodness is omitted from the list of divine attributes; and the omission is not accidental.

This time the emphasis is on the power, the intelligence, and the eternity of God. The Supreme Being is "very powerful" since it "directs so vast and complex a machine," and it is "very intelligent" because "the smallest spring of this machine cannot be equalled by us, who are intelligent beings." Human beings cannot make solar systems, and they also cannot make eyes or ears or stomachs. Since God can produce these things, he must be vastly more intelligent than even the most intelligent men.

As we shall see shortly, Voltaire primarily relies on various forms of the design argument to justify belief in God. However, he realized that, even if it is otherwise unobjectionable, the design argument cannot prove God's eternity. Watchmakers and other "manufacturers" are born and they die. How do we know that the Supreme Designer has no beginning and no end? Voltaire never addresses the latter of these issues, but he has no doubt that he can take care of the former and thus prove God's "infinite duration." To do this, he borrows a version of the cosmological argument found in Locke. God is eternal, Voltaire writes, since he "cannot be produced from nothing, which, being nothing, can produce nothing." Thus, given the existence of something, it is demonstrated that something has existed for all eternity.

This argument is doubly fallacious. Even if it succeeded in proving that there must be an entity that has always existed, it does not follow that this eternal entity is God. Furthermore, the "principle" that something cannot come from nothing does not, in conjunction with the statement that something exists now, yield the desired conclusion that some particular being must always have existed. The conclusion that follows is that at all times there must have been something in existence, which is not at all the same thing as that one and the same thing has always existed. An infinite series of causes, each of whose members is of finite duration, is entirely consistent with the facts that something exists now and that something cannot come from nothing. These criticisms disregard the vagueness and ambiguities in the principle that something cannot come from nothing. It occurred neither to Locke nor to Voltaire that, as it stands, the principle is much too vague to be employed in a serious philosophical argument.

Not only God but matter too is eternal. Voltaire's God is thus a Demiurge rather than a Creator. "My reason alone proves to me a Being who has arranged the matter of this world," he writes in the article "God-Gods" in the *Philosophical Dictionary*. Reason, however, is "unable to prove that he made this matter—that he brought it out of nothing." In the article "Matter" and also in *The Ignorant Philosopher*, he goes further and maintains that reason requires us to hold that matter *is* eternal. In one of his customary stabs at the scholastic philosophers, he remarks that "today we are lucky enough to know by faith that God drew matter from nothingness," but this is not a conclusion warranted by the evidence. Nor is it in fact the view of most religions. In their view the "divine hand" arranged the world out of chaos, not out of nothingness. Belief in the eternity of matter has not "injured the cult of the Divinity in any nation." We are not diminishing the majesty of God if we describe him as "the master of an eternal matter." Not even Genesis teaches creation out of nothing. It simply asserts that the gods (*Elohim*, not *Eloi*) "made heaven and earth," leaving it open whether there was any matter out of which heaven and earth were shaped.

Voltaire's pronouncements on the relations between the Demiurge and the rest of the universe are far from clear. In the article "Infinity" in the *Philosophical Dictionary* he writes that the Supreme Being, by "modifying matter," caused "worlds to circulate in space and form animals, vegetables and metals." He approvingly mentions the view of the Romans that "matter, in the hands of God, was felt to be like clay on the potter's wheel," although he adds that such a comparison is no more than a "feeble image" to express divine power. In *The Ignorant Philosopher*, he remarks that "he cannot conceive that the cause that continually and visibly actuates nature" could have been inactive at any time and that an "eternity of idleness" is incompatible with his other properties. He concludes that the world has probably always "issued from a primordial and necessary cause as light emanates from the sun." Voltaire emphatically disagrees with the teaching of non-Christian religions and of Hesiod and Ovid that before the Divinity's intervention matter was in a state of chaos. "Chaos is precisely contrary to all the laws of nature" and "chaos never existed anywhere but in our heads." As a convinced determinist, Voltaire could have added that, since what goes on in our heads also happens according to laws, in the sense here in question, chaos never exists even in our heads. If initially there was no chaos, there also was not the order we now find in the world. In the course of replying to the charge that belief in the eternity of matter commits him to Manicheism, Voltaire wrote: "Here are stones an architect has not made; he has raised an immense building with them; I don't accept two architects; brute stones obeyed power and genius."

It would appear that Voltaire did believe in one or more datable ordering acts on the part of the Demiurge. Initially, matter was not without order, but the order we now have was imposed on it by the Demiurge. Furthermore, as we shall see later on, Voltaire believed that the Demiurge was involved in the production of every biological structure so that, as far as living organisms are concerned, creation is still going on. The similarity of Voltaire's views to those found in Plato's *Timaeus* is obvious, but, according to most of his interpreters, Plato did not believe that the imposition of order by the Demiurge occurred in time.

THE PROBLEM OF EVIL

In his earlier writings, Voltaire did not hesitate to speak of God as good and just. This was in harmony with his generally optimistic view about the prevalence of both virtue and happiness on the human scene. In the *Philosophical Letters,* in response to Pascal's gloom, Voltaire declared that animals were generally very contented and that many human beings led reasonably happy lives. Rather smugly, he observed that when he looked at Paris or London he saw nothing remotely like the "desert island" to which Pascal had compared our "mute universe." What he saw were "opulent" and "civilized" places where men were "as happy as nature allows." To Frederick the Great he had written in a similar vein in 1738 that "when everything is counted and weighed up . . . there are infinitely more enjoyments than bitterness in this life."

In succeeding years, as his sympathies widened and his observations grew more extensive, Voltaire drastically changed his outlook. The Lisbon earthquake of 1755, in which 15,000 people were killed and another 15,000 seriously injured, finally made him doubt not the existence but the goodness and justice of God. What irritated him beyond measure were the facile attempts to explain why the disaster was in complete harmony with the perfect goodness of God. Bishop William Warburton, an influential Anglican divine (whose main claim to posthumous fame is an attempt to obtain a prosecution of DAVID HUME on charges of blasphemy), asserted that the Lisbon earthquake, "displayed God's glory

in its fairest colors." In a sermon on the cause of earthquakes, John Wesley attributed the disaster to "sin," to "that curse that was brought upon the earth by the original transgression of Adam and Eve." Many Christian apologists claimed that the explanation must be sought in the wickedness of the inhabitants of Lisbon. Jean Jacques Rousseau argued that the earthquake was a just punishment of men who had abandoned a natural country life for the artificial pleasures of big cities. Writing specifically in reply to Voltaire's long poem on the Lisbon earthquake, Rousseau added that, as the only alternative to a suicidal pessimism, we must continue to have faith in the goodness of God—we must believe that in the long run things turn out well and that from a sufficiently broad perspective everything will be seen to make sense.

Voltaire disposed of these and similar "explanations" not only in the poem on the Lisbon earthquake but also in *Candide,* in which the character Doctor Pangloss is a composite of Leibniz, Rousseau, and Alexander Pope. The latter was the author of *The Essay on Man,* in which it had been maintained that really "there are no evils," but if there were any "particular evils, they compose the general good." Nobody had shown that there were more sinners in Lisbon than in London or Paris. Yet Lisbon lay shattered while Paris danced. Even if the adult victims of the earthquake had been such dreadful sinners as to deserve their fate, what about the infants that lay crushed and bloody on their mothers' breasts? Moreover, what happened in Lisbon was only an extreme illustration of the suffering that is the inevitable lot of living things. "All the world," Voltaire writes, "in all its members groans, all born for suffering and for mutual death." The "ferocious vulture" darts upon its "timid prey" and "feasts with joy" on its helpless victim. Its triumph, however, is short-lived. For soon an eagle "with sharply cutting beak devours the vulture." The eagle in turn is reached by a deadly shot coming from a man who not long afterwards lies dying in the dust of a bloody battlefield. There he serves as the food of voracious birds. Beasts and men suffer, almost without ceasing, but men suffer more because, in addition to all their illnesses and misfortunes, they are conscious of their inevitable extinction.

Hence, we must not listen to the optimists who tell us that "all is well" and that the misery of each part composes the happiness of the whole. The universe, Voltaire replies to the optimists, "gives you the lie, and your own heart refutes a hundred times the error of your mind." Pope's "general good" is a "strange thing indeed, composed of the [kidney] stone, the gout, all crimes, all sufferings, death, and damnation." No, evil is very real, and Epicurus was right to insist that its existence rules out a God who is both all-powerful and perfectly good. The problem of evil is "an abyss whose bottom nobody has been able to see," "an inexplicable chaos for those who search honestly," an "unshakable rock" against which the arrows fired by a hundred "bachelors and doctors of divinity" have been totally ineffective. It is a "terrible shelter" for atheists who are wrong in concluding that there is no God but right in questioning his goodness and justice. In one place, in discussing Manicheism, Voltaire seems to incline to the view that God is indeed good but not all-powerful. He tells his imaginary Manicheist that one deity is more economical than two, and he prefers to believe that the true God is the good Ormazd, speculating that possibly this deity "could not do better." He is a "powerful, wise, and good" being but also one who is limited by the materials he works with.

Most frequently in his later works, Voltaire simply regards the entire situation as a baffling mystery that requires us to confess the limits of our understanding. If my understanding is so weak, he wrote, that if I cannot even know "by what I am animated" how "can I have any acquaintance with that ineffable intelligence which visibly presides over the universe?"

THE ARGUMENT FROM DESIGN

Voltaire occasionally has recourse to the cosmological argument for the existence of God not only in Locke's version mentioned earlier but also in the form in which it is found in Samuel Clarke. Voltaire's statement of the argument is greatly inferior to Clarke's formulation, and it is evident that he does not have his heart in this argument, which seems to be too scholastic and metaphysical for his taste. On the other hand, he defends numerous versions of the design argument with great enthusiasm. He regards it as a genuinely empirical argument, and he finds it adequate to the task of proving the finite Demiurge whose existence he champions. Contemporaries like PAUL HENRI HOLBACH who scoff at the argument are castigated at great length. This much despised argument, Voltaire writes, in the article "God-Gods," "is that of Cicero and of Newton. This alone might somewhat lessen the confidence of atheists in themselves."

Many sages, "observing the course of the stars, and the prodigious art that pervades the structure of animals and vegetables," have acknowledged "a powerful hand working these continual wonders." The appeal to final causes is "the most natural" and "for common capacities" the most perfect argument to show that an intelligent being "presides over the universe." As with many other defenders of the argument, both before and after him, the starting point is what we know or supposedly know about the relation between a watch and its intelligent maker. "When I see a watch whose hand marks the hours," Voltaire wrote, "I conclude that an intelligent being has arranged the springs of this machine in order that the hand may mark the hour." If a clock is not made for the purpose of telling the time, he wrote in "Final Causes," also in the *Philosophical Dictionary,* he is prepared to "admit that final causes are nothing but chimeras," adding that he would be content "to go by the name of a fool" to the end of his life. Needless to say, Voltaire did not think that he had to go by the name of a fool to the end of his life. Unlike those who have "willfully shut their eyes to understanding," he gladly admitted that there is design in nature, and, if there is design, then "there is an intelligent cause: there exists a God."

In a passage quoted earlier, Voltaire spoke of "the prodigious art" that pervaded the structures of animals and vegetables. This art is displayed in a great variety of ways but most undeniably and impressively in the construction of bodies of animals and men. "Consider yourself," says Freind, the sage who brings the misguided atheist Birton to his knees: "examine with what art, never sufficiently explored, all is constructed within and without for all your wishes and actions." There is not one "superfluous vessel." The arrangement throughout the body is so artful that "there is not a single vein without valves and sluices, making a passage for the blood." From the roots of the hair to the toes "all is art, design, cause, and effect." It is "audacious madness" to deny that we are here confronted with final causes. A sane person has to admit that the mouth was made to eat and speak with, the eyes "admirably contrived for seeing," the ears for hearing, and the nerves for feeling. Nothing perhaps shows the presence of design more clearly than the arrangement of the reproductive systems in males and females alike and the pleasure associated with the sex act that guarantees the perpetuation of the species. Even Epicurus, the unbeliever, would be obliged to admit that "pleasure is divine" and that pleasure is a "final cause" leading to the incessant introduction of new organisms into the world. "When I see the springs of the human body," Voltaire writes in the relatively skeptical paper "On the Existence of God," "I conclude that an intelligent being has arranged these organs," an intelligent and "superior being" who "skillfully prepared and fashioned the matter." In *The Ignorant Philosopher,* this superior intelligence is referred to as "the supreme artisan" or "workman" who "actuates" the enormous multitude of biological arrangements and who, except for the superiority of his intelligence and skill, is in these respects entirely comparable to human craftsmen.

The order or lawfulness of the universe, especially as it is exemplified in the movements of the heavenly bodies, is just as strong evidence for a supernatural Designer as the purposive character of biological structures. The order of the universe, Voltaire writes in the article "Atheism" in the *Philosophical Dictionary,* "now that it is better known, bespeaks a workman; and so many never-varying laws, announce a law-giver." So far from promoting atheism, Newton's discoveries in mechanics have greatly strengthened the case for a cosmic designer. Voltaire was particularly pleased with his dictum that "as a catechist proclaims God to children, so Newton demonstrates him to the learned." In one place he quite correctly attributes this remark to "a philosophical Frenchman who was persecuted in his own country for asserting as much." This theme is developed in detail in the essay "We Must Take Sides," where he writes: "The unvarying uniformity of the laws which control the march of the heavenly bodies and the movements of our own globe" show that there is "a single, universal and powerful intelligence."

There are three possible ways of accounting for the order in the world. One is blind chance; the second is the view that the order was produced by the heavenly bodies behaving in an orderly fashion; and the third is the postulation of an eternal Orderer or Geometrician. Taking as his illustration one of Johannes Kepler's laws, Voltaire dismisses blind chance as "extreme folly." Surely it is preposterous to maintain that blind chance has produced an arrangement in which "the square of the revolution of one planet is always to the squares of the others, as the cube of its distance is to the cubes of the distances of others, from the common center." Voltaire next rules out the possibility that the planets themselves, or more generally "Nature," are responsible for the order discovered by astrono-

mers. In the "Dialogue Between the Philosopher and Nature," Nature remarks that "she" is no mathematician and that yet everything "in and about" her is "arranged agreeably to mathematical laws." If "your great universal system knows nothing of mathematics," the philosopher responds, and if nevertheless the laws by which "you are regulated" are those of the "most profound geometry," there must necessarily be "an Eternal Geometrician, who directs you, and presides over your operations." Again, in "Atheism" in the *Philosophical Dictionary*, we are presented with the disjunction that "either the planets are great geometricians or the Eternal Geometrician has arranged the planets." The former alternative is plainly absurd, and hence we must embrace the latter.

At times, Voltaire appeals to the fact, or rather what he takes to be the fact, that the universe is a vast machine. "When we see a fine machine," he writes, "we know that there must be a 'good machinist' with 'an excellent understanding.' " This argument is "old, but is not therefore the worse." It should be remarked that it is not identical with the one appealing to the orderly nature of the universe, but it is doubtful that Voltaire perceived the difference between them.

Another version of the design argument is based on copies or reproductions that human beings make of natural objects or collections of such objects. Since the copy required an intelligent cause, we may affirm the same of the original. Voltaire's main illustrations were "orreries," the then newly invented contraptions in which the bodies of the solar system were represented by balls moved by wheelwork. An orrery is "the chef d'oeuvre of the skill of our artisans," and everybody admires Lord Orrery for his invention. Yet it is a very imperfect copy of the solar system and its revolutions. "If the copy indicates genius," how much more must there be in the maker of the original! Similar considerations apply to landscape paintings, drawings of animals, or models in colored wax. They are the work of "clever artists." If this is true of the copies, it must also be true of the original. "I do not see," Voltaire observed, "how this demonstration can be assailed."

There is also the problem of accounting for intelligence. Even a materialist like Holbach cannot deny that there is "some difference between a clod and the ideas of Newton." Intelligent beings like Newton cannot have been "formed" by something blind, brute, insensible, i.e., by matter. It follows that "Newton's intelligence came from some other intelligence." These quotations come from the previously mentioned article "Atheism." The argument is repeated a short time later in a letter to d'Alembert (July 27, 1770). "It seems to me absurd," writes Voltaire, "to derive intelligence from something like matter and motion which are not intelligent." It may be interesting to note that d'Alembert himself, who eventually became a thoroughgoing atheist, accepted this argument in his earlier years.

After this argument one is prepared for the worst, and the worst does not fail to come. What is the purpose of the sun? Most educated people since Copernicus would find this a difficult question, but not so Voltaire in one of his Panglossian moods. "When the atheist lights a candle," he writes, "he admits that it is for the purpose of giving light." He should then similarly admit that "the sun was made to illuminate our part of the universe." Fortunately, however, such Panglossian outbursts are rare. Most of the time, Voltaire confesses that we do not know the purpose of the universe nor presumably that of the sun. In the "Dialogue Between Nature and the Philosopher," the philosopher asks his "beloved mother" why she exists and why, in fact, anything exists. Nature modestly replies that she knows nothing about the matter. The philosopher persists: Why would not "nothing itself" have been preferable to "that multitude of existences formed to be continually dissolved," the animals born to devour others and to be devoured in their turn, the numberless beings whose lives are filled with pain, and the tribes of "reasoning beings" who never or at most rarely listen to reason? For what purpose, he demands, was all this? Leave me alone, Nature replies in effect. "Go and inquire of Him who made me."

The question of the purpose of the universe also arises for Voltaire when he tries to answer the opponents of the design argument who bring up the obvious inperfections in the world as a reason for questioning the wisdom and even the existence of a supernatural designer. Some critics have brought up such phenomena as earthquakes, eruptions of volcanos, and "plains of moving sands." Others have mentioned frightening and poisonous animals like serpents and sharks. And there is, of course, the problem posed by "the woes and crimes of mankind." Voltaire always gave the same answer to such challenges. The various imperfections may show that the designer lacks goodness and concern for the welfare of living things. Perhaps they even show that he is malevolent, but they do not weaken the inference to a designer of *some* kind. "If the

naves of your chariot wheel catch fire," he writes, this does not show that "your chariot was not made expressly for the purpose of conveying you from one place to another." Similarly, the existence of serpents and "so many wicked men worse than serpents" does not show that either serpents or men were not designed. If flies could reason, Voltaire adds, they would undoubtedly complain to God about the existence of spiders, but they would nevertheless admit that the spider's web was arranged in a wonderful manner.

Perhaps the most obvious of the many objections to Voltaire's arguments is that, if all of them were valid, they would not establish the existence of a *single* supernatural intelligence. They would establish a "geometrician," an "architect," an "actualizer," and a "lawmaker." In our experience, it is certainly not the case that a person having one of these skills invariably also possesses the others. Perhaps all four skills or occupations are rolled into one in the Supreme Intelligence, but that is not immediately evident and requires to be proved.

Several of Voltaire's arguments are so glaringly invalid that they can be disposed of in a few words. The inference of a supernatural lawmaker from scientific laws involves a fallacy of equivocation. Laws in the sense of legal regulations do indeed require an intelligent lawmaker, but scientific laws are not laws in the same sense. As has often been pointed out since Voltaire's time, legal regulations are prescriptive while scientific laws are descriptive. Voltaire's "copy" argument is just as threadbare. The fact that a copy like a landscape painting or a model of the solar system is the work of an intelligent being does not show that the original must also have an intelligent cause. If the wind blows bits of paper from a table to the floor and if somebody paints or photographs the resulting scene, the copy is the work of an intelligent cause, but the original is not. In the sense in which "chance" is opposed to design, the original scene is an instance of chance.

Voltaire's argument that intelligent beings can only have been produced by intelligent causes and that hence the Supreme Being must be intelligent rests on the well-worn principle of the scholastics and of Descartes that any attribute of an effect must already have been present in its cause. If this proposition were true, the amoeba would have to have been a mathematician. But one does not have to go to evolution to realize that the principle is false. JOHN STUART MILL gave the example of the liquidity of water and the gaseous character of its components, and there are countless everyday instances concerning parents and children that conflict with the principle. Even if it were true, it still would not give Voltaire a Supreme Intelligence as distinct from an infinite series of intelligent beings, each the cause of its successor. In one place Voltaire declares that an infinite causal series is impossible, but he gives no reason, and in the present context he does not even mention the issue.

The argument based on the similarities between the watch and a biological structure like the eye is not as flimsy, and, in fairness to Voltaire, it must be pointed out that a fully adequate reply was not possible until Charles Darwin's theory of natural selection supplied a naturalistic explanation of what Cleanthes in Hume's *Dialogues Concerning Natural Religion* called "the curious adapting of means to ends" in all living things. However, even before Darwin, several weighty objections, some of them fairly obvious, could be advanced. In the first place, there is a simple but important distinction that Voltaire does not take into account. The distinction is between the assertion that something is *used* for a certain purpose and that it was *designed* for that purpose. If we come to a cave and find signs of habitation in it—beds, cooking utensils, clothes, copies of the Bible and *Playboy*—we are entitled to affirm that it is used as a dwelling. We have no right to infer that it was designed for that purpose. This may in fact be the case—the people living in it or somebody in the past may have dug the cave. However, it may also be a "natural" cave. It may have been produced by purely geological forces. Now, it is certainly true that human beings and various animals *use* their eyes for the purpose of seeing, but it does not follow that the eyes were designed for this purpose or, for that matter, that they were designed at all.

The argument faces a further objection that is so simple and obvious that most people ignore it, feeling that it cannot possibly have any relevance. Hume, fortunately, was not deterred by the simplicity and obviousness of the objection from seeing its force. Evolution aside, we *know* how eyes and other organs are produced. They are produced by natural reproduction, or what Hume called "generation." Design, so far as our observation goes, has nothing to do with it. This common-sense observation leaves, of course, some important questions unanswered. As far as it goes, however, it is absolutely correct and, among other things, it challenges the design theorists to tell us just where and how the alleged designing and "actuating" by the Demiurge

takes place.

Voltaire shows some awareness of this objection and answers it by declaring that the biological parents are not the true cause of the offspring. All offspring are the work of the "eternal manufacturer." Voltaire cannot very well deny that the biological parents play some role in the production of their children, but they are no more than the "blind instruments" of the "eternal manufacturer." Speaking about the "arrangements" within his own body, he insists that he is indebted for them to God and not to his parents. His parents were not his true cause since, when producing him, "they certainly did not know what they were doing." Voltaire's position here is in effect quite similar, in general outline, to that of reincarnationists, who maintain that the familiar biological processes of conception and gestation are not sufficient to bring about a full-fledged human child, and to that of Catholic theologians, who maintain that God's infusion of the soul into the newly formed embryo is an essential element in the production of a human being. The objections that Voltaire would probably have advanced against the reincarnationists and the Catholic theologians are equally applicable to his own contention. What evidence, to begin with, does he have that natural biological causes are insufficient to produce a complete offspring, eyes included? The answer of course is that he has none. He does offer certain arguments, but they beg the question. Thus he argues that the parent organisms, whether they are animals or human beings, do not possess the capacity to "form" their offspring and then concludes that the offspring must have been formed by a superhuman intelligence. Here, "formation" presumably means planning or design followed by "actuation," the way in which a watchmaker designs and actuates a watch. It must be granted that in this sense neither human beings nor animals "form" their children. However, Voltaire's conclusion would follow only if it had been shown that formation is the only means of producing offspring. This assumption is not self-evident, and it is not accepted by the critics of the design argument. Again, Voltaire writes that parent organisms do not know what they are doing when they produce their offspring, and he takes this to be evidence that the parents are not the true cause. But why does ignorance on the part of the parents prevent them from being the true cause of their offspring? We may assume that parent cats are ignorant of the connection between sexual intercourse and pregnancy and that they know nothing about heredity and embryology. We also know that they cannot "form" their offspring the way a watchmaker assembles a watch. None of this, however, shows that the parent cats are not the true cause of their offspring *by means of generation.*

There are additional difficulties in any attempt to maintain that the existence of organisms is the result of the joint efforts of the observable, embodied parents and a supernatural, unobservable intelligence. Voltaire's claim that the parents are the "blind instruments" of the supreme intelligence *seems* to be perfectly intelligible because we can easily think of situations in which certain things are described as the "instruments" of others who are regarded as the true or at least as the decisive cause. We might say, for example, that Greece's ambassador in Washington, D.C., is no more than an instrument of his government. If he orally presents a message to the secretary of state he is not its true cause, even though he may have chosen the precise wording. To take a case in which it might be said that the observable agents are merely the instruments of somebody who is not present, let us consider a performance of *Don Giovanni.* We will assume that the singers, the orchestra, and the staging are superb. It could then hardly be denied that the singers, the orchestra, the director, and the conductor play important roles in bringing about the admirable result; but it would still be true that the main credit belongs to Mozart's score. Without singers, conductor, orchestra, and, for that matter, the opera house, the performance could not have taken place or it could not have been so splendid; and they are certainly not "blind" instruments. Nevertheless, in the end, it is Mozart's score that is the basic and most indispensable factor.

Unfortunately, however, neither this nor any other familiar case of "co-causes" provides us with a model on the basis of which we could give content to Voltaire's claim about the co-causation of organisms by their parents and God. We know what it is like for a composer to compose a score and we also know how the score can be made available to a conductor, the orchestra, and the singers so that they can put on a performance of the opera. On the other hand, we do *not* know what it would be like for a pure intelligence to produce the plan for a new organism. How can a pure intelligence fashion anything like a blueprint? Does such talk have any sense at all? Furthermore, even if this question could be satisfactorily answered, there remains the problem of making the plan available to the "instruments," in this case the

biological parents. How could this be done? What kind of "imprinting" takes place? Where and how? We have not been given a coherent theory unless we are told not only that an intelligent being makes eyes and ears and whole animals but also, at least in outline, *how* this is done. What this objection amounts to is that the word *instrument* has a clear sense only when we are dealing with relations between observable entities and processes. It has lost its sense when one of the entities involved is unobservable. On a few occasions Voltaire himself seemed to recognize as much. In a famous letter to Mme. du Deffand, which has been cited as evidence that Voltaire was secretly an atheist, he speaks approvingly of the opinion of Epicurus and LUCRETIUS that "nothing is more ridiculous than the notion that an unextended being could govern one which is extended," and he adds, referring presumably to the incarnation of God in Jesus, that "combining what is mortal with what is immortal is something most unsuitable." The same surely applies to any supposed "blending" of the contributions of the biological parents with that of the deity to the production of an organism.

Voltaire is aware that, if valid, the design argument gives us an arranger and not a creator; and, since he believes in the eternity of matter, this fact does not disturb him. He is not aware, however, that the designer it would give us is one with a body who needs his body or whose assistants or subordinates need their bodies for "actuating" or "forming" structures like the eye or whole organisms like a cat. If we followed through the machine-maker analogy without stopping before it became too uncomfortable, we would end up with something like heavenly factories of parts and heavenly places for assembling the parts into the finished biological products. The fact that we need one or more *physical* heavenly arrangers is occasionally but only dimly realized by believers when they talk about "the hand" of God, as Addison does in his well-known hymn about the "divine hand" and as Voltaire himself did in the article "God-Gods," in which he refers to the "powerful hand working continual wonders."

The supporter of the design argument is faced with a dilemma, each of whose horns seems to have devastating consequences for his position. If he endows the supernatural arranger with a body, then the arranger could, in principle, "actuate" or "form" biological structures; but educated Western believers find such a position repellent and, what is more, it does seem incredible to almost everybody.

If, on the other hand, the supernatural arranger exists without a body, it is not easy to see how he could engage in actuating biological structures; and it is also not the conclusion that the watchmaker argument would authorize. Teleologists and also some of their critics do not see this predicament because they tend to talk in very general terms of "intelligence" rather than "chance" as the cause of living things. It must therefore be emphasized that intelligence in general is not an entity that can produce anything. Only intelligent *beings* can do this, and they need bodies and tools and preexisting materials.

Turning to the "cosmic" version of the argument, the first thing to note is that in one obvious respect it is much weaker than the "biological" form just discussed. In any complete teleological argument, we may distinguish two stages. The first consists in identifying something as a teleological system; the second in showing that it is the kind of teleological system that is best explained in terms of conscious design. The biological version does at least get to the first stage. For an organ like the eye may in a broad sense be conceded to be a teleological system. Here we at least have an end, namely that of seeing, to which the various internal mechanisms and adjustments seem to be directed. Discussions of this topic have been bedeviled by the ambiguities of such words as *end* and *goal*. However, if not too much is read into this, we may say, following terminology used by a number of contemporary writers on biology, that the activities of the various parts of the eye are "goal-directed," leaving it an open question whether they are also "goal-intended." Now, the first and most basic trouble with the cosmic version of the argument is that it never gets as far as the first stage. To what common end, corresponding to vision, are all the objects in the universe directed? Except for his one regression to pre-Copernican anthropomorphism, when Voltaire told us that the purpose of the sun is to provide light for human beings on the earth, he himself admitted that there is no answer to this question. Voltaire fudged the issue when he called the universe an "admirable machine." There is a popular sense in which the word *machine* is by definition something that was designed to serve a certain purpose. Machines in this sense are "contraptions" or "devices." If it were known that the universe is a machine in this sense, it would indeed follow that it was designed for a purpose by an intelligent being. However, we most emphatically do not know that the universe is a machine in this sense.

This leaves Voltaire with the claim that the order of the world that is described by scientific laws requires an intelligent cause. Such an argument calls for several comments. First of all, it has been questioned whether the statement that the universe is orderly has any content. If it did, it should be possible to describe what a disorderly universe, i.e., a universe that is not governed by laws, would be like. But, as Leibniz already saw and as several contemporary philosophers have emphasized, this is not possible. This objection is not fatal to Voltaire's argument since he would maintain that it is not order as such but the simple and beautiful order described by Newton's laws that shows divine workmanship. The answer to this is twofold. First, we have no means of knowing that the simple order was initially so unlikely that only design would have brought it about. Since the universe occurs only once we cannot say that some other, more complex and less beautiful order, or, for that matter, some simpler and more beautiful order, was more likely. All we can do is note the order that the universe exhibits. In the second place, we have no reason whatever to suppose that the order that characterizes the universe at present did not always belong to it. On the contrary, we appear to have every reason to maintain that objects have always behaved in accordance with the same laws. We do not hesitate to predict that tomorrow or in the next century or millions of years from now objects will still behave in accordance with the laws of mechanics. We also do not hesitate to extrapolate our laws backward to the time of Julius Caesar or the ice age. What reason is there to suppose that, if we were to go still further back in time, the universe would exhibit different laws or no laws at all? Plato and various non-Christian religions, as we mentioned earlier, teach that originally the universe was in a state of chaos, whatever this might be. Such pronouncements are purely arbitrary. Voltaire did not believe in an original chaos but seems to have thought that his Demiurge was needed to transform the original universe with a different (and presumably less admirable) order into its present state. To suppose that at an earlier time the universe was governed by different laws is just as arbitrary as to suppose that it initially was in a state of pure chaos. Voltaire's confusion on this subject is well illustrated in a speech in the "Dialogues Between Posidonius and Lucretius." "You cannot persuade me," Posidonius tells Lucretius, that "the universe put itself into the admirable order in which we now find it." Indeed, not; but why should *anything* have put the admirable order into the universe? Why cannot this order have always been a feature of the universe? Some contemporary physicists maintain that we cannot extend any of our laws to the period before the "big bang," which they regard as a "singularity." This, too, seems arbitrary, but even if such a view is accepted it does not show that before the big bang objects behaved in accordance with other laws. It merely raises such a possibility.

It should be pointed out that we do not have any examples in our experience of intelligent causes, or for that matter of anything else, producing the kind of order now under discussion. Experience, therefore, gives us no guidance about the cause of such order, if indeed it has any. If it could really be demonstrated someday that the order exhibited by the universe at an earlier time was different from what it is today, this by itself would be no evidence whatever for an intelligent cause of such a change. One cannot help feeling that this entire question about the causation of the order or lawfulness found in the world is misguided and the result of the deep-seated belief, even on the part of some of those who have explicitly repudiated it, that the laws discovered by science "regulate" or "control" the world the way legal laws frequently do.

MORTALITY

Locke and the more conservative English deists believed or professed belief in life after death. On this topic Voltaire sided with the more radical deists. In spite of some equivocal and disingenuous passages in certain of his later works, there cannot be the slightest doubt that Voltaire believed that death is the end for man no less than for animals. He considers both of the main forms of survival—the resurrection of the body and the survival of the pure, disembodied mind. Discussions of the resurrection of the body find Voltaire in an ebullient mood. A subject of such gravity must be treated with appropriate reverence. He quite properly takes the word *resurrection* literally. God's production of a replica of my body, even if it ever took place, would not be a resurrection of *my* body. However, once we use the word in its proper sense, it becomes clear that the resurrection of most bodies would not be an easy thing, even for God. Both the Egyptians and the Greeks believed in resurrection, but in Egypt the embalmer's first tasks were to pierce the skull with a small hook and draw out the brain and to clear the entrails. How,

asks Voltaire, "were men to rise again without intestines and without the medullary part by means of which they think?" How were they "to find again the blood, the lymph and the other humors?" It was even more difficult to rise among the Greeks, where the corpse was frequently burned. How can you be restored to life if your body has become "a pound of ashes . . . mingled with the ashes of wood, stuffs and spices"? There is the further problem of children who die in the womb just after receiving their souls. Will such a being rise again as an embryo, a child, or an adult? St. Augustine believed that everybody would be resurrected with a body as it was or would have been at the age of 30. This is an interesting suggestion that has the merit of simplicity, but it invites the question of how a 30-year-old body could be supplied to a child who had died in the womb and who did not go through the intermediary stages to reach the age of 30. Baffling problems are also presented by cannibalism. Some of these, it should be noted, had already puzzled St. Thomas Aquinas. Consider the following situation: A soldier from Brittany, serving in Canada, is short of food and eats an Iroquois whom he had killed the previous day. For two or three months before his death, the Iroquois had been feeding on Jesuits. The soldier consists of Iroquois, Jesuits, and all that he had eaten before. How are all these people going to be resurrected? The problem is particularly acute in the case of the Jesuits, who were digested not once but twice. How could even God accomplish this feat?

If we rule out bodily resurrection, the question becomes whether consciousness by itself can survive. Voltaire's fullest serious discussion of this issue occurs in the *Traité de métaphysique*, the little volume that was not intended to be published in his lifetime. Here, he wrote with complete candor, and he ridicules the notion that thinking and feeling or any kind of mental life could proceed without the body. "I cannot help laughing when I am told that human beings still have ideas after they have lost their sense organs; I would just as readily believe that we could still eat and drink after we have lost our mouth and stomach." God has connected our capacity for thinking with a certain area of the brain, and it is no more possible for thinking to continue without this organ than it is for the song of a bird to continue after its throat has been destroyed in death. God could indeed have supplied both animals and men with an immortal soul, and he could have arranged matters in such a way that this immortal soul could exist independently of the body, just as he could have made human beings with two noses and four hands, and with wings and claws. God *could* have given us an immortal soul, but all indications are that he did not. "I who know that man did not exist yesterday," Voltaire wrote, "should I proclaim that there is a part in him which is indestructible? If I deny immortality to whatever it is that animates a dog, a parakeet or a thrush, how can I attribute immortality to human beings just because we would like it to be so?" Voltaire concedes that he does not possess conclusive proofs, but "all probable evidence" goes against immortality.

These were Voltaire's real and considered views on the subject, but they were not published by him. In his published statements Voltaire professes a complete theoretical agnosticism accompanied by a ringing pragmatic defense of the affirmative position. All these statements occur in the writings of the 1760s and early 1770s when Voltaire had become alarmed about what the spread of atheism might do to society. One of the best-known statements occurs in his polemic against Holbach's *System of Nature.* Holbach's philosophy is accused of "snatching consolation and hope" from suffering mankind. Voltaire grants that "philosophy furnishes no proof of a happiness to come" but insists that it also does not demonstrate the contrary. He then adds a reflection that sounds strange, coming from somebody who had always made fun of the philosophy of Leibniz, including the latter's theory of monads. "There may be in us an indestructible monad," Voltaire wrote, "which feels and thinks, without our knowing anything at all of how that monad is made." He then proceeds to argue, in the spirit of William James' "Will to Believe," that belief in an afterlife has a "prodigious advantage" over unbelief. It is "useful," while unbelief is "baneful." "We are all swimming in a sea of which we have never seen the shore." The unbeliever is like a man who cries out, "You swim in vain, there is no land"; and with his cry he "disheartens me and deprives me of all my strength." It should be noted that Voltaire himself did not believe that there was "land," and yet he was not disheartened in the least and did not lose any of his formidable strength.

The notion of an indestructible monad "inside of us" must have appealed to Voltaire's imagination. It appeared repeatedly in his writings of this period, each time with new embellishments. In one of the "Homilies" that he wrote in the 1760s, advocating natural religion in opposition to both Christianity and atheism, he begins by declaring once again that we are ignorant of "the principle which thinks in us." It follows that we cannot be certain that this "unknown principle" will not survive death. The indestructible monad is now described as a "hidden flame" and "a particle of divine fire." It is entirely "possible" that this divine particle does not die but merely "changes its form" when the body disintegrates. This "possibility" is transformed into a "probability" in the dialogues between Cu-Su, a wise disciple of Confucius, and the skeptical Prince Kou, the son of the King of Lou, which are included as "Chinese Catechism" in the *Philosophical Dictionary.* A thought, Prince Kou begins reasonably enough, "cannot be regarded as something material." It then should not be so difficult to believe that God has placed an "immortal and indissoluble principle" inside all of us. Surely this is not impossible. But if it is possible, "is it not also highly probable? Can you reject so noble a system and one which is so necessary to mankind?" DAVID FRIEDRICH STRAUSS, the great 19th-century German *Aufklärer* who wrote a highly sympathetic study of Voltaire's philosophy, loses his temper over this wretched argument, whose full wretchedness must have been apparent to Voltaire himself. "Somebody who cannot defend immortality in a better way," Strauss wrote, "would edify us more if he openly denied it." In partial extenuation it should be explained that the wise Cu-Su is at once answered by Prince Kou in a most convincing fashion. Although Prince Kou ultimately surrenders, most readers are likely to be far more impressed by his skeptical arguments, one of which, based on the nature of personal identity, is brilliant and original, than by the pious declarations of the ostensible victor.

Rejecting belief in life after death is harmful not only because it "disheartens" people and deprives them of their strength. It is even more damaging because it removes one of the most powerful sanctions against vice and crime. A small number of philosophical unbelievers with a peaceful disposition may not need hellfire as a deterrent. The same, however, is not true of the world's rulers, nor unfortunately of most ordinary men and women. "Eternal hell" may be an illusion, we read in the article "Hell" in the *Philosophical Dictionary,* "but it is a good thing for your servant, your tailor and even your lawyer to believe in it." The "fear of men" is not enough. "Shall we give ourselves up to fatal passions" asks Freind, the sage in *The Sage and the Atheist,* one of the fire and brimstone sermons that occur with increasing frequency in

Voltaire's writings of this period, "and live like brutes, with no other restraint upon us than the fear of men, rendered eternally cruel to each other by their mutual dread?" A man who fears no divine retribution in the hereafter is going to become a "God to himself," and he will sacrifice the whole world to his caprice. A poor and needy atheist "would be a fool if he did not assassinate or steal to get money." If atheism and its companion belief that death is final became common, all the bonds of society would be "sundered," "secret crimes" would inundate the world, and "like locusts" they would "spread over the earth." One cannot help feeling that in these and countless similar passages Voltaire expressed some deep-seated and largely irrational fear. The facts do not seem to bear him out at all. It may be granted that, just as in Voltaire's day, the world is filled with "knaves," with "persons addicted to brutality, intoxication and rapine," and generally with individuals who are cruel and callous. Experience shows that, within rather severe limits, their destructive impulses can be controlled by secular restraints. Fear of punishment in a hereafter seems to be totally ineffective. A cruel believer does not greatly differ from a cruel unbeliever as far as behavior is concerned. The difference lies largely in the kind of rationalization that will be offered.

That the views Voltaire expressed in the *Traité de métaphysique* were his real ones is shown beyond all doubt by remarks about death made to his friends and in his correspondence. His true views also frequently appear in his published writings when keeping potential evil-doers in check is not one of his prime concerns. That death is final and that nothing whatever awaits us afterward is evident both when Voltaire consoles himself and others by the thought that the absence of our consciousness, since it involves no suffering of any kind, is not something to be dreaded and when during fits of depression he likens man to a prisoner awaiting his death sentence. "When the hour arrives," he wrote in one of these moods, "it becomes clear that we have lived to no purpose, that all reflections are vain and all reasoning . . . only wasted words." Such fits of depression were rare, and more commonly Voltaire admonishes us to think about death as little as possible and to get on with the job of living. People who announce death ceremoniously "are the enemies of the human race; we must keep them from ever approaching us." "To cease to love and be lovable," he wrote in a short poem addressed to Mme. du Châtelet, "is a

death unbearable; to cease to live is nothing," and in a letter he repeated that "death is nothing at all—the idea alone is sad."

Although Voltaire missed no opportunity to denounce the atomistic materialism of Lucretius as wildly absurd, it is from Lucretius that he borrowed one idea he seemed to have found particularly consoling. "Why," he asked in the article "Why" in the *Philosophical Dictionary,* "as we are so miserable, have we imagined that not to be is a great ill, when it is clear that it was not an ill not to be before we were born?" This is straight out of Lucretius, and Lucretius is also one of the characters in a discussion concerning immortality in the *Dialogues Between Lucretius and Posidonius,* arguing for the mortality of the soul on the familiar ground that it is so closely tied to the body during life. "The effect at last ceases with the cause," Lucretius remarks, and "the soul vanishes like smoke into air." These are almost the words of the historical Lucretius. Posidonius, who is the ostensible spokesman for Voltaire's philosophy, does not even attempt to answer the argument.

Some of the earlier statements about death were taken from letters to Mme. du Deffand, an exceptionally sensitive old lady who had become blind. In one of his letters to her, Voltaire told of a man who compared us with a musical instrument that cannot produce a sound after it has been broken. This man held it as evidence that human beings had a beginning and an end just like all other animals, like plants and probably everything else in the world. He also taught that our best consolation concerning such evils as aging and death consists in our knowledge that they are inevitable. This man greatly admired the laughing Democritus, and when he became as old as Democritus he followed his master in laughing about everything. It goes without saying that this man was Voltaire himself.

MIRACLES

On the subject of miracles there can be no doubt where Voltaire stood. Miracles are completely at variance with what we know about the working of the world. Belief in miracles is also theologically unsound, and it degrades religion into a form of magic. The miracles reported throughout history are a mixture of fraud and nonsense. Moreover, the nonsense is not usually innocent, because it is used by priests and rulers to keep the common people in ignorance and subjection. Several philosophers, notably the English deists, PIERRE BAYLE, Middleton, and Hume, had written against miracles before Voltaire. Bayle and Hume had raised subtle difficulties that Voltaire ignored, but it was Voltaire's attack that had the most devastating impact. Voltaire had a wonderful eye for the absurd, and he also had vast learning in the history of religions, especially that of Christianity, which supplied him with an endless stream of hilarious illustrations. By the 1760s he had perfected his tongue-in-cheek style, and it was nowhere used to greater effect than in his treatment of miracles. After reading Voltaire, an intelligent reader could not help feeling that only a credulous fool would believe in anything so ridiculous.

Voltaire's various discussions of miracles are deliberately chaotic. He does not state a general thesis that is to be followed by supporting evidence. Instead, case is piled on case, each more absurd than the one before, and yet all of them miracles at one time widely accepted on the basis of supposedly unimpeachable evidence. Voltaire's general objections are mentioned almost as asides, and they are usually accompanied by pious declarations that, although reason may cause philosophers to spurn miracles, revelation and faith are superior guides. Philosophers may exalt "the immutability of the Supreme Being" and the eternity of his laws, but they are clearly mistaken since the histories of most nations are as full of miracles as of natural events. Give me the name of a country where incredible prodigies have not been performed, Voltaire wrote, especially at a time when the people could hardly read or write. It might in fact be laid down as a law that there is an inverse relationship between frequency of miracles and the level of education in any given nation. The number of miracles increases as the level of education declines, and it decreases as the people become more educated.

Voltaire was particularly amused by stories about animals that could talk. Not only could many animals talk in past ages, but they could also make the most accurate forecasts of fateful happenings. No less an authority than Titus Livius reported that one day in the marketplace in Rome an ox cried out to the crowds: "Rome, take care of yourself!" Pliny wrote that, when the tyrant Tarquin was driven from the throne, a dog commented on the event; and Suetonius vouched for the fact that a crow said—in Latin of course—"All is well" when Domitian was assassinated. A horse by the name of Xante told its master Achilles that he would be killed before Troy.

The gift of speech was also occasionally bestowed on fish. The fish Oannes made it a practice to come out of the Euphrates every day to deliver a sermon on its banks. Voltaire laconically observed that fish did not preach any more in his time, although St. Anthony of Padua had preached to the fish. However, that was not a miracle and in any event "such things happen so rarely nowadays, that most people pay no attention to them." The fish, incidentally, listened attentively to St. Anthony's admonitions, but after the sermon they all went their merry ways, much as human beings who ignore the advice of their spiritual guides.

Among both the Romans and the Christians, many people were miraculously cured of illnesses that did not respond to more natural methods. Perhaps the most impressive and best-attested of these cures were performed in Alexandria in the 1st century B.C. by the Roman emperor Vespasian, who is otherwise best remembered for building the Coliseum and for banishing the Stoic philosophers from Rome. What is so remarkable about the cures produced by Vespasian is that he himself had not previously been a believer in miracles. During his visit to Alexandria, two men, one blind and the other paralyzed, presented themselves before the emperor, imploring him to restore them to health. Vespasian modestly replied that he possessed no such healing powers. The two unhappy individuals then told the emperor that the god Serapis had appeared to them, announcing that they would be cured by Vespasian. Moved by their plight, the emperor consented to touch both men, but he warned them that success was most improbable. "Favoring his modesty and virtue," Voltaire writes, "the Divinity communicates to Vespasian his power and that instant the blind man sees and the lame one walks." This twin miracle was performed in the presence of innumerable spectators, Roman, Greek, and Egyptian. It has been preserved in the archives of the empire and is mentioned in all contemporary histories. And yet, Voltaire adds, it has in the course of time come to be universally disbelieved because nobody has "an interest" in the acceptance of its authenticity.

With relish Voltaire enumerated other miraculous cures, including that of a blind man by St. Ambrose. Ambrose had been informed in a dream where the bones of the martyred St. Gervasius and St. Protasius were lying. He promptly dug them up and used the holy relics to cure a blind man in the presence of numerous witnesses. This remarkable event occurred in Milan and is vouched for by no less an authority than St. Augustine, who was in the city at the time. In more recent times the kings of England, right up until William III, daily performed medical miracles. William (reigned 1689–1702) refused to continue the practice and his successors have followed his example. If England should "undergo a great revolution" so that the country once again slides into barbarism and ignorance, we may be confident that miracles will again be performed every day.

Many of the accounts of miracles have an inner lack of logic that makes it quite unnecessary to investigate the supposed evidence. St. Polycarp's last-minute rescue from the flames is a case in point. This miracle took place in the 2nd century, when Polycarp, the bishop of Smyrna, had been condemned by the Romans to be burnt at the stake. Several eyewitnesses heard a heavenly voice calling out to the bishop, "Courage Polycarp! Be strong, show yourself a man!" When Polycarp showed himself a man, the flames were diverted from his body, and a dove, the symbol of the Holy Ghost, flew out of the stake. The jubilations of Polycarp's partisans were, however, premature. Almost immediately after his deliverance from the flames, the luckless bishop had his head cut off. Philosophers will wonder why the executioner's axe was not also deflected.

Another of Voltaire's favorite miracles, which would bring a smile even to the face of a modern pope, concerns King Robert, who had been excommunicated by Pope Gregory V for marrying his godmother, Princess Bertha. After the king was excommunicated, his servants threw his dinner out of the window. This disrespectful treatment of the monarch, though strange enough, does not qualify as a miracle. The miraculous punishment for the incestuous marriage occurred when Queen Bertha was delivered of a goose. "I doubt," Voltaire observed, "if in our time the waiters of the King of France would, if he were excommunicated, throw his dinner out of the window and whether the Queen would give birth to a gosling."

The Romans did not show much interest in bringing the dead back to life. In other countries and among Christians, resurrections have been common. Among the Greeks the resurrections were usually carried out by gods. Hercules, Alcestis, and Pelops were all brought back by the gods. Pelops had been hacked to pieces by his father, and it has not been disclosed how the gods put the pieces of his body back together. Athalide, Mercury's daughter, had the gift of coming back to life at will and

repeatedly made use of it. Er, made famous for later generations by Plato, came back to the world after spending two weeks in hell. Aesculapius, who was chiefly noted for his miraculous treatment of illness, brought Hippolytus back to life. It should be remembered that the Greek gods were physical and that their activities, miraculous or otherwise, could be observed by human beings. In the case of Aesculapius, Voltaire tells us that "we still have documents containing the names of eyewitnesses." Among Christians, resurrections were accomplished not by gods but by saints. St. Francis Xavier, one of the founders of the Jesuit order, who was noted for the vast number of conversions he achieved on his missionary travels to India and the Far East, was spectacularly successful in this field. While in Japan, between 1549 and 1551, Xavier resurrected no less than eight bodies. This feat was altogether remarkable not only because, as Voltaire rightly notes, eight is quite a number, but also because Xavier had lost, or else had never possessed, the gift of tongues, a supernatural gift of a much lower order than that of resurrecting the dead. In his letters from Japan he complained that he felt like a "mute statue" since he could not understand or speak the language of the natives. In the case of Xavier's resurrections, it is important to remember—Voltaire tells us—that they were carried out 15,000 miles from home. Some people, he wryly adds, regard the expulsion of the Jesuits from France as a much greater miracle.

Jesus himself, of course, was no mean resurrector. He resurrected no less than three people—the daughter of Jairus, the son of the widow of Naim, and Lazarus, who had been dead four days. For Christians these miracles have always been "decisive and resplendent" evidence for the divinity of Jesus. If the rest of the world had known about them, it would surely have been instantly converted to Christianity. Unfortunately the rest of the world did not hear about them for at least 200 years. This is as amazing as it is regrettable. Neither the historian Josephus nor the scholarly Philo nor any of the Greek or Roman historians of the time mention even one of these resurrections. What is more, if these sensational events had really occurred, we may rest assured that the Jewish magistrates and especially Pontius Pilate would have undertaken the most minute investigations and obtained the most detailed and authentic depositions. Tiberius had ordered all proconsuls, prefects, and governors of provinces to inform him with exactness of all significant events, and Lazarus as well as the other two beneficiaries of Jesus' supernatural powers would have been interrogated. In the case of Lazarus, Voltaire notes in passing, "not a little curiosity would have been excited" about the fate of his soul during the four days when his body was dead. Suppose that God in our own time should send an ambassador to London and that this ambassador succeeded in raising several men from the dead. Would not everybody be talking about such remarkable occurrences and would not contemporary histories be filled with descriptions of these events and their repercussions? Not only did the world at large not hear about these miracles for 200 years, but fully a hundred years had passed before "some obscure individuals" showed one another writings that contained any mention of these events.

Voltaire was no admirer of the Jews of the Old Testament or, for that matter, of the Jews of any age; but, since the main enemy was Christianity and not Judaism, he delighted to point out that the miracles performed by God on behalf of the Jews were much more stupendous than any of those performed by Jesus. Who would not be impressed by such spectacles as the ten plagues of Egypt, the stopping of the stars in their course over Gibeon and Ajalon, and the sea's opening a passage and suspending its waves so that the Jews could safely go through! Compared to divine interventions on such a scale, miracles like that of the Gadarene swine or the fig tree or even the admittedly mind-boggling resurrection of Lazarus after his brain must already have been totally decayed are paltry. Voltaire approvingly quoted a heretical writer who compared the difference to that between a grand concert and a rustic ditty. Such dangerous reflections have "enchanted" not a few Christians who rashly and audaciously concluded that Judaism and not Christianity was the true religion. Instead of showing the miracles of Jesus "the respect to which they are entitled," these unfortunate men trusted their deceitful reason and maintained that, if God for many ages worked a train of "astonishing and tremendous miracles" in favor of what he himself had pronounced to be the true religion, he would not suddenly cause it to become a false one. For their own good, and for the good of the world, most of the admirers of Judaism have carefully concealed their apostasy from the public, but some misguided priests made no bones about their preference and openly derided the miracles of the New Testament. Suspending his tongue-in-cheek manner, Voltaire relates the case of Nicholas Anthony of Pont-à-Mousson in Lorraine. He first switched

to Calvinism, becoming for a short time a minister in Geneva, and then, not long afterward, was received as a Jew in Venice. He returned to Geneva and proclaimed to the judges and magistrates as well as to the people in the street that the Jewish religion was true, declaring that there was only one god and that Jesus was an impostor. Nicholas Anthony was put in chains and burnt at the stake in Geneva on April 20, 1632.

The most straightforwardly serious passages in Voltaire's articles on the miracles are concerned with the theological unsoundness of any such doctrine. Believing in miracles is an insult to God. It implies that, like a watchmaker who bungled his work, God is required to make repairs in the "immense machine" of the universe. If God is infinitely intelligent, then he foresaw all the unfortunate events that inspire men to pray for the suspension of his laws; and if he too had regarded the events in question as undesirable, he would have fashioned different laws. If it is argued that he failed to foresee the unfortunate events, then he is not infinitely intelligent and hence "he is no longer God." On the other hand, the request for a miracle here and there might not be unreasonable when addressed to a finite deity of the kind favored by Voltaire himself. For in that case God may not know everything and informing him of some unintended mishap might be the signal for rectification.

Also in a serious vein are Voltaire's remarks about the reasons for rejecting the testimony of the witnesses who vouched for the miracles recorded in various holy books. What Voltaire said here resembles Hume's critique, but his challenge was less sweeping and not open to some of the objections leveled at Hume. "In order to believe in a miracle," Voltaire opened one discussion, "it is not enough merely to have seen it." The reason for this is that even careful observers can be deceived. Many "excellent persons" who are in general quite trustworthy "think that they have seen what they have not seen and heard what was never said to them." They thus become witnesses of miracles that did not take place or, if they are suggestible and especially if they have a touch of madness, they may even become the subjects of miracles, for example, miraculous cures. Before paying the slightest attention to such a claim, it is necessary that "the miracle should have been seen by a great number of very sensible people, in sound health, and perfectly disinterested in the affair." When "interest mixes with the transaction," as it almost invariably does in the case of religious believers, "you may consider the whole affair worth nothing." This is so even if a whole nation testifies to the occurrence of the miracle. Above all, the witnesses should have solemnly sworn in writing to what they supposedly witnessed. Voltaire pointed out that in everyday transactions of a very simple kind, such as the purchase of a house, a marriage contract, or a will, we require "minute cautionary formalities" in writing. How much more necessary is the execution of such documents in order to verify "things naturally impossible on which the destiny of the world is to depend." Not one of the miracles described in the Old and New Testaments is supported by anything approximating such evidence. However, even this kind of evidence is not sufficient. For the sake of being fully verified, it would be desirable that a miracle "should be performed in the presence of the Academy of Sciences in Paris, or the Royal Society in London, and the Faculty of Medicine." This is not an unreasonable demand; for surely, if somebody can transform water into wine or resurrect a corpse, he should be able to do this regardless of who is in the audience. In view of the credulity of many scientists and their insufficient experience in detecting fraud, one may fault Voltaire for not requiring that the observers should include skeptical magicians like Houdini or the Amazing Randi.

Both before and since Voltaire's time skeptics have properly raised the question of what different miracles would prove if they had really occurred. It is not at all obvious that they would prove any of the theological assertions of those who champion them. Let us suppose that Jesus really made water into wine and that he really resurrected Lazarus. Such strange performances would no doubt require a revision in some of our common-sense beliefs and also in certain of our scientific theories, but they would not prove the existence of a Creator of the universe and they would also not show that Jesus was his son. Voltaire told of a philosopher who was asked what he would say if he saw the sun stop, if all the dead came back to life, and if all mountains fell into the ocean at the same time. "I would turn Manichean," replied the philosopher, "I would say that there is one principle that unmakes what the other principle has made."

Bibliography

Besterman, T. *Voltaire*. New York: 1969.

Brandes, G. *Voltaire*. Trans. O. Kruger and R. P. Butler. New York: 1930.

Lanson, G. *Voltaire*. Paris: 1910. Eng. trans. R. A. Wagoner. New York: 1960.

Pomeau, R. *La Religion de Voltaire*. Paris: 1956.

Strauss, D. F. *Voltaire: Sechs Vorträge*. Leipzig: 1870.

Torrey, N. L. *Voltaire and the English Deists*. New Haven: 1930.

———. *The Spirit of Voltaire*. New York: 1938.

Voltaire. *Oeuvres complètes*. 52 vols. Ed. L. Moland. Paris: 1877–85.

———. *Correspondance*. 107 vols. Ed. T. Besterman. Geneva: 1953–65.

———. *The Portable Voltaire*. Ed. B. R. Redman. New York: 1949.

———. *Philosophical Letters*. Trans. E. Dilworth. Indianapolis: 1961.

———. *Philosophical Dictionary*. 2 vols. Trans. P. Gay. New York: 1963.

———. *Selected Letters*. Trans. T. Besterman. London: 1963.

PAUL EDWARDS

W

WATSON, JAMES (1799–1874), British publisher of FREETHOUGHT tracts and an important radical reformer during the first half of the 19th century. He was born in Malton, Yorkshire, on Sept. 21. Like many other working-class reformers of the period, Watson attended charity schools from the age of six to twelve. He then did agricultural work for several years to support his mother and other members of his family.

In 1818, at a time of increasing political unrest, Watson moved to Leeds to work as a warehouseman. He joined a group of artisans who studied and debated the writings of radical reformers and freethinkers such as THOMAS PAINE, ELIHU PALMER, the Comte de Volney, and particularly RICHARD CARLILE, who was emerging as a militant champion of infidelity. Watson was by temperament a doer, not a thinker, and in 1822 he went to London to assist Carlile in one of his shops, which was under attack by the Society for the Suppression of Vice. For selling a deist book, Palmer's *Principles of Nature,* in Carlile's shop, he was tried and convicted of blasphemous libel in 1823 and sentenced to one year in Cold Bath Fields prison.

Watson used his prison experience to good effect, reading innumerable freethought and radical publications and engaging in a course of political self-education. After being released in April of 1824, he worked briefly for Carlile, learning the skills of a compositor and printer. He narrowly survived an attack of cholera in 1826, and then became a printer to the wealthy freethinker, JULIAN HIBBERT. From 1827 to 1829, he helped Hibbert issue several important anti-Christian publications.

Watson was an outspoken "infidel" during the late 1820s an early 1830s, although he was more a militant deist than an atheist. But involvement in radical politics, rather than a specific ideological commitment, was what motivated him. Thus, he took part in the Owenite cooperative movement (see ROBERT OWEN), in the agitation for universal suffrage, in trade-union activities, and in the struggle for an unstamped press. He was imprisoned twice during the 1830s for selling illegal penny newspapers, and his own penny paper, the *Working Man's Friend* (1832–33), was one of the best illegal papers of the decade. He also worked closely with William Lovett in the early stages of the Chartist movement.

But despite his involvement in manifold radical activities, Watson's forte was as a publisher, particularly of freethought literature. In the early 1830s, he began to issue many anti-Christian works in cheap editions by writers such as Paine, Palmer, PAUL HENRI HOLBACH, FRANCES WRIGHT, Lord Byron, PERCY BYSSHE SHELLEY, and ROBERT DALE OWEN. In 1834 a bequest of 450 guineas from Hibbert's estate enabled him to expand his business and, from a series of shops in the Finsbury section of London, to issue large quantities of tracts and books.

In 1840 he gave considerable support to HENRY HETHERINGTON, who was tried and convicted of blasphemy for selling Charles Haslam's *Letters to the Clergy of All Denominations.* He also began a close relationship with GEORGE JACOB HOLYOAKE, who succeeded Carlile as the leader of working-class unbelievers. From 1846 to 1854, Watson published Holyoake's *Reasoner,* one of the chief freethought journals of the 19th century. He also helped to found the London Secularist Society in 1853.

Holyoake's purchase of Watson's publishing business in 1854 in effect ended the latter's career as a radical reformer. In 1865, Watson moved with his family to Norwood in south London, where he died in 1874. He is buried in Norwood Cemetery. Watson was a self-effacing reformer of modest abilities who wrote comparatively little. He is best known for his involvement in the struggle to achieve a free press.

Other articles of interest: **Blasphemy Laws.**

Freedom of the Press and Unbelief.

Bibliography

There is no modern biography of Watson. However, the following works contain a brief, rounded view of his life: W. J. Linton, *James Watson: A Memoir* (Hamden, Conn.: 1879); George Jacob Holyoake, *Sixty Years of an Agitator's Life,* 2 vols. (London: 1892); and the *Reasoner* 16 (Feb. 5, 1854).

The following books contain material on different aspects of Watson's life: E. P. Thompson, *The Making of the English Working Class* (London: 1963); Joel H. Wiener, *The War of the Unstamped* (Ithaca, N.Y.: 1969); Thomas Frost, *Forty Years' Recollections* (London: 1880); William Lovett, *Life and Struggles* (London: 1876); and Joseph McCabe, *A Rationalist Encyclopaedia* (London: 1948).

JOEL H. WIENER

WATTS, CHARLES (1836–1906), English freethought writer and publisher, was born in Bristol into a devout Methodist family. He showed an early penchant for public debate, often speaking in favor of temperance and giving dramatic readings. The disavowal of alcohol was based primarily on his Wesleyan upbringing. At the age of 15 his outlook about religion was greatly altered when he heard GEORGE JACOB HOLYOAKE lecture in Bristol. Charles' brother John was also "converted" to SECULARISM by this lecture.

At the age of 16, Charles Watts moved to London, where he soon became friendly with CHARLES SOUTHWELL and Robert Cooper. He joined his brother John in the printing business in 1864. John was then the temporary proprietor of the NATIONAL REFORMER, where Charles soon became subeditor. When John Watts died unexpectedly in 1866, CHARLES BRADLAUGH became the proprietor and Charles remained as subeditor under him until 1877.

Controversy. In 1877, there was a major controversy in the FREETHOUGHT movement in England; the issues were birth control and freedom of the press. Historically, birth control has been a divisive issue for freethinkers. Examples would be DEROBIGNE MORTIMER BENNETT and Anthony Comstock, CHARLES KNOWLTON, and WILLIAM

STEWART ROSS versus Bradlaugh. In 1877, Watts, Bradlaugh and ANNIE BESANT published a new edition of Knowlton's *The Fruits of Philosophy,* an early birth-control book. Without the knowledge of these three, the printer inserted some obscene pictures into some volumes of the edition. The books were seized by the police, and an action for publication of an obscene libel was brought against Watts, Bradlaugh, and Besant. Watts decided to plead guilty, while Besant and Bradlaugh pleaded not guilty, citing freedom of the press (in addition to the fact that they had no knowledge of the insertion of the obscene plates). Watts' action was viewed by Bradlaugh and Besant as a betrayal of the cause of freedom of thought. He broke completely with them, including partnership in the Freethought Publishing Company.

After the break Watts set up his own publishing company, at first known as C. Watts, but later as Watts & Company. The company survived the 1880–90 period by serving as printer for most of the publications produced by W. Stewart & Co., which was run by Ross. Ross and Watts were both against the Malthusianism of Bradlaugh. The two also worked together in the production of the *Secular Review,* from 1882 to 1884. Watts established the British Secular Union in 1878, mostly as an alternative to Bradlaugh's NATIONAL SECULAR SOCIETY.

In 1884 Watts took his family to Canada. He had been asked by the Toronto Secular Society to become their lecturer because of his great skill on the platform. Watts stayed for the next six years. He returned to England in early 1891, upon the death of Bradlaugh. While Watts was in Canada, he single-handedly revived and ran the Canadian freethought movement. Watts lectured widely in both Canada and the northern United States during this period. He also founded and published *Secular Thought,* the most important Canadian freethought magazine (1885–1911). While Watts was in Canada his son, Charles A. Watts, ran the publishing business in England.

Upon the elder Watts' return to England, he was offered the position of leader of the Birmingham Secular Society, which met at Baskerville Hall. The society was undercapitalized and soon found itself in financial difficulty. Watts returned to London, where he continued his publishing and printing business. The formation of the Rationalist Press Association (R.P.A.) in 1896 was a major milestone in the progress of Watts & Company. It marked the beginning of an association that was to last about 60 years and assure the survival of Watts' business. The R.P.A. published its first best-seller in 1900, JOSEPH MCCABE's translation of ERNST HAECKEL's *The Riddle of the Universe*. The great success of this book was exactly what both the R.P.A. and Watts needed; it marked the start of a publishing program that resulted in the sale of hundreds of thousands of cheaply printed free-thought books. The "Cheap Reprint" series was especially popular, while the "Thinker's Library" also sold well.

Watts was described as follows: "A man of handsome presence, he had a massive and shapely head, an open expansive countenance, full-orbed luminous expressive eyes which glowed when activated by emotion, a flexible resonant voice, and a keen dramatic sense, which, had he gone on the stage, would have made him an actor of distinction. These attributes and talents, combined with a full knowledge and mastery of his subjects, won for him a foremost place on the freethought platform as an orator and debator." (J. P. Gilmour; see Bibliography below).

Some of Watts' debates are available in published form, notably those with George Sexton (*Christianity and Secularism: Which Is Better Suited to Meet the Wants of Mankind?* London: Smart & Allen, 1881); with Alexander Jamieson (*Is It Reasonable to Believe in the Existence of a Powerful and Intelligent Being Distinct from the Material Universe?* and *Has Man a Soul That Will Live in a Future State?* Glasgow: R. L. Holmes, 1894); and with B. H. Cowper (*Debate on the Christian Evidences*. London: C. Watts, 1871).

Many of Watts' publications were in the form of pamphlets. These number at least 45, and are now very scarce. Most of them were originally published as articles in one of the freethought journals. Watts also wrote three books: *The Miracles of Christian Belief: A Reply to the Rev. Frank Ballard's "Miracles of Unbelief"* (London: Watts, 1902), *The Meaning of Rationalism and Other Essays* (London: Watts, 1905), and *The History of Freethought* (London: Freethought Publishing Co., about 1877).

Watts was the father of Charles A. Watts (1858–1946) and the grandfather of Frederick C. C. Watts (1896–1953), both of whom carried on the family publishing business and the R.P.A. Charles Watts died in 1906, a year notable for its great losses to the freethought movement (Holyoake, Ross, and JOSEPH SYMES).

Bibliography

Gilmour, J. P. "Charles Watts (1836–1906). A Reminiscence and an Appreciation." *The Literary Guide* (London). Aug. 1935.

[Green, H. L.] "Charles Watts." *Free Thought Magazine* (Chicago). Jan. 1899.

Law, Harriet T. "Charles Watts." *The Secular Chronicle* (Birmingham, England). April 21, 1878.

Ross, W. S. [Saladin]. *Sketch of the Life & Character of C. Watts*. London: W. Stewart & Co., n.d.

Royle, Edward. *Radicals, Secularists and Republicans. Popular Freethought in Britain, 1866–1915*. (Manchester: U. of Manchester Press and Totowa, N.J.: Rowman & Littlefield, 1980).

GORDON STEIN

WELLS, HERBERT GEORGE (1866–1946), British writer. The ATHEISM of H. G. Wells, like that of many other Victorian and Edwardian thinkers, resulted from a collision between his early Christian-fundamentalist upbringing and post-Darwinian science. And, as with many of his contemporaries, the religious images of childhood returned to haunt and embarrass him in later years.

In the case of Wells, the Low Church atmosphere was provided by his mother, Sarah Neal, the daughter of a Midhurst innkeeper. His father, Joseph Wells, was a small-time professional cricketer, an unsuccessful shopkeeper, and a pleasantly irresponsible ne'er-do-well.

Early Life. Herbert George, the youngest of four children, was born at Bromley, Kent, on Sept. 21. His childhood was impoverished and unsettled. He was sent to a local "academy" for a basic primary education. When he was 14 the Wells household broke up. His mother went to work as a housekeeper at Up Park in Sussex, and young Bertie was left largely to care for himself, although he frequently stayed with his mother at Up Park, and later recalled that the house there "abounded in bold and enlightening books" which he was allowed to carry off to his room.

Wells' entire life was punctuated with intervals of illness and convalescence. He himself was of the opinion that some of these early periods of enforced inactivity were responsible for his escape from the semiliterate poverty that seemed destined to be his future. A broken leg, a ruptured kidney, bouts with incipient tuberculosis and diabetes continually broke into his schooling and employment and provided opportunities for him to read and nourish his mind.

After a year at Midhurst Grammar School, he was apprenticed as a draper's assistant, but at the age of 17 he broke his apprenticeship to become a pupil-teacher ("usher") back at Midhurst. This was arranged through the generosity and faith of the headmaster, Horace Byatt, who thereby earned Wells' lifelong gratitude. The position at Midhurst required that he be confirmed in the Church of England. Young Wells submitted himself to the ceremony but with a heavy conscience. He later recalled that he felt as an early Christian might have in being forced to offer a pinch of incense to Divus Caesar. In 1884 he won a government scholarship to the Normal School of Science in South Kensington, where he came under the lasting influence of THOMAS HENRY HUXLEY. Huxley confirmed his earlier "vague and instinctive disbelief in Christianity."

Wells held brief teaching positions at North Wales, Kilburn, and the University Correspondence College at Cambridge, at the same time working toward his bachelor of science at the University of London. He eventually received a doctor of science and an honorary degree of letters from the same institution. As a teacher he was conscientious and well organized, and he was remembered by many of his students as both genial and effective, despite a noticeable cockney accent.

Relations with Women. As soon as Wells had taken his degree at the age of 25, he married his cousin, Isabel, and became a householder in Putney. He had already begun to supplement his teaching income with freelance journalism and short stories. He achieved some prominence with the publication of *The Time Machine* (1895) and *The War of the Worlds* (1898). The marriage, though the culmination of a long and warm friendship, was not satisfactory. Isabel had neither the passion nor the inquiring intellect that Wells thought he was in search of.

Shortly after his marriage Wells formed an attachment with one of his biology students, Amy Catherine Robbins, a young widow. They caused considerable scandal in turn-of-the-century London by openly living together while Wells was still officially married to Isabel. When a divorce was obtained, Wells and Amy Catherine (whom he renamed "Jane") entered into a marriage that lasted formally until her death in 1927. Jane efficiently managed his houses and his business affairs, was a generous and gracious hostess, and the mother of their two sons. Wells himself recognized her as a significant factor in his rise to fame.

But the women in Wells' life could never live up to the fantasies they had inspired. Jane quietly observed a series of liaisons, some of them lasting a decade and resulting in separate households and at least two illegitimate children. At the same time Wells, increasingly wealthy, built and bought houses for himself and Jane: Spade House at Sandgate near Folkestone and Easton Glebe at Little Easton, Sussex. Wells shocked even his fellow Fabians—presumably the "advanced" set— by an affair with one of their daughters, Amber Reeves, with whom he settled for a time in France. The union produced a daughter, and Amber later married someone else. Characteristically, Wells remained cordial with all parties. From 1913 to 1923 Wells maintained an additional household with the noted author and feminist Rebecca West. This union resulted in a son, Anthony.

Three years before Jane's death, when Wells was 58, he began an extended liaison with a European admirer, Odette Keun, who was 36. They met in Switzerland and settled near Cannes. Here he built another "permanent" home. This affair, like the others, eventually soured and broke up in 1933. Odette later published a bitter exposé. There were briefer episodes with Margaret Sanger and Moura Budberg, the baroness von Benckendorff.

None of these affairs was in any way clandestine. Wells early enunciated his advocacy of free love— which he painstakingly kept explaining was not the same as "indiscriminate love." These attitudes spilled over into his novels: *Love and Mr. Lewisham* (1900), *In the Days of the Comet* (1906), and *Ann Veronica* (1909), increasing his popularity and bringing moralistic condemnation upon him. Some of his other novels were autobiographical, at least in part: *Kipps* (1905), *Tono Bungay* (1909), *The Secret Places of the Heart* (1922).

Wells' unconventionality extended beyond his views on sex and marriage. He thought of himself as a socialist (though not a Marxist), and was, for a few years, an influential member of the Fabian Society. He wanted, however, to expand that organization and transform it. He found it an elitist little band of specialists content to promote its influence through research, publications, lectures, and summer schools. He wanted to make it an aggressive political force. In this he found himself opposed by the "old gang," principally Beatrice and Sidney Webb and GEORGE BERNARD SHAW. Wells was unskilled in organizational work and temperamentally unsuited for it. When he failed to carry his motions on the floor of the Fabian Society, he withdrew.

In print, however, his social and political ideas continued to spark discussion. From his *Anticipations* (1901), which first brought him into real prominence, through *A Modern Utopia* (1905) and *The Shape of Things to Come* (1933), he preached a new Platonic order of civilization, a "New Republic" that would have to be brought into existence by "a new mass of capable men," variously referred to as "the Samurai" and the "Open Conspiracy." Perhaps to speed the emergence of such a society he undertook three massive studies: *The Outline of History* (1920), *The Science of Life* (with Julian Huxley and G. P. Wells, 1929), and *The Work, Wealth, and Happiness of Mankind* (1932).

With the approach of World War I, Wells saw the need for a world state, and in the autobiographical novel, *Mr. Britling Sees It Through* (1916), *God the Invisible King* (1917), and other writings he postulated the need for some divine force to bring about a Wellsian world. He later spoke of these references to divinity as a temporary aberration. Though the notion of a supernatural power crops up here and there in Wells' writing, he maintained, on balance, the SECULARISM of his school days.

In his later works Wells pictures man's choice as either controlling the universe, or succumbing to the evil laws of nature. He came to believe that only the threat of complete disaster could move people sufficiently to save civilization. In his *Experiment in Autobiography* (1934) he attempts "the story of how I came upon, and amidst what accidents I doubted, questioned, and rebelled against accepted interpretations of life; and so went on to find the pattern of the key to master our world and release its imprisoned promise."

Wells' influence on his contemporaries, particularly on the younger generation, was pervasive and permanent. His more than 100 books significantly helped to shape the thinking of the 20th century, especially in the matters of popularizing science and liberalizing sexual mores. But as a purely literary figure, his survival is questionable. Late-century readers find his novels plodding and the psychology of his characters overly obvious.

Wells' most lively and permanent contribution would seem to be as a futurist and progenitor of science fiction—called in his time "scientific romance." As a futurist he is given credit for predicting the use of the armored tank and the formation of the League of Nations. It is in these imaginary flights that his scientific background, his fascination with the future, and his yarn-spinning talents find their best combined expression. *The Time Machine, The War of the Worlds, The First Men in the Moon* (1898), *In the Days of the Comet,* and *The Conquest of Time* (1942) all attest to these qualities.

If further evidence were needed, on Oct. 30, 1938, in a New York studio, Orson Welles, as a Halloween prank, broadcast a radio dramatization of *The War of the Worlds* which millions of listeners mistook for a news report. Residents of the northeastern United States sat before their radios in frozen terror or fled in panic, thinking Martians were invading New Jersey. H. G. Wells was reportedly shocked at the news of the broadcast, but the effect was ironically appropriate, since much of his work shows an obsession with man's "fall," the end of the world, or the end of the human race.

As a world-famous public figure Wells visited heads of state, including V. I. LENIN, Joseph Stalin, and Presidents Theodore Roosevelt, Warren Harding, Herbert Hoover, and Franklin D. Roosevelt, seeking hopefully for the "Open Conspiracy" that would bring the world to its senses and prevent future wars. He was generally well received. As a personality he was outgoing and fun-loving. He made friends easily, but he was also quick-tempered and subject to childlike emotional storms. He had few intimates. Nevertheless he maintained a warm relationship with many of his literary colleagues: George Gissing, Joseph Conrad, Henry James, Ford Madox Ford, Stephen Crane, Arnold Bennett, and Shaw.

Despite his always fragile health, Wells remained productive throughout his seventies, though his later works became repetitive and less vigorous. He died in his 80th year on Aug. 13, 1946.

Bibliography

Archer, William. *God and Mr. Wells*. New York: Knopf, 1917.

Belloc, Hilaire. *A Companion to Mr. Wells's Outline of History*. London: Sheed and Ward, 1926.

Brown, Ivor. *H. G. Wells*. London: Nisbet, 1923.

Dickson, Lovat. *H. G. Wells: His Turbulent Life*

and Times. New York: Atheneum, 1969.

Mackenzie, Norman, and Jean MacKenzie. *H. G. Wells.* New York: Simon and Shuster, 1973.

Nicholson, Norman. *H. G. Wells.* London: 1950.

Parrubder, Patrick, ed. *H. G. Wells: The Critical Heritage.* London: Routledge and Kegan Paul, 1972.

Vallentin, A. *H. G. Wells: Prophet of Our Day.* New York: J. Day, 1950.

Wagar, W. Warren. *H. G. Wells and the World State.* New Haven: Yale U. Press, 1961.

Wells, H. G. *The Essex Edition of the Works of H. G. Wells.* 24 vols. London: 1926–1927.

———. *Mind at the End of Its Tether.* London: Heinemann, 1945.

———. *The Outlook for Homo Sapiens.* London: Secker and Warburg, 1942.

Williamson, Jack. *H. G. Wells: Critic of Progress.* Baltimore: Mirage Press, 1973.

WARREN SYLVESTER SMITH

WHEELER, JOSEPH MAZZINI (1850–1898), British author and scholar of unbelief, was born in London, spent his early working years in Edinburgh as a lithographer, and then became acquainted with the FREETHOUGHT press. Wheeler was soon writing articles for the London freethought magazines. He was invited to London by GEORGE WILLIAM FOOTE, who first made Wheeler's acquaintance in 1868. From then on, they were very close friends.

Although Wheeler had little formal education, he had the inquisitive mind and the pertinacity of the successful scholar. From the time he moved to London in the 1870s, Wheeler was most often to be found in the reading room of the British Museum. After years of study there, he became the world's foremost authority on the bibliography of freethought and atheistic books.

Wheeler was also a prolific writer, mostly of articles. He became the subeditor of the FREETHINKER when Foote started that magazine in 1881. He remained subeditor, and was briefly editor while Foote was serving a term in prison for blasphemy. While Wheeler was acting as editor, in 1883, his highly nervous temperament was subjected to an additional strain. He was also worried about Foote's imprisonment. As a result, he had the first of what may be called a "nervous breakdown." He recovered after a convalescence of several months.

The high point of Wheeler's freethought scholarship can be seen in his *Biographical Dictionary of Freethinkers.* It contains identifications of authors of anonymous works whose identity had not been revealed previously. The book is marred by many typographical errors but remains a monument to Wheeler's scholarship.

It is unfortunate that Wheeler's projected *History of Freethought in England* was never completed. A few sections of it were published over the years in the *Freethinker.* The present location of the manuscript is unknown. Wheeler completed several other books, many of which originally appeared as a series of magazine articles. Among these are *Bible Studies* and *Footsteps of the Past,* both of which are mainly anthropological in nature. Wheeler was the coauthor, with Foote, of *Crimes of Christianity* and coeditor, also with Foote, of the English translation of the *Sepher Toldoth Jeschu,* also known as the *Jewish Life of Christ.*

Wheeler died rather suddenly in 1898 after another breakdown. Very little has been written about him.

Bibliography

Wheeler's books are *Biographical Dictionary of Freethinkers of All Ages and Nations* (London: 1889); *Footsteps of the Past: Essays on Human Evolution* (London: 1895); and *Bible Studies: Essays on Phallic Worship and Other Curious Rites and Customs* (London: 1892). There are articles on Wheeler in the *Freethinker,* Oct. 21, 1915 (by A. B. Moss); May 18, 1956 (by Victor E. Neuburg); and an obituary on May 15, 1898. There was also an article the same day in the *Reformer* (London).

GORDON STEIN

WHITMAN, WALT (1819–1892), American poet. See **American Literature, Unbelief in.**

WIXON, SUSAN HELEN (1847–1912), American writer. See **American Literature, Unbelief in.**

WOMEN AND UNBELIEF. A good case can be made, many would say, for the fact that women have been the main support for the churches and the major bulwarks of religion throughout history. Nevertheless, as with many generalizations, this one is not completely true. There were many women who dared to be different and to speak out against religion, or the abuses of religion. A number of these women have been the subjects of separate articles in this Encyclopedia: ANNIE BESANT, VOLTAIRINE DE CLEYRE, EMMA GOLDMAN, HARRIET LAW, EMMA MARTIN, MADALYN MURRAY O'HAIR, ERNESTINE ROSE, and FRANCES WRIGHT.

Other women are treated within longer articles. Examples are Susan B. Anthony, Matilda Joselyn Gage, George Eliot, Elmina Drake Slenker, Susan Wixon, and Elizabeth Cady Stanton. There are still other women, largely unknown to the public, who played a smaller yet still significant role in the history of unbelief. Their names are gathered here for a short discussion of these diverse women who acted at different periods in history and in different locations.

Hypatia Bradlaugh Bonner (1858–1935) was CHARLES BRADLAUGH's younger daughter. After the death of her elder sister, Alice, in 1888, she became her father's main assistant and spent most of her life honoring and perpetuating his memory. She and her husband, Arthur Bonner, formed the publishing company of A & HB Bonner in about 1891, and it lasted until about 1903. They republished many of Bradlaugh's pamphlets in collected volume form, and also published a number of other FREETHOUGHT books and pamphlets. She was briefly a student at the City of London College, until a public outcry was made against having the daughter of a public atheist in attendance. Both Hypatia and Annie Besant had to leave the school, and as a result, all women were refused admittance for a few years.

Hypatia Bradlaugh made her first public speech during 1877, when her father was being prosecuted for having republished *The Fruits of Philosophy*. She taught at the Halls of Science secular schools, and lectured regularly. She was the joint author, with JOHN M. ROBERTSON, of the first full biography of her father: *Charles Bradlaugh: A Record of His Life and Work*. After her father's death, she edited a freethought periodical called the *Reformer*.

Mrs. Bradlaugh Bonner was a delegate to a number of international freethought congresses; her fluency in French was helpful in her reports of the proceedings printed in the British freethought press. Hypatia also wrote several other books, including *The Christian Hell, Christianizing the Heathen* and *Penalties upon Opinion*. Her biography was written by her husband and her son.

Eliza Sharples Carlile (about 1805–1861), born Elizabeth Sharples, was the second (common-law) wife of RICHARD CARLILE. Born into a respectable family, she grew up in Lancashire. She first read Carlile's works after being told by her parents that he was a horrible man. She subsequently visited Carlile in jail, and became emotionally involved with him. After his release from jail and his separation from his wife, Jane, Eliza and Richard lived together as man and wife in what he called "a moral marriage."

Eliza became the first woman freethought lecturer in England (preceded by Frances Wright in America) when she began lecturing at the Rotunda in 1832. For fear of embarrassing her family, she used the name "Isis" or the "Lady of the Rotunda" during her lectures, which were well attended and more scholarly than would have been thought possible from her background. There is suspicion among some scholars that they were written for her by ROBERT TAYLOR. The lectures were subsequently published in *Isis*, a journal she edited.

Eliza gave birth to three children by Richard Carlile. After he died in 1843, she managed to eke out a small living by running a tearoom at which many old radicals gathered. When Charles Bradlaugh was forced to leave home after being accused of ATHEISM by his pastor, Eliza took him in as a boarder.

Helen Hamilton Gardener (1853–1925) was a freethought author and lecturer. Her most popular book was *Men, Women and Gods* (1885), which had a preface by ROBERT G. INGERSOLL. She was born in Virginia, and showed writing ability at an early age. She became known to the public when she made a series of public lectures, still an uncommon thing for a respectable woman to do in those days, especially when religion was criticized. Her three novels were translated into German.

Anne Nicol Gaylor (born 1926) is a second-generation freethinker. She grew up on a farm in Wisconsin, went to the University of Wisconsin, and began a career in journalism. In 1976 she founded the FREEDOM FROM RELIGION FOUNDATION at Madison. This organization was formed by a number of members of the American Atheists who were expelled by Madalyn Murray

O'Hair. Mrs. Gaylor has appeared on many radio and televsion shows to promote what she calls the "nontheist" viewpoint. Her organization publishes a monthly newspaper, *Freethought Today*, and fights for separation of church and state. Mrs. Gaylor is also active in various feminist causes.

Marilla Ricker (1840–1920) was born in New Hampshire. An attorney, she was one of the first women admitted to practice before the U.S. Supreme Court. She was a frequent contributor to the TRUTH SEEKER and offered to donate copies of that magazine and of the complete works of Robert G. Ingersoll to any library that would take them. She wrote a number of books, including *I'm Not Afraid. Are You?*, in which her opinions on religion are made clear.

Matilda Roalfe (1813–1880) was a fighter for freedom of speech and of the press. When a series of blasphemy prosecutions occurred in Edinburgh in 1843, she went there from London and opened a bookshop that sold all of the prosecuted items, plus some of her own. Then she issued a public circular in which she announced her intentions of defying the BLASPHEMY LAWS and was soon prosecuted for selling THOMAS PAINE's *The Age of Reason* and CHARLES SOUTHWELL's *The Oracle of Reason*. Bravely she announced that she would continue to sell them as soon as she was liberated. She served two months in prison for her blasphemy conviction, apparently the only woman ever convicted alone of blasphemy (since the Carlile shopkeepers were in a group or sequential prosecution). After her release, she did indeed continue to sell the proscribed works, but was not prosecuted again. She later married Walter Sanderson and settled at Galashiels, where she died.

Etta Donaldson Semple (1855–1914), born in Illinois, settled in Ottawa, Kansas. There she founded and was president for many years of the Kansas Freethought Association. She edited a freethought magazine called the *Freethought Ideal* in the 1890s, and was a generous benefactor of the sanitarium in Ottawa.

Many other women played smaller roles in the history of unbelief, including Josephine Tilton, Mattie D. Freeman, Mattie Krekel, Lucy Colman, Ella E. Gibson, Lillian Leland, Katie Kehm Smith, Kate E. Watts, the Ingersoll women, and Agnes Wilson Symes.

Bibliography

Bonner, Arthur, and Charles Bradlaugh Bonner. *Hypatia Bradlaugh Bonner: The Story of Her Life*. London: Watts, 1942.

Gaylor, Annie Laurie. "Etta Semple: A Woman of Mystery." *Freethought Today* 2, no. 3 (April/May 1985).

Macdonald, G. M. *Fifty Years of Freethought*. 2 vols. New York: Truth Seeker, 1929.

Putnam, Samuel P. *400 Years of Freethought*. New York: Truth Seeker, 1894.

Stein, Gordon. *Freethought in the United Kingdom and the Commonwealth*. Westport, Conn.: Greenwood Press, 1981.

Wheeler, Joseph Mazzini. *Biographical Dictionary of Freethinkers of All Ages and Nations*. London: Progressive Publishing Company, 1889.

GORDON STEIN

WOOLSTON, THOMAS (1669 or 1670–1733), one of the best-known English deists of the 18th century, was born at Northampton. In 1685 he entered Sidney Sussex College at Cambridge, and in time received his bachelor of arts and bachelor of divinity degrees. He took orders, and became a fellow of the college.

Woolston was a diligent student of the early Church Fathers. In particular, he became a devotee of patristic modes of biblical interpretation, which he found preferable to what he considered the literalism of the preachers of his own time. This preference showed up in his first book, *The Old Apology for the Truth of the Christian Religion Against the Jews and Gentiles Revived* (1705), in which, following some of the Fathers, he interpreted Moses as a "type" of Christ and the Israelites as a "type" of the Christian church. In this typological interpretation, the historicity of Moses and Israel practically disappeared.

During the 1720s Woolston wrote voluminously, particularly in defense of the allegorical method of biblical interpretation. His career reached its climax with the publication, between 1727 and 1730, of six *Discourses on the Miracles of Our Saviour*. The Newtonian world view, as interpreted philosophically by JOHN LOCKE, had been widely accepted by the time Woolston was writing. That acceptance had posed the old questions about miracles in new ways. Locke himself, in *The Reasonableness of Christianity*, had argued that any "reasonable" person would be convinced that Jesus was the Messiah by two kinds of evidence: the internal proof of the moral goodness of Jesus' life, and the two external proofs: the fulfillment of prophecy and the performance of miracles.

ANTHONY COLLINS had already attacked the argument from the fulfillment of prophecy in his *Discourse of the Grounds and Reasons of the Christian Religion* (1724) and *The Scheme of Literal Prophecy Considered* (1727). Later in the century DAVID HUME and Conyers Middleton would attack the argument from miracles in their own way. But Woolston's approach was in many ways the most startling.

Woolston admired the work of the great Alexandrian theologian and exegete Origen, who had employed St. Paul's distinction between letter and spirit as a key to biblical interpretation. "The letter kills," Paul had written, "but the spirit gives life." Origen had perfected the Christian version of the allegorical method as a defense of the "underlying," nonliteral meaning of scripture against pagan attacks. What the pagans found anthropomorphic, crude, or silly became simply the first, the literal, or bodily meaning. Only the truly learned could get at the deeper moral and "spiritual" (or allegorical) meanings. Woolston's treatment of the miracle stories of the New Testament seemed to be following Origen's lead, but his method produced drastically different results. Where for Origen the literal meaning of a text was a first, bodily meaning, for Woolston the literal meaning was one for which he had disdain and contempt.

Woolston announced in his first discourse that "the literal history of many of the miracles of Jesus, as recorded by the evangelists, does imply absurdities, improbabilities, and incredibilities." But when Jesus appealed to his miracles as a witness of his divine authority, he did not, Woolston was sure, refer to these acts done in the flesh, but to "those mystical ones, which he would do in the Spirit." Having made this contrast, Woolston proceeded through story after story, ridiculing the "absurdities" of each, and quoting a variety of Church Fathers about the superiority of the allegorical method.

In the sixth (and final) discourse, Woolston subjected the resurrection narratives to the same treatment, this time having a fictitious rabbi conduct the examination of the evidence. When he then appraised the rabbi's results, he concluded that the difficulties posed should force preachers either to agree with him (that there was no literal, physical resurrection), or else "they must give up

their Religion as well as their Church."

In 1729, Woolston was arrested on a charge of blasphemy. He was convicted, fined 100 pounds, and sentenced to a year's imprisonment. He was granted the relative freedom of the Rules of the King's Bench, but was unable to pay his fine. Furthermore, he refused to retract his published position or to promise to desist from further writing. Under house arrest, he died on Jan. 27, 1733 and was buried in St. George's churchyard in Southwark.

Woolston was something of an enigma to his contemporaries. His first biographer saw him as a "man of probity, understanding and learning," who died "under persecution for religion." But Jonathan Swift, who despised every form of DEISM, wrote in "Verses on the Death of Dr. Swift" about Woolston with characteristic irony:

> He shews, as sure as God's in Gloc'ster,
> That Jesus was a Grand Imposter:
> That all his Miracles were Cheats,
> Perform'd as Jugglers do their Feats:
> The Church has never such a Writer:
> A shame, he hath not got a Mitre!

Most students of the ENLIGHTENMENT have concluded that Woolston's devotion to the allegorical method was a posture, serving as a thin veneer over his attacks on literalistic clergy. His vitriolic sarcasm has offended many, and his unproductive allegorism has seemed strangely dated. Yet in his own way he posed a significant problem. The approach of Hume to the miracle stories was as historically bankrupt as Woolston's. What was needed was an approach that respected the view of "mighty acts" rooted in the 1st-century world view and expressed in 1st-century symbolic modes of writing. While Woolston's ahistorical approach could not fill that need, his posing of the issue of the importance of nonliteral meanings helped later writers find nonallegorical dimensions of which he never dreamed.

Bibliography

Cragg, Gerald R. *Reason and Authority in the Eighteenth Century.* Cambridge: Cambridge U. Press, 1964.

Gay, Peter. *The Enlightenment.* New York: Knopf, 1967.

Kümmel, Werner Georg. *The New Testament: The History of the Investigation of its Problems.*

Trans. S. McLean Gilmour and Howard C. Kee. Nashville: Abingdon, 1972.

Leland, John. *A View of the Principal Deistical writers*. London: 3rd ed., 1757; reprint, New York: 1978.

Life of Mr. Woolston, The. London: J. Roberts, 1733. This work is anonymous.

Stephen, Leslie. *History of English Thought in the Eighteenth Century*. 2 vols. London: 1876; reprint, New York: Harcourt Brace, 1962.

Torrey, Norman L. *Voltaire and the English Deists*. New Haven: Yale U. Press, 1930.

E. GRAHAM WARING

WRIGHT, FRANCES (1795–1858), Anglo-American communitarian, writer, lecturer, and women's-rights advocate, was born in Dundee Scotland, on Sept. 6. Her parents, James Wright, a graduate of Trinity College in Dublin and a linen merchant by trade, and Camilla Campbell Wright, daughter of an English general, died when Frances was two and a half, orphaning her and her older brother Richard and younger sister Camilla. Raised by her aunt, Frances Campbell, first in London and, after 1806, in Dawlish, Devonshire, Frances was a member of the comfortable gentry, with an inheritance to guarantee her later independence. Her brother's death in the Napoleonic Wars drew the two sisters closer, and Camilla was a constant companion in all of Frances' endeavors until her own death in 1831.

Early Life. On reaching 21, in 1816, Frances took her sister to live in the bracing intellectual atmosphere of Glasgow, in the household of her paternal great-uncle, James Milne. Milne was a leader in the Scottish ENLIGHTENMENT's rationalist empiricism, and held the influential position of professor of moral philosophy at the University of Glasgow. Under his direction, Frances studied Epicurean philosophy, read works about the United States and began to compose an essay on Epicureanism, which was later published as *A Few Days in Athens* (1822). In the meantime she had written a play, *Altorf* (1819), which celebrated Swiss independence as a republican confederacy.

Deciding to travel to complete her education, Frances chose not to visit the Continent but rather the United States, which appeared to her an embodiment of the principles of frugal self-government so dear to her Scottish mentors. Introduced to prominent British expatriates by letters from a sister-in-law of Mrs. Milne, Robina Craig Millar (whose husband had died in America in exile for his support of THOMAS PAINE and of revolutionary principles), Frances and Camilla resided in New York for part of 1818 and 1819. *Altorf* was performed there, and Frances felt encouraged to write to the Philadelphia publisher Matthew Carey about printing the play. It had very small sales, but the idea of popular writing had captured Frances. During the remaining months of her visit, she traveled as far west as Buffalo, east across Canada to return to New York City by Lake Champlain, and as far south as Washington, before embarking for England in May of 1820. Her observations on the trip were published in London in 1821 as *Views of Society and Manners in America*.

Although written in the conventional form of a travelogue, *Views* described and praised American political institutions and social habits, contrasting America's republican simplicity favorably with England's aristocratic repression. The only flaws Wright saw were black slavery in the southern states and frivolous female education, which she attributed to America's unfortunate emulation of English practices. The reviews of Wright's book depended mainly upon the reader's political loyalties. Two who approved were JEREMY BENTHAM and the Marquis de Lafayette, both of whom wrote to compliment her on her defense of republicanism.

Wright joined Bentham's household in London briefly in 1821, and then left for France to visit Lafayette and to supervise the translation of the *Views* into French. Between 1821 and 1824, Wright became Lafayette's confidante and sometimes English courier, as the aging revolutionary hero conspired to overthrow the restored Bourbon monarch, Louis XVIII. Although the friendship of the renowned widower and the young Englishwoman attracted criticism, even from his family, Wright's devotion to Lafayette was that of a young enthusiast finding approval for her unconventional interest in political reform and female participation in it. When Lafayette accepted the invitation of the U.S. Congress to revisit, in 1824, the scenes of his triumphs in the American Revolution, the Wright sisters planned to accompany him, despite their family's objections on grounds of propriety. As a solution the sisters traveled independently of the marquis, joining him at various places on his tour.

Interests in Slavery and Model Societies. The 1824 trip changed Wright's life in three important ways. First, she pursued her earlier interest in slavery, including conversations with former presidents THOMAS JEFFERSON and James Madison, whom she met with Lafayette's party. Second, she became aware of the communitarian theories of ROBERT OWEN, who was just completing plans for the purchase of the Rappite properties at New Harmony, Indiana, to establish a model society. Finally, she separated her plans from Lafayette's and chose to remain in the U.S. to begin reform efforts of her own design.

In 1825, Wright published *A Plan for the Gradual Abolition of Slavery in the United States Without Danger of Loss to the Citizens of the South* in the Baltimore newspaper *Genius of Universal Emancipation*. In December, she purchased land in Tennessee on the Wolf River just west of Memphis, and named it Nashoba. She called for slaveowners to bring slaves, who would, through cooperative production, earn enough to purchase their freedom while being educated for freedom and colonization.

Wright's call was answered with the donation of about a dozen slaves, with whom she began clearing the land. She was joined, in 1826, by recruits from the already disintegrating community at New Harmony: an apostate Quaker named Richeson Whitby, an atheistic physician named James Richardson, and, in 1827, by ROBERT DALE OWEN, the son of New Harmony's founder. Ill from overwork in 1827, Wright left with Owen for Europe to seek new recruits, leaving Camilla, Whitby, and Richardson in charge. They soon publicized actions at Nashoba that made Frances Wright's name synonymous with free love. Richardson announced that the community did not recognize the artificial and onerous limitations of marriage and that he had taken one of the mulatto residents as his partner, while Camilla had become pregnant by Whitby.

Hearing the echoes in England, Frances and Robert planned a quick return, having succeeded in recruiting only Frances Trollope and one of her sons to join them at Nashoba. Although Frances Wright had met and impressed Mary Shelley, the young widow was not as as eager as Mrs. Trollope was to visit America. When Wright arrived in Nashoba in January of 1828, she found desolation, from which Mrs. Trollope hastily departed. Riding the crest of the community's notoriety, Wright immediately published a defense of human liberty and a blast against the almost ineradicable bonds of marriage. Religious authority could not, she said, override human inclination; only personal attraction and affection should bind a couple.

Wright's pronouncements could not overcome the real economic problems at Nashoba. She left the site in 1828 for New Harmony, where she and young Owen began joint editorship of the *New Harmony Gazette*. In 1830, she resettled the remaining blacks of the failed venture in Haiti.

Nashoba's collapse in the midst of public abuse convinced Wright that wider public education was required to persuade Americans of the benefits of rational reform. She began lecturing, beginning with Cincinnati in 1828, where she denounced the influence of the clergy on miseducated, timid women. Like her mentor, the senior Owen, Wright believed that rational investigation would lead people to support the liberation of slaves, the education of women and their freedom from unhappy marriages, and the entitlement of laborers to the fruits of their work. The only hindrance to acting on these sentiments was false teaching, most of which was that of the clergy, who preyed especially on susceptible women.

Journalism and Lecturing. In 1829, Wright and Owen moved their journal to New York City, changing its name to the *Free Inquirer*. While Owen did most of the editing work, Wright continued to lecture, both on tour and in their newly purchased Hall of Science, a secular alternative to the Sunday school. Finding a receptive audience among New York artisans, many of whom had already imbibed anticlericalism, Wright and Owen became supporters and publicists for the newly formed Working Men's party. They seconded the demand of workers for free public education, and added that it must be secular and equal for all classes, teaching every child the skills for mental and manual labor.

Wright's lectures quickly became a popular scandal. Her assaults on the clergy (coming in the midst of evangelical revivals), her possible approval of miscegenation at Nashoba, and especially what was considered unfeminine self-publicity in mounting the lecture platform all made her name an epithet representing every ungodly and antisocial principle. The workingmen were excoriated as "Fanny Wright men," perhaps contributing to the defeat of their candidates in the 1829 elections, and Wright's and Owen's educational proposals, which included boarding, were denounced as ploys to steal children from their parents. In the heat of these political struggles, Camilla, living with Owen and Frances, became ill with grief over the death of her child.

Faced with criticism and family crisis, Wright

sailed for France in the summer of 1830, leaving Owen in charge of their paper and promising to send reports of the revolutionary situation in France. The sisters were accompanied by another New Harmony refugee, William S. Phiquepal D'Arusmont, who had come to New Harmony in 1828 to use the reform principles of J. H. Pestalozzi in its school. When Camilla died in Paris in 1831, Wright was devastated and sought to restore herself during the next few years through marriage to D'Arusmont, by whom she had secretly had a child. She continued to develop the ideas formulated in her recent American sojourn.

Wright's marriage to an impoverished reformer 16 years her senior brought only temporary happiness however. At the same time it made her a harsher critic of the restrictions placed on wives by laws supported by religious authority. The family returned to the U.S. in 1835 to check on land investments Wright had made earlier, and she returned to public lecturing, this time on behalf of Andrew Jackson.

With the Owenite communities bereft and with Owen active in Indiana politics, Wright found her most congenial friends in the freethought community that provided an audience for her anticlericalism. Wright approached ABNER KNEELAND, editor of the successful BOSTON INVESTIGATOR, to share his subscription list, and in 1837 she printed six issues of a companion monthly, *A Manual of American Principles*, in Philadelphia.

Unable to regain her previous public attention, Wright returned to the Continent, making frequent trips between 1837 and 1848 to France, the U.S., and Scotland, where she returned to collect an inheritance. During that time, she and D'Arusmont were estranged, and she composed her last work, *England the Civilizer*, "written by A Woman" (1848). The millennial work of a rejected woman, the book claimed that human progress would not occur until women turned their humanitarian impulses from their individual homes to society. Until women overthrew the false religious sentiments that bound them to individual men and learned the true religion of humanity, they would impede reform, Wright wrote.

Returning to the U.S. in 1848 to protect her American investments, Wright was sued for divorce on the grounds that she was incompetent to manage the property in the interests of her family. Alienated from her daughter Sylva, who took her father's side, Wright was awarded in 1850 a portion of her Ohio estate by a Cincinnati judge, who lamented the couple's acrimony. Wright died in Cincinnati in 1852 after a fall on the ice.

Although Frances Wright did not live to see the emancipation of black slaves and better education for women, her courage in defying the conventions about female propriety in order to speak on behalf of both was recognized in later years. For a younger generation of women, whose reform impulses grew out of religious tenets of charity, Wright's devotion to the principles of human equality was troubling, as was her proclivity for self-publicity. Nevertheless, Susan B. Anthony and Elizabeth Cady Stanton, who also came to believe that the clergy were responsible for restricting women to a narrow sphere of home and church, lauded Wright as the first woman to lecture in public on behalf of women.

Other article of interest: **Women and Unbelief.**

Bibliography

Baker, Paul R., ed. *Views of Society and Manners in America.* Cambridge, Mass.: Harvard U. Press, 1963.

Bestor, Arthur. *The Sectarian Origins and the Owenite Phase of Communitarian Socialism in America, 1663–1829.* Philadelphia: U. of Pennsylvania Press, 1970.

D'Arusmont, Frances Wright. *Life, Letters and Lectures: 1834, 1844.* New York: Arno Press, 1972.

Eckhardt, Celia Morris. *Fanny Wright: Rebel in America.* Cambridge, Mass.: Harvard U. Press, 1984.

Harrison, J. F. C. *Quest for the New Moral World. Robert Owen and the Owenites in Britain and America.* New York: Scribner's, 1969.

Hugins, Walter Edward. *Jacksonian Democracy and the Working Class. A Study of the New York Working Men's Movement, 1829–1837.* Stanford, Calif.: Stanford U. Press, 1960.

Leopold, Richard William. *Robert Dale Owen, A Biography.* New York: Octagon Books, 1969.

Owen, Robert Dale. *Threading My Way.* New York: Augustus M. Kelley, 1967; reprint of 1874 edition.

Palmer, Phyllis Marynick. "Frances Wright: Case Study of a Reformer." Ph.D. dissertation, Ohio State University, 1973.

Perkins, A. J. G., and Theresa Wolfson. *Frances Wright, Free Enquirer.* New York: Harper, 1939.

Pessen, Edward. *Most Uncommon Jacksonians;*

The Radical Leaders of the Early Labor Movement. Albany: State U. of New York Press, 1967.

PHYLLIS PALMER

Y–Z

YAROSLAVSKI, EMEL'YAN MIKHAILO-VICH (1878–1943), Russian atheist, whose real name was Miney Izrailevich Gubel'man. He was born in Chita, Siberia. The son of a Jewish deportee—his father had been banished to Siberia for trying to evade military service—and one of ten children, Yaroslavski was drawn into the revolutionary movement at the age of 17 or 18.

Political Activism. In 1898, the year of its founding, Yaroslavski joined the Russian Social Democratic Labor party (R.S.D.L.P.) to which the present-day Communist party of the Soviet Union [C.P.S.U.] traces its origin. He gained his first revolutionary experience in Social Democratic circles in Chita and organized the first Marxist revolutionary group among the workers of the Trans-Baikal Railway. In 1901 he went to Berlin and Paris and established contact with Russian emigrés associated with the journal *Iskra*. He played an active and prominent role in the 1905 Revolution, carrying out various party mandates in St. Petersburg, Tver, Nizhni Novgorod, Odessa, Yaroslavl, and Moscow. Arrested in 1907 after the fifth R.S.D.L.P. congress, Yaroslavski was sentenced to five years imprisonment in Gornyy Zerentuy and subsequent settlement in eastern Siberia.

After the February Revolution in 1917, Yaroslavski became a member of the Yakutsk Committee for Public Safety and later chairman of the Unified Yakutsk Soviet of Workers' and Soldiers' Deputies. In July Yaroslavski began working in the military organization of the Moscow City Committee of the R.S.D.L.P. During the October Revolution he was a member of the Moscow Military-Revolutionary Committee and the first military commissar of the Kremlin. Advancing rapidly in the hierarchy of C.P.S.U., Yaroslavski held numerous party posts in Moscow and Siberia and served as editor or editorial staff member of a number of newspapers and journals, including *Sotsial-Demokrat, Pravda, Bol'shevik* (forerunner of the present-day journal *Kommunist*), *Istoricheskiy zhurnal*, and *Istorik-Marksist*. Eventually Yaroslavski rose to the position of secretary of the Communist party Central Committee and membership in the Central Committee, the Party Control Commission, and the Central Executive Committee of the U.S.S.R.

As a leading figure among the older Bolsheviks and head of the All-Union Society of Exiles and Former Political Convicts, as well as in his capacity as party historian and member of the board of directors of the Lenin Institute, Yaroslavski became a logical target during the Stalin purges. In the words of the historian A. L. Sidorov, after Stalin's famous letter to the historical journal *Proletarskaya revolyutsiya* in 1931, "E. M. Yaroslavski in particular was subjected to criticism" and "had to acknowledge his mistakes, both imaginary and real."

Unlike many fellow-historians and old Bolsheviks however, Yaroslavski (who, it goes without saying, demonstrated the necessary "flexibility" in his views and writings) was lucky and escaped the worst. As a matter of fact, while his party career went into an eclipse during the 1930s, Yaroslavski wrote on such sensitive topics as the party purge—practically on the eve of the first great wave of the purges that were to decimate the ranks of the intelligentsia in Soviet Russia. In 1939 he regained his Central Committee membership; and for his work as a party member, historian, publicist, and propagandist, Yaroslavski was elected to the U.S.S.R. Academy of Sciences and awarded the Order of Lenin and the State Prize. When he died in 1943, he was buried in a place of honor at the Kremlin wall in Red Square.

Antireligious Propagandist. In both the Soviet Union and the outside world Yaroslavski is best known for his role in the antireligious campaign conducted by the Soviet government after the October Revolution. In the words of a Soviet biographer Yaroslavski was a "fighter against religion," "not an ordinary atheist," but "the commander of the antireligious front." It was Yaroslavski who headed the League of the Militant Godless, established in 1925, and in 1928 he announced an ambitious "antireligious five-year-plan." Although this plan, like the plans for the development of the national economy, fell short of its targets, the results were nevertheless impressive.

By 1932 the League of the Militant Godless boasted a membership of 5.5 million; eventually it attained a membership of 17 million. From 1922 to 1941 Yaroslavski was also the editor-in-chief of the newspaper *Bezbozhnik* (atheist, or godless), whose circulation eventually reached 350,000. From 1925 to 1932 he edited a journal of the same title; both publications, along with the more scholarly *Antireligioznik* (antireligionist; 1938 circulation, 60,000), were supposed to help Soviet citizens overcome the vestiges of religion and enable them to develop a scientific-materialist *Weltanschauung*.

Yaroslavski, in fact, was the chief organizer of the grandiose effort of the Soviet regime to stamp out any and all traces of religion. In addition to atheistic newspapers and journals published on a regular basis, there were countless lectures and exhibits attacking religion and developing the perspectives of ATHEISM, and at the beginning of the 1930s Soviet printing presses were turning out antireligious pamphlets at the rate of more than four million copies a month. Evidently Yaroslavski firmly believed in the efficacy of such measures. At one point he confidently predicted that after the completion of the second "antireligious five-year-plan" (that is, by 1937), all churches in the Soviet Union would be closed.

How grossly mistaken Yaroslavski was in his belief that under socialism the phenomenon of religion would soon disappear was revealed by the results of the (still unpublished) 1937 census—taken a year after the achievement of socialism had been officially proclaimed in the Stalin constitution of 1936. To the consternation of the authorities, the census showed that some 80 million Soviet citizens—approximately 57 percent of the total population—still professed to hold religious beliefs. It is a measure of the embarrassment of the Soviet regime that no such question was included in subsequent censuses.

Indirect evidence of the continuation of religion as a powerful social force in Russian life was supplied by the Soviet regime during World War II. While persecution of religion in the U.S.S.R. in various forms has continued intermittently to the present day—there was a particularly vicious antireligious campaign under Khrushchev during the years 1959–1964 that resulted in the closing of many churches—the grandiose and ambitiously conceived organizational campaigns associated with the work of Yaroslavski during the 1920s and 1930s came to a sudden end in 1941 within a few months after the Nazi attack on the U.S.S.R.

The League of the Militant Godless, like the Comintern on the political plane a few years later, was dissolved, and such publications as *Bezbozhnik* and *Antirelgioznik* were suspended. A number of Russian Orthodox seminaries were reopened, theological literature began rolling off government presses in the Soviet Union, and in 1944 the office of the Moscow Patriarch was again filled on a permanent basis for the first time since 1925. All of these concessions were made in return for the support given by the Russian Orthodox church to the Soviet regime during its great hour of need, that is, the "great patriotic war" against the Nazi invaders.

However, if in recent years the Soviet regime has refrained from mounting the kind of all-out campaign against religion enthusiastically endorsed by Yaroslavski and others in the 1920s and 1930s and by Khrushchev later, it is as much from a sense of futility as from gratitude. Perhaps recent Soviet leaders have come to appreciate the truth of the observation made by A. V. Lunacharski, who was People's Commissar for Education during the 1920s. "Religion is like a nail," Lunacharski said during a moment of despair in the early 1930s, "the harder you hit it, the deeper it goes in."

According to Yaroslavski's own testimony, his desire to become involved in a crusade against religion developed even before the October Revolution. He evidently conceptualized his first book on the subject of religion well before 1917, although *Bibliya dlya veruyushchikh i neveruyushchikh* ("The Bible for Believers and Nonbelievers"), initially written in the form of separate chapters for the newspaper *Bezbozhnik,* did not appear until late 1922. The book became a standard weapon in the arsenal of atheist propaganda in the U.S.S.R. By 1959 it had appeared in at least 11 editions in Russian alone. Another successful book by Yaroslavski on religion was *Kak rodyatsya, zhivut i umirayut bogi i bogini* ("How Gods and Goddesses Are Born, Live and Die"), a comparative history of religion from an atheistic point of view. Yaroslavski's most important writings on religion and atheism have been collected in his *O religii* ("On

Religion").

Yaroslavski's basic stance on religion is easily summarized: He began with the proposition that religion "poisons the brain" and produces an "incorrect" and "mutilated" understanding of the world and human relationships. Religion is harmful because it sanctions slavery and is an obstacle to social progress and the creation of a more rational and better world. He ended with the conclusion that religion and communism are irreconcilable. "Religion," he wrote in *Religion in the USSR,* "acts as a bandage over the eyes of man, preventing him from seeing the world as it is. It is our task to tear off this bandage and to teach the masses of workers and peasants to see things correctly, to understand what does exist and what does not, so as to be able to rebuild this world to fit the needs of the workers and peasants. We must, therefore, convince the masses that Communism and religion cannot go together, that it is not possible to be a Communist and at the same time believe in devils or gods, in heavenly creatures, in the Virgin Mary, in the saints, in pious princes and princesses, bishops, and landowners, who have been canonized by the priests."

Perhaps the life of Yaroslavski is best summarized by Fëdor Dostoevski's remark that only in Russia could atheism become a kind of religion.

Other articles of interest: **Propaganda, Antireligious. Russia and the Soviet Union, Unbelief in.**

Bibliography

Bociurkiw, B. R., and J. W. Strong, eds. *Religion and Atheism in the USSR and Eastern Europe.* Toronto and Buffalo: U. of Toronto Press, 1975.

Bourdeaux, Michael. *Religious Ferment in Russia.* London: Macmillan, 1968.

Conquest, Robert. *Religion in the USSR.* New York: Praeger, 1968.

Curtiss, J. S. *The Russian Church and the Soviet State.* Boston: Little, Brown, 1953.

de la Saudee, J. de Bivort. *Communism and Anti-Religion.* London: Burns, Oates and Washbourne, 1938.

Haward, Max, and W. C. Fletcher. *Religion and the Soviet State: A Dilemma of Power.* New York: Praeger, 1969.

Kolarz, Walter, *Religion in the Soviet Union.* New York: St. Martin's Press, 1961.

Marshall, Richard, Jr., et al., eds. *Aspects of Religion in the Soviet Union 1917–1967.* Chicago: U. of Chicago Press, 1971.

Powell, David E. *Antireligious Propaganda in the Soviet Union.* Cambridge: MIT Press, 1975.

Timasheff, Nicholas S. *Religion in Soviet Russia, 1917–1942.* New York: Sheed and Ward, 1942.

Yaroslavski, E. *Bolshevik Verification and Purging of the Party Ranks.* Moscow-Leningrad: Cooperative Publishing Society of Foreign Workers in the U.S.S.R., 1933.

Yaroslavski, F. [sic]. *Religion in the USSR.* New York: International Publishers, 1932.

ROLF H. W. THEEN

ZOROASTRIANISM. See Devil, Unbelief in the Concept of the.

Appendices

The appendices that follow are as complete as the editorial staff could make them as *The Encyclopedia of Unbelief* went to press. When a blank space appears under a heading, it means that reasonably correct information could not be obtained. A question mark indicates that the information is a reasonable guess. The use of the abbreviation for *circa* (c) indicates that the date was one during which an organization, publisher, or periodical existed, but it may not be the initial or final year of its existence.

The officers or heads of organizations, founders or proprietors of publishing companies, and editors of periodicals are the most important people associated with a particular entity, even though many others may have contributed significantly. Therefore, the names under the heading "Remarks" are not exhaustive; a name that appears in capital letters refers to an article in *The Encyclopedia of Unbelief.*

Any reader who can supply missing information or the location of copies of periodicals marked with an asterisk (*) should write:

Dr. Gordon Stein, Editor
The Encyclopedia of Unbelief
P.O. Box 4996
Culver City, CA 90231

APPENDIX 1: BIBLIOGRAPHY OF UNBE-
LIEF. The literature of unbelief is much more extensive than the average reader would imagine. The best way to locate that literature—other than by consulting the bibliographies at the end of each article in the *Encyclopedia of Unbelief*—is to use bibliographies pertaining to a particular field or a specific subject within a field. This appendix lists the most important bibliographies, as well as a few important biographies that contain bibliographies. A number of important histories of freethought and unbelief are also included, since they provide many titles of publications important in the field.

Allen, Don Cameron. *Doubt's Boundless Sea: Skepticism and Faith in the Renaissance.* Baltimore: Johns Hopkins University Press, 1964.

Becker, Karl. *Freigeistige Bibliographie.* Stuttgart: Verlag der Freireligiösen Landesgemeinde Württemberg, 1971.

Besterman, Theodore. *A Bibliography of Annie Besant.* London: Theosophical Society in England, 1924. Not as complete for the freethought period of her life as the reader might wish.

Bonner, Hypatia Bradlaugh, ed. *Catalogue of the Library of the Late Charles Bradlaugh.* London: H. Bradlaugh Bonner, 1891.

Bonner, Hypatia Bradlaugh, and John M. Robertson. *Charles Bradlaugh: A Record of His Life and Work.* 2 vols. London: T. Fisher Unwin, 1894. The section on Bradlaugh's political career is by Robertson.

Brown, Marshall G., and Gordon Stein. *Freethought in the United States: A Descriptive Bibliography.* Westport, Conn.: Greenwood Press, 1978.

Buckley, George T. *Atheism in the English Renaissance.* 1932. Reprint. New York: Russell & Russell, 1965.

Budd, Susan. *Varieties of Unbelief.* London: Heinemann, 1977.

Burr, Nelson R., in collaboration with the editors, James Ward Smith and A. Leland Jamison. *A Critical Bibliography of Religion in America.* 2 vols. Princeton, N.J.: Princeton University Press, 1961.

Collis, David, compiler. *Catalogues 1–10.* Corby, England: David Collis, 1969–71. These catalogues offer scarce freethought material for sale and serve as good bibliographies for some areas of freethought

[Foote, George William]. *Catalogue of the Library of G. W. Foote.* London: P. J. & A. E. Dobell, 1916. Dobell's Catalogue No. 251 for February 1916 may be somewhat disappointing to the freethought reader since much of the material is related to Foote's literary interests.

Gillett, Charles Ripley, compiler. *The McAlpin Collection of British History and Theology.* 5 vols. New York: Union Theological Seminary, 1927–30. Useful for early deistic works, those published before 1700.

Gilmour J. S. L. "A Freethought Collection and Its Predecessors." *The Book Collector* (London) 11 (1962): 184–96. Gilmour was the owner of one of the best freethought collections in England, which is now dispersed.

Gimbel, Richard. *Thomas Paine: A Bibliographical Checklist of Common Sense, with an Account of Its Publication.* New Haven, Conn.: Yale University Press, 1956.

Goss, C. W. F. *A Descriptive Bibliography of George Jacob Holyoake, with a Brief Sketch of His Life.* London: Crowther & Goodman, 1908. The "Sketch" is by Holyoake's daughter, Emilie Marsh.

Gould, F. J. *The Pioneers of Johnson's Court.* London: Watts, 1929. Deals with the founders of the Rationalist Press Association.

——. *The History of the Leicester Secular Society.* Leicester, England: Leicester Secular Society, 1900.

Grugel, Lee. *George Jacob Holyoake: A Study in the Evolution of a Victorian Radical.* Philadelphia: Porcupine Press, 1977.

Istoriia Pravoslaviia i Rússkogo Ateizma. Moscow: Izdatelstvo Akademia Nauk USSR, 1960.

Koch, G. Adolph. *Republican Religion: The American Revolution and the Cult of Reason.* New York: Henry Holt, 1933. Reprinted under the title *Religion of the American Enlightenment.*

Lechler, Gotthard V. *Geschichte des englischen Deismus.* Stuttgart: Cotta'scher Verlag, 1841. Reprint. Stuttgart, W. Germany: Georg Olms.

McCabe, Joseph. *A Biographical Dictionary of Ancient, Medieval and Modern Freethinkers.* Girard, Kans.: Haldeman-Julius Publications, 1945. Useful for names and dates of freethinkers.

——. *A Biographical Dictionary of Modern Rationalists.* London: Watts, 1920. This publication supplies names and dates.

——. *The Life and Letters of George Jacob Holyoake.* 2 vols. London: Watts, 1908.

Macdonald, George E. *Fifty Years of Freethought, Being the Story of the Truth Seeker, with the Natural History of Its Third Editor.* 2 vols. New

York: Truth Seeker Co., 1929. The story of freethought in the United States from 1873 until 1925. Reprint. New York: Arno, 1972.

McGee, John Edwin. *A History of the British Secular Movement*. Girard, Kans.: Haldeman-Julius Publications, 1948. Quite useful, covering 1840–1922, with a brief update to 1946.

Mauthner, Fritz. *Der Atheismus und seine Geschichte im Abendland*. 4 vols. Stuttgart & Berlin: Deutscher Verlags-Anstalt, 1922. Reprint. Stuttgart, W. Germany: Georg Olms, 1966.

Morais, Herbert M. *Deism in Eighteenth Century America*. New York: Columbia University Press, 1934. Reprint. New York: Russell & Russell, 1960.

National Library of Wales. *A Bibliography of Robert Owen, the Socialist, 1771–1858*. Aberystwyth: National Library of Wales, 1925. This is the greatly enlarged second edition.

Nethercot, Arthur. *The First Five Lives of Annie Besant*. Chicago: University of Chicago Press, 1960. This is the first half of a two-volume biography, ending with Besant's conversion to theosophy. The second volume is called *The Last Four Lives of Annie Besant*. University of Chicago Press, 1963.

Neuburg, Victor E. "The Reading of the Victorian Freethinkers." *The Library* (London) 28 (1973): 191–214.

Orr, John. *English Deism: Its Roots and Its Fruits*. Grand Rapids, Mich.: Wm. B. Eerdmans, 1934. Probably the best introduction to British deism.

Osnovy Nauchnogo Ateizma. Moscow: Izdatelstvo "Kniga," 1966.

Post, Albert. *Popular Freethought in America, 1825–1850*. New York: Columbia University Press, 1943. Reprint. Octagon, 1974.

Putnam, Samuel P. *Four Hundred Years of Freethought*. New York: Truth Seeker Company, 1894. Important and very detailed in its coverage of American freethought organizations.

Ratcliffe, S. K. *The Story of South Place*. London: Watts, 1955. A history of an important Ethical Culture and Humanist society.

Rationalist Press Association. *Catalogue of the Library of the Rationalist Press Association*. London: Watts, 1937.

Redwood, John. *Reason, Ridicule and Religion: The Age of Enlightenment in England, 1660–1750*. London: Thames & Hudson, 1976.

[Robertson, John M.]. *Catalogue of the Library of J. M. Robertson*. London: Hodgson's, 1933.

Catalog No. 14 of the 1932–33 auction season for a sale that occurred on April 26, 1933. The catalog gives little detail, with most of the freethought materials being listed as lots only.

Robertson, J. M. *The Dynamics of Religion*. 2nd ed. London: Watts, 1926. The first edition was published under the pseudonym "M. W. Wiseman" (London: The University Press, 1897). It is a history of deism in England.

———. *A History of Freethought, Ancient and Modern, to the Period of the French Revolution*. 2 vols. London: Watts, 1936. This and the following book are the most comprehensive and ambitious histories of freethought yet undertaken. The coverage is uneven, but they remain masterpieces of scholarship.

———. *A History of Freethought in the Nineteenth Century*. 2 vols. London: Watts, 1929.

Royle, Edward. *Radicals, Secularists and Republicans: Popular Freethought in Britain, 1866–1915*. Manchester: Manchester University Press, 1980. A fine piece of scholarship.

———. *Victorian Infidels*. Manchester: Manchester University Press, 1974. This covers the 1840–1865 period in England.

Sayous, Edouard. *Les Déistes Anglais et le Christianisme Principalement depuis Toland jusqu'à Chubb (1696–1738)*. Paris: G. Fischbacher, 1882.

Stein, Gordon. *Freethought in the United Kingdom and the Commonwealth: A Descriptive Bibliography*. Westport, Conn.: Greenwood Press, 1981.

———. *Robert G. Ingersoll: A Checklist*. Kent, Ohio: Kent State University Press, 1969.

Stephans, Hildegard, compiler. *The Thomas Paine Collection of Richard Gimbel in the Library of the American Philosophical Society*. Wilmington, Del.: Scholarly Resources, 1976. A reproduction of the catalog cards of the collection.

Taylor, G. H. *A Chronology of British Secularism*. London: National Secular Society, 1957. A useful pamphlet for dating events.

Tribe, David. *100 Years of Freethought*. London: Elek Books, 1967. This covers the 1850–1950 period.

———. *President Charles Bradlaugh, M.P.* London: Elek Books, 1971. Based upon Bradlaugh's papers, which were long thought to be lost.

Trinius, J. A. *Freydenker Lexicon*. 4 vols. Leipzig: Berglegts Christoph Gottfried Corner, 1759–65. Reprinted in one folio volume in Turin: Bottega d'Erasmo, 1966.

[Truelove, Edward]. *Catalogue of Books from the Library of the Late Edward Truelove*. London: Executors of the Estate of E. Truelove, 1900. Sale catalog of the large freethought library of an important freethought publisher and bookseller.

Vercruysse, Jeroom. *Bibliographie Descriptive des Écrits du Baron d'Holbach*. Paris: Minard, 1971. An important bibliography for an author who is extremely difficult to catalogue.

Warren, Sidney. *American Freethought, 1860–1914*. New York: Columbia University Press, 1943. Reprint. New York: Gordian Press.

Watts, Charles. *History of Freethought*. London: Watts, n.d. [1885?]. Published also by Watts under the title *Freethought: Its Rise, Progress and Triumph*.

Wheeler, Joseph Mazzini. *A Biographical Dictionary of Freethinkers of All Ages and Nations*. London: Progressive Publishing Co., 1889. Extremely useful, even though marred by careless proofreading.

Whyte, Adam Gowans: *The Story of the R.P.A. (1899–1949)*. London: Watts, 1949. A history of the Rationalist Press Association.

Appendix 2: MEETINGS OF UNBELIEVERS

Unbelievers have assembled many times in the past. These meetings were often local or statewide, but sometimes they were national or international. This appendix lists different types of meetings, from regular annual meetings of small organizations to irregular, worldwide meetings. The only kinds of gatherings that are excluded are regular weekly or monthly meetings of established unbelief groups, that is, membership meetings. Only special annual meetings of these groups are listed. Information about regular membership meetings may be found in **Appendix 3: Organizations of Unbelief.**

The following list is arranged chronologically. It cuts across both countries and organizations. The date at which the first annual meeting of a particular organization was held is the one under which all meetings of that group appear. The list is comprehensive but not exhaustive.

Date	Location	Organization/ Conference	Type of meeting	Remarks
1836	Saratoga Springs, New York	United Moral and Philosophical Society	organizational	ABNER KNEELAND, Benjamin Offen, organizers. Subsequent annual meetings in New York, 1837–41 (except 1839, in Rochester, N.Y.).
1845	New York	Infidel Society	organizational	Transactions published as *Meteor of Light* (Boston: J. P. Mendum, 1845). Annual meetings held in New York in 1846 and 1847.
1854	Hartford, Connecticut	Hartford Bible Convention		Transactions published as *Proceedings of the Hartford Bible Convention* (New York: 1854).
1857	Philadelphia	Infidel Assn. of the U.S.	organizational	Proceedings published as *Minutes of the Infidel Convention* (Philadelphia: 1857).
1867	[unknown]	Free Religious Assn.	organizational	O. B. Frothingham, ROBERT DALE OWEN, organizers.
1876	Philadelphia, Chicago, et al.	National Liberal League American Secular Union	annual	The league and union merged soon after formation; 25 annual meetings held from 1876 to 1904.
1877	New York	N.Y. Freethinkers' Assn.	annual	
1878	Watkins Glen, New York	N.Y. Freethinkers' Assn.	convention	Proceedings published.

Date	Location	Organization/ Conference	Type of meeting	Remarks
1880	Brussels	Intl. Fed. of Societies of Free Thought (I.F.F.)	annual congress 1	Report in DEROBIGNE MORTIMER BENNETT's *An Infidel Abroad* (New York: Liberal & Scientific Publishing House, 1881).
1881	London	I.F.F.	annual congress 2	
1883	Amsterdam	I.F.F.	annual congress 3	CHARLES BRADLAUGH attended. Reports in the NATIONAL REFORMER.
1885	Antwerp, Belgium	I.F.F.	annual congress	
1892	Madrid	I.F.F.	annual congress	
1893	Chicago	I.F.F.	annual congress	SAMUEL PORTER PUTNAM's *Four Hundred Years of Freethought* (see Appendix 1) has a report.
1900	Paris	I.F.F.	annual congress	The FREETHINKER 20 (1900), pp. 637, 653, has a report.
1902	Geneva	I.F.F.	annual congress	
1904	Rome	I.F.F.	annual congress	Full report published in French. Report in J. B. Wilson's *A Trip to Rome* (Lexington, Ky.: James E. Hughes, 1905).
1904	St. Louis	Congress of Progressive Thought		Proceedings published as *Report of the International Congress for Progressive Thought* (New York: 1905).
1905	Paris	I.F.F.	annual congress	
1906	Buenos Aires	I.F.F.	annual congress	Report in *La Prensa* and *Diccionario Biografico de los Libres Pensadores de Argentina* (1910).
1907	Prague	I.F.F.	annual congress	Full report published in Czech, short report in French.
1910	Brussels	I.F.F.	annual congress	

Date	Location	Organization/ Conference	Type of meeting	Remarks
1912	Munich	I.F.F.	annual congress	Report published as *Congress Proceedings*.
1913	Lisbon	I.F.F.	annual congress	Report published as *Congress Proceedings*.
1915	San Francisco	Rationalist Assn. of North America	congress	Also called Panama/Pacific Congress. Report published.
1925	New York City	Freethinkers of America	annual	Held almost annually, 1925–69.
1941	various U.S. cities	American Humanist Assn.	annual	Held annually until the present.
1949	Madras	Indian Rationalist Assn.	organizational	
1952	various European cities	Intl. Humanist and Ethical Union	annual	Held annually until the present.
1956	various U.S. cities	American Rationalist Fed.	annual	Held annually, usually in Chicago, until the present.
1967	various U.S. cities	American Atheists	annual	Held annually until the present.
1968	Bombay	Indian Secular Society	organizational	
1972	Vijayawada, India	1st World Atheist Conference		GORA, convener and host.
1978	various U.S. cities	Freedom from Religion Foundation	annual	Held annually, often in Madison, Wis., until the present.
1980	Vijayawada, India	2nd World Atheist Conference		Lavanam, convener and host.
1981	various U.S. cities	Council for Democratic & Secular Humanism	annual	Papers published in *Free Inquiry*. Paul Kurtz, chairman.
1983	Helsinki	3rd World Atheist Conference		Erkki Hartikaian, convener and host.
1985	Vijayawada, India	4th World Atheist Conference		Lavanam, convener and host.

APPENDIX 3: ORGANIZATIONS OF UN-BELIEF

This appendix lists the names of organizations whose primary purpose is the furtherance of unbelief or that exist for social, literary, or ideological discussion of unbelief. Also given are dates of formation and dissolution and the main headquarters of the organization, when this information is known. Groups still active are noted.

English-speaking countries appear first, followed by South Africa, India, Latin American republics, European nations, and Israel. Two international organizations complete the list. Within each country, the list is presented chronologically by date of founding.

For annual or special meetings of unbelief groups, see **Appendix 2: Meetings of Unbelievers.**

It should be noted that many unbelief organizations outside the United States, especially in Latin America and Western Europe, were sponsored by Masonic Lodges. Especially notable was the Grand Orient Lodge of France, also important in Latin America. However, no effort has been made to include Masonic Lodges, as there were thousands, and, strictly speaking, they were not unbelief organizations.

Dates	Organization	Headquarters	Remarks
		United States	
1790–c1791	Universal Society	Philadelphia	A deistical society.
1795–c1795	Society of Ancient Druids	Newburgh, NY	A deistical society.
c1795–c1809	Theophilanthropists	Philadelphia	A deistical society.
1796–c1806	Deistical Society	New York	ELIHU PALMER, founder.
c1796–c1800	Theophilanthropic Society	Baltimore	A deistical society.
1828–c1835	Free Enquirers	New York	ROBERT DALE OWEN, FRANCES WRIGHT, founders.
1829–39	Moral Philanthropists	New York	
1830–40	1st Society of Free Enquirers	Boston	ABNER KNEELAND, founder.
1836–41	United Moral and Philosophical Society for Diffusion of Useful Knowledge	Buffalo?	GILBERT VALE, secretary.
1840–45	Boston Discussion Society	Boston	
1842–?	Society of Free Enquirers	New York	
1845–47?	Infidel Society for the Promotion of Mental Liberty	New York	
1850–1970s	Freien Gemeinden	Milwaukee	Large, multicity organization.
1876–1920s	National Liberal League (#1)	Philadelphia	SAMUEL P. PUTNAM, secretary.

Dates	Organization	Headquarters	Remarks
c1877–c1880?	Skandinaviske Fritenkerforening	Chicago?	Norwegian/American.
1883–1920s?	Am. Secular Union	Chicago	E. Reichwald, secretary.
1892–94	Freethought Fed. of Am.	New York	Samuel P. Putnam, secretary.
1900–05	Myl etojai Teisybes	Chicago	Lithuanian/American
c1900–c1905?	Zveza Slovenskih Svobdomiselv Ameriki	Chicago	Slovenian/American.
1907	Czech Rationalist Fed.	Chicago	Large, multicity organization, still slightly active.
1908–c1908	Circulo Giordano Bruno	Chicago	Italian/American.
1924–1930s	Am. Rationalist Assn.	Chicago	P. Ward and F. Steiner.
1925–c1975	Freethinkers of Am.	New York	JOSEPH LEWIS, founder.
1925	Am. Assn. for the Advancement of Atheism	New York	CHARLES L. SMITH: dormant after 1936
1941–active	Am. Humanist Assn.	Buffalo	Publishes the *Humanist*.
1945–1950s	National Liberal League (#2)	New York	
1947–81	United Secularists of Am.	Clifton, NJ + Oakland, CA	Published *Progressive World*.
1954–active	Am. Rationalist Fed.	St. Louis	Only organizations can belong.
1962–active	Am. Atheists (Society of Separationists)	Austin, TX	MADALYN MURRAY O'HAIR, founder. Has also been located in Baltimore and Honolulu.
1978–active	Freedom from Religion Foundation	Madison, WI	Anne Gaylor, founder.
1980–active	Council for Democratic & Secular Humanism	Buffalo	Paul Kurtz, founder; publishes *Free Inquiry*.
1982–active	Atheists United	Los Angeles	
1984–active	Academy of Humanism	Buffalo	Paul Kurtz, founder.
19*–active	International Humanist & Ethical Union	Utrecht, Netherlands	

Dates	Organization	Headquarters	Remarks
		United Kingdom	
1776–?	Deistic Chapel	London	David Williams, founder.
1821–c1830	Zetetic Societies	Edinburgh	
1842–43	Anti-Persecution Union	London	Founded to help blasphemy defendants.
1843–?	London Atheistical Society	London	
1853–c1855	London Secular Society	London	
c1855–62	Fleet Street House	London	GEORGE JACOB HOLYOAKE, founder.
1866–active	National Secular Society	London	CHARLES BRADLAUGH, founder.
1870	Scottish Secular Union		
c1870–1890s	Halls of Science	London and other cities	Branches of NATIONAL SECULAR SOCIETY.
1872–active	Leicester Secular Society	Leicester	Josiah Gimson, founder.
1877–c1891	Birmingham Secular Society	Birmingham	
1878–1880s?	British Secular Union	London	CHARLES WATTS, founder
c1878?–1880s	Glasgow Eclectic Institution	Glasgow	
1888–c1888	London Secular Fed.	London	GEORGE WILLIAM FOOTE, founder.
1898–active	Rationalist Press Assn.	London	Charles Watts, C. A. Watts, founders.
18??–?	Edinburgh Secular Society	Edinburgh	
1901–?	North of England Secular Fed.		Became British Secular League.
?–1963	South Place Ethical Society	London	MONCURE CONWAY, principal leader.
1963–active	British Humanist Assn.	London	
1970s?	Belfast Humanist Group	Belfast	

Dates	Organization	Headquarters	Remarks

Canada

Dates	Organization	Headquarters	Remarks
1884	Canadian Secular Union	Toronto	R. C. Adams, president.
188?	Pioneer Club	Montreal	
188?	General Freethought Assn.	Toronto	
c1928	Rationalist Society	Winnipeg	
1939	Rationalist Club	Regina	W. A. Waddell, president.
1967	Humanist Assn. of Canada	Vancouver, moved to Ottawa	
1970s?	Society of Prairie Atheists	Biggar, Saskatchewan	
1982	Assn. Rationaliste du Québec	Montreal	

Ireland

Dates	Organization	Headquarters	Remarks
188?	Irish Secular Society	Dublin	

Australia

Dates	Organization	Headquarters	Remarks
1865	Newcastle Secular Society	Newcastle	
1871	Spiritualist & Freethought Propagandist Assn.	Melbourne	
1876	Adelaide Secular & Free Discussion Society	Adelaide	
1882–c1894	Australasian Secular Assn.	Melbourne	Thomas Walker, JOSEPH SYMES, lecturers.
1882–84	Liberal Assn. of N.S.W.	Sydney	
c1883–1888	Brisbane Freethought Assn.	Brisbane	
1885	So. Australian Freethought Society	Adelaide	
1886	Australasian Freethought Union	Sydney	George Douglas, leader.
c1892	Gympie Secular Society	Gympie, Queensland	Wallace Nelson, lecturer.

Dates	Organization	Headquarters	Remarks
1894	Sydney Progressive Lyceum	Sydney	J. Rose, leader.
1912-active	Rationalist Assn. of N.S.W.	Sydney	Published *Rationalist News;* became Rationalist Society of Australia.
1919	Rationalist Society of Victoria	Melbourne	Became N.S.W. Humanist Society.
1960-active	Sydney Humanist Group	Sydney	Became N.S.W Humanist Society.
1961-active	Humanist Society of Victoria	Melbourne	Publishes *Victorian Humanist.*
1965	Council of Australian Humanist Societies		
1966	(Australian) National Secular Society		Lasted less than one year.
1971-active	Atheist Foundation of Australia	Gunerache (near Adelaide)	Publishes *Australian Atheist.*
1971-80	Atheist Society of Australia	Sydney	Published *Atheist Journal,* 1971–80.
1973	Freethinkers' Assn. of N.S.W.		
1978-79	Secular Society of Victoria		Became Victorian Secular Soc. for a few months before dissolution.

New Zealand

Dates	Organization	Headquarters	Remarks
1855-59	Auckland Secular Society	Auckland	Archibald Campbell, founder.
1870	Dunedin Mutual Improvement Assn.	Dunedin	
1876	Eclectic Society		
1878-90	Freethought Assn.	Dunedin	Charles Bright, lecturer.
1881	Canterbury Freethought Assn.	Christchurch	
1881-1890s	Freethinkers of Wellington	Wellington	Later Wellington Freethought/ Secular Society
1884	Auckland Rationalist Assn.	Auckland	

Dates	Organization	Headquarters	Remarks
1884	N.Z. Freethought Federal Union		ROBERT STOUT, president.
1923-active	N.Z. Rationalist Assn.	Auckland	Publishers *NZ Rationalist & Humanist*.
1968-active	Humanist Soc. of N.Z.	Christchurch	

Republic of South Africa

1888-1890s?	Freethought Assn.	Port Elizabeth	
1956?-1976	Rationalist Assn. of S.A.	Johannesburg	Published *The Rationalist*.
1979-active	Humanist Assn. of S.A.	Cape Town	Publishes *South African Humanist*.

India

1875-94	Hindu Freethought Union	Madras	Published *Philosophical Inquirer*.
1925-44	Self-Respect Movement	Madras	Became Dravidian Fed.
1930-31	Anti-Priestcraft Assn.	Bombay	Became Rationalist Assn. of India.
1931	Rationalist Assn. of India	Bombay	Published *Reason*.
1936?-active	Atheist Centre	Vijayawada	GORA, founder.
1944-active	Dravidian Fed.	Madras	PERIYAR, founder.
1948	Radical Humanist Movement	Bombay	M. N. Roy, founder
1950-active	Indian Rationalist Assn.	Madras	Publishes *Freethought* and *Indian Rationalist*.
1960	Indian Humanist Union	Lucknow	Publishes *Humanist Outlook*.
1968	Indian Secular Society	Bombay	A. B. Shah, founder.
1979	Indian Atheist Centre	New Delhi	Publishes *Indian Atheist*.

Argentina

1902	Fed. Anti-Clerical Intransigente des Libres Pensadores	Buenos Aires	
1904?	Comité Nacional des Libre Pensadores	Buenos Aires	

Dates	Organization	Headquarters	Remarks
1909	Liga Nacional de Mujeres Librepensadores	Buenos Aires	

Brazil

	Liga Anticlerical	São Paulo, Parana	

Chile

c1900	Liga de Libre Pensadores		
c1900	Circulo de Propaganda Anti-Clerical	Santiago	

Cuba

1893	Victor Hugo Society	Havana	

El Salvador

c1900	Liga Centro-America des Libre Pensadores	San Salvador	

Guatemala

c1900	Sociedad de Libre Pensadores		

Mexico

c1925	Fed. de Libre Penser	Mexico City	Branches.

Peru

1890	La Liga des Libre Pensadores		

Uruguay

c1900	Asociación de Propaganda Liberal	Montevideo	

Austria

1848	Deutschösterreichische Freidenkerbewengung	Vienna	
1894	Ethische Gesellschaft	Vienna	
1909	Monistenbund in Österreich	Vienna	
active	Freidenkerbund Österreichs	Vienna	

Dates	Organization	Headquarters	Remarks
	Belgium		
1869-80	Féd. des Sociétés des Libres Penseurs	Verviers	Socialist
1874-80	Féd. Rationaliste Belge		Socialist.
1875	Féd. Rationaliste	Charleroi	
1877-80	Féd. des Sociétés rationalistes	Brussels	
1889	Féd. des Sociétés du Libre Pensée du Centre	Centre?	Socialist.
1895	Vlaame Federatie van Vrijdenkers		
1905-06	Féd. des Libres Penseurs	Nivelles	Branches (all organizations in Belgium).
1905-07	Féd. des Libres Penseurs	Limbourg	
1908	Féd. Rationaliste	Mons	
	Czechoslovakia		
1904-active	Volná Myślenka	Prague	Branches.
	Bund Proletarischer Freidenker		Branches.
	Unie Socialistickych Svobodnych Myslitelu		Branches, socialist.
	Ustredni Svaz Volnych Myslitelu		Branches.
	Denmark		
189?	Fritanker Assn.	Copenhagen	
	Finland		
active	Finnish Freethought Union	Helsinki	Many branches.
	France		
1906	Union des Libres Penseurs		Branches.
1930-active	Union Rationaliste	Paris	Branches

Dates	Organization	Headquarters	Remarks
?-active	Assn. Nationale des Libres-Penseurs de France	Paris	Branches.
?-active	Féd. Française de la Libre Pensée		Branches.
?-active	Union des Athées	Bellenaves	Branches.

Germany

Dates	Organization	Headquarters	Remarks
1859-active	Bund freier religiöser Gemeinden Deutschlands	Breslau	
1881-active	Deutscher Freidenker Bund	Frankfurt	
1892	Deutsche Gesellschaft für ethische Kultur	Berlin	
1905-c1936	Verein der Freidenker für Feuerbestattung	Berlin	
1906	Deutscher Monistenbund	Jena	Moved to Hamburg.
1907	Kartell der freiheitlichen Vereine	Munich	
1908-1932	Gemeinschaft proletarischer Freidenker	Leipzig	Socialist: published *Atheist*.
?-c1933	Volkbund für Geistesfreiheit	Leipzig	
?-c1933	Bund des freigeistegen Jugend Deutschlands	Magdeburg	Published *Freigeistige Jugend*.
?-c1933	Bund sozialistischer Freidenker	Leipzig	Published *Der Sozialistische Freidenker*.

Italy

Dates	Organization	Headquarters	Remarks
	Giordano Bruno	Rome	
	Fed. de Libri Pensadores	Ticino	
	Assn. Razionalista Lega Antireliogiosa	Pisa, Ferrara, Livorno	Branches.

Luxembourg

Dates	Organization	Headquarters	Remarks
	Luxemburgische Freidenkerbund		

Dates	Organization	Headquarters	Remarks

Netherlands

Dates	Organization	Headquarters	Remarks
1856	Dagaraad	Amsterdam	
188?	Vrij Woorde		
	Libre Pensée	The Hague	

Norway

Dates	Organization	Headquarters	Remarks
active	Human-Etisk Forbund		

Portugal

Dates	Organization	Headquarters	Remarks
c1925	Portuguese Freethought Fed.		Branches.

Soviet Union

Dates	Organization	Headquarters	Remarks
1925-29	League of the Godless	Moscow	Became League of Militant Godless.
1929-41	League of Militant Godless	Moscow	Branches; published *Atheist;* division: Young Atheists.
1964-active	Institute of Scientific Atheism	Moscow	Offers study, degrees.

Spain

Dates	Organization	Headquarters	Remarks
c1883	Liya Anti-Clerical	Barcelona	Branches.
1886	Union Espanola de Libre Pensadores	Madrid?	Branches.

Switzerland

Dates	Organization	Headquarters	Remarks
1800s-active	Libre-Pensée de Genéve	Geneva	
1800s-active	Libres Penseurs Polonais	Geneva	
1867-defunct	Freethought Society	Caronge	
1913	Freidenkerbund	Bern	
active	Assn. Vaudoise de la Libre Pensée	Lausanne	
active	Freidenker-Vereinigung der Schweiz	Zurich	Union of several groups.
active	Freidenker-Union	Basel	Many regional groups.

Dates	Organization	Headquarters	Remarks
	Sweden		
active	Förbunder för Religionsfrihet	Stockholm	Branches.
c1890	Swedish Freethought Fed.		Branches.
	Israel		
c1978-active	Israel Secular Humanist Assn.	Tel Aviv	
	International		
1880	Intl. Fed. of Freethinkers	Brussels	Became World Union of Freethinkers.
1880-active	World Union of Freethinkers	Brussels	

Appendix 4: Publishers of Unbelief

This appendix lists publishers, their headquarters, and dates of operation. Included are publishers from all over the world whose *primary* purpose was to issue books or pamphlets about religious unbelief. Those who published only materials *against* unbelief are not listed. Publishers of magazines and newspapers will be found in **Appendix**

5: Periodicals of Unbelief. Publishers who at one time issued books or pamphlets about unbelief but then published other materials are included.

Entries are by country, beginning with English-speaking nations.

A dagger (†) appears before the names of all major freethought publishers. An arrow (→) indicates that the location of a publisher changed from one city to another.

Note: *Freethought* is abbreviated FT.

Publisher	Location	Dates	Remarks
		United States	
A. Kneeland/Investigator	Boston	1832-38	ABNER KNEELAND, founder.
†J. P. Mendum	Boston	1838-1904	Successor to Kneeland's *Investigator.*
†Truth Seeker Co.	New York San Diego	1873-present	DEROBIGNE MORTIMER BENNETT, founder.
†Freethought Press Assn.	New York	c1926-68	JOSEPH LEWIS, founder.
†Peter Eckler Pub. Co.	New York	c1882-1928	Eckler was a printer prior to founding.
C. P. Farrell	Peoria, IL.→ Washington, D.C. → New York	1877-1925	Major publisher of ROBERT G. INGERSOLL.
American Atheist Press	Austin, TX	1964-present	MADALYN MURRAY O'HAIR, founder.
Prometheus Books	Buffalo	1970-present	Paul Kurtz, founder.
J. W. Bouton	New York	c1870-c1900	Mostly anthropological works.
Ironclad Age	Indianapolis	c1880-c1898	J. R. Monroe, founder.
Blue Grass Ptg. Co.	Lexington, KY	c1890-c1905	C. C. Moore, founder.
G. Vale	New York	c1836-c186	Important early FT publisher.
Wright & Owen	New York	1825-c1835	FRANCES WRIGHT, ROBERT DALE OWEN, founders.
A. J. & G. W. Matsell	New York	c1835-c1840	
H. D. Robinson	New York	c1832-c1835	Publisher of the "New York Philosophical Library" series.
Calvin Blanchard	New York	c1850-c1860	

Publisher	Location	Dates	Remarks
Columbian Press	New York	c1795-?	First American FT publisher.
T. & J. Swords	New York	c1795-?	Major publisher of THOMAS PAINE.
†E. Haldeman-Julius	Girard, KS	1915-51	Publisher of the Little Blue Books.
A. K. Butts	New York → NJ	c1870-c1875	Mostly pamphlets.
C. P. Somerby	New York	c1870-c1875	Absorbed into the Truth Seeker Co.
American Secular Union	Chicago	1883-c1902	Mostly pamphlets.
Open Court Pub. Co.	Chicago → La Salle, IL	1887-present	Works on the origins of religion.
Independent Publications	Paterson, NJ	c1975-present	Pamphlets only.
Friendship Liberal League	Philadelphia	1947-c1970	Pamphlets only.
American Rationalist	St. Louis	1953-present	Pamphlets only.
Gordon Press	New York	c1975-?	Reprints of FT books.
Freidenker Pub. Co.	Milwaukee	c1872-1917	German-lang. FT works.
August Geringer	Chicago	c1877-?	Czech-lang. FT works.
Václav Šnajdr	Cleveland	c1880-?	Czech-lang. FT works.
Rosický	Omaha	c1880-?	Czech-lang. FT works.
Bárta-Letovský	St. Louis	c1880-?	Czech-lang. FT works.
Raivaaja Pub. Co.	Fitchburg, MA	c1900-10	Finnish-lang. FT works.
Työmis Society	Superior, WI	c1900-10	Finnish-lang. FT works.
Vilho Leikas & Co.	Calumet, MI	c1900-10	Finnish-lang. FT works.
Forskaren Pub. Co.	Minneapolis	c1900-c1910	Swedish-lang. FT works.

United Kingdom

Publisher	Location	Dates	Remarks
D. I. Eaton	London	1794-c1812	Thomas Paine's works; Daniel Isaac Eaton, proprietor.
†R. Carlile	London	1818-43	RICHARD CARLILE, proprietor

Publisher	Location	Dates	Remarks
Holyoake & Co.	London	1853-63	GEORGE JACOB & AUSTIN HOLYOAKE, proprietors.
†Austin & Co.	London	1864-74	Austin Holyoake, proprietor.
†James Watson	London	1843-53	
G. H. Reddalls	Birmingham	c1875-?	Pamphlets only.
Truth Seeker Co.	Bradford	1897-c1920	J. W. GOTT, proprietor; pamphlets only.
H. Hetherington	London	1840-49	Important FT publisher.
M. Roalfe & Co.	Edinburgh	1842-44	Matilda Roalfe, proprietor; pamphlets only.
Abel Heywood & Sons	Manchester	1835-c1890	Important; mostly pamphlets.
†Edward Truelove	London	1852-93	
Annie Besant & Charles Bradlaugh	London	1875-77	CHARLES WATTS also involved.
†Freethought Pub. Co.	London	1877-90	ANNIE BESANT, CHARLES BRADLAUGH, proprietors.
†R. Forder	London	1891-1903	Robert Forder, proprietor.
†Progressive Pub. Co.	London	1881-99	GEORGE WILLIAM FOOTE, proprietor.
Freethought Pub. Co.	London	1899-1908	G. W. Foote; successor to Progressive Pub. Co.
†Pioneer Press	London	1908-present	G. W. Foote, proprietor.
†C. Watts/Watts & Co.	London	1877-present	Charles Watts, proprietor.
A. & H. B. Bonner	London	1891-1903	Charles Bradlaugh's daughter, Hypatia Bradlaugh Bonner, and her husband, Arthur Bonner, were the founders.
†W. Stewart & Co.	London	c1882-1906	WILLIAM STEWART ROSS, proprietor.
Thomas Scott	Ramsgate	c1870-1879	Mostly pamphlets.
†Rationalist Press Assn.	London	1900-present	
South Place Ethical Society	London	c1950-present	

Publisher	Location	Dates	Remarks
G. Standring	London	c1900–c1920	George Standring, proprietor.

Canada

Publisher	Location	Dates	Remarks
Secular Thought	Toronto	1885–1911	Charles Watts, J. Spencer Ellis, founders.

Australia

Publisher	Location	Dates	Remarks
Sydney Freethought Press	Sydney	c1888	WILLIAM WHITEHOUSE COLLINS, founder.
Sydney Lyceum Committee	Sydney	c1886	
William Rowney	Brisbane	c1886	
Thomas Walker	Melbourne	c1882	
Australasian Secular Assn.	Melbourne	c1888	
Rationalist Assn. of Australia	Melbourne	c1935	
Rationalist Assn. of New South Wales	Sydney	1912	
Joseph Symes/ *Liberator*	Melbourne	1884–c1890	JOSEPH SYMES, founder.
A. T. Wilson	Melbourne	c1890–1904	Agnes Wilson, founder, was Symes' wife.
George Robertson	Melbourne, Sydney	1880s	
W. H. Terry	Melbourne	c1877–c1882	Freethought/spiritualist.
E. W. Cole	Melbourne		
W. C. Rigby	Adelaide	c1880	

New Zealand

Publisher	Location	Dates	Remarks
Joseph Braithwaite	Dunedin	c1879	
R. Shannon	Christchurch	c1880	
Rationalist Assn.	Auckland	c1940–present	Pamphlets.

India

Publisher	Location	Dates	Remarks
Suyamariadai Iyakkam (Self-Respect Movement)	Madras	1925–present	After 1944 known as Dravida Kazhagam (Dravidian Federation).

Publisher	Location	Dates	Remarks
Indian Rationalist Assn.	Madras	1950-present	
Indian Renaissance Institute	Bombay	1948-present	
Atheist Centre	Vijayawada	1969-present	GORA, Lavanam, founder/director.
Periyar Publications/Thinker's Forum	Tiruchirappalli	c1970-present	PERIYAR's Self-Respect publications.

Argentina

Publisher	Location	Dates	Remarks
Propaganda Liberal	Buenos Aires	c1913	
L. J. Rosso	Buenos Aires	c1917-c1927	

Brazil

Publisher	Location	Dates	Remarks
Igreja e Apostolado Positivista do Brasil	Rio de Janeiro	c1880-c1967	Major positivist publisher.

Mexico

Publisher	Location	Dates	Remarks
Libertad	Mexico City	c1880	
Soria	Mexico City	c1921	

Peru

Publisher	Location	Dates	Remarks
Ligue des Libres Pensadores	Lima	c1890	

Uruguay

Publisher	Location	Dates	Remarks
Asociación de Propaganda Liberal	Montevideo	1920-25	

Austria

Publisher	Location	Dates	Remarks
Anzengruber Verlag	Vienna	c1912	
†Freidenker Bund	Vienna	c1926	

France

Publisher	Location	Dates	Remarks
†Éditions de L'Union Rationaliste	Paris	1930-present	
†Éditions de L'Idée Libre	Herblay	c1920-present	
Éditions du Pavillon	Paris	c1968-?	

Publisher	Location	Dates	Remarks
L'Anti-Cléricale	Paris	c1880	
Letouzey & Ané	Paris	c1886	
†Éditions Rationalistes	Paris	c1935-?	
†Éditions Rieder	Paris	c1930-?	

Germany

Publisher	Location	Dates	Remarks
U. Bod Verlag	Berlin	c1925	
A. Kröner	Leipzig	c1910	
Verlagsanstalt Proletarischer Freidenker	Leipzig	1919-33	
†Freidenker Verlag	Leipzig	c1922-c1926	
†E. Oldenburg	Leipzig	c1918-c1923	
IHW Dietz	Berlin	c1922	
Verein der Freidenker für Feuerbestattung	Berlin	1919-33	
Freireligiöse Gemeinde	Hamburg	c1925	
Freireligiöse Landesgemeinde Württemberg	Stuttgart	c1947-present	
Volkesbund für Geistesfreiheit	Leipzig	c1926	
Konrad Beisswanger	Nuremburg	1914	
Neuer Frankfurter Verlag	Frankfurt	1900	
Verlag Unesma	Leipzig	1907-33	
Urania-Verlag	Leipzig	1919-33, 1945	
JBDK-Verlag	Berlin	c1978	
Hamburger-Kulturverlag	Hamburg	1947-60?	
H. Freistühler	Schwerte	c1947	
Szczesny-Verlag	Munich	c1958-68	

Publisher	Location	Dates	Remarks
	Netherlands		
†*Dageraad*	Amsterdam	1853-c1935	
†Roode	Amsterdam		
†J. Van Loo	Amsterdam	c1920	
NH Luigies & Zonen	Rotterdam	c1925	
†Uitgave B.O.O.	Zandvoort		
J. Emmering	Amsterdam	c1931	
Fakkel	Amsterdam	c1923	
Lenfring	Amsterdam	c1913	
L. J. Vermeer	Amsterdam	c1904	
P. C. Wezel	Haarlem	c1894	
	Belgium		
De Jongh	Antwerp	c1934	
	Soviet Union		
†Mysl'	Moscow	c1980	
Nauka	Moscow	c1970-present	
†Muzei istorii religii i ateizma	Leningrad	c1970-present	

Note: All publishers are government owned, so the names may be meaningless.

Publisher	Location	Dates	Remarks
	Sweden		
Svea	Stockholm	c1879	
Loonström	Stockholm	c1884	
Björck & Börjesson	Stockholm	c1907	

Appendix 5: Periodicals of Unbelief

This appendix lists magazines and newspapers whose *primary* purpose was to further religious unbelief. Publications of a political, economic, or nationalistic character are not listed, since they had other primary purposes. (Therefore, I have excluded Communist, socialist, libertarian, anarchist, and fraternal-order publications.) Mimeographed newsletters of unusual importance are included.

The presentation is by country of publication, beginning with English-speaking countries; periodicals are listed alphabetically within each country.

The basic information given for each periodical is all that was available. In some cases, neither the editor's name nor the exact dates of publication are known. Where names do appear, only one or two of the most important or most recent are given.

In a number of cases, no copy of the periodical is known to have survived. An asterisk (*) precedes the names of those publications of which I have been unable to locate a single copy.

An arrow (→) indicates that the location of a periodical changed from one city to another.

Note: *The,* or its equivalent, is omitted from titles. The language of a periodical is given only when it would not be obvious from the name of the country.

Publication	Location	Dates	Remarks
United States			
Age of Reason	New York	1848-51	Ed., Peter Eckler; semi-mo.
Age of Reason	New York	1937-68	Ed. JOSEPH LEWIS.
American Atheist	Baltimore → Honolulu → Austin, TX	1963-present	Ed., MADALYN MURRAY O'HAIR.
American Freeman	Girard, KS	1922-51	Ed., EMANUEL HALDEMAN-JULIUS; newspaper.
American Freethinker	Baltimore	1963-65	See *American Atheist*.
American Humanist Assn. Bull.	Yellow Springs, OH	1953	
American Rationalist	Chicago → St. Louis	1956-present	Ed., Gordon Stein; semi-mo.
American Rationalist Federation Bull.	St. Louis	1956-c1960	Irregular.
Appeal to Reason	Thousand Oaks, CA	1964-c1966	Monthly.
Arbitrator	New York	19?-19?	Ed., Floyd Dell; mo.
Atheist	New York → San Diego	1953-present	Eds., Charles Smith, J. H. Johnson.
Atheist Connection	Culver City, CA	1982-83	Ed., Ron Nelson; mo.
Atheists United Newsletter	Sherman Oaks, CA	1983-present	
Atomic Era	Weissport, PA	c1940-c1950	Monthly.
Beacon	New York	1836-46	Ed., GILBERT VALE; mo.

Publication	Location	Dates	Remarks
Biblical Errancy	Enid, OH → Springfield, OH	1983-present	Ed., Dennis McKinsey; mo.
Blätter für Freies Religiöses Leben	San Francisco → Philadelphia	1856-77	Ed., F. Schueneman-Pott; German.
Blue Grass Blade	Lexington, KY	1884-1910	Eds., Charles C. Moore, J. E. Hughes; wkly.
Boston Investigator	Boston	1831-1904	Eds. ABNER KNEELAND, H. Seaver; wkly. paper.
Comet	New York	1832-33	Eds., H. D. Robinson, S. J. W. Taber; wkly.
Comet	Weissport, PA	1946-c1955	Monthly.
Common Herd	Dallas	1909-40	Ed., Richard Potts; quart.
Common Sense	New York		See *Age of Reason*.
Correspondent	New York	1827-29	Ed., George Houston; wkly.
Critic and Guide	Girard, KS	1947-51	Ed., E. Haldeman-Julius; mo.
Crucible	Seattle	1916-32	Weekly, monthly.
Crucible	Cass Lake, MN	1966-c1977	Ed., Garry deYoung; mo., semi-mo.
Debunker	Girard, KS	1928-32	Ed., E. Haldeman-Julius; continuation of *H-J Monthly*.
Delaware Free Press	Wilmington	1830-33	
Dial	Cincinnati	1860	Ed., MONCURE CONWAY; mo.
Dixie Rationalist	Clanton, AL	1960	Monthly.
Ethical Outlook	New York	c1956-present?	Bi-monthly.
Ethical Record	Philadelphia → New York	1888-present	Monthly.
Exit	New York	1969-c1972	Ed., Martin J. Martin; irreg.
Fable Buster	Seattle	c1944-c1949	Monthly.
Fackel	New York → Baltimore	1843-47; 1848-50	Ed., Samuel Ludvigh
Fact	Rockford, IL	1959-c1962	Ed., Ralph Blois; irreg.

Publication	Location	Dates	Remarks
Fact Digest	Rockford, IL	1960	Quarterly.
Forskaren	Minneapolis	1893-1924	Swedish.
Free Enquirer	New Harmony, IN → New York	1825-35	Until 1829, *New Harmony Gazette*; eds., FRANCES WRIGHT, ROBERT DALE OWEN.
Free Humanist	Philadelphia	1960-63	
Free Humanist	Baltimore → Honolulu	1963-64	Ed., Madalyn Murray O'Hair.
Free Inquiry	Buffalo	1980-present	Ed., Paul Kurtz; quart.
Free Lance	Toledo	1924	Ed., Karl Pauli; quart.
Free Mind	Portland, OR → Buffalo	1946-present	Bi-monthly.
Freethinker	Philadelphia	1959-60	1960-63, *Free Humanist*.
Freethinker's Magazine	Buffalo	1882-94	Ed., H. L. Green; mo.
Freethought	San Francisco	1888-91	Eds., S. P. PUTNAM, G. Macdonald.
Freethought Commentary	Paterson, NJ	1977; 1980	Ed., Carl Shapiro; quart.
Freethought Ideal	Ottawa, KS	c1893-c1900	Ed., Etta Semple.
Free Thought Magazine	Chicago	1894-1903	Ed., H. L. Green.
Freethought Opinion	Paterson, NJ	1974-75	Ed., Carl Shapiro.
Free Thoughts	El Segundo, CA	c1960-c1961	Irregular.
Freethought Today	Madison, WI	1983-present	Ed., Anne Gaylor; newspaper.
Freidenker	New York	1872-?	Ed., Fred. Leiss; German.
Freidenker	Milwaukee → New Ulm, MN	1872-1931	German, mo.
Freie Vort/Free Word	Milwaukee	1932-c1972	German and English, mo.
Friends of Robert G. Ingersoll	Peoria, IL	1982-83	Newsletter.
GALA Review	San Francisco	1978-present	Gay Atheist League of America.
Gay Atheist	New York	1984-present	
Godless World	Oakland, CA	1931	Ed., Martin S. Charles.

Publication	Location	Dates	Remarks
Grandpappy's Almanac	Erie, MI	1961-c1963	Ed., Karl Pauli.
Haldeman-Julius Monthly	Girard, KS	1924-28	See *Debunker*.
Haldeman-Julius News-Letter	Girard, KS	1939-c1940	Weekly.
Haldeman-Julius Quarterly	Girard, KS	1926-28	Quarterly.
*Herald of Reason & Common Sense	Poughkeepsie, NY	1835	Ed., Jesse Torrey, Jr.
Hornet	Fork, NC	c1923?-c1955	Monthly.
Humanist	Yellow Springs, OH→ San Francisco → Amherst, NY	1941-present	Ed., Lloyd Morain; mo., bi-mo.
Humanist Century	San Diego, CA	1980-present	Ed., Frank Mortyn; mo.
Humanist Community News	San Jose, CA	c1982	Irregular.
Humanistic Judaism	Farmington Hills, MI	1977-present	Ed., Sherwin Wine; quart.
Humanist Pulpit	Minneapolis	1927-c1932	Ed., J. H. Dietrich.
Humanist Quest for Truth	Brighton, CO	1978-present	Ed., Jane Cathryn Conrad.
Humanist Reporter	Chicago	c1961-?	Newsletter.
Humanist Soc. Berkeley, CA	Berkeley	c1968-?	Newsletter.
Humanist Soc. Metro. N.Y.	New York	1983-present	Newsletter.
Humanists of the Southwest	Phoenix	1978	Newsletter.
Humanist Voice	Dallas	c1982-present	Newsletter.
Humanist World Digest	Berkeley		Before 1952, *Humanist World*.
Humanitarian Review	Los Angeles	1903-11	Ed., Singleton W. Davis.
Humanity	Kansas City	c1895-c1898	
Iconoclast	Washington, DC	1870-71	Ed., Lester Ward; mo.
Iconoclast	Indianapolis	1882-?	Monthly.
Independent Pulpit	Waco, TX	1882-1901	Ed., J. D. Shaw; mo.
Index	Toledo → Boston	1870-86	Eds. F. E. Abbot, B. F. UNDERWOOD.

Publication	Location	Dates	Remarks
Infidel Pulpit	Boston	1881-?	Ed., George Chainey; semi-mo.
Ingersoll Memorial Beacon	Chicago	1904-c1913	Ed., W. H. Maple; mo.
Iron-Clad Age	Indianapolis	1881-98	Ed., J. R. Monroe; wkly.
Joseph McCabe Magazine	Girard, KS	1930-c1931	Eds., J. McCABE, E. Haldeman-Julius; mo.
J. of Art, Science, Philosophy	St. Paul	c1972-73	Ed., Garry deYoung.
Know Thyself	Girard, KS	1923-24	Ed., W. Fielding; mo.
*Liberal	Liberal, MO	1881-89	Ed., George Walser.
Liberal	Philadelphia	1947-c1970	Friendship Liberal League.
Liberal Advocate	Rochester, NY	1832-34	Ed., Obediah Dogberry (pseud?).
Liberal Iconoclast	Chicago	?-c1937	
Liberal Press or Anti-superstitionist	Philadelphia	1828	
Liberal Review	Chicago	1904-06, 1918	Eds., T. B. Wakeman, M. M. Mangasarian.
*Libre Pensée	Jeanette, PA	c1900	French?
Light of Reason	Indianapolis	c1890	Annual.
*Little Freethinker	Snowville, VA/Chicago?	1892-93	Ed., Elmina Drake Slenker.
Lookout	Seattle	c1962-c1966	
Louisville Skeptic	Louisville	1838	Ed., R. K. M. Ormsby.
*Loxias	Chicago	1908-c1921	Greek weekly paper.
Lucifer	Milwaukee→Madison, WI	1882-98	*Arminia* after 1896; German.
Man	New York	1878-84	Ed., T. B. Wakeman.
Manas	Los Angeles	c19?-c1960	
March of Mind	Cincinnati	1828	
Militant Atheist	Girard, KS	1933	Ed., Joseph McCabe; mo. paper.

Publication	Location	Dates	Remarks
*Mirror	Newburgh, NY	1798-99	Deistic; wkly.
Modern Thinker	New York	c1930-c1935	Monthly.
*Mohawk Liberal	Little Falls, NY	1833-34	Ed., L. Windsor Smith.
Murray Newsletter	Honolulu	1964-65	Ed., Madalyn Murray.
New Perspective	Philadelphia	1966-c1968	
Northern California Secular Soc. Collectanea	San Francisco	c1969-c1972	
Open Mind	Belleville → Newark, NJ	1960-c1961	
Pacific Coast Free-Thinker	San Francisco	1879	Ed., Byron Adonis.
People's Press	Chicago	c1896-c1905	Ed., E. Lenau.
Pfaffenspiegel	Chicago	1906-11	German; anticlerical; mo.
Pleasure Boat	Portland, ME	c1844-c1850	Ed., Jeremiah Hacker; mo.
Pokrok	Chicago → Racine, WI	1867-78	Ed., Joseph Pastor; Czech.
*Progressive Age	Grand Rapids, MI	c1886	Ed., VOLTAIRINE DE CLEYRE.
Progressive Forum	Los Angeles	1923-30	Ed., Charles Calhoun; mo.
Progressive World	Clifton, NJ → Los Angeles → Oakland, CA	1947-81	Ed., H. R. Orr; United Secularists of America; bi-mo.
Prospect: View of the Moral World	New York	1803-05	Ed., ELIHU PALMER.
Queen Silver's Magazine	Inglewood, CA	1923-32	Ed., Queen Silver; irreg.
Quester	Austin, TX	197?-c1978	Ed., Garvin Chastain, mo.
Radical	Boston	c1863-?	Ed., Sidney H. Morse.
Rationalist	Chicago	1912-c1916	Ed., M. M. Mangasarian.
Rationalist	Philadelphia	1947	
Rationalist News	Rockford, IL	c1959-c1960	Ed., Ralph S. Blois.
Rationalist News	St. Louis	c1956-c1963	Am. Rationalist Fed.; irreg.
Rationalist Reporter	New York	c1959	Rationalist Press Assn.

Publication	Location	Dates	Remarks
Regenerator	Fruit Hills, OH	1844-48	Ed., Orson S. Murray.
Religious Humanism	Yellow Springs, OH	c1966-present	Ed., Paul Beattie.
Repartee	New York	c1968-c1972	Ed., Martin J. Martin; irreg.
Rip Saw	South Bend, IN	c1955-c1965	Ed., Virgil McClain; mo.
San Diego Humanist	San Diego	c1972-present	Newsletter.
SEA Journal	Fresno, CA	1975-present	Ed., W. H. Young; mo.
Secularist	Cicero, IL	c1950-c1958	Monthly.
Secularist	Newark, NJ	1960-c1961	Monthly.
Secular Subjects	St. Louis	1948-present	Ed., Eldon Scholl; mo.
*Self-Examiner	Goshen, OH	1843	Ed., Aaron Hinchman.
Separationist Newsletter	Leavittsburg, OH	1979	Bi-monthly.
Seymour Times	Seymour, IN	1879-81	See *Iron-Clad Age*.
Sky Rover	Mercedes, TX	c1976	
Society of Separationists	Austin, TX	c1967-present	Became *Insider's Newsletter*.
Southern Humanist	Cocoa Beach, FL	c1974-c1975	Bi-monthly.
South-West Freethinker's News	Dallas	1954	
Standard	New York	c1923-?	N.Y. Soc. for Ethical Culture.
Svobodna Skola	Oak Park → Berwyn, IL	1897-present	Czech Rationalist Schools; Czech.
Svojan	Chicago	1894-1924	Czech.
Svornost	Chicago	1875?	Ed., F. B. Zdrubek; Czech.
Tax the Church	Austin, TX	c1966	Newsletter; mo.
Temple of Reason	New York → Philadelphia	1800-03	Deistic; mo.
*Temple of Reason	Philadelphia	1835-37	Ed., Russell Canfield.
Theophilanthropist	New York	1810-11	Deistic.
Thinker	New York	c1928-c1932	Monthly.

Publication	Location	Dates	Remarks
Torch of Reason	Silverton, OR → Kansas City	1896-1903	Ed., T. B. Wakeman; pub. of Liberal University; newspaper.
Truth Seeker	Paris, IL → New York → San Diego	1873-present	Founded by D. M. BENNETT; wkly.
Vek Rozumu	New York → Berwyn, IL	1910-present	Ed., Victor Cjecka; mo.; Czech.
Vesmir	Okla. City → Chicago	1909-21	Ed., Frank Iska; Czech.
Voice of Freedom	Milwaukee	1932-c1972	See *Freie Wort*.
Voice of Freedom	Nashville	c1952-c1959	
Voice of Reason	New York	1981-present	Ed., Edd Doerr.
Volcano	Salem, MO	c1966-c1968	
Western Examiner	St. Louis	1834-35	Ed., John Bobb.
*World As It Is	Rochester, NY	1836	Ed., Luke Shepherd.

United Kingdom

Publication	Location	Dates	Remarks
Agnostic	London	1885	Ed., Charles A. Watts.
Agnostic Annual	London	1886-1905	Ed., CHARLES WATTS; annual.
Agnostic Journal (& Secular Review)	London	c1888-89 (1889-1906)	Ed., W. S. ROSS; joined with *Secular Review* in 1889 to form joint title.
*Christian Warrior	London	1842-43	Ed., RICHARD CARLILE.
*Church	London	c1838	Ed., Richard Carlile.
Counsellor	London	1861	Ed., G. J. HOLYOAKE; see *Reasoner*.
Essex Forum	Brentwood, England	1970-?	Essex Council of Humanist Groups.
Ethical Record	London	1895-present	South Place Ethical Society.
Fight	London	1934	
Free Enquirer	London	1761	Ed., PETER ANNET; deistic.
Free Mind	London	1947-48	Student Rationalists.

Publication	Location	Dates	Remarks
Freethinker	London	1881-present	Eds., G. W. FOOTE, CHAPMAN COHEN.
Free-Thinkers' Information for the People	Glasgow	1842-43	Ed., HENRY HETHERINGTON.
Freethinker's Magazine & Review	London	1850-51	
Freethought News	Bradford	1947-50	Ed., F. J. Corina; mo.
Gauntlet	London	1833-34	Ed., Richard Carlile.
Humanist (New Humanist)	London	1956-72 (1972-present)	Formerly *Literary Guide; New Humanist* after 1972; Rationalist Press Assn.; mo., quart.
International Humanist & Ethical Union Info. Bulletin	London	c1953-?	Newsletter.
Investigator	London	1843	Ed., CHARLES SOUTHWELL.
Isis	London	1832	Ed., Eliza Sharples Carlile.
Journal of Radical History	Nottingham	1983-present	Irreg.; about THOMAS PAINE.
Lancashire Beacon	Manchester	1842	Ed., Charles Southwell.
Leicester Reasoner	Leicester		Ed., F. J. Gould.
Liberal	London	1879	Ed., G. W. Foote.
Lion	London	1828-29	Ed., Richard Carlile; about ROBERT TAYLOR.
Literary Guide & Rationalist Review	London	1885-1956	R.P.A.; founder, Charles A. Watts.
London Investigator	London	1854-59	Eds., R. Cooper, CHARLES BRADLAUGH.
Moralist	London	1823	Ed., Richard Carlile.
Movement	London	1843-45	Ed., G. J. Holyoake; wkly.
National Reformer	London	1860-93	Eds., Charles Bradlaugh, Joseph Barker, J. M. ROBERTSON.
Newgate Monthly Magazine	London	1825	Edited from prison.

Publication	Location	Dates	Remarks
New Humanist	London	1972-present	See *Humanist*.
Oracle of Reason	Bristol	1841-43	Eds., Charles Southwell, G. J. Holyoake.
Our Corner	London	1883-88	Ed., ANNIE BESANT; wkly.
Philalethian	London	1833	Ed., ROBERT TAYLOR.
Plain View	London	1944-65	Ed., H. J. Blackham; Ethical Union.
Plebian	Edinburgh	1844	Ed., Matilda Roalfe.
Poor Man's Guardian	London	1831-35	Ed., Henry Hetherington.
Present Day	London	1883-86	Ed., G. J. Holyoake.
Progress	London	1883-87	Ed., G. W. Foote.
Prompter	London	1830-31	Ed., Richard Carlile.
Propagandist	London		Ed., W. H. Johnson ("A. Collins").
Question	London	1968-80	Rationalist Press Assn.; annual.
Rationalist Annual (RPA Annual)	London	1908-26 (1927-67)	Annual.
Rational Review	London	c1963-c1964	Monthly.
Reason	London	1898-c1899	Ed., George Standring.
Reasoner	London	1846-72	Ed., G. J. Holyoake; titles included *Counsellor, Secular World, English Leader;* wkly., mo.
Reformer	London	1893-1904	Ed., J. M. Robertson; mo.
Republican	London	1819-26	Ed., Richard Carlile.
Republican	London	c1876-c1884	Ed., George Standring.
Scourge	London	1834-35	Ed., Richard Carlile.
Secular Chronicle	Birmingham	1872-79	Ed., HARRIET LAW.

Publication	Location	Dates	Remarks
Secularist	London	1876-77	Eds., G. J. Holyoake, G. W. Foote.
Secularist	Bradford	1902-?	Ed., H. Percy Ward.
Secular Review	London	1876-89	Eds., G. J. Holyoake, Charles Watts, G. W. Foote, W. S. Ross; became *Agnostic Journal* in 1889.
Secular Review	Nottingham	1958	Monthly.
Secular World	London	1862-64	See *Reasoner*.
South Place Magazine	London	1895-c1910	South Place Ethical Society.
Thinker's Digest	London	c1949	R.P.A.; quart.
Thomas Paine Soc. Bulletin	Nottingham	c1966-c1972	Ed., R. W. Morrell.
Truthseeker	Bradford	1894-c1905	Ed., J. W. GOTT.

Canada

Publication	Location	Dates	Remarks
Atheism in Canada	Toronto	1983-present	Ed., Louise Goueffic.
Avenir	Montreal	1847-57	Anticlerical, French.
Both Sides	Alymer, Ont.	1875	
Freethought Journal	Toronto	1877	
Humanist in Canada	Vancouver	1967-present	Humanist Soc. of Canada; quart.
Pays	Montreal	1910-21	Anticlerical; French.
Raison	Montreal	1979-present	Ed., Gabriel Dubuisson; French.
Rationalist	Vancouver	1914-?	Ed., E. V. Cook.
Secular Thought	Toronto	1885-1911	Founder, Charles Watts; wkly. mo., bi-mo.
Victoria Humanist	Victoria	1964-67	Quarterly.

Australia

Publication	Location	Dates	Remarks
Adelaide Secular & Free Discussion Society's Review	Adelaide	1878-79	Ed., Henry Oliver; mo.

Publication	Location	Dates	Remarks
Atheist Journal	Lidcombe No., NSW	1973–c1977?	Ed., Alan Rickard.
Australian Atheist	Adelaide	1971–?	Pub. by Atheist Foundation of Australia.
Australian Humanist	Adelaide	1968–75	Ed., Bruce Muirden; quart.
Australian Rationalist	Malvern, Vic.	1969–c1975	Ed., W. Glanville Cook; mo.
Australian Rationalist Quarterly	Melbourne	1980–present	Rationalist Soc. of Australia; quart.
*Freedom	Brisbane	1883	Ed., W. Taylor; mo.
Freedom	Sydney	1889–90	Ed., W. W. COLLINS; mo.
*Freethinker & NSW Reformer	Sydney	1886	Ed., W. W. Collins; semi-mo.
Freethought	Sydney	1880–81	Ed., E. Cyril Haviland; mo.
Freethought	Melbourne	1939–44	Ed., J. S. Langley; mo.
*Glow-Worm	Melbourne?	1869–70	Ed., B. S. Naylor; spiritualist and freethought; mo.
*Ingersoll News	Sydney	c1946–48	Ed., H. Scott Bennett.
*Liberal	Sydney	1882–84	Eds., G. Lacy, C. Bright; wkly.
Liberator	Melbourne	1884–1904	Ed., JOSEPH SYMES; wkly.
*Progressive Spiritualist & Freethought Advocate	Melbourne	1873–74	Ed., John Tyerman; wkly.
Queensland Rationalist Soc.	Brisbane	c1966	Newsletter.
Rationalist	Melbourne	1924–69	Ed., J. S. Langley; became *Australian Rationalist* in 1969; mo.
Rationalist News	Chippendale, NSW	1967–present	Ed., Ron Marke; bi-mo.
*Reformer	Melbourne	1880–83	Ed., Joseph Wing; mo., semi-mo.
Ross's Monthly	Melbourne	1915–23	Ed., Robert S. Ross; mo.
*Spiritual Inquirer	Sandhurst, Vic.	1874–75	Ed., J. Wing; spiritualist and freethought; wkly.
*Stockwhip	Sydney	1875–77	Ed., J. E. Kelly; became *Satirist;* wkly.

Publication	Location	Dates	Remarks
Victorian Humanist	E. Malvern, Vic.	1967-?	Ed., M. Beadnell.
Viewpoints	Winston Hills, NSW	c1976-?	NSW Humanist Society.
Westralian Secularist	Perth	c1958-?	Monthly.

New Zealand

Publication	Location	Dates	Remarks
*Auckland Examiner	Auckland	1857-60	Ed., Charles Southwell.
*Echo	Dunedin	1869-73; 1880-83	Ed., ROBERT STOUT; wkly., mo.
*Examiner	Christchurch	1907-17	Ed., W. W. Collins; mo. bi-mo.
*Freethought Review	Wanganui	1883-85	Ed., JOHN BALLANCE; mo.
New Zealand Humanist	Auckland	19?-1964	Merged with *NZ Rationalist;* mo.
New Zealand Humanist	Christchurch	c1975-?	Newsletter of Humanist Soc. NZ.
New Zealand Rationalist	Auckland	1939-64	Merged with *NZ Humanist;* mo.
New Zealand Rationalist & Humanist	Auckland	1964-present	Monthly.
*Rationalist	Auckland	1885-86	Ed., J. Evison ("Ivo"), wkly.
*Tribune	Christchurch	1894-95	Ed., W. W. Collins.
Truthseeker	Auckland	1927-39	Became *NZ Rationalist;* mo.

South Africa

Publication	Location	Dates	Remarks
Humanist Assn. South Africa	Joubert Park	c1983-present	Newsletter; bi-mo.
Rationalis/Rationalist	Johannesburg	1956-76	English, Africaans; mo.
*Reflector	Capetown	c1881	Ed., Thomas Walker.
South African Humanist	Joubert Park	1979-present	S.A. Humanist Assn.; mo.

India

Publication	Location	Dates	Remarks
Aayudh	Bombay	1977-present	Marathi; bi-mo.
Age of Atheism	Visakhapatnam	1974-79	Ed., Jayagopal; Atheist Soc. of India.

Publication	Location	Dates	Remarks
Arivu Vazhi	Madras?	1975-present	Tamil; mo.
Atheist	Vijayawada	1969-present	Ed., Lavanam; Atheist Centre; mo.
Atheist Society of India	Visakhapatnam	1972-?	Newsletter; mo.
Charvaka	Vijayawada	1976-79	Telugu; ed., "TR."
Freethought	Madras	1970-83?	Indian Rationalist Assn.
Humanist Outlook	Lucknow	1966-present?	Indian Humanist Union.
Indian Rationalist	Madras	1952-65	Indian Rationalist Assn.
Insaan	Vijayawada	1956-62	Hindi; ed., Lavanam.
*Kudi Arasu	Madras?	1924-?	Tamil; ed., PERIYAR.
Modern Rationalist	Madras	c1973-present	Ed., K. Eeramani.
Nasthika Margum	Vijayawada	1977-present	Telugu; ed., "Mythri."
Nasthika Mitra	Vijayawada	1979-present	Telugu; ed., Y. Phanu; quart.
Nasthika Yugam	Visakhapatnam	1972-79	Telugu; ed., Jayagopal.
*Pakutharivu	Madras	1935-?	Tamil; ed., Periyar.
*Philosophical Inquirer	Madras	1878-c1888	Tamil, English; Ed., M. Mudaliar; wkly.
Radical Humanist	Bombay → Calcutta → New Delhi	1937-present	Eds., M. N. Roy, V. M. Tarkunde; mo.; called *Independent India,* 1937-48.
Reason	Bombay	1931-46	Eds., C. L. D'Avoine, R. V. Karve.
*Sangam	Vijayawada	1949-52; 1960-67	Telugu; eds., GORA, Lavanam.
Secularist	Bombay	1969-present?	Ed., A. B. Shah.
Sinthanayaian	Madras?	1974-present	Tamil; ed., V. Anaimuthu.
Viduthalai	Madras?	1931-present	Tamil; ed., Periyar; daily newspaper.
Vikasam	Hyderabad	1975-present	Telugu; ed., M. V. Ramamurti.
Yukthivadi	Iranjalakuda	1929-present	Malayalam; ed., M. C. Joseph.

Publication	Location	Dates	Remarks
Yukthi Vicharanam		1976-present	Malayalam.

Ceylon/Sri Lanka

Ceylon Rationalist Ambassador	Colombo	1966-72	Ed., Abraham Kovoor; annual.

Argentina

Giordano Bruno	Buenos Aires?	1895	
Infierno	Buenos Aires	1902-05	Anticlerical.
Infierno Lucifer	Porto Allegro	c1908	
Liberal	Buenos Aires?	c1908	
Progreso	Buenos Aires	c1908-12	Ed., Francisco Gicca.

Bolivia

Radical	La Paz	c1908	

Brazil (Portuguese)

Lanterna	São Paulo	c1908	Ed., E. Dias.
Livre Pensador	São Paulo	c1908	Ed., "Mota."
Lucifer	Pôrto Alegre	c1908	

Chile

Espiritu Libre			
Idea	Santiago?	1904-?	
Ley			
Radical	Temuco	1912-14	

Colombia

Thalia		c1910	

Cuba

Espiritu del Siglo	Santiago	c1890	

Ecuador

Alborada	Río Bamba	c1910	

Publication	Location	Dates	Remarks
El Salvador			
America Central	Santa Anna	c1890	
Guatemala			
Noticias	Guatemala City	c1910	
Quetzal	Guatemala City	c1910	
Mexico			
Liberal Poblano	Mexico City	c1962-?	Newspaper.
Libre Pensador	Mexico City	1870-?	Monthly.
*Partido Liberal	Mexico City	c1885-94	
*Revista Positiva	Mexico City	1901-14	Ed., Augustin Aragon.
*Universal	Mexico City?	c1888-94	
Voz de Juarez	Mexico City	c1956-?	Newspaper.
Paraguay			
Voz del Siglo	Asunción?	c1910	
Peru			
Libre Pensamiento	Lima	c1910	
Razón	Trujillo	c1908	
Tiempo	Lima	c1908	
Puerto Rico			
Conciencia Libre	Ponce	1910-21	Weekly.
Trinidad			
Progress		c1890	Ed., E. Dos Santos.
Uruguay			
Capital	Montevideo	c1890	
Despertar	Río Negro	c1908	
Estudio	Montevideo	c1890	

Publication	Location	Dates	Remarks
Liberal	Montevideo	c1910	Ed., Belén Sarraga de F.
Libre Pensamiento	Montevideo?	c1908	
Paysandu	Montevideo	c1890	
Verdad	Montevideo	c1908	
Austria (German)			
Besinnung	Vienna	c1955	Quarterly.
Freidenker	Vienna	c1913-33; 1948-present	
Geist & Gesellschaft	Vienna		Combined with *Freidenker*.
Kirchenfreie	Graz	c1955-present	
Belgium			
Almanach Populaire	Brussels	c1910	French; anticlerical.
Diogenes		c1955	Flemish; quart.
Pensée	Brussels	c1905-c1965	French.
Pensée et Action	Brussels	c1957	French.
Pensée et les Hommes	Brussels	c1958-present	French; monthly.
Vrijdenker		c1955	Flemish; mo.
Czechoslovakia			
Havlicek	Prague	c1930-?	Monthly.
Nova Skutecrost	Prague		
Volna Myslenka	Prague	c1910-?	Weekly.
Finland			
Ajatuksen Vapaus	Tampere	1937-39	Ed., Hugo Lehtinen.
Vapaa Ajattelija	Turku; Helsinki	1940-41; 1945-present	Monthly; 8 per year.
Vapaa Ajatus	Helsinki	1910-17	Ed., S. E. Kristianson.
Wapaita Aatteita	Kuopio	1889-90	Eds., M. Canth, A. B. Mäkelä.

Publication	Location	Dates	Remarks
		France	
Bulletin du Cercle Ernest-Renan	Paris	c1952	
Bulletin Rationaliste	Lyon	c1950	
Cahiers du Cercle Ernest-Renan	Paris	c1952	
Cahiers Rationalistes	Paris	c1930-present	Published by Union Rationaliste.
Calotte	Gennes	c1864	
Candide	Paris	1865	Ed., M. Tridon.
Courrier Rationaliste	Paris	c1953	Monthly.
Defense de l'Homme	Paris	c1957	
Europe et Laïcité	Paris		
Idee Libre	Herblay → Meaux		
Libre Pensée	Paris	1866	Became *Pensée Nouvelle*.
Libre Pensée	Marseilles	c1972	Quarterly.
Libre-Pensée Intégrale	Puch	c1925	
Libre Pensée Nantaise	Nantes	c1974	
Morale Independente	Paris	c1855	Ed. Louis A. Martin.
Pensée Nouvelle	Paris	c1868	
Raison	Paris	c1957	Ed., René Labregere.
Revue Encyclopedique	Paris	1866	
Tribune des Athées	Bellenaves	c1980-present	Quarterly.
		Germany, East and West	
Atheist	Nuremberg	1905-c1933	
Es Werde Licht	Munich	c1914	
Freidenker	Berlin → Bonn	?-1933; c1946-present	

Publication	Location	Dates	Remarks
Freie Jugand	Berlin	c1914	
Freie Wort	Frankfurt	c1914	Ed., Max Henning.
Freigeistige Aktion		1957-present	Publisher, Deutscher Volks-bund f. Geistesfreiheit.
Freigeistige Wort	Nuremberg	c1947	
Freireligiöse	Mannheim	1947	
Freies Menschentum	Wiesbaden	c1948	Bi-monthly.
Funke	Bremen	c1970	
Geistesfreiheit	Werigerode	c1970	Ed., G. Tschirn.
Humanist	Ludwigshafen	c1963-present	
Lichtstrahlen	Berlin	1890	
Mitteslunsblatt der Frei-religiösen Landesgemeinde Bayern	Nuremberg	c1947	
Monatsschau: Freigeistige Gemeinschaft Berlin	Berlin	c1949	
Quell	Munich	c1948	

Hungary

Publication	Location	Dates	Remarks
Pesti Naplo	Budapest	c1904	

Italy

Publication	Location	Dates	Remarks
Acacia	Rome	c1910	
Asino	Rome	c1910-25	
Don Basilio	Rome		
Libero Pensiero Internationale	Rome	c1904	
Ragione	Rome	c1918-present	Publisher, "Giordano Bruno"; newspaper became magazine.
Secolo	Milan	c1910	

Publication	Location	Dates	Remarks
Luxembourg			
Freie Wort / Libre Penseur	Luxembourg	c1954-?	German and French; mo.
Freie Gedachte	Luxembourg	c1950	
Netherlands			
Dageraad	Amsterdam	1856-19?	
International Humanism	Utrecht	c1965-?	
Maandblad de Vrije Gedachte	Rotterdam	1970-present	Successor to *Vrijdenker;* mo.
Mens en Wereld	Utrecht	c1957	
Moralist	Antwerp	c1935-present	Bi-monthly.
Vrijdenker	Amsterdam	1943-c1970	Successor to *Dageraad;* newspaper; semi-mo.
Norway			
Human-Etikk	Oslo	19?-present	Ed., Levi Fragell; bi-mo.
Poland			
Argumenty	Warsaw	c1956-present	Monthly.
Euhemer			
Fakty i Mysli	Bydgoczez	c1958	Weekly.
Glos Wolnych	Bydgoczez	c1957	
Horyzontz	Cracow?	c1910	
Panteon	Paris (exiled Poles)	c1906	Polish League of Freethought.
Polski Wolnymysliciel	Warsaw	1926-c1936	
Wolny Mysl	Warsaw?	1906-c1908	Ed., A. Niemojewski.
Wolnymysl	Warsaw?	1920-28	
Portugal			
Revista de Estudio Livres	Lisbon	c1910	

Publication	Location	Dates	Remarks
Seculo	Lisbon	c1910	
Vanguardia	Lisbon	c1908	
Voz Publica	Oporto	c1908	

Romania

Adevéral	Bucharest	c1904	

Soviet Union

Agitator	Moscow	19?-present	
Antireligioznik	Moscow	192?-1941	Publisher, League of the Militant Godless.
Bezbozhnik	Moscow	1924-41	Publisher, League of the Militant Godless.
Lyudina i Svit	Kiev?	1964	Ukranian; publisher, Knowledge Society.
Nauka i Religiya	Moscow	1959-present	Successor to *Antireligioznik*.
Voivnichii Ateist	Kiev?	1961-64	Ukrainian; mo.; became *Lyudina i Svit*.
Voprosy Ateizma	Kiev	1964-?	Annual.
Voprosy Istorii Religii i Ateizma	Moscow	?-c1965	Publisher, Institute of History; annual.
Voprosy Nauchnogo Ateizma	Moscow	1966-present	Publisher, Institute of Scientific Atheism, annual.
Yezhegodnik Muzeya Istorii Religii i Ateizma	Leningrad	1958-64	Annual.

Spain

Dominicales del Libre Pensamiento	Madrid	1894-c1910	Ed., Fernando Lozano ("Demófilo").
Tramontana	Barcelona	1894-c1895	Ed., D. José Llunas.
Tronada	Barcelona		

Publication	Location	Dates	Remarks
Sweden			
Fri Ord	Stockholm	1900-03	Publisher, Freedom Union.
Fritänkaren	Stockholm?	1897	
Fri Tanke	Johanneshov	c1954	Förbund för Religionsfrihet.
Gudinna	Stockholm?	c1920	
Human-Etiska Förbundet	Enskede	19?-present	Bi-monthly.
Ny Sanning	Stockholm?	1895-97	Succeeded by *Fritankaren.*
Switzerland			
Freidenker	Aarau → Basel	c1917-present	German; called *Befreiung* in 1950s.
Libre Penseur	Lausanne	c1972?	French.
Lumiére	Geneva	c1901	French; ed., M. Fulpius.
Rationaliste	Geneva	c1860-c1865	French.
Israel			
Breira Humanistit	Tel Aviv	1977-present	Hebrew version of *Israel Humanist Alternative.*
Israel Humanist Alternative	Tel Aviv	1977-present	English.
Israel Humanist Review	Tel Aviv	1981-present	English.
Egypt			
al-'Usur	Cairo	1927-31	Arabic; ed., Isma'il Mazhar.
Lebanon			
al-Duhur	Beirut	1931-33	Arabic; ed., Ibrahim Haddad.
Japan			
Iunri	Yokahama	1910-?	Ed., Y. Oyama.

Index

This Index covers only the text of the Encyclopedia. The front matter and appendices are not indexed. Titles of periodicals and books are italicized.